The Credentialing Handbook

Sheryl Deutsch, CPCS
President/Senior Consultant
Quality Management Options, LLC
Colorado Springs, Colorado

Christine S. Mobley, CMSC, CPCS
President
C. Mobley & Associates, LLC
Colorado Springs, Colorado

AN ASPEN PUBLICATION®
Aspen Publishers, Inc.
Gaithersburg, Maryland
1999

Library of Congress Cataloging-in-Publication Data

Deutsch, Sheryl.
The credentialing handbook / Sheryl Deutsch, Christine S. Mobley.
p. cm.
Includes bibliographical references and index.
ISBN 0-8342-0933-0 (alk. paper)
1. Allied health personnel—Certification—Handbooks, manuals, etc. 2. Medical staff—Rating of—Handbooks, manuals, etc.
I. Mobley, Christine S. II. Title.
[DNLM: 1. Credentialing handbooks. W 49 D486c 1999]
RA396.A1D48 1999
610.69—dc21
DNLM/DLC 98-55685
for Library of Congress CIP

Orders: (800) 638-8437
Customer Service: (800) 234-1660

Editorial Services: Greg Balas
Library of Congress Catalog Card Number: 98-55685
ISBN: 0-8342-0933-0

Printed in the United States of America

1 2 3 4 5

This book is dedicated to our credentialing colleagues and friends nationwide who share our desire to promote quality patient care through quality credentialing practices.

Table of Contents

Contributors

Special thanks to the following individuals who contributed forms for inclusion is this book.

Lynn Buchanan, CMSC, CPCS
President, Buchanan & Associates Consulting
Former Director, Medical Staff Services
Columbia-Continental Division, Denver, CO

Carolyn Burnham, CMSC, CPHQ
Medical Staff Services Team Leader
Children's Hospital, San Diego, CA

Elizabeth Carroll-Gonzalez
Director, Medical Staff Services
Columbia Medical Center–West, El Paso, TX

Rachael Deming
Director of Professional Services
Stanford University Hospital, Stanford, CA

Suzanne Edwards
Manager, Quality Improvement
St. Francis Cabrini Hospital, Alexandria, LA

Gloria Holden
Director
Greater Arizona Central Credentialing Program, Phoenix, AZ

Peggy LeFors
Administrative Director, Medical Staff Services
Desert Regional Medical Center, Palm Springs, CA

Gizelle Loveland, CMSC, CPCS
Manager, Credentialing
Group Health Cooperative, Seattle, WA

Luetta Luman, CMSC
Director Medical Staff Services/Centralized Credentialing Services
Sutter Health, Sacramento, CA

Margie Margolis, CMSC, CPHQ
Director Medical Staff Services, Quality Manager
Good Samaritan Hospital, Los Angeles, CA

Jeanna McIntosch, CPCS
Manager, Medical Staff Services
Columbia Memorial Medical Center of Jacksonville, Jacksonville, FL

Jeanne Etheridge McNeil
Former Director, Physician Services
Columbia Retreat Hospital, Richmond, VA

Kathleen Morris, MS, CPHQ, RRA
Administrative Director Quality Management
Columbia Adventura Hospital and Columbia Miami Heart Institute, Miami, FL

Cecile Mosher, CMSC
Manager, Medical Staff Services
St. Vincent Hospital, Worcester, MA

Christine Otto, CMSC, CPHQ, CPCS
Former Administrative Director, Quality and Medical Staff Services
Cedars-Sinai Medical Center, Los Angeles, CA

Susan Parker
Former Administrative Assistant, Credentialing
Colorado Springs Health Partners, Colorado Springs, CO

Carol Penciaro, CPHQ, CSMC
Director, Medical Affairs
Boulder Community Hospital, Boulder, CO

Paula Petersen
Director
Fairview System Credentialing, Minneapolis, MN

Cindy Radcliffe, CMSC
Director, Medical Staff Services
Western Medical Center Hospital–Anaheim, Anaheim, CA

Jodi Schirling, CMSC
Director QA/UM, Medical Staff Services
Alfred I. duPont Hospital for Children, Wilmington, DE

Linda Seyfert, CMSC
Credentials Manager
Penrose Health Care System, Colorado Springs, CO

Patricia Strasberg, MS, CMSC, CPCS
Director Medical/House Staff Services
University Hospital, Stony Brook, NY

Carol Walker
Former CEO
National Credentialing Forum, Colorado Springs, CO

Christina Wiggins-Giles, MS, CMSC
Principal
Medical Staff Solutions, Pepperell, MA

About the Authors

Sheryl Deutsch is President and Senior Consultant of Quality Management Options, LLC, Colorado Springs, Colorado, a consulting firm that has specialized in the development and implementation of quality management and improvement programs for the past 10 years. She works with hospitals, ambulatory, physician group, and managed care organizations and has designed credentialing programs for major insurance and managed care companies. Her expertise has been used to prepare for accreditation surveys by the Accreditation Association for Ambulatory Health Care, Joint Commission on Accreditation of Healthcare Organizations (Joint Commission), and the National Committee for Quality Assurance (NCQA). Having worked in health care since 1967, she has watched and been involved in the developing quality programs, accreditation processes, and credentialing activities. Her work in the managed care field is the basis for many presentations made on a national basis. She is also assistant editor of *Medical Staff Management Forms, Policies, and Procedures for Health Care Providers* (Aspen Publishers, 1995). Her background is in nursing, and she is a Certified Provider Credentialing Specialist (CPCS) by the National Association of Medical Staff Services (NAMSS).

Christine S. Mobley, President of C. Mobley & Associates, LLC, Colorado Springs, Colorado, is a consultant and educator for medical staff/provider services management in hospitals, managed care organizations, and credentialing verification organizations (CVOs) with 25 years' experience in her profession. Following a 15-year career in hospital medical staff services, she now consults in all areas of credentialing, medical staff governance, related office systems, and personnel support, including Joint Commission and NCQA accreditation compliance assessment/survey preparation. She is an NCQA surveyor for CVOs and is on the OPUS Advisory Board for *Credentialing across the Continuum*. She is the editor of *Medical Staff Management Forms, Policies, and Procedures for Health Care Providers* (Aspen Publishers, 1995) and has authored several publications for the NAMSS. She is a NAMSS past president, is currently on the NAMSS faculty, and holds current certification as a Certified Medical Staff Coordinator (CMSC) and a Certified Provider Credentialing Specialist (CPCS). She is a frequent presenter nationwide at conferences and seminars.

Foreword

The health care revolution has dramatically changed the way health care services are provided to patients in the United States. Both physicians and health care organizations have been forced to rethink their previous care delivery models and develop new models to meet the needs of the current managed care environment. New sets of standards and regulations have been developed in response to this changing health care environment.

Outcomes measurements and performance-based reappraisal are now an integral part of our health care delivery system. The role of the credentialing specialist has expanded as requirements for objective measurement of performance have increased. Licensing, accrediting, and certifying agencies now require definitive documentation that practitioners are indeed competent to perform the types of clinical services they have been credentialed to perform.

The Credentialing Handbook is a well-organized, comprehensive, concise book that will guide the credentialing specialist through the ever-changing requirements related to appointment and reappointment. Sheryl Deutsch and Christine Mobley have done an excellent job of developing a handbook that can be used as a comprehensive training manual for the novice and as an excellent resource for the most seasoned credentialing expert. *The Credentialing Handbook* offers a useful blend of theory and practical operational guidelines. It contains multiple examples of both implementation models and implementation forms that can be used as the basis for establishing a new credentialing program or improving a current program.

The book gives the credentialing specialist the knowledge necessary for establishing credentialing programs in a variety of health care settings and throughout an integrated delivery system. Those credentialing issues that are common across various health care settings have been aggregated and are discussed in single chapters or sections. Those credentialing issues that vary from setting to setting have been addressed in specific chapters or sections such as "Credentialing in Hospitals" and "Credentialing in Ambulatory and Managed Care." For those organizations that currently incorporate multiple health care settings and provider relationships, an integrated credentialing model is of utmost importance.

A new phase of the health care revolution in the United States is underway. Health care organizations, practitioners, and providers will be selected on the basis of objective measurements of performance and verification of the individual practitioner's qualifications and competencies. Credentialing specialists will be integral players in this changing paradigm, and *The Credentialing Handbook* provides the information necessary for their success.

Peter Leeson, DO, Medical Director
Leeson Consulting Group/Healthcare
Consulting Services
San Luis Obispo, California

Preface

Welcome to the world of credentialing. Whether you are a beginner or an experienced person involved with credentialing, we hope you will find this book a useful resource. The intent of this book is to provide basic information about the credentialing process and to identify the activities that will make the job of the credentialing professional easier, more productive, and more satisfying.

As experienced credentialers, we find we are constantly challenged to keep up with changes in the health care environment. Too much is happening too fast for any of us to ignore what is happening in relation to the credentialing of health care practitioners, regardless of the environment. It is an exciting time to be in this field with so many opportunities. Many individuals, however, enter the profession with little or no experience, preparation, education, or support. This book should answer questions, provide direction, and stimulate thinking about the possibility of a better way.

Sheryl Deutsch
Christine S. Mobley

Acknowledgments

The completion of this book would not have been possible without the contributions and support of many people whom we would like to acknowledge and thank. First, we wish to thank all those who contributed exhibits to this book; otherwise, we would still be creating forms and duplicating good work that is already out there. Names are listed in the "Contributors" section. Our great appreciation to Chris Wiggins-Giles for authoring Chapter 9 and coauthoring Chapter 2. Our heartfelt thanks to April Atkins, Lynn Buchanan, Royce Dent, and Chris Otto for their dedication in reviewing the chapters and giving us the constructive criticism we needed (over and over again). We appreciate all the individuals at the various accrediting organizations who answered our many questions regarding standards. A special thank you to our typists Gloria Alvarez, Linda Allison, Judy Tracy, and flowchart wizard Don King (or we would still be typing). We want to express our sincere thanks to Dr. Peter Leeson for writing the Foreword to this book and giving it support from the medical profession. We missed working with Jack Bruggeman at Aspen on this book, but we appreciate Marsha Davies' perseverance in pushing and prodding us to keep up with deadlines.

We appreciate the support and encouragement of our good friends and relatives, some of whom still do not understand what we do but encouraged us anyway. And to our husbands, David and Jerry, thank you for your love and willingness to support us through a *second* publishing project. We owe you big time!

Finally, to each other we owe a debt of gratitude for sticking with this project—and more, for maintaining our mutual respect for one another and our friendship beyond our business relationship. This was a tough one, but we made it.

Acknowledgments

CHAPTER 1

Overview of Credentialing

INTRODUCTION

Health care services, organizations, and delivery systems are evolving and changing at an increasingly rapid rate. Thirty years ago, health care was focused on physicians who provided care in their office and at hospitals. Today, health care is provided in a wide variety of ambulatory settings in addition to the hospital, and by a wide variety of specialized practitioners, and it is driven by numerous factors, not the least of which is managed care. Costs, federal and state law, concern and demand for high-quality care, and litigation have played roles in changing health care. And, as health care has changed, so too has credentialing activity.

The intent of this book is to provide basic information about the credentialing process and to identify the activities that will make the job of the credentialing professional easier, more productive, and more satisfying. The dynamics in our field today make it nearly impossible to stay abreast of all aspects of our profession. Many individuals enter the profession with little or no experience, preparation, or support. This book should answer questions, provide direction, and stimulate thinking about the possibility of a better way.

HISTORY OF CREDENTIALING

The history of credentialing can probably be traced back to the early 1900s, when the American College of Surgeons created minimum standards for physicians and surgeons privileged to practice in hospitals. Those standards referred to a "staff" composed of physicians practicing in the hospital, limited that staff to physicians and surgeons who had completed the appropriate training in their respective fields, and required them to be worthy in character. Those minimum standards also required the staff to initiate, and have adopted by the governing board, rules, regulations, and policies regarding

- staff meetings; review of clinical experience at regular intervals within the various departments, such as medicine, surgery, and obstetrics
- written, accurate, and complete records for all patients
- supervised diagnostic and therapeutic facilities, such as a clinical laboratory and/or X-ray department, available for study, diagnosis, and treatment of patients[1]

How the hospitals and staff of that period determined that the physicians were graduates in good standing, legally licensed to practice, competent in their respective fields, and worthy in character is unknown, but at least the foundation was laid for a credentialing process that has continued to evolve and expand.

We can trace accreditation credentialing standards to the mid-1970s with the Joint Commission Hospital Accreditation program. The Joint

Commission's credentialing standards then were not what they are today; like everything else, they have undergone substantial change. Credentialing staff in hospitals in the 1970s did not have to be concerned with reappointment, privilege delineation, or primary source verification. It was basically a time when copies of training certificates, board certification, state licenses, and Drug Enforcement Administration (DEA) certificates were collected and placed in a credentials file along with some type of application form. Very few fair hearings were held, probably because there were few decisions to cause dispute. There were few allied health professionals (AHPs) practicing in a hospital environment, and podiatrists did not generally have hospital privileges. The allopathic (MD) and osteopathic (DO) practitioners practiced at separate hospitals and did not cross into each other's territory. There was no quality assurance as we know it today. The medical record department initiated various audits of common practices in treatment and procedures and reported statistics to the medical staff. Organized committees included executive, credentials, bylaws, medical records, maybe one or several audit committees, a utilization review committee, and departments/sections when medical staffs were too large to meet as a whole. There was little managed care, and what managed care activity there was did not affect or concern hospitals. Some hospitals had typed lists of medical staff rosters. More sophisticated hospitals with data-processing assistance could generate a data-processing roster with hard-copy updates. Physicians frequently practiced in a solo office or with a small, specialized group, and the majority of health care was provided in the physician office and in a hospital.

In the 1980s, we began to see more detailed credentialing standards from the Joint Commission that included the requirement for primary source verification (end of the 1980s), a requirement for a privilege laundry list, and a two-year reappointment process. Computers replaced electric typewriters, credentialing software surfaced, and the Health Care Quality Improvement Act was passed in 1986.[2] Fair hearings became more commonplace, as there were more opportunities to deny or suspend privileges and/or membership on the basis of more standards, rules, and peer review. Some medical societies began to offer a verification service for the local hospitals and physicians practicing in the community. Managed care organizations were increasing in size and in number, and the National Committee for Quality Assurance (NCQA) began accrediting health maintenance organizations (HMOs).

The 1990s have brought us more of the 1980s activities as well as the beginning of on-line verifications services, diverse types of credentials verification organizations (CVOs), a more organized privilege delineation process with core privileges and bundling of privileges, the introduction of privileging into the ambulatory setting, required use of the National Practitioner Data Bank (NPDB), many AHPs seeking access to hospitals, and multiple accreditation programs. Organizations have developed express credentialing processes that can speed up the review and approval steps using clearly defined criteria. A significant increase in managed care, accreditation of managed care organizations and credentialing requirements for practitioners in managed care networks and panels has brought a new dimension to credentialing activities. Managed care organizations may delegate credentialing activities of verifying and collecting data and/or completing the credentialing process to hospitals, independent practice associations (IPAs), and CVOs. Capitation (a payment arrangement on a per-member basis for a given number of patients assigned to a practitioner[3]) has resulted in questions about quality of care and quality of practitioners' care. With questions about quality come increased requirements to assure competency and qualifications. With the increase in diverse organizations that are credentialing practitioners (hospitals, managed care, ambulatory care, medical group practices, etc.) and systems/networks seeking multiple accreditation and certifications, credentialing professionals are truly becoming experts in their field.

WHAT IS CREDENTIALING?

Credentialing may be defined as the process by which an organization (e.g., a hospital, managed care organization, or physician group) determines whether an applicant is qualified for association, membership, employment, and/or the practice of specific clinical privileges being requested. The credentialing process is focused on verification of adequate training, experience, licensure, and competence, and the assessment of the data and information collected to determine if a practitioner is qualified and competent to render acceptable quality of care to patients.

A *credential* is a certificate, letter, or award given to an individual that represents that he or she has the knowledge or right to exercise certain activities, or authority, or function in a specific position. Medical credentials that are identified, verified, and reviewed against criteria include

- state license
- Drug Enforcement Agency (DEA) certificate
- training and education
- specialty status and/or certification
- health care affiliations
- request for privileges that are organization specific

Additional information commonly gathered as part of credentialing activities includes:

- continuing medical education (CME) depending on state or organizational requirements
- malpractice insurance coverage
- existence of malpractice claims or judgments or other actions that might relate to the ability to render appropriate and quality care
- work history
- statement as to disciplinary activity, physical and mental status, criminal record, lack of impairment

Most credentialing is completed at the time that an individual applies for membership, association, or employment and/or requests clinical privileges and is referred to as initial application, appointment, or credentialing. Recredentialing and/or reappointment commonly occurs every two years and involves the collection, verification, and review of nonstatic credentials and information such as licenses, DEA, and insurance coverage. Credentials provide the proof and support for the right of a practitioner to provide care. *Collection of data does not constitute credentialing.* The information must be reviewed *and* a decision made relevant to qualifications and competency before a practitioner is considered to be credentialed.

WHY CREDENTIAL?

Institutions and organizations have a responsibility to patients to exercise due care when determining membership, affiliation, and employment and/or awarding clinical privileges. The process enables a hospital, managed care organization, employer, or other health care entity to make formal evaluations and determinations based on quality to ensure that quality care is provided. It is a risk management tool in that it encourages selection of qualified health care practitioners. Credentialing functions are required by health care accreditation organizations and have been further mandated by regulatory requirements and case law.

The driving forces for credentialing activity in a health care environment include

- quality
- accreditation standards and requirements
- risk management
- customer and payor expectations

- regulatory requirements
- case law

Quality

Competent, qualified practitioners provide quality patient care. Health care organizations are responsible for protecting their patients from practitioners who are incompetent, inadequately trained, or unethical. A prudent organization identifies criteria, collects data, and evaluates the data before making a decision about its relationship with a practitioner. Standards and criteria reflect the commitment of an organization to an affiliation with practitioners who practice quality health care delivery. Affiliating with a practitioner before review of credentials, making exceptions to criteria, and refusing to deny participation does not reflect a commitment to quality. Any doubts about an individual's competence to practice medicine should be addressed in the beginning of the process, with a final determination made only after all questions have been answered or situations resolved.

Accreditation Standards and Requirements

All health care accreditation organizations have credentialing standards. Some of the organizations have very specific credentialing standards, while others simply require the organization to identify and implement a credentialing and/or privileging process. Of the major accrediting organizations, the Joint Commission and the American Osteopathic Association (AOA) have been surveying health care organizations for the longest time. Newer to the scene are the National Committee for Quality Assurance (NCQA), which emerged as managed care became more prominent in the health care industry; the Accreditation Association for Ambulatory Health Care (AAAHC); and the Utilization Review Accreditation Commission (URAC). The American Medical Association and American Osteopathic Association (AOA) are the newest players in the accreditation field as they develop standards for physician office practices. Chapter 2 of this book includes detailed descriptions of these accrediting organizations.

Risk Management

Risk avoidance is another driving force behind credentialing activities. Organizations are at risk if practitioners are allowed to see and treat patients before credentialing. Ignoring signs and symptoms (caution flags) identified during initial credentialing or after a relationship is established also increases risk. There is an increased risk if the process of credentialing is not followed according to policies and bylaws or if a practitioner is declared to be competent and have qualifying credentials but is subsequently found to be incompetent. Avoiding unnecessary risk to patients, as well as to the organization, starts with a thorough credentialing process.

Meeting Customer and Payor Expectations

As consumers of medical care become more educated and more concerned about the cost of health care, it becomes increasingly important that organizations be able to assure the public that they are being prudent in their credentialing activities. Background checks and ongoing competency evaluation help assure consumers that they are receiving the best care that is available to them. Payors of health care are also very involved in defining expectations of the care available for the covered lives in their program. This is especially the case in the managed care industry, where payors decide which managed care organizations to contract with on the basis of whether the organization meets their standards.

Regulatory Requirements

Numerous federal and state requirements must be taken into account when credentialing practitioners. The government's conditions for participation are the basis for evaluation in those organizations that treat Medicare/Medicaid patients. The Health Care Quality Improvement Act of 1986 provided immunity for peer review and established the National Practitioner Data Bank (NPDB). State requirements for practitioner credentialing differ from state to state. It is important that organizations and credentialing professionals be aware of and understand requirements of federal and applicable state statutes.

Case Law

Legal actions provide direction for credentialing activities, as the courts have determined accountability for care rendered. Starting with *Darling v. Charleston Community Memorial Hospital* (1965),[4] the courts have held that hospitals have a corporate duty to select competent physicians and to monitor patient care. In 1989, with *Harrell v. Total Health Care, Inc.,*[5] the courts extended responsibility for credentialing into the managed care sector. It is clear that health care entities have a responsibility for the quality of care provided by the independent medical staff members or contracted physicians, and there is a clear legal foundation for credentialing activities.

A partial listing of cases that direct and/or support credentialing processes follows:

- *Darling v. Charleston Community Memorial Hospital* (1965). This landmark case initiated the corporate negligence doctrine, which holds hospitals responsible for the negligent acts of their employees and physicians and states that hospitals have a corporate duty to monitor patient care provided in the facility.[6] The hospital was found to be negligent in its failure to supervise treatment of the patient, to require consultation and in its selection and appointment of the physician to their medical staff.
- *Mitchell County Hospital Authority v. Joiner* (1972).[7] In this case, the hospital governing board denied its liability for the inadequate performance of a medical staff member. Its basis was the practitioner license and the recommendation made by the medical staff. The court found that the medical staff acted as an agent of the governing board in screening applicants and thus did not relieve the institution from liability.[8]
- *Robins v. Magovern* (1979).[9] In Robins vs. Magovern, a physician who was denied privileges brought action under antitrust and state law. The court found that medical staff committee records are discoverable, that objective criteria contained in bylaws must be carefully and thoroughly adhered to, and that hospitals may determine proper limitation on competition with the hospital and surrounding areas.[10]
- *Rule v. Lutheran Hospitals and Homes Society of America* (1987).[11] A verdict of $650,000 in this case was supported by the hospital's failure to investigate qualifications of the attending physician before granting privileges. The physician's privileges had been limited at another hospital for the procedure performed.[12]
- *Johnson v. Misericordia Community Hospital* (1981).[13] The Wisconsin Supreme Court affirmed that hospitals are obliged to review credentials carefully before granting privileges. In this case, it was found that the hospital had not adhered to its own established procedures and that hospital supervision of the appointment process is mandatory, not optional.[14]
- *Elam v. College Park Hospital* (1982).[15] In Elam vs. College Park Hospital, the California Court of Appeals held that a hospital must review physicians and that if it fails in the performance of this duty, it may be held liable for the malpractice of physicians who are not employees or agents.[16]
- *Harrell v. Total Health Care, Inc.* (1989). In this case the applicability of corporate negligence doctrine to an HMO was considered. The Missouri Court of Appeals found that

the HMO had been negligent in credentialing and that although the HMO did not directly render patient care, it did have a corporate responsibility to select qualified competent physicians.[17]

- *McClellan v. Health Maintenance Organization of Pennsylvania* (1992).[18] In Pennsylvania, the courts also ruled that an HMO must select competent physicians. Their finding was based, not on corporate negligence, but on common law related to exercising reasonable care when rendering services.[19]

Case law related to credentialing has become fairly extensive. Organizations and credentialing professionals should be cognizant of the decisions that affect or direct their credentialing activities.

WHO IS CREDENTIALED?

The authors have adopted NCQA's definitions when referring to individuals, institutions, or organizations in health care. In this book, the term *practitioners* will refer to individuals (physicians, podiatrists, dentists, nurses, clinical psychologists, etc.) who provide health care services. These individuals are commonly required to be licensed as defined by law. The term *providers* will refer to organizations that provide services (e.g., a hospital, pharmacy, or home health agency).

In managed care and hospital environments, many practitioners who provide or participate in the care of patients do so independently. The ability to practice independently is determined by both their licensure and the organization. Practitioners may be employed by, affiliated with, or contracted by an organization. Those who do not practice independently are required to practice under supervision as defined by the organization. These factors and determinations are used to identify categories of caregivers, such as medical staff and affiliated or allied health staff.

Individual state laws may also define which practitioners may or may not qualify for hospital medical staff membership and/or who must be credentialed. A hospital must decide which practitioners are part of the organized medical staff.[20] Within some organizations, employed individuals who also provide care independently, as allowed by their license and the organization, may be required to apply as an allied health professional or may be eligible for medical staff affiliation.

Accreditation requirements and eligibility for affiliation, membership, or privileges determine who must be credentialed. But internal processes (bylaws, policies, etc.), and external sources such as state and federal law also affect the determination. Traditionally, those independent practitioners who are eligible for both medical staff membership and clinical privileging in a hospital are medical doctors (MDs), osteopathic doctors (DOs), dentists (DDSs, DMDs), and podiatrists (DPMs). Those credentialed as affiliated practitioners or as allied health practitioners traditionally include practitioners such as nurse practitioners (NPs), clinical psychologists (PhDs), certified nurse anesthetists (CRNAs), and physician assistants (PAs). Determining the category and type of each affiliated provider and practitioner is the first step in determining who is credentialed.

Accreditation and regulatory requirements are reviewed against identified categories and types of practitioners to determine required credentialing. As a general rule, anyone who is granted clinical privileges or who will be allowed to provide patient care without supervision (i.e., an independent practitioner) is addressed in all accreditation credentialing standards. Some organizations and accrediting agencies do not require credentialing of affiliated practitioners or allied health practitioners. To some extent, this is a matter of how the organization defines credentialing. In the strictest sense, any review of qualifications for any practitioner or provider by any member of the organization could be considered credentialing. This book concentrates on credentialing activities as traditionally defined, which are usually accomplished by the medical staff office in a hospital and by designated credentialing staff in ambulatory and managed care organizations and which focus on practitioners and providers who are licensed.

Accreditation standards, state and federal regulations, and internal policy and procedure will determine the extent of credentialing activity for practitioners and providers. With the emergence of new types of practitioners and the increased use of physician extenders or other allied health practitioners, the health care industry will constantly be evaluating what types of individuals they need within their organizations to provide health care services. It is important that good processes be in place to evaluate the need for new types of practitioners, as well as to evaluate credentials and competence. The types and categories of practitioners and providers and how they are credentialed are discussed in more detail later in this book.

ORGANIZATIONS THAT CREDENTIAL

In the past, most credentialing was done in hospitals for physicians applying for appointment to the medical staff. But credentialing activity now occurs in a wide variety of health care organizations. Health maintenance organizations (HMOs), preferred provider organizations, independent practice associations, medical groups, clinics, and ambulatory care centers commonly perform credential reviews. Today, any health care organization that affiliates with practitioners or providers is probably involved in credentialing activities.

CREDENTIALING STEPS AND ACTIVITIES

Although credentialing activities and procedures can vary substantially between organizations, there are basic steps common to most processes. These are

- development of program structure
- application
- collection and verification of data and information
- evaluation of data and information
- decision-making process
- ongoing monitoring and evaluation of competence
- recredentialing/reappointment/reappraisal

The macro flowchart in Figure 1–1 outlines the basic steps followed in credentialing a practitioner. Chapters 3 and 4 give detailed information about each step of the credentialing process in hospitals and in ambulatory and managed care organizations, respectively.

Development of Program Structure

Before any credentialing activity can take place, the program structure must be identified. Answers to questions of who will be credentialed, how they will be credentialed and what credentials or qualifications will be collected and evaluated provide the basis for the program. Regulations, accreditation standards, and case law direct many components of the credentialing process, but many organizations choose to go beyond the requirements and implement a process that they hope will *ensure* affiliation with competent, fully qualified practitioners and providers.

The credentialing program structure identifies:

- purpose
- scope
- authority and accountability for decision and outcome
- criteria, standards, or qualifications for membership, affiliation, association, or employment
- required and optional credentialing steps and activities, including prescreening, application, information collection, verification, evaluation, decision making, and monitoring
- required documentation

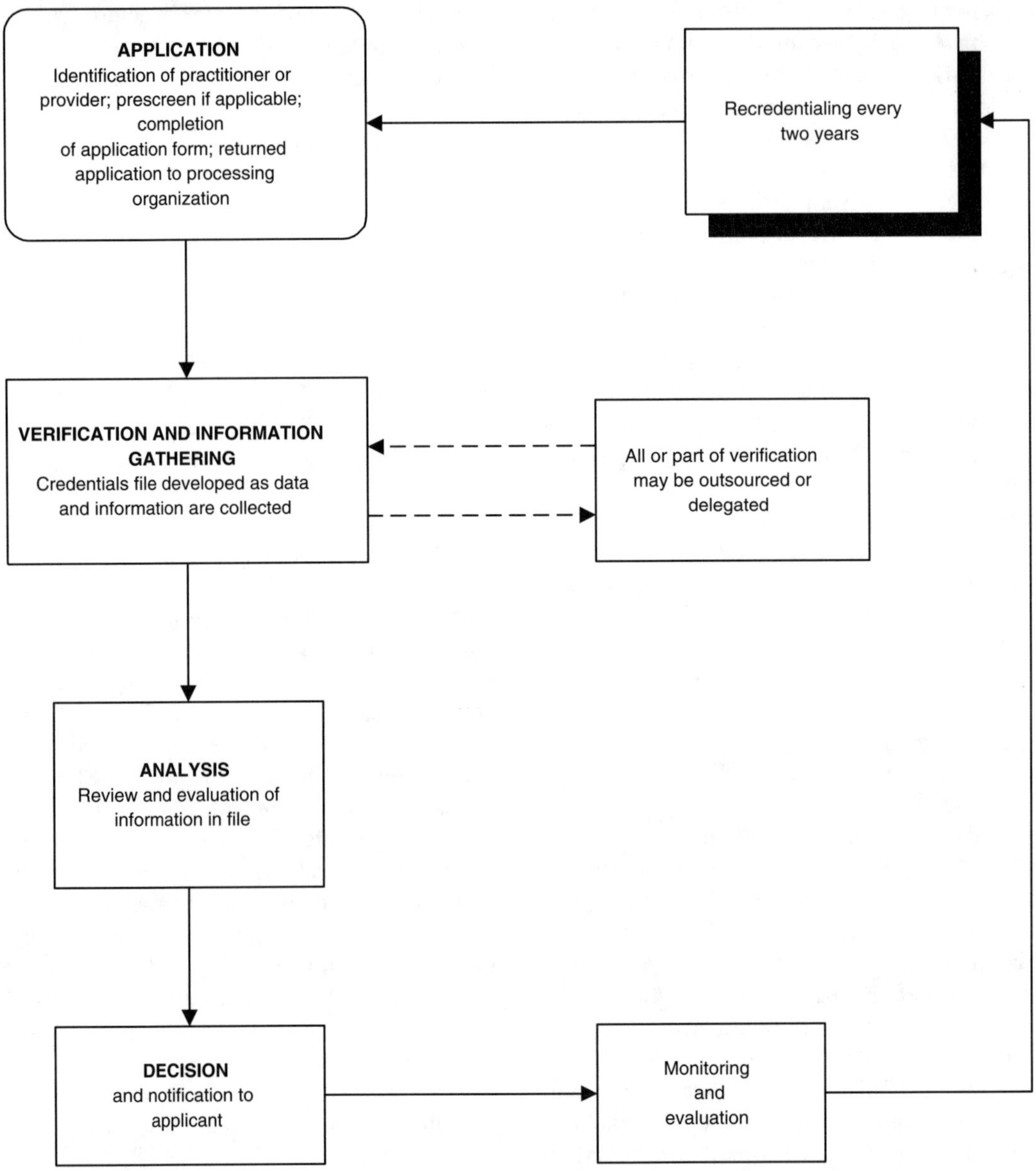

Figure 1–1 Basic Credentialing Process Steps. Courtesy of C. Mobley & Associates, LLC, and Quality Management Options, LLC, Colorado Springs, Colorado.

Application

The application step may involve identification and or screening of potential applicants or may begin with a request for an application. The application is a formal document that allows an applicant to provide information about experience and qualifications. It is common practice to require an applicant to sign a release of liability and an attestation that all information in the application is complete and correct. The application step is considered to be complete once an application with required attachments is returned and reviewed for completeness and the information is entered into a tracking system (manual or automated).

Collection and Verification of Data and Information

This credentialing step involves the collection and verification of information related to the experience, qualifications, and competence of the applicant. Some information may simply be identified (e.g., work history); while other information (e.g., license or education) is verified with the issuing agency or organization. This step may be completed

- within the organization by credentialing staff
- by outsourcing work to a credentials verification organization (CVO)
- through delegation to another organization
- by a centralized system verification service

The collection and verification step is considered to be complete once all required information has been collected and placed in a credentials file.

Evaluation

The person responsible for collecting information and assembling the credentials file performs the first evaluation. A checklist or summary profile is completed that identifies the file contents. The profile or summary will often highlight any items or information that do not appear to comply with criteria. Caution flags (a warning to slow down and use caution because further review or consideration of the information is indicated) are identified. In the hospital, the file is evaluated by a department or department chair to determine whether qualifications match requested privileges. The bylaws of the medical staff outline accountability for this function. In managed or ambulatory care, a peer review committee, credentials committee, or other designated entity may complete the peer review (review by an individual with like or similar training, education and qualifications).

Although review by a credentials committee is not required by hospital accreditation standards, many organizations use a designated credentials committee to review files, evaluate against criteria, and make a recommendation. Hospital credentials committees must forward recommendations to the medical executive committee, which is responsible for recommendations to the governing body.

Decision-Making Process

Hospitals accredited by the Joint Commission are required to forward recommendations from the medical executive committee to the governing body for a decision. Governing bodies in other health care organizations may choose to delegate the decision to the credentials committee or to another designated committee or entity. If the applicant is rejected or if the appointment or privileges are limited, the applicant may have the right to a fair hearing appeals mechanism.

Ongoing Monitoring and Evaluation of Competence

Applicants who are credentialed, appointed, and/or granted privileges are notified of the decision and are subject to ongoing monitoring and evaluation to ensure competence. A practitioner profile is developed from information collected through quality/performance improvement activities.

Recredentialing/Reappointment/Reappraisal

Currently, the major health care accrediting organizations require a reevaluation of credentials every two years. Information gathered through the monitoring and evaluation activities and nonstatic information (information that is subject to change, such as licensure, certification, or malpractice insurance) is subject to review.

DIFFERENCES BETWEEN CREDENTIALING ACTIVITIES IN HOSPITALS AND MANAGED CARE ORGANIZATIONS

Some credentialing professionals and health care administrative staff believe that there are few differences between credentialing activities in the hospital and in managed or ambulatory care settings. But while it is true that the basic activities of collecting and verifying information are much the same, numerous differences affect the process. These include

- *Number of Practitioners Credentialed*—A medium-sized hospital usually has a medical staff of several hundred physicians who are credentialed. In a medium-sized managed care organization or an integrated system that has a managed care plan, it would not be unusual to find 1,500 to 3,000 practitioners and providers who are credentialed.
- *Scope*—Facilities and organizations that deliver or provide for health care services (providers) may be credentialed by managed care organizations, but are not part of hospital credentials activity.
- *Bylaws versus Contracts*—The bylaws, rules and regulations, and policies and procedures are the documents that dictate relationships, parameters, and credentialing steps for a hospital medical staff. In managed and ambulatory care, there is a formal contract or letter of agreement that defines the relationship between the organization and the practitioner or provider. The contract or agreement does not detail specific information related to credentialing but instead outlines credentialing criteria and/or references the organization's credentialing plan, policy, and procedure.
- *Accrediting Organizations and Standards*—There are numerous differences in both the scope and the focus of the various health care accrediting organizations and in their credentialing standards and requirements. Chapter 2 of this book includes information about the various accreditation organizations and their credentialing standards.
- *Appointment*—The end result of the credentialing and privileging process in hospitals is appointment to a medical or allied health staff. In the ambulatory and managed care arena (except possibly in some staff-model HMOs), there is no organized medical staff. Practitioners commonly become part of a network or panel on the basis of their contract with the organization.
- *Privileging*—Although Joint Commission network accreditation standards are moving toward requirements for privileging in ambulatory care, currently there is little privileging activity outside of hospitals (an exception being ambulatory surgical centers, which privilege their practitioners in much the same way as hospitals).
- *Physician Office Site Visits and Medical Record Review*—The credentialing process for managed care often involves site visits to physician offices and provider facilities before a credentialing decision. Unless they are part of an integrated system that includes a managed care organization, hospitals do

not use information about the physician office practice in their credentialing decisions.

- *Temporary Status or Temporary Privileges*—Recognition of a practitioner on a temporary or provisional basis while credentials are being processed is not often practiced in ambulatory and managed care and is not recognized by NCQA. Some hospitals grant temporary privileges for practitioners to see patients before completion of the initial credentialing process. (Standards require at least primary source verification of licensure and current competence before granting privileges.)
- *Economic Credentialing*—Economic credentialing is not a consideration that hospitals have traditionally included in their credentialing process, but it has been used in managed and ambulatory care for some time. Much of the information related to managed care affiliation deals with utilization and economic factors and thus affects credentialing and contracting activities and decisions.
- Recredentialing—While both the Joint Commission and NCQA require an evaluation of competence of practitioners for recredentialing, NCQA also requires results from three of six additional sources of information: member satisfaction surveys, facility reviews, medical record review, utilization management, member complaints, and information from quality improvement activities.
- *Verification Time Frame*—Although timely processing of credentials is a Joint Commission requirement for hospitals, it is defined in numbers of days (180) by NCQA. Hospital credentialing completion times are defined in its bylaws.
- *Roles and Responsibilities*—Credentialing professionals in the hospital are usually part of the medical staff office and provide both credentialing and support services for members of the medical staff organization. In managed and ambulatory care, the credentialing professional is more likely to be involved in only credentialing activities and to work in, or in conjunction with, the provider services department.
- *Delegation of Credentialing Activities or Process*—Although it is becoming increasingly popular to delegate or to outsource verification activities, hospitals do not delegate the credentialing process. Managed and ambulatory care, on the other hand, may delegate verification or the entire credentialing activity to another organization.

There are other, more subtle differences between credentialing activities in hospitals and managed care organizations that have more to do with accreditation compliance. These will be discussed in more detail in Chapters 3 and 4 of this book.

CREDENTIALING PRACTICES

A comprehensive credentialing program should minimally provide for

- initial credentialing, appointment, and recredentialing procedures
- a uniform set of selection criteria managed care organizations (MCOs) or membership and privileging criteria (hospitals)
- verification of credentials against criteria
- corrective action and fair hearing plan
- monitoring and evaluation of professional performance, clinical competence, and judgment

Basic Principles

Basic principles of credentialing should apply regardless of the accrediting organization or the environment where health care is provided. Over time, basic principles have evolved, and the following are universally accepted as standard practice.

- *The process should be applied consistently for all practitioners.* Each organization should ensure a credentialing process that is clearly defined and consistently applied for every applicant. Exceptions made for one individual and not for another who may have the same or similar credentials could result in liability or charges of discrimination. If exceptions are made to general credentialing and/or privileging criteria, they should be documented to include the reason and the alternative identified for meeting the defined criteria. An objective process that evaluates credentials and information against criteria reduces additional risk to individuals or groups that review and evaluate credentials.
- *The burden of proof is on the applicant.* Additional information that is required and requested of the applicant is that applicant's responsibility to obtain and provide. Nonresponse or refusal to provide the information that is requested should be considered a voluntary withdrawal of application (as opposed to denial). An organization should have a defined process for request of information, additional requests, or follow-up if information is not received, with time frames for each action.
- *The benefit of doubt should go to the patient, not the applicant.* If there are substantial concerns about the quality of care that may be provided by a practitioner, the organization should carefully consider potential results for patient care that may result in an adverse outcome and should act accordingly.
- *Credentialing is the basis of quality and, properly done, decreases risk.* A quality credentialing process is of benefit to the patient as well as to the organization. Qualified, competent practitioners provide quality care.
- *Credentialing should be completed before contract or privileging.* NCQA standards do not recognize provisional or temporary credentialing. They require the entire credentialing process to be completed before a practitioner can begin seeing health plan members. Hospitals and ambulatory and managed care organizations that are not accredited by NCQA should carefully consider any provisions for temporary approval to ensure that a practitioner not fully competent or qualified cannot negatively affect patient care.

Critical Elements

Critical elements of an effective credentialing process are

1. A documented plan that identifies
   - the scope of the process
   - each step in the credentialing and privileging process
   - responsibility and accountability for all activities
   - required documents
   - a category/status designation for all practitioners and providers
2. Criteria that
   - are objective and quantifiable
   - define qualification
   - are used on a consistent basis
3. A standardized application process that is consistently implemented and understood by all involved in the process
4. A process of collecting and verifying data and information, with
   - express or expedited processing as the norm, rather than the exception
   - established production and turnaround time standards
   - file management policies
5. A review, evaluation, and approval process that
   - provides for peer evaluation
   - functions in a timely manner
   - requires a file summary/profile
   - uses trigger criteria for caution flags
   - regularly orients all involved in the process to function, responsibilities, and options available

- requires effective meeting function for all committees
- does not rubber-stamp credentials on the basis of previous recommendations or recruitment requests
- uses a CVO if that is determined to be the most productive and cost-effective practice

6. A recredentialing, reappraisal, reappointment process that
   - is initiated and completed on a two-year cycle
   - is consistent for all categories and types of practitioners and providers
   - identifies accountability for data collection of practitioners; performance monitoring
   - uses information from ongoing evaluation and monitoring activities
7. A privileging process that
   - defines site, location, and scope of privileges
   - uses privilege forms reflecting core competency and special privilege categories
8. Consideration of delegation whenever possible and appropriate

Documents

Documents commonly found in an office responsible for credentialing activities that support the credentialing process include

- *Medical Staff Bylaws Rules and Regulations*—Bylaws, rules, and regulations are documents required by the Joint Commission for hospitals. Qualifications for membership and the credentialing process are identified in bylaws. The rules and regulations include specifics about patient care.
- *Credentialing Plan/Manual*—A formal document used by ambulatory and managed care organizations and by hospitals that want to define the process, steps, parameters, and "how-tos" of the credentialing process.
- *Policies and Procedures*—Most organizations develop policies and procedures addressing specific aspects of their credentialing (and privileging, as applicable) process. Standard forms and letters are developed and included in the document.
- *Fair Hearing Plan*—The fair hearing plan or appeals process is often a supplemental appendix to the medical staff bylaws, or the credentials plan. If not, it may be developed as a stand-alone document.
- *Rules and Regulations/Policies for Allied Health*—A document specifically addressing allied health may be developed as an alternative to integrating the requirements, policies, procedure forms, and so forth into other documents.
- *Medical Staff Organization or Committee Function Manual*—If not part of the bylaws or credentialing plan, this manual outlines the composition and functions of all committees.

Accountability and Reporting Structure

In hospitals, the medical staff office is charged with the responsibility for all credentialing and medical staff functions. In the ambulatory and managed care settings, the activities are usually the responsibility of the quality management or provider relations staff/department. Some organizations assign credentialing to the human resources or contracting departments. Regardless of location, it is necessary to establish reporting relationships that ensure that all activities take place independently of employment and/or contract services. All positions responsible for or involved with credentialing activities should report along the same lines of organizational structure. Additional information about accountability and reporting structure can be found in Chapter 11 of this book.

CREDENTIALING IN TRANSITION: CHALLENGES AND OPPORTUNITIES

Credentialing activity has greatly expanded during the 1990s, and as we head into the next millennium, some of the challenges faced in this century have been overcome, some continue, and there are some ahead about which we do not yet know. Some of the challenges lie in the processes used to credential practitioners and providers, and some relate to who is being credentialed. It is becoming increasingly difficult for the credentialing professional to stay abreast of the various accreditation and regulatory requirements and changes. However, with challenges come opportunities for those in the credentialing profession to expand their repertoire of expertise. As credentialing professionals educate and prepare themselves to meet the demand and needs of organizations that credential, they are developing and positioning the profession to respond to the market's need for specific expertise. For many, this means stepping "out of the box"—going from a comfort zone of many years' credentialing in the hospital to looking at other opportunities, within either integrated networks or systems or the ambulatory or managed care environment. Opportunities for the credentialing profession are greater now than they ever have been. It is currently estimated that there is a greater demand for credentialing expertise than a supply of qualified individuals in the credentialing profession.

The traditional job security of being able to work within the same organization and in the same position for many years is becoming more scarce. Individuals must continue to monitor the challenges that health care organizations are facing, anticipate change, evaluate change as it relates to their position, and educate their organization in the area of their expertise.

Some of the trends that have been part of the 1990s will continue into the year 2000 and beyond and should be anticipated and understood by those who expect to continue working in the credentialing field. These include

- *Integrated Health Care Systems and Networks*—Health care delivery systems are changing. Today there are systems composed of several facilities offering a variety of services. There are health care delivery systems that include practitioners, facilities, and payors. Credentialing activity may occur in individual facilities or at a centralized location for the entire system or network. Various accreditation programs may apply to a network.
- *CVOs*—Increasingly, health care organizations are looking at delegating or outsourcing the verification component of the credentialing process to a commercial or medical society CVO or to a centralized verification office of a health care delivery system.
- *Delegation*—Although many managed care organizations are currently delegating all or part of their credentialing process, this trend will probably continue and expand to other health care organizations.
- *Express (Fast-Track) Credentialing Process*—With an increasing number and type of practitioners, increasing demand for credentialed practitioners, and new requirements related to timing, an express credentialing process has become popular. As "shortcuts" are identified and implemented, the express process will become the norm rather than the exception.
- *Paperless Credentials File*—As health care delivery systems grow and increasing numbers of organizations require and duplicate activities, it is increasingly advantageous to eliminate duplication of paperwork to the extent possible. Using information systems and networked software allows less paper to be transmitted and/or filed.
- *Allied Health Practitioners*—Increasingly, more allied health staff and/or physician extenders are being used in the health care delivery system. What is termed "alternative health care delivery" today is gaining acceptance, and insurers are increasingly paying for service by these practitioners. The scope of credentialing will expand, as will criteria to accommodate the various types of practitioners providing health care.
- *Greater Interaction among Hospitals, Managed Care Organizations, and Practitio-*

ners—As hospitals and ambulatory and managed care organizations move forward, there is increasing concern about duplication, and interest in cooperative efforts is growing.

- *Ongoing Competency Evaluation*—As the diversity in types of health care practitioners increases and the location of practice changes, it will continue to be a challenge to define criteria and to identify how competency will be evaluated both initially and at the time of recredentialing. Whether or not accrediting organizations will continue a mandatory two-year recredentialing requirement, it will be necessary to define how competency is evaluated.
- *Impairment/Harassment*—Physician impairment, substance abuse, and sexual harassment are widely recognized issues. Laws, policies, and procedures have been enacted and are increasingly enforced through courts and organizations. Effective means of rehabilitation and methods of monitoring a practitioner once the impairment is identified will continue to be a challenge for those in the credentialing profession.

Those involved in the credentialing profession cannot expect to have their positions or the environment around them stay the same for very long. Being open to change and the challenges ahead and, more importantly, being able to predict the challenges ahead will enable credentialing professionals to be effective in their jobs.

NOTES

1. *Medical Staff Briefing* (Marblehead, MA: Opus Communications, March 1997), 5.
2. 42 U.S.C. §§11101–11152.
3. R. Rognehaugh, *The Managed Health Care Dictionary* (Gaithersburg, MD: Aspen Publishers, Inc., 1996), 27.
4. 211 N.E. 2d 253 (Ill. S. Ct. 1965).
5. W.L. 153066 (Mo. Ct. App. 1989).
6. K. Cartwright, *Physician Credentialing and Peer Review Answer Books* (Gaithersburg, MD: Aspen Publishers, Inc., 1995), 10.
7. 189 S.E. 2d 412 (Ga. 1972).
8. Cartwright, *Physician Credentialing,* 10.
9. 83 F.R.D. 79 (W.D. Pa. 1979).
10. G. Roger, *Legal Aspects of Health Care Administration* (Gaithersburg, MD: Aspen Publishers, Inc., 1996), 380.
11. 835 F. 2d 1250 (8th Cir 1987).
12. Roger, *Legal Aspects,* 252.
13. 301 N.W. 2d 156 (Wis. S. Ct. 1981).
14. Roger, *Legal Aspects,* 252.
15. 183 Cal. Rptr., 156 (Cal. Ct. App. 1982).
16. G. Pozgar, *Legal Aspects of Health Care Administration* (Gaithersburg, MD: Aspen Publishers, Inc., 1996), 210.
17. P. Younger, *Legal Answer Book for Managed Care* (Gaithersburg, MD: Aspen Publishers, Inc., 1996), 76.
18. 604 A. 2d 10053 (Pa. 1992).
19. Younger, *Legal Answer Book,* 176.
20. *Medical Staff Credentialing* (American Hospital Publishing, 1994), 7.

Chapter 2

Accreditation, Regulation, Bylaws, and Contracts

OVERVIEW

The foundation for credentialing is the desire to ensure quality and to comply with regulatory requirements, accreditation standards, organizational bylaws, and individual contracts. Credentialing has been evolving over more than 40 years. Legal actions involving and affecting the credentialing process have increased since 1965 with *Darling v. Charleston Community Memorial Hospital,*[1] in which the hospital was found negligent in its selection and appointment of the attending physician. Credentialing is also affected by federal and state statutory laws and regulations as well as court decisions. All states have licensure laws, and many have antidiscrimination, peer review, and any-willing-provider laws. The Health Care Quality Improvement Act of 1986[2] contains both reporting requirements and immunity provisions that impact credentialing. Medicare conditions of participation include specific credentialing criteria. Health care accrediting organizations require specific activities related to determining qualifications and competency of affiliated practitioners. Additionally, hospital medical staff bylaws address credentialing requirements and may be considered a binding contract. To be effective in their work, credentialing professionals must be cognizant of the standards and requirements that affect and direct their activities.

ACCREDITATION

The concept of health care accreditation started in 1919, when the American College of Surgeons formally established the Hospital Standardization program. In 1951, the Joint Commission on Accreditation of Hospitals (JCAH) was formed to carry on the program and traditions established by the college.[3]

Currently, the Joint Commission on Accreditation of Healthcare Organizations (Joint Commission) evaluates and accredits more than 18,000 health care organizations and programs, including hospitals, health care networks, and health care organizations that provide ambulatory care, behavioral health, home care, and long-term care services. As the oldest and largest accrediting body in health care, the Joint Commission acts as an independent not-for-profit organization.[4]

Additional accrediting organizations have emerged in response to the rapidly developing health care market. Physicians, purchasers, and consumers of health care have urged that systems be established to ensure quality of care and to provide comparative data related to outcomes. Organizations established with the purpose of responding to demands for accountability in the managed care sector include the Utilization Review Accreditation Commission (URAC) and the National Committee for Quality Assurance

(NCQA). Also providing voluntary accreditation programs to health care organizations are the Accreditation Association for Ambulatory Health Care (AAAHC), the American Osteopathic Association (AOA), the Commission on Accreditation of Rehabilitation Facilities (CARF), and the American Medical Association (AMA) through its American Medical Accreditation Program (AMAP).

Purpose of Accrediting Organizations

Health care accrediting organizations have an underlying purpose and commitment to contribute to the quality of patient care, and they have designed standards to promote quality. AAAHC states that "improving the quality of medical, surgical and dental care to America's patients is the bottom line goal of this entire exercise in external accreditation."[5] The Joint Commission's ambulatory care standards state, "As the health care field moves toward measuring and improving its performance the [accreditation] handbook provides you with standards that you can use today to assess and improve your own performance. By helping you focus on doing the right things right the first time and every time this resource will support your ongoing performance improvement efforts across the organization, the key to enhancing the quality and value of health care services."[6] Increasingly, health care organizations are being held responsible by numerous outside forces for the quality of care that is provided within them and by the people affiliated with them, whether they are employees or independent providers of care.

Each of the accrediting organizations currently performs on-site surveys to determine compliance with written standards. Although credentialing standards have varying levels in terms of detail, credentialing is an important component of the current health care accrediting organizations. The Joint Commission, NCQA, and AOA have the most definitive credentialing standards. These organizations publish the intent of each standard, as well as scoring guidelines to help health care organizations better understand how to comply with the standard and what will be reviewed during the survey process. Detailed information relating to the survey process is found in individual accrediting handbooks. Each health care organization should have applicable accreditation manuals and handbooks and should refer to those books for detail involving the survey process and compliance factors.

The Impact of Accreditation on Credentialing Activities

One of the major impacts and driving forces behind credentialing activities is the voluntary health care accreditation process. The degree to which accreditation standards address credentialing activities varies significantly between accreditation organizations. Some accrediting organizations have very detailed credentialing standards in addition to prescribing, in varying degrees of detail, how to achieve compliance with the standards. Other accrediting organizations have much less definitive standard requirements allowing more discretion and scope in the implementation of a credentialing program. No matter what an accrediting organization requires in terms of credentialing standards, a health care organization may choose to exceed the intent of the standards and require more detail or scope than its accrediting organization. The purpose of both accrediting organizations and those requesting accreditation is concern for quality patient care. Credentialing standards come into play as a basis for quality. A practitioner or provider who is not qualified or competent will not be able to render quality patient care. Many Joint Commission surveyors and Dennis O'Leary, MD, the president of the Joint Commission, have been quoted as saying that accreditation requirements and standards should not be the only reason an organization performs an activity. Standards are written to support and promote quality patient care. Organizations requesting accreditation should refer to the standards and to the processes in place to comply with those standards in that light.

Individuals who are critics of activities and processes in their health care organization often blame the accrediting process. But an organization should be able to differentiate for these individuals the activities required by the accreditation standards and the activities required by the organization through its bylaws and policies. Often practitioners within an organization are not aware that many of the rules that govern their ability to practice have been developed internally by either the governance of the organization or the governance of the medical staff. Some organizations continue to comply with standards that were originally required by an accrediting agency but are no longer applicable. They may have decided that even though an accrediting agency no longer requires a particular activity, they want to continue the requirement. At times organizations are not aware that the standards have changed and that new options are available. A formal review of compliance with standards should question the need to continue activities for which standards have been changed or deleted. It is always a good idea to review credentialing activities against accreditation standards on a regular basis and choose either to include the reason or need to continue an activity or to revise or delete components of the process and activities.

Organizations That Accredit

Organizations that provide accreditation services to health care include

- Accreditation Association for Ambulatory Health Care (AAAHC)
- Utilization Review Accreditation Commission (URAC)
- The American Medical Association through the American Medical Accreditation Program (AMAP)
- American Osteopathic Association (AOA)
- Commission on Accreditation of Rehabilitation Facilities (CARF)
- Joint Commission on Accreditation of Healthcare Organizations (Joint Commission)
- National Committee for Quality Assurance (NCQA)

Accreditation Association for Ambulatory Health Care (AAAHC)

History. AAAHC was incorporated in Illinois as a not-for-profit corporation on March 22, 1979. Its purpose, as stated in its certificate of incorporation, is to "organize and operate a peer based assessment, education, and accreditation program for ambulatory health care organizations as a means of assisting them to provide the highest achievable level of care for recipients in the most efficient and economically sound manner."[7]

Scope of Services. AAAHC accreditation is available to ambulatory care organizations that meet eligibility criteria. These include ambulatory health care clinics, ambulatory surgery centers, birthing centers, college and university health services, community health centers, dental group practices, diagnostic imaging centers, health maintenance organizations (HMOs), hospital-sponsored ambulatory clinics and surgery centers, multispecialty group practices, office surgery centers and practices, radiation oncology centers, and urgent/immediate care centers.[8]

Core Standards. The core standards of the AAAHC accreditation process are

1. Rights of Patients
2. Governance
3. Administration
4. Quality of Care Provided
5. Quality Management and Improvement
6. Clinical Records
7. Professional Improvement
8. Facilities and Environment

In addition to the core standards there are fourteen adjunct standards specific to specialty services that may be provided in the ambulatory care setting.[9]

Credentialing. Credentials standards are outlined under the governance standard and titled "assignment of credentials."[10]

(American Accreditation Health Care Commission)—Utilization Review Accreditation Commission (URAC)

History. URAC was established in December 1990 by an initiative led by the American Managed Care and Review Association (AMCRA), a trade association for utilization review firms, health maintenance organizations, and provider organizations. In 1994, URAC announced its plan to develop an accreditation program for those health care entities that were ineligible for NCQA accreditation. Its focus between 1994 and 1996 was the evolving utilization review industry. Standards for utilization review were developed and implemented for those organizations applying for voluntary accreditation. Organizations interested in this accreditation include those offering utilization review services, such as HMOs, preferred provider organizations, and other managed care systems. In March of 1997, URAC changed its corporate name to the American Accreditation Health Care Commission, Inc. (AAHCC).[11] The acronym *URAC* is currently being used, and a name change is being considered for late 1998 or early 1999.[12]

Scope of Services. Currently, URAC offers accreditation programs in three areas:

1. provider networks and health plans
2. utilization management
3. workers' compensation and managed care

All organizations offering managed care services are eligible for URAC accreditation, including health maintenance organizations (HMOs), preferred provider organizations (PPOs), physician hospital organizations, (PHOs), independent practice associations (IPAs), physician organizations (POs), single specialty networks, and other managed care entities.[13] A new product line has been developed that will specifically address credentialing in health care networks. This modular program will allow for review of only the credentialing component of an organization.[14]

Core Standards. The five basic areas addressed by the current Provider Network and Health Plan standards of URAC are

1. Participation and Management
2. Utilization Management
3. Quality Management
4. Provider Credentialing
5. Member Participation and Protection

Credentialing. The Provider Network and Health Plan accreditation program includes a core standard for credentialing. The standards for Utilization Management and Worker's Compensation managed care accreditation do not specifically address credentialing. The new modular credentialing accreditation will use the credentialing standards of the Provider Network and Health Plan program.

American Medical Association (AMA)

History. In 1996, the American Medical Association (AMA) house of delegates approved implementation of the American Medical Accreditation Program (AMAP). AMAP is a voluntary, comprehensive accreditation program that measures and evaluates individual physicians against national standards, criteria, and peer performance. The program was to be implemented in some states during 1997, but negotiations with the state medical societies, which were to administer the program, continued in 1998. It is anticipated that only a few programs will be operational by 1999. The AMAP accreditation may be used by hospitals and health plans in the accrediting and/or credentialing of their physicians. Physicians participating in the AMAP program agree to have the results of the review and the accreditation decision available for those health plans and hospitals identified by the physician (if these entities agree to participate in AMAP). Hospitals and plans receive copies of information required by the accrediting organizations, such as the Joint Commission, NCQA, and URAC.

Scope of Services. AMAP plans to survey physicians through their office settings. AMA markets the program as one developed *by* the medical profession *for* the medical profession.

Core Standards. Core standards include

1. Physician Credentials
2. Personal Qualifications (ethics, continuing medical education, peer review, and self-assessment)
3. Environment of Care
4. Clinical Performance and Patient Results[15]

Credentialing. The standards for the AMAP program will be a combination of some of the credentialing standards from NCQA, URAC, and the Joint Commission, in addition to other data that might be required by AMAP. It is anticipated that the program will be rolled out in two phases: phase 1 will include the evaluation of physicians in the areas of credentialing, personal qualifications, and office site visits, and phase 2 will consist of clinical performance and patient care outcomes.[16]

American Osteopathic Association (AOA)

History. The AOA Hospital Accreditation Program began addressing hospitals in 1945. Osteopathic hospitals requesting evaluation and those approved for intern training were inspected on an annual basis. In 1966, Medicare conditions of participation were established, and in 1967, a new program was enacted in which AOA "approved" hospitals were known as "accredited and approved for intern and/or residency training." The division of Hospital Accreditation was organized in 1983.[17] Today, the AOA Health Care Facilities Accreditation Program continues to conduct surveys, has "deemed status" with Medicare, and has published a complete revision of its accreditation requirements, *Accreditation Requirements for Health Care Facilities, 1998–1999.*[18]

In addition to the hospital accreditation program, AOA is currently developing an accreditation program for osteopathic physicians that will be offered as a membership benefit and function in much the same way as the AMA's physician accreditation program (AMAP). It is called the American Osteopathic Accreditation Program (AOAP).

Scope of Services. AOA provides accreditation for laboratories and for hospitals that are

- designated as osteopathic institutions or
- mixed staff, with professional staff composed of both osteopathic and allopathic physicians[19]

AOAP plans to collect and verify information including

- credentials
- continuing medical education credits
- clinical performance measures and patient satisfaction
- office inspections[20]

The areas addressed in the AOA Health Care Facilities Accreditation Program are

1. Organizational Management
2. Support Services
3. Patient Diagnosis and Therapeutic Services

Credentialing. The credentialing standards and requirements are outlined in the "Organizational Management" section and are divided into categories for

- allied health practitioners
- medical staff
- human resources management

Commission on Accreditation of Rehabilitation Facilities (CARF)

History. CARF is a private, not-for-profit organization that grew out of the need for medical and vocational rehabilitation programs to promote quality care for people with disabilities and others in need of rehabilitation. Approximately

10 years before the formation of the commission, two national associations representing providers in the rehabilitation industry began developing standards for their respective memberships. In 1966, the two groups, the Association of Rehabilitation Centers and the National Association of Sheltered Workshops and Homebound Programs, formed CARF.[21]

Scope of Services. CARF accredits rehabilitation programs in long-term care facilities, hospitals, hospital-based skilled nursing facilities, and skilled nursing facilities that provide significant therapy. Each year, separate standards manuals are produced for

- behavioral health
- employment and community services
- medical rehabilitation

CARF has a cooperative accreditation agreement with the Joint Commission to avoid any duplication surveys in organizations accredited by the Joint Commission.

Core Standards. Core standards of the CARF accreditation are

1. Promoting Organizational Quality
2. Promoting Program Quality
3. Promoting Outcome Measurement and Management

There are also specific standards related to comprehensive inpatient categories, spinal cord, pain management, brain injury, and outpatient programs.

Credentialing. When surveying facilities, programs, and/or services, CARF makes no distinction between employees and nonemployees. The various programs require that there be a formal credentialing process but are not prescriptive. Some standards refer to a hospital credentialing process as being acceptable.

Joint Commission on Accreditation of Healthcare Organizations (Joint Commission)

History. The American College of Surgeons was created in 1913, with one of the stated purposes being hospital standardization. Between 1913 and 1916, the college found it necessary to reject 60 percent of the applicants for fellowship because the 50 case records required from each applicant provided insufficient information to determine clinical competence. As a result, a foundation gift was obtained and used to launch a hospital standardization program. The money was used to bring together 300 surgical fellows from every state, as well as 60 leading hospital superintendents, to discuss existing conditions and improvements necessary to ensure proper care and treatment of patients. In 1919, the American College of Surgeons formally established the hospital standardization program. In 1951, the American College of Physicians, the American Hospital Association, the American Medical Association, and the Canadian Medical Association joined with the American College of Surgeons to form Joint Commission on Accreditation of Hospitals, which functioned as an independent, nonprofit organization. In 1959, the Canadian Medical Association withdrew to participate in the development of its own program, and the Joint Commission began to offer the first accreditation to hospitals. The organization has since changed its name to the Joint Commission on Accreditation of Healthcare Organizations to more accurately reflect the growing scope of organizations it accredits.[22]

Scope of Services. The Joint Commission currently offers the following accreditations:

- Ambulatory Care Accreditation, to include outpatient surgery facilities, rehabilitation centers, and infusion centers
- Behavioral Health Care Accreditation (formerly Mental Health Care), for organizations with services including care of individuals with behavioral/mental disorders,

mental retardation or developmental disabilities, and chemical dependency
- Home Care Accreditation, for those organizations that provide home health care, personal care and support, hospice, respiratory therapy, pharmaceutical services, and/or medical equipment services
- Hospital Accreditation, to include general, psychiatric, rehabilitation, children's, and other specialty hospitals
- Long-Term Care Accreditation, for nursing homes and acute care facilities
- Health Care Network Accreditation, for health plans, integrated delivery systems, physician-hospital organizations, independent practice organizations, and other health care delivery networks
- Clinical Laboratory Accreditation
- Preferred Provider Organization Accreditation

Core Standards. Joint Commission standards are classified into three functional areas as applicable to the specific accreditation. The first set of functions is patient focused and includes

1. Patients' rights and organizational ethics
2. Assessment of patients
3. Continuum of care
4. Care of patients
5. Education

The second set, organizational focused functions, includes

6. Improving Organization Performance
7. Leadership
8. Management of the Environment of Care
9. Management of Human Resources
10. Management of Information
11. Surveillance, Prevention, and Control of Infection

Structures with functions apply to some but not all of the accreditations. These include

12. Governance
13. Management
14. Medical Staff
15. Nursing

Credentialing. Location of credentialing standards varies according to the accreditation process. The majority of credentialing standards for hospitals are found in the Medical Staff standards. Those for Ambulatory and Network Accreditation are found in the Human Resources standards.

Standards related to the credentialing process may be found in the functions of

- Medical Staff
- Improving Organization Performance
- Leadership
- Management of Human Resources
- Governance

National Committee for Quality Assurance (NCQA)

History. NCQA was established in 1979 by the Group Health Association of America (GHAA) and the American Association of Foundations for Medical Care (new AMCRA) and was governed by the HMO industry. In 1990, NCQA became a separate, independent entity that focused on external quality review of managed care organizations. In 1996, NCQA introduced its certification program for credentials verification organizations (CVOs) and accreditation for managed behavioral health care organizations. In 1997, the Physician Organization Certification Program was introduced to certify physician organizations.[23]

Scope of Services. Currently, NCQA has accreditation and certification programs for

- Accreditation of Managed Care Organizations
- Accreditation of Managed Behavioral Health Care Organizations

- Certification for Credentials Verification Organization
- Certification of Physician Organizations
- New Health Plan Accreditation

NCQA accredits prepaid managed care organizations such as HMOs, physician organizations, and Medicaid programs that meet the eligibility criteria. Eligible organizations must have a process that is designed to monitor, evaluate, and improve the quality of care provided to their members. They must also have access to necessary clinical information for members, must provide or arrange to provide comprehensive services through an organized delivery system, and must have been in operation for at least 18 months.[24]

The New Health Plan Accreditation is available for health plans less than 18 months old that are required by their corporate office and/or by state regulations to be surveyed.

A CVO is eligible for certification if it is a stand-alone vendor of credentials verification services, a medical society, an independent practice association, a medical group, or other organization that collects and verifies practitioner credentials information. CVOs may be certified for one or all specific credentialing elements (a total of 10). A managed care organization contracting with a NCQA-certified CVO (for all 10 elements) is considered to be compliant with NCQA verification requirements and is not required to perform oversight of certified elements. (Additional information about CVOs and delegation may be found in Chapter 10 of this book.)

The new program of physician organization certification (POC) will work much the same way as the CVO certification. Physician organizations that perform their own credentialing functions will have an opportunity to be certified, and the managed care companies with which they do business will be able to delegate the credentials function without oversight.

Core Standards. Core standards for managed care organizations, managed behavioral health care organizations, and New Health Plan accreditation are

1. Quality Management and Improvement
2. Utilization Management
3. Credentialing and Recredentialing
4. Members' Rights and Responsibilities
5. Preventative Health Services
6. Medical Records[25]

CVO certification elements include

1. application processing
2. board certification/education
3. Drug Enforcement Administration (DEA)/controlled dangerous substance registration
4. hospital privileges
5. license to practice
6. malpractice claims history
7. malpractice insurance
8. Medicaid/Medicare sanctions
9. National Practitioner Data Bank (NPDB) query
10. sanctions against licensure[26]

Physician organization certification elements are the same as the core standards for managed care organization and managed behavioral health care accreditation.

Credentialing. Credentialing has been a core component of NCQA's accreditation program since its inception. The standards are prescriptive and include scoring guidelines. The 1998 NCQA accreditation standards scoring guidelines assign credentialing standards an overall score of 10 percent.

CREDENTIALING STANDARDS OF HEALTH CARE ACCREDITATION ORGANIZATIONS AND PROGRAMS

This section addresses, in general terms, the credentialing standards of health care accreditation organizations and their various programs outlined above. The standards for each organization are not specifically quoted because they may change from year to year. In addition, any organization that is seeking or maintaining accreditation should always reference the most current copy of the credentialing standards. Tables 2–1 and 2–2 at the end of this section outline 1998–99 information for easy reference. Contact information for individual organizations is listed in Exhibit 2–1 at the end of this section.

Accreditation Association for Ambulatory Health Care (AAAHC)

Because ambulatory health care organizations do not have a medical staff organization, AAAHC credentialing standards (listed in the "Governance" section) require that all credentialing provisions and decisions be made by the governing body of the accredited organization. All decisions are to be made on the basis of professional peer evaluations, but the standards are not specific as to how peer evaluations should be carried out.

The standards require "expeditious" processing of applications but are not specific as to time frame. The time frame for reappointment is not specified, but the standards do require that clinical privileges be granted for a specific period of time. AAAHC requires that credentials be verified and is not specific with regard to primary source verification, that is, the issuing source of the credential. The information collected for an evaluation of a candidate must include the basic components of licensure, training and education, description of privileges requested, information acquired by external resources (e.g., NPDB), and information related to liability, claims history, and malpractice insurance.

AAAHC allows delegation of its credentialing activities, but while the information provided by another organization may be used as part of the credentialing process, it cannot be relied upon exclusively. AAAHC does not require the ambulatory care organization to maintain copies of all of the primary source materials. If credentials verification is delegated, the organization can accept a statement by the verifying organization as to the correctness and completeness of information obtained and is not required to maintain copies of primary source materials.[27] (See more on delegation in the section "NCQA Managed Care Organization Accreditation" below.)

Utilization Review Accreditation Commission (URAC)

URAC Health Care Practitioner standards are primarily based on the credentialing chapter of the current National Network Standards of URAC. The standards address credentialing activities for

- structure of the network's credentialing oversight process
- contents of credentialing applications
- requirements for primary and secondary verification of credentialing information
- oversight of delegated credentialing activities

In addition to requiring a credentialing plan, the standards relating to verification indicate whether primary or secondary sources are required or acceptable. Verifications of training, licensure, board certification, liability coverage and claims are outlined. NPDB queries, if any, are also to be obtained, along with professional references (if used), hospital privileges, and disciplinary actions (if any). Recredentialing is required every two years and includes verification of board certification (if expired), liability history since last credentialed, current licensure (state, DEA, state controlled, if applicable), liability insurance coverage, disciplinary actions (state and/or federal), and recent work history. Time frames are identified for applications (no older than one year) and verifications no older than 180 days (except for those of education or hospital privileges).

Delegation and subdelegation arrangements are accepted and defined. Delegation requires a contractual agreement between parties as well as a quarterly status report and annual reviews of credentialing activities to include random audits representing at least 25 percent of the network's entire delegated population.[28]

American Medical Accreditation Program (AMAP)

As part of the AMAP accreditation process, compliance with 10 credentialing standards is reviewed. To obtain accreditation, compliance with 5 is required:

1. medical school graduation (with qualification)
2. current, active unrestricted licensure
3. current, unrestricted DEA
4. lack of disciplinary action within the last five years by licensing or federal agency
5. no record of felony or fraud convictions

Supplemental standards relate to

- training program completion
- board certification/recertification
- professional liability claims experience
- record of disciplinary action in NPDB

An additional section addresses continuing medical education and AMA's Physician's Recognition Award, state requirements, and/or credit in the primary specialty of practice.

American Osteopathic Association (AOA)

American Osteopathic Association (AOA) Health Care Facilities Accreditation Program

Credentialing standards for AHPs, medical staff, and others who are contracted or providing services are outlined in the "Organizational Management" section. Credentialing requirements for osteopathic physicians include

- licensure
- training/education
- current competence
- health status
- information about other facilities where the applicant did or does have privileges, professional liability actions, continuing medical education, insurance, reductions or limitation in privileges or membership at another hospital, and procedure logs with outcomes to support privilege requests.[29]

American Osteopathic Accreditation Program (AOAP)

AOA is considered a primary source for verification of osteopathic physicians for

- residency training
- board certification
- continuing medical education

The proposed AOAP plans to help AOA members demonstrate training and qualifications to managed care plans, using a system much like that of the AMAP program.[30]

Commission on Accreditation of Rehabilitation Facilities (CARF)

CARF standards require an organization to have a credentialing and privileging process for its rehabilitation physicians. The standards require that a mechanism be documented to determine each physician's privileges through a formal credentialing process. CARF does not prescribe how a credentialing process should work, stating only that there must be evidence that the physician being credentialed has expertise in rehabilitation and physical medicine through training or experience. The Human Resource standards state that staff should meet appropriate legal, licensing, registration, or certification requirements established by the respective professional group.[31] Primary source verification is not specified. The *1998 Standards Manual and Interpretive Guidelines for Medical Rehabilitation*[32] requires verification of the background of personnel at the time of hire. The organization is to act on the information received, obtain verification of the accuracy of the information received, and receive information from the NPDB as applicable.[33]

The Physician Services standards require specific credentials for program medical directors. These include board certification, licensure, and demonstrated experience and training. Experience and training are defined as residency in physical medicine and rehabilitation, a related fellowship, or at least two years' experience as a collaborative team member in a comprehensive rehabilitation program.

Joint Commission on Accreditation of Healthcare Organizations

Joint Commission Hospital Accreditation Program

Hospitals were the first organizations to be accredited by the Joint Commission. In general, the additional programs developed by the Joint Commission have used the hospital credentialing standards as a baseline, some adding requirements specific only to that program.

Credentialing standards found in the Medical Staff function section of the accreditation manual describe four criteria on which all credentialing standards are based.

1. current licensure
2. relevant training or experience
3. competence
4. ability to perform the privileges requested[34]

The Joint Commission is very prescriptive about these criteria. The intent of the standards, scoring guidelines, and explanations of what is to be expected when a hospital is surveyed are all given in the accreditation manual. The Joint Commission requires primary source verification for many of the elements contained in the four core requirements. Because the hospital standards require and refer to a defined medical staff organization, the standards are prescriptive regarding peer review for initial appointment and reappointment, as well as requiring involvement by an executive committee. The governing board is designated as the approval authority for all recommendations regarding privileging and membership.

A primary element of the hospital medical staff standards is the requirement for clinical privileging for the specific procedures to be performed and the treatment of specific disease modalities for patients who are admitted. An important element in the credentialing/privileging process is the participation in privileging by the designated medical staff departments (for those hospitals that are departmentalized versus nondepartmentalized). If the hospital is nondepartmentalized, the responsibility of defining privileges and related criteria is delegated to the executive committee acting as a "department of the whole." The standards include provisions for temporary privileges that may be granted for a specific period of time if approved by medical staff and hospital leadership (as defined in the individual organization's bylaws).

The standards do not specifically address "delegation," although they allow credentials verification by an outside source. The information must be evaluated internally, and all decisions with regard to recommendations and approvals are the responsibility of the hospital. The standards include guidelines for the organization's use of an outside agency to acquire the verification components (see Chapter 10 of this book).

Time frames are specified, with initial appointments granted for up to two years and reappointments for medical staff membership and clinical privileges required every two years. (Note: At this writing, the Joint Commission, through its Professional Technical Advisory Committee—Hospital Accreditation Program (PTAC-HAP), is considering a recommendation originating from the National Association Medical Staff Services (NAMSS) to reconsider the reappointment standard and its two-year requirement. It is anticipated that if the reappointment standards are rewritten, some means of ongoing monitoring, evaluation, and update of nonstatic credentials such as license, malpractice insurance, and board certification will still be required in some form.)

Those components for which primary source verification is required are noted in the standards along with other information that is accepted in lieu of primary source verification, namely information from the AMA physician master file and the Federation of State Medical Boards (FSMB).

Finally, the standards require a fair hearing and appeal process that relates in part to any credentialing decisions negatively affecting a practitioner's ability to care for patients independently.

Joint Commission Ambulatory Care Accreditation

The requirements related to credentialing licensed independent practitioners are found in both the leadership and the human resource standards. Because there is no required medical staff organization in an ambulatory care organization, the responsibility for making appointments, reappointments, and granting clinical privileges for licensing independent practitioners falls upon the leadership of the ambulatory care organization. The four core criteria identified in Joint Commission hospital accreditation (current licensure; relevant training or experience; current competence; and health status, or ability to perform) are also required for ambulatory care organizations. The general rules for verification in hospital accreditation standards also apply. Ambulatory care accreditation requires that clinical privileges be reviewed or revised every two years.

The leadership standards address the use of physician assistants to provide anesthesia. Qualifications are listed for these physician assistants, including the requirement that they be supervised by an anesthesiologist or qualified operating physician, dentist, or podiatrist.

Joint Commission Managed Behavioral Healthcare Accreditation

The Joint Commission published a *Comprehensive Accreditation Manual for Behavioral Health Care* in 1997.[35] The credentialing criteria are outlined in the Human Resources (HR) standards. Required components when evaluating a behavioral practitioner's background are

- current license
- training and certificate
- experience
- competence

Joint Commission Healthcare Network Accreditation

Credentialing standards for networks are described in the "Management of Human Resources" chapter of the Joint Commission's *Accreditation Manual for Health Care Networks.*[36] One of the goals of the human resources function is to provide for competent staff, including licensed independent practitioners, who can be obtained through employer-employee relationships, contracts, or other arrangements. The functions of assessing, maintaining, and improving the competence of these individuals are also addressed to include ongoing, periodic competence assessment and evaluating continuing abilities.

The network standards refer to "network leaders" as the formal authority to approve credentialing criteria, appointment, and reappointment. The four core credentialing criteria (listed in the previous hospital accreditation section) are also required. In addition, an applicant is required to provide a chronological work history covering at least the past five years. This requirement is unique to the Network accreditation program.

Because delineated "clinical privileges" are not required in a network environment as they are in hospitals, the network standards require evidence of "ability to perform requested professional activities" as opposed to the "clinical privileges" required in the hospital standards. Additional standards require the evaluation of clinical records in office practices of those sites where practitioners are being considered for reappointment. The practitioner's specific information from performance improvement activities at reappointment is compared to aggregate information.

Standards have been proposed for network accreditation programs to define a process to grant clinical privileges for those licensed independent practitioners who practice in network settings other than the network's components. This may include the physician office setting.

The caps on those standards requiring specific privileges may be lifted by the year 2000. At that time, network accreditation surveys by the Joint Commission will include the review and evaluation of privileges granted to the licensed independent practitioners in non-network settings. For now, surveyors will be looking at the process that organizations are using to define privileges.[37]

Joint Commission Home Care Accreditation

There are no requirements to credential participating practitioners in the Joint Commission's *Accreditation Manual for Home Care*.[38] However, the "Management of Information" section does require that the home care organization verify licensure of the patient's physician from whom orders are accepted. Home care agencies may find that they need to comply with new credentialing requirements of the Health Care Financing Administration (HCFA) conditions of participation even if they are accredited by the Joint Commission. Specific licensure, education, and continuing education requirements are being proposed for home health physicians and other caregivers.[39]

Joint Commission Long-Term Care Accreditation

Human resource standards for long-term care facilities require that an organization have a credentialing process that includes the Joint Commission's four basic criteria (evidence of current licensure, relevant training and/or experience, current competence, and ability to perform privileges requested). The requirements for primary source verification are the same as for hospitals accredited by the Joint Commission. If the facility is owned by a hospital that is accredited by the Joint Commission, verifications done by the hospital are allowed. Either a letter attesting to the verifications or actual copies provided are acceptable. In addition, the practitioner's training, experience, and expertise should match what he or she is doing at the long-term facility. Reappointment is required every two years.[40]

Joint Commission Preferred Provider Accreditation

Preferred provider organization accreditation includes credentialing standards for preferred provider organizations that assume responsibility for the credentialing review of any of the practitioners on their panel. The standards follow the guidelines for hospital accreditation credentialing standards.

National Committee for Quality Assurance (NCQA)

The standards for managed care organizations precede those for the other three types of organizations to be discussed in this section, namely behavioral health care, credentialing verification, and physician organizations. The standards for the managed care organizations are the basis for those used in the other three accreditation and certification programs.

NCQA Managed Care Organization Accreditation

NCQA standards for a managed care organization require a credentialing and a recredentialing process for practitioners and providers practicing within its delivery system. The standards require a designated credentialing committee or other review body that makes direct recommendations regarding credentialing activities. If the review body is a decision-making body, the standards indicate that it is not necessary to delay approval of these practitioners until the recommendation or decision has been reviewed by the governing body.[41] NCQA does not recognize any type of provisional or temporary credentialing based on an incomplete credentials file. Information that is verified/collected for credentialing purposes may or may not require verification from the primary source, and is indicated for each criterion. Information collected and verified includes license, DEA certificate, education and training, status of privileges at a designated hospital (refers to primary admitting facility), board certification as applicable, Medicare and Medicaid sanctions, adequate malpractice coverage, and professional liability claims. The standards are very prescriptive about which sources are acceptable for verifying the information. (See also Chapter 5 of this book for additional information.)

A unique characteristic of the NCQA credentialing standards is the requirement for practitioner attestation on the application verification of the information within 180 days, including the time that a final credentialing decision is made. The standards are also explicit about what information is to be included on the application; reasons for any inability to perform functions, lack of present illegal drug use (or whatever language is used, based on an organization's interpretation of the ADA) requirements history of licensure loss; felony convictions by the applicant and/or loss or limitation of privileges or disciplinary action; and attestation that the application is correct and complete. NCQA requires that additional information be included in the files such as NPDB queries (if applicable), information from the FSMB, and Medicare/Medicaid sanctions. As of April 1997, information on Medicare and Medicaid sanctions is included in the NPDB report. An on-site office visit for all primary care practitioners, including obstetricians/gynecologists, must be completed as part of the initial application process.

NCQA standards require recredentialing at least every two years. In addition to the collection and verification of nonstatic information (license), office site reviews are again required to include primary care practitioners (PCPs) if seeing more than 50 plan members, obstetrician/gynecologists (if they are considered PCPs by the organization), and high-volume specialists, as defined by the organization. The recredentialing process is required to obtain and use three of the following six sources of information as part of individual practitioner review:

1. member complaints
2. information from quality improvement activities
3. utilization management
4. member satisfaction
5. medical record review
6. site visit[42]

As part of the policies for credentialing and recredentialing of physicians, podiatrists, dentists, and chiropractors, the standards include the prerogative of the practitioner to review information submitted in support of his or her application. If any information is received from a verifying source that is different from that submitted by the practitioner, the practitioner is to be notified of that discrepancy and allowed to comment and/or correct any information.

Delegation of the credentials verification process as well as the credentialing decision is allowed. A managed care organization may delegate either or both. Delegation requires a written agreement that describes the delegation activities. If the delegated entity makes credentialing decisions, the managed care organization must retain the right to decline a practitioner or provider. Any part of the credentialing process that is delegated to another organization requires some oversight in the form of an annual audit that includes 5 percent or 50 of the files, whichever is less. An exception to this oversight requirement is described in the CVO certification information.

Credentialing standards also address organizational providers with which the managed care organization intends to contract. Examples include hospitals, home health agencies, and skilled nursing facilities. The requirements to credential these organizations include confirmation that the provider has been accredited by an appropriate organization and holds a current license to provide care. If the provider has not been approved by an accrediting body, the managed care organization must develop and implement standards of participation. Provider information (i.e., current accreditation, licensure) is reconfirmed every three years.[43]

NCQA New Health Plan Accreditation

The credentialing standards and requirements for new health plans follow the guidelines for Managed Care Organization Accreditation.

NCQA Managed Behavioral Health Care Accreditation

Practitioners including psychiatrists, physicians certified in addiction medicine and other nonphysician practitioners who specialize in behavioral health are affected by the behavioral health care credentialing standards. The credentialing standards and requirements follow those of a managed care organization. The one difference in standards is that site visits of intended high-volume behavioral health practitioners are required before these practitioners are accepted into a network.[44]

NCQA Credentials Verification Organization (CVO) Certification

Because CVOs are considered delegated entities, the information and criteria for their certification matches that of the managed care and behavioral health credentialing verification standards. Information verified by the CVO, as well as the attestations signature on the application form, can be no older than 120 days at the time it is forwarded to the managed care organization. This allows 60 days for the managed care organization to complete its review and decision. The 1998 CVO standards address only the verification of information on the application.

NCQA Physician Organization Certification

The credentialing standards for physician organization certification are the same as those for managed care organizations, including the 180-day time frame.

The following guidelines in Tables 2–1 and 2–2 outline initial credentialing and recredentialing activities of the major accreditation organizations. Exhibit 2–1 provides contact information for credentialing organizations.

STATE AND FEDERAL STATUTORY LAWS REGULATING CREDENTIALING

In addition to accreditation and case law, credentialing activities are directed by state and federal laws and regulations.

State Law

There are laws and regulations on a state-by-state basis that involve and affect credentialing activities. It is vital that staff responsible for credentialing activities be informed and current on all requirements for their particular state. Types of laws and regulations that may be applicable include

- antidiscrimination
- any-willing-provider
- licensure
- peer review
- disclosure of selection criteria
- economic profiling

State antidiscrimination laws are often similar to federal antidiscrimination laws and pro-

Table 2–1 Accreditation Guidelines Related to Credentialing Activities

	Joint Commission—Hospitals 1998 Standards	*NCQA—Managed Care 1998 Standards*	*URAC 1997 Standards*	*AAAHC 1998–99 Standards*
Credentialing Program documentation	Most typically delineated in bylaws, rules, and regulations that are adopted by the medical staff and approved by the governing body and that also address • fair hearing and appellate review mechanisms • description of the medical staff organization, including categories of membership Documentation, which may be in the form of bylaws, rules and regulations, or a policy • must specify that the governing body grants membership and privileges following review of recommendations submitted to it by the medical executive committee • must outline the mechanisms used for appointment; required information should include data on qualifications such as licensure and training or experience, and data on actual performance	Must address • scope of practitioners covered • criteria • primary source verification of information used to meet criteria • process used to make decisions • extent of any delegated arrangements • right of practitioner to review information • process for notification if information obtained by MCO differs from that provided by practitioner • right of the practitioner to correct erroneous information • medical director or other directs responsibility and participation in the credentialing program • process to ensure confidentiality	The credentialing plan is to include • purpose and scope of program • committee responsibility • responsibilities of committee members, credentialing staff, and the medical/clinical director • criteria, standards, and requirements • documentation required • levels of review and actions taken at each level • verification of credentials • file maintenance of history of sanctions and disciplinary actions • statement of nondiscrimination • initial and recredentialing P&P • appeals P&P • confidentiality and conflict of interest • process to amend plan • procedures for rejecting a practitioner at time of application • use of outcome performance measures	Not specified

	• must include a description of each mechanism that is detailed enough to permit tracking of the procedural steps • must specify time limits for each step of the process Applicants must be informed of bylaws, rules and regulations and policies regarding the application process, and must agree in writing to be bound by them			
Application	The bylaws, rules and regulations, and policies define the information to be provided by the applicant to include at least • previously successful or currently pending challenges to, or voluntary relinquishment of, any licensure or registration • voluntary or involuntary termination of medical staff membership or voluntary or involuntary limitation, reduction, or loss of clinical privileges at another hospital • involvement in a professional liability action (circumstances specified in bylaws, rules and regula-	Application must be completed to include a statement regarding • reasons for any inability to perform essential function of position • lack of present illegal drug use • history of loss of license and felony convictions • history of loss or limitation of privileges or disciplinary activity • attestation to correctness and completeness of application	Application completed to include • personal information • practice information, including federal tax ID, primary office address, and access and availability information • education, training, work history for last five years • professional and hospital affiliations • licensure, certification, and registration information • professional liability insurance information • professional liability claims history • history of sanctions • disclosure of physical, mental, or substance abuse problem that would impede ability to provide care	Application for initial privileges should provide sufficient evidence of • training • experience • current competence

continues

Table 2–1 continued

	Joint Commission—Hospitals 1998 Standards	*NCQA—Managed Care 1998 Standards*	*URAC 1997 Standards*	*AAAHC 1998–99 Standards*
	tions, and policies); at a minimum, final judgments or settlements		• statement of completeness, veracity, and release of information Application may not be older than 1 year when presented to the credentialing committee	
Scope of program	All medical staff members and all others with delineated clinical privileges that are subject to department bylaws, rules, and regulations	The scope of practitioners is defined by the MCO. It must include but is not limited to • MDs • DOs • DDSs • DPMs • DCs • other licensed independent practitioners with whom it contracts or employs and who treat members outside the inpatient setting	According to the organization's written credentialing plan	Each member of the health care organization, including AHPs
Criteria	The mechanisms designed for appointment provide for professional criteria that are uniformly applied to all applicants for membership and for privileges. The criteria	Must be specified in the credentialing document to include the primary source verification used to meet the criteria	Must be specified in the credentialing plan document	Specific criteria for credentialing and recredentialing are specified by the governing

	constitute the basis for granting membership and privileges and must pertain to • current licensure • relevant training and experience • current competence • ability to perform the privileges requested			body on the basis of the size and complexity of the organization
Primary source verification	Whenever feasible, primary source verification is completed for • licensure • specific training • experience • current competence	MCO verifies with primary source • license to practice • status of clinical privileges at hospital designated as the primary admitting facility • education and training; if board certified, education and training are not verified; if not board certified, highest level of education is verified • board certification, if applicable • history of liability claims	Primary source verification of • medical or other professional license • hospital privileges With the exception of education and hospital privileges, all verification information should be no older than 180 days when presented to the credentials committee	Credentials are to be verified according to procedures established in the bylaws, rules, and regulations
Additional information obtained	The organization is encouraged to consider additional information concerning the applicant from other sources, including the FSMB and AMA master file	Additional information to be included in the credentials file/identified in application: • work history • NPDB report • sanction or limitation on licensure • DEA or CDS certificate • malpractice insurance	Verification by primary or secondary method of • education and training • board certification • professional liability history for past five years • DEA	Information to be obtained for evaluation includes • education and training • peer evaluation

continues

Table 2–1 continued

	Joint Commission—Hospitals 1998 Standards	*NCQA—Managed Care 1998 Standards*	*URAC 1997 Standards*	*AAAHC 1998–99 Standards*
	Hospitals are also required to query the NPDB at time of initial appointment and granting of privileges	• previous sanction activity by Medicare and Medicaid • documentation of a structured review evaluating site (office) • documentation of evaluation of medical recordkeeping practices	• professional liability insurance coverage • disciplinary actions taken under state or federal regulation • work history for past five years	• current state license • DEA • NPDB as applicable • other pertinent information, which may include claims history, license revocation or suspension, probationary status, refusal or cancellation of liability coverage, complaints or adverse action reports, actions related to privileges, conviction of a criminal offense, and problems that might affect ability to practice

Decision-making process	Department directors are responsible for recommending clinical privileges for each member of the department and for determining of the qualifications and competence of department or service personnel who are not licensed independent practitioners and who provide patient care services. The medical executive committee makes recommendations to the governing board, who determines membership and privileges	A credentials committee is designated to make recommendations regarding credentialing decisions. The committee must include representation by practitioners practicing in the MCO. Practitioners are considered to be credentialed after decision of the Credentials Committee.	A credentials committee is established that has authority for credentialing and is accountable to the governing body or to corporate management. Membership must include representatives from quality management, network management, and utilization management departments. Review process includes review by staff, identification of files requiring additional review, review of summary information by committee, approval or disapproval based on criteria, documentation of all actions, and notification of applicant	The governing body, either directly or by delegation, makes initial appointment, reappointment, and assignment or curtailment of privileges on the basis of professional peer evaluation
Term of credentialing cycle	No more than two years	Two years	Two years	Privileges are granted for a specified period of time
Other	Recommendations for appointment to the medical staff and granting of privileges includes information provided by a peer or peers of the applicant	MCO must have P&P for altering the conditions of participation with the MCO on the basis of issues of quality of care and service, including an appeal process	A medical director or clinical director must be responsible for clinical aspects of the program The network must employ, contract, or appoint an adequate number of credentialing staff who are knowledgeable about credentialing	Credentials file must be maintained for each member to include • initial application • reapplication • verifications • privileges granted

continues

Table 2–1 continued

Joint Commission—Hospitals 1998 Standards	*NCQA—Managed Care 1998 Standards*	*URAC 1997 Standards*	*AAAHC 1998–99 Standards*
	P&P must outline initial and ongoing assessment of organizational providers Delegation requires oversight of the delegated activity, a mutually agreed upon document, retention of the right to approve, terminate, or suspend individual practitioners or providers, evaluation of delegated agency's capacity to perform, and an annual evaluation of activities	Credentials file must include • application that is signed and dated • copies of licenses, residency certificate, board certification, DEA, proof of liability insurance, and claims history • verifications • results of database queries • professional references • correspondence • documentation of actions Network must ensure confidentiality of information	• other pertinent, required information The process may not be fully delegated

Note: MCO, managed care organization; P&P, policy and procedure; FSMB, Federation of State Medical Board.

Source: Data from *1998 Hospital Accreditation Standards,* Joint Commission on Accreditation of Healthcare Organizations; *MCO Surveyor Guidelines for the Accreditation of Managed Care Organizations,* 1998, National Committee for Quality Assurance; *1997 National Health Care Practitioner Credentialing Standards,* Utilization Review Accreditation Association; and *1998–1999 Accreditation Handbook for Ambulatory Health Care,* AAAHC.

Table 2–2 Accreditation Guidelines Related to Quality and Recredentialing Activities

	Joint Commission—Hospitals 1998 Standards	*NCQA—Managed Care 1998 Standards*	*URAC 1997 Standards*	*AAAHC 1998–99 Standards*
Terminology used in relation to quality measurement activities	PI&E—Performance Improvement and Evaluation	QIM—Quality Improvement and Management	QM—Quality Management	Quality Management and Improvement and Quality of Care Provided
Quality activities	The executive committee makes recommendations to the governing body pertaining to the participation of the medical staff in organizational performance improvement activities	The QIM program provides the framework within which the MCO assesses and improves the quality of clinical care and the quality of service	Outcome and performance measurements used in credentialing/ recredentialing of health care practitioners are included in the written credentialing plan as applicable	Appointment/ reappointment and clinical privileges are based upon professional peer evaluation
Who is responsible for quality activities	When medical staff clinical departments exist, the director of each department is responsible for • clinically related activities • continuing surveillance of the professional performance of all individuals in department who have delineated clinical privileges • recommending clinical privileges for each department member • continued assessment; improvement of quality of care and services	The credentialing committee or other review body designated by the governing body is responsible for evaluation of information as it relates to recredentialing. The QI function is responsible for collection and sharing information related to • credentialing • member complaints • UM • medical records review	Not defined in standards	The governing board may be involved directly or may delegate to a peer-based quality management and improvement program

continues

Table 2–2 continued

	Joint Commission—Hospitals 1998 Standards	*NCQA—Managed Care 1998 Standards*	*URAC 1997 Standards*	*AAAHC 1998–99 Standards*
	Each department makes recommendations regarding professional criteria for privileges that pertain to current competence and the ability to perform the requested privileges When these departments do not exist, the Executive Committee takes this responsibility.			
Who is reviewed	Current competence is evaluated for all medical staff members and all others with delineated clinical privileges that are subject to department bylaws, rules, regulations, etc., at time of reappointment	The scope of practitioners is defined by the MCO. It must include but is not limited to: • MDs • DOs • DDSs • DPMs • DCs • other licensed independent practitioners with whom it contracts and employs and who treat members outside the inpatient setting	As defined in the organization's written credentialing plan	Each member of the health care organization, to include AHPs

When/how often activity occurs	Every two years as part of recredentialing Continuous assessment and improvement of quality of care and services	Every two years as part of recredentialing Ongoing development of practitioner's profile	As defined in the organization's written credentialing plan	Every two years as part of reappointment Peer evaluation of current competence
How reviewed	Department chair evaluation Individual case review (peer review) Profiles Outcome studies Other PI activities	Profiles QI activities Peer review	Not defined in standards	Not defined in standards
What is reviewed	Demonstration of current competence is based upon • results of performance improvement activities • peer recommendation • department or clinical service recommendation PI functions requiring medical staff participation include • medical assessment and treatment of patients • use of medications • use of blood and blood components • use of operative and other procedures • efficiency of clinical practice patterns	Performance monitoring information collected to reappraise professional performance, judgment and clinical competence must include at least three of the following six sources: • member complaints • information from QI activities • UM • member satisfaction • medical record reviews • site visits	Not defined in standards	The standards specify specific quality improvement activities but do not require that results be incorporated into the reappointment review

continues

Table 2–2 continued

	Joint Commission—Hospitals 1998 Standards	*NCQA—Managed Care 1998 Standards*	*URAC 1997 Standards*	*AAAHC 1998–99 Standards*
	• significant departures from established patterns of practice • education of patients and families • coordination of care • accurate, legible, timely completion of medical records Appraisal for reappointment is based on ongoing monitoring of information concerning • professional performance • judgment • clinical or technical skills			

Note: QI, quality improvement; UM, utilization management; MCO, managed care organization; PI, performance improvement.

Source: Data from *1998 Hospital Accreditation Standards,* Joint Commission on Accreditation of Healthcare Organizations; *MCO Surveyor Guidelines for the Accreditation of Managed Care Organizations,* 1998, National Committee for Quality Assurance; *1997 National Health Care Practitioner Credentialing Standards,* Utilization Review Accreditation Association; and *1998–1999 Accreditation Handbook for Ambulatory Health Care,* AAAHC.

Exhibit 2–1 Contact Information Credentialing Organizations

Accreditation Association for Ambulatory Health Care, Inc. (AAAHC)
9933 Lawler Avenue
Skokie, IL 60077-3708
Telephone: 847-676-9610
Fax: 847-676-9628

American Accreditation Health Care Commission/Utilization Review Accreditation Commission (URAC)
1130 Connecticut Avenue, NW, Suite 450
Washington, DC 20036
Telephone: 202-296-0120
Fax: 202-296-0690
Web site: http://www.urac.org

American Medical Accreditation Program (AMAP)
c/o American Medical Association
515 North State Street
Chicago, IL 60610
Telephone: 312-464-4817
Fax: 312-464-5706
Web site (American Medical Association): http://www.qmo_assn.org

American Osteopathic Association (AOA)
142 East Ontario Street
Chicago, IL 60611
Telephone: 312-280-5800
Fax: 312-280-3860
Web site: http://www.am_osteo_assn.org

Commission on Accreditation of Rehabilitation Facilities (CARF)
4891 East Grant Road
Tucson, AZ 85712
Telephone: 520-325-1044
Fax: 520-318-1129
Web site: http://www.carf.org

Joint Commission on Accreditation of Healthcare Organizations
One Renaissance Blvd.
Oakbrook Terrace, IL 60181
Telephone: 630-792-5000 (main telephone number)
Customer Service: 630-792-5800
Web site: http://www.jcaho.org

National Committee for Quality Assurance (NCQA)
2000 L Street, NW, Suite 500
Washington, DC 20036
Telephone: 202-955-5697
Web site: http://www.ncqa.org

hibit discrimination on the basis of color, race, national origin, religion, age, or physical disability. These laws may affect a preapplication process and regulate the wording of questions on an initial application. Antidiscrimination laws should also be considered in relation to interviews of applicants.

Some states have enacted any-willing-provider laws that apply to managed care organizations. These laws vary from state to state, but many require managed care organizations to consider all classes of practitioners (e.g., podiatrists or nurse midwives) as potential participants. Any-willing-provider laws are developing as physicians push to prevent managed care plans from dropping or excluding practitioners and providers. Professional qualifications and compliance with preestablished criteria are still applicable under these laws, and currently no state requires a managed care organization to accept every physician meeting criteria.[45]

All states have hospital and medical practice licensure laws. Hospital licensure may include regulatory provisions for credentialing criteria. Some states indicate that accreditation by the Joint Commission constitutes compliance with hospital licensure law and preempts state inspection. Others, such as California, complete a state inspection in conjunction with the the Joint Commission survey. Medical practice laws govern issuance and maintenance of practitioner licenses. The credentialing professional must know how to access information related to licenses for purposes of verification and determination of any action related to the license. Some states have different departments or agencies responsible for different types of practitioners. Others have consolidated licensure activity.

Peer review statutes have been enacted in most states. The purpose of these laws is to grant some form of immunity to practitioners who participate in peer review activities (even though the Health Care Quality Improvement Act of 1986 provides protection at the federal level). Legal counsel for each health care organization usually interprets state-applicable peer review statutes and provides information specific to individual organizational function. The credentials committee activities, minutes, and credentialing process may be protected under state peer review regulation.

Disclosure of selection criteria is required of managed care organizations in some states. And some states have enacted regulations related to the "economic profiling" of practitioners. This is a term that is used when consideration is given to financial information.

Federal Law*

Several federal laws affect credentialing activities. These include

- Americans with Disabilities Act[46]
- Health Care Quality Improvement Act
- Medicare Conditions of Participation
- Health Maintenance Organizations Act[47]

Americans with Disabilities Act

See Chapter 9 of this book for details about the impact of the Americans with Disabilities Act on credentialing activities.

**Source:* This section was written by Christina Wiggins-Giles, MS, CMSC, Principal, Medical Staff Solutions, Pepperell, Massachusetts.

Health Care Quality Improvement Act (HCQIA)

HCQIA was enacted in 1986. A "credentialing" case, *Patrick v. Burget*[48] in Astoria, Oregon, provided the impetus for this legislation. Dr. Patrick was a member of an orthopedic group practice in Astoria. He practiced at the only hospital in town with the other members of his group. Dr. Patrick decided to leave the group and establish his own practice. The hospital initiated a peer review investigation into Dr. Patrick's cases at the hospital, and the resulting action was the removal of his privileges. He sued the members of the group practice and the hospital on the basis of antitrust, claiming that the other physicians conspired to terminate his privileges. As it was the only hospital in the town, loss of hospital privileges would drive him out of practice. This case became very well known because it established, for the first time, that negative peer review and credentialing processes are not immune from federal antitrust laws. The defendant physicians had argued that their conduct should be immune from liability because of the state statutes that govern the procedures that hospitals may use to grant or deny staff privileges.[49] The final decision in *Patrick v. Burget* was made in 1988, when the U.S. Supreme Court held that a credentialing decision made in accordance with the state of Oregon's peer review statute was not a state-mandated action because the state did not actively supervise such activity. Thus, the participants in the peer review process were not granted immunity from antitrust liability.[50]

The legislation that initiated the HCQIA was successful because the U.S. Congress was convinced that medical malpractice litigation in the country was increasing and that there was a need to improve the quality of medical care by protecting the public from incompetent physicians. Congress believed that effective professional peer review keeps incompetent practitioners from moving from hospital to hospital or state to state. Thus, the act built into its proposed wording incentives and protection for those physicians and dentists who participate in peer review activities as long as certain requirements are fulfilled. The intent of the legislation was to improve the quality of health care by encouraging hospitals, state licensing boards, and other health care entities, including professional societies, to identify and discipline those who engage in unprofessional behavior and to restrict the ability of incompetent physicians, dentists, and other health care practitioners to move from state to state without disclosure or discovery of their previous damaging or incompetent performance.

The act encourages and supports professional review activity by physicians and dentists by providing immunity from private damages in civil suits under federal or state law, providing that the professional review action regarding professional competence or professional conduct of a physician or dentist has been taken

- in the reasonable belief that the action was in the furtherance of quality health care
- after a reasonable effort to obtain the facts of the matter
- after adequate notice and hearing procedures are afforded to the physician or dentists involved or after such other procedures as are fair to the physician or dentist under the circumstances
- in the reasonable belief that the action was warranted by the facts known, after such reasonable effort to obtain facts and after meeting the notice and hearing requirement[51]

The immunity provided by the act applies only to "professional review actions" that are based on the competence or professional conduct of a physician if that conduct affects or could adversely affect the health or welfare of a patient or patients. A disciplined physician or dentist has the right to sue; however, the court may award attorney's fees and court costs to the defendants if the suit is determined to be frivolous, unreasonable, without foundation, or in bad faith.

National Practitioner Data Bank (NPDB). The second component of HCQIA is the NPDB, a national information clearinghouse that collects and releases certain information related to the professional competence and conduct of physicians, dentists, and, in some cases, other health care practitioners. The NPDB represents the portion of the law that was included to enhance professional review activities by making certain information concerning medical malpractice payments and adverse actions available to eligible entities and individuals.

Data bank information is an important supplement to the credentialing process because of the information it contains (see below). It is intended to augment the process, not replace it. Information that can be obtained includes:

1. *Medical Malpractice Payments*—Entities, including insurance companies, making a payment as a result of a medical malpractice action or claim must report that action to the NPDB.
2. *Licensure Action Taken by Licensing Boards*—Disciplinary action based on reasons relating to a physician's or dentist's professional competence or conduct taken by a state licensing board is reported by that licensing board.
3. *Action Taken against Clinical Privileges*—Adverse actions taken against a physician/dentist's clinical privileges based on professional competence or conduct as a result of a peer review action. These include
   - a denial, revocation, suspension, limitation in clinical privileges that is in place for longer than 30 days
   - a surrender or restriction of clinical privileges by a physician/dentist currently under investigation
4. *Action Taken against Society Membership*—Adverse actions taken against membership of a physician or dentist when action was reached through a formal peer review process and when the action was based on the practitioner's professional competence or professional conduct[52]

It is important to remember that the information obtained from the NPDB is to be used only as a basis for further investigation. The NPDB report should supplement other information collected during the credentialing process such as the findings from performance improvement studies, peer recommendations, verification of training and experience, and relationships with patients and colleagues. The information on the report should not be used as the sole basis for an action. Users of the information in the NPDB reports need to educate themselves concerning the information contained in the report. For example, settlement of a medical malpractice claim may occur for a variety of reasons that do not necessarily reflect negatively on the professional competence or conduct of a practitioner. A payment made in settlement of a medical malpractice action or claim should not be construed as a presumption that medical malpractice has occurred.

Confidentiality of Data Bank Information. Information reported to the NPDB is considered confidential and may not be disclosed to any unauthorized person or entity. The reports may not be shared with another health care entity. Each health care entity entitled to query the NPDB establishes an authorized agent, either someone in the organization or a CVO representative, who is authorized to query the NPDB on behalf of the organization.

A hospital or managed care organization may disclose the information received to those individuals/review bodies within the organization that have a responsibility to perform a review of credentials. Both the individual who receives the report and those officials of the hospital or managed care plan responsible for the review of the information (i.e., Credentials Committee, Medical Executive Committee, Medical Director, CEO, or Board of Trustees) are allowed access. However, if there is a delegated credentialing agreement, or if a CVO is used, *an individual query for each organization must be completed.* Queries may not be shared between organizations. The report received by or for an organization may be used only by or for that organization.

The Office of Inspector General of the Department of Health and Human Services (HHS) has been delegated the authority to impose civil monetary penalties on those who violate the confidentiality provisions of this law. For *each* violation of confidentiality, a civil money penalty of up to $10,000 can be levied. In any case in which it is determined that more than one party was responsible for improperly disclosing confidential information, a penalty up to the maximum $11,000 limit can be imposed against each responsible individual, entity, or organization.[53]

Access to Data Bank Information. NPDB reports are available to

1. Hospitals requesting information
   - concerning a practitioner on the medical staff,
   - concerning a practitioner to whom they have granted clinical privileges, or
   - with respect to professional review activity
2. Health care entities (including hospitals)
   - that have entered or may be entering employment or affiliation relationships with a practitioner to which the practitioner has applied for clinical privileges or appointment to the medical staff, or
   - with respect to professional review activity
3. Practitioners requesting information about themselves
4. Boards of medical examiners or other state licensing boards
5. Attorneys or individuals representing themselves under limited circumstances
6. Persons or entities requesting information in a form that does not identify any particular entity or practitioner[54]

Neither the general public nor medical malpractice payers may currently receive information from NPDB.

Eligible Entities. Entities entitled to participate in NPDB must certify their eligibility to the NPDB in order to report to and/or query the NPDB. A health care entity must provide health care services *and* engage in professional review activity through a formal peer review process for the purpose of furthering quality health care in order to be considered eligible.

Summary. To be eligible to *query* the NPDB, an entity must be

- a board of medical examiners or other state licensing board,
- a hospital,
- a professional society that engages in professional review activity through a formal peer review process, or
- another health care entity that provides health care services *and* engages in formal peer review activity through a formal peer review process.

To be eligible to *report* to the NPDB, an entity must be

- authorized to make a medical malpractice payment for the benefit of a health care practitioner, or
- a state licensing board, or
- a health care entity that takes an adverse clinical privileging action as a result of professional review, or
- a professional society that takes an adverse membership action as a result of professional review.

A hospital is the only health care entity that is required to query the NPDB. It must query

- at the time that a physician, dentist, or other health care practitioner applies for a position on its medical staff or for clinical privileges at the hospital, *and*
- every two years on all physicians, dentists, and other health care practitioners who are on its medical staff or who have clinical privileges at the hospital, *and*
- whenever a practitioner requests additional privileges or temporary privileges.[55]

Hospitals are the only health care entities with mandatory requirements for querying the NPDB. The biennial query can be made at the time of reappointment and clinical privilege redelineation, but at least every two years. Although it is common practice to query at the time of reappointment, there is no requirement to match the two activities. Hospitals must also query the NPDB when a practitioner requests additional privileges or expansion of current privileges or submits an application for temporary privileges. Hospitals may query any time they wish with respect to professional review activity.[56]

Failure To Query. Failure to query as required by the guidelines may give a plaintiff's attorney, or a plaintiff representing him- or herself, access to NPDB information on that practitioner for use in litigation against the hospital.[57] Failure to report by hospitals and other health care entities is subject to an investigation by the Secretary of HHS. If HHS determines that a health care entity has substantially failed to report information in accordance with Title IV requirements, the name of the entity will be published in the *Federal Register*, and the entity will lose the immunity provisions of Title IV with respect to professional review activities for a period of three years, commencing 30 days from the date of publication in the *Federal Register*.[58]

Help from NPDB. HHS publishes a *National Practitioner Data Bank Guidebook*[59] that includes all the information required to understand who can access and how to access the NPDB. The guidebook includes the most commonly asked questions and answers relevant to how the NPDB works and what to do when faced with a particular situation concerning a practitioner. The NPDB may be reached through its NPDB Help Line: 1-800-767-6732. The NPDB Help Line is staffed weekdays, except federal holidays, between 8:30 A.M. and 6:00 P.M. (5:30 P.M. Fridays) Eastern Time and offers recordings on frequently asked questions seven days a week, 24 hours a day (Figure 2–1).

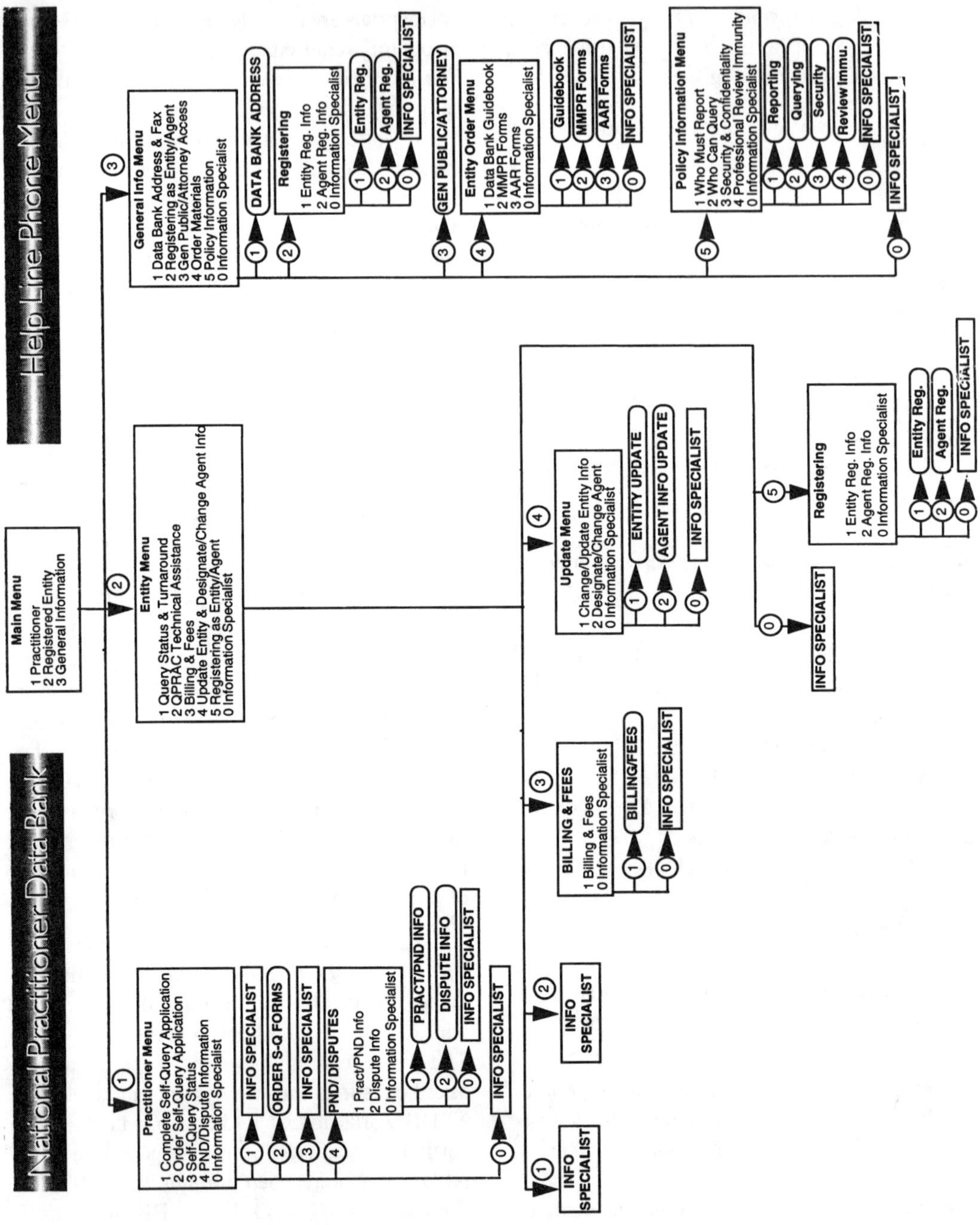

Figure 2–1 NPDB Help Line Phone Menu. *Source:* Reprinted from Department of Health and Human Services, Health Resources and Services Administration.

The Data Bank Help Line assists users with

- entity registration
- electronic funds transfer account registration
- agent designation
- submission of complete and accurate reports and queries
- compliance with federal regulations
- technical questions relating to QPRAC software
- obtaining the *NPDB Guidebook*, entity registration materials, the current version of QPRAC software and *QPRAC Users' Manual*, fact sheets on various topics, and other materials such as the NPDB annual report, the newsletter, and any forms currently in use.

Accessing NPDB. An eligible health care entity may access NPDB (submit queries) using free NPDB software called QPRAC. Entities submit electronic queries to the NPDB via modem or via diskette by mail. Paper queries are no longer accepted by the NPDB. Responses to modem submission of queries are transmitted to the querying entity via the same data transmission network. Responses to diskette submissions are mailed to the querying entity at its address of record in the NPDB computer system.

QPRAC (version 3.0 or higher) functions on any IBM-compatible PC operating under MS-DOS with a minimum of 2 megabytes of available RAM or MS Windows with a minimum of 4 megabytes of RAM. The software operates on personal computers with a hard drive and a floppy disk drive. QPRAC software is available only on 3½-inch high density diskettes.[60]

Query Fees. Fees are charged for all queries to the NPDB except for self-queries by practitioners. The query fee is based on the cost of processing requests and providing information to eligible entities. As of March 1998, fees are

- *electronic query*: payment by credit card (MasterCard or VISA) or EFT (electronic funds transfer), $4.00 per query; payment by check, $8.00 per query
- *diskette query:* payment by credit card or EFT, $7.00 per query; payment by check, $11.00 per query[61]

In the near future, diskette queries will be discontinued, and all queries will have to be submitted electronically. The NPDB accepts payment by one of two electronic payment methods: credit card (Master Card or VISA), EFT, or by check.

Health Care Financing Administration (HCFA) Medicare Conditions of Participation

HCFA is the government organization that oversees the Medicare program. The program, enacted as a result of the Title XVII of the Social Security Act of 1965, provided health care benefits for Medicare (the aging population) and Medicaid (the poor population) patients. For hospitals to receive reimbursement for these programs, they are required to comply with federal regulations called the conditions of participation.[62] If a hospital is accredited by the Joint Commission or AOA, it may be granted "deemed status." Deemed status indicates that an organization meets Medicare's conditions of participation and that no additional surveys are required. However, HCFA does conduct validation surveys for a small percentage of hospitals that have been recently surveyed by the Joint Commission in an effort to substantiate compliance.

Currently the conditions of participation regulations specifically address credentialing standards, and all conditions are addressed in some form by the Joint Commission in its medical staff standards. The regulations require the governing body to establish criteria for the selection of members of a medical staff and state that members must have the appropriate character, competence, training, experience, and judgment. The regulations also require the medical staff to conduct periodic appraisals of medical staff members.

Credentialing elements of the Medicare conditions of participation include requirements for

- procedures for determining that personnel providing patient care services are properly licensed
- verification of licensure
- appointment by the governing board
- a quality assurance program that includes evaluation of contracted services
- periodic appraisal of medical staff members
- credentials review at time of appointment
- medical staff organization and accountability
- bylaws that address duties, qualification, and privileges of each medical staff category

Hospitals that are not Joint Commission accredited are subject to oversight by the state surveying agency (department of health), which acts as an agent of HCFA.[63]

In late 1997, proposed changes to the conditions of participation were published. Some relate to medical staff organization, board certification status, and supervision of certified registered nurse anesthetists (CRNAs). At the time of this writing, no changes have yet been enacted. All new and revised regulations are available in the *Federal Register*, an official government publication available through subscription.

Health Maintenance Organizations Act

On December 19, 1973, the president signed the Health Maintenance Organization Act, giving official federal support to HMOs and subjecting them to regulating control.

The key points of the act are that it

- provides federal recognition of HMOs as legal entities
- authorizes funds to encourage HMO development ($325 million over a five-year period)
- prescribes standards for HMO organization and the services offered
- overrides some state legislation that is a barrier to development of HMOs
- requires most employers to offer their employees the opportunity to select a qualified HMO as an alternative to their present employees' health benefit plans if approached by an HMO that serves the area where their employees live (known as the *dual option* or *multiple option*)[64]

A manual was produced in 1989 by HCFA that outlined operating rules and procedures for HMOs applying for federal qualification under the Act. Credentialing is addressed as part of the Quality Assurance Program requirements. The introduction to credentialing states:

> The judgement and technical skills of individual practitioners provide the foundation of the delivery system. A QA program is not effective in fostering quality health care for enrollees unless it assures that the physicians and other health care professionals are qualified to perform their services and that facilities are safe and well equipped. Thus, a program to validate the credentials of physicians and other health care professionals applying to participate in the HMO is a sign of organizational commitment to quality.[65]

Requirements include

- recruitment of physicians with demonstrated performance consistent with the HMO's standard of practice
- identification of indicators of quality
- risk-adverse evaluation of such factors as malpractice payments, convictions, suspensions, and sanctions
- NPDB query
- recredentialing
- validation of credentials
- evaluation of facilities in which patients receive care
- medical recordkeeping evaluation

BYLAWS AND CONTRACTS AS THE LEGAL BASIS FOR ACTIVITIES AND DECISIONS*

Bylaws and contracts also form a basis and provide direction for credentialing activities.

Hospital Medical Staff Bylaws

The majority of medical staff members, governing bodies, and hospital administrators concur that medical staff bylaws are binding. Some state courts have held that the bylaws are a contract or are legally binding only if they say so. A number of states have recognized that medical staff bylaws create a contract between the hospital and the medical staff and may be enforced as such. Decisions supporting the idea of medical staff bylaws as a contract have been made in Maryland, Iowa, Texas, Illinois, Wisconsin, Missouri, Tennessee, Maine, Indiana, Alaska, and South Dakota. However, courts in several other states, including Ohio, Georgia, and New York, have not recognized medical staff bylaws as contracts.[66] Many medical staffs function as if the bylaws are a binding contract; however, most bylaws do not contain language to the effect that they constitute a contract. In 1995, the Organized Medical Staff Section (OMSS) of the AMA passed a resolution to strengthen medical staff bylaws. The AMA/OMSS issued sample bylaws language, as did many of the individual state medical societies. The AMA's language proposes that "In consideration of the mutual promises and agreements contained herein, these bylaws, when approved by the medical staff and adopted by the hospital governing body, constitute a mutually binding contract that cannot be unilaterally amended by any party." Hospital bylaws should address the effect of the medical staff bylaws and whether they constitute a binding contract between the hospital and the members of the medical staff. This is an important issue and should be included in all of the appropriate medical staff documents.

Medical staff bylaws usually document the credentialing process for appointment, reappointment, and initial granting and renewal of privileges. Many bylaws outline the process in general and include specifics included in rules and regulations, policies, or a medical staff credentialing manual. The current trend is to reference the credentialing process in the bylaws and detail the process in a credentialing manual. This has been found to be effective since the amendment process for any change in bylaws is often cumbersome or time consuming. The Joint Commission hospital standards allow credentialing information to be included in the bylaws, rules, and/or policies. Exhibit 2–2 contains a sample table of contents for a medical staff credentialing manual.

The Joint Commission hospital accreditation standards require that medical staff bylaws include provisions for

- an executive committee
- a fair hearing and appeals mechanism for individuals with clinical privileges
- mechanisms for corrective action
- categories of medical staff membership[67]

The current Joint Commission accreditation manual should be consulted for details relating to these requirements.

Contract Issues in Hospitals

An additional "issue" relevant to hospital medical staff bylaws has to do with whether a contracted physician or practitioner is governed by the provisions in his or her contract with the hospital or by the medical staff bylaws. Hospitals may execute employment or exclusive practice contracts with practitioners. Many contracts include a statement that if medical staff membership is required, loss of membership will result in termination of the contract. They should also address the effect of termination of the contract on membership and privileges.

**Source:* This section was written by Christina Wiggins-Giles, MS, CMSC, Principal, Medical Staff Solutions, Pepperell, Massachusetts.

Exhibit 2–2 Sample Table of Contents for a Medical Staff Credentialing Manual

continues

Exhibit 2–2 continued

Courtesy of Buchanan and Associates Consulting, Morrison, Colorado.

Exclusive contract arrangements are used for a variety of reasons: to improve the efficiency of the hospital, to standardize procedures, to increase patient satisfaction, to ensure availability of specific services, to contain costs and to improve the quality of care. Court decisions regarding exclusive contracts generally recognize the discretion of the hospital board and its responsibility for the hospital to be conducted as a business. Courts around the country have recognized that a hospital governing body has the right to enter into exclusive contracts that will preclude competing physicians who are otherwise qualified from obtaining staff privileges in the affected specialty area.

Issues that should be discussed and defined concerning exclusive contracts include the following:

1. What role does the medical staff have in determining the need for an exclusive contract, the continuation of such a contract, or the transfer of an exclusive contract from one contracting entity to another?
2. Do the bylaws and the contract contain language to address termination/reduction of privileges due to the expiration or termination of a contract?
3. Will the medical staff members who have exclusive contracts be allowed a fair hearing procedure relevant to maintaining privileges for other than quality-of-care reasons if the contract is terminated?
4. Does the wording used in the medical staff bylaws relating to exclusive contracts coincide with the wording in the exclusive contract and ensure that the rights of the medical staff member with privileges are consistently protected in both documents? The bylaws should also make it clear that when a contract and bylaws conflict, the contract will prevail.
5. Will the hospital need to close certain services/departments if an exclusive contract with a physician group or specific physician is executed?

Managed Care Agreements/Contracts

Managed care organizations usually execute agreements with the physicians, practitioners, and providers included in their panel or network. The agreement (usually called a participating physician agreement or contract) outlines the understanding between the parties and imposes legal support and requirements for both. The agreement may include compensation and rate-setting provisions and usually includes language requiring compliance with the policies and procedures of the managed care organization. A common provision acknowledges that the managed care organization may impose obligations regarding quality of care provided to members and has the right to oversee and review quality of care. The agreement may spell out credentialing criteria and requirements, may include them as an attachment, or may simply reference a required compliance with "Plan Credentialing Policies and Procedures." Inclusion of credentialing requirements in an agreement may allow a managed care organization to terminate a physician who breaches the agreement without benefit of hearing or due process.

Common credentialing requirements included in managed care agreements are

- maintenance of license to practice medicine
- possession of a current federal DEA registration number with a local address
- status as a medical staff member in good standing at a managed care organization contracted hospital (or a statement identifying who will provide coverage if the practitioner is not a member of a hospital medical staff)

- possession and maintenance of malpractice insurance

The agreement should describe in detail all duties and responsibilities of participating physicians and list the services and care to be rendered in the office setting. Each managed care organization develops its own office practice criteria that may include requirements related to

- availability of services (office hours, evening and weekend coverage, telephone coverage, wait time)
- minimum medical record and documentation standards
- Occupational Safety and Health Administration (OSHA) compliance
- ability to accept and serve new patients

Agreements that detail credentialing requirements and physician rights and responsibilities support the credentialing process. If language is not specific, or if it refers only to current policy and procedure, the difficulty of requiring compliance with criteria is increased.

NOTES

1. 211 N.E.2d 253 (Ill. S. Ct. 1965).
2. 42 U.S.C. §§1101–11152.
3. *Briefings on Credentialing* (Marblehead, MA: Opus Communications) 5, no. 12 (December 1996).
4. Joint Commission web site, http://www.jcaho.org.
5. *Accreditation Handbook for Ambulatory Health Care, 1996–97* (Skokie, IL: Accreditation Association for Ambulatory Health Care).
6. *Accreditation Manual for Ambulatory Care, 1996–97,* Vol. 1 (Oakbrook Terrace, IL: Joint Commission on Accreditation of Healthcare Organizations).
7. *Accreditation Handbook for Ambulatory Health Care,* 79.
8. *Accreditation Handbook for Ambulatory Health Care,* 7.
9. *Accreditation Handbook for Ambulatory Health Care,* 5.
10. *Accreditation Handbook for Ambulatory Health Care,* 21–22.
11. "AAHCC/URAC General Information Packet" (Utilization Review Accreditation Association, Washington, DC, 1997).
12. The Commission, URAC representative telephone interview, October 1998.
13. "AAHCC/URAC Accreditation" (Utilization Review Accreditation Association, Washington, DC, 1997, brochure).
14. Utilization Review Accreditation Association, Washington, DC, June 1997.
15. *American Medical Accreditation Program: Accreditation Standards and Criteria* (Chicago: American Medical Association, 1997.
16. *Briefings on Credentialing* (Marblehead, MA: Opus Communications), 5, no. 12 (December 1996).
17. G. Reuther, Reprinted from "AOA Hospital Accreditation on Program Special Report," *DO* (January 1991).
18. *Accreditation Requirements for Health Care Facilities, 1998–1999* (Chicago: American Osteopathic Association).
19. *Accreditation Requirements.*
20. *Medical Staff Briefing* (Marblehead, MA: Opus Communications) (March 1998), 7–8.
21. *The CARF History* (Tucson, AZ: Commission on Accreditation of Rehabilitation Facilities, 4).
22. S. Lindsey and C. Orsund-Gassoit, *Medical Staff Management* (Gaithersburg, MD: Aspen Publishers, Inc., 1990).
23. P. Kongstvedt, *Managed Health Care Handbook,* 3rd ed. (Gaithersburg, MD: Aspen Publishers, Inc., 1996), 604.
24. *1998 Standards for Accreditation of Managed Care* (Washington, DC: National Committee for Quality Assurance).
25. *Standards for Accreditation of Managed Care.*
26. *Standards for Certification of Credentials Verification Organizations* (Washington, DC: National Committee for Quality Assurance, 1998).
27. *Accreditation Handbook for Ambulatory Health Care, 1998–1999* (Skokie, IL: Accreditation Association for Ambulatory Health Care).
28. *National Health Care Practitioner Credentialing Standards* (Washington, DC: Utilization Review Accreditation Association, 1997).

29. *Accreditation Requirements for Health Care Facilities, 1998–1999.*
30. *Accreditation Requirements for Health Care Facilities, 1998–1999.*
31. Commission on Accreditation of Rehabilitation Facilities representative, telephone interview, September 1998.
32. *Standards Manual and Interpretive Guidelines for Medical Rehabilitation 1998* (Tucson, AZ: Commission on Accreditation of Rehabilitation Facilities).
33. Commission on Accreditation of Rehabilitation Facilities representative, telephone interview, September 1998.
34. *1998 Accreditation Manual for Hospitals* (Oakbrook Terrace, IL: Joint Commission on Accreditation of Healthcare Organizations, 1998).
35. *Comprehensive Accreditation Manual for Behavioral Health Care 1997* (Oakbrook Terrace, IL: Joint Commission on Accreditation of Healthcare Organizations).
36. *1997 Accreditation Manual for Health Care Networks* (Oakbrook Terrace, IL: Joint Commission on Accreditation of Healthcare Organizations).
37. *Accreditation Manual for Health Care Networks,* 75.
38. *Accreditation Manual for Home Care* (Oakbrook Terrace, IL: Joint Commission on Accreditation of Healthcare Organizations, 1995).
39. *Credentialing across the Continuum* (Marblehead, MA: Opus Communications) (April 1997), 11.
40. *Credentialing across the Continuum* (Marblehead, MA: Opus Communications) (February 1997), 12.
41. *Standards for Accreditation of Managed Care,* 145.
42. *Standards for Accreditation of Managed Care,* 170.
43. *Standards for Accreditation of Managed Care,* 177.
44. *Standards for Accreditation on Managed Behavioral Health Care Organizations (Interim Version)* (Washington, DC: National Committee for Quality Assurance, 1996).
45. B. Strama, "Credentialing and Managed Care Organizations: The Legal Issues" (presentation at the NAMSS Institute, Kansas City, MO, March 1997).
46. Pub. L. No. 101–336.
47. Health Maintenance Act of 1973, 42 U.S.C. § 300 et seq.
48. 108 S. Ct. 1658 (1988).
49. G. Pozgar, *Legal Aspects of Health Care Administration* (Gaithersburg, MD: Aspen Publishers, Inc., 1996), 140.
50. Pozgar, *Legal Aspects,* 668–669.
51. *National Practitioner Data Bank Guidebook,* Pub. No. HRSA-95-255 (Rockville, MD: U.S. Department of Health and Human Services, 1996).
52. *National Practitioner,* C-1.
53. *National Practitioner,* NPDB News, February 1998, 3.
54. *National Practitioner,* A-5.
55. *National Practitioner,* D-1.
56. *National Practitioner,* D-2.
57. *National Practitioner,* D-1.
58. *National Practitioner,* D-11.
59. *National Practitioner.*
60. *National Practitioner,* D-8.
61. *National Practitioner,* G-1–G-2, *NPDB Newsletter* (February 1998).
62. 42 C.F.R. 482.12 (ah) (6).
63. *Medical Staff Briefing* (Marblehead, MA: Opus Communications, 1996), 11.
64. Health Maintenance Organization Act of 1973, 42 U.S.C. § 300 et seq., Pub L. No. 93 222.
65. HCFA A-Pub 77, Title 13, Public Health Service Act.
66. J. Hall and K. Rieger, "Aligning the New Health Care System: Physicians Hospitals, Plans and Management Organizations" (paper presented at the National Health Lawyers Association, Oklahoma City, OK, March 1997).
67. *1998 Accreditation Manual for Hospitals.*

CHAPTER 3

Credentialing in Hospitals

OVERVIEW

This chapter will cover only those credentialing processes that relate to hospitals. This information specific to verification of each component in the application and reapplication process can be found in Chapter 5. Additional information specific to privileging and proctoring can be found in Chapter 6. This chapter will discuss processes used in credentialing practitioners that are based upon applicable accreditation standards as well as industry standards. The chapter also includes who is credentialed, when individuals are credentialed, roadblocks that may cause a need for additional documentation and/or evaluation, how information is requested, review and approval process, and how hospitals respond to requests for information.

Credentialing in hospitals has evolved over the years. As discussed in Chapter 1, over the last 30 years or so there have been many changes in the industry. We have seen a greater sophistication in technology that has added to the efficiency of the credentialing operations. There has been an increase in requirements from federal, state, and accreditation organizations, and the industry has to keep learning what the expectations are externally as well as adapting internal policies, procedures, and bylaws to coincide with all of the regulations and accreditation standards. The credentialing process has, in many cases, become more cumbersome because of the increase in requirements. At the same time, the quality of credentialing processes has increased information available for review, and better technology is available. There is more accountability as different individuals or groups of individuals are included in the evaluation and approval process. The accountability has also increased as federal, state, and accreditation requirements stipulate additional verifications or evaluations to be sought and reviewed.

Although procedures for processing credentialing components vary greatly from organization to organization, the concepts are basically the same in any hospital. Any physicians or other practitioners eligible to apply for medical staff membership and/or clinical privileges and any other licensed independent practitioners or unlicensed allied health professionals (AHPs) who may be defined in the hospital's plan of providing services must go through a credentialing/approval process. Some hospitals have a medical staff plan that in collaboration with the hospital defines the services to be provided in the hospital and the classifications of practitioners who will be allowed to apply and provide patient care services. Those so classified may include AHPs, who may fall into one of several categories defined by the hospital and medical staff.

The components of hospital credentialing include

- initial appointment (preapplication is optional)
- reappointment (every two years)

- privileging (or defined scope of services for those nonmedical staff members who may be required to have physician supervision and not to act independently in the services they provide)
- ongoing monitoring and evaluation
- due process (used when adverse recommendations are made or actions taken)

In the initial appointment and reappointment process, completion of an application and attestation that information provided is correct and current are required, as well as the gathering of verification to support the information on the application, evaluation, and final action. Assignment of clinical privileges is based on request by the applicant, determination that criteria related to the clinical privileges requested have been met, evaluation of any supportive documentation, recommendation, and action. The ongoing evaluation (e.g., reappointment) includes data collection as defined by the organization and review and action at any time that a questionable pattern of care or trends or a sentinel event involving an individual is identified.

Some new trends in the 1990s may have begun in the 1980s but are more prominent now. One is the increased use of external organizations or companies to collect verification information for the hospitals. These include credentials verification organizations (CVOs) of all types and may even include a hospital system centralized credentialing office created in an effort to reduce duplication. Another trend is "express credentialing," which uses a fast-track method of reviewing "clean" files and signing them off individually as opposed to waiting for each committee and/or board meeting to occur. Express credentialing is discussed later in this chapter. Centralized verification is discussed further in Chapter 10. As will be evident in this chapter, there are numerous ways to process a file for appointment, reappointment, or privileging. Organizations must choose the credentialing method that works best for them on the basis of their needs, staffing, budget, and other resources.

ACCREDITATION—JOINT COMMISSION AND AMERICAN OSTEOPATHIC ASSOCIATION

Hospitals are primarily accredited by either the Joint Commission on Accreditation of Heathcare Organizations (Joint Commission) or the American Osteopathic Association (AOA).

The Joint Commission offers voluntary accreditation programs for acute care hospitals as well as specialty-type hospitals and for all of the programs and/or organizations that may be affiliated with hospitals, such as ambulatory care, home health, and long-term care. The AOA's Healthcare Facilities Accreditation Program (also voluntary) surveys acute care hospitals and several other health-related organizations that are primarily osteopathic. Some hospitals providing Medicare and Medicaid services may choose to be surveyed by the state component of the Health Care Financing Administration (HFCA) in lieu of any accreditation by either of the two voluntary accreditation programs mentioned above. Additional information on these and other accreditation programs is found in Chapter 2. Because the vast majority of hospitals are accredited by the Joint Commission, references to accreditation standards in this chapter refer to the Joint Commission.

Accreditation standards serve as a basis for developing hospital-specific language in medical staff bylaws, rules and regulations, and policies and procedures to ensure that only qualified practitioners gain access to provide hospital patient care and that their patient care activities are monitored and evaluated on an ongoing basis. Hospitals usually expand upon these required standards to put in place a quality credentialing program specific to their needs in terms of patient care services offered.

CRITICAL DOCUMENTS AND ELEMENTS IN THE CREDENTIALING PROCESS

Numerous documents and elements in the credentialing process are critical for providing a quality credentialing program. They include

- bylaws of the medical staff organization
- rules and regulations
- credentials policy and procedure manual
- delineated clinical privileges
- allied health manual
- corrective action/fair hearing plan
- file content and maintenance
- data management system

Bylaws of the Medical Staff Organization

The bylaws define the formal organization of the medical staff including its structure and responsibilities within each defined area of the medical staff organization. It is the "what" of the organization. From those bylaws, any rules, policies, procedures, or guidelines are developed to more fully elaborate on how the organization will function—that is, the "how," the "when," and the "where." Every hospital medical staff organization is required to have bylaws. The Joint Commission standards outline all of the necessary components to be included. The organization may define additional components that are unique to that organization and need to be defined in a formal document.

Hospitals do not have to follow a standard format when organizing their medical staff bylaws. Some hospitals have a very comprehensive set of bylaws that include all of the requirements that the Joint Commission or AOA standards state must be included in bylaws, rules, or policies. Other hospitals have a very brief set of bylaws (often less than 30 pages) and include areas of procedural requirements in separate policy manuals or plans. The current trend is to reduce the size of the bylaws document itself and attach supplemental documents or plans. One reason that hospitals have for a division between a short set of bylaws with the attached separate manuals is that the voting process for amendments to the bylaws has been traditionally cumbersome, requiring a ballot to the medical staff. If hospitals keep the credentialing manual or fair hearing plan separate, the procedure for making any revisions in the supplemental documents is generally a recommendation for approval at the executive committee level. They become effective once approved by the board. Also, in many hospitals, the information contained in the medical staff bylaws is considered to be more or less permanent and to require little change throughout the years, and the information that may be subject to change according to current industry standards or accreditation requirements is put in the form of "working" documents separate from the actual bylaws.

A word of advice about bylaws of the medical staff organization is that hospitals should be certain that the medical staff is following the information outlined and required in the medical staff bylaws and associated documents. One of two options is suggested. Either the leadership of the medical staff organization must work to support and enforce the bylaws, or the medical staff organization must change the bylaws to reflect what is actually being practiced. During the accreditation survey process, surveyors will compare the written document to actual practices, and the two need to be in sync. More important, when legal action is pending (fair hearing or lawsuits), the organization will be scrutinized to determine that bylaws/related documents were followed as written.

The following areas within medical staff bylaws are related to the credentialing process:

- qualifications for medical staff membership
- categories of medical staff
- medical executive committee
- medical staff departments
- credentials committee

Qualifications for Medical Staff Membership

The bylaws will define the membership of the medical staff organization by stating who is eligible to apply for medical staff membership.

There are two components to hospital credentialing. One is qualifications for medical staff membership, and the other is qualifications for clinical privileges. The credentialing process is necessary for either of these components. In other words, it is possible for a physician or other practitioner as defined by the medical staff bylaws to apply for medical staff membership and/or clinical privileges. All individuals who are going to be members of the medical staff will also have clinical privileges. One exception is physicians who are retired honorary or emeritus members. Another may be administrative staff: by definition, they usually do not have clinical privileges, but they can maintain their medical staff membership (as discussed further in this chapter). Any individual who has clinical privileges only and not medical staff membership is usually classified as temporary, as locum tenens (see Chapter 6), or as an AHP. The medical staff membership component differs from the clinical privileges component in that it involves "citizenship" privileges: in other words, involvement by an individual in an organization that allows him or her the opportunity to vote, serve on committees, chair a department, serve as an officer of the medical staff, or, possibly, take on duties of medical administration. Such prerogatives of membership are defined in the medical staff bylaws and can vary from hospital to hospital.

The bylaws will define what types of practitioners are eligible for medical staff membership. We have come a long way from the days when medical staff membership was offered only to MDs or DOs. When there were more osteopathic hospitals, DOs were not frequently members of the staff of allopathic hospitals, and vice versa, but today there is a mixture of MDs and DOs on medical staffs, and DDSs from general dentists to oral surgeons are generally considered members of the medical staff. In many hospitals, podiatrists are now members of the medical staff. In specialty hospitals such as psychiatric hospitals, psychologists may qualify as medical staff members.

It is not necessary to have admitting privileges to be a member of the medical staff. For example, radiologists or pathologists are members of the medical staff, but by definition of their specialty, they do not generally have admitting privileges. The same is true for psychologists. They can be members of a medical staff of a hospital that has psychiatric services, but they will not necessarily have admitting privileges. Most states do not license psychologists for admitting privileges at this time. However, in California, where the psychologist's license does allow admitting privileges, hospitals must decide if their criteria will include admitting privileges. Some of the aforementioned specialists may actually end up as members of an allied health staff as opposed to a medical staff. Again, the bylaws are going to define who qualifies for medical membership and clinical privileges and who qualifies for clinical privileges only (e.g., allied health staff).

Categories of Medical Staff

Medical staff organizations define categories of membership based on varying degrees of citizenship privileges, tenure on the staff, clinical activities, or other nonclinical criteria. As part of the credentialing process, medical staff members are assigned a membership category. Hospitals use a variety of medical staff categories to define different categories of medical staff members within the organizational structure. Some hospitals still use the more traditional terminology for their categories; other hospitals have changed the names of the categories and have added some newer categories to reflect variances in practice patterns for medical staff members that will be discussed further in this section. Typical titles commonly used for medical staff categories are *provisional, courtesy, ancillary, associate, active, administrative, consulting, affiliate, honorary, emeritus, retired, locum tenens, resident, fellow, house staff,* and *student*. The complexity of the medical staff organization may also determine how many categories of membership will be defined.

To generalize the types of categories that a hospital may choose to define for its membership, we have chosen to discuss specific characteristics of certain categories without assigning specific category titles (e.g., *active, courtesy*), since title definitions vary so much. Again, organizations may choose to consolidate some of these groups or expand to have more categories.

A hospital can define a category specifically for new medical staff members, or these members can be assigned a category on the basis of other things such as anticipated activity level or a particular affiliation with a hospital. Some hospitals use the term *provisional* in front of another category name to indicate that the individual is new to the staff. The bylaws will define the specific period of time that an individual can have this designation or remain in an initial appointment category (no longer than two years per Joint Commission).

Some hospitals differentiate physicians who either are more actively involved at the hospital or have been on the medical staff for a certain period of time. Hospitals can categorize physicians according to a hierarchy whose top level is what most term *active staff.* This term usually indicates that an individual has a high degree of patient activity (as defined) in the hospital and/or has been on the staff for a period of time. The bylaws define how much time is required in the "step" categories to attain different levels (e.g., *provisional* to *associate* to *active*). The active category often includes more "citizenship" privileges, such as right to vote, hold office, or be eligible for department chairmanship, or admit, and may include other preferential benefits that other staff categories do not have, such as convenient operating room time, lower staff dues, and admitting priority. Some medical staff bylaws allow members to initially be appointed to this level. Bylaws often require that a physician have a minimum number of patient contacts per year to maintain or obtain this category level. Some hospitals have an affiliate-type category for those who may not have an acute practice but who have clinic activity (associated with the hospital), must have an affiliation to comply with a managed-care contract, need a referral, and/or have a consultation practice only.

A category of limited clinical activity can be defined for those medical staff members who do not practice primarily at a given hospital. Numbers of patient contacts can be limited for these categories. Categories for limited activity do not usually permit the opportunity to vote, hold office, or hold any other leadership position such as committee or department chair. The emergency department call list may or may not stipulate a requirement for this category depending upon how the medical staff organization views emergency call participation (as a privilege or as a nuisance). This category may also be used to assign to practitioners who, for whatever reason, cannot meet the requirements of more active categories. Such practitioners are placed in this category either permanently or until they can again meet the requirements for a more active category (e.g., by increasing patient activity). This category may be limited to those practitioners who perform consultations only or to those who primarily hold administrative positions.

For different reasons, practitioners may decrease their activity at a hospital to the point that they no longer have any patient contacts. Some hospitals will place them in a holding category (inactive) and give them an opportunity (usually a year) to have some patient contacts before they consider the lack of activity a voluntary resignation. If that happens, the practitioner can usually reapply later should his or her practice patterns change. Hospitals that have no minimum activity requirements will not need this type of category.

The following practitioner characteristics should be considered in defining categories, taking into consideration whether they apply to the medical staff organization:

- provision of specific services on a consulting basis, with or without active involvement in the organization
- expertise that is not provided locally
- admitting privileges
- involvement with the medical staff organization that is medical administrative with or without clinical privileges
- level of activity within the hospital
- former service on the active staff; now retired from clinical practice
- special designation by the medical staff for outstanding contributions for someone no longer actively involved
- reduced obligations (emergency department call, committee appointments, etc.) following service on staff for a defined period of time; and has current active service

- enrollment in a postdoctoral training program (residents or fellows) in a teaching institution; no eligibility for another category; license or registration with the appropriate licensing board
- possession, for whatever reason, of clinical privileges for a specific period of time but normally no active practice at the hospital (or possibly in the process of applying for permanent membership and privileges)

Other qualifications may be added to the above list, but this is an example of the types of information to be defined and assigned to particular categories of medical staff.

Nonclinical privileges that may be attached to different categories of practitioners may include voting, holding office (chief of staff or president, chief-elect, secretary, etc.), priority admitting status, no admitting, committee membership, committee chairmanship, department or section chairmanship or other officer position, level of patient activity and/or admissions, participation in hospital-sponsored continuing medical education, and emergency department call.

Medical Executive Committee

The only medical staff committee required by the Joint Commission is the executive committee. The Joint Commission standards outline the functions of the executive committee. The standards for the executive committee that pertain to credentialing (which should be defined in the bylaws) include making recommendations to the governing board for its approval that relate to

- the mechanism used to review credentials and to delineate clinical privileges
- recommendations of individuals for medical staff membership
- recommendations for delineated clinical privileges for each eligible individual
- participation of the medical staff in organizational performance activities
- mechanisms by which medical staff membership may be terminated
- mechanisms for fair hearing procedures
- acting on reports and recommendations from medical staff committees, clinical departments, and assigned activity groups[1]

Medical Staff Departments

Medical staff departments play a crucial role in the credentialing process as well. Again, the Joint Commission outlines responsibilities for the departments relative to credentialing. The standards indicate the department leadership role, although in larger organizations the department chair will often use other members of the department in the credentialing review and recommendation process. Specific standards that relate to departmental obligations for credentialing include

- recommending to the medical staff the criteria for clinical privileges in the department
- recommending clinical privileges for each department member
- conducting continuing surveillance of the professional performance of all individuals with clinical privileges in the department
- assessing and improving the quality of care[2]

If there are no medical staff departments, the executive committee as a whole carries out these functions.

Credentials Committee

Although not a required committee by accreditation standards, many hospitals have a credentials committee to facilitate the credentialing review function. The committee is primarily involved with the evaluation of initial appointments and reappointments, and requests for change or additions in staff categories and/or clinical privileges; it may also be involved in investigation processes for medical staff members, or funneling of peer review information to the medical executive committee. Because a credentials committee is charged primarily with credentialing activities, it often has more time than an executive committee to thoroughly evaluate and investigate information surrounding requests for appointment, reappointment, or other changes in privileges. The bylaws or policies define the composition of the credentials committee, which may be a representation of the major services provided in the hospital and may or may not include department leadership. It is recommended that members of the credentials committee be different from those who serve on the executive committee so that no member is evaluating and voting twice on any individual. The credentials committee is discussed further in Chapter 7. The credentials committee function can also include the development of forms, policies, and procedures that relate to any component of the credentialing processes; these forms are then forwarded and reviewed by the medical staff leadership (executive committee, department leadership).

Rules and Regulations

The rules and regulations cover the specifics of patient care that is provided within the organization. General requirements still found in most medical staff rules and regulations include

- specific provisions for medical care
- admission requirements
- consultations or patient care
- patient discharge information
- autopsy protocol

Medical Records

The medical records section is contained in most rules and regulations and outlines the requirements for the dictations, informed consent, progress and postop notes, orders, and so forth, that are required in the Joint Commission's management-of-information standards. This section will also contain information concerning delinquent medical records (i.e., records not completed within the time frame required). There is usually a notification/reminder process detailed in this section of the rules and regulations. Some processes include a suspension of a practitioner's privileges if the delinquencies are not corrected in a timely manner. Medical record delinquency information is often used at the time of reappointment when physician activity is being reviewed for consideration of reappointment.

Department-Specific Rules and Regulations

In hospitals that have departments, many departments have their own rules and regulations and/or policies and procedures. Often the departmental rules and regulations are included as an appendix to the general rules and regulations and address those issues that are specific to each department and may vary from department to department. It is important that departmental rules not supersede general medical staff rules and regulations or the medical staff bylaws. However, the medical staff bylaws may direct each department to develop rules with regard to emergency call coverage. Therefore, each department's rules and regulations would outline what that department requires in terms of emergency department call by its members. The departmental rules and regulations may also contain information with regard to criteria for specific privileges that need to be met before a physician can be considered for those privileges. The criteria may define additional documentation that is required to apply for certain privileges. Any rules that apply in general to the entire medical staff should be located in the general rules and regulations, and again only those items that are specific to departments should be contained within departmental rules and regulations.

Credentials Policy and Procedure Manual

As stated earlier, the credentialing requirements and procedures are often contained in a medical staff credentialing policy and procedure manual as opposed to being described in detail in the medical staff bylaws. If a hospital has a medical staff credentials policy and procedures manual, reference should be made to it in the bylaws. Sample language might state, "Credentialing will be done according to policies and procedures that are outlined in the medical staff credentialing policy and procedure manual, as appended to the bylaws." As with any plan or manual that is appended to the bylaws, there should be some statement in the bylaws as to how such plans or manuals will be reviewed, revised, and approved. Changes may be recommended by the executive committee to the governing board for approval or may be amended at any regular general staff meeting without a previous notice. These options eliminate the cumbersome amendment process associated with amendments for the bylaws. Regardless of the process used, the governing board must always be the final approval body. As with the medical staff bylaws, neither the medical staff nor the governing body may unilaterally amend, approve, or create bylaws-related documents.

If the medical staff credentialing procedures are outlined in a policy and procedure manual, the same table of contents can also be used to develop the credentialing section of the medical staff office policy and procedure manual, which contains the detailed procedures for carrying out that which is required by the medical staff manual.

Identify Required Procedures

Policies and procedures are developed to give structure to the process and to identify specific activities and responsibilities. A policy is a statement of fact or a requirement that outlines a process that must be followed or a standard that should be maintained. The policy statement may be one sentence or several paragraphs.[3] A procedure is a set of instructions that describes how a policy will be achieved. Procedures do not exist without a policy statement. The procedure details how a process will be followed and should list the easiest or most productive set of activities that will result in effective performance.[4] Policy and procedure formats are frequently identified by the organization, and a standard format is followed by all departments. A detailed table of contents should outline all of the required procedures for any credentials-related activity within the hospital. The major components of such a policy and procedure manual should contain the initial appointment, granting of clinical privileges, and reappointment. Some fair hearing plans are included in the credentialing manual and others are separate. See Exhibit 2–2 in Chapter 2 for a credentialing manual's table of contents.

It is important to be consistent with all processes concerning any credentialing procedures. Therefore, the more detailed a plan can be, the more easily the procedures can be carried out in the same manner for each individual medical staff member or prospective medical staff member. This is especially important when potential adverse recommendations are made—for example, when a fair hearing process is requested in that the approved process that is outlined must be followed to protect the medical staff organization from accusations that the approved process was not followed or consistent.

The medical staff office policy and procedure manual that contains all of the credentialing procedures should include the forms, letters, flowcharts, and so forth associated with each process. It is important to keep this information updated, to follow the procedures consistently, and to review the manual periodically to be sure it meets the needs of the medical staff organization.

A good way to create a medical staff office credentialing policy and procedure manual is to elaborate on the related items from the bylaws and/or the medical staff credentials policy manual and begin a table of contents similar to the one shown in Exhibit 2–2. Include all related information and forms for each area, and create a table of contents that reflects the information collected. As procedures are added or deleted, be sure to update any of the manuals where this information is found.

Identify Process Steps

It is recommended that flowcharts of the processes and steps be developed that include time frames and accountability for each step. A flowchart is an effective tool because it includes each step of the process. It is also an effective tool for educating anyone with involvement or interest in the credentialing process. Flowcharts can identify major steps (macro flowcharts) or may be very detailed, identifying all possibilities (micro flowcharts). It may be easier to create a macro flowchart with the major steps and then to go back and fill in all of the decision trees and other related steps for each process. Flowchart examples are included later in this chapter. As mentioned later in the next section, any credentialing process defined for AHPs needs to be outlined in detail either in the rules and regulations or in an allied health manual so that there is consistency in the processing of these individuals for appointment and reappointment or for the granting of clinical privileges. Included in the written policies and procedures should be flowcharts to assist in the understanding and education of each process defined. Figure 3–1 is a sample initial application flowchart.

Identify Required Documents

Processes described in the medical staff credentials policy and procedure manual will refer to numerous documents. These will more than likely be explained in more detail in the medical staff office policy and procedure manual. The most common are

- preapplication packet
  - introduction letter
  - criteria outline
  - request for application
  - response letter
- application packet
  - cover letter, including requirements and checklist of attachments
  - application form
  - delineation of clinical privileges and criteria
  - attestation (may be included in the application form)
  - release of liability (also used for recredentialing; may be included in the application form)
  - letters for second request or additional information
- information and verification
  - letters requesting information (accompanying questionnaire optional)
  - letters requesting verification (accompanying questionnaire optional)
- analysis and decisions
  - documentation of department, committee, and board action
  - letters to applicant about board action
- reappointment
  - cover letter
  - reappointment application or update information forms (software summary sheet)
  - activity profile
  - clinical privilege delineation
- other
  - tracking status of applications
  - file completion checklist
  - proctoring forms
  - temporary privilege forms

Allied Health Manual

Since most AHPs are not members of the hospital medical staff, policies and procedures specific to AHPs can be defined in a separate allied health manual. Reference should be made in the bylaws to such a manual. A manual for AHPs can look very similar to that for the medical staff, although AHPs will not necessarily be afforded all of the rights and privileges of medical staff members, so there will be some differences. For example, AHPs generally are not assigned different categories (e.g., active, courtesy) according to their activity level in the hospital but are credentialed for privileges or through a job description. They do not have officers, department chairs, voting rights, or emergency department call for the most part. However, there should be some categorization of the AHPs allowed to prac-

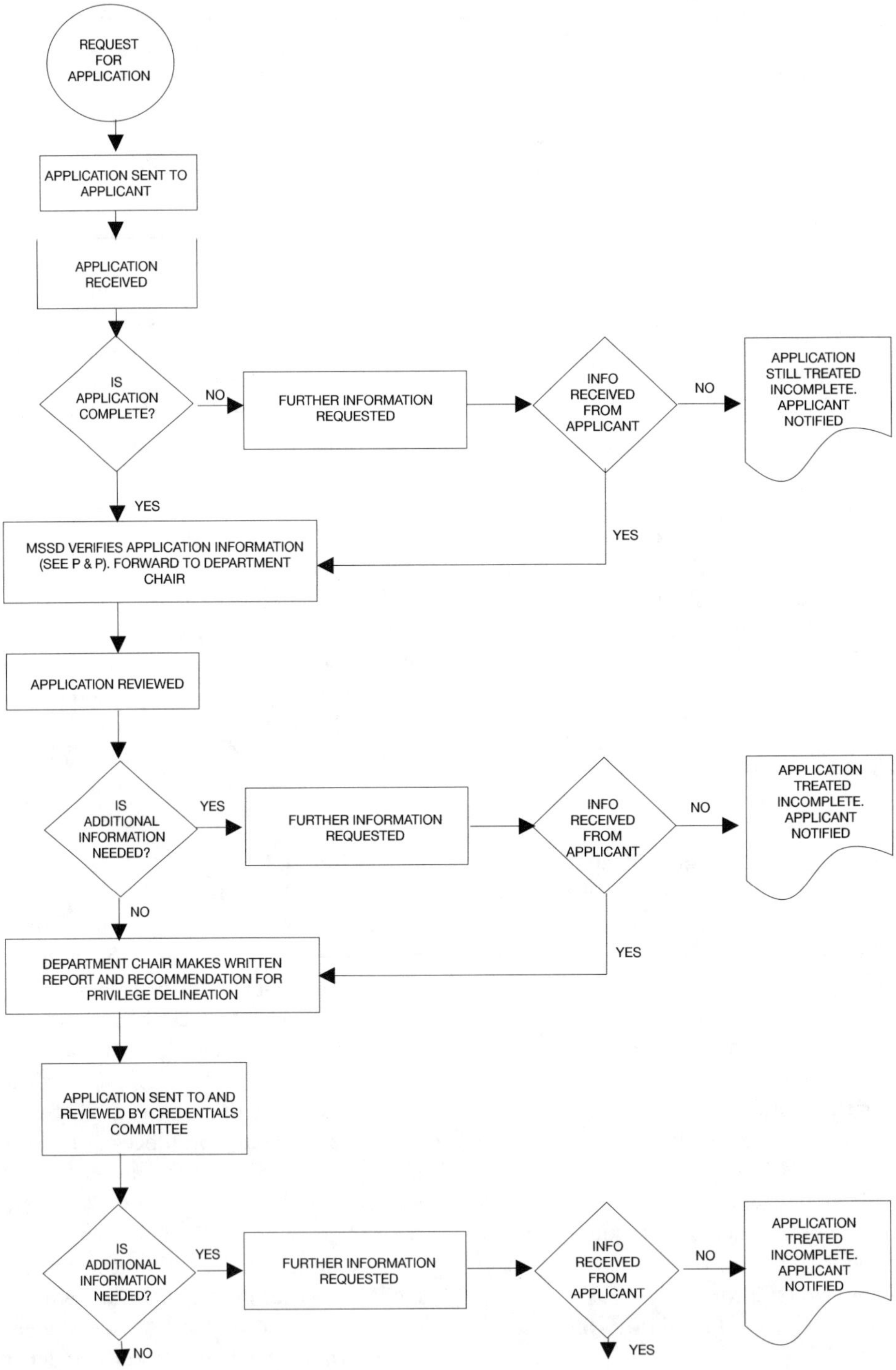
REQUEST FOR APPLICATION
APPLICATION SENT TO APPLICANT
APPLICATION RECEIVED
IS APPLICATION COMPLETE?
NO
FURTHER INFORMATION REQUESTED
INFO RECEIVED FROM APPLICANT
NO
APPLICATION STILL TREATED INCOMPLETE. APPLICANT NOTIFIED
YES
YES
MSSD VERIFIES APPLICATION INFORMATION (SEE P & P). FORWARD TO DEPARTMENT CHAIR
APPLICATION REVIEWED
IS ADDITIONAL INFORMATION NEEDED?
YES
FURTHER INFORMATION REQUESTED
INFO RECEIVED FROM APPLICANT
NO
APPLICATION TREATED INCOMPLETE. APPLICANT NOTIFIED
NO
YES
DEPARTMENT CHAIR MAKES WRITTEN REPORT AND RECOMMENDATION FOR PRIVILEGE DELINEATION
APPLICATION SENT TO AND REVIEWED BY CREDENTIALS COMMITTEE
IS ADDITIONAL INFORMATION NEEDED?
YES
FURTHER INFORMATION REQUESTED
INFO RECEIVED FROM APPLICANT
NO
APPLICATION TREATED INCOMPLETE. APPLICANT NOTIFIED
NO
YES

continues

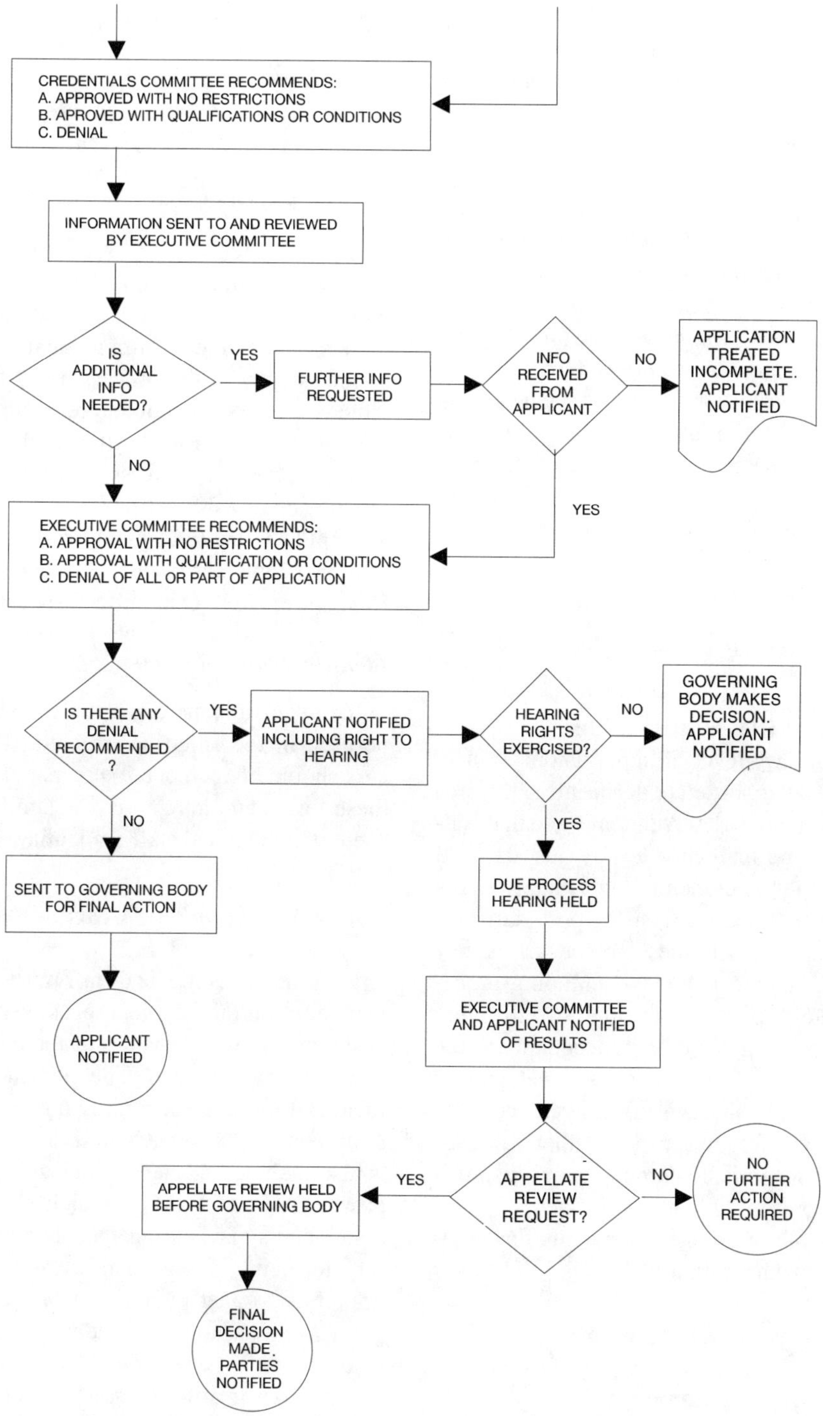

Figure 3–1 Initial Application Flowchart. Courtesy of C. Mobley & Associates, LLC, and Quality Management Options, LLC, Colorado Springs, Colorado.

tice in a hospital that relate to their licensure or certification and other criteria. The hospital should categorize those who may practice independently, those who may practice under direct or general supervision from a designated physician, and those who by contract or scope of services defined will be able to provide patient care. The terminology used by each organization will vary. Terms used include *physician-sponsored AHP, dependent AHP, licensed and supervised AHP, medical assistant, medical associate, physician extender,* and *independent AHP*. Also important in the definitions are those specific classifications of individuals whom the hospital allows to provide services; for example, *registered nurse, operating room technician, perfusionist, physician assistant, nurse practitioner, clinical social worker, psychologist,* and *certified registered nurse anesthetist.*

Identify Required Procedures

Because options are available to hospitals regarding how AHPs function within the organization (state law, level of supervision defined, etc.), it is very important to define all of the procedures involving AHP credentialing so that consistency can be maintained. The hospital will most likely not be credentialing as many AHPs as medical staff members, so support staff may not be as familiar with these procedures as they are with the medical staff credentialing procedures. In addition, there are often two different AHP credentialing procedures, depending on the category of AHP (independent vs. dependent, or supervised vs. unsupervised); this can contribute to the less frequent use of either category and can cause confusion among support staff if the procedures are not clearly defined.

An example of a table of contents for an allied health manual might include

- definitions of AHPs (approved classification)
- definition of categories
- requirements for establishing new categories
- application and appointment process
- privileges
- temporary privileges
- reappointment
- suspension or termination
- corrective action/due process
- functional policies and procedures

Identify Process Steps

As mentioned in the "Credentials Policy and Procedure Manual" section, any credentialing process defined for AHPs needs to be outlined in detail in an allied health manual so that there is consistency in the processing of these individuals for appointment and reappointment. Included in the written policy and procedures should be flowcharts to assist in the understanding of each process defined. See Figure 3–2 for a sample AHP with Clinical Privileges/Medical Staff Reviews and Figure 3–3 AHP with Job Description/AHP Committee Review.

Identify Required Documents

Identification and copies of all documents to be used in the allied health credentialing process should be included in the manual. Many of these forms and letters may be similar to those used in the medical staff credentialing process.

Corrective Action/Fair Hearing Plan

Every hospital medical staff must have a corrective action/fair hearing process that is defined in the medical staff bylaws or the credentialing or fair hearing manual. The current trend is to include it in the credentialing manual. It is a requirement of the Joint Commission standards. It is also included in the Health Care Quality Improvement Act of 1986,[5] which outlines those components of a hearing appeals process necessary for being in compliance and receiving the immunity to peer review that the act provides. Most hospitals have legal counsel who assists the medical staff in developing their corrective action and fair hearing plan. More detailed information is contained in Chapter 9 of this book. AHPs have a separate plan from that of the medical staff.

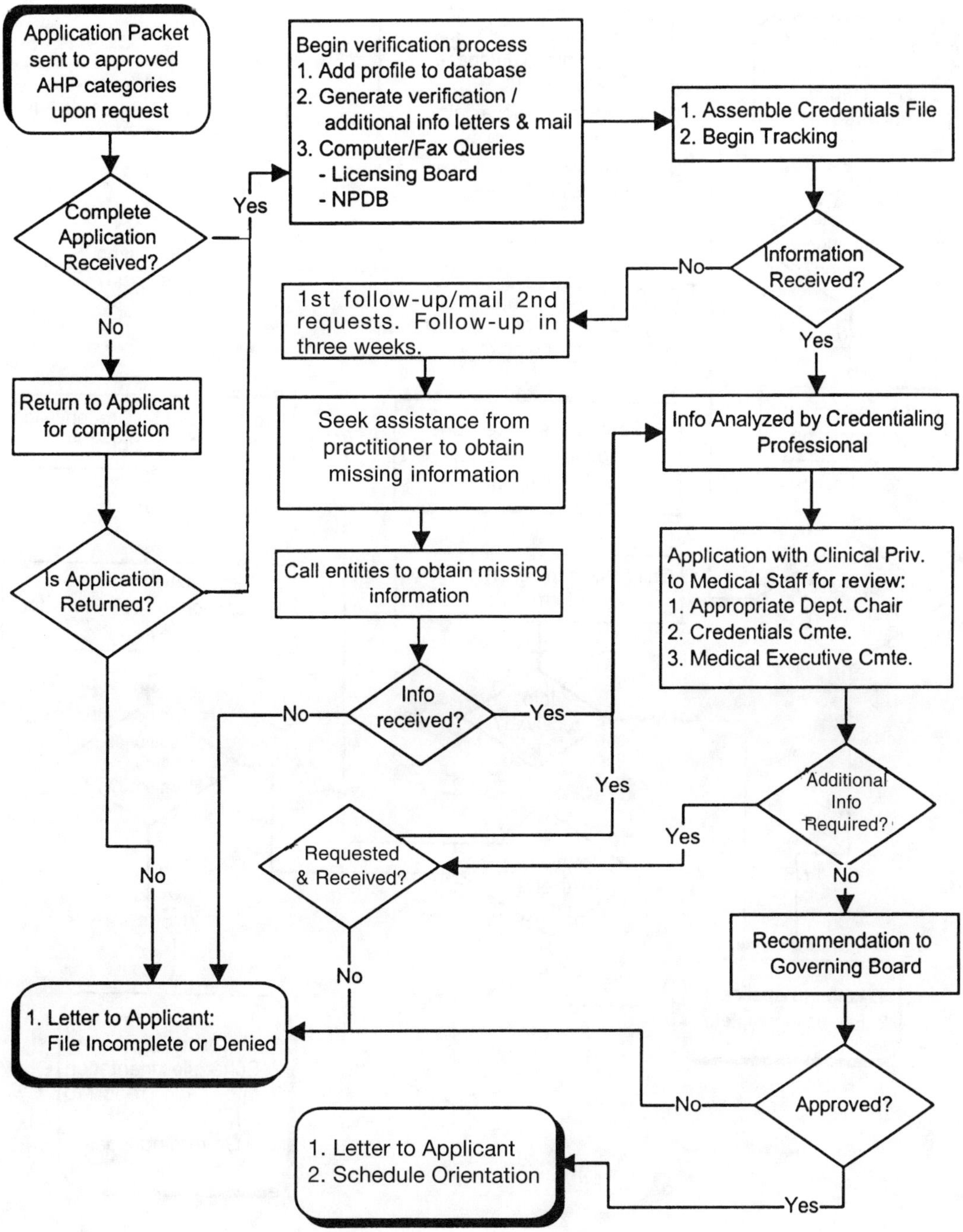

Figure 3–2 AHP Initial Appointment Flowchart for AHP with Clinical Privileges/Medical Staff Review. Courtesy of C. Mobley & Associates, LLC, and Quality Management Options, LLC, Colorado Springs, Colorado.

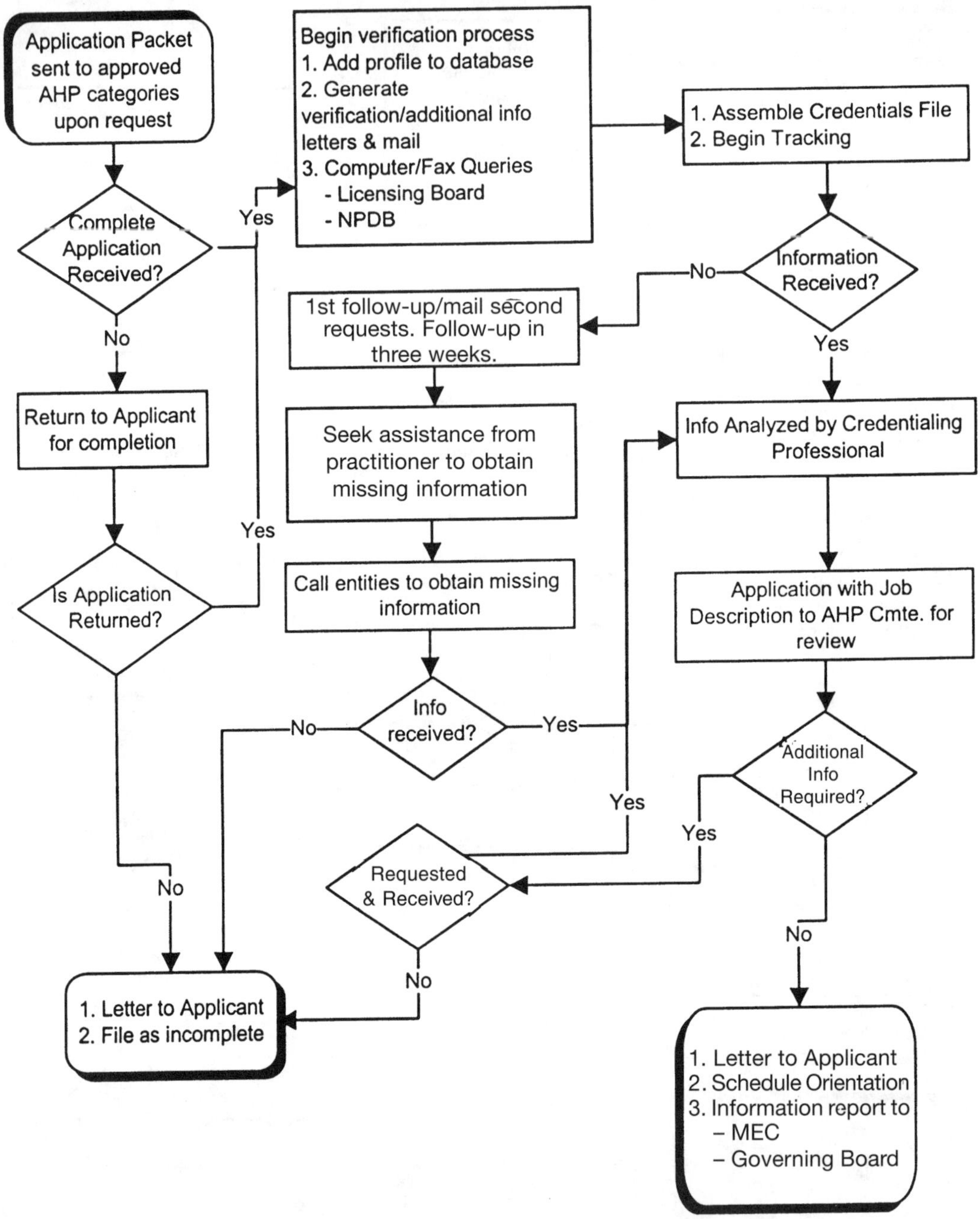

Figure 3–3 AHP Initial Appointment Flowchart for AHP with Job Description/AHP Committee Review. Courtesy of C. Mobley & Associates, LLC, and Quality Management Options, LLC, Colorado Springs, Colorado.

Identify Required Components

The Health Care Quality Improvement Act has specific components defined for fair hearing, many of which hospitals had in place before the Act became law in 1986. Some hospitals had to refine and add to their fair hearing and appellate review section of the bylaws or manual when the Act was passed. See Chapter 9 for an example of a table of contents for a fair hearing plan or a fair hearing section in the medical staff bylaws.

Identify Process Steps

It is imperative that the processes under the corrective action, fair hearing, and appellate review outlines be very clearly defined, with all steps included. When any kind of adverse corrective action or recommendation occurs that may result in summary or automatic suspension or denial, revocation, limitation, or suspension of privileges, the process must be well defined so that the individual in question is treated fairly by those involved in the processes and in the eyes of the law. Chapter 9 defines in more detail the corrective action, fair hearing, and appellate processes. This is another area where flowcharts are very beneficial in identifying the processes.

File Setup and Maintenance

There must be an individual credentials file for each practitioner.

Contents of a Credentials File

All kinds of credentials files are available in the market today. Some hospitals use only a manila file folder to store all information. However, that can be very cumbersome because numerous pieces of paper are usually maintained in a credentials file. It is suggested that a divided file folder be used, with tabs for each section. Usually the divided file folder has some kind of fastener at the top or on the side so that papers can be attached to the appropriate section and not get lost in the file or fall out. Medical staff office personnel need to be comfortable with the way they have organized the credentials file. Often the files do not all look the same because different people managed the department and may have implemented a different filing process for the information contained in the credentials file. If the decision is made that all files need to be reorganized, it is suggested that once a file design is decided upon, one of two options be considered: (1) a major reorganization of the files, which might require bringing in temporary help with credentialing background, or (2) reorganization of groups of files, using the reappointment schedule so that the project is spread out over a period of time, and done by the current staff in the department. The time frame within which your reappointment must occur will guide which approach to use. A medical staff office policy regarding file organization is also a good idea.

Contents of a credentials file should include

- the initial application and all supporting documentation, including the approval letter
- all reappointment information and supporting documentation, including department assessment/recommendation and the reappointment letter
- clinical privileges and all supporting documentation
- all information with expiration dates, including licensure, National Practitioner Data Bank (NPDB), Drug Enforcement Administration (DEA) certification, and insurance coverage
- any correspondence that is not included anywhere else
- if a software program is used, a copy of the profile information that is currently included on each practitioner in the system

Hospital preference, legal advice, and state statutes regarding protection and confidentiality of peer review information will determine where sensitive information such as investigations, NPDB reports, internal risk management information, claims history, quality performance improvement reports, and other sensitive information should be kept. Sometimes this information is kept in the quality management department or can be included in a separate file folder within the credentials file that is marked "confidential" and references the state statutes that protect the information contained within. Legal counsel can assist in determining where this information should reside.

File Organization

File folders should be labeled with the last name first and should include the credentials (MD, DO, DDS); they can be color coded for department or specialty. For purposes of this next section, it will be assumed that people will use the divided file folders with fasteners to separate information within each section and/or pockets in each section for information to be maintained.

Information should always be filed with the most current information on top. If tabs are not used in each section, the order listed in each section should be considered. The following is a suggested format for filing information in divided file folder sections:

- *Section 1*—current appointment letter on top (may be initial appointment or reappointment but should include all appointment/reappointment letters)
- *Section 2*—clinical privileges/job description (for some AHP classifications), tabs within this section should include
  - tab—current privilege delineation form and any other current privileges not included on the privilege form (including a letter to a practitioner approving privileges, e.g., single and/or temporary privileges)
  - tab—documentation for any privileges requested
  - tab—old privilege delineation lists
- *Section 3*—dated information with expirations
  - tab—state license verification (most current on top)
  - tab—Drug Enforcement Agency (DEA)/Controlled Dangerous Substance (CDS) (state pharmacy) license (most current on top)
  - tab—malpractice insurance (most current on top)
  - tab—NPDB query reports (most current on top) (unless located in a "protected" file)
  - tab—board certification (some boards expire and physician must be recertified)
  - option—a tab on top of this section may include just the most current information for each of the above categories plus tabs for each individual category that contains outdated information. This way, it is easier to access the most current information that is all on top in this section. This tab could be entitled "Current." Also see the section "Purge Policy" below.
- *Section 4*—reappointment information
  - tab—most current reappointment application on top, with supporting documentation underneath; suggest most current computer demographic summary on top of reappointment application
  - tab—outdated reappointment and supporting documentation
- *Section 5*—correspondence/miscellaneous
  - tab—internal correspondence
  - tab—external correspondence
  - tab—miscellaneous
- *Section 6*—initial appointment
  - tab—application form
  - tab—medical school
  - tab—internship
  - tab—residency/fellowship
  - tab—professional references
  - tab—hospital references
  - tab—continuing medical education
  - tab—miscellaneous application, information

It is suggested that an empty file folder be in the front section of the file to drop-file any information in between the reappointments. The information can be filed at the time the file is pulled to begin the reappointment process for that practitioner. It also keeps one from having to pull the credentials file numerous times to file the information.

Purge Policy

Some hospitals have a purge policy that allows them to shred or otherwise dispose of information in the credentials file that is no longer relevant. The credentials file can get very full of outdated information that is seldom, if ever, referred to at a later date. Examples include expirables such as license, DEA, insurance coverage and older reappointment information. It is suggested that legal counsel be consulted with regard to purging the information or at least taking out old, outdated information and placing it into another file that can be stored somewhere other than the current credentials file. There are software programs on the market that will scan the information and save it to a disk that can easily be downloaded if a hard copy is needed later.

A rule of thumb is to not keep anything older in the file than the last reappointment cycle in terms of reappointment application, practitioner profile information, and dated information (license, insurance, etc.). Files should contain all privileging information, the original application and supporting information, and all correspondence that indicates when membership privileges and so forth were initially approved and subsequently reviewed. Some hospitals can microfilm or scan the information and then dispose of the hard copy. If an organization has a purge policy, it should be approved by the medical staff and governing board and included in the medical staff office policy and procedure manual.

Delineated Clinical Privileges and Criteria

Clinical privileges are essential in the credentialing process and outline the procedures and/or treatments that are available to practitioners who meet specific criteria for all of the privileges that are delineated. Chapter 6 of this book is entirely devoted to clinical privileges.

Data Management System

A computer system that is user friendly and meets the needs of the medical staff organization and support personnel can be a huge benefit to both productivity and easy access of needed information. Some hospitals use an internal system that is designed through their information management systems department. Some hospitals have purchased a commercial software program designed specifically for the medical staff organization and all of its components. Either method can be beneficial as long as the users have the ability to make changes and to keep up with the information that they are required to maintain. Many software companies have excellent credentialing software. Many of these companies advertise in *SYNERGY*, the publication of the National Association Medical Staff Services (NAMSS) in Lombard, Illinois. Different systems have different capabilities, and which system is best depends on what the user needs.

Analysis of Needs/Evaluation of Software

If purchasing a credentials software system, an analysis of needs should be completed. Chapter 12 of this book includes a section that addresses evaluation of credentialing software requirements. Additionally, it is important to understand and use a backup system (daily or weekly), no matter what kind of software is used. Also, an operations manual and policies and procedures for the software system and its backup process are important to have, since problems do occur but may be resolved by consulting an operations manual.[6]

Information Maintenance

It is important to have a policy and procedure on maintaining updated information in the software program as well as whose responsibility it is. Most input occurs at the time of initial processing. However, there are ongoing updates for reappointment; changes in privileges or categories; committee appointments; officer, committee, or chair appointments; dated information; and changes of board certification status. Address, phone, and fax changes come in from time to time, and it is important to keep that information up to date, since address labels and rosters/directories are generated from the computer system.

Any information that expires and is reverified needs to be updated as soon as possible. Many software systems track expirations and generate letters requesting updated copies or produce a list of expired information; therefore, it is important to keep that information current in the system.

STEPS IN THE CREDENTIALING PROCESS

Step 1: Application Request

The application request is a process used to determine if a physician or other prospective member of the medical staff is qualified to make application for medical staff membership and/or privileges. If the practitioner does not meet the criteria, an application is not provided (see sample criteria below).

This process is used in some geographic areas where a high number of requests for medical staff applications occur. Hospitals may want to accept only those practitioners they know are going to use their hospital. Some organizations do not find it necessary to have an application request process because almost everybody who applies for membership and/or privileges meets the qualifications and subsequently becomes a member of the staff.

The application request process is generally an administrative process. Eligibility can be determined through objective criteria established by the medical staff and used by medical staff office personnel to determine whether the individual should receive an application. Examples of criteria to meet qualification to receive an application are the following:

1. Is the person currently licensed in the state?
2. Does the person carry the minimum malpractice insurance that is required by the hospital?
3. In terms of specific privileges, is the individual board certified or board qualified (if the medical staff requires this certification or qualification)?
4. Is a geographic distance required within which the individual must live and/or have an office (for response time)?
5. Other questions that could be answered with a "yes" or "no."

Figure 3–4 shows a macro process for application requests.

Characteristics of a Successful Process

It is important that an application request process be used consistently for everybody who requests an application.

Options

The application request process can be accomplished in several ways.

1. Have a completely separate abbreviated form that is completed by the prospective member.
2. Questions are asked over the phone by medical staff services personnel and documented. If the individual meets the qualifications, an application packet is sent to the individual.
3. A preassessment or preapplication questionnaire is sent out with the application packet, along with instructions that the prospective applicant should first fill out the questionnaire. Instructions state that if all answers to the questions are "yes" or "no" (depending on how they are asked), the applicant can proceed with completion of the application and return it to the medical staff office.

Exhibit 3–1 is an example of a hospital's preapplication questionnaire; on the basis of the

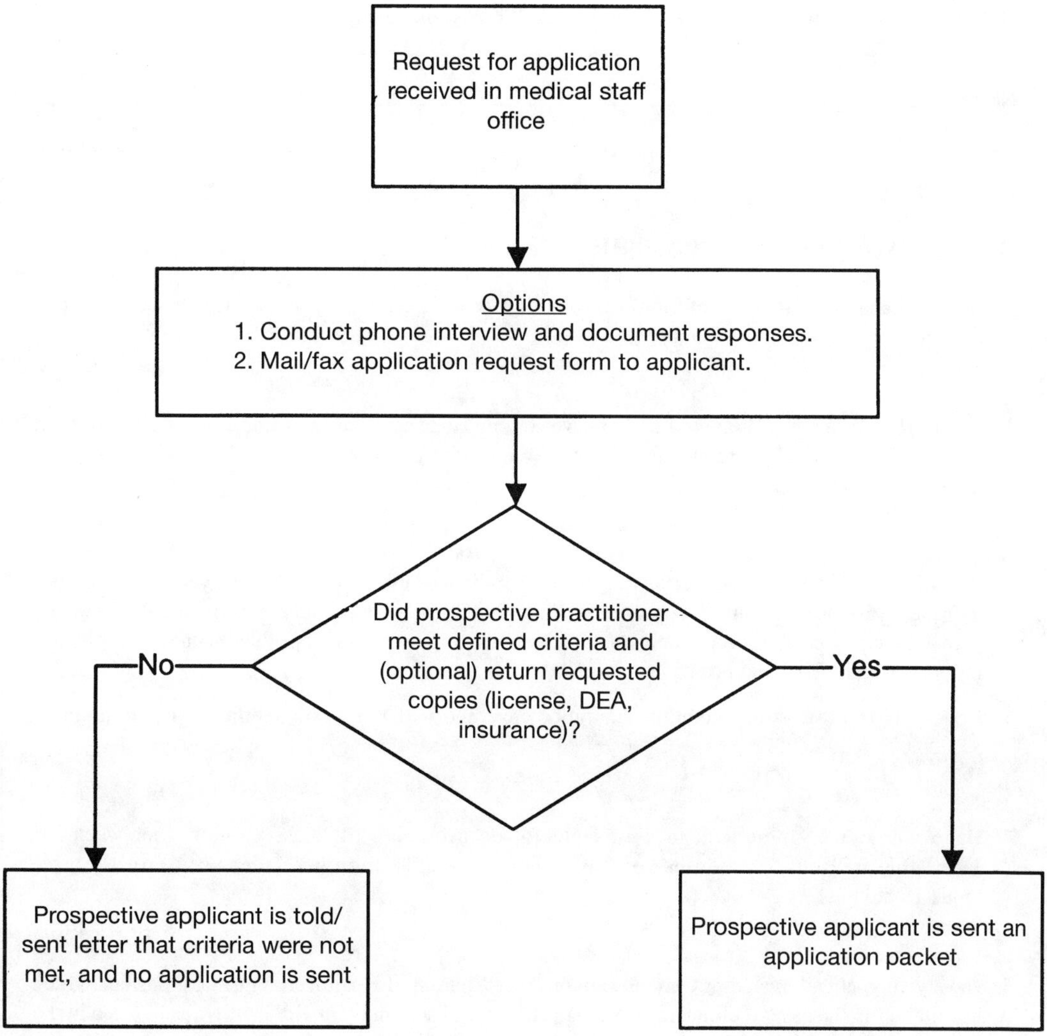

Figure 3–4 Application Request Flowchart. Courtesy of C. Mobley & Associates, LLC, and Quality Management Options, LLC, Colorado Springs, Colorado.

Exhibit 3–1 Preapplication Questionnaire for Medical Staff Membership

Name: ____________________

Current Address: ____________________

Current Phone: ____________________ Practice Specialty: ____________________

QUALIFICATIONS FOR MEMBERSHIP

1. Are you licensed in the State of California and (if practicing clinical medicine, dentistry or podiatry) do you have a federal DEA number?

   ☐ YES ☐ NO

2. Are you board certified or admissible; or have completed an approved residency; or have practiced in your field in a hospital accredited by the Joint Commission on Accreditation of Healthcare Organizations for ten years?

   ☐ YES ☐ NO

   Applicants for off-site ambulatory care privileges only may also qualify with one year post-graduate training in primary care in an approved hospital and 24 months practice experience. Practitioners with ambulatory care privileges only do not have admitting or in-patient privileges unless they obtain full staff membership and privileges.

3. Do you have professional liability insurance coverage with limits of liability at a minimum of $1,000,000/$3,000,000?

   ☐ YES ☐ NO

4. Have you actively practiced in your field for an average of at least 20 hours per week for 18 of the previous 24 months (or have completed a 12-month residency within the previous 18 months)?

   ☐ YES ☐ NO

5. Have you practiced in a Joint Commission on Accreditation of Healthcare Organizations accredited hospital, or in the case of clinical psychologists, a multidisciplinary health facility (as defined in the Department of Psychiatry Rules and Regulations), at least two of the previous five (5) years?

   ☐ YES ☐ NO

   This requirement is waived for applicants for off-site ambulatory care privileges only.

6. Except for consulting staff applicants and physicians assigned specific times to be at the facility, i.e., Emergency Room physicians, do you plan to reside and practice within 35 miles or 45 minutes (surface travel time) of Sutter General, Sutter Memorial, or Sutter Center for Psychiatry?

   ☐ YES ☐ NO

   Exceptions to this requirement may be granted where the applicant or Medical Staff member provides and maintains in the Medical Staff Office a written agreement for coverage of his patients by a Senior Staff member who meets the geographic requirements.

continues

Exhibit 3–1 continued

7. For clinical psychologists, do you hold a Ph.D. or Psy.D. degree in clinical psychology?

☐ YES ☐ NO

8. Please check the privileges you wish to request:

- ☐ Anesthesia
- ☐ Diagnostic Imaging & Radiation Oncology
- ☐ Family Practice (Please check Medicine also, if you wish to have privileges in the Critical Care Units or EKG interpretation. Please check Pediatrics also for other than normal newborns.)
- ☐ Emergency Medicine
- ☐ Laboratory Medicine
- ☐ Medicine
- ☐ Obstetrics/Gynecology
- ☐ Pediatrics
- ☐ Psychiatry
- ☐ Surgery

I certify that I meet the criteria for membership as outlined in this pre-application questionnaire. I understand that completing this questionnaire in no way obligates the hospital and/or medical staff to afford me medical staff membership or privileges.

I hereby release from liability any representatives of the hospital and its medical staff for their acts performed in good faith and without malice in connection with evaluating my request for medical staff membership and privileges at Sutter Community Hospitals, and I hereby release from liability any and all individuals and organizations who provide information to the hospital, or its medical staff in good faith and without malice concerning my professional competence, ethics, character and other qualifications, and I hereby consent to the release of such information.

________________ ____

DATE SIGNATURE

IF YOU MEET THE ABOVE SUTTER COMMUNITY HOSPITALS MEDICAL STAFF BYLAWS REQUIREMENTS FOR MEMBERSHIP AND PRIVILEGES, PLEASE CONTINUE. IF YOU **DO NOT MEET** THE ABOVE REQUIREMENTS, PLEASE DO NOT CONTINUE BEYOND THIS PAGE. WE THANK YOU FOR YOUR INTEREST; IF, HOWEVER, AT A LATER DATE YOU FIND YOU DO MEET OUR QUALIFICATIONS FOR MEDICAL STAFF MEMBERSHIP AND PRIVILEGES, PLEASE DO NOT HESITATE TO RE-APPLY.

Courtesy of Sutter Community Hospitals, Sacramento, California.

answers the physician can assess whether he or she is eligible to apply for medical staff membership privileges. This questionnaire can also be used as a telephone questionnaire. The medical staff office can ask these questions, fill them in, and date and sign the questionnaire, but the attestation paragraphs will need to be removed as well as the paragraph below the signature. Another option is for the medical staff office to request this information over the phone. If the practitioner meets the criteria, this completed form can be sent with the application packet for the applicant to sign and return with the completed application packet.

If the prospective member does not meet the qualifications to receive an application, a letter is sent to the individual stating why the criteria were not met. This action is not considered a denial and does not entitle the individual to due process, which is another advantage to the application request process. It is not reportable to the NPDB because it is not a denial based on evaluation of clinical judgment or evaluation of adverse action that has taken place in the past. (This type of information is evaluated during the initial application process.)

If no application request process is used, it may be determined at some point during the initial appointment procedure that someone does not meet one or more of the qualifications listed in the bylaws. If appointment for privileges and membership is denied on the basis of not meeting one or more of the qualifications or if sufficient adverse information is received, the individual may be entitled to a fair hearing process on the basis of bylaws language.

If the individual meets the criteria outlined that have been previously approved by the medical staff, he or she receives an application. This does not mean that the individual will be ensured medical staff membership and privileges but simply that he or she now has the opportunity to apply for membership and clinical privileges.

Documentation of the Process

The application request process is documented in the bylaws or credentialing manual (policies and procedures). If an application request process is used, regardless of whether it is a form or a documented phone conversation, this information is made part of the credentials file. If the individual does not meet the criteria, so that no subsequent credentials file is kept for this individual, a list can be kept of all initial inquiries for a record of the requests.

There are no accreditation standards related to the application request process; it is strictly an individual organization's option as to whether it would be beneficial to have such a process.

Assessment of Application Request Process

If an organization uses an application request process, it should periodically assess the value of the process. The organization needs to ask itself if individuals were identified through this process who did not meet the criteria and therefore did not receive an application packet. If so, the application request process was able to separate those individuals who did not qualify to make application. Another question to ask is: Even if all individuals who went through the application process did receive an application packet, was the information that was received in the application request process more beneficial to the organization than if it had been received at a later date?

Step 2: Initial Application Process

Characteristics of a Successful Process

A Good Application Form. There is a saying that "you get what you ask for." This applies to an application form in that the hospital wants to obtain as much information as possible about the applicant in order to make an informed decision about the applicant's competence to provide patient care. Hospitals have the option of requesting as much or as little information as possible. If the right questions are not asked or little detail is requested, it is probable the applicant will not provide any unsolicited, additional information. If the application is not comprehensive enough, valuable information may be missed.

A Thorough Review Process. Even though the medical staff office personnel evaluate the information received, the medical staff is responsible and accountable for reviewing all of the available information. They should not rely solely on the evaluation of support staff but have an obligation to review the file thoroughly when it is presented to them and to request additional information if necessary. No review individual or group should rubber-stamp a recommendation, for they each have an obligation as defined in the bylaws to evaluate the information presented to them. There should be periodic orientation for any new committee or department members involved in the credentialing review process so that they thoroughly understand their role in this important function.

An Informed and Educated Governing Board. Governing boards often rely upon the recommendation of the medical staff without really understanding the steps in the application process. Each new board member should be oriented to the process used by the medical staff to verify the information provided and how that information is evaluated. It is also important for them to be familiar with the accreditation requirements that relate to any part of the credentialing process. They are ultimately accountable for the decision-making process and should be comfortable with the recommendations they receive from the medical staff and with taking action on those requests.

Well-Defined Membership and Privilege Criteria. Well-defined criteria about who can apply for clinical privileges and membership and a good understanding of the expectations should one be appointed to the medical staff will help to avoid any confusion. The criteria, once approved by the medical staff and board, should be supported in the review and approval process, with no exceptions made unless extenuating circumstances are defined and thoroughly evaluated. The verification process for information on the application form is fairly routine for all organizations, although the methods of verification vary. However, privileging criteria can vary greatly, and it is to the organization's advantage to have well-defined privileging criteria to allow for a more thorough evaluation both at initial appointment (when the individual may be relatively unknown) and on an ongoing basis once the individual has been granted privileges to provide patient care.

Well-Organized and Knowledgeable Support Staff. It is crucial that the support staff who work with the medical staff organization be knowledgeable individuals and that they understand the credentialing process and its impact on the quality of patient care provided. There is a great deal of work to be done before a credentials file is ready for review by the medical staff and ultimately the governing board. Well-established policies and procedures will assist greatly in providing the mechanism needed to process the application in a timely and thorough manner. Even though some support staff may understand the process better than anyone on the medical staff, in administration, or on the governing board, it is important that they encourage, educate, and support those involved in the review and approval process.

Tracking System. Most credentialing software packages include a tracking system. If no software is used, a manual system can be established or a handwritten form can be kept noting receipts, requests, and so forth. This enables the medical staff office to know at any time where the application is in the process.

The Application Form

A variety of application forms are used in the industry today. Many states, through collaborative efforts, have designed an application for use by any health care organization within the state. Many CVOs have designed their application for use by any client who uses their services. And in 1997, the Medical Society Credentialing Verification Organizations of America (MSCVOA) invited major players from the health care industry to collaborate on a set of core credentialing data that could be used by anyone needing assistance developing an application form. Some of the groups represented in this collaborative effort were: numerous medical societies that had CVOs, the Joint Commission, the National Committee for Quality Assurance (NCQA), the Utilization Review Accreditation Commission (URAC), NAMSS, the Federation of State Medical Boards (FSMB), American Association of Health Plans (AAHP), and Medical Group Management Association (MGMA).

The length of the application form has expanded as organizations have felt the need to know more information about a practitioner. Two-page application forms have turned into 20-page application forms. One of the reasons for this is that many organizations are credentialing practitioners for both hospitals and managed care organizations, requiring information that may be unique to one or the other. The information on application forms can vary from "nice to know" to "need to know" to "required by accreditation standards."

NCQA is referenced because many managed care organizations delegate the verification component to hospitals that will need this information. In many cases, the information on application forms is very similar but the format differs widely.

Exhibit 3–2 is the core credentialing data form that the MSCVOA collaborative group designed for use by all health care organizations. Below is an explanation of each section with the notation of whether the information in each section is "nice to know," "need to know," or an accreditation requirement. Unless otherwise indicated, "accreditation requirement" refers to either the Joint Commission or NCQA. Detailed information about the verifications, including Joint Commission and NCQA requirements, can be found in Chapter 5.

Section 1: Personal Information. Nice to know/need to know. Much of the information contained here is information needed by an organization and provides local demographics about the individual. Some of the nonbusiness information requested, such as home address and spouse name, may or may not be completed by the applicant. Organizations may want to list this information under "optional." In general, most applicants are willing to fill out this section in its entirety.

Section 2: Education, ECFMG. Need to know/accreditation requirement. This section lists the school or schools (medical/dental/graduate professional) where individuals obtained their medical or other degree and is usually the earliest credential that is verified by organizations. The Educational Commission for Foreign Medical Graduates (ECFMG) license or certification number is often the only way to verify a foreign medical graduate. Many foreign medical schools cannot be verified, so accreditation organizations have accepted the confirmation of an ECFMG certification without collecting information from the graduate and/or foreign medical school. The ECFMG certification is the primary way for a foreign graduate to enter a formal training program within the United States.

Section 3: Training. Need to know/accreditation requirement. This section lists all training (internships/residency/fellowships/preceptorships) required for a specific specialty in the area in which the practitioner will practice. Because an individual may enter several training programs before completing a program, it is important to ask whether the program was successfully completed. There are many reasons for not completing a particular program, and this is an item that organizations should be evaluating. It is also important to ask for the month as well as the year of all information requested to assist in determining if there are gaps in practice periods.

Section 4: Licensure. Need to know/accreditation requirement. This section asks for all current as well as past professional state licenses. Verifying past licenses with either the individual state licensing board or FSMB may produce any adverse information from the past that will be beneficial for organizations to know.

Section 5: Certifications and Registrations. Need to know/accreditation requirement. If a physician has a license to prescribe narcotics, he or she is required to have a DEA number. CDS

Exhibit 3–2 Core Credentialing Data

THIS MUST BE COMPLETED IN FULL & TYPED OR PRINTED LEGIBLY

SECTION ONE
PERSONAL INFORMATION

Name ____
Last First Middle

Other Name(s) By Which You Have Been Known: ______________________

Dates This Name Was Used: From ☐☐-☐☐-☐☐☐☐ To ☐☐-☐☐-☐☐☐☐

Other Name(s) By Which You Have Been Known: ______________________

Dates This Name Was Used: From ☐☐-☐☐-☐☐☐☐ To ☐☐-☐☐-☐☐☐☐

Home Address ____
No. and Street City State Zip

Home Telephone (_____) ______________________

Primary Office Address ____
No. and Street City State Zip

Primary Office Telephone (_____) ______________________

Fax Number (_____) ______________ E-Mail Address ______________

Address To Which All Correspondence Should Be Sent ______________________
No. and Street City State Zip

Social Security Number ☐☐-☐☐-☐☐☐☐ Birth Date ☐☐-☐☐-☐☐☐☐

Place of Birth ______________ Citizenship ______________

If Not American Citizen, Status and Visa Number ______________________

Gender: ☐ Male ☐ Female

US Military Service/Public Health (attach copy of DD214)

From ☐☐-☐☐-☐☐☐☐ To ☐☐-☐☐-☐☐☐☐

Location ______________ Branch of Service ______________

From ☐☐-☐☐-☐☐☐☐ To ☐☐-☐☐-☐☐☐☐

Location ______________ Branch of Service ______________

SECTION TWO
EDUCATION

(MEDICAL/DENTAL/GRADUATE PROFESSIONAL SCHOOLS, LIST ALL, COMPLETED OR NOT)

School Name ______________ Degree Awarded ______________

Mailing Address ____
No. and Street City State Zip

Dates Attended (month, day, year) From ☐☐-☐☐-☐☐☐☐ To ☐☐-☐☐-☐☐☐☐

Graduation Date (month, day, year) ☐☐-☐☐-☐☐☐☐

continues

Exhibit 3–2 continued

School Name ______________________ Degree Awarded ______________________

Mailing Address ____
No. and Street City State Zip

Dates Attended (month, day, year) From □□-□□-□□□□ To □□-□□-□□□□

Graduation Date (month, day, year) □□-□□-□□□□

School Name ______________________ Degree Awarded ______________________

Mailing Address ____
No. and Street City State Zip

Dates Attended (month, day, year) From □□-□□-□□□□ To □□-□□-□□□□

Graduation Date (month, day, year) □□-□□-□□□□

SECTION THREE
TRAINING

INTERNSHIP/RESIDENCIES/FELLOWSHIPS/PRECEPTORSHIPS
(LIST ALL, COMPLETED OR NOT. IF YOU REQUIRE ADDITIONAL SPACE, ATTACH SEPARATE SHEET)

Institution ____

Complete Mailing Address ____
No. and Street City State Zip

From □□-□□-□□□□ To □□-□□-□□□□

Type of Training/Specialty ____

Your Program Director's Full Name ____

Current Program Director (if known) ____

Was the program successfully completed? □ Yes □ No

Institution ____

Complete Mailing Address ____
No. and Street City State Zip

From □□-□□-□□□□ To □□-□□-□□□□

Type of Training/Specialty ____

Your Program Director's Full Name ____

Current Program Director (if known) ____

Was the program successfully completed? □ Yes □ No

Institution ____

Complete Mailing Address ____
No. and Street City State Zip

From □□-□□-□□□□ To □□-□□-□□□□

Type of Training/Specialty ____

Your Program Director's Full Name ____

Current Program Director (if known) ____

Was the program successfully completed? □ Yes □ No

continues

Exhibit 3–2 continued

SECTION FOUR
LICENSURE

(LIST ALL CURRENT PROFESSIONAL LICENSES; EXAMPLES OF "TYPE" OF LICENSE ARE MD, DO, DPM, DDS, DMD, ETC)

If you are an International Medical Graduate, are you: ECFMG Certified? ☐ Yes ☐ No

USMLE/ECFMG Number ☐☐-☐☐-☐☐☐☐ Certification Issue Date ☐☐-☐☐-☐☐☐☐

List all current professional licenses:

State	Type	Number	Original Date of Issue	Expiration Date
			☐☐-☐☐-☐☐☐☐	☐☐-☐☐-☐☐☐☐
			☐☐-☐☐-☐☐☐☐	☐☐-☐☐-☐☐☐☐
			☐☐-☐☐-☐☐☐☐	☐☐-☐☐-☐☐☐☐

List all past professional licenses:

State	Type	Number	Original Date of Issue	Expiration Date
			☐☐-☐☐-☐☐☐☐	☐☐-☐☐-☐☐☐☐
			☐☐-☐☐-☐☐☐☐	☐☐-☐☐-☐☐☐☐
			☐☐-☐☐-☐☐☐☐	☐☐-☐☐-☐☐☐☐

SECTION FIVE
CERTIFICATIONS AND REGISTRATIONS

(LIST ALL CURRENT CERTIFICATIONS AND REGISTRATIONS)

Federal DEA Number ______________________________

Date Issued ☐☐-☐☐-☐☐☐☐ Expires ☐☐-☐☐-☐☐☐☐

Federal DEA Number ______________________________

Date Issued ☐☐-☐☐-☐☐☐☐ Expires ☐☐-☐☐-☐☐☐☐

Controlled Dangerous Substance (CDS) Number __________ Date Issued ☐☐-☐☐-☐☐☐☐

Controlled Dangerous Substance (CDS) Number __________ Date Issued ☐☐-☐☐-☐☐☐☐

Specialty ______________________________ Board Certified? ☐ Yes ☐ No

If No, are you qualified to sit for the examination? ☐ Yes (attached confirmation letter) ☐ No

Board Name ____________________ Date of Initial Certification ☐☐-☐☐-☐☐☐☐

Date of Most Recent Certification ☐☐-☐☐-☐☐☐☐

Date Qualified ☐☐-☐☐-☐☐☐☐ Qualification Expires ☐☐-☐☐-☐☐☐☐

Sub Specialty ______________________________ Board Certified? ☐ Yes ☐ No

If No, are you qualified to sit for the examination? ☐ Yes (attach confirmation letter) ☐ No

Board Name ____________________ Date of Initial Certification ☐☐-☐☐-☐☐☐☐

continues

Exhibit 3–2 continued

Date of Most Recent Certification ☐☐-☐☐-☐☐☐☐

Date Qualified ☐☐-☐☐-☐☐☐☐ Qualification Expires ☐☐-☐☐-☐☐☐☐

Sub Specialty ______________________ Board Certified? ☐ Yes ☐ No

If No, are you qualified to sit for the examination? ☐ Yes (attach confirmation letter) ☐ No

Board Name ______________________ Date of Initial Certification ☐☐-☐☐-☐☐☐☐

Date of Most Recent Certification ☐☐-☐☐-☐☐☐☐

Date Qualified ☐☐-☐☐-☐☐☐☐ Qualification Expires ☐☐-☐☐-☐☐☐☐

CPR CERTIFICATIONS:

Are you certified in CPR?	☐ Yes (attach copy of certificate(s) ☐ No	Expiration Date ☐☐-☐☐-☐☐☐☐
Check classification(s):	☐ Basic Life Support (BLS)	Expiration Date ☐☐-☐☐-☐☐☐☐
	☐ Advanced Cardiac Life Support (ACLS)	Expiration Date ☐☐-☐☐-☐☐☐☐
	☐ Health Care Provider (Core C)	Expiration Date ☐☐-☐☐-☐☐☐☐
	☐ Advanced Trauma Life Support (ATLS)	Expiration Date ☐☐-☐☐-☐☐☐☐
	☐ Neonatal Advanced Life Support (NALS)	Expiration Date ☐☐-☐☐-☐☐☐☐
	☐ Pediatric Advanced Life Support (PALS)	Expiration Date ☐☐-☐☐-☐☐☐☐
	☐ Other	Expiration Date ☐☐-☐☐-☐☐☐☐

SECTION SIX
ACADEMIC APPOINTMENTS

School Name ______________________

Location ______________________

Rank/Position ______________________

Inclusive Dates: From ☐☐-☐☐-☐☐☐☐ To ☐☐-☐☐-☐☐☐☐

School Name ______________________

Location ______________________

Rank/Position ______________________

Inclusive Dates: From ☐☐-☐☐-☐☐☐☐ To ☐☐-☐☐-☐☐☐☐

School Name ______________________

Location ______________________

Rank/Position ______________________

Inclusive Dates: From ☐☐-☐☐-☐☐☐☐ To ☐☐-☐☐-☐☐☐☐

continues

Exhibit 3–2 continued

SECTION SEVEN
HEALTH CARE AFFILIATIONS

List all hospitals/health system affiliations where you have been employed, practiced, associated, or privileged for the last ten (10) years for the purpose of providing patient care. If there is insufficient space, continue in section seventeen. Do not list affiliations that were part of your training (internship, residency, fellowship). Your response must include the reason(s) for any termination or discontinuance of practice, privileges, employment, or association at any of the named health care facilities.

Facility Name ______________________________

Complete Mailing Address ______________________________
No. and Street City State Zip

Department/Service ______________________________

Dates of Appointment: From □□-□□-□□□□ To □□-□□-□□□□

Staff Category ______________________________

Reason for Discontinuance ______________________________

Facility Name ______________________________

Complete Mailing Address ______________________________
No. and Street City State Zip

Department/Service ______________________________

Dates of Appointment: From □□-□□-□□□□ To □□-□□-□□□□

Staff Category ______________________________

Reason for Discontinuance ______________________________

Facility Name ______________________________

Complete Mailing Address ______________________________
No. and Street City State Zip

Department/Service ______________________________

Dates of Appointment: From □□-□□-□□□□ To □□-□□-□□□□

Staff Category ______________________________

Reason for Discontinuance ______________________________

Facility Name ______________________________

Complete Mailing Address ______________________________
No. and Street City State Zip

Department/Service ______________________________

Dates of Appointment: From □□-□□-□□□□ To □□-□□-□□□□

Staff Category ______________________________

Reason for Discontinuance ______________________________

Indicate which of the above is your "current primary admitting facility" (where you currently spend the greatest portion of your time).______________________________

____

continues

Exhibit 3–2 continued

SECTION EIGHT
OTHER PROFESSIONAL WORK HISTORY

List chronologically all professional work history for the past five (5) years not included previously under academic appointments or health care affiliations (i.e., clinics, solo practice, employment, or practice). Account for all time gaps of thirty (30) days or more.

Name and Nature of Affiliation: ______________________________

Complete Mailing Address ______________________________
No. and Street City State Zip

From ☐☐-☐☐-☐☐☐☐ (Month Day Year) To ☐☐-☐☐-☐☐☐☐ (Month Day Year)

Reason for Discontinuance ______________________________

Name and Nature of Affiliation: ______________________________

Complete Mailing Address ______________________________
No. and Street City State Zip

From ☐☐-☐☐-☐☐☐☐ (Month Day Year) To ☐☐-☐☐-☐☐☐☐ (Month Day Year)

Reason for Discontinuance ______________________________

Name and Nature of Affiliation: ______________________________

Complete Mailing Address ______________________________
No. and Street City State Zip

From ☐☐-☐☐-☐☐☐☐ (Month Day Year) To ☐☐-☐☐-☐☐☐☐ (Month Day Year)

Reason for Discontinuance ______________________________

Name and Nature of Affiliation: ______________________________

Complete Mailing Address ______________________________
No. and Street City State Zip

From ☐☐-☐☐-☐☐☐☐ (Month Day Year) To ☐☐-☐☐-☐☐☐☐ (Month Day Year)

Reason for Discontinuance ______________________________

Name and Nature of Affiliation: ______________________________

Complete Mailing Address ______________________________
No. and Street City State Zip

From ☐☐-☐☐-☐☐☐☐ (Month Day Year) To ☐☐-☐☐-☐☐☐☐ (Month Day Year)

Reason for Discontinuance ______________________________

continues

Exhibit 3–2 continued

SECTION NINE
PROFESSIONAL LIABILITY INSURANCE

(Submit current face sheet of policy)

Present Carrier's Name ______________________________

Complete Address ______________________________
No. and Street City State Zip

Policy Number ______________________ Coverage Amounts ______________

Dates of Coverage From □□-□□-□□□□ To □□-□□-□□□□

Prior Carriers (during the past five (5) years). If there is insufficient space, please use section 17.

Prior Carrier's Name ______________________________

Complete Address ______________________________
No. and Street City State Zip

Policy Number ______________________ Coverage Amounts ______________

Dates of Coverage: From □□-□□-□□□□ To □□-□□-□□□□

Prior Carrier's Name ______________________________

Complete Address ______________________________
No. and Street City State Zip

Policy Number ______________________ Coverage Amounts ______________

Dates of Coverage: From □□-□□-□□□□ To □□-□□-□□□□

1. Have you ever been denied professional liability insurance or has your coverage ever been cancelled?

□ Yes* □ No

2. Within the last five (5) years, are there currently pending or have there been final judgments or settlements involving your professional practice?

□ Yes* □ No

*If "Yes", please provide the following information for each situation on a separate sheet. This would include final settlements or judgments where no liability was assigned to you.

a) name of insurance carrier

b) policy number

c) name, address, and age of claimant or plaintiff

d) nature and substance of claim

e) date and place at which claim arose

f) amounts paid, if any, and date and manner of disposition, judgment, settlement, or otherwise

g) date and reason for final disposition, if no judgment or settlement

continues

Exhibit 3–2 continued

SECTION TEN
CURRENT PROFESSIONAL PRACTICE

Primary Specialty of Practice: ______________________________

Subspecialty(s): ______________________________

____

____

Secondary Specialty of Practice: ______________________________

Subspecialty(s): ______________________________

____

____

____

Do you wish to be listed as: ☐ Primary Care Provider ☐ Specialist ☐ Both

If you are a primary care physician, list special diagnostic or treatment procedures performed in your office(s):

____

____

____

____

Medicare ID # ______________ Medicaid ID # ______________

National Provider Identification Number (NPID—formerly UPIN) ______________

Are you a member of an IPA? ☐ Yes ☐ No If Yes, complete the following:

IPA Name ______________________________

IPA Address ______________________________

IPA Telephone ( ) ______________________________

Are you currently accepting new patients into your practice? ☐ Yes ☐ No

Are you willing, in the future, to accept new patients? ☐ Yes ☐ No

List any restrictions on your practice:

____

____

____

____

____

continues

Exhibit 3–2 continued

SECTION ELEVEN
OFFICE BILLING INFORMATION: PRIMARY OFFICE

Complete mailing address ____
No. and Street City State Zip

Office Telephone ( ) ____________________ Fax ( ) ____________________

Type of practice:

☐ Solo

☐ Partnership Name of Partner(s) ____________________

☐ Single-Specialty Group Name of Group/Specialty ____________________

☐ Multi-Specialty Group Name of Group/Specialty ____________________

☐ Other Specify ____________________

Group/Corporate Name as it appears on your W-9 (if applicable) ____________________

Name of Office Manager ____________________

Name of Nurse Coordinator/Manager ____________________

List name, specialty and phone number of physicians covering your practice in your absence. Your practice must provide 24-hour coverage; attach an additional sheet, if necessary:

Name ____________ Spec. ____________ Phone ____________

Name ____________ Spec. ____________ Phone ____________

Name ____________ Spec. ____________ Phone ____________

Language(s) in which you are fluent ____________________

Language(s) in which office staff are fluent ____________________

Any other resources for translation? ____________ Languages ____________

Does the office have wheelchair or handicapped access? ☐ Yes ☐ No

Does the office have other services for the disabled? (TTY, ASI, mental/physical impairments, etc.)
☐ Yes ☐ No

List services ____________________

Office Hours:	Monday	______ am	to	______ pm
	Tuesday	______ am	to	______ pm
	Wednesday	______ am	to	______ pm
	Thursday	______ am	to	______ pm
	Friday	______ am	to	______ pm
	Saturday	______ am	to	______ pm

Make checks payable to ____________________

Payment Address ____
No. and Street City State Zip

Telephone ( ) ____________________ IRS Tax ID # ____________________

continues

Exhibit 3–2 continued

SECTION ELEVEN
OFFICE BILLING INFORMATION: OFFICE NUMBER 2

Complete mailing address ______________________________
No. and Street City State Zip

Office Telephone ( ) ______________ Fax ( ) ______________

Type of practice:

☐ Solo

☐ Partnership Name of Partner(s) ______________

☐ Single-Specialty Group Name of Group/Specialty ______________

☐ Multi-Specialty Group Name of Group/Specialty ______________

☐ Other Specify ______________

Group/Corporate Name as it appears on your W-9 (if applicable) ______________

Name of Office Manager ______________

Name of Nurse Coordinator/Manager ______________

List name, specialty and phone number of physicians covering your practice in your absence. Your practice must provide 24-hour coverage; attach an additional sheet, if necessary:

Name ______________ Spec. ______________ Phone ______________

Name ______________ Spec. ______________ Phone ______________

Name ______________ Spec. ______________ Phone ______________

Language(s) in which you are fluent ______________

Language(s) in which office staff are fluent ______________

Any other resources for translation? ______________ Languages ______________

Does the office have wheelchair or handicapped access? ☐ Yes ☐ No

Does the office have other services for the disabled? (TTY, ASI, mental/physical impairments, etc.)
☐ Yes ☐ No

List services ______________

Office Hours:	Monday	______ am	to	______ pm
	Tuesday	______ am	to	______ pm
	Wednesday	______ am	to	______ pm
	Thursday	______ am	to	______ pm
	Friday	______ am	to	______ pm
	Saturday	______ am	to	______ pm

Make checks payable to ______________

Payment Address ______________________________
No. and Street City State Zip

Telephone ( ) ______________ IRS Tax ID # ______________

continues

Exhibit 3–2 continued

SECTION ELEVEN
OFFICE BILLING INFORMATION: OFFICE NUMBER 3

Complete mailing address ____
No. and Street City State Zip

Office Telephone ( ) ____________________ Fax ( ) ________________

Type of practice:

☐ Solo

☐ Partnership Name of Partner(s) ____________________

☐ Single-Specialty Group Name of Group/Specialty ____________________

☐ Multi-Specialty Group Name of Group/Specialty ____________________

☐ Other Specify ____________________

Group/Corporate Name as it appears on your W-9 (if applicable) ____________________

Name of Office Manager ____________________

Name of Nurse Coordinator/Manager ____________________

List name, specialty and phone number of physicians covering your practice in your absence. Your practice must provide 24-hour coverage; attach an additional sheet, if necessary:

Name ____________________ Spec. ______________ Phone ______________

Name ____________________ Spec. ______________ Phone ______________

Name ____________________ Spec. ______________ Phone ______________

Language(s) in which you are fluent ____________________

Language(s) in which office staff are fluent ____________________

Any other resources for translation? __________ Languages ______________

Does the office have wheelchair or handicapped access? ☐ Yes ☐ No

Does the office have other services for the disabled? (TTY, ASI, mental/physical impairments, etc.)
☐ Yes ☐ No

List services ____________________

Office Hours:	Monday	______ am	to	______ pm
	Tuesday	______ am	to	______ pm
	Wednesday	______ am	to	______ pm
	Thursday	______ am	to	______ pm
	Friday	______ am	to	______ pm
	Saturday	______ am	to	______ pm

Make checks payable to ____________________

Payment Address ____
No. and Street City State Zip

Telephone ( ) ____________________ IRS Tax ID # ____________________

continues

Exhibit 3–2 continued

SECTION TWELVE
PRACTICE INFORMATION ADDENDUM

Do you or your business entity own, operate, manage or participate in any medical enterprise or business? If Yes, explain on separate attachment.

☐ Yes ☐ No

Please provide the following information for each office location; does this office have:

Lab Services ☐ Yes ☐ No

☐ On Site ☐ Reference Lab

Name of Reference Lab ______________________________

CLIA Waiver # ______________________________

CLIA Identification # ______________________________

Does this office have the following: (Check all that apply)

☐ Radiology ☐ EKG

☐ Audiology ☐ Treadmill

☐ Sigmoidoscopy ☐ Other

List all independent licensed non-physicians working out of this office, by name, provider type and license #:

Name ______________________________

Provider Type ______________________________

License # ______________________________

Name ______________________________

Provider Type ______________________________

License # ______________________________

continues

Exhibit 3–2 continued

SECTION THIRTEEN
REFERENCES

Please list three (3) peers who have personal knowledge of your current clinical abilities, ethical character, and ability to work cooperatively with others. These should be individuals who will provide specific written comments on these matters upon request. The named individuals must have acquired the requisite knowledge through observation of your professional practice over a reasonable period of time.

Examples of professional references are other practitioners in the same field and/or other practitioners in your specialty. None of your references should be relatives or current professional associates.

If your training was completed within the past three (3) years, you may list your Program Director(s) as professional reference(s). If you have been out of training for more than three (3) years, it is important to name individuals who have not been listed in any other part of the application.

1. Name ____________________

   Mailing Address ____________________
   No. and Street City State Zip

2. Name ____________________

   Mailing Address ____________________
   No. and Street City State Zip

3. Name ____________________

   Mailing Address ____________________
   No. and Street City State Zip

4. Name ____________________

   Mailing Address ____________________
   No. and Street City State Zip

continues

Exhibit 3–2 continued

SECTION FOURTEEN
DISCLOSURE INFORMATION

Have any of the following ever been, or are currently in process, either on a *voluntary or involuntary basis: denied, revoked, suspended, reduced, limited, placed on probation, not renewed or relinquished for disciplinary reasons?

All "Yes" answers require full explanation on a separate page.

1. Medical license in any state	☐ Yes	☐ No
2. Other professional registration/licensure	☐ Yes	☐ No
3. State Controlled Substance Registration	☐ Yes	☐ No
4. Federal DEA Registration	☐ Yes	☐ No
5. Membership on any hospital/medical staff	☐ Yes	☐ No
6. Clinical privileges	☐ Yes	☐ No
7. Participation in the Medicare/Medicaid program	☐ Yes	☐ No
8. Other health care organizations (surgicenter, managed care, PPO, PHO, MSO, etc.)	☐ Yes	☐ No
9. Professional society membership	☐ Yes	☐ No
10. Board certification	☐ Yes	☐ No
11. ECFMG certification	☐ Yes	☐ No
Additional Information A. Have you been convicted of a felony?	☐ Yes	☐ No

*A voluntary relinquishment or voluntary non-renewal is for disciplinary reasons when the relinquishment or non-renewal is done to avoid an adverse action or preclude an investigation or is done while the licensee is under investigation related to professional conduct.

1) Are you able to perform the procedures and the essential functions of the position for which you have applied or requested privileges, with or without reasonable accommodation, according to accepted standards of professional performance and without posing a direct threat to patients? ☐ Yes ☐ No

2) Are you currently engaged in the illegal use of drugs?* ☐ Yes ☐ No

3) Have you used illegal drugs within the last 2 years?* ☐ Yes ☐ No

*If you are making application to a governmental entity, you have the right to elect not to answer questions 2 & 3, if you have reasonable cause to believe that answering may expose you to the possibility of criminal prosecution.

continues

Exhibit 3–2 continued

SECTION FIFTEEN
ATTESTATION

All information and documentation submitted by me in this application is correct and complete to my best knowledge and belief.

I acknowledge that any material misstatements in or omissions from this application may constitute cause for denial of my application for staff membership or participation.

A copy of this original statement as signed by me shall have all the same force and effect as the signed original.

Name (print): ______________________________

Signature: ______________________________

Date: ______________________________

continues

Exhibit 3–2 continued

SECTION SIXTEEN
REQUIRED COPIES

PLEASE INCLUDE A COPY OF THE FOLLOWING WITH THIS APPLICATION:

☐ Current state license(s) (wallet card)

☐ State Controlled Dangerous Substance Certificate (if applicable)

☐ Current federal DEA registration

☐ Board Certification Certificate or qualifying letter
Copies may be obtained through your respective specialty board.

☐ Current Professional Liability Insurance face sheet
A copy may be obtained from your individual carrier and/or your agent.

☐ Standard ECFMG certificate (if applicable)
International medical graduates requiring a copy of their certificate should contact the:
Educational Commission for Foreign Medical Graduates
3624 Market Street
Philadelphia, PA 19104

☐ Emergency Care Training Certificates (CPR, BLS, ACLS, HCPC, ATLS, NALS, PALS, etc.)

☐ Photo identification. Four (4) prints of a recent photograph (either black & white or color) for identification purposes.

☐ Curriculum Vitae

continues

Exhibit 3–2 continued

SECTION SEVENTEEN
ADDITIONAL INFORMATION

THIS PAGE IS FURNISHED FOR YOUR CONVENIENCE IN PROVIDING ADDITIONAL INFORMATION. PLEASE MAKE AS MANY COPIES OF THIS PAGE AS YOU REQUIRE TO FULLY ANSWER ALL QUESTIONS.

Note: ECFMG, Educational Commission for Foreign Medical Graduates; IPA, independent practice association; PPO, preferred provider organization; PHO, physician-hospital organization; MSO, management service organization; UPIN, unique provider identification number; CPR, cardiopulmonary resuscitation; CLIA, Clinical Laboratory Improvement Act.

Courtesy of National Credentialing Forum, Colorado Springs, Colorado.

licenses are required by some states. Check individual states for requirements.

There may be multiple board certification, and it is important to know whether a particular board requires recertification. Historically, the period has been every 7 to 10 years for those boards that require recertfication.

Cardiopulmonary resuscitation (CPR) certification is the only component in this section that is not an accreditation requirement. However, organizations may require CPR certification by everyone or by designated specialties that would most likely be in a position to use CPR, and it is therefore relevant for meeting privileging criteria.

Section 6: Academic Appointments. Nice to know. This information can be helpful in determining where individuals spent some of their time if not in private practice or if in addition to active practice. It may also serve as information required by NCQA with regard to "work history" (see section 8). Verification of this information is optional.

Section 7: Health Care Affiliations. Need to know/accreditation requirement. Most hospitals will want to verify all current and past hospital affiliations. This requirement falls under the Joint Commission category of "current competence," since most hospitals will give some kind of evaluation when they respond to the request for information. NCQA requires only verification of a primary admitting facility, although managed care organizations may decide to verify all that are listed. However, this information in conjunction with section 8 could be used to verify a work history for the previous five years. The time limit mentioned (the last five years) is optional; organizations can decide how far back they want to go.

Section 8: Other Professional Work History. Need to know/accreditation requirement (NCQA). This information may vary from section 7 in that it often lists practice affiliation and/or employment that may be separate from general health care affiliations. NCQA does require a work history for the past five years. The statement at the top of this section with regard to accounting for time gaps of 30 days or more is an option, although it is a good idea for organizations to determine what time lapse is acceptable without a need to know what the practitioner was doing during that period of time.

Section 9: Professional Liability Insurance. Need to know/accreditation requirement. NCQA requires information on professional liability insurance coverage and any claims history within the last five years. The Joint Commission requires verification of whatever is outlined in the bylaws; most medical staffs have a requirement for professional liability insurance. In addition, the Joint Commission does require a minimum of information with regard to final judgments or settlements. The question about denial of coverage is optional, but most organizations request this information, since it could provide insight into any problems encountered with canceled insurance. The same reason exists for requesting prior insurance carrier information: this information might be needed to obtain the five-year claims history.

Section 10: Current Professional Practice. Need to know. This information is primarily for the benefit of managed care organizations, although hospitals may find it useful information. The unique provider identification number (UPIN) and the Medicare and Medicaid ID numbers are often requested by the billing department of the hospital.

Section 11: Office Billing Information. Primary office information is need to know. This information is used primarily in managed care organizations, although hospitals might be interested in the section regarding other languages spoken. Secondary and tertiary office information is need to know. See previous section.

Section 12: Practice Information Addendum. Need to know. This information is primarily used by managed care organizations. The last bullet regarding licensed nonphysicians working out of the office may be useful to hospitals and managed care organizations if these individuals apply to the allied health staff.

Section 13: References. Need to know/accreditation requirement (the Joint Commission). The number of references required by an organization is optional. The Joint Commission's reference to peer references states that recommendations given should be from those who have firsthand knowledge of the applicant and who, preferably, are in the same specialty but at least have the same license.[7] Whether to require or exclude program directors depending on how long someone has been out of training is optional for each organization to decide. Also, any stipulation about references from relatives or current professional associates is an individual organization decision.

Section 14: Disclosure Information. Need to know/accreditation requirement. Basically, the first section regarding "voluntary or involuntary" language and the questions in numbers 1 through 6 and number 8 are referred to in Joint Commission standards. The phrase "placed on probation" is not accreditation language. NCQA standards refer to any sanctions or limitations on licensure and would pertain to numbers 1 through 4, and specific standards relate to number 7. All questions are relevant information and in the best interest of organizations to ask. Number 1 at the bottom of the page refers to Joint Commission and NCQA language, and number 2 is specific language from NCQA. Both accreditation organizations defer exact statement or inquiry about health matters to the specific organization, on the basis of legal requirements such as the Americans with Disabilities Act and legal advice.

Section 15: Attestation. Need to know/accreditation requirement. NCQA requires an attestation to all of the information provided on the form. The Joint Commission has no standard related to an attestation but requires compliance with bylaws and agreement to no fee splitting.

Section 16: Required Copies. Need to know/accreditation requirement. The first six items are required by both accrediting organizations in terms of verification. Some require primary source verification; others (CDS, DEA, and liability insurance face sheet) require only that a copy be provided and not necessarily that it be verified. See Chapter 5 of this book for more specific information. The last three items are optional as required by the individual organization.

Section 17: Additional Information. This page allows space for the practitioner to give any explanations requested throughout the application form.

Release of Information

All applications have some type of release of information that is also signed by the applicant. This can include many different items, such as

- attestation (as seen in the credentialing data)
- agreement to appear for any interviews if requested
- acknowledgment of receipt and reading of medical staff bylaws, rules and regulations, and policies and procedures, and agreement to abide by same.
- authorization of the hospital to verify all information included in the application
- statement releasing from liability the hospital, its medical staff, and their authorized representatives in obtaining the information necessary to the credentialing review process
- statement releasing providers of "good faith" information
- recognition that applicant has the responsibility of producing adequate information for proper evaluation
- agreement to not participate in any form of illegal fee splitting

See Exhibit 3–3 for example of an attestation, release, and consent form.

Exhibit 3–3 Sample Attestation, Release, and Consent Form

Application for Appointment to the Medical Staff—

NAME: ______________________________ DATE: ______________

I FULLY UNDERSTAND THAT ANY SIGNIFICANT MISSTATEMENT IN OR OMISSIONS FROM THIS APPLICATION CONSTITUTE CAUSE FOR DENIAL OF APPOINTMENT OR CAUSE FOR SUMMARY DISMISSAL FROM THE MEDICAL STAFF. ALL INFORMATION SUBMITTED BY ME IN THIS APPLICATION (INCLUDING ATTACHMENTS) IS TRUE TO MY BEST KNOWLEDGE AND BELIEF. I AGREE TO UPDATE THIS APPLICATION SHOULD THERE BE ANY CHANGE IN THE INFORMATION PROVIDED.

In making this application for appointment to the Medical Staff of this Hospital, I acknowledge that I have received and read the Medical Staff Bylaws, Rules and Regulations, and that I am familiar with the Guiding Principles for Physician-Hospital Relationships of the California Medical Association and the Principles of Medical Ethics of the American Medical Association. I agree to be bound by the terms thereof if I am granted membership or clinical privileges, and I further agree to be bound by the terms thereof without regard to whether or not I am granted membership or clinical privileges in all matters relating to the consideration of my application for appointment to the Medical Staff.

By applying for appointment to the Medical Staff I hereby signify my willingness to appear for the interviews in regard to my application and authorize the Hospital, its Medical Staff and their representatives to consult with administrators and members of medical staffs of other hospitals or institutions with which I have been associated and with others, including but not limited to past and present malpractice carriers, professional societies, specialty boards and professional schools and training programs who may be material to an evaluation of my professional qualifications and competence to carry out the clinical privileges requested as well as my moral and ethical qualifications for staff membership. I hereby release from liability all representatives of the Hospital and its Medical Staff for their acts performed in good faith and without malice in connection with evaluating my application and my credentials and qualifications, and I hereby release from any liability any and all individuals and organizations who provide information to the Hospital, or its Medical Staff, in good faith and without malice concerning my professional competence, ethics, character and other qualifications for staff appointment and clinical privileges, and I hereby consent to release of such information.

I hereby further authorize and consent to the release of information by representatives of this Hospital, or its Medical Staff, to other hospitals and healthcare facilities, or their medical staffs, licensing boards and medical associations on request regarding any information the Hospital and the Medical Staff may have concerning me as long as such release of information is done in good faith and without malice, and I hereby release from liability the Hospital, its Medical Staff and their authorized representatives to the full extent permitted by law for so doing. Nothing in this document shall be construed as limiting or superseding any immunities otherwise provided by law.

I understand and agree that I, as an applicant for Medical Staff membership, have the burden of producing adequate information for proper evaluation of my professional competence, character, ethics and other qualifications and for resolving any doubts about such qualifications. I agree that further verification of my identity may be obtained if deemed necessary by the Hospital, by use of my photograph. I will not participate in any form of illegal fee-splitting.

SIGNATURE OF APPLICANT: ____________________ DATE: ______________

Courtesy of Children's Hospital, San Diego, California.

The Application Packet

The application packet will include the application form and other forms as required by internal policies and documents. Those most often included are

1. a cover memo or letter providing directions or explanation to the applicant (this information could be included on the front page of the application form rather than being in a separate letter)
2. the application form
3. privilege delineation forms and criteria
4. an attestation, if not part of the application
5. a release form, if not part of the application
6. copy of the medical staff bylaws, general rules and regulations, department rules and regulations and any supplemental documents to the bylaws, such as fair hearing plan and credentialing policies and procedures
7. any forms requiring signature or other information as outlined in hospital policy

The application packet may be given or sent to the applicant by the medical staff office or by some other designated centralized credentialing organization, such as a commercial or medical society CVO or a corporate or system credentialing office.

See Exhibit 3–4 for a sample cover letter to the applicant. The application packet should include a cover letter or statement as to the application information that should be completed and returned. See above list for examples. A curriculum vitae may also be requested.

Complete Application Criteria

The application should not be considered complete until or unless all information requested or required has been received. Bylaws should define a "completed application," which involves more than just the completion of the application itself, and should state that "the application is not complete unless all information verified and requested is received for adequate review." The bylaws or policies could also contain a statement pertaining to review by all medical staff and board components and noting that, at any step in that process, additional information can be requested by the applicant or other sources. If such information is not received, the application is considered incomplete.

The reason for defining a completed application is that if additional information is not received, rather than denying the application on the basis of all information not being received, one can consider the application incomplete, so that denial or acceptance is a nonissue. Any incomplete application should not be processed through all review groups because information is missing that could make a difference in the outcome if it were available. (See the section "Voluntary Withdrawal of Application" below.)

Returned application packets should be reviewed and compared against criteria to ensure that all required and requested information has been submitted. Such criteria would address

- all sections on the application completed
- explanation of any gaps in time
- explanation of any litigation
- explanation of any "yes" answers
- signed and dated attestation, release forms
- legible copies of any license, insurance coverage, and so forth requested
- other signed information required by policy
- clinical privilege form and any required documentation for specific clinical privileges

Exhibit 3–5 is a sample checklist that can track information sent and received. The 180 days at the bottom is optional. Each hospital can define its own number unless it has a delegated arrangement with a managed care organization requiring a time limit (either 120 or 180 days, depending upon the agreement).

Verification and Information-Gathering Process

Detailed information about what needs to be verified and options for verification can be found in Chapter 5 of this book. The verification pro-

Exhibit 3–4 Application Letter to Physicians

Name
Address

Dear Doctor ______________:

Thank you for requesting an application for membership to the Medical Staff of the Hospital of the Good Samaritan.

Enclosed you will find an application packet that you need to complete and return to the Medical Staff Office in its entirety. We will commence the application process on receipt of the completed packet. This process usually takes three to five months.

It is important that you **include the full name and address of your training institutions and, if possible, the names of your department and service chief. Applications will not be processed if any portion of the application packet is returned incomplete.**

There is a **four hundred dollar ($400.00) nonrefundable processing fee, and your completed application must be accompanied by a check in that amount made payable to Medical Staff of The Hospital of the Good Samaritan. Applications will not be processed if the fee is not submitted.**

In addition, copies of the following documents should be included with your completed application:

- Current California medical license
- Current DEA certificate
- Current professional liability insurance coverage ($1,000,000/$3,000,000)
- Recent photograph
- Radiology/fluoroscopy/X-ray certificate (if applicable)
- ECFMG certificate (if applicable)
- Current copy of ACLS/BCLS
- Copies of continuing medical education credits for the past two years
- Board certification in your principal field of practice by a recognized specialty board

Please be mindful when completing your request for clinical privileges sheet to **request only those privileges for which you can document training and recent experience.**

You will also find enclosed copies of both the Hospital and the Medical Staff Bylaws, Rules and Regulations. We advise that your signature on the **Statement of Applicant** indicates that you have received these documents, are familiar with them, and agree to abide and be bound by the same.

Again, thank you for your interest in membership to the Medical Staff of The Hospital of the Good Samaritan.

Sincerely,

, M.D.
Chairman, Credentials Committee

Courtesy of The Hospital of the Good Samaritan, Los Angeles, California.

Exhibit 3–5 Applicant Checklist

Name of Applicant: ____________________ Specialty ____________________
Date Application Received: ____________________ Complete: ____________________

State License: ____________________ Verified: ______ Yes ______ No
Expires: ____________________
DPS Registration: ____________________
Expires: ____________________
DEA Registration: ____________________
Expires: ____________________

Board Certified: ______________ Yes _____ No _____ In Process
Name of Board: ____________________
Date of Certification: ______________ Expiration: __________ Recert.: ________
Malpractice Insurance Carrier: ____________________
Amt. of Coverage: ____________________ Expiration date: ______________
Need to verify ECFMG: ______ Yes ______ No Date Queried: ______ Received: ______

Need the following to be queried:

	Queried	2nd Request	Received
National Practitioner Data Bank:	______	______	______
Federation of St. Medical Boards:	______	______	______
TSBME or Other:	______	______	______
Premedical Education:	______	______	______
Medical Education:	______	______	______
Internship:	______	______	______
Residency:	______	______	______
Fellowship/Other:	______	______	______
Hospital Affiliations:			
____________________	______	______	______
____________________	______	______	______
____________________	______	______	______
____________________	______	______	______
____________________	______	______	______
Peer References:			
____________________	______	______	______
____________________	______	______	______
____________________	______	______	______

COMMENTS/NOTES ____

____

___All information provided by the applicant and verification done within 180 days

Note: TSBME, Texas State Board of Medical Examiners; DPS, Department of Public Safety.

Courtesy of Columbia Medical Center–West, El Paso, Texas.

cess may be done internally by the organization's credentialing staff, contracted to an outside organization such as a CVO, or performed at a system level by some form of internal centralized verification service. More information on the centralized verification options can be found in Chapter 10.

Internal Process. Requests for verification and other information are generated, usually from a software or word-processing program that generates letters and forms, to go to the various organizations and individuals from which verifications and references will be sought. In general, organizations are asked to verify the dates when the applicant was affiliated with them, in addition to commenting on the competency of the individual for the privileges requested. Hospitals must also decide if they are going to send the applicant's privilege delineation request to training programs, hospital affiliations, and professional references and ask as part of their investigation process whether the referenced individual/organization believes the applicant is qualified for the privileges requested. See Chapter 5 for sample letters. At a minimum, most hospitals do elect to include the completed privilege delineation when sending reference verification letters to other acute care facilities. It is a traditional way in which to seek confirmation of current competency covering the full scope of clinical privilege requests by the applicant.

Policy will dictate whether professional references can come from former associates or should be from persons unaffiliated with the applicant in any formal way. There are two schools of thought. An affiliate or an associate may not be totally objective about the recommendation, whether it is negative or positive. On the other hand, that individual may have firsthand knowledge about the applicant's qualifications. If this type of reference is acceptable, be sure there are also references from individuals who are not affiliated through practice or formal association with the applicant. Some hospital policies state that professional references will exclude training program directors because information will come from those directors when verifying training and education. If any peer reference is not received, the hospital needs a policy as to whether it will request additional names from the applicant or consider the nonreply from the requested reference as a "caution flag" and follow up as to why the professional reference is not responding.

It is possible that in verifying certain training or education programs, there may be difficulty locating a foreign medical school or hospital reference. Again, the organization needs to define whether options are available if that original information cannot be verified, including acceptance of the ECFMG verification (see Chapter 5). The Joint Commission's intent statement in the verification section of its hospital accreditation standards states that reasonable efforts should be made to obtain the information from primary sources and to document those efforts.[8]

Primary source verification refers to getting information directly from the issuing source. The Joint Commission defines whether primary source verification is required or what acceptable alternatives there are to primary sources. Further detail is contained in the discussions of each of the verification components in Chapter 5 of this book.

Hospitals need a policy for second requests and possibly third requests for the information. In addition, a time frame should be established whereby a second request and/or subsequent notices are sent to the reference individual or organization. See the section "Voluntary Withdrawal of Application" below.

The hospital needs to decide whether it is going to send a reference/verification letter asking for a response and take what it gets or send an evaluation form (which could be included in the letter) and request that the form be completed and returned. Regardless of the policy of the hospital requesting the information, every hospital usually has a policy as to how it is going to respond to reference requests. If the hospital verifying the information sends an evaluation form and receives a letter in response, it needs to decide if it will accept that information in a standard response format in lieu of the evaluation form it originally sent. It usually has no choice in the matter. It could require the applicant to have someone at the other organization complete the form.

A copy of the release form signed by the applicant should accompany every request for information. See Chapter 5 for sample reference requests.

External Requests for Verification. As mentioned above, hospitals that send for references and verifications also receive requests to verify information for an applicant at another organization. The policy will dictate whether various types of evaluation forms will be completed manually by somebody in the medical staff office or whether a computer-generated letter will be sent with specific information such as how long the practitioner has been on staff, what the practitioner's category and/or status is, what department he or she belongs to, and whether he or she is in good standing. Usually a form letter is sent unless there has been some formal action taken, in which case legal counsel is usually consulted or has already drafted a letter to be sent to any organizations requesting information on that practitioner. Such policies should be outlined in the credentialing manual.

Another option for answering a request for a reference is to send a medical staff roster with limited information on a regular basis to those organizations (other hospitals, CVOs, managed care organizations) that routinely request a reference from the hospital. This concept was developed as a result of the requirement for managed care organizations, and CVOs that were delegated managed care organization verifications, to have all hospital affiliation current within 180 days. Some hospitals prefer to print a limited roster to save time in answering individual requests. Other hospitals are hesitant to provide that information in general to many organizations. If the roster is going to be distributed, limited information should be available, such as

- name of practitioner, license (MD, DO, DDS, etc.)
- category (active, courtesy, affiliate, other)
- initial appointment date
- a cover letter stating that physicians named on the roster are in good standing at that hospital

The roster should be dated and have the hospital name on it.

Hospitals who do provide rosters with this kind of information need to determine how they will handle any physicians who have had adverse action taken against them. We suggest that any of those names be pulled out of the roster, with a specific directive to the requesting hospital that before any information on the following physician can be given to the hospital, a release of information from that physician is required. See Chapter 5 for additional information on rosters.

Staff Analysis of Information Received

Completeness. In most hospitals, a medical staff office or some individual designated within the department or another department will manage the process of initial appointment. It is generally that individual's responsibility to review all the information when it is first submitted to clarify any issues that are identified before the medical staff is asked to review the application. The person reviewing the information needs to understand what the hospital is looking for and where to go with questions and/or concerns.

As the verified information is returned, an assessment is made to determine whether everything requested has been received, information is still missing that needs to be requested, or any information that is returned requires additional documentation or clarification. If the verification is verbal (over the phone), the information is documented in writing, signed, and dated. This information is kept with the application in the credentials file.

Caution Flags. In reviewing the information and verifications received, the following are examples of what should be evaluated and may raise a caution flag:

- gap in time—all time should be accounted for since graduation from medical school or its counterpart for other degrees. As mentioned earlier, the application and/or policies should state the acceptable time period that would not need to be verified (in days, weeks, or months).
- any unanswered question or incomplete section on the application
- any potential adverse comments from any of the references, training programs, hospital affiliations, and so forth that are received
- evasive information given on a reference form—for example, a reference that does not comment at all on the competency of the individual being evaluated but only states affiliation
- a difference in the dates confirmed from what is contained on the application (this may be a typo and may easily be corrected by reconfirming with the applicant or reference respondent)
- any claims, judgments, or lawsuits filed (the medical staff may have a policy as to what they consider serious lawsuits versus "nuisance suits" and may not want to evaluate or be concerned with any payment under a certain amount of money (e.g., $5,000).
- any information with regard to revocation, suspension, denial, voluntary withdrawal, investigation, or other matters of an adverse nature
- noncompletion of a training program at any institution
- any felony conviction

Any one of these caution flags does not in and of itself mean that there is a particular problem. It is information that should be pointed out to the medical staff review individuals and committees so that they can determine if further information is required from the source of the reference or the applicant or both.

Medical Staff Review Process

When the credentials file is ready for review by the medical staff, it should include any preapplication information, the application itself, any information that was requested to accompany the application (copy of license, photo, other information), all verified information, the clinical privilege form, any required or volunteered documentation, continuing medical education information, and any documentation of phone verification in lieu of written verifications.

Medical staff policy will dictate whether interviews with new applicants are or may be required should any review individual or committee at any point have questions that they believe would be best answered by a personal interview. Some hospitals routinely conduct an interview with all new applicants as a means of getting to know them on an individual basis and have the applicant meet one or several of the groups of peers who are reviewing their application request. Other hospitals request interviews only when they have specific reason. The medical staff office generally schedules the interviews between the new applicant and whichever group or individual requests the interview. Some organizations place the burden of scheduling one-on-one interviews directly on the applicant.

The order of the medical staff review processes varies among organizations and seems to vary depending on the area of the country or the particular community. Usually, the credentials file first goes to the department chair for review. In some hospitals, the file may go to the credentials committee before the department review.

There can be as many levels of application review as bylaws and policies define. It is important to understand that at any time during the review process, up to and including the evaluation/review by the governing board, additional information can be requested from the applicant or other sources. (See the section "Express Credentialing Process" near the end of this chapter for sample review and approval worksheets.)

Department Review. Although the Joint Commission standards indicate that it is the chair's responsibility to make any recommendations regarding appointment, reappointment, or clinical privilege criteria, a department chair often will utilize other members of his or her department to involve them in the review process. Files can be referred to a subcommittee or section chair (e.g., in specialties such as cardiology or gastroenterology that are part of the department).

It is recommended that the credentials file not go to the entire department. If an adverse recommendation is sent to the credentials committee or executive committee, it should not come from the department as a whole. Legal counsel should be sought when deciding how many people to involve at the department-level process in this review, on the basis of concerns such as restraint of trade and conflict of interest.

If a credentials committee does exist, the function of the department committee and the function of the credentials committee differ. The department should always be responsible for reviewing whether the individual is qualified for the clinical privileges being requested. The department chair and any delegated review body within the department have the prerogative to request any additional information that may be helpful or needed in making that determination. Even though the whole file is reviewed at the department level, some information can be delegated as a credentials committee review responsibility. It is a good idea for the medical staff office individual responsible for reviewing the files to meet with the department chair and review each file, pointing out any information that the support staff is questioning. Medical staff members not familiar with the credentials file may need some assistance in their review.

Credentials Committee Review. Many hospitals have a credentials committee, and although not required, it serves a very useful purpose in that it is primarily involved with the evaluation of initial appointments, reappointments, and requests for change or additions in staff category or clinical privileges. The committee reviews all of the other information that has been submitted, such as malpractice insurance coverage, relationship evaluations, and any nonclinical issues. If the credentials committee reviews the file before the department does, it could also be responsible for determining that everything has been submitted for review, regardless of who is going to be reviewing what component. The credentials committee also has the option of requesting additional information from the applicant or the references before making an informed recommendation to the next level of review. The medical staff office personnel should meet with the credentials committee chair before files go to the credentials committee in case any questions or special information needs to be relayed to the chair before the committee meeting (see Chapter 7 of this book for more detail).

Medical Executive Committee Review. Once the file reaches the executive committee, the recommendations of the department and credentials committee (if one exists) are reviewed, and a recommendation is made to the governing board. If the medical staff is not departmentalized or is without a credentials committee, the executive committee will probably perform a more intense review. Unless any problems have been earlier identified or unless someone on the executive committee brings forth additional information, the executive committee will generally rely on the recommendation made to it and then forward its recommendation to the governing board (see Chapter 7).

Governing Body Action

The governing board is required by the Joint Commission to act on all applications for medical staff membership and clinical privileges. It is the governing board that "approves" all credentialing actions. Up to that point, all medical staff actions are to "recommend," but the governing board "approves." In some hospitals, there may be a subcommittee of the governing board that looks at the credentials file and then makes a recommendation to the board through a consent agenda.

A summary of the credentials file or a list of actions to be considered according to appointment, reappointment, or change in privileges can go to the governing board. There is variation in what governing boards like to see with regard to credentialing information. The norm for most hospitals is that the medical staff office has the responsibility of producing a medical staff report (see Chapter 7).

Notification to Applicant and Others

Following governing board approval, the applicant is notified in writing of the action taken by the governing board. All appropriate hospital departments and/or medical staff are additionally notified of the applicant's approval. Information can be included in a medical staff newsletter, if one exists, that lists all the new appointments to the medical staff.

With regard to notification to hospital department personnel, several methods may be considered, depending upon resources:

- A memo may be sent to all departments following each board meeting with additions, deletions, and corrections.
- Internal e-mail notification may be used.
- New medical staff rosters, which would contain any changes in medical staff information, may be produced on a routine basis and distributed.
- Other internal information systems may be updated to include the new information.
- Information may be included in an employee newsletter.

Any computer system should also be updated with the governing board approval date and anything else that needs to be included and has not previously been entered into the computer.

Adverse Action

Should an adverse recommendation result from the medical staff review process, most bylaws state that the applicant must be notified of the adverse recommendation before final action by the governing board.

Some medical staff bylaws allow adverse recommendations to go directly to the board. Once the board has taken action to deny privileges and/or membership, the applicant is notified about the denial and allowed to appeal that denial through the fair hearing process. Either way, it is important to understand that the process used is defined in the bylaws or the fair hearing plan. Follow it. (See Chapter 9 for the general process to be followed in fair hearing procedures.)

Voluntary Withdrawal of Application

The burden of proof is on the applicant! If information is missing, it is the applicant's responsibility to help obtain that information so that a review process can take place. A policy and procedure needs to state that if additional information is requested from the applicant, the applicant is given a certain amount of time to submit the information. If it is not submitted within the stated time frame, a certified letter needs to be sent to the applicant stating that if the information is not received by a certain date, the application will be considered to be voluntarily withdrawn. It will be considered incomplete and will not be processed. This keeps the organization from having to reject the application and, possibly, going through a fair hearing process. It is also not reportable to the NPDB.

When such a certified letter is sent to the prospective applicant, the same letter should also be sent by regular mail. If someone did not want to accept the certified letter, there would be no way of proving that the information was received because the letter would be returned. If, however, the letter was also sent regular mail and not returned, it could be assumed that someone did receive the letter.

Time Frame for Initial Application Process

The time frame for the initial application process varies widely depending upon the time it takes to verify information and the time it takes for all the department, committee, and board reviews to take place. The process can take anywhere from 60 to 180 days. The bylaws or policies should have some provisions with regard to time frame so that applications are not delayed unnecessarily. Unlike NCQA, which requires a 180-day time frame, the Joint Commission does not require a specific time frame to complete the process other than adherence to whatever is stated in the bylaws.

The medical staff needs to determine how current it thinks the information should be for proper review to take place. This is where hospitals differ in the amount of time they allow for an application to be processed. Some bylaws and policies state that if an application takes longer than the period of time defined in the bylaws or policies, information older than a certain number of days needs to be reverified. Additionally, any information gathered early in the process that has since expired (e.g., licensure, DEA, insurance) is reverified so that all dated information is current at the time of the peer review process.

Step 3: Reappointment

Reappointment is the process of evaluating a practitioner's professional behavior and clinical competence for the previous two years, using internal as well as external sources to obtain the needed information for a thorough evaluation. The Joint Commission requires a reappointment process to occur at least every two years and specifies that reappointment to the medical staff and renewal and/or revision of clinical privileges is based on information concerning the individual's professional performance, judgment, and clinical or technical skills.[9]

Those practitioners who have honorary or emeritus type status (without clinical privileges) are not required to go through the reappointment process. They do not have any privileges, so there would be no reason for information to be verified regarding clinical competence for the continuation of clinical privileges. Physicians who are retired do not carry malpractice insurance, and many do not keep their licenses current either. Figure 3–5 is a flowchart showing steps in the reappointment process.

Characteristics of a Successful Process

Three crucial characteristics of a successful reappointment process are

1. *Timely process.* It is important to complete reappointments in a timely manner. This is important not just because of the Joint Commission two-year requirement but because most hospitals stagger reappointments on a monthly or quarterly basis, and it is easier when the defined schedule can be maintained.
2. *Sufficient information for performance evaluation.* The primary reason for reappointment is to be able to evaluate a practitioner's performance and make a determination whether to continue to grant the requested clinical privileges. This information can be obtained internally if the practitioner has been actively involved in patient care. If not, the hospital relies more heavily on information from outside sources, such as other hospitals' references and NPDB reports.
3. *Current privilege delineation forms.* It is important that clinical privilege delineation forms be current and that practitioners complete a new form for several reasons. Privilege forms can be updated often, depending on how frequently privileges are added. Practitioners should have the most up-to-date forms with all of the current privileges available to request. This is also the time when practitioners can de-

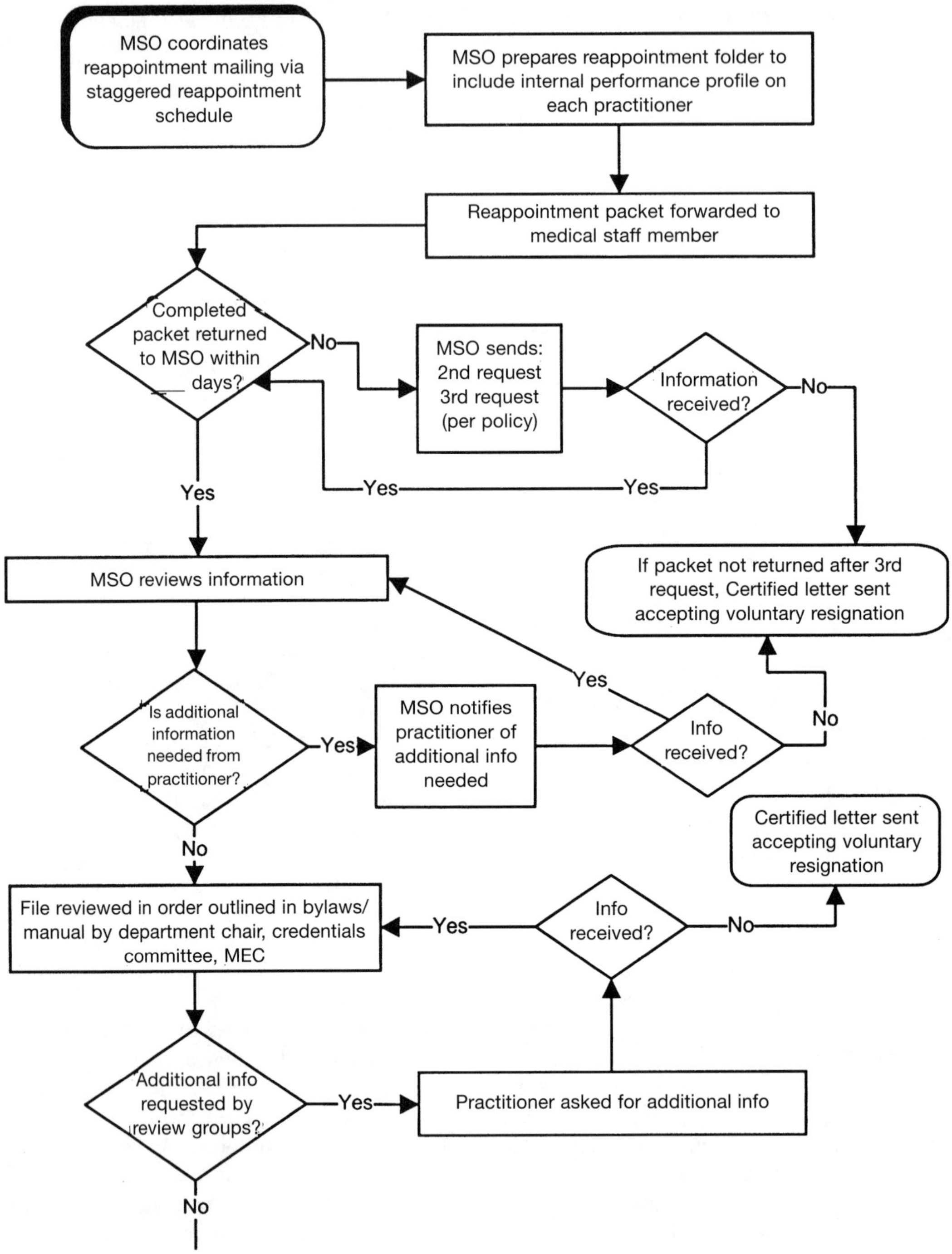
MSO coordinates reappointment mailing via staggered reappointment schedule
MSO prepares reappointment folder to include internal performance profile on each practitioner
Reappointment packet forwarded to medical staff member
Completed packet returned to MSO within ___ days?
No
MSO sends: 2nd request 3rd request (per policy)
Information received?
No
Yes
Yes
Yes
If packet not returned after 3rd request, Certified letter sent accepting voluntary resignation
MSO reviews information
Yes
Is additional information needed from practitioner?
Yes
MSO notifies practitioner of additional info needed
Info received?
No
No
Certified letter sent accepting voluntary resignation
File reviewed in order outlined in bylaws/ manual by department chair, credentials committee, MEC
Yes
Info received?
No
Additional info requested by review groups?
Yes
Practitioner asked for additional info
No

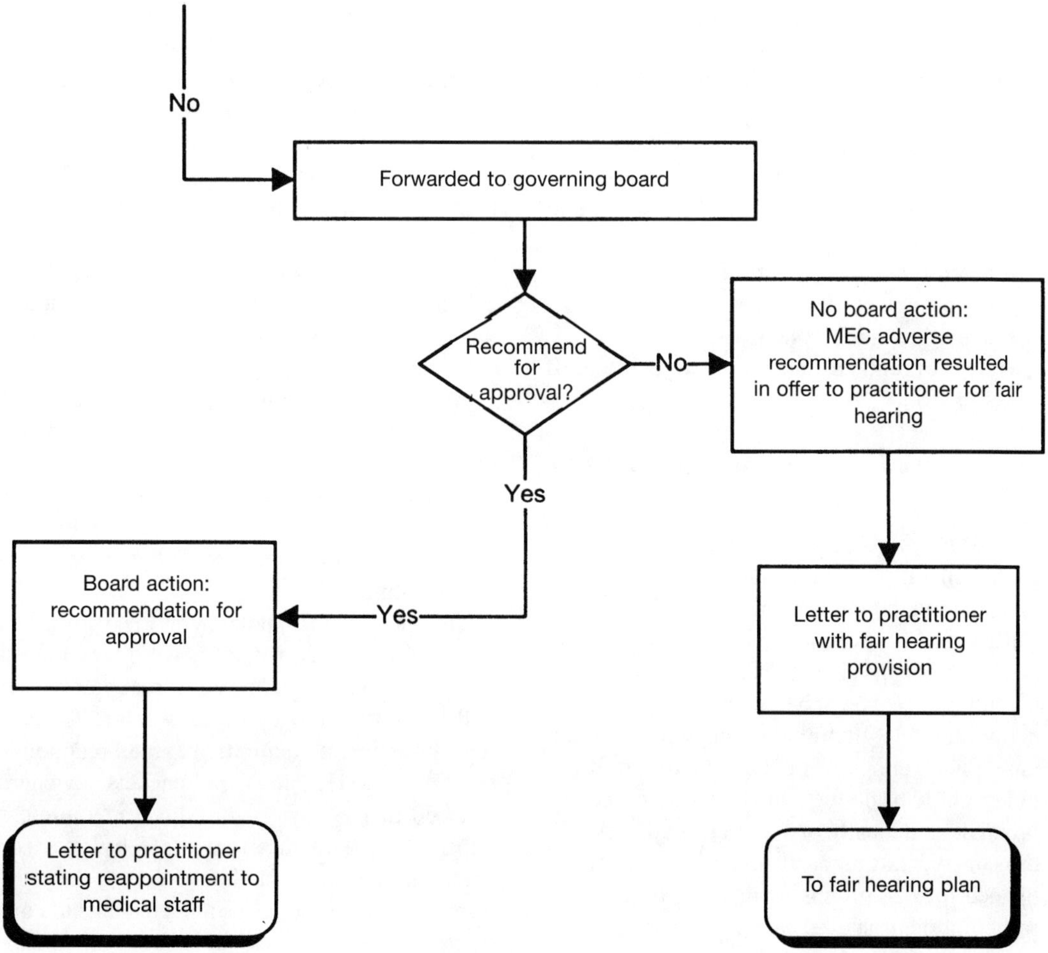

Note: MSO, medical staff office; MEC, medical executive committee.

Figure 3–5 Reappointment Process. Courtesy of C. Mobley & Associates, LLC, and Quality Management Options, LLC, Colorado Springs, Colorado.

lete privileges they do not want so that, when approved, the form will reflect only the current privileges granted.

Other characteristics have already been identified in the "Step 2: Initial Application Process" section and should be referenced. They include

- a good reapplication form
- a thorough review process
- a good tracking system
- well-organized and knowledgeable staff support

Schedule and Time Frame for Reappointment Process

Most hospitals do reappointments on a staggered schedule to better integrate this process with all the other responsibilities of the medical staff office or credentialing professional. Depending upon the size of the medical staff, reappointments can be scheduled over a two-year period quarterly, monthly, semiannually, or annually. For example, a small medical staff of 100 or less could be divided into two groups and one group done annually or six months apart within the same year. A medical staff of 1000 could be divided into 24 groups, with approximately 42 reappointments started each month or 120 each quarter. Each hospital needs to decide how best to stagger its reappointments and still be able to maintain other work activities: in other words, reappointment processing should be part of the ongoing activities. Otherwise, a huge reappointment "project" could generate a concentrated time effort that could jeopardize other routine activities such as meeting management and processing initial appointment requests, or requests for temporary privileges, which are more sporadic and need to be addressed when they occur.

How to divide the medical staff reappointments also presents some options. This can be done by alphabet, birth dates, license expiration (if state licenses expire at different times, often on birth date), department, or specialty for large medical staffs. If done by department or specialty, the department/section chairs have to be prepared to evaluate a majority or all of their colleagues in a concentrated period of time. This can have advantages, especially if the department/specialty can schedule its privilege delineation revision before the reappointment cycle. All current privilege forms in the credentials file will then be the same and will reflect all privileges currently available in that department. This option may work better for smaller medical staffs in terms of the department chair's time commitment to evaluate each department member over a 30- to 60-day time period.

Another option is to reappoint by birth date or some other mechanism that mixes the various specialties over a two-year period. This option requires department chairs to evaluate various department members (monthly, quarterly, etc.) over a year or two and spreads the labor intensity over time.

The number of reappointments to be processed at a time and a history of knowing how long it will take to process a group of reappointments will determine how many days before the current appointment's expiration to mail reappointment packets. Hospitals mail packets anywhere from 60 to 180 days before the reappointment expiration. The medical staff bylaws (or credentialing manual) should define the time frame for reappointment. Time elements to consider when deciding how far ahead to mail packets are

- time for practitioner to complete the reapplication form and return to the medical staff office (second or third requests may be necessary, depending on the facility's policy)
- processing time (for gathering information and verifications)
- time for evaluation by medical staff office (for obtaining additional information if necessary)
- time for medical staff review process (for the department, credentials committee [optional], and medical executive committee to obtain additional information if necessary)
- time for governing body review/approval (for obtaining additional information if necessary)

Some reappointments may not be able to be completed within the two-year time frame. Regardless of the reason, the Joint Commission expects 100 percent compliance with the standard (score 1). They expect that if the governing board has not acted on a reappointment within the two-year time limit, performance has been reviewed through the peer review process at some level within the two-year period from the last reappointment. A legitimate reason for not meeting the two-year requirement is that an investigation based on information received has extended the time. Compliance may be jeopardized if practitioners do not return their information on time, if the medical staff office is late in getting the packets distributed or processed when returned, or if the medical staff is delinquent in its review process.

The Reappointment Form

Two options are available regarding forms. A hospital (or its contracted CVO) can use the traditional reappointment application form, which is very similar to the appointment application form except that "static" information (i.e., information that does not change, such as initial training) is not included. Or a computer physician profile summary can be sent to the practitioner, requesting that any changes be made on the summary and returned. If a computer summary is used, an addendum needs to be sent that asks about all of the required Joint Commission information relative to malpractice judgments/settlements; involuntary/voluntary revocation, limitation, reduction, or loss of clinical privileges or hospital membership; earlier or current pending challenges to licensure or registrations (or voluntary relinquishment of these); and a statement regarding the ability to practice the privileges requested. In addition to the required accreditation information, a profile summary (with an addendum) or reappointment form should include

1. personal information update (address, phone, fax)
2. additional training
3. new board certifications/recertifications
4. current hospital affiliations (if part of the evaluation process per medical staff policy)
5. professional references (if part of the evaluation process). Note here that if the practitioner does not have any peers who will be involved in the formal medical staff review process (persons with the same credentials, such as MD/DO, DDS/DMD, or DPM), references from someone with the same credentials must be obtained. Also, the Joint Commission's explanation of the term *peer* states that it is "advisable" that an individual competency evaluation be made by someone from the same specialty when possible but is not required.[10]
6. indication to request any changes in privileges, staff category, or appointment (voluntary resignation, which, if requested, does not require completion of the form, just a dated signature)
7. continuing medical education participation
8. current information on state/DEA licensure and malpractice coverage (expiration dates, amount of insurance coverage)
9. dated and signed attestation, consent, and release

Exhibit 3–6 is a sample reapplication form.

The Reapplication Packet

The reappointment packet should include

- A cover letter that may request copies of information to be returned with the reappointment form (e.g., license, DEA, insurance face sheet with amounts of coverage and expiration dates). If a hospital is updating all expired information as it expires, it is not necessary at reappointment to request that information again. Another option is a reapplication fee. If there is one, a reminder to return a check with the packet is included.
- A reapplication form or computer profile summary with addendum (explained above) to include attestation and consent/release form.

Exhibit 3–6 Reappointment Application

Do you wish to apply for reappointment to the medical staff?

YES _____ NO _____

Please mark changes below as appropriate.

1. UPDATE OF PROFILE DATA		
Name:	Staff Class:	
Specialty: Subspecialty:		
Area(s) of Special Interest:		
Current Office Address:		
Office Phone:	Office Fax:	
Corporate Name:		
Home Address (For Emergencies Only):		
Home Phone:		
California License #:	Expiration Date:	
D.E.A. Number:	Expiration Date:	
UPIN #:		
Tax ID #:		
Medi-Cal Prov #:		
Applicant Name: **Doc Test**		
Professional Liability Carrier:	Policy Number:	Exp Date:
Amount of Coverage (Minimum Required $1 Million/$3 Million):		
Type of Board Certification:	Date Cert.:	Date Expires:
( ) Check here if certification or recertification has occurred within last two years. **(If so, please attach a copy of Board Recertification Letter.)**		

continues

Exhibit 3–6 continued

If Boards are Pending—Date Orals Taken: ________
Date Written Taken: ________

Certificate of Special Competency ________ Date Certified: ________
Active Candidacy: Yes: No:

Do you hold a Radiography/Fluoro. Certificate? (Dentists Excluded)
No: ________
Yes: ________ (Please attach a copy)
Certificate #: Expiration Date:

Hospitals at which you hold Active, Associate, or Provisional status. (Please indicate staff status and provide address if not local):

________________________ ________________________
________________________ ________________________
________________________ ________________________
________________________ ________________________

Foreign Languages Spoken:
Other: ____

Professional College/Academy/Society Memberships: ________________________
____

2. PRIVILEGES (See attached copy of current privilege sheet)

( ) I request that my clinical privileges remain the same.
( ) I request deletion of the following privileges:
____
( ) I request additional privileges (request must be accompanied by documentation of training and experience within the last three-year period and will not be considered without required documentation): ________________________
____

(ATTACHED PRIVILEGE REQUEST FORM MUST BE COMPLETEDAT EACH REAPPOINTMENT. REFER TO THE FORM FOR ADDITIONAL REQUIREMENTS, IF APPLICABLE.)

3. STAFF CLASSIFICATION REQUESTED

( ) I request to remain at my current classification of
( ) I request to be changed to the following (if I meet criteria for same):
( ) Honorary ( ) Senior ( ) Associate
( ) Courtesy ( ) Consultant {Assisting only}
( ) I request transfer to Affiliate Category (Category carries no privileges to practice at Children's Hospital.)
( ) Other:

continues

Exhibit 3–6 continued

4. PLEASE ANSWER THE FOLLOWING QUESTIONS		
If you answer "YES" to any of the following questions, please provide the status of any such matter regardless of whether the outcome is/was for or against you. The only exception to this will be as specifically mandated by a court order.		
	YES	NO
1. Have you had any voluntary or involuntary relinquishment of membership or have you had any voluntary or involuntary relinquishment, or limitation, reduction, or loss of clinical privileges at any other health care entity? (Do not include temporary suspension for medical records or privileges dropped at time of reappointment.)		
2. Do you have any pending disciplinary action by the medical staff or its departments or committees at any other hospital?		
3. Have you had any adverse judgments in the past two years?		
4. Do you have or have you had any successful or currently pending adverse actions at this time or in the last three years regarding licensure, DEA certification, professional liability insurance, professional organization, administrative agencies, faculty appointment, criminal/civil complaints related to medical practice?		
5. Have you voluntarily relinquished any such licensure, registration, membership or faculty appointments?		
6. Have you been involved in a professional liability action within the last three years? Or are you currently involved in a professional liability action? (If "YES," please give details on the attached "Professional Liability Action Explanation.")		
7. Are there any conditions of your mental or physical health (including history of substance dependency) which may affect your ability to meet professional standards related to your medical qualifications?		

continues

Exhibit 3–6 continued

5. PEER REFERENCES

Please provide the names and addresses of TWO PEER REFERENCES who are knowledgeable of your current competency. These individuals do not need to be members of Children's Medical Staff, but must have the same licensure (M.D., D.D.S., etc.) and SHOULD NOT BE PRACTICE ASSOCIATES.

Name: ______		Name: ______	
Address: ______		Address: ______	
City: ______	St: ______	City: ______	St: ______
Zip: ______	Phone: ______	Zip: ______	Phone: ______

6. APPLICANT'S ACKNOWLEDGMENT AND AGREEMENT:

I agree to maintain an ethical practice, to provide for continuous care of my patients, and to discharge Medical Staff, Departmental, Committee and Hospital functions for which I am responsible. I agree to appear, if requested, before Medical Staff officers and Medical Staff committees for interviews or inquiries regarding this reappointment application. I agree to notify the Hospital of any action taken by the Medical Board of California which affects the status of my California license. I verify that the information on this reappointment form is true and complete to the best of my knowledge. I agree to promptly advise the medical staff of Children's Hospital, San Diego, of any changes to this information which may occur prior to my next reappointment.

APPLICANT'S SIGNATURE: ______________________ DATE: __________

Courtesy of Children's Hospital, San Diego, California.

- A copy of current privilege delineation and a blank one to be completed. This gives practitioners the opportunity either to delete privileges that they no longer need or to add privileges that they did not have previously. (Note that this can be done at other times also, but some find it more convenient to request at reappointment. In addition, reappointment is a reminder for practitioners to review what privileges they currently have. They may see privileges they no longer need or want due to practice changes that they might not otherwise consider.)
- Any hospital-specific forms to be completed (e.g., signature cards)

See Exhibit 3–7 for sample cover letter.

Exhibit 3–7 Reappointment Application Letter

Dear Doctor __________________:

RE: REAPPOINTMENT TO STAFF/RETURN DEADLINE:

Reappointment at ______________ Hospital for all medical staff members is conducted on a rotational basis every 21 months (not to exceed an appointment period of 24 months).

The requirements of the Joint Commission on Accreditation of Healthcare Organizations mandate critical reappraisal of a physician at the time of reappointment. To assist us in meeting that requirement we would request that you complete the forms enclosed and supply the information as noted on the listing entitled "Additional Documentation Required for Reappointment Application." To assist you in completing these forms, the following informational items have been included:

(1) Breakdown of requirements by medical staff classifications
(2) Activity profile

Please be advised that information from the data summary sheet will be considered in all deliberations regarding your reappointment and staff classification. Should you feel that the information on the data summary sheet is not accurate, please indicate accordingly on the data summary sheet with appropriate documentation regarding additional utilization or committee attendance.

ADDITIONALLY, PLEASE NOTE THAT INFORMATION FROM QUALITY IMPROVEMENT ACTIVITIES IS PROFILED IN THE QUALITY IMPROVEMENT DEPARTMENT AND REVIEWED AT THE TIME OF REAPPOINTMENT. IF YOU WISH YOU MAY CONTACT THE QUALITY IMPROVEMENT DEPARTMENT AT ________________________ TO ARRANGE A TIME TO REVIEW THOSE DATA PRIOR TO YOUR REAPPOINTMENT.

Any questions regarding the reappointment process can be directed to ________________________. Packets should be forwarded to Medical Staff Services, (address) city, state, zip code. Thank you for your cooperation in this matter.

Sincerely,

Courtesy of Children's Hospital, San Diego, California.

Complete Reappointment Application Criteria

Detailed information with regard to what needs to be verified and options for verification can be found in Chapter 5 of this book. The verification process is one that may be done internally by the organization's credentialing staff, contracted to an outside organization such as a CVO, or carried out at a system level by some form of internal centralized verification service. More information on the centralized verification options can be found in Chapter 10.

Verification and Information-Gathering Process

Internal Process. This section under "Step 2: Initial Application Process" should be referred to, since the information defining a completed application is the same for the most part. Information in that section relevant to reappointment includes

- request for verification
- professional references (if used at reappointment other than the committee/department peer review process)
- second- and third-request policy
- hospital references (if used at reappointment)

Exhibit 3–8 is a sample reappointment evaluation form that includes reviews by medical staff office and medical staff.

For reappointment, information must be collected internally relative to performance activity that is practitioner specific. This includes clinical activity review (performance and statistics for admissions, consults, etc.) as well as compliance with any bylaws-specific requirements (e.g., meeting attendance, minimum or maximum admissions for certain staff categories, emergency department call compliance). For details on the practitioner profile, see Chapter 8 of this book.

External Requests. Bylaws, policies, or procedures will define what verifications and information must be collected at reappointment. Some of the information is outlined by accreditation standards, but some options exist. For example, the accreditation standards require verification of competency, and hospitals must decide the best way for them to obtain this. Internal performance activity is a good method. In addition, some hospitals will request information from other hospitals and/or professional references on all practitioners. Some hospitals will solicit references from other hospitals and/or professionals only if the practitioner is not active at their hospital. Again, it is a matter of policy according to what the medical staff believes it needs for a thorough evaluation upon which to make a recommendation. For details on external verifications, see Chapter 5.

Staff Analysis of Information Received

Completeness. As outlined in the "Step 2: Initial Application Process" section, medical staff office or other designed support personnel will first review the information received and request any additional information that is needed. It is important for personnel to determine if there are any requests for change in staff category, appointment status (some may indicate their desire not to be reappointed), and/or clinical privileges (deletions or additions) and if any attached documentation is required for new privileges requested. See the "Step 2: Initial Application Process" section for other staff analysis that relates to reappointment. Exhibit 3–9 is a sample letter for missing information.

Caution Flags. Information that may cause concern or at least be flagged for medical staff reviewers includes

- privileges that were not requested before if they require additional documentation that is not submitted with the revised privilege form or if they are not consistent with training/specialty
- neutral or negatively toned reference letters from other hospitals and/or peers

Exhibit 3–8 Reappointment Evaluation Form

Name ____________________ Department ____________________

Specialty ____________________ Staff Category ____________________

1 Current Licensure
Verified ☐ **Yes** ☐ **No**
Expiration Date: ________

2 Current DEA Licensure
Verified ☐ **Yes** ☐ **No**
Expiration Date: ________

3 National Practitioner Data
Bank Verified ☐ **Yes** ☐ **No**
NPDB Clear ☐ **Yes** ☐ **No**
If NO, see appended: ________

4 Malpractice Insurance Verified ☐ **Yes** ☐ **No**
Insurance Clear ☐ **Yes** ☐ **No**
If NO, see appended ________

5 Current ACLS Certificate
(if applicable) ☐ **Yes** ☐ **No**
Expiration Date: ________

6 Current Radiography
Fluoroscopy/X-ray ☐ **Yes** ☐ **No**
Certificate (if applicable)
Expiration Date: ________

7 CME Hours Appended ☐ **Yes** ☐ **No**

8 Attendance Requirements Met

	19	19		
Department			☐ **Yes**	☐ **No**
Gen. Staff			☐ **Yes**	☐ **No**

9 Hospital References Verified ☐ **Yes** ☐ **No**

10 Peer References Verified ☐ **Yes** ☐ **No**

11 Physician Activity Appended ☐ **Yes** ☐ **No**

12 Quality Management Activity Data
Appended ☐ **Yes** ☐ **No**

13 ________ Suspension Days in Past Two Years

14 Current Proctor Status: ________

15 Change in Privileges Requested
Add ________

Delete ________

Withdrawn ________

16 Change in Staff Category Requested
by Practitioner ☐ **Yes** ☐ **No**

Requested Category
-Meets Bylaws Requirements for
Requested/Current Staff
Category ☐ **Yes** ☐ **No**

17 Board Certification Status ________

COMPLETED BY ____________________ ____________
Medical Staff Coordinator *Date*

continues

Exhibit 3–8 continued

BASIC MEMBERSHIP FACTORS

To be completed by Department Chair

The following is an analysis of the practitioner's professional performance obtained through the verification of references contained in his/her reappointment application and the review of his/her Quality Management Activities at HGS or other facilities where he/she is clinically active.

1 Has the applicant had sufficient activity within the past 2 years consistent with the requested staff category?

☐ **Yes** ☐ **No**

2 Based on a QA & I activity this applicant's professional performance is satisfactory.

☐ **Yes** ☐ **No**

3 Has the applicant satisfactorily maintained coverage for his/her patients?

☐ **Yes** ☐ **No**

4 Does the applicant adhere to ethical standards?

☐ **Yes** ☐ **No**

5 Does the applicant work satisfactorily with hospital personnel, peers and patients?

☐ **Yes** ☐ **No**

6 Does the applicant adhere to the requirements in the Bylaws, Rules and Regulations including appropriate use of consultants?

☐ **Yes** ☐ **No**

7 Are suspensions for incomplete medical records within acceptable parameters as defined in the Rules and Regulations?

☐ **Yes** ☐ **No** ☐ **N/A**

8 Have you observed or been informed of any physical or behavioral conditions that have or may affect the practitioner's ability to perform professional and medical staff duties appropriately?

☐ **Yes** ☐ **No**

9 Have you any knowledge of erratic or intemperate behavior on the part of this applicant?

☐ **Yes** ☐ **No**

Summary Comments ________________________________

____

____

CLINICAL PERFORMANCE FACTORS

To be completed by Department Chair

1 Has the applicant adequately met his responsibility to provide Emergency Room coverage?

☐ **Yes** ☐ **No** ☐ **N/A**

2 Is this applicant's quality of care consistent with community/HGS standards?

☐ **Yes** ☐ **No**

3 If applicable, do you feel the applicant's professional liability history may have an effect on the quality of care provided to patients?

☐ **Yes** ☐ **No**

If yes, please specify: ________________________________

____

____

Summary Comments: ________________________________

____

____

____

continues

Exhibit 3–8 continued

CLINICAL PRIVILEGING FACTORS

To be completed by Department Chair

1 Has this applicant maintained educational skill levels and demonstrated competency sufficient to continue to exercise the range of clinical privileges requested?

☐ **Yes** ☐ **No**

2 Has this applicant demonstrated technical skills and judgment sufficient to continue to exercise the range of clinical privileges requested?

☐ **Yes** ☐ **No**

3 Are new clinical privileges substantiated by evidence of experience and/or training sufficient to warrant approval?

☐ **Yes** ☐ **No** ☐ **N/A**

PROCTORING STATUS

To be completed by Department Chair

1 Continue current proctoring status?

☐ **Yes** ☐ **No**

Reason: ______

2 Initiate proctoring for new privileges

☐ **Yes** ☐ **No**

3 Proctoring waived ☐ **Yes** ☐ **No** Reason ______

Summary Comments ______

CONCLUSIONS

To be completed by Department Chair

A detailed record of basic responsibilities and performance from various sources has been reviewed and the following recommendation(s) are made:

☐ Reappointment with no change in category and privileges as requested.

☐ Active ☐ Courtesy ☐ Affiliating
☐ Consulting ☐ Adjunct ☐ House Physician

☐ Reappointment with no change in category and modification of privileges as requested.

☐ Additions ☐ Deletions

☐ Reappointment with change in staff category to ______

Reason ______

Other Recommended Actions:

☐ Request for new privileges denied

☐ Request for new privileges withdrawn

☐ Request for staff category denied

Reason ______

☐ Reappointment NOT Recommended

Reason ______

Date ______ *Signature, Section Chair* ☐ *N/A*

Date ______ *Signature, Department Chairman or Designee*

APPROVED

Medical Staff Chairman ______ Date ______

Board of Trustees ______ Date ______

Note: ACLS, Advanced Cardiac Life Support; CME, continuing medical education.

Courtesy of The Hospital of the Good Samaritan, Los Angeles, California.

Exhibit 3–9 Missing Information Letter

Date

Name
Address

RE: FOLLOW-UP REAPPOINTMENT

Dear Doctor ____________:

When the materials you returned in your reappointment packet were reviewed, it was noted that the following items either were not included or need to be completed, as noted below:

[ ] Reappointment form incomplete and/or unsigned (see attached)
[ ] Privilege list incomplete and/or unsigned (see attached)
[ ] Consent/Confidential form unsigned (see attached)
[ ] Documentation of current DEA registration
[ ] Documentation of current California medical license
[ ] Documentation of category 1 CME hours for the past two years
[ ] Documentation of current professional liability insurance coverage
[ ] Documentation of current training for orthopedic privileges
[ ] Documentation of Peds Board Certification (copy of certificate)
[ ] Brief explanation of malpractice action indicated on form

These materials must be returned for your reappointment packet to be considered complete and subsequently to be presented for review to the appropriate supervisory committee.

Please be aware that your immediate completion and return of the above are necessary to ensure the processing of your reappointment within the time frame mandated by the Medical Staff Bylaws.

If you have any questions regarding your appointment, please call our office.

Thank you.

Sincerely,

Credentials Coordinator

Note: CME, continuing medical education.

Courtesy of Children's Hospital, San Diego, California.

- an NPDB report on adverse actions and/or malpractice settlements
- information on the reapplication form/addendum indicating adverse action, as indicated by a "yes" or a "no" answer, depending on how the question is worded

Medical Staff Review Process

The review process outlined for the medical staff in bylaws will be the same for reappointment as appointment. The information reviewed will vary, however. At reappointment, the evaluation is concentrated on what has occurred within the past two years, including internal hospital activity as well as external activity. Please refer to the medical staff review process in the section "Step 2: Initial Application Process" as a guide. The following processes are mentioned here to discuss any components unique to the reappointment process.

Department Review. The department chair (with designated section chiefs as an option for larger departments) should look closely at the clinical privileges requested. With or without defined minimum numbers of treatments or procedures performed for more invasive and/or high-risk procedures and/or core privileges, the department chair has the prerogative to request additional information from the practitioner and/or the hospital (for further information regarding any internal reviews, reports, profiles, etc.). For those practitioners who are active in the hospital, most of the peer review will concentrate on internal performance evaluation. Further investigation can be warranted on the basis of information or verifications gathered.

Credentials Committee Review. The credentials committee can be charged to review those issues relating to bylaws, rules/regulations, and policy compliance. Based on this information, recommendations for change in staff category may be made if someone did or did not meet compliance. For example, if someone did not meet a minimum requirement to maintain active status, he or she may be assigned to another category that does not provide as many prerogatives as the previous category, or if someone's patient activity has increased, he or she may be eligible for an active status as defined by the facility.

Medical Executive Committee Review. This committee's function for reappointment review is basically the same as in initial appointment (see the section "Step 2: Initial Application Process").

Governing Body Action

Action by this group for reappointment recommendations from the medical staff is basically the same as in initial appointment. However, if some practitioners' reappointments are not ready for final action by the governing board, the board should be provided with a list of practitioners who are due and the reason for the delay. The information should also include assurance that peer review is in process to avoid noncompliance with the two-year reappointment standard. The board should expect those names to reappear at their next meeting and extend the current appointment appropriately. (See additional information in the section "Step 2: Initial Application Process.")

Notification to Applicant and Others

Action for this section is basically the same as in initial appointment (see the Section "Step 2: Initial Application Process"). The letter to the practitioner should include effective dates of current appointment (a two-year period) and any approved changes in privileges or category.

See Chapter 6 of this book for distribution of clinical privilege lists to appropriate hospital departments or areas. Also, any changes in the computer profile should be made to reflect the reappointment process (e.g., effective reappointment dates, any expiration updates to license or insurance, NPDB query). A copy of the reappointment letter to the practitioner should be filed in the credentials file.

Adverse Action

Any adverse recommendation from the medical executive committee would be handled in the same way as outlined in the section "Step 2: Initial Application Process." The difference between initial appointment and reappointment denial of clinical privileges and/or membership is that if denial occurs at reappointment, unless the practitioner has his or her clinical privileges suspended, he or she continues to practice with current privileges until the fair hearing process is concluded and action is taken by the governing board.

Voluntary Resignation from Medical Staff

If the practitioner does not supply the required information, including additional information from what was required in the routine process, a second request (third request at option of organization) should be sent by certified mail, stating that if the information is not received by a certain date, a voluntary resignation from the medical staff will be accepted. As long as this voluntary resignation is not in lieu of an investigation, it is not a reportable event to NPDB. For example, if someone does not return his or her reapplication packet or if there is missing information that is requested and not returned (not related to a formal investigation), a voluntary resignation is a "benign" process. A voluntary resignation can be one way that a hospital can avoid noncompliance with the Joint Commission standard for the two-year maximum reappointment period. If the practitioner does not return the packet soon enough to process within the two-year limit, he or she can be voluntarily resigned from the staff and required to reapply as an initial appointee.

CREDENTIALING ALLIED HEALTH PROFESSIONALS (AHPs)

AHPs are those individuals who provide patient care services but are not members of the medical staff and generally are not employees of the hospital, although this will vary according to hospital services offered (see further explanation of hospital-employed AHPs later in this section). AHPs are defined by the organization. The category may also include contracted services. Possession of a license and the level of supervision, if any, defined by law and by the hospital will determine whether AHPs should have delineated clinical privileges or other scope of services defined (job descriptions, practice protocols).

Although the Joint Commission does not specifically address AHPs in its medical staff standards, it does require that "any individuals permitted by law *and the hospital* to provide patient care services independently in the hospital have delineated clinical privileges, whether or not they are medical staff members."[11] Therefore, any practitioners who fall under this category of LIPs must comply with the standards. This category is usually very limited (e.g., clinical psychologists).

Other than the Joint Commission definition above for an LIP who must go through medical staff clinical privileging process, all other categories of AHPs, including any defined hospital employees or contracted services, are processed according to guidelines or procedures that are unique to each individual organization. There are several options for hospitals to make a decision on how to allow these individuals access to patient care. This section will provide as much information as possible to assist organizations in making that decision. It will also address the various classifications and the credentialing process in general. Chapter 6 will discuss clinical privileges, job descriptions, and scope of services in more detail. A section on contracted services at the end of Chapter 6 more specifically describes that component of credentialing as well.

Many of the processes for AHPs are very similar to those for medical staff members. The process for medical staff members should be reviewed when establishing guidelines for AHPs. However, this section will address those policies and procedures specific to AHPs that will probably not be found in other sections of this chapter.

Category Definition

The following are different categories of AHPs and the options that may be available to an organization for credentialing them.

1. Licensed independent AHP (non-MD, non-DO)
   - allowed by license and by hospital to practice independently
   - contracted service
   - hospital employee
   - sponsor may or may not be required
2. Licensed supervised AHP
   - although possibly allowed by licensure to practice independently, not allowed by hospital to practice independently
   - allowed by hospital to practice with some defined physician supervision
   - contracted service
   - hospital employee (with physician supervisor)
   - sponsor usually required if not employed by physician or hospital
   - physician employee (with physician supervisor)
3. Nonlicensed AHP (may or may not hold some kind of certificate)
   - required supervision by a medical staff member
   - employed by a physician and required supervision
   - contracted service with supervision

Each state defines licensure and/or certification and also whether licensures or certifications of AHPs allow for independent practice. It is important to check with state laws before defining categories of AHPs and how they will be processed through the system.

Supervisor/Sponsor

In some hospitals, all or some defined AHP categories require a physician sponsor. This does not necessarily require that the sponsor directly supervise the AHP, but the AHP needs the sponsorship to gain access to the hospital. Other hospitals may not require physician sponsorship, but the individual, once credentialed, will be treating patients only at the request or order of the attending physician on the medical staff, and that attending physician will have the supervisory responsibility, however defined by the organization. Some AHPs (e.g., psychologists) have their own private patients who may require hospitalization. Patients are admitted by a medical staff member who also provides the medical workup and any care or treatment not within the scope of the license or privileges of the AHP.

For AHPs who are employees of a medical staff member (e.g., scrub techs, physician assistants) some degree of supervision by the medical staff member will be defined by the organization in accordance with applicable law. Generally, the application form includes a statement or addendum that is signed by the employing physician who is requesting the AHP to have hospital access and agrees to the defined responsibilities of the supervising physician. Exhibit 3–10 is a sample statement by a supervising physician that can be used or modified to suit the individual organization's need. This statement of supervision should be signed each time the AHP's hospital access is renewed (biannually at reappointment or according to other time/process defined).

Regardless of what forms are used, the supervision statement should include the following components:

- acceptance of responsibility for the performance of the supervised AHP
- proof of professional liability coverage (if applicable)
- copy of any certificate issued to the supervising physician by a state licensing board that may be required for specific employed AHP categories (e.g., physician assistants)
- agreement to notify a hospital authority should the AHP's employment or working relationship with the supervising physician be terminated

Exhibit 3–10 Statement by Supervising Medical Staff Member

Name ____

Allied Health Professional

Name ____

Supervising Medical Staff Member—PRINT NAME

In accordance with the AHP Rules and Regulations:

1. I hereby accept full legal and ethical responsibility for the performance of all duties and acts performed by the above-named individual, whom I have employed as a ___________________.
2. I hereby request approval to allow the above-named individual to perform the tasks described on the appropriate scope of services as defined by the hospital.
3. I assume responsibility for the professional liability insurance coverage of the Allied Health Professional. Verification of this coverage is hereby established in the form of the attached correspondence from my insurance company (ATTACH COPY).
4. If applicable, attached is a certificate issued to me by the state licensing board indicating my approval to supervise an Allied Health Professional in the type and scope of practice for which this application is made.
5. I agree to immediately *notify* the Medical Executive Committee, *in writing*, in the event my approval to supervise an Allied Health Professional is removed, limited or otherwise altered by action of the state licensing board or in the event of any notification of investigation of my supervision by the board, or *if there is a change in employment status of the Allied Health Professional.*
6. I agree to comply with all regulations of the state licensing board and/or Columbia Medical Center with respect to the supervision of the Allied Health Professional, specifically including such regulations as have been (or may, from time to time, be) adopted by said board and the Hospital with respect to

   a. billing for the services of the Allied Health Professional

   b. requirements for supervision of the Allied Health Professional with respect to the type and scope of services approved for the Allied Health Professional to perform by the board

   c. requirements for identification of the Allied Health Professional while rendering medical services. It is understood that compliance with such regulations shall be considered a necessary but not a sufficient condition for the continuing approval of the Medical Executive Committee of the performance of services by the Allied Health Professional in the hospital.
7. I understand that the right of the Allied Health Professional to render medical services within the hospital shall be contingent upon my continued membership on the Medical Staff. If I terminate my staff membership, or if my membership is suspended or revoked, the Allied Health Professional's privileges shall automatically be terminated. Similarly, if my privileges are restricted, the Allied Health Professional's privileges shall be restricted accordingly.

________________________________ ____________________

Signed Date

Courtesy of Columbia Medical Center–West, El Paso, Texas.

Degrees of supervision may need to be defined, since that could help determine the category to which each AHP will be assigned. For example, direct supervision (in the operating room as a scrub tech) would classify someone as dependent or very limited in scope. A certified registered nurse anesthetist (CRNA) may need only to have access to an anesthesiologist on call and may be able to practice with enough autonomy to require delineated clinical privileges similar to an anesthesiologist's. This example can be classified as general supervision.

Medical Staff versus Human Resource Function

Traditionally, the medical staff office has been the place where all non–hospital-employed providers of care were credentialed. As the types of individuals seeking AHP status and the total number of individuals seeking AHP status increase, many hospitals have evaluated whether all these individuals need to go through the medical staff office and a medical staff credentialing process. As defined earlier in this chapter, LIPs who are also allowed by license and by the hospital to practice independently are the *only* individuals (other than MDs, DOs, and DDSs) required by the Joint Commission to be processed through medical staff credentialing mechanisms because of the necessity of delineated clinical privileges. Even if an AHP does not require a medical staff credentialing process including delineated clinical privileges, the medical staff office may still be involved in processing the appointments and reappointments of other AHPs within the hospital. If AHPs are not required to have clinical privileges on the basis of the Joint Commission standards, they may have a defined job description or scope of services that is very similar to an employee job description. The job description or scope of services is very straightforward, defining exactly what the individual is and is not allowed to do and the requirements for eligibility to perform the assigned duties or scope of services. Chapter 6 will more fully define the clinical privileges or job descriptions that can be used for AHPs.

Often, the human resources department is agreeable to processing certain categories of AHPs, since it is familiar with some of the information that is collected, such as license verifications, certificates, and current cardiopulmonary resuscitation (CPR) certification. Human resources may not do primary source verification unless required individually by the organization; there are no external requirements for primary source verification to be done unless the individual is applying for delineated clinical privileges or unless Joint Commission human resource standards require it for certain categories of employees. When the internal guidelines for AHP appointments and reappointments require primary source verification, the human resources department may not want to be involved in the process.

Another option to consider is a department other than medical staff or human resources to process individuals who do not have to go through a medical staff credentialing process. For example, the nursing department can process nursing AHPs who are working as supervised individuals employed by a physician on the medical staff.

The question arises regarding whether nonphysician practitioners who are employees of a hospital that also has an AHP classification for the same kind of practitioners from outside the organization (e.g., clinical psychologists, CRNAs) also have to be credentialed by the medical staff or other defined mechanism as AHPs. Unless they are defined as LIPs, a status that requires medical staff credentialing, the process can be considered duplicative, although a hospital human resource evaluation can include components different from those of a medical staff credentialing process. Hospitals struggle with whether to credential some non-LIPs through the medical staff in addition to the human resource mechanism. If they are not credentialed through the medical staff, there should be a component in the annual employee appraisal that includes medical staff participation in the evaluation of the care given to patients. The important point here is that there should be consistency in the review and evaluation process for like individuals, regardless of their entry into patient care. Human resources is responsible for other hospital employee evaluation factors, such as compliance with human resource policies for all employees, obtaining copies of current license, required physicals, and safety and disaster training.

Table 3–1 shows a grid for suggested processing through either human resources or the medical staff privileging process for the various classifications of AHPs in terms of licensure, supervision, and means of accessing the hospital. If human resources does not process those AHPs where indicated, the medical staff office can process them through an AHP committee or other defined mechanism that does not require medical staff credentialing.

AHP Committee

In many hospitals, there is an AHP committee or interdisciplinary practice committee that functions like the medical staff credentials committee. They review the application and periodic assessment of all credentialed AHPs. It is suggested that those individuals reviewed and approved (through job descriptions or scope of service defined) by an AHP committee be reported to the medical executive committee for information, but no formal action is required by the medical staff, since they do not have clinical privileges. When new categories of AHPs are approved by the hospital's governing board, the medical staff can be asked to review the category as well as the proposed job description or defined scope of services. If the new category is for an LIP, the medical staff needs to be involved in development and approval of privileges and

Table 3–1 Processing Grid for AHPs

	Employed by Hospital	*Contracted with Hospital*	*Licensed, Nonphysician Not Employed or Contracted with Hospital*	*Employed by MS Member, Activity in Hospital*
No state license	HR	HR	N/A	HR
State license and hospital requires direct supervision	HR	HR	HR	HR
State license and hospital requires indirect or general supervision	HR or MS	HR or MS	HR or MS	HR or MS
State license and hospital does not require supervision. LIP as defined by state law and the hospital	MS	MS	MS	MS

Note: HR, human resources department; MS, medical staff.

Courtesy of C. Mobley & Associates, LLC, and Quality Management Options, LLC, Colorado Springs, Colorado.

criteria. An AHP committee should have a membership composed of representatives from nursing, human resources, a physician or physicians in a specialty that may use a high number of AHPs (e.g., a psychiatrist from a behavioral health or psychiatric unit that uses clinical psychologists and licensed social workers), administration, the medical staff office, and surgery (if there is an adequate number of AHPs working in surgery, such as perfusionists, scrub techs, CRNAs, and nurse midwives). (Any of these individuals could chair the committee, although if it is considered a medical staff committee, it should be chaired by a physician.) The function of this committee is to review and make recommendations with regard to new categories of AHPs requested, to define criteria for each category of AHP, review the information submitted by the AHP applicant, to verify or delegate verification of any required documentation from the application, and to make a recommendation for approval to the medical staff or governing body.

File Setup and Maintenance

An individual credentials file should be set up for each AHP. (See earlier section on file setup and maintenance in this chapter.) Exhibit 3–11 is a sample file order specifically for AHPs. A similar setup can be used with those tabs that are pertinent for any specific group of AHPs. It is possible that a six-section file folder will not be needed and that some sections can be combined. If a regular manila file folder is used, appropriate tabs should be used so that information can be accessed easily. For example, there should be a tab for a physician sponsor/supervisor statement, which would not be one of the tabs in the medical staff member's file. If an AHP does

Exhibit 3–11 Order of Membership Application File for AHPs

I. Original Application and Backup
   1. Signature sheet from initial application
   2. AHP application
   3. Reference/verification documentation

II. Annual Update Application
   1. Most current annual update (same order as in original application)
   2. Previous annual updates (in the following order)
      a. Signature sheet from annual update
      b. Annual update application
      c. Annual update backup information
      d. Reference/verification documentation

III. License/Certification/Registration Documentation
   1. Current license/certification/registration
   2. Current verification from appropriate agency/board
   3. Current National Practitioner Data Bank Information
   4. Current CME documentation
   5. Expired information in the order listed in 1–4

IV. Professional Liability Insurance Information
   1. Current insurance certificate
   2. Current claims history information from carrier
   3. Current claims history information from practitioner
   4. Expired insurance with previous claims history

V. Practice Prerogatives
   1. Current category description containing practice prerogatives
   2. Previous prerogative information
   3. Proctoring documentation
   4. Temporary services documentation (if any)

VI. Correspondence in Chronological Order
   1. All correspondence regarding the practitioner (to and from)

Note: CME, continuing medical education.

not have clinical privileges but has a job description or scope of services defined, that information should be under a specific tab labeled *Job Description* or *Scope of Services.*

Initial Application Process

AHPs are subject to an appointment and a reappointment/reevaluation process very similar to the medical staff organization's. An AHP manual should define a uniform process that is used for all categories or each category of AHPs within a hospital. When an AHP makes a request for an application, the hospital must first determine if that is an approved AHP category. If it is not, the prospective applicant should be told that that it is not an approved category of AHP, and no application packet should be provided to the individual. If it is an approved AHP category, the applicant receives an application packet that should include

- cover letter (see Exhibit 3–12)
- AHP application
- AHP general policies, rules and regulations, or other documents outlining the AHP scope of services provided at the hospital
- a supervising/sponsoring physician statement (if applicable)
- the clinical privileges, job description, or scope of services for the appropriate AHP category
- other information that may apply to a specific category of AHPs or to all AHPs making application

Application Form

A variety of application forms are used in the industry today. Different application forms may be used to accommodate the type of information gathered in the credentialing of AHPs. Most hospitals use one uniform application for all AHPs, indicating that the applicants should fill out those portions that are applicable to them. The form is very similar to the medical staff application form in that AHPs may also be trained, boarded, and licensed and may have professional liability insurance, references, and hospital affiliations. Exhibit 3–13 is an example of one type of application form that can be used. "Supervising physician" may or may not be applicable to particular categories of AHPs. A form like this could be used and the words "if applicable" inserted in those sections that might or might not apply to all AHPs. See the earlier section, "Supervision/Sponsor."

In general, applications should include information from high school onward, since some AHPs may have only a high school diploma. Others may get their training through undergraduate degrees. This is information not usually requested on a medical staff application. A physician supervisor statement would also be included in some AHP applications. See sample Exhibit 3–10 for a sample form.

Verification and Information-Gathering Process

AHP manuals should outline what information is to be collected for each group or category of AHPs. The organization must decide whether primary source verification is required or whether copies of licenses, certificates, and other such documents are acceptable. (LIPs going through a medical staff clinical privilege process are subject to the same primary source requirements as the medical staff.)

When AHPs are granted clinical privileges and credentialed through the medical staff, a query must be made to the NPDB. AHPs who do not have delineated clinical privileges do not require a query, but the organization has the option of querying for those individuals if they choose (see the NPDB guidelines[12] in Chapter 5 for additional information).

In verifying licensure for an AHP, some state licensing boards are all-inclusive and provide information on any license granted within that state. Other states have separate licensing boards for each specific license. If the physician licensing board does not license AHPs, it may be able to provide the phone number or additional information needed to contact other licensing boards.

Exhibit 3–12 Response to AHP Application Request Letter

Date
Name
Address
RE: Allied Health Professional Application

Dear Allied Health Professional:

Thank you for requesting an application for membership to the Allied Health Professional (AHP) Staff of The Hospital of the Good Samaritan.

Enclosed you will find an application packet that you need to complete and return to the Medical Staff Office in its entirety. We will begin the application process after receiving the completed packet. This process usually takes three to five months. Applications will not be processed if any portion of the application packet is returned incomplete, which will delay processing. **All questions must be answered completely.**

There is a $150 nonrefundable processing fee, and your completed application must be accompanied by a check in that amount made payable to **Medical Staff of The Hospital of the Good Samaritan**. Copies of the following documents should be included with your completed application:

- current California licensure or certificate
- current professional liability insurance coverage
- recent photograph
- current ACLS/BCLS **(required for AHPs working in Critical Care areas)**
- copies of continuing medical education credits for the past two years

Again, thank you for your interest in The Hospital of the Good Samaritan. If you have any questions, please contact ____________________, Credentials Coordinator, in the Medical Staff Office at ____________________.

Sincerely,

NAME
TITLE

Note: ACLS, advanced cardiac life support; BCLS, basic cardiac life support.

Courtesy of The Hospital of the Good Samaritan, Los Angeles, California.

Exhibit 3–13 AHP Application

Please TYPE or PRINT all information. Applications will not be processed if any portion is not returned or is incomplete. Please include the APPLICATION FEE of one-hundred dollars ($100.00). Please attach a recent photograph.

PERSONAL INFORMATION

Last Name | First Name | Middle Initial | Date of Birth

Office Address | City | State | ZIP Code

Home Address | City | State | ZIP Code

Office Telephone Number | Home Telephone Number

Answering Service Number

Birthplace | Birth Date | Social Security Number

Sex | Marital Status | Name of Spouse

EDUCATION

Begin with HIGH SCHOOL, then COLLEGE/UNIVERSITY/OTHER SCHOOLS—Use additional sheet (Attachment "A") if needed:

Name of School | Degree/Certificate | Dates Attended—From and To

Address | City | State | ZIP Code

Name of School | Degree/Certificate | Dates Attended—From and To

Address | City | State | ZIP Code

SEMINARS/ SPECIAL COURSES

Name/Subject | Place | Date(s) | Credits

Name/Subject | Place | Date(s) | Credits

CONTINUING EDUCATION

Submit documentation of continuing education courses attended and hours during the past two years (Attachment "B"). Emphasis should be placed upon those programs most closely related to your current specialty and privileges.

continues

Exhibit 3–13 continued

LICENSURE/ CERTIFICATION

PLEASE ATTACH A COPY OF ALL LICENSES/REGISTRATIONS/ CERTIFICATES.

California License/Certificate Number   Date Issued   Expiration Date

BCLS Number   Date Issued   Expiration Date

ACLS Number   Date Issued   Expiration Date

Other State Licenses/Certificates past and present:

Type   State   Number   Date Issued   Expiration Date

Type   State   Number   Date Issued   Expiration Date

BOARD CERTIFICATION

Board Certified Specialty   Certificate Number

Date Issued   Expiration Date

Board Certified Specialty   Certificate Number

Date Issued   Expiration Date

Board Eligible Specialty   Eligibility Expiration Date

If not certified, have you failed an examination? Yes ☐ No ☐ If *Yes*, provide explanation on Attachment "C".

SUPERVISING PHYSICIAN

Indicate **all** physicians who currently provide/previously provided direct supervision during the last five years; list others on Attachment "D".

Name   Specialty   Supervised From   To

Address   City   State   ZIP Code

Name   Specialty   Supervised From   To

Address   City   State   ZIP Code

continues

Exhibit 3–13 continued

PROFESSIONAL LIABILITY INSURANCE

Please submit a copy of the Certificate of Insurance showing policy holder, coverage, limitations and expiration date (Attachment "E"). Please complete the following:

Carrier ______ Agent ______ Name of Insured ______

Address ______ City ______ State ______ ZIP Code ______

Telephone Number ______ Coverage Amount ______ Expiration Date ______

Have there been or are there currently pending any malpractice claims, suits, judgments, settlements or arbitration proceedings involving your professional practice? YES ☐ NO ☐

If you answered *Yes* to the above, please provide the following information on Attachment "F":

- DATE SUIT OR CLAIM WAS INITIATED
- YOUR ACCOUNT OF THE CASE
- CURRENT STATUS OF THE CASE
- NAME OF PATIENT(S)
- YOUR INVOLVEMENT WITH PATIENT(S)
- DATE OF DETERMINATION (IF REACHED)

If you answer *Yes* to either of the following questions, please provide the details on Attachment "F":

Have you ever been denied professional liability coverage or had coverage canceled? YES ☐ NO ☐

Has your liability insurer refused to renew your policy or placed limitations on the scope of your coverage, or has any carrier expressed intent to deny, cancel, not renew or limit your coverage? YES ☐ NO ☐

I attest that my Professional Liability Insurance covers the scope of my practice (i.e., to include all privileges being requested with this application) at The Hospital of the Good Samaritan.

CORRECTIVE ACTION

In the past two years, have any of the following been, or are currently in the process of being denied, revoked, suspended, reduced, limited, placed on probation, not reviewed, or voluntarily relinquished? If you answer *Yes* to any of the following, please provide a full explanation on Attachment "G".

- LICENSE/CERTIFICATE IN ANY STATE YES ☐ NO ☐
- OTHER PROFESSIONAL REGISTRATION OR LICENSE YES ☐ NO ☐
- MEMBERSHIP ON ANY HOSPITAL STAFF YES ☐ NO ☐
- PRACTICE PRIVILEGES YES ☐ NO ☐
- OTHER INSTITUTIONAL AFFILIATION OR STATUS THEREOF YES ☐ NO ☐

continues

Exhibit 3–13 continued

CORRECTIVE ACTION (continued)	• PROFESSIONAL OFFICE	YES ☐ NO ☐
	• PROFESSIONAL SOCIETY MEMBERSHIP OR FELLOWSHIP	YES ☐ NO ☐
	Has any action, including investigation, been undertaken, whether still pending or completed, against you by any governmental agency or law enforcement body for your alleged failure to comply with laws, statutes, regulations, or other legal requirements which may be applicable to the practice of your profession or to your rendition of services to patients?	YES ☐ NO ☐
	Have you voluntarily withdrawn an application for staff membership while under formal or informal investigation?	YES ☐ NO ☐
	Have you been charged or convicted of a criminal offense?	YES ☐ NO ☐
TEACHING APPOINTMENTS	List any teaching appointments which you currently hold or have held in the past (list additional on Attachment "H"). Name of Institution Position Faculty Director Dates Address City State ZIP Code	
HEALTH STATUS	If you answer *Yes* to any of the following, please provide a full explanation on Attachment "I".	
	Do you presently have a physical or mental health condition, including alcohol or drug dependence, that affects or may reasonably progress within the next two years to the point of affecting your ability to perform professional duties appropriately within the scope of the privileges requested?	YES ☐ NO ☐
	Have you had any such condition in the past that is now resolved without the need for continuing therapy or medication?	YES ☐ NO ☐
	Are you taking medication or in therapy for a condition which could affect your ability to perform professionally if discontinued?	YES ☐ NO ☐
	Have you been hospitalized or received any other type of institutional care in the past for a health-dependency problem?	YES ☐ NO ☐

continues

Exhibit 3–13 continued

HEALTH STATUS (continued)	Most Recent Physical Exam: ____________________ Date Performed by Telephone Number Significant Findings: ____________________ ____________________
HOSPITAL/ HEALTH CARE FACILITY AFFILIATIONS	Please list all current and previous affiliations beginning with current; list additional on Attachment "J". ____________________ Name of Facility Telephone Number Position Dates ____________________ Address City State ZIP Code ____________________ Name of Facility Telephone Number Position Dates ____________________ Address City State ZIP Code ____________________ Name of Facility Telephone Number Position Dates ____________________ Address City State ZIP Code
PEER REFERENCES	Please list the names of two (2) practitioners in your specialty, preferably members of the AHP Staff of this hospital. ____________________ Name of Practitioner Telephone Number ____________________ Address City State ZIP Code ____________________ Name of Practitioner Telephone Number ____________________ Address City State ZIP Code
PREVIOUS PRACTICE	List all previous practices or positions not otherwise listed on this application, including office, hospital, clinic and military. Begin with the most recent and list others in reverse chronological order. List additional on Attachment "K". ____________________ Name of Practice/Institution Position Dates ____________________ Address City State ZIP Code

continues

Exhibit 3–13 continued

SPECIALTY	I am applying for the following approved Allied Health Professional Staff Category. Please mark only one. ☐ Dental Assistant ☐ Nurse Coordinator ☐ Nurse Midwife ☐ Nurse Practitioner ☐ Operating Room Technician ☐ Oral & Maxillofacial Surgery Assistant ☐ Perfusionist ☐ Physician Assistant ☐ Speech Pathologist
APPLICANT STATEMENT	In making this application, I: • fully understand that any misstatements on or omissions from this application constitute cause for denial of appointment or summary dismissal from the AHP Staff. • attest that all information submitted by me on this application and its attachments is true to the best of my knowledge and belief. • acknowledge that I have received and read the Bylaws, Rules and Regulations of the Medical Staff and of the Hospital, and agree to be bound by the terms of the Bylaws, Policies, Procedures, Rules and Regulations of the Medical Staff and the Hospital as they may pertain to my actions and duties, if I am granted AHP Staff membership or practice privileges. • bear the burden of producing adequate information for proper evaluation of my professional competence, character, ethics, and other qualifications, and for resolving any doubts about such qualifications. • acknowledge that the evaluation of my application, credentials, qualifications and conduct will be done initially upon application and randomly during my HGS affiliation. • authorize the Hospital, its Medical Staff and their representatives, in order to evaluate my professional qualifications, competency and ethical qualification, to consult: – Administrators and the Medical Staff of other hospitals or institutions with which I have been associated. – past and present professional liability carriers who may have information regarding my professional competence. – all records and documents, including medical records at other hospitals or other institutions. • release from liability all representatives of the Hospital, including members of the Medical Staff, for their acts performed in good faith and without malice in connection with all evaluations. • release from any liability any and all individuals and organizations who provide information to the Hospital, its Medical Staff or representatives, in good faith and without malice, and release from liability this Hospital, its Medical Staff and representatives for doing so. • signify my willingness to appear for any interviews or inquiries regarding this application. • authorize and consent to the release of information by this Hospital, its Medical Staff or representatives to other hospitals, medical associations, and other interested persons, who possess my written authorization, upon request regarding any information the Hospital or Medical Staff may have

continues

Exhibit 3–13 continued

APPLICANT STATEMENT (continued)	as long as such release of information is done in good faith and without malice, and I hereby release from liability this Hospital, its Medical Staff or its representatives for so doing. • understand that all information concerning patients is strictly confidential. • recognize that all evaluations, inquiries and responses to inquiries regarding my professional competence and qualifications shall be carried out in a professional and ethical manner, with due regard for appropriate confidentiality and the information at issue. I further agree to the following terms of the Evaluation Procedure: • I recognize that the granting of privileges is dependent upon the individual professional competence and ethical practice of my supervising physician (if any) and myself in keeping with the qualifications, standards and requirements set forth in the Medical Staff Bylaws, Rules and Regulations. • I understand that the Hospital Medical Staff must evaluate my supervising physician (if any) for professional competence and qualifications, and make appropriate recommendations to the Board of Trustees, and that such responsibility extends to both the processing of this application and continuing assessment of my performance. • I understand that it will be necessary to investigate the professional training, experience, conduct and judgment of my supervising physician (if any), and that it may be necessary to consult other hospitals, schools, professional societies, liability insurance carriers, practitioners and other persons or institutions. • I agree to provide copies of patients' records from other facilities upon request of the Interdisciplinary Practices Committee if deemed relevant in the evaluation of this application. • I agree to submit to a physical or mental health examination acceptable to the Interdisciplinary Practices Committee or Medical Executive Committee upon request as deemed relevant to determine compliance with health status requirements. I further agree to maintain an ethical practice, to provide for continuous care of patients, and to discharge such functions for which I will be responsible as an Allied Health Professional who is granted privileges. ____________________ AHP Applicant Signature Date
APPROVAL OF APPLICATION	____________________ Chairman, Interdisciplinary Practices Committee Date ____________________ Chairman, Credentials Committee Date ____________________ Chairman, Department of Date ____________________ Chairman, Medical Executive Committee Date ____________________ Board of Trustees Date

Courtesy of The Hospital of the Good Samaritan, Los Angeles, California.

Analysis, Review, and Action Process

Once information is received to support the application, an evaluation process begins. Exhibit 3–14 is a sample evaluation form that can be used to determine whether all of the information has been received.

How the AHPs in general or certain categories are to be reviewed and approved will determine the evaluation process. Either the medical staff office or another designated department will gather the information to support the application. If the application is not going through a medical staff review process that includes delineated clinical privileges, it can be processed in either of the following ways:

1. It can be reviewed by human resources or other department, approved, and sent for information to the medical staff and governing board.
2. It can be reviewed by the medical staff office or another department, presented to the committee that reviews AHPs, and sent to the medical staff for review or information and to the governing board for information or approval. It should be noted here that in the case of dependent AHPs when little or no verification is received regarding competency other than from the supervising/sponsoring physician, the individual can be deemed to have met the criteria or not met the criteria. When the criteria are well defined, it is possible that no approvals will be needed other than a designated committee/individual to determine that the individual meets the criteria. In that case, the names may be sent to a medical staff group or governing board for information only.

If the AHP is licensed and allowed by the hospital to practice independently without supervision, or if that category of AHP has delineated clinical privileges, the application is processed through the medical staff and the governing board. This will require a recommendation from the medical staff to the governing board for approval.

Following review and approval that is required for AHPs, the applicant is notified of acceptance or rejection. As with new medical staff appointees, appropriate hospital departments need to be notified and any appropriate updates made to a computer database.

Once approved as an AHP, the AHP should be required to attend a new employee hospital orientation program or those components that would be appropriate. For example, this could include an orientation to the surgical suite, where all of the rules that apply to employees would also apply to a scrub tech working with a supervising physician. Orientation could also include other units or services of the hospital where the AHP will function, such as the emergency department. An orientation to medical records may be pertinent for all AHPs. The hospital should make a list and add to the policies those portions of an orientation that should take place for AHPs.

Reappointment Process

As defined earlier, whatever mechanism (committee, review process, approval, etc.) is used for the initial appointment process should also be used for the reappointment or reappraisal process.

Either a reappointment/reappraisal form or a profile that is printed from the credentialing software is forwarded to the AHP. If a profile is used, a questionnaire should be included that asks about any adverse or other action taken that has occurred in the last two years. In addition, the applicant should be asked to update any of the information on the profile if necessary. Using a profile keeps the AHP from having to complete information that the organization most likely already has in its database (see Exhibits 3–15 and 3–16).

For those AHPs going through the medical staff reappointment process, it must occur at least every two years, according to Joint Commission standards. All other AHPs may be processed every two years as well or at shorter intervals, de-

Exhibit 3–14 Checklist for AHPs

Applicant Name: ____________________ Employee: YES or NO (Circle)

AHP Category: ____________________ Human Resource Contact: ______________

Division: ____________________ New Appointment: ______________

Department: ____________________ Temporary Privileges: ______________

Reappointment: ______________

DOCUMENTS	DATE REQUESTED/ SENT	DATE RECEIVED
1. Application		
2. Specified Services/Privileges Form		
3. Curriculum Vitae		
4. Current License(s) / Certificate(s)		
a. STATE ______ EXPIRES ______		
b. STATE ______ EXPIRES ______		
c. STATE ______ EXPIRES ______		
5. (PA, NP, RNCS, CNMW ONLY FOR Nos 5, 6 & 7) Mass State Controlled Substances Certificate		
6. Federal DEA Certificate EXPIRES: ______		
7. Prescriptive Guidelines with Supervising Physician		
8. (PA ONLY) a. Supervising Physician Agreement		
b. Letters from BRM-RE: Supv. Physician (2)		
9. Education and Training a.		
b.		
c.		
d.		
10. Professional Liability Insurance a. Face Sheet/Certificate		
b. Claims Experience		
I		
II		
III		
11. Specialty Board Certification/Accreditation a.		
b.		
12. National Practitioner Data Bank		

continues

Exhibit 3–14 continued

DOCUMENTS	DATE REQUESTED/ SENT	DATE RECEIVED
13. References		
Member(s) of Same Discipline a.		
b.		
Physician(s) a.		
b.		
14. Other Institutional Affiliations a.		
b.		
c.		
d.		
15. Summary of Clinical Work		

Note: BRM, Board of Regulatory Medicine; NP, nurse practitioner, PA, physician assistant; RNCS, registered nurse clinical specialist.

Courtesy of St. Vincent Hospital, Worcester, Massachusetts.

Exhibit 3–15 Licensed or Registered Health Practitioner Reappointment Application

I wish to apply for reappointment to the University Hospital Staff as a Licensed or Registered Health Practitioner. I am currently a faculty member in the Department of ________________ in the SUNY at Stony Brook School of Medicine/Dental Medicine.

1. PERSONAL INFORMATION

Name ____

Last Name *First Name* *Middle Initial*

Office Address ____

Street *City* *State* *ZIP*

Office Phone ( )

Home Address ____

Street *City* *State* *ZIP*

Home Phone ( ) ____________

Marital Status ______________ Name of Spouse ______________________

2. CURRENT PRACTICE INFORMATION

Practice limited to ____

Practicing with whom and nature of affiliation ______________________

____

Name(s) of partner(s) *(if applicable)* ______________________

____

____

Has the nature of your practice changed in the last two years? ____ No ____ Yes

If yes, how ____

____

3. CONTINUING EDUCATION

A. List all activities which you have attended or for which you have received credit in the past two years.

____

____

____

B. Professional Recognition (offices held, honors) ______________________

____

____

C. Have you participated in documented basic CPR training? ____ No ____ Yes

BLS: ____

____

Name of sponsoring organization *Date of Expiration*

ACLS: ____

____

Name of sponsoring organization *Date of Expiration*

continues

Exhibit 3–15 continued

4. MEDICAL STAFF AFFILIATION ADDITIONS/DELETIONS
(i.e., hospitals, health care facilities, HMOs)

Please indicate any changes in your staff affiliations that have occurred in the last two years.

Street *City* *State* *ZIP*

Additions ____

____

____

Deletions ____

____

____

5. ACADEMIC APPOINTMENTS (*University Affiliations*)
Please list any changes in teaching appointments in the last two years.

Institution Position/Rank

____

____

6. PROFESSIONAL SANCTIONS
In the last two years:

A. Has your license to practice your specialty in any jurisdiction been or in the process of being denied, revoked, suspended, reduced, not renewed or voluntarily relinquished? ____ No ____ Yes

B. Has your membership and/or clinical privileges been reduced, suspended, revoked, or not renewed at any other hospital or health care institution? ____ No ____ Yes

C. Has your employment at any hospital or health care institution ever been suspended, diminished, revoked, or not renewed? ____ No ____ Yes

D. Have you been denied membership or renewal thereof, or been subject to disciplinary action in your specialty? ____ No ____ Yes

E. Are you the subject of any pending professional misconduct proceeding? ____ No ____ Yes

F. Except for violations, have you been convicted of committing an act constituting a crime under New York State Law, Federal Law or a law of another jurisdiction which, if committed within this state, would have constituted a crime under New York State Law? ____ No ____ Yes

G. Have you ever been found guilty of professional misconduct, as defined in the Education Law of the State of New York, or unprofessional conduct as defined by the Board of Regents? ____ No ____ Yes

If the answer to any of the above questions is "**Yes,**" please give full details on a separate sheet of paper.

continues

Exhibit 3–15 continued

7. LIABILITY INSURANCE
Do you consent to the release of information to the hospital from your present or any past malpractice insurance carrier? ____ No ____ Yes

A. Are there any malpractice actions pending against you in this or any other state? ____ No ____ Yes

B. Have any judgments in a malpractice action been entered against you in this or any other state? ____ No ____ Yes

C. Have you entered into a settlement of any malpractice action brought against you in this or any other state? ____ No ____ Yes

If the answer to questions A, B, or C is "**Yes,**" please give full details on a separate sheet of paper including dates, name of case, the substance of any charge, and allegations or findings.

8. PHYSICAL AND MENTAL HEALTH
Attached is a form for you to give to your personal physician to complete and return to the Medical Staff Office. This form must be submitted for your application to be considered complete.

9. RESPONSIBLE UNIVERSITY HOSPITAL STAFF PHYSICIAN/DENTIST
I am the direct supervisor of this applicant for the privilege of treating patients at University Hospital and support this request for reappointment.
Comments: ____

____

____
Name (Print) Department

____
Signature *Date*

All the information contained in this application is complete and accurate, I fully understand that any significant misstatement or omissions from this application may constitute cause for denial of reappointment or cause for summary dismissal from the Medical Staff of University Hospital as a Licensed/ Registered Health Practitioner. I agree to report any changes in health status that would affect my ability to practice medicine and changes in staff membership status at other hospitals or health care institutions during the next two years.

____ ____________________
Signature *Date*

continues

Exhibit 3–15 continued

MEDICAL STAFF REAPPOINTMENT
DECISIONS, RECOMMENDATIONS AND ACTIONS
FOR LICENSED/REGISTERED HEALTH PRACTITIONERS

CREDENTIALS COMMITTEE	After reviewing statements of the applicant and results of our evaluations, the Credentials Committee hereby: _____ Recommends for Reappointment. _____ Recommends that application for reappointment be denied for the following reasons: ________________________________ Signed ____________________ Date __________ *Chairman, Credentials Committee*
DEPARTMENT CHAIRMAN	After review of the report of the Credentials Committee, I, as Department Chairman, hereby recommend to the Medical Board that: _____ The application be approved as recommended by the Credentials Committee. _____ The application be denied. Signed ____________________ Date __________ *Department Chairman*
MEDICAL BOARD	After review of the application, the evaluation by the Credentials Committee, and recommendations of the Department Chairman, the Medical Board of University Hospital hereby: _____ Grants Reappointment. _____ Terminates Medical Staff appointment as of ____________ *Date* Signed ____________________ Date __________ *President, Medical Board*
V.P. For Health Sciences	______ Grants Reappointment. ______ Terminates Reappointment Signed ____________________ Date __________ Vice President for Health Sciences State University of New York at Stony Brook

Note: BLS, basic life support; ACLS, advanced cardiac life support, CPR, cardiopulmonary resuscitation.

Courtesy of University Hospital, State University of New York at Stony Brook, Stony Brook, New York.

Exhibit 3–16 AHP Evaluation Form

NAME	*SPECIALTY*
DEPARTMENT	*PHYSICIAN SUPERVISOR*

1	Current Licensure Verified	☐ Yes	☐ No	☐ N/A	
2	National Practitioner Data Bank Clear	☐ Yes	☐ No		______
3	Malpractice Insurance Verified Clear	☐ Yes	☐ No		______
4	Current BCLS Certificate (if applicable)	☐ Yes	☐ No	☐ N/A	______
5	ACLS Certificate (if applicable)	☐ Yes	☐ No	☐ N/A	______
6	CEU Hours Appended	☐ Yes	☐ No	☐ N/A	______
7	Hospital/Clinic/Healthcare References Verified	☐ Yes	☐ No	☐ N/A	______
8	Supervisor Evaluations Appended	☐ Yes	☐ No		______
9	Peer References Verified	☐ Yes	☐ No	☐ N/A	______
10	Quality Management Activity Data Appended	☐ Yes	☐ No	☐ N/A	______
11	Change in Privileges/Job Description Requested	☐ Yes	☐ No	☐ N/A	______

Add ______________________________

Delete ______________________________

☐ Approved ☐ NOT Approved—Reason ______________________________

Department Chairman	*Date*	*Chairman, Medical Staff*	*Date*
Board of Trustees	*Date*		

Note: BCLS, basic cardiac life support; ACLS, advanced cardiac life support; CEU, continuing education unit.

Courtesy of The Hospital of the Good Samaritan, Los Angeles, California.

pending on the organization's policies. Some hospitals process the supervised and nonindependent AHPs on an annual basis to parallel the employee evaluation time period. For the physician-employed AHP, this can be a fairly simple process that requires the supervising or employing physician to complete an evaluation and confirm that the individual is still employed by the physician. It is also advisable to have the appropriate hospital supervisor or someone at the management level in the area where the AHP is working fill out an evaluation as well. Any current licensure or insurance coverage would also need to be forwarded by the employing physician. Additional reference letters are not necessary unless an organization requires them.

Exhibit 3–17 is an example of a performance evaluation form that could be filled out by either hospital management or a supervising physician.

It is important for licensed AHPs with clinical privileges to have an evaluation or a peer reference at reappointment from someone else who is in the same specialty or has the same license as that AHP. For example, a clinical psychologist should have a peer reference from another clinical psychologist by either individual letter or documentation in committee minutes of attendance by someone in that specialty. This is a Joint Commission requirement.[13]

Adverse Action

Grounds for initiating routine, summary, or automatic suspension of an AHP's services or privileges need to be defined in the AHP manual. In addition, the actions that can be taken and by whom also need to be defined. Generally, AHPs do not have the same rights to a medical staff fair hearing and appeals process, even if they have clinical privileges, although some type of grievance procedure may be available to AHPs (according to AHP policy) if some adverse action is recommended. The grievance procedure might allow the affected AHP to provide evidence or make a statement or be interviewed by a designated committee or group of individuals that would then evaluate the information and make a final recommendation to the designated committee (e.g., the medical executive committee or AHP committee). If there is a sponsoring or supervising physician, that individual should also be involved in the grievance process. With regard to any NPDB reports for adverse action against an AHP who does not have clinical privileges granted by the medical staff, reporting that action to the data bank is optional for the hospital. (See the NPDB guidelines for further information.)

If any adverse action is taken and a relationship with the AHP is terminated, the areas in the hospital where he or she normally practices should be notified that he or she no longer has the privileges or authority to be working in the hospital.

EXPRESS CREDENTIALING PROCESS

In general, most applications that are processed are fairly routine in that the practitioners making application meet the criteria that the organization has developed and approved and no "caution flags" are identified. While the majority of the applications are processed without incident, hospitals have found over the years that more of their time is spent evaluating the smaller percentage of applicants who do not have a "clean" file. Within the last few years, many hospitals have considered and/or developed a process to expedite the processing of those applications or reappointments that meet certain criteria as established by the organization. The term for this process is *express credentialing* or *fast-track credentialing*. Other reasons for organizations wanting to institute an express credentialing process are that

- organizations wish to expedite the credentialing process when feasible
- organizations wish to eliminate temporary privileges, at least as they relate to the initial application process
- not all governing boards meet on a monthly basis

Exhibit 3–17 AHP Performance Evaluation

____________________________ ____________________________

Allied Health Professional Supervising Physician

____________________________ ____________________________

Patient's Name Patient's History #

* *

PART I—CLINICAL COMPETENCE (please complete applicable box)
(If you mark "yes" please provide information)

	Requirement Met	
NURSE ANESTHETIST (CRNA)	**YES**	**NO**
Anesthesia record complete		
Possesses knowledge of and practices sterile technique		
Shares knowledge of case with surgical team		
Maintains proper dress code		
Interaction with team members and patients is satisfactory		
Demonstrates ability to interpret problems		
Demonstrates ability to initiate appropriate intervention		
Handles emergency situations efficiently		
SURGICAL SCRUB TECHNICIAN	**YES**	**NO**
Possesses knowledge of and practices sterile technique		
Maintains proper dress code		
Interaction with team members and patients is satisfactory		
Knowledgeable of instrumentation		
OR PHYSICIAN'S ASSISTANT	**YES**	**NO**
Possesses knowledge of and practices sterile technique		
Shares knowledge of case with surgery team (patient history, etc.)		
Maintains proper dress code		
Interaction with team members and patients is satisfactory		
CERTIFIED NURSE MIDWIFE	**YES**	**NO**
Demonstrates the ability to perform multi-system assessment		
Demonstrates the ability to interpret problems		
Demonstrates the ability to initiate appropriate intervention		
Manages and delivers normal vaginal delivery		
Interprets external and internal fetal monitoring		
Demonstrates efficiency in an emergency situation		

continues

Exhibit 3–17 continued

	Requirement Met	
NURSE PRACTITIONER (ARNP)	**YES**	**NO**
Demonstrates the ability to perform multi-system assessment		
Demonstrates the ability to interpret problems		
Demonstrates the ability to initiate appropriate intervention		

PART II—CONDUCT AND HEALTH EVALUATION

	Acceptable	Unacceptable
Relationship with others	_____________	_____________
Patient relationship	_____________	_____________

Has this Allied Health Professional ever shown signs of any drug or alcohol problems?
_____ No _____ Yes. If yes, please attach details.

OVERALL EVALUATION: _____ Above Average _____ Average _____ Below Average

Completed by: ________________________________

Position: ________________________________

Note: OR, operating room; ARNP, advanced registered nurse practitioner.

Courtesy of Memorial Medical Center, Jacksonville, Florida.

- some medical staff departments or committees do not meet on a monthly basis

Sometimes an application may be completed and ready for the review process but take more time to get through the medical staff and governing board review and approval process simply because of waiting time for the various groups to meet.

The express process eliminates the waiting period for the majority of the applications and reapplications. Using this process also saves committee time and involves fewer people in a routine review of an application. For this to be successful, the department chairs, committee chairs, medical executive committee, and governing board need to be willing to delegate, if necessary, this review to one or several individuals who represent each of the review components. The department cannot neglect this responsibility, since it is a Joint Commission requirement that the chair is responsible for reviewing and recommending. However, in larger organizations, there may be a section or division chief with specialty privileges in the same area as the applicant. That individual may be asked to do a more involved review at the department chair's request. The credentials committee chair may opt to review all such files designated as "express" or to delegate on a monthly basis some type of rotation for members of the credentials committee to share in this responsibility. The chief of staff or president of the medical staff does have the obligation to sign off on these files and should not delegate this responsibility unless he or she is not available. The president-elect or vice chief of staff reviews and signs off on behalf of the medical executive committee. The governing board can delegate this responsibility to the chief executive officer of the hospital to act on its behalf.

A first step in the process is for the medical staff to determine what objective criteria they consider must be met for a practitioner to be eligible for the express process. Exhibits 3–18 and 3–19 are examples of criteria defined by a medical staff, including required approvals regardless of whether the process is express. The criteria should be objective enough so that a medical staff office person can review and make the recommendation to the department chair or credentials representative (whoever reviews the file first). Another important component in this process is for everyone involved to understand that if someone at any point along the way has a question or concern that was not raised before, the file will go back into the standard routine for processing, which allows full committee and/or board review.

Figure 3–6 is a flowchart that details the express credentialing process. One important consideration is that if at any point along the way the designated reviewer does not look at the file before a designated committee or board meeting, the file is not held up but is simply put into the standard process of taking the file to the committee. For example, if the department chair reviews a file that is tagged for express process and agrees and signs off on the file, it is then ready for a credentials committee representative to review. If the designated credentials representative does not review the file before the next credentials committee meeting, the file is taken to the credentials committee. If the committee decides that the file is still considered an express process file, the file is then given to the chief of staff for review and signature, rather than being held for the medical executive committee meeting. The same scenario applies to the medical executive committee and governing board.

Using this process, it is conceivable that once a file was complete and ready for the medical staff and governing board review process it could be hand-carried to four individuals (the department chair, the credentials committee representative, the chief of staff, and the chief executive officer) and approved within hours or days as opposed to weeks or months. Again, if for any reason anyone questions anything in the file, it automatically comes out of the express process and is processed routinely with other files at the committee meetings.

As shown in Exhibit 3–19, if any of the review individuals sign off on the express process, their signature is required on the form. If, however, the file is not considered an express file, the medical staff office can document the date of the meeting on the review sheet in an effort to eliminate unnecessary signatures. The minutes of any meeting where a file was reviewed and action was taken serve as the official record. This process eliminates blank signature lines that may not get signed. The privilege delineations should be signed by the department chair, since often they are distributed to other areas of the hospital, and the signature signifies a formal review.

If files are processed by express method, then at the subsequent meeting of the credentials or committee executives, a list is available "for information only" that the named files have been reviewed and approved via the expressed credentialing process before the meeting date.

The medical staff may want to periodically review the criteria they have established for appointment and reappointment express processes and make any revisions to reflect current policy or standards.

Exhibit 3–18 Initial Appointment Evaluation Form

Physician Name: Appointment Year:
Department: Specialty:

MEDICAL STAFF OFFICE REVIEW:

Criteria Evaluation:	Standard	Express
	(Circle One)	
1. Do any hospital affiliation letters indicate adverse information or potential concerns?	Yes	No
2. Do any peer reference letters indicate adverse information or potential concerns?	Yes	No
3. Are there any malpractice actions in the last five years?	Yes	No
4. Does physician have more than one active medical license?	Yes	No
5. Does applicant have any criminal convictions?	Yes	No
6. Are there any reports of disciplinary actions, licensure restrictions or investigations that are current or in the past?	Yes	No
7. Are there any reports listed on the National Practitioner Data Bank?	Yes	No
8. Are there any privilege requests that are not consistent with the specialty and training?	Yes	No
9. Is there any criterion that is not met for specific clinical privileges requested?	Yes	No
10. Is there any other negative or questionable information contained in the application that might require further investigation/discussion?	Yes	No
11. Is any information from CMSO/profile missing or are any problems noted?	Yes	No
12. Is any licensure (state, DEA, DPS) and/or malpractice insurance coverage not current?	Yes	No

Comments: ____

____

______________________ ______________________

Medical Staff Office Signature Date

DEPARTMENT CHAIR REVIEW:

Based on information received relating to licensure, training, experience, malpractice history competency evaluation and ability to practice the privileges requested, the Applicant's competency, professional performance, judgment, and technical skill appear to be satisfactory within the limits of the clinical privileges requested, and if contrary evidence exists, reasons must be documented.

Comments: ____

____

____ Recommend appointment to medical staff with clinical privileges as requested

____ Recommend appointment to medical staff with clinical privileges as specified on Privilege Request Form

____ Do Not Recommend appointment to medical staff or clinical privileges requested

____ Express ____ Standard review recommended.

______________________ ______________________

Department Chair Signature Date

______________________ ______________________

Additional Signature at Chair's Request Date

Note: CMSO, Columbia Medical Services Organization; DPS, Department of Public Safety.

Courtesy of Columbia Medical Center–West, El Paso, Texas.

Exhibit 3–19 Reappointment Evaluation Form (Committee, Board action applies to initial appointment and reappointment)

Physician Name: Reappointment Year:
Department: Specialty:

MEDICAL STAFF OFFICE REVIEW:

Criteria Evaluation: Standard Express (Circle One)

1. Do any hospital affiliation letters indicate adverse information or potential concerns?	Yes	No	
2. Do any peer reference letters indicate adverse information or potential concerns?	Yes	No	
3. Are there any malpractice actions in the last five years?	Yes	No	
4. Does physician have more than one active medical license?	Yes	No	
5. Does applicant have any criminal convictions?	Yes	No	
6. Are there any reports of disciplinary actions, licensure restrictions or investigations that are current or in the past?	Yes	No	
7. Are there any reports listed on the National Practitioner Data Bank?	Yes	No	
8. Are there any privilege requests that are not consistent with the specialty and training?	Yes	No	
9. Is there any criterion that is not met for specific clinical privileges requested?	Yes	No	
10. Is there any other negative or questionable information contained in the application that might require further investigation/discussion?	Yes	No	
11. Is any information from CMSO/profile missing or are any issues noted?	Yes	No	
12. All licensure (state, DEA, DPS) and malpractice insurance coverage current?	Yes	No	
13. Any bylaws noncompliance?	Yes	No	
14. Change in category? If yes, number of patient contacts, if applicable.	Yes	No	To: ____
15. Changes in privileges request? (See Privilege Form)	Yes	No	

____

____

______________________________ ______________________________
Medical Staff Office Signature Date

DEPARTMENT CHAIR REVIEW:

Based on primary hospital, peer references and performance assessment and improvement data available for review, the Applicant's competency, professional performance, judgment, and technical skill are satisfactory within the limits of the clinical privileges requested, and further, based on these references, and/or personal knowledge, there is no evidence of any change in Applicant's health status which would adversely affect his/her competence within the scope of the clinical privileges requested/granted. There is no evidence before the department contrary to this statement. (If contrary evidence exists, reasons must be documented.)

Comments: ____

____

____ Recommend reappointment to medical staff with clinical privileges as requested
____ Recommend reappointment to medical staff with clinical privileges as specified on Privilege Request Form
____ Do Not Recommend appointment to medical staff or clinical privileges requested
____ Express ____ Standard review recommended.

continues

Exhibit 3–19 continued

Department Chair Signature ____________ Date ____________

Additional Signature at Chair's Request ____________ Date ____________

Signatures on prior page and below signify that the candidate's application has been reviewed and validated/verified, that there are no reasons to withhold staff membership according to provisions of the medical staff bylaws and that approved privileges have been justified by validated training or documented expertise unless otherwise stated.

CREDENTIALS COMMITTEE/DESIGNEE REVIEW, RECOMMENDATION:

____ Recommend reappointment to medical staff with privileges as requested
____ Recommend reappointment to medical staff with privileges as specified on Privileges Request Form.
____ Do Not Recommend reappointment to medical staff or privileges requested

EXPRESS REVIEW: ____________________________
Chair/Designee Signature Date

or

STANDARD REVIEW: ____________________________
Date of Credentials Committee Meeting

EXECUTIVE COMMITTEE/CHIEF OF STAFF REVIEW, RECOMMENDATION:

____ Recommend reappointment to medical staff with privileges as requested
____ Recommend reappointment to medical staff with privileges as specified on Privilege Request Form
____ Do Not Recommend reappointment to medical staff or privileges requested

EXPRESS REVIEW: ____________________________
Chief of Staff Signature Date

or

STANDARD REVIEW: ____________________________
Date of Executive Committee Meeting

GOVERNING BOARD ACTION:

____ Approve reappointment to medical staff with clinical privileges as requested
____ Approve reappointment to medical staff with privileges as specified on Privilege Request Form
____ Do Not Approve reappointment to medical staff or clinical privileges requested

EXPRESS REVIEW: ____________________________
CEO/DESIGNEE Signature Date

STANDARD REVIEW: ____________________________
Governing Board Meeting Date

FOR MEDICAL STAFF OFFICE USE ONLY:

☐ Standard Letter
☐ Standard Letter noting changes requested/approved
☐ Letter noting changes with further action required

Note: CMSO, Columbia Medical Services Organization; DPS, Department of Public Safety.

Courtesy of Columbia Medical Center–West, El Paso, Texas.

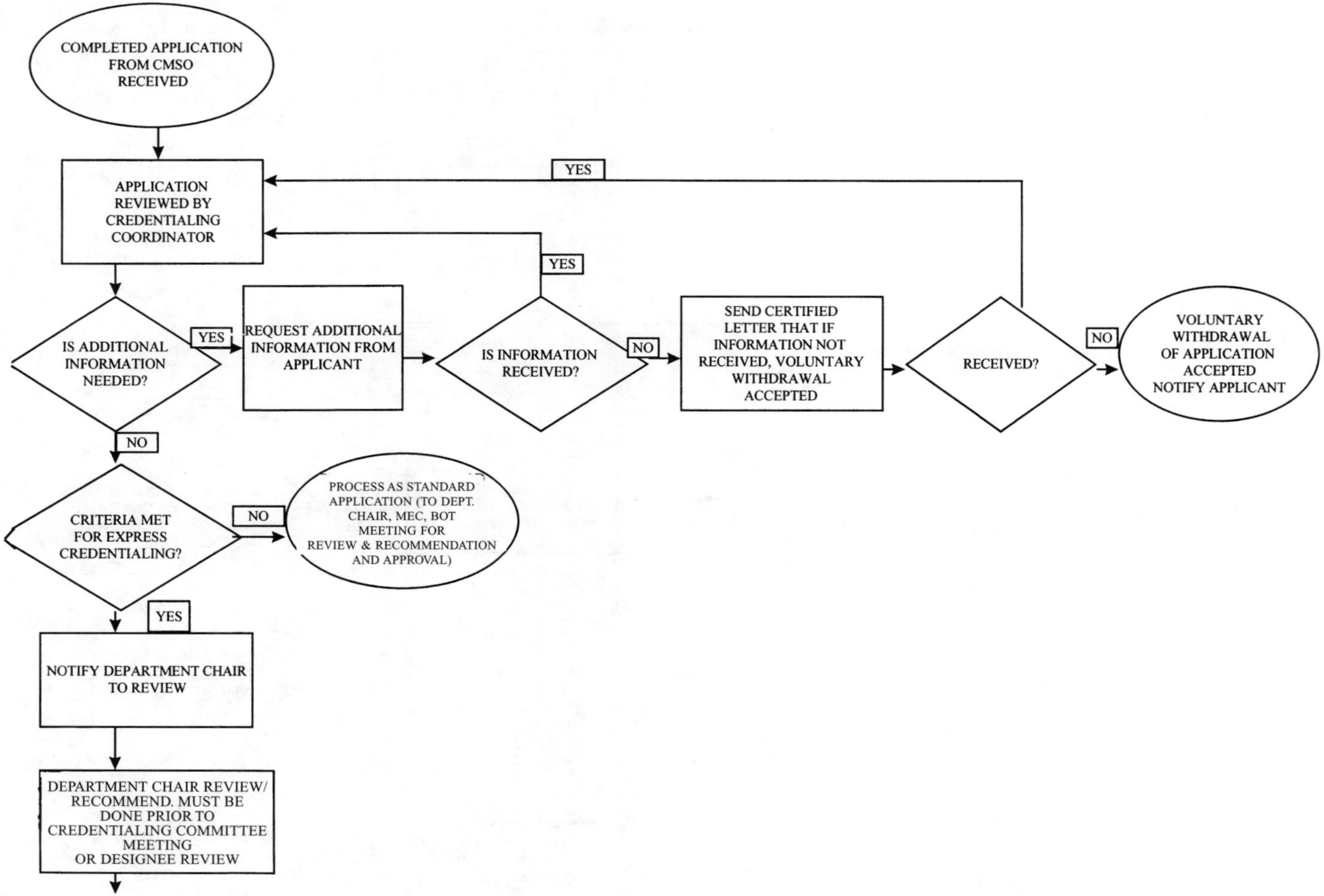

Figure 3–6 Express Credentialing Flowchart. Courtesy of Columbia Medical Center–West, El Paso, Texas.

continues

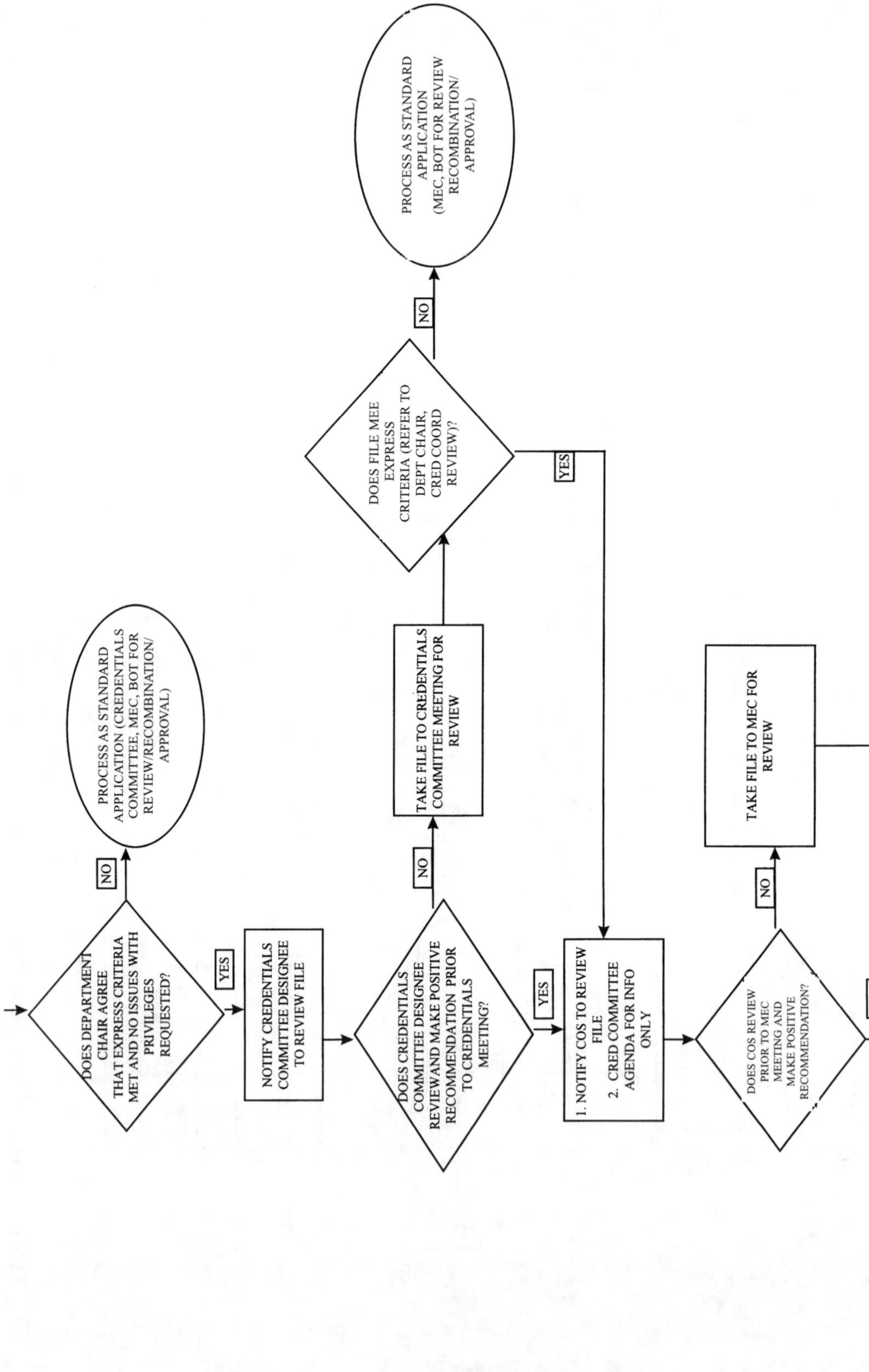
DOES DEPARTMENT CHAIR AGREE THAT EXPRESS CRITERIA MET AND NO ISSUES WITH PRIVILEGES REQUESTED?
NO
PROCESS AS STANDARD APPLICATION (CREDENTIALS COMMITTEE, MEC, BOT FOR REVIEW/RECOMBINATION/ APPROVAL)
YES
NOTIFY CREDENTIALS COMMITTEE DESIGNEE TO REVIEW FILE
DOES CREDENTIALS COMMITTEE DESIGNEE REVIEWAND MAKE POSITIVE RECOMMENDATION PRIOR TO CREDENTIALS MEETING?
NO
TAKE FILE TO CREDENTIALS COMMITTEE MEETING FOR REVIEW
DOES FILE MEE EXPRESS CRITERIA (REFER TO DEPT CHAIR, CRED COORD REVIEW)?
NO
PROCESS AS STANDARD APPLICATION (MEC, BOT FOR REVIEW RECOMBINATION/ APPROVAL)
YES
YES
1. NOTIFY COS TO REVIEW FILE
2. CRED COMMITTEE AGENDA FOR INFO ONLY
DOES COS REVIEW PRIOR TO MEC MEETING AND MAKE POSITIVE RECOMMENDATION?
NO
TAKE FILE TO MEC FOR REVIEW
YES

continues

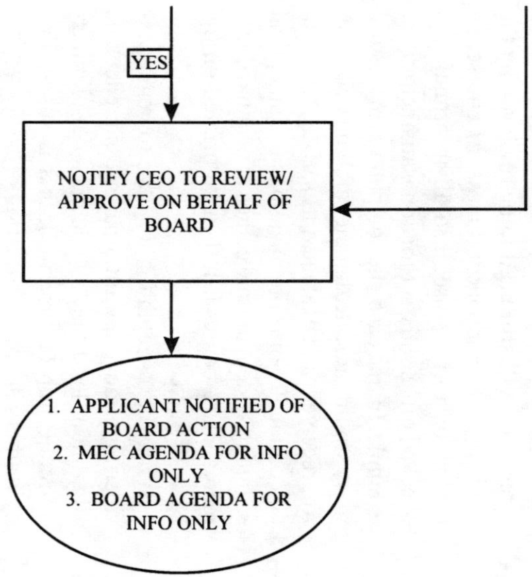

Note: MEC, medical executive committee; BOT, board of trustees; CMSO, Columbia Medical Services Organization; COS, chief of staff; Cred Coord, credentialing coordinator.

PAPERLESS CREDENTIALS FILE

The paperless credentials file is now in use by some managed care organizations that contract with a certified CVO that maintains all of the hard-copy information. The managed care organizations have a summary of that information that they keep within their organization. Hospitals are beginning to think about the paperless credentials file and how they might eliminate some of the unnecessary paper. Much of the paper that is contained in a credentials file is there because of "old-school thinking" that the more paper, the better. Often information is collected that is not required. For example, some hospitals still receive copies of certificates of training and education and board certification. Because of the Joint Commission primary source standard, verifications must be received from the issuing source. Information also needs to be collected directly from the state licensing board with regard to currency of license and any sanctions or stipulations. Therefore, it is not necessary to maintain copies of anything when documented verification from the primary source is present in the credentials file.

As many hospitals begin to use external CVOs or internal credentialing verification departments, we suggest that they look at what information could be maintained in a central location and avoid much duplication throughout a system. This can be especially beneficial to those systems that use credentialing software that provides a practitioner profile listing all the information that has been verified and the date it has been verified. For example, if no adverse or negative information regarding malpractice claims history, licensure, and NPDB queries is received, only confirmation that the information is current, clear, and/or in good standing is needed. If hospitals use a centralized process, it is suggested that they audit whatever group is collecting and housing some of these verifications. This may be more easily done in a local community where a local CVO is involved or in an office or department within a health care delivery system that is doing all the verifications for all of the system components. The audit could be done to make sure that information on the practitioner profile summary is in fact in the file and that no information is there that would require any evaluation.

As the Joint Commission becomes more sophisticated in its use of technology, it is already seeing that in some hospitals it is looking at information on a computer to verify what is in a credentials file. It may want to see one or two files to verify that the information is in fact in the file. If this information is housed in a central location, when the list of files is given to the medical staff office to pull for the credentials file review, the hard copies may be pulled for backup on site to the information that the surveyor is reviewing on the computer screen.

It may be a while before hospitals are comfortable about eliminating some of the paperwork that traditionally has been maintained in each individual credentials file. In interviews with Joint Commission personnel, we have been told that surveyors know they may be reviewing information from a computer system as opposed to looking at a hard-copy file. Obviously, any information such as hospital training and peer references will still need to be reviewed by the medical staff component, unless, of course, an evaluation form is used and all information is checked off as satisfactory or unsatisfactory, for example. In that case, the computer profile summary would indicate that the reference was sent for, received, and evaluated as satisfactory with no comment. Some organizations use an optical scanning system to store copies of original documents. Hard copies can then be printed on the basis of need.

It may be a stretch for hospitals to begin considering a move toward a paperless credentials file, but at least they should consider eliminating collection of paperwork that is superseded by primary source verification.

NOTES

1. *1998 Hospital Accreditation Standards* (Oakbrook Terrace, IL: Joint Commission on Accreditation of Healthcare Organizations), 243–244.
2. *1998 Hospital Accreditation Standards,* 245.
3. *Developing a Policy and Procedure Manual for the Medical Staff Services Department* (Lombard, IL: National Association Medical Staff Services, 1995).
4. *Developing a Policy and Procedure Manual,* 4.
5. 42 U.S.C. §§ 11101–11152.
6. V. Searcy and V. Jackson (paper presented at the conference of the National Association Medical Staff Services, Pittsburgh, PA, October 1998.
7. *1998 Hospital Accreditation Standards,* 255.
8. *1998 Hospital Accreditation Standards,* 254.
9. *1998 Hospital Accreditation Standards,* 258.
10. *1998 Hospital Accreditation Standards,* 255.
11. *1998 Hospital Accreditation Standards,* 234.
12. NPDB Guidebook, Pub. L. No. HRSA-95-255 (Rockville, MD: U.S. Department of Health and Human Services, 1996).
13. *1998 Hospital Accreditation Standards,* 255.

CHAPTER 4

Credentialing in Ambulatory and Managed Care

OVERVIEW

Health care is increasingly being delivered in settings other than hospitals and through alternative care delivery systems. These may include health maintenance organizations (HMOs), preferred provider organizations, point-of-service products, freestanding ambulatory surgical centers, physician-hospital organizations, or other systems, networks, and integrated entities that are composed of physicians, hospitals, ambulatory care facilities, and insurance plans. As with hospitals, all of these organizations share the goals of providing quality patient care services and reducing the organizational liability to the extent possible. A well-structured and implemented credentialing process is an important element in obtaining these goals, regardless of the setting or the organizational structure. In general, the credentialing activities in ambulatory and managed care are different from those carried out in hospitals. We have therefore developed this separate chapter to address basic credentialing activities in managed and ambulatory care. Readers who are working in ambulatory or managed care settings will also benefit from review of information in Chapter 3, since additional ideas can be gained from many of the hospital processes and forms.

Because a physician may be affiliated with an ambulatory practice, several hospitals, and numerous different types of insurance plans, he or she may be credentialed and recredentialed numerous times. This major duplication of effort creates inefficiencies that may tempt an organization to shorten the credentialing process or to rely entirely on another organization's process. But an abbreviated or unsupervised delegation of the credentialing process undermines liability protection and seldom results in a panel of appropriately credentialed practitioners and providers. Therefore, it is very important for credentialing professionals to identify all requirements specific to their setting to ensure that their process meets organizational, regulatory, and accreditation requirements so that the result of their efforts is assurance of affiliation with competent practitioners and providers. A number of major accrediting organizations offer voluntary accreditation to managed and ambulatory care organizations, including

- Accreditation Association for Ambulatory Health Care
- Joint Commission on Accreditation of Healthcare Organizations (Joint Commission)
- National Committee for Quality Assurance (NCQA)
- Utilization Review Accreditation Commission

While many managed and ambulatory care organizations are not accredited, most states have statutes that govern or regulate their activities. Accreditation is becoming the norm among managed care organizations, and integrated systems may be accredited by several organizations and affected by numerous statutes and requirements. Accrediting organizations, statutes, and regulations are discussed in detail in Chapter 2.

Managed and ambulatory care relationships with practitioners are commonly outlined in a contract or agreement with practitioners and providers. These contracts, along with organizational policies and procedures, provide the structure for credentialing activities. Alternative health care delivery systems that "manage" some aspect of health care delivery are referred to as *managed care organizations* in this chapter. Ambulatory care in this chapter relates to those facilities outside of hospital systems in which patient care is rendered, such as a physician office or a surgical center. Integrated networks or systems are those organizations made up of two or more entities, commonly including a hospital and a managed and/or ambulatory care organization. This chapter addresses activities for managed and ambulatory care organizations and those integrated systems that include managed and ambulatory care components.

The scope of credentialing is often much broader in ambulatory and managed care than in hospitals. Practitioners include both physicians and allied health professionals (AHPs) who either directly provide health care as employees or enter into a contract with a managed care organization to provide care for its enrollees. In some instances, a practitioner will be employed by a physician group that has a contract with a managed care organization and will be credentialed by the physician group, by the managed care organization, and by one or more hospitals. Also included in the scope of credentialing by managed care organizations are providers of care. A provider is a facility in which service is rendered, such as a pharmacy, a mammography/radiology center, a physical therapy outpatient unit, or an ambulatory care surgical center. Accreditation and state statutes may require credentialing of providers as well as practitioners.

As practitioner and provider activities in managed care organizations and ambulatory settings are governed by contracts rather than bylaws, it is necessary for organizations to identify and implement clear plans, policies, and procedures that include criteria and basic qualifications for participation. It is common practice to determine compliance with criteria before execution of a contract in the managed and ambulatory care arena. Development of a plan, criteria, policy and procedure, and site visits will be addressed in this chapter, along with details related to basic credentialing steps.

There are six basic steps in the credentialing process for managed and ambulatory care organizations:

1. need evaluation
2. application
3. verification and information gathering
4. analysis and decision
5. recredentialing
6. maintenance and problem resolution

It is common for managed or ambulatory care organizations to define the scope of practice and of their network. A need evaluation determines how many practitioners with specific qualifications are in specific geographic locations and how many practitioners and providers of care will be reviewed for possible acceptance into the network. The organization may also utilize a formal preapplication process as part of its need evaluation.

The application and verification information-gathering processes do not differ greatly between hospitals, managed care, and ambulatory care organizations. But some additional types of information are gathered. For example, an HMO that is accredited by NCQA will perform facility site visits and medical record audits in the practitioner offices and use that information in making credentialing and recredentialing decisions.

In the absence of an organized medical staff, the credentials analysis and decision process may be delegated by the governing body to a credentials or peer review body. NCQA, the accrediting body for managed care organizations, requires that participating practitioners give advice to those making credentialing decisions. An express process is common and relatively easy to implement if no privileging is involved. A less onerous and involved due-process procedure is usually found in managed and ambulatory care settings than in hospitals. As the relationship is contractual, termination of the relationship may be affected by other aspects of the contract than those specifically having to do with credentialing or recredentialing activities.

In managed and ambulatory care settings, reappointment is commonly completed every two years. The recredentialing process includes the practitioner's completion of a questionnaire, followed by verification of the regulatory aspects of practice. Member/patient complaints, medical record review, patient satisfaction utilization patterns, care delivery, and results of additional facility audits may be collected and reviewed as part of the recredentialing process.

The credentialing process is a critical one that should be initiated when a practitioner is recruited. If the credentialing activities are not complete at the time that the practitioner or provider is ready to sign the contract, the contract should include a provision indicating that final agreement is contingent upon successful completion of the credentialing process. (NCQA accreditation standards do not allow practitioners or providers to render services or establish an affiliation until credentialing is complete.) Credentialing is a newer activity in managed and ambulatory care than in hospitals, and the accrediting organizations have less history and experience in evaluating credentialing activities than the Joint Commission. Nonetheless, credentialing is rapidly growing and changing and requires increasing levels of knowledge and expertise.

DEFINITIONS AND TYPES OF AMBULATORY AND MANAGED CARE ORGANIZATIONS

In the broadest sense, managed and ambulatory care organizations are those entities that deliver or are involved with provision of health care services in settings outside of the hospital. Numerous definitions and acronyms that are specific to health care are used by these organizations. Those that may be necessary for the credentialing professional to know are listed in Exhibit 4–1.

What Is Ambulatory Care?

Ambulatory care is defined as "healthcare services that are rendered on an outpatient basis or to patients who are not confined overnight in a healthcare institution."[1] Examples of ambulatory care entities or settings include physician medical group practices, freestanding ambulatory surgical centers, health service facilities at a college or university, endoscopy centers, and urgent/immediate care centers. An ambulatory center is defined as "the environment for providing healthcare services that is consistent with the definition of ambulatory care."[2]

What Is Managed Care?

In previous years, the term *managed care* brought to mind a Health Maintenance Organization or HMO. In the 1980s, an HMO was defined as an organized health care system that provided health care to members in return for a preset amount of money.[3] Managed care was focused on lowering the cost and utilization of health services while maintaining a certain level of quality. Defining managed care today is much more difficult. At the very least, it is a system of health care delivery and financing mechanisms that is focused upon managing cost, quality, and access to care.[4] The common characteristics of managed care organizations include

- a panel of affiliated or contracted practitioners and providers
- limitation of benefits if a noncontracted provider/practitioner is used
- an authorization system

Exhibit 4–1 Common Acronyms and Definitions

Alternative Delivery System (ADS)
A managed care organization such as an HMO, a PPO, or an IPA.

Ancillary Services
Supplemental services that may be performed on an outpatient basis, including radiology, pharmacy, and laboratory services.

Any-Willing-Provider (AWP) Laws
Laws, found in many states, that establish a policy related to managed care organizations in that state. Most require that a provider who is "willing to join" a network be allowed to do so if basic provisions are met.

Ambulatory Surgery Center (ASC) or Ambulatory Surgical Unit (ASU)
Center outside of the hospital providing surgery on a same-day basis, usually of a fairly uncomplicated nature. Some standards differentiate these units from centers that are hospital affiliated by referring to them as "freestanding" units or centers.

Access
Terminology used within managed care that defines the ability of a member or patient to obtain services at the time that they are needed. *Access* may refer to telephone access, to the ability to schedule an appointment, or to physical access at the physician's office.

Availability
Terminology used in managed care organizations that refers to the number of physicians, practitioners, and providers who are available to patients and members for covered services.

Capitation
Money paid/received on a per-member basis rather than on actual cost of service. A physician who receives capitation payments from a managed care organization is paid a specific amount for each assigned member regardless of the number of visits, tests, or other services rendered or not rendered.

Clinic Without Walls (CWW)
An organization or network with medical groups at various locations. The organization usually provides professional management services to the medical groups, such as staffing, purchasing, or centralized billing and accounting.

Contracted Practitioner/Provider
A practitioner, entity, institution, or facility having a contractual agreement to provide specific services.

Credentials Committee
A committee established by the governing body to carry out credentialing (and privileging as applicable), including the evaluation of credentials and the determination of credentialing and recredentialing status for eligible, employed, and contracted practitioners and providers.

Exclusive Provider Organization (EPO)
A type of managed care in which patients must see the physicians who are contracted with the managed care organization in order to obtain coverage for their health care.

Delegated Services
Activities granted by contract to a qualifying entity having the ability to perform specific functions on behalf of the ambulatory or managed care organization. Functions may include credentialing, utilization management, and quality improvement activities.

Foundation
A nonprofit integrated delivery system. A foundation is made up of physicians and hospital(s) and usually exists in states that do not allow physicians to be directly employed by hospitals or in states that have laws prohibiting corporate practice of medicine.

Group Practice Without Walls (GPWW)
The same as a clinic without walls, but involving practitioners.

Health Plan Employer Data Information Set (HEDIS)
A group of performance measures developed through the National Committee for Quality Assurance (NCQA) for the purpose of evaluating health plans. NCQA-accredited health plans use HEDIS measures as part of their quality program. Payors and customers support the program as an effort to provide standardized data and to allow comparison between plans.

Health Maintenance Organization (HMO)
An organization that manages the health care services provided to members in return for a fixed

continues

Exhibit 4–1 continued

premium, which is usually prepaid. To qualify as an HMO the organization must have (1) an organized system for providing health care within a specific geographic area; (2) basic and supplemental health maintenance and treatment services; and (3) a voluntarily enrolled group of members (patients). There are four types of HMO models: group model, staff model, network model, and independent practice association (IPA) model.

Indemnity Insurance
The traditional type of insurance, in which coverage is provided against loss of health or injury.

Independent Practice Association (IPA)
A term used to define both a type of HMO model and a physician organization that contracts with a managed care plan to deliver services. The IPA contracts with individual physicians and other practitioners to provide services for which they receive capitation. The IPA usually involves numerous specialties but may be set up as a primary care IPA or a single-specialty IPA. An IPA may also be the physician component of a physician hospital organization.

Management Service Organization (MSO)
An organization usually formed to provide specific services to physician office practices. Services may include billing and accounting, staffing, computer support, purchasing or other services that are more cost-effective or productive when provided by a group than when provided on individualized basis. They may also be formed as a means to contract with managed care organizations.

Member
Term frequently used by managed care organizations to refer to their enrollees or those insured by the organization.

Physician Hospital Organization (PHO)
Organization formed between physicians and a hospital in which the hospital provides management and contracting services. A PHO may involve all members of a hospital staff or may be a closed panel and involve only those who are determined to be eligible for membership.

Plan
A generic term for a managed care organization.

Per Member Per Month—PMPM
A method frequently used to quantify data. Refers to the payment made to a practitioner for providing care (as defined in an agreement or contract) for each enrolled member (in his or her practice) each month.

Point-of-Service (POS)
A plan that allows members to choose the form of service at the time it is needed. Normally, there is an HMO or HMO-like system as well as an indemnity plan. Unlike many managed care plans, POS plans allow the member to use out-of-plan services and practitioners, but at a higher rate of payment.

Preferred Provider Organization (PPO)
An organization that contracts with practitioners to provide services on a discounted basis. A PPO usually offers a wider variety of access to practitioners but is not usually considered to be as cost-effective as an HMO.

Practitioner
An individual who usually is licensed and is qualified to practice as a health care professional. Physicians are referred to as *practitioners* by NCQA.

Primary Care
The general medical care provided by family practitioners, internal medicine physicians, and pediatricians.

Privileges
The authorization granted to an individual practitioner to perform specific patient care functions (including diagnostic, therapeutic, medical, dental, pediatric, psychological, and surgical services) at a specified site(s) within the limits of license, registration, and certification.

Provider
By NCQA's 1997 definition, institutions or organizations providing services. Examples include hospitals, pharmacies, and other facilities, institutions, or organizations.

Source: Data from *Surveyor Guidelines for the Accreditation of Managed Care Organizations,* © 1997, NCQA; R. Rognehaugh, *Managed Health Care Dictionary,* © 1996, Aspen Publishers, Inc.; and P. Kongstvedt, *Managed Care Handbook,* 3rd ed., © 1996, Aspen Publishers, Inc.

Examples of managed care organizations today include HMOs, preferred provider organizations, medical foundations, and the numerous forms of integrated delivery networks and systems formed between physicians, hospitals, and health care insurers.

What Is Integrated Delivery?

Integrated delivery is a system or network of health care practitioners and/or providers that is organized to span a broad range of services.[5] It may provide a complete range of health care services, obtain an HMO license, or negotiate agreements with health care insurers for the organization's practitioners and providers within the system.[6] Figure 4–1 outlines some of the possible relationships between physicians, hospitals, and health plans. This outline does not address all of the possibilities of organizations that are currently involved in providing managed and ambulatory health care services. It does include the more common entities that have been defined in Exhibit 4–1.

HISTORY OF CREDENTIALING ACTIVITIES IN AMBULATORY AND MANAGED CARE

Until the mid- to late 1980s, there was very little credentialing activity outside of hospitals. There had been no significant legal case indicating that credentialing needed to be performed outside of hospitals, there were few regulations, and accreditation was still in developmental stages.. It was considered very acceptable for ambulatory organizations to "piggyback" onto hospital credentialing determinations, since it was widely felt that hospitals completed a detailed review of physician credentials. A physician's affiliation with a hospital meant that he or she was qualified and competent to practice medicine. Most managed and ambulatory care organizations gathered demographic information but did little or no verification. This changed with the advent of the Health Care Quality Improvement Act of 1986[7] and the development of Joint Commission and NCQA accreditation programs. Concerns about the ability of a patient to obtain quality care within a managed care system resulted in demands by payors and the government that managed care organizations affiliate with only high-quality credentialed providers. It is currently an industry standard that practitioners hired, contracted with, or designated as the preferred providers for a managed care organization be fully credentialed by that organization. In recent years, courts have increasingly held that managed care plans have a responsibility to ensure quality of care delivery. Once the Joint Commission implemented an accreditation specific to ambulatory care, credentialing activity independent of the hospital quickly developed. Because integrated systems and networks are commonly affiliated in the same manner with a managed care organization, there is increasing activity across the continuum.

THE CREDENTIALING PROCESS

Critical Elements

The aspects of the credentialing process that will determine its effectiveness and the ability of the organization to minimize liability are

- structure and accountability
- credentialing plan and related policies and procedures
- principles
- contracts and contractual relationships
- criteria
- process steps

Structure and Accountability

A managed or ambulatory care organization that engages in credentialing activity should ensure a strong structure for the program credentialing activities and should clearly identify accountability for the process. The steps involved include

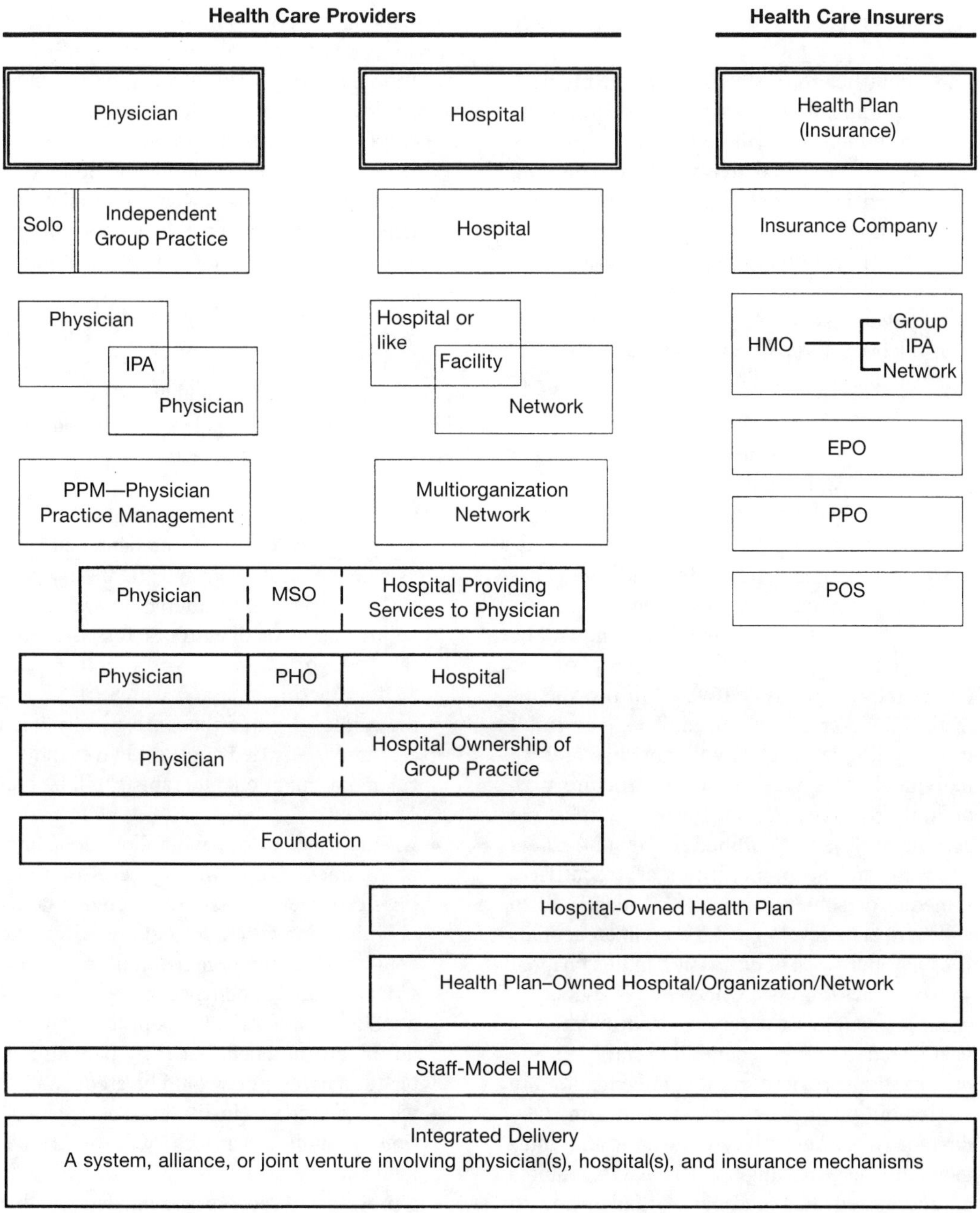

Note: For abbreviations refer to Exhibit 4–1.

Figure 4–1 Managed and Integrated Care Entities. Courtesy of C. Mobley & Associates, LLC, and Quality Management Options, LLC, Colorado Springs, Colorado.

1. identification of the structure that will be used
2. identification of the scope of the program
3. determination of how issues, disputes and disagreements will be handled
4. if an integrated delivery system is present, identification of any issues related to integration
5. determination of who will make key decisions (including those that have legal implications)
6. identification, development, and approval for the process, policies, procedures, and criteria

Identifying the Credentialing Structure. There are usually fewer departments, physicians, and committees involved in credentialing in managed and ambulatory care organizations than in hospitals or integrated systems. In establishing, developing, or reorganizing the credentialing structure, it is necessary first to identify who will be specifically involved in each step of the credentialing process and who will provide direction for everyone involved. This may result in a very simple structure with only two or three individuals or a very complex structure with multiple reporting levels. Basic activities and accountabilities are outlined in Figure 4–2. As structure and accountabilities are identified, someone or some group will be identified to collect data to develop and maintain credentials files. For purposes of discussion in this chapter, whoever does this task, whether an individual, a group of people, or an entire department, will be referred to as the credentialing staff. In some organizations, review and recommendation are carried out by an individual such as a medical director (if accountability is given to that individual by the governing board). NCQA requires an accredited managed care organization to designate a credentialing committee.[8] The review and recommendation structure should always include appropriate practitioners and not rely solely on administrative staff. The governing board may determine that they will be the only entity that may approve credentials, but it is not uncommon for a governing board to delegate to a review body that meets more frequently and that is more actively involved with practitioners. More information related to structure may be found in Chapter 11 of this book.

Once identified, the structure should be outlined in a flowchart that reflects accountability for each major component. This chart should be included in the credentials plan book or document.

Defining the Scope. Once the credentialing program structure is identified, the scope of the credentialing program should be defined. When identifying program scope, considerations and decisions should take into account

- types and general categories of practitioners and providers that will be credentialed, such as categories of primary care and specialist, or categories of allopathic and osteopathic: inclusion of chiropractors as a separate category, as specialists, or as allied health practitioners; and which (if any) of the midlevel practitioners, e.g., physician assistants, certified nurse midwives, physical and occupational therapists will be credentialed
- whether credentialing will follow along lines of contracts and claim payments or along lines of patient contact (e.g., credentialing only those practitioners and providers who contract with the organization or all individuals who have patient contact); if by contract, a hospital radiologist probably would not be credentialed, but if by patient contact, the radiologist would be credentialed
- which providers (institutions or organizations providing services) will be credentialed
- if providers of care are credentialed, whether employees or licensed caregivers working for providers will be credentialed
- whether all or part of the credentialing process will be delegated
- whether privileging will be a component of the program

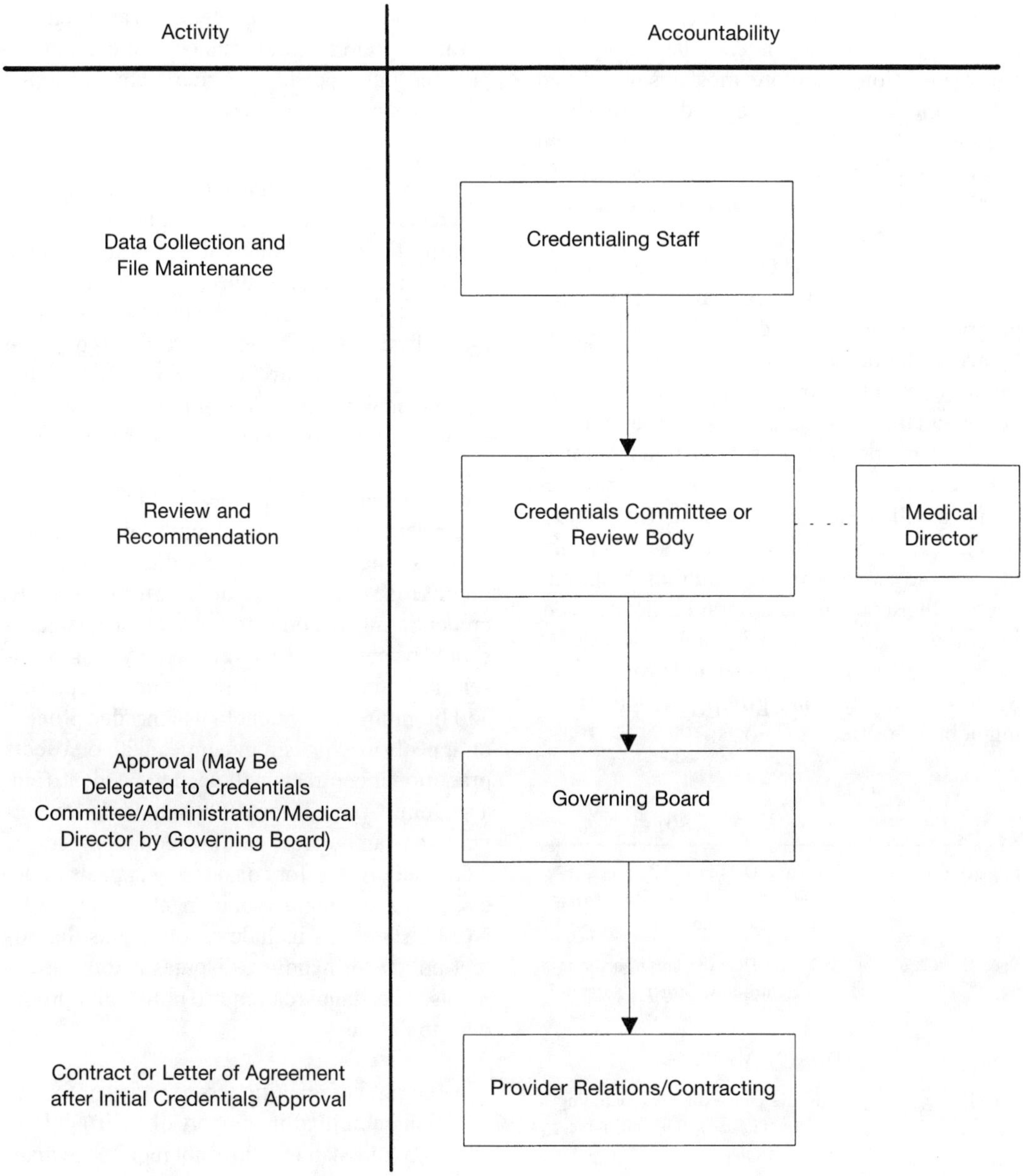

Figure 4–2 Structure for Credentialing Process in Managed and Ambulatory Care. Courtesy of C. Mobley & Associates, LLC, and Quality Management Options, LLC, Colorado Springs, Colorado.

Most organizations do not credential practitioners who have no independent relationship with the organization. Therefore, most hospital-based practitioners would not be credentialed by a managed care organization. But if an organization "promotes practitioners" or includes them in marketing literature, they should be credentialed.

If the organization is accredited or involved with a program such as CHAMPUS or a Medicare/Medicaid Risk Contract, the scope of the program may already be defined to some extent by accreditation standards, regulations, or the service contract. An organization may choose to go beyond the scope defined by accreditation or a contract but not to do less. If an organization is not accredited and has no contractual requirements, it will need to identify the driving factors behind its program and, on the basis of its goals, identify the scope of its credentialing program.

Once the scope of the program is determined, it should be documented in such a way as to clearly identify all practitioner and provider categories. In a physician group practice, scope might be identified as follows:

Category	*Type*
Primary Care	MDs and DOs in family practice (FP), internal medicine (IM), pediatrics (Ped)
Specialty Care	MDs and DOs in ob/gyn, orthopedics, urology, surgery, dermatology
Associate	DDSs, DPMs, DCs
Allied	All physician extenders including physician assistants and nurse practitioners

In an ambulatory surgical unit, scope might be identified as follows:

Category	*Type*
Physician	MDs, DOs, DDSs, DPMs, DCs
Allied Health	All other licensed individuals rendering care to patients

All practitioners and providers who are included in the program scope are subject to credentialing policies and procedures. Criteria are developed for each category and type.

Handling Issues, Disputes, and Disagreements. When determining the structure and scope of credentialing, the organization will need to identify the process that will be used to handle and resolve issues, disputes, and disagreements. A formal mechanism may be identified for handling physician concerns, disagreements between integrated components in a network, internal disagreement with a decision, or physician disputes related to credentialing decisions. A determination should be made related to the extent to which the organization plans to deal with disputes and disagreements before development of processes, policies, and procedures. If a due process or a mechanism to appeal decisions related to credentialing is going to be made available, it should be developed and reviewed by legal counsel and integrated into practitioner orientation and literature. The extent to which a due process or appeals mechanism integrates with or affects practitioner contracts will need to be identified. The Joint Commission 1998 standards for networks and ambulatory care accreditation[9] require a defined process for considering appeals to decisions to terminate appointment. The 1998/99 NCQA standards include requirements that affect policy for handling disputes and disagreements. The standards require policy and procedure to define

- the right of practitioners to review information submitted in support of their application (this standard does not require the managed care organization to allow practitioners to review references or information that is peer review protected)
- the process for notifying practitioners if information collected by the managed care organization differs substantially from the information submitted by the practitioner
- the practitioners' right to correct erroneous information[10]

Identifying Issues Related to Integrated Systems and Networks. If the credentialing activities are taking place in an integrated system or network, it will be necessary to clearly define where and how each step will occur. A key factor is identification of the governing structure for the network because determination or final credential decisions will be the responsibility of the governing body. Data collection may take place in numerous locations, and the review and recommendation process may be centralized. Individual components of the organization may complete activities of data collection, review, and recommendation separately. Often political aspects are involved in centralizing functions for which individual components of the organization have been responsible. Integration of activities and centralization of credentialing may result in a more productive process or may slow everything down. Duplication of efforts and standardization of process are major challenges faced by organizations that continue decentralized operations. Chapter 10 of this book addresses centralized credentialing activities.

Making Key Decisions. Identification of the decision makers and key individuals who will be involved in the credentialing process should be made by the governing board and/or administrative staff. It is strongly recommended that legal review be obtained during the identification of program structure and for review of processes, policies, procedures, and criteria. In most organizations, a medical director or medical advisor will play a key role in credentialing and be responsible for the appropriate processing of credentials, making exceptions to the process and ensuring peer review as required. All administrative and management staff should know and understand who is accountable for the credentialing process and should be aware of who is able to make decisions, possible exceptions in the process, and who may resolve any issues that occur. Inevitably, a practitioner will be identified and recruited, and then pressure brought to bear on credentialing staff because of a specific network requirement or key client request. A request may be made for exceptions to criteria, policy requirements, or turnaround time because of the importance of the practitioner to network development. The structure of credentialing should identify the individuals that will be held accountable for any possible exceptions.

Plan Policies and Procedures

Development of the credentialing plan and related policy and procedures involves several steps:

- identification of the credentialing process that will be used by the organization, along with a description of the process
- list of key components of the credentialing plan
- identification of the policies and procedures that will be required
- identification of documents that will be used as part of daily credentialing activities

Identifying Credentialing Process Steps. The organization will need to review requirements for its process and then identify the steps that will be implemented. Although prescreen or preapplication is not required by accreditation or regulation, it may be determined to be useful. Delegation will also affect the flow of the process, so the organization should determine its applicability and/or the extent to which it should be used.

Once major process steps are identified, it is recommended that a flowchart be developed that includes time frames and accountability for each step. A flowchart is an effective tool in that it requires clear identification of each step and brings to light possible issues and problems. It also is an effective tool for educating everyone with involvement or interest as to the complexity, time frames, and accountabilities for the process. Flowcharts may be *macro flowcharts* that identify only major steps or *detailed flowcharts* that identify all possibilities. Figure 4–3 is an example of a macro flowchart identifying common steps in an ambulatory care credentialing

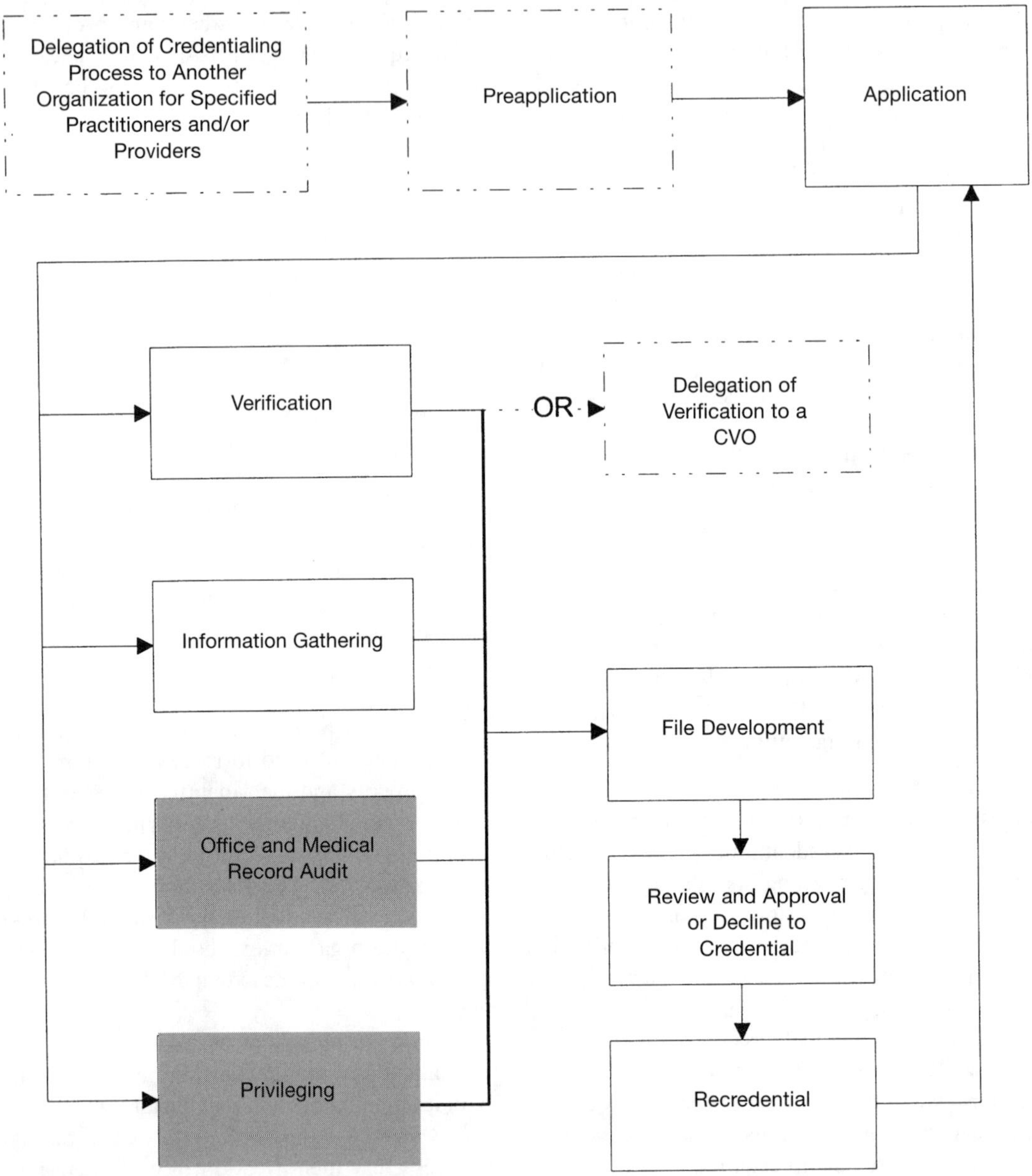

Key
Indicates an optional process
Indicates process that may be applicable to some but not all organizations
CVO, credentials verification organization.

Figure 4–3 Credentialing Process Flowchart. Courtesy of C. Mobley & Associates, LLC, and Quality Management Options, LLC, Colorado Springs, Colorado.

process. Once a macro flowchart is completed, a more detailed flowchart can be developed that identifies time frames for each activity and accountability.

Identifying Required Documents. At minimum, an initial application form and a recredentialing application form will be required to support the credentialing process. Numerous other documents may also be developed and used. The most common are

1. Preapplication packet
   - introduction letter
   - criteria outline
   - request for application
   - response letter
2. Application packet
   - cover letter, including requirements and checklist of attachments
   - application form
   - privileges, if applicable
   - attestation
   - release of liability (also used for recredentialing)
   - letters for second request or additional information needed
   - as applicable, notification of right to review information
3. Information and verification packet
   - letters requesting information
   - letters requesting verification
   - file summary
4. Forms to document analysis and decision
   - documentation of committee process and decisions
   - letters to applicants of committee decisions (including notification of right to appeal, as applicable)
5. Recredentialing packet
   - cover letter
   - recredential questionnaire form
   - profile
6. Other
   - tracking status of applications
   - file completion checklist
   - site visit audit tool, if applicable
   - medical record audit tool, if applicable
   - forms related to delegation, if applicable

Once identified and developed, a procedure relating to use of each form or letter should be completed and the form and procedure added to the credentialing plan document or notebook.

Identifying Required Policies and Procedures. Policies and procedures are developed to give structure to the credentialing process and to identify specific activities and responsibilities. In the managed and ambulatory care settings, most contracts or letters of agreement with individual practitioners and providers will reference the organizational policy and procedure. The credentialing process requirements and criteria are not commonly detailed outside of these policies and procedures. A policy is a statement of fact or a requirement that outlines a process that must be followed or a standard that should be maintained. The policy statement may be one sentence or several paragraphs.[11] A procedure is a set of instructions that describes how a policy will be achieved. Procedures do not exist without a policy statement. The procedure outlines how a process will be followed and should list the easiest or most productive set of activities that will result in effective performance.[12] Standard policy and procedure formats are frequently identified by the organization and followed by all departments. A standard format such as the example in Exhibit 4–2 helps ensure that all necessary information is identified when a policy and procedure is developed.

Each organization will identify the specific policies and procedures that will be included in its credentialing program. Common policies and procedures that are developed for credentialing activities include

- preapplication process
- application process
- recredentialing process
- evaluation of credentials/decision making
- right to appeal
- suspension and termination

Exhibit 4–2 Sample Policy and Procedure Format

TITLE:		P&P Section and #:
ATTACHMENTS:		PAGE _____ of _____
EFFECTIVE DATE:	APPROVED BY: DATE:	
POLICY STATEMENT:		
PROCEDURE:		

REVIEWED BY:			REVIEWED BY:			REVIEWED BY:		
DATE:			DATE:			DATE:		
REVISION	YES	NO	REVISION	YES	NO	REVISION	YES	NO

Courtesy of C. Mobley & Associates, LLC, and Quality Management Options, LLC, Colorado Springs, Colorado.

- confidentiality
- access to information

and, as applicable,

- office site visits
- medical record audits
- delegation
- express process

A credentialing program may have few or numerous policies and procedures, and they may be brief or very detailed depending upon their use within the organization and the goals of the department.

Development or review of current policies and procedures begins with identification of the topics or areas for which the organization wishes to have written policy and procedure statements. Credentialing staff who are familiar with or closely associated with that aspect of the process complete the initial writing of the draft policy and procedure. Information may be obtained from other like organizations or may be developed on the basis of the desired outcome of the process. Once the draft policy and procedure is completed, it is forwarded to the credentials committee or other review body within the organization, which is charged with the responsibility for credentials activity. Following its review and approval, final approval is obtained from the governing board. Exhibit 4–3 is a sample policy and procedure for physician recredentialing.

Policies should be reviewed and updated on a regular basis. This review process should occur on an ongoing basis, once a year, or every two years. Revisions or entirely new policies and procedures may be necessary as

- new activities or steps are added to the process
- steps or activities are deleted from the process
- new practitioner or provider categories (e.g., alternative medicine practitioners and providers) are integrated into the plan
- improved or more productive steps to complete an activity are identified
- responsibilities are added or changed

In summary, the identification, development, and update of policies and procedures should be an ongoing process and should be detailed enough to provide clear direction for all individuals involved in credentialing activities.

The Credentialing Program Document. The credentialing document clearly identifies the structure, scope, responsibility, and accountability for the credentialing program. It is the document that includes all required information about the credentialing program. It includes policies, procedures, and standard forms and serves as both an orientation/reference tool and evidence of compliance with accreditation requirements for documentation of the process. The documents should

- comply with all applicable regulations and accreditation standards
- include all applicable criteria
- include policies and procedures that will ensure objective, consistent application of criteria
- identify the mechanisms for credentialing and recredentialing activities

Common components of a credentialing program document are

- scope of the credentialing program
- structure and accountability
- definitions
- credentialing process
- credentialing criteria
- policies and procedures

and, as applicable,

- privileges
- proctoring
- office site visits and medical record audit
- delegation activity and relationships

Exhibit 4–4 is a sample table of contents for a credentialing program document.

Exhibit 4–3 Sample Credentials Program Policy and Procedure

Title: Physician Recredentialing Process		P&P Section and #: Recredential 04
Attachments: 04a Recredential Information Form 04b Profile		Page 1 of 2
Effective Date: 01/01/99	Approved by: Approval date:	Credentials Committee 10/10/98 Governing Board 12/15/98

Policy:

- All physicians who have been credentialed, are under contract, or are providing primary or specialty care to Plan members will be recredentialed every two years. Within this policy, *physician* will include MDs, DOs, DPMs, DDSs, and DCs.
- Review of information against criteria and standards by the credentials committee will result in a recommendation regarding continued participation to the governing board.

Procedure:

1. 120 days before expiration of current credentials cycle:
   a. The Recredential Information Form and packet will be forwarded to the physician.
   b. The Profile will be forwarded to Quality Management for completion of applicable sections.
2. Should the completed Information Form not be returned within 20 days of distribution, a reminder notice will be forwarded to the physician.
   a. The reminder will include an outline of consequences should the form not be completed and returned by the date, which is 30 days before the end of the current credentials cycle.
   b. Failure to complete the process may result in termination by the Plan.
3. Upon receipt, the information will be reviewed against criteria for the complete recredential packet. If noncompliance is identified, required information will be obtained by phone, or a letter outlining missing information will be forwarded to the physician.
4. Credentials staff will verify primary source:
   a. license with the state medical board
   b. professional liability coverage and history of malpractice action during the past cycle with the liability carrier(s)
   c. status of hospital privileges with the hospital identified as primary admitting facility
   d. board status, if any change during this cycle, with applicable board
5. Credentials staff will collect information including:
   a. copy of current Drug Enforcement Administration (DEA) certificate
   b. attestation statement
   c. details or explanation related to activity identified in the Information Form
6. A National Practitioner Data Bank query will be completed.
7. The quality file and profile will be updated to include reports/information, as applicable, related to
   a. results of access/availability audit(s)
   b. results of medical record audit(s)
   c. results of site visit audit
   d. results of patient satisfaction survey(s)

continues

Exhibit 4–3 continued

   e. number of patient/member complaints
   f. number of primary care physician (PCP) changes
   g. utilization data
   h. results of peer review
   i. clinical competence
8. Credential staff will complete a review of the file, complete checklist, and schedule:
   a. review of file by the medical director and the credentials committee if it appears that there is noncompliance with any criteria
   b. review of file by credentials committee if file is complete and there is compliance with all criteria
9. The credentials committee will review the credentials and quality files and evaluate activity. A recommendation related to continued participation will be completed on the basis of peer evaluation of all information presented.
10. The governing board will be the authority to approve continued participation.
11. The credentialing staff will notify the physician of the governing board decision by letter, and a copy will be included in the credentials file.
12. The credentialing staff will notify all appropriate departments/individuals of the decision.

<table>
<tr><td colspan="3">Reviewed by:

Date:</td><td colspan="3">Reviewed by:

Date:</td><td colspan="3">Reviewed by:

Date:</td><td colspan="3">Reviewed by:

Date:</td></tr>
<tr><td>Revision:</td><td>yes</td><td>no</td><td>Revision:</td><td>yes</td><td>no</td><td>Revision:</td><td>yes</td><td>no</td><td>Revision:</td><td>yes</td><td>no</td></tr>
</table>

Courtesy of C. Mobley & Associates, LLC, and Quality Management Options, LLC, Colorado Springs, Colorado.

Exhibit 4–4 Sample Table of Contents for Credentialing Program Document

Courtesy of C. Mobley & Associates, LLC, and Quality Management Options, LLC, Colorado Springs, Colorado.

Principles

Several widely held principles are the basis of a credentialing program. Identification of underlying principles for the credentialing program results in a program that will be closely aligned with the organization's culture, strategic plan, and overall goals. Examples of principles that may be adopted include the following:

- Credentialing must always be accomplished before establishment of a contractual relationship.
- The burden of proof is on the applicant.
- Rework or duplication is avoided whenever possible.
- The benefit of the doubt will go to the patient and not the applicant.
- Credentialing is the basis of quality.
- There must be consistency in all decision-making processes.
- The practitioner has a right to know why and how decisions are made.

Identification of principles may be completed through a formal process or may simply develop over time as key leaders in the organization make decisions related to credentialing activities and how the process will work. If principles are formally identified or documented, they should be shared with all individuals and committees involved with, or making decisions relating to, the credentialing process.

Contracts and Contractual Relationships

In most ambulatory and managed care relationships, a contract or letter of agreement, rather than organizational bylaws, formalizes the relationship between the organization and the practitioners or provider. The contract or agreement is important in light of growing regulations. At a minimum, the contract/agreement

- defines terms used in the contract
- describes termination provisions
- outlines the rights and obligations of entities or parties
- establishes the legal relationship between the parties
- provides structure for, and evidence of, intentions.[13]

Types of Agreements/Contracts. There are two types of agreements/contracts between a practitioner and a health care organization. The relationship between the two parties will be either one of employment or one of independent contracting. Different regulations affect the two types of relationships. The employment contract takes into account

- antidiscrimination issues
- income tax withholding requirements
- employment laws
- labor relations
- unemployment compensation obligations[14]

Common provisions in agreements/contracts for both employment and independent contractor relationships include

- provider obligations
- payment methods
- relationship of the parties
- insurance and indemnification
- termination and suspension
- declarations[15]

Agreements/contracts are also executed with providers or health care organizations by integrated delivery system or networks. The same categories that are applicable to practitioner agreements are found in organizational agreements.

Contract Language That Affects the Credentialing Process. Three common components found in agreement/contract language affect the credentialing process. These relate to

- compliance with organizational programs, policies, and procedures
- requirements related to credentialing criteria
- termination or change in relationship

Contractual requirements for compliance with programs, policies and procedures of the organization will differ depending upon the focus of the organization. If the focus is on compliance, language will be worded to require that compliance. If the focus is on cooperation, the language will be softer and will encourage rather than require participation. From the viewpoint of the credentials activities, it is preferable that compliance with the credentials program, policies, and procedures be required. Language may require or indicate the need for cooperation with programs including member grievance and appeals, quality assurance, utilization, and risk management as well as credentialing. Some contracts require compliance only with the utilization program or utilization and quality assurance, the assumption being that credentialing is a component of the quality assurance program. This approach does not provide strong direction or support for credentialing activities. It is recommended that the credentialing policies and procedures be specifically noted in contract language.

The agreement or contract should clearly define the practitioner's responsibilities for compliance with the credentialing program. A sample of common contractual language is "Practitioner agrees to participate in and abide by the policies and procedures governing quality and utilization management. The practitioner will comply with all determinations rendered by these programs."

The inherent problem with contract language is that either it is so detailed that the contract becomes unwieldy or it is so brief (as above) that the practitioner is not familiar with the specific requirements of the programs. It is preferable to have brief language with the attachment or distribution of a summary page of eligibility criteria and an overview of programs along with a listing of specific practitioner obligations. The organization must understand that if changes are made to the program, practitioners are to be notified.

Detailed contract language includes requirements that are specifically related to credentialing criteria. Common examples include a requirement that the practitioner have professional liability insurance or be board certified in the appropriate specialty. Sample language for compliance with credentialing criteria might be as follows:

> Practitioner agrees that at all times during the terms of this Agreement, he or she shall:
>
> 1. Maintain in good standing a license to practice medicine in the State of __________
> 2. Possess a current valid federal drug administration registration certificate (exceptions to this requirement would be noted)
> 3. Maintain professional liability insurance with coverage no less than ______________ (amount determined to be applicable would be identified by the organization)
> 4. Be a member in good standing of the medical staff of ___________ hospital, with unrestricted admitting privileges
> 5. Be board certified by a member board of the American Board of Medical Specialties (ABMS)[16]

The third aspect of agreement/contract language that affects credentialing is the one addressing termination or change in relationship. Two types of termination clauses may be included in a contract: *for cause* and *without cause*. More common is termination without cause. This type of clause normally allows a 90-day notice. A without-cause clause in a contract allows the organization to terminate the relationship without explanation or discussion. Usually no due process is offered to the practitioner or provider that is being terminated. It is unclear whether, in the long term, courts will uphold a without-cause termination. It has already been challenged in the case *Texas Medical Association v. Aetna Life Insurance*[17] and *Texas Medical Association v. Prudential Life Insurance Company of America.*[18] The physicians who had been terminated under a without-cause contract brought a suit related to the validity of the clause. Ultimately the federal court dismissed the case and the physicians did not win an appeal. A with-cause termination provision allows termination of a contract for negative credentialing decisions and/or negative quality findings. Of course, National Practitioner Data Bank (NPDB) reporting requirements would not be affected by either a with- or a without-cause provision.

Numerous legal issues are related to contract language. Credentialing staff should be familiar with language in their practitioner and provider contracts and should ensure that contract staff know and understand credentialing policies, procedures, and criteria. Additional information related to contract issues may be found in two other Aspen volumes: *Physician Organizations and Medical Staff Contracts Rights and Liabilities* (Volume 2), by the Aspen Health Law and Compliance Center,[19] and the chapter entitled "Legal Issues in Provider Contracting" in Peter Kongstevdt's *Managed Health Care Handbook.*[20]

Criteria

Types and Categories of Criteria. To maintain an effective credentialing program that is objective and has a consistent decision making process, it is necessary to have written criteria. In managed and ambulatory care, criteria may be categorized as either *participative* or *evaluative*. Participative criteria are those requirements that must be met to participate in the plan or to enter into or maintain the relationship. Participative criteria are those that can be objectively measured. An example of a participative criterion would be a license to practice medicine. Evaluative criteria are those that require judgment or assessment to determine compliance. An example of an evaluative criterion would be evaluation of malpractice history. Review, against evaluative criteria, of malpractice history of two physicians with the same number of cases might have two different outcomes. Although the number of cases was the same, a judgment might be made to accept one physician and deny participation to the other on the basis of professional peer review of the cases.

Criteria are developed to apply to both initial and recredentialing decisions. Additionally, criteria are delineated for types of practitioners and providers. Criteria may also be identified for medical record review, the preapplication process, application acceptance, the complete file, and delegation, including analysis and oversight of a delegation process.

Criteria should be

- specific to the type of practitioner or provider service
- worded so that compliance is measurable to the extent possible
- specific as to applicability
- specific as to how compliance with the criteria will be verified or measured
- as applicable, specific about acceptable sources for verification of compliance with the criteria

Criteria for Medical Doctors, Osteopathic Doctors, Podiatrists, Dentists. History, status, activity, and other data addressed by participatory criteria for medical and osteopathic doctors, podiatrists, dentists, and chiropractors commonly address the following:

1. License to practice
    - current
    - unrestricted
    - in state where currently practicing
2. Medical training
    - specific to the area of practice
3. Hospital privileges
    - at a hospital in geographic area or a hospital contracted with the managed care organization to which the practitioner is applying
    - admitting privileges, as appropriate
    - in good standing

    (Note: Criteria frequently specify "active status." The categories of activity at hospitals differ from one hospital to the next. A physician may have admitting privileges, ability to see and treat patients in the hospital setting, and privileges in good standing but not be categorized as having an "active status." Of interest is not the designation of category by a hospital but whether privileges are in good standing.)

4. Drug Enforcement Administration (DEA) Certificate
   - current
   - unrestricted
   - with address in state where physician is practicing

   (Note: Some organizations make specific exceptions to a DEA requirement.)
5. Professional liability insurance
   - current
   - amount of coverage deemed acceptable by the organization (amount may differ according to specialty)
6. Board certification
   - certification in the appropriate specialty may be required by some organizations; if required, exceptions to include new graduates that are not yet eligible for certification need to specified

History, status, and activity data addressed by evaluative criteria include the following:

1. History of malpractice claims
   - time frame (number of years for which information will be considered)
   - current activity
   - filing of claims versus settlement of claims
   - outcome (death, permanent disability, amount of payment made on practitioner's behalf)
2. Continuing education (usually tracked only if organization delineates privileges)
   - hours specifically related to state board requirement
   - education pertaining to area of practice
3. Attestation
   - physical and mental status
   - lack of impairment
   - ability to perform duties required

   (Note: These areas should comply with the requirements of the Americans with Disabilities Act.)
4. Practice
   - coverage arrangements and credentials of practitioner providing coverage
   - ability to provide routine office procedures (e.g., drawing blood, immunizations, pap smears, EKG)
   - availability, ability to accept new patients
5. Office site visit and medical record review
   - numerous aspects of physician office and medical recordkeeping practice may be reviewed. Criteria should be specifically worded to measure compliance in all areas required by the organization. The section "Facility Site Visits and Medical Record Audits" later in this chapter covers this topic in more detail.
6. Activity
   - restrictions or actions (including loss) related to affiliations or memberships (may be related to medical and/or civil actions)
   - limitations, sanctions, or disciplinary actions
   - felony convictions
   - Medicare/Medicaid sanction information
   - consideration of information included in NPDB report (if eligible to query)
7. Supportive of philosophy and concepts
   - of managed care
   - of the organization

Exhibit 4–5 shows sample criteria for initial participation by a primary care physician with an Health Maintenance Organization (HMO).

Recredentialing Criteria. In recredentialing, the participative criteria are mainly the initial criteria for which compliance may have changed during the two-year credentials cycle. The evaluative criteria are mainly concerned with performance data. An example of information that changes would be professional liability insurance. The practitioner may have changed the limits, the carrier of the policy, or the coverage during the credentialing cycle. Each organization must identify those areas that it feels are the basis of determining the capability of a practitio-

Exhibit 4–5 Sample General Criteria for Primary Care Physician Participation

1. Current, unrestricted license to practice in the state in which the application is submitted
2. Current, valid, unrestricted DEA registration
3. Current professional liability coverage not less than $1 million/$3 million
4. Current, unrestricted clinical and admitting privileges granted by a participating hospital located in the service area
5. Board certification by the American Board of Medical Specialties or the American Osteopathic Association in the physician's practicing specialty. Exception will be considered for physicians who are actively involved in preparation for certification.
6. Absence during the past five years of
   - disciplinary actions affecting license
   - felony convictions
   - sanctions by regulatory agencies
   - suspension, restriction, or termination of hospital privileges
7. No more than three malpractice claims and/or settlements during past five years. Exception may be considered following peer review of case detail submitted by applicant and with approval by risk manager.
8. Absence of evidence that applicant might be unable to perform the duties for which he or she wishes to contract.
9. Agreement to
   - provide routine office care and procedures Monday through Friday between the hours of 9:00 A.M. and 5:00 P.M.
   - arrange coverage only with practitioners credentialed by the Plan
   - accept no less than 500 new patients during the next 12 months
10. A grade no less than 80 percent for office audit and no less than 75 percent for medical record audit

Courtesy of C. Mobley & Associates, LLC, and Quality Management Options, LLC, Colorado Springs, Colorado.

ner to render services within it or under its contractual agreement. Of course, applicable accreditation credentialing standards and state and federal regulations will also affect the determination of recredentialing criteria to be used.

The criteria addressed in recredentialing for MDs, DOs, DPMs, and DDSs are

1. license
2. hospital privileges
3. DEA certificate
4. professional liability insurance
5. board certification (changes related to) and for-current-cycle-only information
6. malpractice activity
7. continuing education (if privileges are delineated)
8. attestation of physical and mental status and ability to perform required duties
9. practice
10. activity: actions, limitations, sanctions, losses, etc., of affiliations, felony convictions, memberships, etc.

Exhibit 4–6 outlines sample criteria for practitioners in a medical group practice.

Criteria for Allied Health. Ambulatory or managed care organizations may have relationships or contracts with practitioners who do not independently provide service or who do not fall into the organizational scope of services as a physician category. Some allied health or nonphysician practitioner categories are physician extenders, nurse practitioners, psychologists and other behavioral health professionals, physical therapists, and certified nurse midwives. Criteria for allied health categories are often not as extensive or detailed as for licensed independent

Exhibit 4–6 Criteria and Standards for Medical Group Practice

General Criteria and Standards*

1 Each primary and specialty physician submitting an application shall meet the following standards:
   a. A current unrestricted license to practice medicine or osteopathy
   b. Current staff membership, clinical privileges, and admitting privileges granted by hospital within the service area
   c. Board certification or qualified by training with a minimum of two years accredited residency training and a total of three years minimum of internship and residency, in the appropriate specialty
   d. Sound moral character, absence of felony convictions, and in good professional standing in the community (initially evaluated by references)
   e. No suspension or exclusion from Medicare or Medicaid during the past three years
   f. Provision of quality, appropriate and timely care (initially evaluated through review of references, malpractice history and other information as deemed necessary)
   g. Professional liability coverage within minimum limits of $1 million/3 million
   h. Valid unrestricted DEA certificate
2. Each licensed practitioner submitting an application shall meet the following criteria:
   a. Current unrestricted license
   b. Absence of felony convictions, absence of any convictions related to the practice granted by license, sound moral character, and in good professional standing in the community
   c. Provision of quality, appropriate, and timely care (initially evaluated through review of references and malpractice history of both individuals and the agency with whom they are associated)

   * If no license is required under state statutes, the minimum level of training and experience is determined through the national organization representing the specialty.
3. The following requirements must be met in order for the Credentials Committee to recommend acceptance:
   a. Acceptable compliance with general criteria.
   b. The Committee may deny participation to any practitioner having three or more malpractice incidents within the previous five years.
   c. The Committee may deny participation to a physician that is qualified for but has chosen not to obtain Board Certification.
   d. Exceptions can be made by the Credentials Committee due to needs of the group.

Continued Participation and Recertification Review

1. It is the responsibility of each physician and licensed practitioner to maintain compliance with general criteria and to inform administration of changes in status of any information.
2. The following materials will be requested and reviewed for recertification status every two years:
   a. Recertification application
   b. Review and update of clinical privileges
   c. Current medical licensure
   d. Inquiry regarding malpractice incidents for previous two years
   e. Other information or material determined to be applicable by the Credentials Committee
3. Recertification will be referred with a recommendation from the Credentials Committee to the Board of Directors if any of the following are determined:
   a. Failure to maintain compliance with general criteria
   b. Failure to maintain clinical privileges at a participating hospital within the service area

continues

Exhibit 4–6 continued

c. The physician has engaged in conduct in violation of state law or standards of ethical conduct governing the practice of medicine in the state of which he/she was disciplined or otherwise censured or is under investigation with respect to such conduct
d. Suspension or exclusion from Medicare or Medicaid
e. Any other circumstances in which the Credentials Committee believes that acceptance or retention of the practitioner would not be in the best interests of the group
f. Performance evaluation during participation will be conducted by the Professional Review Committee and/or the Credentials Committee

Courtesy of Colorado Springs Health Partners, P.C., Colorado Springs, Colorado.

practitioners. Participatory criteria for allied health professionals address

1. License to practice
   - current
   - unrestricted
   - in state where practicing
2. Degree
   - appropriate to profession
   - from accredited institution
   - specific to area of practice
   - minimum level determined by the national organization representing the specialty
3. Professional liability insurance
   - current
   - amount specified by organization
4. DEA certificate (if applicable)
   - current
   - unrestricted
5. Experience
   - specified experience in area of specialty
6. Supervision (if required)
   - completion of supervision agreement with a physician who is credentialed by the organization

Evaluative criteria address

1. History
   - malpractice
   - restrictions
   - criminal or felony convictions
2. Suspension or exclusion from Medicare or Medicaid
3. Information included in NPDB report as applicable

Criteria may be developed that are specific to each individual specialty within an allied health category (e.g., specific to psychologists, physician assistants, etc.) or may be developed for the overall category of allied health practitioners.

Criteria for Facilities. Some managed care organizations credential organizational providers of care or facilities because of requirements by NCQA. Others credential providers because of concern about contracting with a facility about which no information has been collected and reviewed. Facilities that may be credentialed include

- ambulance services
- ambulatory surgical centers (freestanding)
- birthing centers (freestanding)
- diagnostic imaging centers
- dialysis centers
- home health care
- hospices
- hospitals
- laboratories (independent or mobile)
- local health departments/clinics (city or county)
- medical equipment/supply firms
- pharmacies

- radiology (freestanding facilities or portable services)
- residential treatment centers
- rural health clinics
- skilled nursing facilities
- sleep study centers
- transplantation centers
- urgent care facilities

Participative criteria for a facility address

1. appropriate current state license
2. existence and status of appropriate certifications
3. existence and status of appropriate accreditation(s)
4. current certificate of insurance disclosing amount of coverage that is compliant with managed care organization requirements

Evaluative criteria may address

1. status with state and federal monitoring bodies
2. past and pending litigation/claims
3. volume of procedures performed
4. clinical record review

As with allied health, criteria for facilities may be general to the overall category of providers/facilities or specific to each facility type with which the organization has a relationship or contract. Exhibit 4–7 includes sample criteria for a freestanding radiology facility.

Criteria for denial of affiliation. Specific criteria for denial of affiliation may be identified and outlined in the credentialing plan document as a specific policy and procedure outlining the actions and steps involving denial. If criteria for denial are used, they may address

1. failure or refusal to provide necessary and relevant information
2. the willing and/or deliberate submission of inaccurate or misleading information
3. loss of professional license
4. loss of DEA certification
5. loss of hospital privileges at primary admitting facility
6. sanction by Medicare or Medicaid
7. history or incidents of malpractice claims that are judged to be of concern or that are negatively related to the ability to treat patients
8. loss or deliberate termination of professional liability insurance coverage
   - reduction in limits of professional liability insurance
   - coverage below required limits

Additional criteria may be added related to activity that results in restrictions, sanctions, or failure to maintain required relationships or certificates.

If criteria for denial of privileges are used, and the organization queries the NPDB, it is recommended that the criteria and/or credentialing plan document include a statement that specifies action related to denial. Should denial occur related to quality or physician competency, it is a reportable event, and policy and procedure should ensure the reporting process.

Exceptions. If the credentialing process is not followed consistently, it becomes very difficult for an organization to justify decisions. If the organization identifies specific instances in which an exception will be made on a regular basis, the exception should become part of the criterion statement. One example might be "DEA certificate required for all independent practitioners, with the exception of pathology and radiology." Board certification is another common requirement that results in exceptions. Board certification should not be established as a criterion unless the organization is in a position to deny practitioners who are not board certified. If it is a requirement, exceptions may be necessary for specific specialties and the length of time since completion of their training.

A number of managed care organizations have developed a review process of malpractice history in which accountability and level of review are specified. This process assigns parameters to determination of an "acceptable history." The thought process behind this approach is that the organization as a whole has increased liability if

Exhibit 4–7 Criteria for Radiology Facility

DEFINITION

A freestanding radiology facility is an independent organization that performs diagnostic and/or therapeutic procedures involving the use of radiological materials. The services provided include the full spectrum of radiology, mammography, and radiation exams and procedures.

CRITERIA

1. Minimum certification and license requirements:
   a. current department of health (DOH) certificate.
   b. DOH radioactive materials permit for disposal of isotope-tracking materials (if invasive procedures are performed)
   c. state business license
   d. current Food and Drug Administration radioactive materials license, if applicable.
2. All radiologists will be board certified or will obtain board certification within two years of affiliation with facility and will hold current license.
3. Emergency support policy, procedures, plans, and equipment will be maintained at the facility. The emergency cart will be maintained in accordance with plan/organization standards.
4. Any practitioner using conscious sedation will be privileged to do so.
5. The facility will maintain a current general liability and malpractice policy.

Courtesy of Group Health Cooperative, Seattle, Washington.

malpractice history is significant and that exceptions to a criterion of "no significant malpractice history" should be minimized. Parameters for data, review, and determination are identified, outlined, and included in the credentials plan. A sample decision matrix for malpractice history review is shown in Table 4–1.

Steps in the Credentialing Process

There are six basic activities or steps related to the credentialing process in ambulatory and managed care organizations:

1. need evaluation
2. application process
3. verification and information gathering
4. analysis and decision-making process
5. recredentialing
6. maintenance and problem resolution

Step 1: Need Evaluation

Plans, networks, or practices may be in a development or a maintenance mode. In a development mode, practitioners and providers are being actively identified and recruited. In a maintenance mode, only specific specialties or practitioners in specific geographic areas are being recruited or accepted for affiliation. An organization that wishes to limit the size of its network, is not accepting applications in all specialties, or wishes to screen out those who do not meet absolute criteria may find a screening process to be of use.

Scope of Practice/Network Development. Many ambulatory and managed care organizations have a network development plan. The plan identifies the scope of services that are offered by the organization or through the benefit package. It identifies the geographic area in which services are provided and the number of practitioners and providers that are required. The distribution of specific specialties within that geographic area and the number of providers per specialty to be recruited on the basis of the membership or access to the facility are also part of the plan. On the basis of this network design and plan, the number and specialty mix of practitio-

Table 4–1 Sample Review and Decision Matrix for Malpractice History

	Pending Claims	*No Judgments or Settlements*	*Judgment, Settlement Less Than $250,000, No Permanent Disability or Loss of Life*	*Settlement More Than $250,000, with Permanent Disability or Loss of Life*
One or two claims or settlements during past 5 years	Review and recommendation by medical director. Decision by credentialing committee	Review and recommendation by medical director. Decision by credentialing committee	Review and decision by credentialing committee	Review and recommendation by credentialing committee. Decision by administration
Three to five claims or settlements during past 5 years	Review and recommendation by medical director. Decision by credentialing committee	Review and decision by credentialing committee	Review by risk management with recommendation to credentials committee who make decision	Review and decision by administration
More than five claims or settlements during past 10 years	Review by medical director with risk manager recommendations made to administration, who determines action	Review by risk manager and medical director with recommendation to credentials committee, who make decision	Review and decision by administration	Review and decision by administration

Note: Review for highest activity level applies; therefore, a practitioner with a pending claim and/or settlement of $500,000 would be reviewed by the credentials committee, and a decision would be made by administration.

Courtesy of C. Mobley & Associates, LLC, and Quality Management Options, LLC, Colorado Springs, Colorado.

ners and providers who are offered contracts are identified. An organization that is in a recruitment mode and actively looking at numerous practitioners and providers may not find a screening process to be of value. An organization that is in a maintenance mode and adding few practitioners may find a screening process to be helpful.

Screening Process. The purpose of a screening or preapplication process is to ensure that applications are not offered to practitioners and providers who

- are not going to meet organizational objectives
- are not qualified and will not meet criteria
- are not of the specialty or in the location that matches a network need

If an organization elects to use a screening process, interested potential applicants contacting the organization are prescreened either by phone or through a written questionnaire format. The organization provides some basic information to the potential applicant about requirements. This may include information related to

- the network design, panel size, specialty mix, and scope of services
- the risk/incentives/payment program (if applicable)
- administrative/contract requirements
- credentialing criteria

All of this information does not need to be provided to potential applicants, but many organizations find that access to information before completion of an application assists in weeding out those who will not, in the long term, complete the process and be offered a contract. The preapplication questionnaire or application request form includes questions and requests for information such as

- specialty and scope of services provided
- basic credentials and background
- knowledge of or experience with managed care, quality management, and utilization management
- ability and availability to see new patients

In a prescreening process, *an application is not given to a potential applicant until it is determined that the applicant will be able to comply with core credentialing criteria and will pursue execution of a contract.* Information provided and questions asked should relate to the goal of screening and should not address "nice-to-know" information. The potential applicant should understand the purpose of the process, and it should be used consistently.

Once the prescreen is completed, a determination is made relative to offering an application. If an application is distributed, completed, and returned, the entire credentialing process should be completed unless the application is voluntarily withdrawn by the practitioner or provider.

If a prescreening process is adopted, it is recommended that the process, procedure, and all related documents be reviewed by legal counsel. Exhibit 4–8 lists information that might be included in a letter or provided during a telephone screen interview. Exhibit 4–9 is an example of a preapplication questionnaire.

Any-Willing-Provider Laws. Common to managed care plans and networks is the concept of planned network development and limitation of the number of practitioners and providers who are affiliated with the organization. Approximately 35 states now have statutes that relate to network development.[21] These statutes are known as "any-willing-provider" legislation. They are so called because they relate to a network being required to accept a provider who is willing to accept and comply with the requirements for participation. Statutes differ according to state, type of network, and the providers and practitioners to which they may apply. Some any-willing-provider laws deal exclusively with pharmacies. Others include physicians, who have pushed legislation to prevent managed care plans from excluding or dropping practitioners. There are a number of different types of any-willing-provider statutes:

- any-willing-pharmacy statutes
- any-willing-provider statutes in which the network is required to accept providers who meet requirements
- freedom-of-choice statutes (which prohibit plans from requiring members to use only designated providers)
- open-panel requirements (which restrict a plan's ability to use exclusive contracts with providers)[22]

In light of the scope of any-willing-provider statutes and the various possibilities, it is important that credentialing professionals be aware of all applicable statutes that may affect their prescreening process, network development plan, or recruitment efforts.

Step 2: Application Process

The application process starts at the time an application packet is given to a practitioner or provider and ends once the completed application is received and placed in a file and the credentials staff initiates the information verification process. The flowchart in Figure 4–4 shows steps in the application process.

Exhibit 4–8 Information Included in Letter or during Telephone Screening Interview

It is the policy of (name organization) to screen potential applicants through use of a questionnaire. Questions may be answered by phone or may be completed in writing by a physician interested in obtaining a participation contract with (name organization).

Credentialing criteria that are used by (name organization) to determine if a physician will be credentialed and offered a participation contract include requirements for

1. Current unrestricted medical license in the state of ___________________
2. Current unrestricted DEA
3. Professional liability insurance in the amount of ______________________
4. Absence of significant history of malpractice activity, restrictions or sanctions, felony convictions, or finding of unprofessional conduct
5. Admitting privileges at XYZ hospital(s)
6. Ability to accept 350 new patients
7. Office located within the _________________ Plan geographic area

If you comply with these criteria, you are invited to request a telephone interview or to complete and return a questionnaire.

Our Medical Director will review the information provided. If it appears that you will substantially comply with our requirements and if you provide care in a specialty category that is currently required by the network development plan, an application will be made available. If we will not be forwarding an application, you will be notified of the reason.

Thank you for your interest.

Courtesy of C. Mobley & Associates, LLC, and Quality Management Options, LLC, Colorado Springs, Colorado.

Exhibit 4–9 Preapplication Questionnaire

Name ____________________ Specialty ____________________; Board Certified ☐ yes ☐ no

Office Address ____

Office Telephone (_____)__________________ Office Fax (_____)__________________

Screening Questions:

1. Do you have a current unrestricted state license? ☐ yes ☐ no
   If yes; # ______________________________
2. Do you have a current DEA with categories approved as 2, 2N through 5? ☐ yes ☐ no
3. Do you have current professional liability insurance? ☐ yes ☐ no
   If yes, company ____________________________ coverage amount ______________
4. How many malpractice claims have been filed against you in the last five years? ____________
5. How many total malpractice claims have been filed since your graduation from medical school?
   ____
6. Are there any restrictions or sanctions against any professional license, registration, membership, or certification that you now hold or have held in the past five years? ☐ yes ☐ no
7. Have you ever been sanctioned by Medicare, Medicaid, or similar agency? ☐ yes ☐ no
8. Have you ever been convicted of or pleaded no contest to any felony charges against you? ☐ yes ☐ no
9. Have you ever been found by a state professional disciplinary board to have committed unprofessional conduct as defined in applicable state provisions? ☐ yes ☐ no
10. Do you have or are you in the process of applying for medical staff privileges at a local contracted hospital? ☐ yes ☐ no
    If yes, which hospital(s) ______________________________________
11. Do you currently have the ability to add new patients to your practice? ☐ yes ☐ no
    If yes, what is the estimated volume that could be added during the next year? ______________

____________________________________ ____________________________________
Signature Date

____
Printed Name

I understand that this preapplication is not an application for privileges or network or staff affiliation. I understand that the information is used to determine eligibility for the credentialing process and that it is applied without discrimination. I understand that I must meet minimum criteria in order to be considered an applicant.

Information provided by ______________________________________ and documented by ______________________________ and verbally attested to by ______________________________

Criteria met? ☐ yes ☐ no If no, which criteria ______________________________________

Application will be forwarded: ☐ yes ☐ no Provider notified by: ☐ letter ☐ phone call ☐ other

Courtesy of Group Health Cooperative, Seattle, Washington.

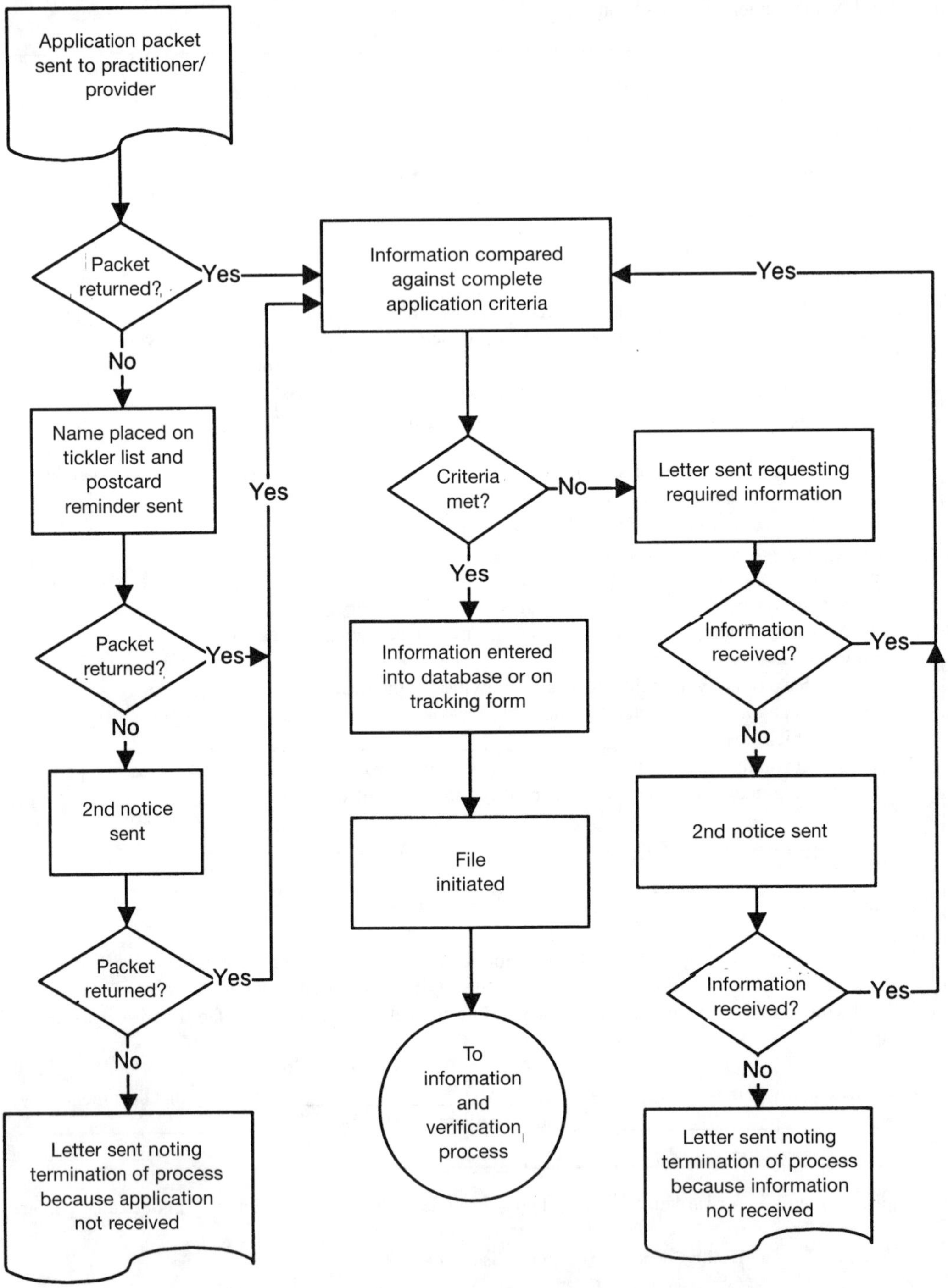

Figure 4–4 Application Process Flowchart. Courtesy of C. Mobley & Associates, LLC, and Quality Management Options, LLC, Colorado Springs, Colorado.

Characteristics of a Successful Application Process. A number of elements are common to a successful application process, including

- *Use of a universal application.* Using one common application form is a productive use of practitioners' time and effort. Applications have proliferated and become longer. It is not uncommon for a practitioner to be asked to complete applications that are 10 to 15 pages long. Applications are often developed for a physician category, an allied health category, and a facility/organization category. Some organizations use the same application for their physician and allied health categories. Others develop numerous applications specific to practitioner and provider categories. A successful program uses one form and cooperates with community and statewide efforts to develop and use one standard form.
- *Template letters and forms.* Forms and letters common to the process are developed as templates and entered into a computer word-processing program. This ensures a standardized outcome. Most credentialing software programs include preformatted letters and forms, which often can be customized.
- *Tickler file.* A tickler file is a very helpful tool in the application process. Information in the file allows the credentials staff to track distribution, status, and receipt of all forms. It is not uncommon for an applicant to delay completion and return of the application packet or to return the packet incomplete. Use of a tickler file ensures that any identified turnaround times for reminders or requests for further information can be met. The tickler file can also provide information related to numbers of packets distributed and returned, those meeting and not meeting criteria, and those requiring termination of the process.
- *Single point of entry for all requests and receipt of material.* It is not uncommon for the practitioner or provider to have all initial contact with recruitment and/or contract staff. As a result, staff other than those responsible for credentialing sometimes become involved in the initial application process. In large organizations, there may be numerous points of entry for requests, and if the organization employs practitioners as well as contracting through a health plan, there may be several points of contact. A single point of entry ensures that requests are handled consistently and in a timely manner, that information is entered into the tracking system, and that compliance with time lines is maintained.
- *Tracking system.* A tracking system provides information related to the number of applications requested, returned, or requiring additional information and to dates that affect turnaround times. Most credentialing software packages include a tracking system. If a credentialing software package is not used, a tracking system within the word-processing program used can be established. In its simplest form, a handwritten chart noting dates of distribution, receipts, and requests constitutes a workable tracking system. Information and data obtained from the tracking system can and should be included in management reports.
- *Orientation and education of all staff responsible for/involved with/affected by the process.* Everyone that will play a role in the application process should understand and agree to all criteria, time lines, and steps involved. As already noted, other areas of the organization, including recruitment, human resources and contracting, may be involved in the application process. It is important that everyone understand his or her level of authority and scope of action specifically related to credentialing.
- *Defined application packet for each practitioner/provider category.* All materials to be included in an application packet should be clearly identified and specific to the category. If materials are filed in various locations or not clearly identified, it is probable that incomplete packets will be distributed.

- *Established criteria for "complete application."* It is important to have clearly understood requirements of acceptance for an application to be processed. Initiating the information and verification process when the materials are incomplete will significantly slow the overall process. The next step should not be initiated until all information in the application is complete. Sample criteria for a complete application might be
  1. all questions answered
  2. attestation signed and dated within two weeks of receipt date
  3. liability release signed and dated
  4. copy of DEA certificate attached that is current and issued to address in the state of __________
  5. completed malpractice claim form for each claim identified in application

The Application Form. Currently, there is no such thing as the one perfect application form. One of the reasons that a universal form has not yet been developed is that health care organizations' credentialing requirements and criteria vary, often due to the line(s) of business they offer. In developing or revising an application form, the first step is to identify all information that is *required* to complete the credentialing process. A second list of information may then be added that includes information that is "nice to know" but not required for the final decision. Common headings or categories in applications used in managed and ambulatory care are given in Exhibit 4–10. The examples listed under each heading are not all-inclusive but are provided to summarize information that might be included under that heading. The reader should also review Exhibit 3–2 in the previous chapter. This form was developed for use by health care organizations and is the first national effort at standardization.

The Application Packet. An application packet will include a number of forms:

- a cover memo or letter
- the application
- privilege requests forms (as applicable)—see Chapter 6 for additional information relating to ambulatory privileges
- an attestation statement if it is not part of the application
- release forms, including
  - –agreement authorizing release of information/release from liability
  - –credentials verification organization (CVO) release (as applicable)
  - –office visit/medical record review release (as applicable)
- a checklist of materials to be returned with the completed application
- explanation of malpractice or litigation history
- recruitment or orientation materials
- sample contract or letter of agreement
- information related to payment or claims processing

Exhibit 4–11 is a sample cover letter, Exhibit 4–12 a sample attestation statement, Exhibit 4–13 a sample release form, Exhibit 4–14 an application checklist, Exhibit 4–15 a malpractice claims explanation, and Exhibit 4–16 a sample tracking form.

Complete Application Criteria. Returned application packets should be reviewed and compared against criteria to ensure that all required and requested information has been submitted. Criteria should address

- all fields completed/all questions answered
- explanation of any gaps in work history
- explanation of any litigation
- explanation for any questions answered "yes"

Exhibit 4–10 Common Components of Ambulatory and Managed Care Practitioner Applications

1. Instructions
   - requirements for completion of application
   - list of documents to be attached to the application
   - contact names and phone numbers for questions
2. Demographics
   - practitioner name
   - birth date
   - birthplace
   - social security number
3. Practice information
   - name of practice/clinics/affiliation
   - primary office address, phone number, fax number
   - secondary office address, phone number, fax number
   - billing address
   - patient appointment telephone number
   - federal tax ID number
   - office manager
   - Medicare and Medicaid numbers and unique provider identification number (UPIN) if applicable
   - list of practitioners who will be accepting call
   - office hours
4. Education
   - undergraduate education: name and address of institution, degree obtained, graduation date, address
   - medical/professional education: name and address of institution, degree obtained, graduation date, address
   - internship: name and address of institution, name of program director, type of internship, specialty, dates
   - residency: institution, program director, type of residency, specialty, dates
   - fellowships
   - preceptorship
5. Licensure, registration, and certification
   - state professional license; number, issue and expiration date
   - Educational Commission for Foreign Medical Graduates (ECFMG) number; date issued
   - DEA number, expiration date—copy requested
   - board certification: specialty, date obtained
   - other certifications
6. Work history
   - chronological list of all work history and activity; name, address, and dates (usually includes instruction to explain any gap in work/education history)
7. Professional liability
   - current liability carrier—copy of certificate requested
   - previous liability carrier: address, policy number, per-claim amount dollars, aggregate amount dollars, dates of coverage
   - malpractice history
8. Affiliations and references
   - hospital affiliations: name, address, status, appointment date
   - peer references
9. Attestation
   - statement that information is complete, accurate, and current
   - acknowledgment that omissions and misstatements may constitute denial or dismissal
10. Ability to practice
    - confirmation that there are no impairments related to the ability to practice
    - felony conviction

Courtesy of C. Mobley & Associates, LLC, and Quality Management Options, LLC, Colorado Springs, Colorado.

Exhibit 4–11 Sample Application Cover Letter

Date

Name
Address

Dear____________________________

Thank you for your interest in XYZ Health Plan. We have received your request for an application and enclosed you will find an application packet.

All forms must be fully completed and returned with copies of all requested information attached before we can start processing your application. It is important to answer all questions and to provide full addresses and complete names with titles. Once all information is received, the credentialing process will take from two to four months to complete.

You will find a sample contract and a fee schedule specific to your specialty in the packet. Should you have any questions about this material, please feel free to contact _____Name_____ in the _____department_____ at _____phone number_____.

Please return your completed application packet in the prestamped envelope provided. Again, thank you for your interest in XYZ Health Plan.

Sincerely,

Name
Title

Courtesy of C. Mobley & Associates, LLC, and Quality Management Options, LLC, Colorado Springs, Colorado.

Exhibit 4–12 Sample Attestation Statement

By my signature, I certify that all information in this application and its attachments is truthful, correct, and complete to the best of my knowledge and belief. I understand that the intentional submission of false or misleading information or the withholding of relevant information is grounds for termination as a participating provider with XYZ Health Plan. I agree to notify XYZ Health Plan of any changes to the information provided within sixty (60) days of that change.

____________________________ ____________________________
Applicant's Signature Date

____
Printed Name (or typed)

Courtesy of C. Mobley & Associates, LLC, and Quality Management Options, LLC, Colorado Springs, Colorado.

Exhibit 4–13 Agreement Authorizing Release of Information and Release from Liability

Authorization To Obtain and/or Release Information

I authorize and give permission for XYZ organization, its agents, representatives, and employees, to consult with any third party who may have information about me including references named in my application and persons, hospitals, institutions, or practices with which I have been associated to obtain information regarding my professional competence, ability to deliver safe and efficient quality care, professional education and training, licensing, certification, character, ethical qualifications, ability to work cooperatively with others, professional liability claims history, and/or insurance or other qualifications for the purpose of evaluating my initial application or for ongoing evaluation. This authorization includes the right to inspect all records and documents that may be pertinent to an evaluation of my qualifications and competence. I further authorize XYZ organization to discuss with my current and prior insurers my professional liability insurance and my professional liability claims history.

I authorize XYZ organization, its agents, representatives, or employees, to release to other hospitals, medical personnel, medical associations, state or federal agencies, professional review organizations, or peer review bodies any information they may require or request concerning my professional competence and conduct, ability to deliver safe and efficient quality care, ethics, character, and other professional qualifications, as long as such release of information is done in compliance with law and professional ethics.

This authorization will remain in effect until it is revoked in writing by me.

Release from Liability

I hereby release, indemnify, and agree to hold harmless XYZ organization, its agents, representatives, and employees, and any person or entity who or which provides information described above.

I agree that a photocopy of this document will serve as a duplicate original.

____________________________ ____________________________

Applicant Signature Date

____

Please Type or Print Name

Courtesy of C. Mobley & Associates, LLC, and Quality Management Options, LLC, Colorado Springs, Colorado.

Exhibit 4–14 Application Checklist

Practitioner Name ____________________ Specialty ____________
☐ APPLICATION REQUESTED: Date: ____________ By: ____________
☐ APPLICATION RETURNED: Date: ____________ Attestation Date: ____________
Additional Information Required: Date Requested: ______ Date Received: ____________
☐ Meets criteria for complete application: Date verification initiated: ____________

VERIFICATIONS/QUERIES	DATE REQUESTED	SECOND REQUEST OR FOLLOW-UP	RECEIVED *INDICATES CAUTION FLAG
State License # Expiration Date / /			
_____ NPDB Query			
Professional Liability Insurance Company Name: _____ Requested from Practitioner or _____ Requested from Carrier			
Status of Hospital Privileges Primary Admitting Hospital: Other Hospital:			
Malpractice History: _____ Requested from Carrier or _____ NPDB Query			
Board Certification: _____ yes _____ no If Yes, Which Board			
Education: Name of School:			
ECFMG			
DOCUMENTS/INFORMATION OBTAINED			
DEA Certificate # Expiration Date / /			
Work History			
UPIN Number: PIN Number:			
Complete Application with Explanation of All Yes Answers			

Note: NPDB, National Practitioner Data Bank; ECFMG, Educational Commission for Foreign Medical Graduates; DEA, Drug Enforcement Administration; UPIN, unique provider identification number.

Courtesy of C. Mobley & Associates, LLC, and Quality Management Options, LLC, Colorado Springs, Colorado.

Exhibit 4–15 Malpractice Claim Information

(One sheet must be completed for each claim made against you, regardless of outcome or status; photocopy as needed)

NAME(S) OF PLAINTIFF(S): ______________________________

NAME(S) OF DEFENDANT(S): ______________________________

DATE OF INCIDENT: ______________ DATE OF FILING: ______________

WHAT WAS/IS YOUR INVOLVEMENT? (Medical Details)

____

____

____

SUMMARIZE THE PLANTIFF'S COMPLAINT: ______________________________

____

STATUS OF CASE (Check One): RESOLVED ☐ PENDING ☐

IF RESOLVED:

A. DATE RESOLVED:

B. RESOLUTION (Check One):

☐ 1. DISMISSAL WITHOUT PAYMENT ON YOUR BEHALF

☐ 2. SETTLEMENT BEFORE TRIAL

a. AMOUNT PAID TO PLAINTIFF ON YOUR BEHALF:____________

☐ 3. TRIAL DECISION

☐ DISMISSED ☐ SETTLED

a. WHAT WAS THE DECISION?______________________________

b. AMOUNT PAID ON YOUR BEHALF: ______________________________

OTHER INFORMATION ABOUT THIS CASE: (Use the back of this sheet if additional space is needed.) ______________________________

____

____

____

____

NAME (print or type) ______________________________

SIGNATURE:______________________ DATE:______________________

Your application will not be processed if this form is incomplete or if you have had a claim and this form is not attached to the application.

Courtesy of C. Mobley & Associates, LLC, and Quality Management Options, LLC, Colorado Springs, Colorado.

Exhibit 4–16 Sample Tracking Form for Applications in Process

Updated: dd/mm/yy By: Page _____ of _____

Applicant Name: Last, First, Title	Date Application Mailed	Follow-up Information Request	Second Request Information Received
Specialty	Application Received	Info Received	Termination of Process
Contact Phone #	Date on Attestation	Second Request for Information	Complete
Smith, John, MD Family Practice 000-000-0000	02/05/99 03/10/99 03/06/99	N/A	03/12/99
Thomas, Joe, DO Family Practice 000-00-0000	02/15/99 02/25/99 02/24/99	02/26/99 03/10/99 N/A	3/12/99
Feelgood, Tom, MD Urology 000-000-0000	02/19/99 03/12/99 03/10/99	03/13/99 04/11/99 incomplete 04/12/99	05/10/99

Courtesy of C. Mobley & Associates, LLC, and Quality Management Options, LLC, Colorado Springs, Colorado.

- signed and dated attestation
- signed and dated release form
- legible copies of
  - –professional liability insurance coverage
  - –professional license if requested (copy not required by NCQA)
  - –DEA certificate

Step 3: Verification and Information Gathering

Detailed information related to verification and data and information collection can be found in Chapter 5. Figure 4–5 is a flowchart showing steps in the verification and information-gathering process.

Characteristics of a Successful Verification and Information-Gathering Process. A successful verification and information-gathering process includes

- *Identification of a standard file format and content.* When credentials files are consistently organized using the same format, there is less chance of missing information.

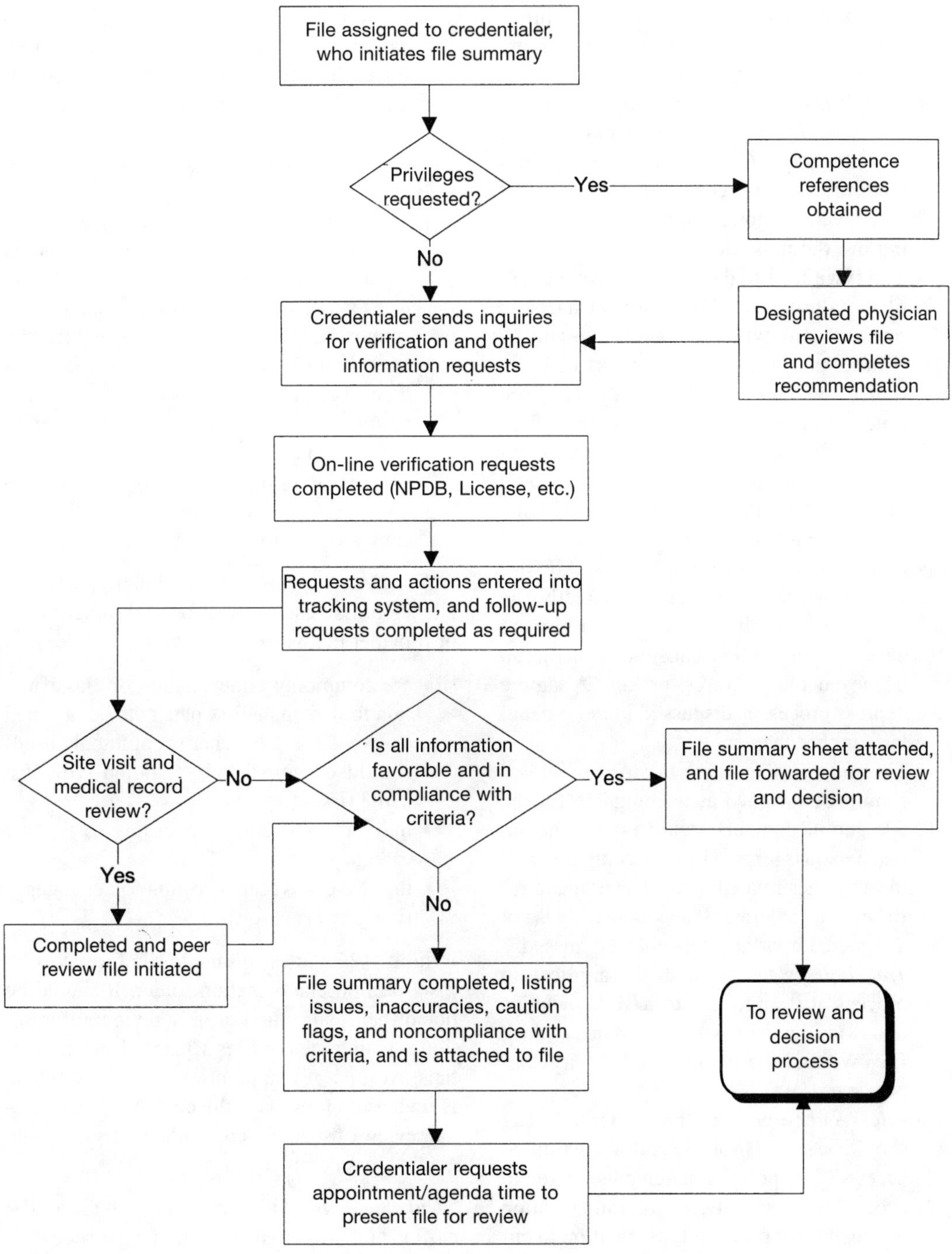

Figure 4–5 Verification and Information-Gathering Process Flowchart. Courtesy of C. Mobley & Associates, LLC, and Quality Management Options, LLC, Colorado Springs, Colorado.

Files are easier to review, and adding information as it is collected becomes a more productive activity.

- *Established and monitored verification and turnaround time standards.* Organizations accredited by NCQA are required to complete the *entire* credentialing process (of which verification and information gathering are the most time consuming components) within 180 days following signature of the attestation. Therefore, turnaround time standards with associated requirements if times are not met will support completion of credentialing within the required time. If an organization is not accredited through NCQA, it should still identify expectations related to all activities and should identify steps that will be taken if time frames are not met.
- *Express process for "clean" files.* All files do not have to be handled in exactly the same way. Ones that meet all criteria and have no information causing concern can be moved into an express process. A sample express process is discussed in more detail later in this chapter.
- *Accountability for each file.* An individual should be assigned as accountable for the file and its contents regardless of whether that person is responsible for completing all the activities related to verification and information gathering. If accountability is not assigned, important steps may be missed.
- *Tracking system.* As with the application process, it is important to have knowledge of and ability to report on the status of each file. Without these data, productivity cannot be tracked.
- *File security policy.* The credentials file should be stored in an area allowing limited access. Clear policies/statements related to access confidentiality, storage, and location of sensitive or protected information to ensure that confidentiality will not be violated must be in place and enforced.
- *Acceptable verification sources identified for each criterion.* As part of the criteria development process, an acceptable verification source should have been identified for each criterion. Information can be obtained from numerous sources, some more complete and reliable than others. Several accreditation organizations specify acceptable sources.
- *Verifications completed and information requested only for required criteria.* Some organizations obtain information and/or request verification for information that is not supported by criteria or that is required by accreditation, regulations, or internal standards. For example, NCQA standards do not require an organization to verify education if a physician is board certified. Collection of "nice-to-know" or "maybe need-to-know" information is time consuming and causes confusion if not done consistently.

File Development. An individual credentials file should be established for each practitioner or provider that is being credentialed. Files

- are commonly either manila or classification folders that allow papers to be fastened (two-holed top fastener is commonly used)
- should be consistently labeled with last name first
- may be color coded according to type or category
- may have tabs (classification folder) categorizing information

Exhibit 4–17 shows an sample file format using a six-section classification folder. It should be noted that quality and/or peer review information is maintained in files separate from credentials. At time of reappointment, the quality file is reviewed along with the credentials file. Legal review of standard credential and quality file content is recommended.

File Summary. The final activity in the verification and information-gathering process is completion of a file summary. The purpose of the file summary is to provide key information for the reviewer. The staff member who has processed the file completes a formal review of the

Exhibit 4–17 Sample File Format Using Six-Section (Two-page) Classification Folder

1. Applications	2. License/Certification
• Most recent on top • Applications divided by colored sheets File summary Application or reappointment request Release forms Copy of approval letter	• Most recent on top License DEA

3. Training	4. Insurance/Claims
AMA physician master file (if applicable) Board certification Training verification, certificates	Policy Claims history Information/correspondence related to insurance/claims

5. Affiliations/References	Other
Hospital affiliations Practice affiliations References (as applicable)	Correspondence

Note: If privileges are applicable, they may be filed in tab 2, and License/Certification may be combined with Insurance/Claims. AMA, American Medical Association; DEA, Drug Enforcement Administration.

Courtesy of C. Mobley & Associates, LLC, and Quality Management Options, LLC, Colorado Springs, Colorado.

file once all information has been verified and obtained. At that time, a file summary is completed. The file summary should provide concise, specific information related to contents of the file and compliance with criteria. Exhibit 4–18 is a sample file summary.

Step 4: Analysis and Decision-Making Process

The analysis and decision-making process starts once the credentials file is complete and ends with status notification to the practitioners. In the ambulatory and managed care settings, there are numerous ways to complete analysis, review, and determine the credentialing status of practitioners and providers. Most organizations use a credentials committee, although review by committee is not always a requirement. Some organizations allow review by a medical director who makes a direct recommendation to a management or steering committee or the governing board. Requirements for the process come from accreditation standards. Figure 4–6 is an analysis and decision-making flowchart using an express process (which is explained in more detail later in this chapter) and a formal credentials committee.

Exhibit 4–18 File Summary

Name ______________________________ Specialty ______________________________

☐ APPLICATION REQUESTED Date __________

☐ APPLICATION RETURNED (meets criteria for complete application) Attestation Date __________

	Copy in File	**Verification Received**	**Requires Review**
State License			
DEA Certificate			
NPDB			
Professional Liability Insurance			
Hospital Privileges			
Malpractice History			
Education			
Board Certification			
ECFMG			
Work History			

☐ yes ☐ no Privileges reviewed and recommended by designated peer
☐ yes ☐ no Sanctions, restrictions or other positive information identified
☐ yes ☐ no Compliance with all criteria
☐ yes ☐ no Eligible for Express Process

File Audit completed by ______________________ Date ______________________

☐ Review by Medical Director (Express Process) Date ______________________
☐ Credentials Committee Date ______________________
☐ Governing Board Date ______________________
☐ Approved ☐ Disapproved
☐ Practitioner Notified Date __________ By ______________________
☐ Contract Management Notified Date __________ By ______________________

Courtesy of C. Mobley & Associates, LLC, and Quality Management Options, LLC, Colorado Springs, Colorado.

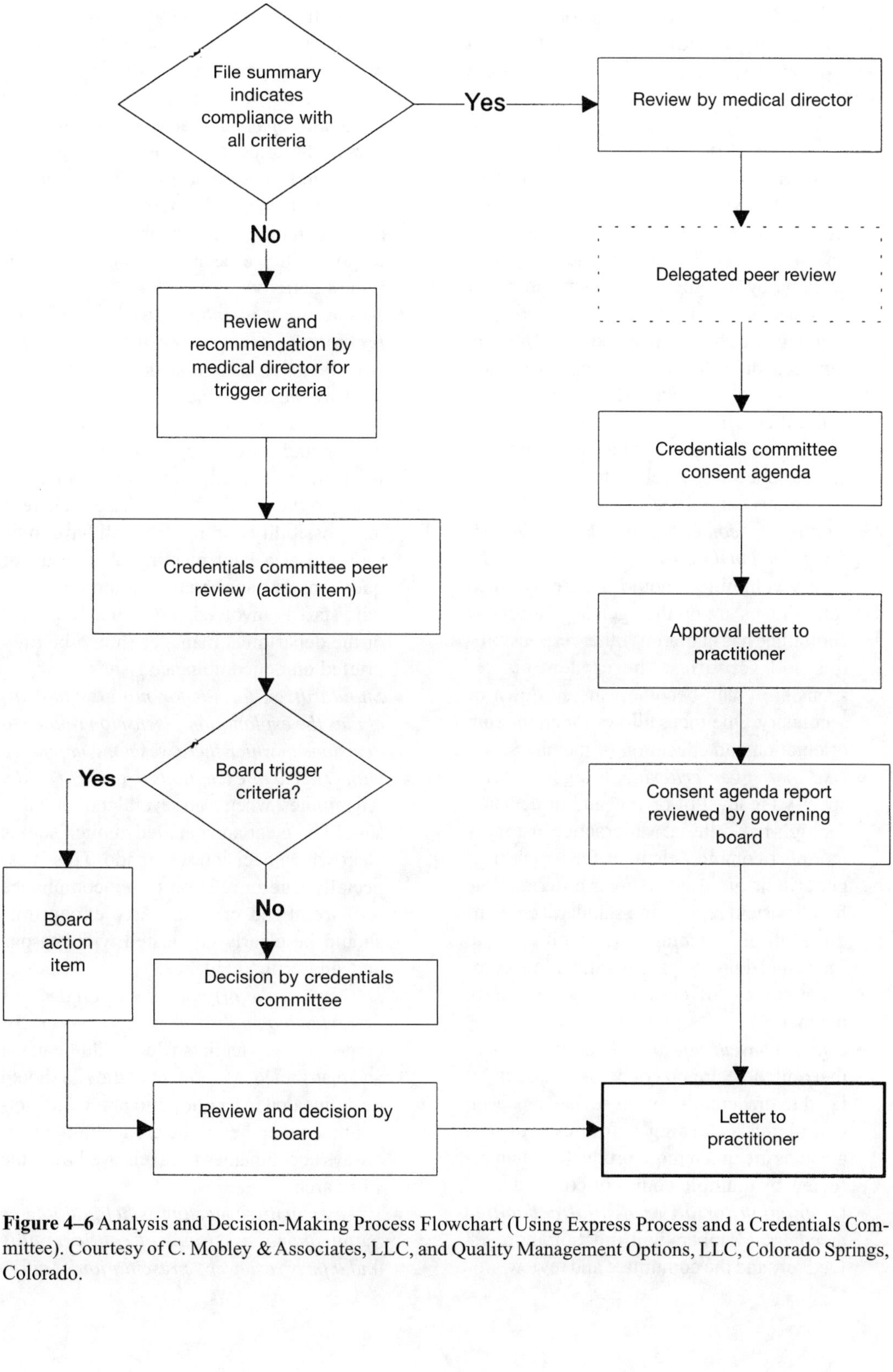

Figure 4–6 Analysis and Decision-Making Process Flowchart (Using Express Process and a Credentials Committee). Courtesy of C. Mobley & Associates, LLC, and Quality Management Options, LLC, Colorado Springs, Colorado.

Characteristics of a Successful Analysis and Decision-Making Process. Characteristics of a successful analysis and decision-making process include

- *Delegation of final decision by the governing body to a credentials committee or other designated body if there is compliance with clearly worded preestablished criteria and review by peers.* Requiring review and final decision by the governing body can result in a very time-consuming process, as governing bodies have full agendas and a fairly rigid schedule. A decision to approve practitioners and providers who are compliant with all criteria and are reviewed by peers (using preestablished criteria) may be delegated to a lower level or specifically to a credentials committee.
- *One review committee that has as its primary function the credentialing process.* The review committee should meet only when action items are on the agenda. If a review committee has numerous other responsibilities and activities, the credentials responsibility can become watered down or secondary. One focus allows for an indepth orientation and education of members.
- *Use of trigger criteria.* Trigger criteria specify the level of review and/or decision for high-risk criteria. Malpractice history is the most common element for which trigger criteria are used. Trigger criteria allow for consistent review and standardized handling of all noncompliance with criteria. They speed up the process and allow complete review of credentials in a timely manner.
- *Use of consent agendas.* If all criteria are met and there are no concerns or issues related to credentials, and if review has been completed according to policy, consent agendas are much more productive than rereview by multiple bodies or committees.
- *Orientation for all credential committee members.* Members will function more effectively and the committee and review process will be more productive if all members clearly understand the committee's function, requirements, and responsibilities.
- *Concise, written accountability for each credentialing committee member.* All members of the credentialing or review committee should understand their rights and responsibilities; whether they have a vote or are functioning in a support role, and their responsibility, especially in relation to peer review activity.
- *If there is noncompliance with criteria, file presentation at committee by the credentials staff member who was most involved in working the file.* Presentation by the person who was most involved in collecting information and for developing the files allows for further discussion and questioning relating to the information gathered. There is less possibility that the file will have to be returned at a later meeting as a result of questions not answered. If a large credentials staff is involved, a designated person or the department manager should be fully briefed on noncompliance issues.
- *Standardized format for minutes that includes the explanation/discussion related to decisions in which there was noncompliance with criteria or exceptions to criteria made.* All minutes, when read several months later, should be clear and detailed enough so it is clear why a decision was made. This is especially true in relation to noncompliance with required criteria. Any exceptions should be clearly delineated with reasons and supporting evidence.
- *Delivery of the original file to credentials or review committee or peer reviewer.* No copies of a credentials file should be made and distributed. Movement of the file should be delineated in a policy and procedure noting that a member of the credentialing staff always accompanies files removed from the work area.
- *If the committee meeting is held on line or by telephone, assurance of confidentiality and a peer reviewer's presentation of infor-*

mation directly from the original file. Action items are outlined (on line or in a packet forwarded to members before the meeting). Information is presented by the file peer reviewer, and all members are polled for their response to each action item. There is an increased demand by committee members for meetings that are outside of the traditional/formal gathering in one location to make decisions. It is possible to complete committee business on line or by telephone if all aspects of confidentiality, ability to discuss vital information, and discussion of action items are appropriately addressed.
- *Appropriate communication of findings and decisions in a timely manner and using standard format.* Once the final decision relating to the credentialing action is made, everyone who has a need to know should be informed. The practitioner or provider should be informed of the outcome and next steps as applicable.

The Credentials Committee. As noted earlier, it is not always a requirement that there be a formal credentials committee. Accreditation standards and program structure dictate the review process. The following information will relate to the review body of credentials information and will refer to this body as a *credentials committee*. The credentials plan document should include information related to the analysis and decision-making process and should define the review committee and/or committee structure.

A credentials committee will most likely have membership including

- practitioners who can act in a peer review capacity and who are representative of the practitioners that are affiliated with the organization; the review body may be multidisciplinary, or there may be several separate committees addressing types of practitioners (e.g., high-volume specialists)
- representative from legal/risk management
- representative from clinical quality
- representative from provider relations or contracting
- credentials manager or director
- representative from administration
- designated minute taker

The key roles and responsibility of the credentials committee include

- review, recommendation, and possibly approval of practitioners and providers who meet all credentialing criteria
- review and recommendation related to practitioners and providers who do not meet criteria
- development of policies and procedures related to credentialing
- recredentialing
- appeals process, if applicable

The plan policy and procedure related to the committee should spell out

- the voting method
- confidentiality of information
- minutes' requirements
- frequency of meetings
- any other requirements related to the committee structure

Caution Flags. Caution flags are those pieces of data or information that should send up warning signals to the credentialing staff and the reviewers. Caution flags require additional review and possibly indicate that additional information should be obtained. Common caution flags include the following:

1. Overall application
    - discrepancies within the application
    - unanswered questions on the application
    - discrepancies between information in the application and verifications or other information obtained during the credentialing process
    - gaps in time intervals for training and education or work that are not explained
2. Training
    - training or certification different from the requested specialty or area of practice
    - questionable or unknown foreign school
    - excessive training (e.g., two residencies in the same specialty)

3. Work history and affiliation
   - no longer affiliated with a hospital or other health care organization in the area
   - excessive movement from job to job
   - no hospital affiliation
4. License and certificates
   - limited DEA schedule
   - restrictions
   - current investigation
   - numerous state medical licenses during a four- to five-year period
5. References
   - negative references
   - references with a specific statement that a telephone contact should be made
   - questions answered with a fair or below-average rating
6. Professional liability coverage and history
   - numerous cases filed
   - cases involving death or major disabilities
   - high settlement amounts
   - cases associated with adverse publicity
   - cases associated with regulatory agencies
   - insurance liability limits lower than standard for that specialty
   - frequent change in professional liability carrier or very short-term professional liability

Caution flags do not mean that a practitioner should be declined or that the credentialing process should be stopped, but they should require review and detailed discussion related to the information at several levels. If an express process is used, identification of caution flags should require specific review by the credentials committee or other designated review body.

Trigger Criteria. An organization may choose to develop trigger criteria for those components that are not clearly objective, or for which some decision-making elements will be involved: for example, acceptance of practitioners with a limited DEA schedule or with insurance limits that fall below specified criteria amounts. Organizations that have identified one level of insurance coverage may find that certain specialties commonly have lower levels of coverage or that a limited DEA is acceptable in certain circumstances. Another area that is often addressed with trigger criteria is number of malpractice claims and settlements. Malpractice claims may be reviewed regardless of outcome, whether they were closed or whether a payment was made. A malpractice history does not mean that the practitioner should not be accepted or credentialed, but it probably requires further detailed review.

Trigger criteria specify the level of review and decision making for "exceptions" to evaluative criteria. They help ensure continuity of decisions and the appropriate involvement in high–risk-assuming decisions. Table 4–2 is an example of trigger criteria for initial application. In this example, the organization has determined that a practitioner who has a current restriction or sanction to a license or certificate that will affect his or her ability to practice must be reviewed and that the decision will be made only at the governing board level, whereas a limited DEA with no state medical board sanctions can be reviewed by the medical director with the recommendation made to the credentials committee. The credentials committee can, in this case, approve credentials for this practitioner without governing board review. This same format can be developed for two levels of review.

Table 4–1 earlier in this chapter showed a sample review and decision matrix for malpractice history. Trigger criteria with a specified level of review help to ensure a standardized process and minimize inappropriate or high-risk exceptions.

Step 5: Recredentialing

The recredentialing process takes place on a regular cycle, the most common period being two years. It is initiated four to eight months before the end of the current cycle. The flowchart in Figure 4–7 outlines steps in the recredentialing process.

Recredentialing involves collection of information that has changed since the last credentialing decision. Common recredentialing questionnaire components address

Table 4–2 Sample Matrix Review for Trigger Criteria: Initial Application

Element	*Medical Director Review with Recommendation to Credentials Committee*	*Credentials Committee Review with Recommendation to Governing Board*	*Governing Board Review and Determination*
License or certification restrictions and/or sanctions	Limited DEA with no state medical board sanctions	History of restriction or sanction for any license or certificate that has been lifted	Current restriction or sanction to a license or certificate that will affect ability to practice
Negative reference(s)	Medical director will contact reference(s) and outline possible issues and concerns for discussion with credentials committee		
Insurance limits below criteria requirements ($1 million/$3 million)	No less than $500/$1 million; no history of malpractice claims; in practice for at least seven years	No less than $500/$1 million; history of 1 or 2 malpractice claims; in practice for at least five years	Self-Insured; limits less than $500/$1 million; three or more malpractice claims; in practice for less than five years
Malpractice claims and settlements	Cases over 10 years old with no activity in preceding 10 years; one or two cases in preceding 10 years that were dropped/closed or in which settlement did not exceed $100,000	Any open malpractice case; one case within preceding 10 years that resulted in mortality; one to five claims in past 10 years in which settlement exceeded $100,000 but was less than $500,000; three or four claims during past 10 years	More than 5 claims during past five years; more than one case that resulted in mortality; one to five claim(s) in past 10 years in which settlement(s) exceeded $500,000

Courtesy of C. Mobley & Associates, LLC, and Quality Management Options, LLC, Colorado Springs, Colorado.

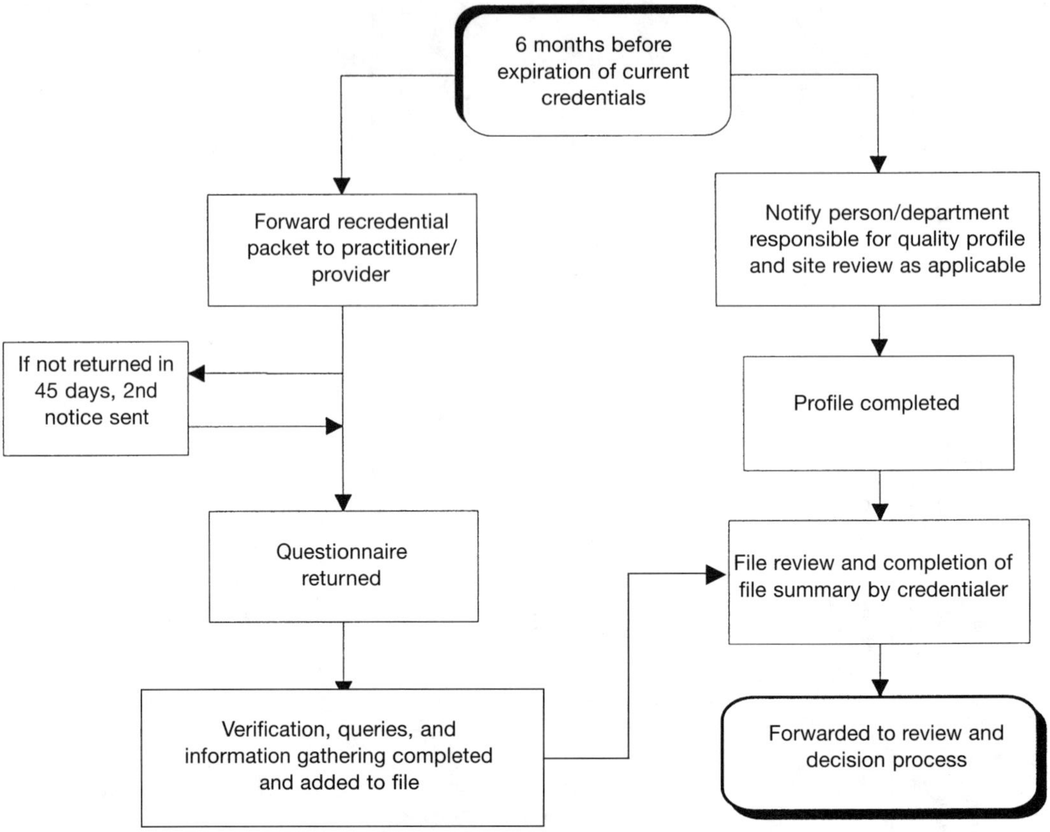

Figure 4–7 Recredentialing Flowchart. Courtesy of C. Mobley & Associates, LLC, and Quality Management Options, LLC, Colorado Springs, Colorado.

- changes and updates in demographic information
- changes and updates in license and certificates
- changes in hospital affiliation
- updated educational and continuing medical education information, if applicable to privileges or change in board status
- changes in board certification information
- claim and liability issues
- sanctions or disciplinary actions
- quality-of-care concerns

Criteria for the recredentialing process should not be in conflict with or different from criteria used in the initial application process. The steps in verification and information gathering for recredentialing are the same as those taken during the initial process. The focus of recredentialing is activity since the previous credentialing review and decision. Information previously considered should not be revisited. The key or vital element in recredentialing is collection of information related to the delivery of patient care. At the time of initial appointment, a decision is made based on history and information from other organizations or institutions. At the time of recredentialing, there should be information available related to care rendered for, or within, the organization. Chapter 8 contains more detailed discussion related to performance improvement and development of a profile for use during recredentialing. Site visits and medical record review are addressed in detail later in this chapter.

Characteristics of a Successful Recredentialing Process. Recredentialing activities are most successful when the following have been implemented.

- *Recredentialing is completed within the specified time frame.* The cardinal element of a successful recredentialing program is that the process be completed within the identified time frame (e.g., two years). If the cycle is two years, all practitioners and providers should have verification and review completed and a decision rendered by the time the current two-year cycle ends.
- *The recredentialing decision is closely integrated with the quality program and information-gathering process.* A large part of the recredentialing decision should be based upon evidence of activity and competence. Information gathered through quality or performance assessment activities and documented in the form of a profile provides evidence of competence.
- *The recredentialing cycle and decision are independent of the contracting process.* Some organizations try to match the credentialing and contract cycles. As contract terms vary from six months to indefinite and are based on a business relationship, renewal should not be integrated into the recredentialing decision.
- *Recredentialing activity is evenly distributed during the year.* There should be continuous recredentialing work occurring. This can be accomplished through the recredentialing of 1/24 of the practitioner and provider network on a monthly basis or 1/8 every quarter. It is an almost impossible task to recredential the entire network at one time.
- *If the practitioner is an employee of the organization, the recredential process matches the timing of the employment review process.*
- *There is a policy and procedure related to handling verification and information requests that are not completed within 120 days and for handling questionnaires that are not returned in a timely manner.* Staff and committee members must have a defined process for dealing with nonresponse to requests. If a practitioner or provider does not complete and return a questionnaire, a process must be implemented to terminate the relationship. If verifications cannot be completed in a timely manner, actions to ensure timely completion of the process are indicated.
- *There is a clear understanding and a defined process related to production of performance improvement and other quality data.* All staff involved with development of a practitioner profile should understand their role and responsibility. As this often involves several departments, a cooperative relationship is essential.
- *There is a standard profile format that includes quality, performance, and activity data.*

Recredentialing Trigger Criteria. Many of the same trigger criteria used for an initial process could be used for recredentialing. They address areas such as

- aggregate malpractice claims settlements or judgments
- changes in coverage to be less than the required limit
- new malpractice cases resulting in mortality or permanent disability

Additional triggers that may be developed for recredentialing relate to performance improvement or quality. These include

- member complaints
- disenrollment
- medical record review score
- facility site review score
- peer review cases

- utilization management noncompliance
- percentage patient satisfaction
- compliance with access standards

Forms Related to Recredentialing. The recredentialing packet is made up of a cover letter, the recredentialing questionnaire, and any supporting or orientation materials related to the recertification process that the organization chooses to include. Exhibit 4–19 is a sample cover letter that provides instructions and lists information that should be completed, attached, and returned. This cover letter also provides information related to a site visit and medical record review. Exhibit 4–20 is an outline for a recredentialing and continued participation policy and includes specific criteria and actions related to continued participation. Exhibit 4–21 is a physician-recredentialing questionnaire. The physician-recredentialing questionnaire is commonly repopulated with existing information before its distribution. The practitioner is then asked only to make corrections or changes and to complete the section related to medical/legal information.

Step 6: Maintenance and Problem Resolution

Once the review and decision are completed, the credentials file goes into a maintenance mode. This may be a totally manual system or may be integrated with a software tracking system or a paperless credentialing process.

File Maintenance. The key aspect of file maintenance is a policy that addresses access, control, and confidentiality. Access to files should be limited to those with a "need to know." These include the members of the credentialing staff, the medical director, and, to a limited extent, those in administration involved with problem resolution. It does not include recruitment, contracting, or provider relations staff members. Files, as a general statement, should not be checked out or moved from one area to another without a member of the credentials staff in attendance. Accountability for files should be outlined to include storage in a locked area and in locked files. If quality and peer review files are stored as part of the credentials file or in the same area, they should be easily separated.

Legal counsel can provide information related to coverage of credentialing files by state peer review statutes. A component of all orientation programs should always be the issue of confidentiality. The credentials committee members, medical directors, and credentialing staff should understand that all information learned during the credentialing process is strictly confidential and may not be shared outside of the work area. Some credentials committees require that a confidentiality statement be signed as part of the orientation process.

Tracking. A credentials file tracking system should be in place regardless of whether it is entirely manual, part of a software program, or a combination of both. It is essential that the credentialing staff have a listing of all files and the status of each file. A categorization process may be implemented to track status of a file, such as the one described on page 217.

Exhibit 4–19 Recredential Cover Letter

Date:

Name:
Address:

Dear Doctor ________________:

To maintain and continue your status with _____________, your participation is required in the recredential process every two (2) years.

To initiate the process:

1. You complete, sign, and return the enclosed forms.
2. You submit updated copies of the following documents:

____ Current DEA certificate
____ Current professional liability insurance, including company, policy number, expiration dates, and limits

Provider relations staff will be contacting your office to schedule a site visit, which includes a medical record audit.

When your recredentialing has been completed, the Credentials Committee will notify you. Please direct questions you may have about the process to your provider relations contact. For your information, we have also enclosed a summary of primary care physician criteria.

Thank you for your cooperation and continued support.

Sincerely,

____
Signature Title

Courtesy of C. Mobley & Associates, LLC, and Quality Management Options, LLC, Colorado Springs, Colorado.

Exhibit 4–20 Recredentialing and Performance Evaluation

All participating physicians will be recredentialed every two years. The following materials will be obtained and reviewed.

1.0 Recredentialing questionnaire

2.0 Primary source verification of:
- 2.1 Current unrestricted state medical license
- 2.2 Hospital privileges
- 2.3 Current unrestricted DEA certificate
- 2.4 Board certification, as applicable
- 2.5 Current malpractice insurance coverage, according to criteria
- 2.6 Professional liability claims history for past two years
- 2.7 Medicare and Medicaid sanctions

3.0 Signed attestation of ability to perform contracted services

4.0 Review of information from:
- 4.1 The National Practitioner Data Bank
- 4.2 State board of medical examiners regarding sanctions

5.0 Other information taken into consideration:
- 5.1 Numbers of types of member complaints during past two years
- 5.2 Results of quality reviews by peer review committee
- 5.3 Primary care provider changes due to quality issues
- 5.4 Results of facility on-site visit
- 5.5 Medical record review findings
- 5.6 Utilization management data
- 5.7 Results of member satisfaction surveys
- 5.8 Cooperation with managed care policies and staff

Performance Evaluation:

Evaluation of quality of health care delivery and clinical competence will be conducted by the peer review committee, who will make a recommendation related to recredentialing to the credentials committee. The credentials committee will determine compliance as applicable and recommend one of the following:

- recredentialing, or
- recommend recredentialing with provision to administration, or
- recommend termination to administration.

Courtesy of C. Mobley & Associates, LLC, and Quality Management Options, LLC, Colorado Springs, Colorado.

Exhibit 4–21 Physician-Recredentialing Questionnaire

Name ______________________________ Birth Date: ______________
(First) (MI) (Last) (MD/DO, etc.)

Main Office: ______________________________
Street Address, Suite #

____
City, State, ZIP

Phone: ______________________ Contact Person: ______________

Office Days: ☐ Monday ☐ Tuesday ☐ Wednesday ☐ Thursday ☐ Friday ☐ Saturday

Office Hours: ________ ________ ________ ________ ________ ________

Second Office: ______________________________
Street Address, Suite #

____
City, State, ZIP

Phone: ______________________ Contact Person: ______________

Office Days: ☐ Monday ☐ Tuesday ☐ Wednesday ☐ Thursday ☐ Friday ☐ Saturday

Office Hours: ________ ________ ________ ________ ________ ________

Changes in Business Arrangement during Last Two (2) Years

☐ Legal partnership/professional corp. ☐ Solo practice
☐ Associate ☐ Employee

Names of new partners or associates: ______________________________

Names of physicians with whom you share on-call coverage: ______________________________

____

____

Changes in Professional Education/Qualifications Obtained during Past 2 Years

Fellowship in: Specialty: __________ Hospital: __________ From: __________ To: ________

Certified by: American Board of ____________ # ____________ Date: ____________

Recertified by: American Board of ____________ # ____________ Date: ____________

continues

Exhibit 4–21 continued

CURRENT HOSPITAL PRIVILEGES

Hospitals	Status
______________________	____________
______________________	____________
______________________	____________

MEDICAL/LEGAL INFORMATION

If you answer YES to any of the questions contained in this section, PLESE ATTACH A DETAILED, WRITTEN EXPLANATION.

Since your last credentials review:	Yes	No
1. Have there been any disciplinary actions or investigations against you by any state licensing board?	☐	☐
• Are there any actions/investigations in process?	☐	☐
• Have you voluntarily surrendered your medical license?	☐	☐
2. Has your DEA registration been denied, revoked, suspended, restricted, reduced, or nonrenewed?	☐	☐
• Are there any investigations/actions in process?	☐	☐
• Have you voluntarily surrendered your DEA registration?	☐	☐
3. Has your professional liability coverage been canceled, limited, denied, or nonrenewed?	☐	☐
4. Have your privileges at any hospital been denied, suspended, reduced, revoked, or put on probation?	☐	☐
• Are any investigations in process?	☐	☐
• Have you resigned from any hospitals?	☐	☐
5. Have you been investigated, suspended, sanctioned, or otherwise restricted from participating in any federal or state health insurance program?	☐	☐
6. Have there been any criminal proceedings against you?	☐	☐
7. Do you suffer from any illness, injury, or health condition (physical or mental) that limits or impairs your ability to safely provide medical services as outlined in your contract?	☐	☐
8. Have any of the following occurred?	☐	☐
• lawsuits dismissed/dropped	☐	☐
• lawsuits pending	☐	☐
• settlements or judgments	☐	☐
• other____________	☐	☐

(If "YES" to #8, please provide on a separate sheet the date of occurrence, name/age of parties involved, statement of events, basis of suit, and insurance carrier.)

AGREEMENT/ATTESTATION

I understand and agree that submission of this questionnaire in itself does not constitute continuation of my contract. I hereby attest that all information submitted in this questionnaire is true to the best of my knowledge and belief.

____
Signature Date

Courtesy of C. Mobley & Associates, LLC, and Quality Management Options, LLC, Colorado Springs, Colorado.

- Category I: Initial application requested by/forwarded to practitioner
- Category II: Application received and file initiated
- Category III: Initial two-year credentialing cycle
- Category IV: Recredential cycle
- Category V: Suspended
- Category VI: Terminated or contract not renewed

Tracking systems can be very detailed, providing a great deal of information with ability to print numerous types of management reports, or very simple, involving only names, status, and number in each category.

Coordination with Recruitment, Contracting, and Employment Activities. It is important that an organization clearly identify the communication, responsibility, and accountability between credentialing staff and those in recruitment and contracting positions or responsible for employment activities. A policy and procedure should ensure that a credentialing decision will be made before a contract is executed, an offer of employment is made, or the practitioner is allowed to see patients. There are numerous legal ramifications and risk factors associated with allowing a practitioner to initiate patient contact before the validity of all credentials and qualifications is determined. Although many organizations that are in a strong recruitment mode do not follow this process, the risks to the organization can be significant.

Due Process. Most organizations will include a due-process or appeal mechanism in their credentialing policies and procedures, and in 1998 NCQA implemented standards requiring a limited due process.[23] In ambulatory and managed care, *due process* relates to a practitioner's right to enter a complaint or appeal or to request review of a decision. Many managed and ambulatory care organizations do not offer due process for the initial credentialing decision. Physicians who are denied initial credentialing may challenge the decision on the grounds of interference in business relationships or anticompetitive issues. It is important that a legal review of decisions related to offering due process be obtained.

It is advisable to review and comply with the Health Care Quality Improvement Act of 1986 requirements for physician due-process rights if there is ever the possibility of excluding a physician for reasons related to competency. Compliance with the act's requirements will allow the organization to avail itself of the immunity clause.[24] Some organizations will wish to use a due process to maintain good relations with their practitioners and may even go so far as to encourage use of a review process for concerns, questions, and issues. Further detail related to due process can be found in Chapter 9.

Termination and Summary Suspension. Most contracts include language that outlines specific events that may result in automatic termination or summary suspension. Events that may be reason for automatic contract termination frequently relate to specific credentialing criteria. Examples include

- revocation, suspension, or voluntary relinquishment of the medical license, professional liability insurance coverage, or DEA certificate
- incomplete, inaccurate, or untruthful information submitted on an application or recredentialing questionnaire
- loss or relinquishment of privileges at the primary admitting or practice facility
- Medicare/Medicaid sanction
- felony conviction

In cases of contract termination, the practitioner is not commonly availed of the right to a hearing or review.

The events leading to summary suspension may be outlined in a contract and are not as clear-cut as the events that may result in contract termination. Summary suspension occurs as the result of an action on the part of the practitioner that requires immediate intervention to protect life or reduce the possibility of eminent damage to health or safety of another individual. This may relate to competence or to the impairment of a practitioner. In the case of a summary suspension, the circumstances are reviewed, and the due-process policy is invoked. Exhibit 4–22 is a sample policy statement related to termination of participating physicians and the appeals process.

Characteristics of a Successful Credentialing Process

In summary, a number of key elements define a successful credentialing process. These include

- a concise written credentialing plan, policy, and procedure
- detailed specific criteria
- clear accountability
- medical involvement in the form of a medical director and/or peer review
- management support
- defined relationship with the governing body
- organized credentials file
- a credentials or review committee educated with regard to its function and the policies and procedures that govern it
- compliance with identified turnaround times
- ongoing recredentialing activities that occur within a specified time frame for each practitioner and provider
- defined communication and interaction between recruitment, contracting, human resources, and credentialing staff
- a dedicated credentialing staff committed to compliance with the credentialing plan and its policies and procedures

FACILITY SITE VISITS AND MEDICAL RECORD AUDITS

Organizations may choose to complete facility or site review visits and audits before contracting with a practitioner or provider. If the organization is accredited or is seeking accreditation through NCQA, it is required by accreditation standards to complete the site visit and medical record audits before credentialing. NCQA requires a structured review of the quality of a facility where care is provided.[25] Figure 4–8 flowcharts facility and medical record audits. Although there is no requirement, if there is going to be any medical record review (whether for quality or for compliance with NCQA standards), the review should take place at the same time as the site or facility visit.

Key Elements

Key elements of the facility site visit and medical record reviews are

- written plan, policies, and procedures
- specific criteria
- standardized audit format
- standards for acceptable plan/network participation

Written Plan, Policies, and Procedures

In determining elements of the plan and required policies and procedures, the first decision is to identify components that will be reviewed during the site visit. Common components reviewed are

- appearance and adequacy of facility
- access and availability
- medical recordkeeping practices
- safety and risk management
- ancillary services

Once components are identified, the next step is to determine which aspects of each component will be reviewed. Sample aspects of review of the appearance and adequacy of facility are

- parking arrangements
- handicap accessibility
- appearance and comfort of waiting room
- number of exam rooms

Sample elements of availability and accessibility are

- wait time for appointments
- wait time in office

Exhibit 4–22 Sample Policy for Termination of Participating Physicians and the Appeals Process

POLICY

Noncompliance with credentialing criteria and qualifications for participation in the plan may result in a recommendation for suspension and/or termination of a participating physician for cause. In accordance with the Medical Service Agreement, the physician may be suspended or terminated for failure to continue to meet the credentialing criteria. (In addition, the Medical Service Agreement may be terminated without cause, as described in the Agreement.)

SUSPENSION/TERMINATION

Recredentialing may be deferred and a participating physician may be suspended or terminated under any of the following

1. Failure to maintain compliance with general criteria
2. Failure to maintain medical staff and clinical privileges at a participating hospital within the service area or to maintain use of participating hospitals for the majority of his/her practice
3. Multiple and significant quality of care issues that result in a recommendation by the quality improvement committee to suspend or terminate the participation agreement
4. Felony or other act involving dishonesty, fraud, deceit, or misrepresentation
5. Engagement in conduct that violates state law or standards of ethical conduct governing medical practice or investigation with respect to such conduct
6. Refusal to execute a Medical Service Agreement
7. Documented circumstances related to performance, such that the credentialing committee believes that retention of the physician would not be in the best interest of the plan or its members

PROCEDURE

Suspension and Termination for Cause and the Appeals Process:

If a physician is terminated for cause, he/she may request a review of the decision by an appeals committee. Within 30 working days following receipt of notification of the decision, the involved physician must request that the decision be reconsidered by an appeals committee. The request for reconsideration must be in writing and must set forth in detail those matters that the involved physician believes were improperly considered. The appeals process is applicable to only participating physicians.

APPEALS COMMITTEE

1. The appeals committee shall consist of the senior medical director (or his/her designee), two physicians currently participating in quality assurance and utilization management programs and who did not serve on the committee that rendered the decision being appealed, a member of the professional relations staff, and a member representing administration. The medical director will identify and appoint the members of the appeals committee.
2. The appeals committee will meet only to review written appeals by a participating physician who disagrees with a decision related to suspension or termination for cause.
3. Minutes will be taken at all meetings and maintained in such a manner as to ensure confidentiality.
4. A decision shall be by vote of the majority of members and shall be binding and final.

Guidelines Used by the Appeals Committee

1. The appeals committee will select one of its members to serve as chairperson for the meeting.
2. Proper notice will be given to the physician stating date of the appeals meeting.
3. The appeals committee review shall be designed to reevaluate the initial decision as an administrative decision to suspend or terminate the involved physician on the basis of the information available to it. Every aspect of the hearing should be designed to result in a decision that is fair to the involved physician.
4. In the event that the appeals committee's decision upholds the original determination for suspension or termination, the participation status shall cease in compliance with contract language and as outlined in original letter of notification.
5. In the event that the appeals committee's decision is not to suspend or terminate, the physician shall continue as a participating practitioner of the plan.

Courtesy of C. Mobley & Associates, LLC, and Quality Management Options, LLC, Colorado Springs, Colorado.

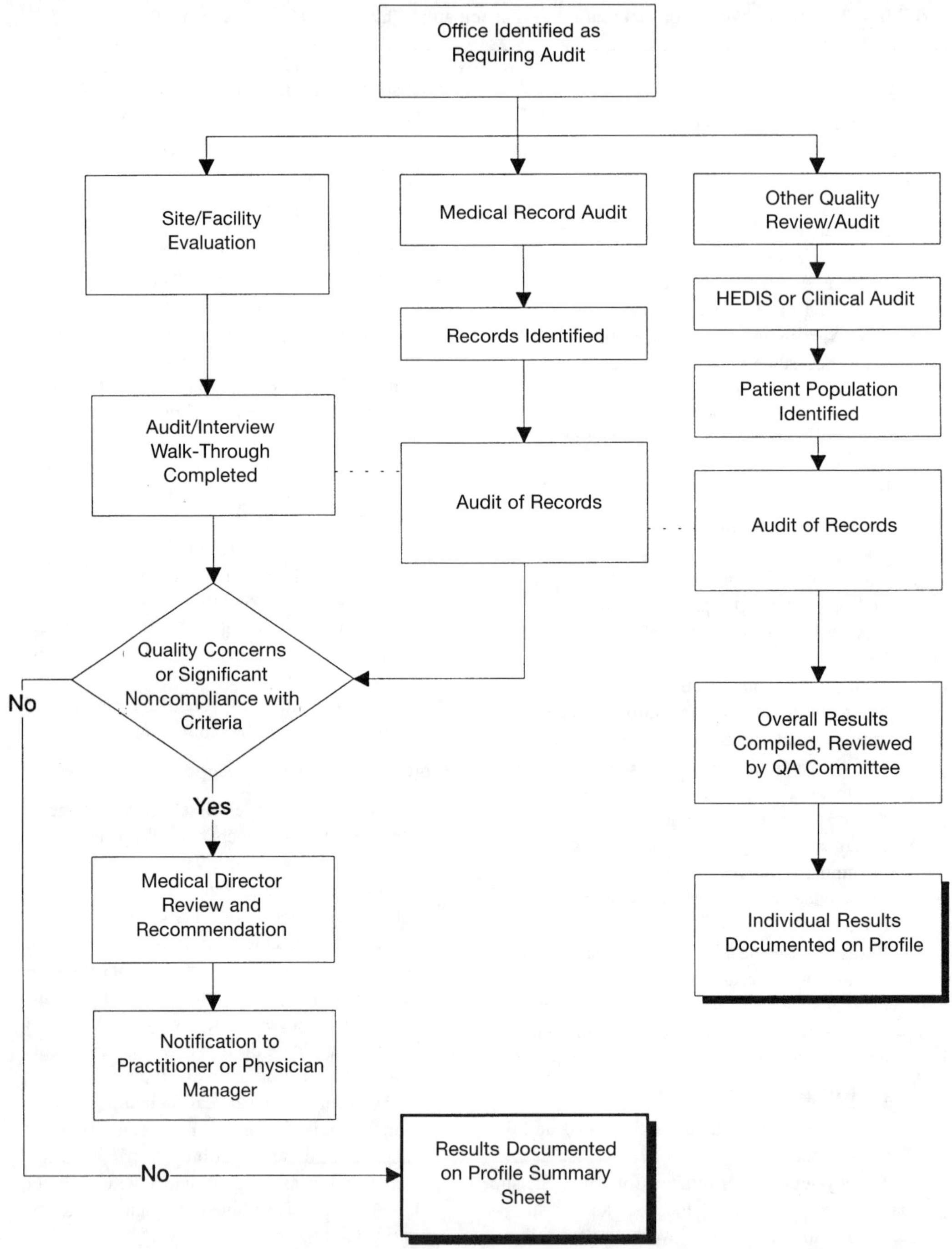

Note: HEDIS, Health Plan Employer Data Information Set.

Figure 4–8 Facility and Medical Record Audit. Courtesy of C. Mobley & Associates, LLC, and Quality Management Options, LLC, Colorado Springs, Colorado.

- phone system
- after-hours phone system and coverage
- appointment system
- management of walk-in appointments

There are numerous aspects that could be reviewed for each component. It is important to determine:

1. What *must* we know?
2. Is this "need to know" or "nice to know"?
3. Who will use the information?
4. Will the information allow us to draw a conclusion regarding acceptable performance?

Criteria

Once the components and aspects of review have been identified, the next step is to identify criteria for each aspect. Criteria are statements by which a judgment can be formed or a conclusion drawn. They must be both objective and measurable.

Standardized Audit Format

Once criteria are identified, they are formatted into a standard audit tool. An effective audit format is one in which the reviewer will have few opportunities for more than one clear choice. For example, adequate seating in the waiting area might be defined as a number of chairs equaling the total number of appointments per day divided by 4.

Standards for Acceptable Plan/Network Performance

Development of the criteria and the audit format includes identification of the measurements of acceptable performance. At the outcome of a review, there should be a standardized measurement methodology that allows a decision to be made related to acceptable performance. This is often accomplished through use of a scoring system in which points are assigned to each element or standard.

Facility Site Visit Review Criteria and Audit; Medical Record Criteria and Audit

Exhibit 4–23 is a sample audit tool that includes criteria statements and ends with standards for acceptable performance. Exhibit 4–24 is a sample medical record audit format that includes criteria and standards for acceptable performance.

Options and Decisions

A number of options are available to support site visit review and audits, and determination will have to be made regarding the following:

1. *Facility and medical record review process may be delegated to another organization.* There are now numerous organizations that provide facility and medical record reviews for NCQA-accredited organizations. An organization that is large and has numerous participating practitioner contracts may find that delegation is a viable option.
2. *Credentials requirement for reviewers and the reporting relationship within the organization.* Individuals involved in site audits may be nurses (both RNs and LPNs), provider relations staff, or administrative assistants. The organization will need to determine the extent of decision making it wishes to allow, determination of quality of care, and the credentials required.
3. *The number of medical records to be reviewed for each practitioner and the method to be used for identifying records.* The sample format in Exhibit 4–24 shows 10 questions for a review of 10 records. This allows for a total of 100 points, making measurement against performance standards easier. Review of only one or two records will in all probability not provide enough information for determining quality of content.
4. *Policies and procedures indicating how results will be documented and any follow-*

Exhibit 4–23 Sample Facility Site Review Criteria and Audit

OFFICE ADDRESS: ____________________ PHONE NUMBER: ____________________

PARTICIPATING PHYSICIANS AT THIS ADDRESS: ____________________

____

REVIEW BY: ____________________ DATE: ____________________

Date of First Review		Recredential Review Date		PCP		Pediatrics		OB/GYN		Specialist

1.0 FACILITY: APPEARANCE AND ADEQUACY

CRITERIA	COMPLIANCE			SCORE	
	YES	NO	N/A	WEIGHT	SCORE
1.1 Address and office signage clearly visible				3	
1.2 Office handicapped/wheelchair accessible				3	
1.3 At least one handicapped-equipped restroom				3	
1.4 Patient rights and responsibilities posted in waiting area				2	
1.5 No-smoking sign posted in waiting area				2	
1.6 Adequate seating in waiting area (no. of chairs equaling total no. of appointments per day divided by 4)				2	
1.7 Parking adequate (one space for every three chairs in waiting area and minimum of one handicapped space)				2	
1.8 Patient education materials available for patients				3	
1.9 Waiting area free of dirt, dust, and clutter; well lighted and ventilated				2	
1.10 Exam room provides for patient privacy, including curtains				3	
TOTAL POINTS FOR FACILITY				**25**	

2.0 ACCESS AND AVAILABILITY					
CRITERIA	COMPLIANCE			SCORE	
	YES	NO	N/A	WEIGHT	SCORE
2.1 24-hour/seven-day-a-week answering service, answering machine with notification system or beeper				3	
2.2 Minimum of 25 hours per week of scheduled office hours				2	
2.3 On-call coverage provided by same specialty and qualifications				3	
2.4 Minimum of two phone lines				2	
2.5 Response to urgent calls within 30 minutes				3	
2.6 Tickler system for follow-up appointments				3	
2.7 Average waiting room time less than 30 minutes				2	
2.8 At least one appointment slot available for urgent appointment				2	
TOTAL POINTS FOR ACCESS AND AVAILABILITY				**20**	
3.0 MEDICAL RECORDKEEPING					
3.1 Confidentiality policy related to recordkeeping				2	
3.2 Records accessible only to staff				3	
3.3 Individual record for each patient				3	
3.4 Each record clearly identified with patient name and ID no.				2	
3.5 Each sheet in record identified with patient name				2	
3.6 Record can be identified and obtained within one hour of a request				3	
3.7 Written release is required for copying records				3	
3.8 Records are organized and filed in a consistent manner				2	
TOTAL POINTS FOR MEDICAL RECORDKEEPING				**20**	

continues

Exhibit 4–23 continued

4.0 SAFETY AND RISK MANAGEMENT					
CRITERIA	COMPLIANCE			SCORE	
	YES	NO	N/A	WEIGHT	SCORE
4.1 Fire extinguishers present and function checked within past six months				3	
4.2 Syringe and needle disposal system that is tamper resistant and protects against needlesticks				3	
4.3 Disposable gloves available for all staff				2	
4.4 No patient access to prescription pads, medication samples, or syringes				3	
4.5 Emergency kit easily available, and documentation shows checked within prior week				3	
4.6 Written policy and procedure for disposal of infectious waste				3	
4.7 All containers (including cleaning supplies) clearly labeled				3	
4.8 At least one CPR-certified staff member on during regular business hours				3	
4.9 Controlled medications locked, accessible only to licensed staff, current dispensing record displayed				3	
4.10 Medications reviewed for expiration date at minimum monthly but more frequently acceptable				2	
4.11 Exits clearly identified and with emergency lighting				2	
TOTAL POINTS FOR SAFETY AND RISK MANAGEMENT				**30**	
5.0 ANCILLARY SERVICES					
5.1 Blood specimen drawn/blood handlers must wear disposable gloves				3	
5.2 CLIA certificate or waiver posted and current				2	
5.3 Policy and procedures for test equipment inspection/calibration/effective function				2	

CRITERIA	COMPLIANCE			SCORE	
	YES	NO	N/A	WEIGHT	SCORE
5.4 Evidence that inspection/calibration and function testing completed in compliance with policy and procedures				3	
TOTAL POINTS FOR ANCILLARY SERVICES				**10**	

Reviewer Comments:

RESULTS:	
1.0 FACILITY: APPEARANCE AND ADEQUACY	
2.0 ACCESS AND AVAILABILITY	
3.0 MEDICAL RECORDKEEPING	
4.0 SAFETY AND RISK MANAGEMENT	
5.0 ANCILLARY SERVICES	
TOTAL	

	A score of 65–79 points requires completion of a written action plan to address deficiencies.
	A score less than 65 points results in a report to the Credentials Committee that participation is not recommended.
	Copy of findings given to: ______________________

Note: CPR, cardiopulmonary resuscitation; CLIA, Clinical Laboratory Improvement Act

Courtesy of C. Mobley & Associates, LLC, and Quality Management Options, LLC, Colorado Springs, Colorado.

Exhibit 4–24 Sample Medical Record Criteria and Audit

Physician # ____________ Date of Review ____________ Reviewer ____________

	1	2	3	4	5	6	7	8	9	10	TOTAL # YES
PATIENT ID NO.											
NO. OF VISITS DURING PAST YEAR											
STANDARDS:											
1. Allergies are noted in a prominent place.											
2. Entries are dated and provider is identified.											
3. Entries are legible.											
4. Chief complaint or purpose is recorded for each visit.											
5. A diagnosis is recorded for each visit.											
6. A treatment plan is recorded for each visit.											
7. Entry signed by physician/ practitioner for each visit.											
8. Documentation of follow-up instruction.											
9. Current medications listed.											
10. Blood pressure recorded yearly.											
										Total	

Reviewer Comments ____________

Less than 70 total points requires completion of written action plan to address deficiencies.

Copy of findings given to:

Courtesy of C. Mobley & Associates, LLC, and Quality Management Options, LLC, Colorado Springs, Colorado.

up required. When quality-of-care concerns or major discrepancies with criteria are identified during the review, a process for communication of these problems and concerns to the practitioner and/or staff must also be identified.

5. *Authorization and consent for review of medical records before contract.* (Since the time of the first precontractual site review, the plan will have no members with records for review.) Some practitioner offices allow review of medical records if the reviewer signs a confidentiality statement. Others copy records and black out all identifying information. If the activity has been delegated to a review organization, the same set of records may be reviewed and results provided to numerous clients.
6. *For NCQA-accredited organizations, identification of high-volume specialists for recredentialing review.* This can be accomplished through claims data, benchmarking, or another method that can be validated by the organization.
7. *Time frames.* NCQA now accepts site visits conducted within the two years previous to the recredentialing decision.[26] This decision was made in an effort to reduce duplication of credentialing activity. Thus, an organization can now complete a single site visit and fulfill requirements related to other quality mandates.
8. *Scheduling.* A two-year scheduling matrix will allow work distribution and enhance productivity through the ability to schedule visits within the same geographic area.

EXPRESS PROCESS

Since temporary/provisional status does not comply with NCQA standards, a business decision may need to be made to develop an express process. Those practitioners meeting all criteria can be given participation consideration in a shorter time than the standard two to three months involved in the credentialing process. The basis of an express credentialing process should be

- shortened time frame from receipt of application to time of decision
- compliance with *all* criteria
- review of file outside of normal committee process

Figure 4–9 is a sample flowchart for an express credentials process. If it is used, a policy and procedure should be developed addressing each step. An organization using an express process will need to identify steps to obtain required information and verification within a short turnaround time. One option may be use of an online verification service. The policy and procedure should take into account all applicable regulatory requirements and accreditation standards.

ALLIED HEALTH PROFESSIONALS (AHPs)

For the purpose of this section, AHPs are defined as practitioners providing patient care who are licensed and are not physicians. Examples of practitioners in this category include social workers, clinical psychologists, nurse midwives, and physician assistants. In the ambulatory and managed care settings, it is necessary to determine a category for all practitioners. The "physician" category may include podiatrists, dentists, psychologists, and so forth, or these practitioners may be categorized as AHPs. The credentials plan should define practitioner categories and all types of practitioners that fall within each category. Once categorization has been completed, it is necessary to identify applicable regulatory and accreditation standards and the requirements related to the allied health category. NCQA has few requirements for AHPs, such as physician assistants and nurse midwives who are not categorized as primary caregivers. If an organization determines that its AHPs are to be credentialed, all of the same steps outlined to this point are applicable. All policies, procedures, and forms must include statements related to the category, and review and approval mechanisms must be clearly identified. Credentials information that is gathered and verified for AHPs includes

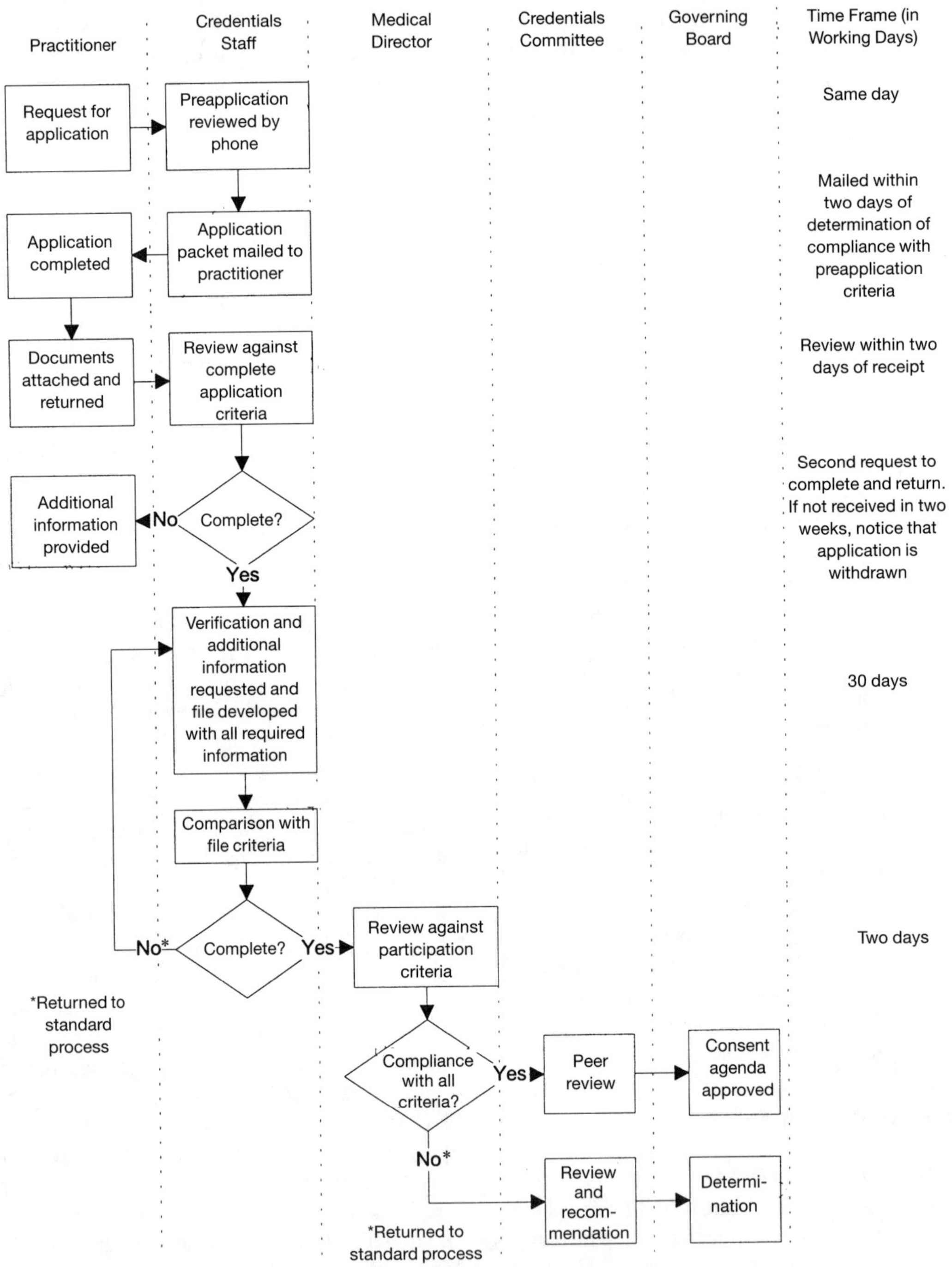

Figure 4–9 Credentials Flowchart for Express Process. Courtesy of C. Mobley & Associates, LLC, and Quality Management Options, LLC, Colorado Springs, Colorado.

- education and training
- health care affiliations
- professional practice
- licensure, registration, and certification information
- professional liability insurance
- NPDB as applicable if entity is eligible to query
- history of restrictions, sanctions, and loss of a license or certificate
- DEA (as applicable)
- felony conviction

FACILITY CREDENTIALING

In addition to credentialing practitioners, organizations that are seeking accreditation through NCQA must accredit their provider panel. As a result, hospitals, ambulatory surgical centers, home health agencies, and other facilities are included in the credentialing process. The scope of provider review includes all facilities with which the organizations contract. Therefore, reviewed organizations may include

- ambulance services
- birthing centers
- durable medical equipment providers
- hospitals—all sizes, types, and specialties
- freestanding laboratories
- local health departments/clinics (city or county)
- long-term care, including hospices, nursing homes, and skilled nursing facilities
- pharmacies
- centers and facilities offering radiology services
- residential care facilities for chemical dependency
- rural health clinics
- freestanding surgical centers
- sleep study centers

Key elements related to facility provider certification are

1. policies and procedures that include criteria and standards of participation
2. structure, accountability, and oversight
3. verification that the provider is in good standing with all applicable state and federal regulatory bodies
4. analysis and decision related to certification
5. review and certification before initial contracting and at least every two years thereafter

Information that can be verified and may be addressed by provider criteria and standards includes

- accreditation status
- Medicare/Medicaid certification
- Medicare/Medicaid sanction information
- state license verification
- specialty-specific certification

Many of the same options and decisions that apply in development of facility and medical record audits also apply to facility credentialing.

CHALLENGES, ISSUES, AND OPPORTUNITIES

Temporary Approval

Unlike hospitals, in the ambulatory and managed care settings, temporary approval is not used and does not comply with NCQA standards. This issue requires careful consideration if the credentialing process is delegated in full to a hospital that uses temporary privileges.

Assessing the Effectiveness and Productivity of Credentialing Activities

It is wise to periodically assess the effectiveness of credentialing activities and the productivity of all staff members. This can be accomplished through

- audits, which can be internal, external, or through the corporate office of a system or network

- benchmarking for best practice identification
- a quality initiative or reengineering project
- management productivity reports comparing current practices against standards
- comparison of all current activities against program plan policy and procedure and accreditation requirements
- networking with credentialing professionals in other organizations

---

NOTES

1. R. Rognehaugh, *The Managed Health Care Dictionary* (Gaithersburg, MD: Aspen Publishers, Inc., 1996), 10.
2. Rognehaugh, *Managed Health Care Dictionary*, 10.
3. P. Kongstvedt, *The Managed Health Care Handbook,* 2nd ed. (Gaithersburg, MD: Aspen Publishers, Inc., 1993), 13.
4. P. Kongstvedt, *The Managed Health Care Handbook,* 3rd ed. (Gaithersburg, MD: Aspen Publishers, Inc., 1996), 996.
5. Kongstvedt, *Managed Health Care Handbook,* 996.
6. Rognehaugh, *Managed Health Care Dictionary,* 96.
7. 42 U.S.C. §§ 11101–11152.
8. *Surveyor Guidelines for the Accreditation of Managed Care Organizations, 1998–99* (Washington, DC: National Committee for Quality Assurance, 1998).
9. *Standards for Networks and Ambulatory Care Accreditation* (Oakbrook Terrace, IL: Joint Commission on Accreditation of Healthcare Organizations, 1998).
10. *Surveyor Guidelines.*
11. *Developing a Policy and Procedure Manual for the Medical Staff Services Department* (Lombard, IL: National Association of Medical Staff Services, 1995).
12. *Developing a Policy and Procedure Manual,* 4.
13. Aspen Health Law Center, *Physician Organizations and Medical Staff Contracts, Rights, and Liabilities,* vol. 2 (Gaithersburg, MD: Aspen Publishers, Inc., 1996), 7:1–7:2.
14. Aspen Health Law Center, *Physician Organizations,* 7:4.
15. Kongstvedt, *Managed Health Care Handbook,* 851–863.
16. Aspen Health Law Center, *Physician Organizations,* 7:85–7:86.
17. No. 93-060950 (165th District Court, Harris County, Texas).
18. No. 93-065003 (80th District Court, Harris County, Texas).
19. Aspen Health Law Center, *Physician Organizations.*
20. Kongstredt, *Managed Health Care Handbook.*
21. B. Stama, "Legal Aspects of Credentialing" (presentation at the National Association of Medical Staff Services Institute, Kansas City, October 1997).
22. Strama, "Legal Aspects" (handout accompanying presentation), 34.
23. *Accreditation of Managed Care Organizations* (Washington, DC: National Committee for Quality Assurance, 1998).
24. Strama, "Legal Aspects" (handout accompanying presentation), 27.
25. *Accreditation of Managed Care Organizations.*
26. *Credentialing Standards Interpretation Update* (Washington, DC: National Committee for Quality Assurance, March 18, 1997).

Chapter 5

The Verification and Information-Gathering Process

OVERVIEW

The verification and information-gathering process may be the most time consuming of the credentialing steps. Once a credentialing application is received and determined to be complete, verification and information gathering are initiated. The purpose of these activities is to obtain information that will support the credentialing and privileging decisions. In most cases, the accrediting organization specifies information to be obtained and information that must be verified according to either standards or standard intent. The Joint Commission on Accreditation of Healthcare Organizations (Joint Commission) and the National Committee for Quality Assurance (NCQA) also identify how information is to be verified. It is the responsibility of the credentialing professional to request, obtain, review, and file all information required by the organization's bylaws, rules and regulations, plan, and/or policy and procedure. Because many items can be verified or obtained by numerous methods, it is important that the organization determine which is the most productive and cost-effective for their program, at the same time meeting the intent of the applicable accreditation standards.

Information in this chapter relates to credentialing standards for Joint Commission and NCQA-accredited/certified organizations only, since the two of them together represent the majority of accredited/certified health care–related organizations.

VERIFICATION AND INFORMATION-GATHERING ACTIVITIES

Verification is the process of validating information. Health care organizations usually validate, to the extent possible, the credentials of the practitioners and providers who submit applications. Most accrediting organizations, including the Joint Commission, NCQA, the American Osteopathic Association (AOA), and the Utilization Review Accreditation Commission (URAC), require that specific credentials and information be obtained, reviewed, and verified.

Process steps in a verification and information-gathering process are outlined in Figure 5–1.

A number of acceptable methods may be used for verification, including:

- *written*—the verifying entity forwards a written response to a request
- *copies*—a copy is submitted/obtained that is usually reproduced from an original document
- *verbal*—the verifying entity provides a verbal response (usually by phone) to a request
- *on line*—information is verified through use of an on-line service
- *visual inspection*—a document is provided for visual inspection but not for inclusion in the credentials file

Accreditation standards may require primary source verification and may specify the source(s)

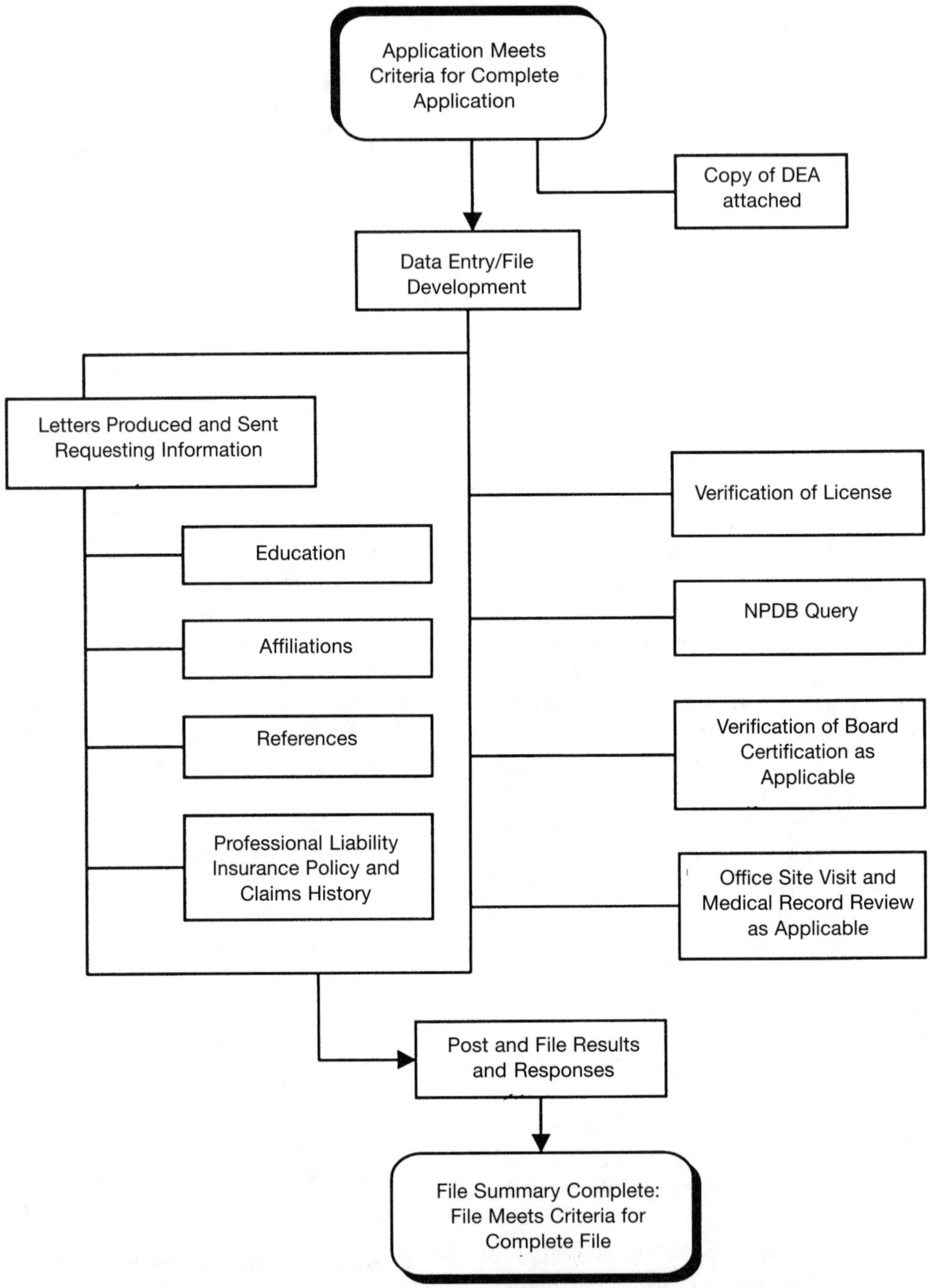

Note: DEA, Drug Enforcement Administration; NPDB, National Practitioner Data Bank.

Figure 5–1 Verification and Information-Gathering Flowchart. Courtesy of C. Mobley & Associates, LLC, and Quality Management Options, LLC, Colorado Springs, Colorado.

that can be considered primary. Most standards require that verifications be obtained in a timely manner, and NCQA specifies time frames in which they must be obtained. It is important that credentialing professionals understand the requirements, activities, and the options available for verification and information-gathering activities.

Primary Source Verification

Primary source verification is defined by NCQA as "the process in which an organization validates credentialing information from the organization that originally conferred or issued the credentialing element to the practitioner."[1] The Joint Commission defines it as "the original source of a specific credential that can verify the accuracy of a qualification reported by an individual healthcare practitioner."[2] When information is verified, a primary source is the preferred source, but at times verification from a primary source is not feasible or timely. For example, physicians trained in other countries may provide names, addresses, and phone numbers for educational institutions attended, but responses to requests may not be printed in English, may not be obtained in a timely manner, or may not be received at all. In this case, the Educational Commission for Foreign Medical Graduates (ECFMG) provides information that, although not primary source, is considered acceptable for verification of medical education by most organizations. Accreditation requirements relating to primary source verification differ from one accrediting agency to another. The credentialing professional should be cognizant of all verification requirements of applicable accreditation standards.

Verification and information may be obtained using one or a combination of resources. The entire process may be completed internally, or all or a portion of it may be outsourced. Credentials verification organizations (CVOs), centralized verification services (CVSs), and the American Medical Association (AMA) Physician Masterfile are currently the resources most commonly used to support this process.

The AMA Physician Masterfile

The AMA Physician Masterfile (also known as the AMA profile) meets some of the specific primary source verification requirements of the Accreditation Association for Ambulatory Health Care (AAAHC), the Joint Commission, URAC, and NCQA. AMA Physician Masterfiles are available for doctors of medicine (MDs) and most doctors of osteopathic medicine (DOs). Information on the Masterfile includes

- medical school (date of graduation)
- residency training history
- licenses granted (initial years)
- current licenses (status)
- national board certification
- American specialty board certification—American Board of Medical Specialties (ABMS) board, sub-board, etc. (initial year granted and expiration dates)
- disciplinary actions taken by state licensing boards and federal agencies, including Medicare/Medicaid
- Drug Enforcement Administration (DEA) status
- government service affiliation (as a physician)
- gender, birthplace, birth date[3]

The Physician Masterfile does not include any competency verification, so if it is used by Joint Commission–accredited hospitals, additional information will most likely need to be obtained.

Use of a Physician Masterfile may decrease costs of verification activities. A paper or diskette file can be obtained for $12 with a turnaround time of 10 to 15 business days and an express fax copy for $20 with a turnaround time of three business days.[4] Organizations may find a cost benefit analysis to be effective in determining the most productive and cost-effective method of verification.

CVO and CVS Profiles

Many CVOs (external to a system) and CVSs (internal to a system) verify information and then provide summary information about the verification (in the form of a profile) to clients. The profile indicates what elements were verified, gives the method used, date verified, and the source. Copies of any information related to competency, as well as questionable or negative findings, are usually forwarded with the profile. Some clients (usually managed care organizations) accept the profile and negative findings only, and other clients (usually hospitals) want copies of all information received in addition to a profile.

COMMUNICATION

Requests and responses may be obtained verbally, on line, or in a written form. Usually, any communication method is considered acceptable but must be documented.

Verbal versus Written Verification

Verbal verification (usually by telephone) is considered acceptable by most organizations. Documentation of verbal verification should include

- the element being verified
- the source, including name and title of person providing the verification
- the date the verification is obtained
- the name of the person requesting/obtaining verification

Verification by telephone is usually used on a limited basis because of the time involved and the expense of playing long-distance telephone tag. But it can be very effective when turnaround time becomes a factor. Exhibit 5–1 is a sample form used to document telephone verification. NCQA considers electronic credentialing files acceptable as long as appropriate evidence of verification within acceptable time periods can be identified.

Letters

Computer-generated standard form letters are the most common method used to request verifications not available on line. Exhibits 5–2 through 5–7 are sample letters used to request verification of license, medical education, board certification, affiliation, professional peer reference and training. If a credentialing software program containing standard verification letters is not available, letters can be developed and entered into word-processing software as templates.

When a letter or written documentation is obtained or returned, it should be stamped as "received" with the date. Some organizations also require an initial or signature of the person responsible for receipt and review/file/data entry or next activity step.

Considering the vast amount of paperwork involved in verification, the credentialing professional should not get bogged down in extra pieces of paper. Verification requests do not require a cover letter or a separate questionnaire. "Simple and quick" should always be the motto for this task. Inclusion of a self-addressed stamped return envelope increases the possibility that the information will be completed and returned.

On-Line Verification

Some specialty certification boards and state medical boards now have on-line verification available. If the credentialing professional has on-line capability, this verification option is worth pursuing. Exhibits 5–8 and 5–9 list boards with on-line verification services as of this writing.

Exhibit 5–1 Documentation of Telephone Verification

Practitioner Name: ______________________ Specialty: ______________

Element; Organization or Institution Contacted	Source: Name and Title	Verified by	Date and Time	Comments
Medical School: ______ Year graduated: ______			Date ______ Time ______	
Internship: ______ Dates: From ______ To: ______			Date ______ Time ______	
Residency: ______ Dates: From______ To: ______			Date ______ Time ______	
Medical License: ______ Number: ______ Effective Dates: ______			Date ______ Time ______	Restrictions/Actions ☐ Yes ☐ No
Hospital Privileges: ______ ______ Date of Appointment: ______			Date ______ Time ______	Status: ______
Board Certification: ______ Date Issued: ______			Date ______ Time ______	
Professional Liability Insurance: ______ ______ Policy Number: ______ Amounts of Coverage: ______ Dates of Coverage: ______			Date ______ Time ______	Claims History ☐ Yes ☐ No

Courtesy of C. Mobley & Associates, LLC, and Quality Management Options, LLC, Colorado Springs, Colorado.

Exhibit 5–2 License Verification Request

Letterhead

Date

Board of Medicine
Address
City, State, Zip

RE: ______________________________ (Physician)
______________________________ (License Number)

We have received an application from the above-referenced physician. Please provide information and confirmation regarding licensure. A Release from Liability statement and a self-addressed stamped envelope are enclosed for your response.

License number above is correct: Yes ___ No ___

License was granted: ______________________________
Date

The license will expire: ______________________________
Date

Is the license current and in good standing? Yes ___ No ___

Has the license for this physician ever been suspended or revoked or has any other action been related to it? Yes ___ No ___

If yes, please explain: ______________________________
____

Verified by: ______________________________

______________________________ ______________________________
Title Date

Courtesy of C. Mobley & Associates, LLC, and Quality Management Options, LLC, Colorado Springs, Colorado.

Exhibit 5–3 Medical Education Verification Request

Letterhead

Date

Registrar
Medical School
Address
City, State, Zip

RE: _________________________ (Physician)

We have received an application from the above-referenced physician. We require verification of the information provided by the applicant regarding your institution.

Thank you for your help. A self-addressed stamped envelope and a Release from Liability statement are enclosed.

Date of graduation: __________________________________

Degree obtained: ____________________________________

Comments: ____

____

____

Verified by: ____

____________________________________ ____________________________________
Title Date

Courtesy of C. Mobley & Associates, LLC, and Quality Management Options, LLC, Colorado Springs, Colorado.

Exhibit 5–4 Specialty Board Certification Verification Request

Letterhead

Date

American Board of ____________________
Address
City, State, Zip

RE: _______________________ (Physician)

We have received an application from the above-referenced physician. Please confirm the status of certification. A Release from Liability statement and a self-addressed stamped envelope are enclosed for your response.

Dr. __________________ was board certified by this organization on __________________ (Date)
in the specialty of __________________.

This certification will expire on ______________________ (Date) .

Verified by: ____

____________________________ ____________________________
Title Date

Courtesy of C. Mobley & Associates, LLC, and Quality Management Options, LLC, Colorado Springs, Colorado.

Exhibit 5–5 Hospital Affiliation Verification Request

Date

Hospital
Address
City, State, Zip

RE: ______________________________ (Physician)

We have received an application from the above-referenced physician stating that he/she has been affiliated with your hospital. Please provide confirmation of this information and comments regarding your experience.

Your help is greatly appreciated. A Release from Liability statement and a self-addressed stamped envelope are enclosed.

Dr. ____________________________ was granted privileges on ____________________________
Name Date

He/she has current privileges: Yes ___ No ___

If no, please give date and reason: ____

Staff category: ____

Were privileges or medical staff membership ever suspended, revoked, or limited? Yes ___ No ___

If yes, please explain: ____

Please indicate competence:	Outstanding/ Very Good	Average	Fair/Poor
Knowledge and understanding in his/her field	_____	_____	_____
Interpersonal relationships with patient, staff and peers	_____	_____	_____
Maintenance of medical records	_____	_____	_____

Comments (including explanation of average, fair, or poor checks): ______________________________

Signed: ____________________ Title: __________ Date: __________

Courtesy of C. Mobley & Associates, LLC, and Quality Management Options, LLC, Colorado Springs, Colorado.

Exhibit 5–6 Professional Peer Reference Request

Date

Name
Address
City, State, Zip

RE: ________________________________ (Physician)

Dear Dr. ______________________:

We have received an application from ________________________ in which the physician lists you as a reference. Your completion of the following questionnaire will be greatly appreciated.

A Release from Liability statement and a self-addressed stamped envelope is enclosed. Thank you for your help and attention.

1. Number of years I have known this physician: ______________

2. We are: social friends ___; friends from medical school, internship, or residency ___; professional associates ___; other ____

3. For the following categories, I would rate this physician to be:

	Outstanding/ Very Good	Average	Fair/Poor
Ethical conduct	____	____	____
Sense of responsibility	____	____	____
Medical knowledge	____	____	____
Professional judgment and skills	____	____	____
Recordkeeping	____	____	____
Patient management	____	____	____
Physician/patient relationship	____	____	____

4. My perception of this physician's dedication, integrity, and honesty is: ____________________
____

5. I am aware of problems that might affect this physician's ability to care for patients related to:

Health/Disability	Yes ___	No ___
Emotional stability	Yes ___	No ___
Alcohol or drugs	Yes ___	No ___

Other ____

6. Additional comments (including yes answers and average, fair, or poor evaluation): ___________
____

Signature ______________________________ Date ______________________________

Courtesy of C. Mobley & Associates, LLC, and Quality Management Options, LLC, Colorado Springs, Colorado.

Exhibit 5–7 Training Verification Request

Letterhead

Date

Program Director
Address
City, State, Zip

RE: ______________________________ (Physician)

Dear Dr. ______________________:

We have received an application from ______________________ in which the physician indicates completion of (internship, residency, fellowship) at your institution. A copy of the clinical privileges requested is enclosed. Your completion of the questionnaire will be greatly appreciated.

A Release from Liability statement and a self-addressed stamped envelope are enclosed. Thank you for your help and attention to this matter.

1. __________(program) from_____(mo/yr) to____(mo/yr).

2. Was program completed? Yes____ No____

3. For the following categories, I would rate this physician to be:

	Outstanding/ Very Good	Average	Fair/Poor
Basic clinical knowledge	____	____	____
Competence and skill	____	____	____
Professional judgment	____	____	____
Medical recordkeeping	____	____	____
Patient management	____	____	____
Cooperativeness	____	____	____
Ethical conduct	____	____	____
Ability to understand/speak English	____	____	____
Sense of responsibility	____	____	____

If your evaluation is fair/poor, please clarify with further comments: ____________________
____

4. I am aware of problems that might affect this physician's ability to care for patients related to:

Health/disability	Yes____	No____
Emotional stability	Yes____	No____
Alcohol or drugs	Yes____	No____
Other	Yes____	No____

continues

Exhibit 5–7 continued

5. Has the applicant ever been subject to any corrective or disciplinary action such as admonition, reprimand, suspension, or termination? Yes ____ No ____

6. Has the applicant ever been a defendant in a medical malpractice action? Yes ____ No ____

7. Is the applicant qualified for the privileges requested? Yes ____ No ____

8. REPORT IS BASED ON:
   A. Close personal observation _____
   B. General impression _____
   C. Composite of evaluations by supervisors _____
   D. Other (explain below)

9. RECOMMENDATION:
   A. Recommend highly without reservation _____
   B. Recommend as qualified and competent _____
   C. Recommend with some reservation _____
   D. No comment _____
   E. Do not recommend _____

10. Additional comments (including explanation of any adverse answers): ____________________
____
____
____

Signature: ______________________ Date: ______________________

Title: ______________________ Printed Name: ______________________

Courtesy of C. Mobley & Associates, LLC, and Quality Management Options, LLC, Colorado Springs, Colorado.

TIME FRAMES AND TRACKING SYSTEM

Organizations should identify turnaround time standards for response to requests for verification or information, as well as a procedure for second requests on follow-up actions. One missing piece of information can stop the entire credentialing procedure if it is vital to the decision-making process. A tickler file or tracking system should be in place to ensure that all requests are tracked and that a follow-up action occurs for any information not received within the time frame specified by the organizational standards. The procedure should also outline consequences or alternatives if a response is not received. Some organizations enlist practitioner support in obtaining information.

NCQA has very specific requirements for verification time frames that are outlined in their scoring guidelines. NCQA surveyors review dates of verifications that require a time frame and determine if they were obtained within the 180 days before the credentials decision. If a written verification is obtained, the 180-day time limit starts with the date on the letter or document, not the date the information is received. If a managed care organization delegates to a CVO, NCQA standards require that verification be no older than 120 days at the time it is submitted to

Exhibit 5–8 Medical Specialty Boards with On-Line Verification

American Board of Family Practice	www.abfp.org
American Board of Internal Medicine	www.abim.org
American Board of Medical Genetics	www.faseb.org/genetics/abmg/abmgmenu/htm
American Board of Pediatrics	www.abp.org
American Board of Preventive Medicine	http://members.aol.com/abmnet/indes.html

Exhibit 5–9 State Medical Boards with On-Line Verification Available

Arizona	www.docboard.org/doc_find/doc_find.htm
California	www.docgoard.org/doc_find/doc_find.htm
Colorado	www.dora.state.co.us/medical/main_verification-htm
Florida	www.fdhc.state.cl.us
Georgia	www.sos.state.ga.us
Indiana (password registration required)	www.ai.org./hpb
Iowa	www.docboard.org/doc_find/doc_find.htm
Kansas	www.docboard.org/doc_find/doc_find.htm
Maine	www.docboard.org/doc_find/doc_find.htm
Maryland	www.docboard.org/doc_find/doc_find.htm
Massachusetts	www.docboard.org/doc_find/doc_find.htm
Minnesota	www.docboard.org/doc_find/doc_find.htm
Missouri	www.ecodev.state.mo.us/pr.healarts
New York	www.nysed.gov
North Carolina	www.docboard.org/doc_find/doc_find.htm
Ohio	www.state.oh.us/med/
Oklahoma (DO)	www.docboard.org/doc_find/doc_find.htm
Oklahoma (MD)	www.osbmls.state.ok.us
Texas	www.docboard.org/doc_find/doc_find.htm
Utah	www.commerce.state.ut.us
Vermont	www.docboard.org/doc_find/doc_find.htm
Virginia	www.dhp.state.va.us

Note: Information also can be accessed through www.docfinder.com.

the managed care organization; this allows 60 days for review and decision by the managed care organization.

VERIFICATION AND INFORMATION-GATHERING ELEMENTS

An organization may obtain information or verification for numerous elements. Some are directed by accreditation standards, others by regulation, and many by standard practice or needs of the organization.

Verification Guidelines for the Joint Commission and NCQA

Table 5–1 outlines the verification guidelines for the Joint Commission and NCQA. As previously stated, verification and information-gathering activities are the most time-consuming activity of the credentialing process. It is important to carefully review regulatory and accreditation requirements to ensure compliance. Those items not required should be reviewed on a periodic basis. Identification of the value added, cost to produce and maintain, and reason the information is obtained should be included in the evaluation.

The elements most commonly verified or obtained are:

- ability to perform privileges requested/ability to perform essential functions
- application for membership/application or reapplication form
- board certification status
- civil and criminal history
- clinical privileges
- continuing medical education
- disciplinary actions
- DEA certificate and State Pharmacy certificate
- hospital references
- licensure
- malpractice history
- medical record review
- Medicare and Medicaid sanction activity
- member satisfaction/member complaint information
- NPDB query
- office assessment/site review
- peer references
- professional liability insurance coverage
- quality performance improvement activities/data
- training—professional and postgraduate school
- training—internship, fellowship, residency, postdoctoral
- utilization management
- work history/experience

Following is a grid, for each item listed above, of information that is commonly verified or obtained. The reader should reference the most recent accreditation standards, as they may have changed. The verification and information elements are outlined to include information related to

- purpose/description
- sources for verification or information (Unless otherwise indicated, sources pertain to both Joint Commission and NCQA.)
- Joint Commission and NCQA accreditation requirements/guidelines
- frequency of verifying/obtaining
- applicability
- comments/considerations/issues

Table 5–1 Initial Verification Guidelines of the Joint Commission and NCQA

Verification	*Joint Commission Guidelines*	*NCQA Guidelines*
Education		
Medical school	Yes	If no residency or board certification
Internship	Yes	No
Residency	Yes	If program completed and no board certification
Fellowship	Yes	No
ECFMG	If applicable	If no U.S. residency completed and graduated from a foreign medical school after 1986
Licensure and certification	Yes	Yes
Current appropriate state licensure	Per medical staff bylaws, rules, and regulations	
DEA certificate	Per medical staff bylaws, rules, and regulations	As applicable
State pharmacy certificate		If applicable
Specialty board certification	If applicable	If stated on application
Professional liability Insurance coverage	Per medical staff bylaws, rules, and regulations	Yes
Experience	For evaluation of privileges	No
Work history	No	Yes (stated on application or CV. Gaps over one year should be clarified in writing.)
Malpractice history of claims resulting in settlement or judgment on behalf of practitioner	Per medical staff bylaws, rules, and regulations	Yes
Competence/ability to perform clinical functions	Per medical staff bylaws rules, and regulations	No
All hospitals		
Individuals personally acquainted with professional and clinical performance	Yes	No
Continuing medical/ professional education	Per medical staff bylaws, rules, and regulations	No
Affiliations	Per medical staff bylaws, rules, and regulations	Status of clinical privileges at primary hospital

continues

Table 5–1 continued

Information and Data Gathering	*Joint Commission Guidelines*	*NCQA Guidelines*
Completed application for membership	To include a statement that – no health problems exist that could affect practice – practitioner agrees to abide by bylaws and rules and regulations and to provide continuous care for patients – practitioner consents to inspection of records/ documents and interview (if requested) – any challenges to any licensure or registration, or voluntary or involuntary relinquishment of such licensure or registration – any voluntary or involuntary termination of medical staff membership, or limitation reduction, or loss of clinical privileges	To include statements regarding – reasons for any inability to perform essential functions (with or without accommodation) – lack of present illegal drug use – history of loss of license and felony convictions – history of loss or limitations of privileges or disciplinary activity – attestation to correctness and completeness of the application
National Practitioner Data Bank query	Yes, per Health Care Quality Improvement Act of 1986	Yes
Sanctions or limitations on licensure	Yes	Yes
Medicare/Medicaid sanction activity	Per medical staff bylaws, rules, and regulations	Yes
Confirmation that no health problems exist that could affect practice	Yes	See statements to be included in application above
Structured site review of offices of all potential primary care and ob/gyn practitioners	No	Yes
Medical recordkeeping evaluation of all potential primary care and ob/gyn practitioners	No	Yes

Courtesy of C. Mobley & Associates, LLC, and Quality Management Options, LLC, Colorado Springs, Colorado.

Ability To Perform Privileges Requested/Ability To Perform Essential Functions

<table>
<tr><th colspan="2">PURPOSE/DESCRIPTION</th></tr>
<tr><td colspan="2">To evaluate and/or determine if any health problems exist that could affect clinical practice and whether further corroboration or investigation is needed on the basis of the information provided.</td></tr>
<tr><th>SOURCES FOR VERIFICATION/INFORMATION</th><th>ACCREDITATION</th></tr>
<tr><td><ul><li>Questions included on the application/reapplication forms and information must be completed by the applicant.</li><li>At appointment, the answers must be confirmed by a training program director/or chief of services or chief of staff at another hospital where applicant has privileges or a currently licensed physician designated by the hospital (Joint Commission).</li><li>At reappointment, the answers must be confirmed at least by a countersignature by the department director (or by the chief of staff at a nondepartmentalized hospital) (Joint Commission).</li></ul></td><td><ul><li>The Joint Commission requires that the applicant's ability to perform privileges be evaluated.</li><li>NCQA does not require verification, but a statement is to be included on the appointment and reappointment form regarding any inability to perform the essential functions of the position, with or without accommodation.</li></ul></td></tr>
<tr><th>FREQUENCY</th><th>APPLICABLE FOR</th></tr>
<tr><td><ul><li>At initial review</li><li>At reappointment/recredential or reapproval</li></ul></td><td><ul><li>Medical staff and allied health practitioners (AHPs) as applicable (hospital)</li><li>Physicians and other licensed independent practitioners (LIPs) (managed care)</li></ul></td></tr>
<tr><th colspan="2">ADDITIONAL COMMENTS, CONSIDERATIONS, AND ISSUES</th></tr>
<tr><td colspan="2"><ul><li>Both accreditation organizations address the Americans with Disabilities Act (ADA) with regard to this requirement; statements made on an application may vary according to applicable legal requirements of the ADA (NCQA), and allowing the hospital to determine the applicability of the ADA to its medical staff will not be inconsistent with that hospital's efforts to comply with the (Joint Commission). (See also information on the ADA in Chapter 9 of this book.)</li><li>In this area, NCQA also asks for a statement on the application regarding lack of present illegal drug use, with the same notation regarding the ADA. It has issued a classification regarding an acceptable statement to fulfill this requirement that reads, "Is there anything that may currently adversely affect your ability to exercise, or would require an accommodation in order for you to safely and competently exercise, the clinical privileges requested?"</li><li>Information may be obtained by use of questions on the application/reapplication forms or comprehensive health questionnaire. It is up to the organization how much or how little information they will require and how they will interpret the ADA requirements. (The ADA refers to employees, and in many cases health care practitioners are not employees.)</li><li>The Joint Commission standards related to this requirement include any LIPs with clinical privileges. The hospital determines if it is going to ask the same questions of an AHP who is not independently licensed and whether it will request confirmation by any listed reference or by a supervisor or sponsoring physician.</li></ul></td></tr>
</table>

Application for Membership/Application or Reapplication Form

PURPOSE/DESCRIPTION	
To obtain data and information from the practitioner. All practitioners must complete a standardized, approved application form before initiation of the credentialing process.	
SOURCES FOR VERIFICATION/INFORMATION	**ACCREDITATION**
The application form and related attachments provided are compared with information and verifications obtained by the organization.	Both the Joint Commission and NCQA require an initial application and specify the components to be included (see below).
FREQUENCY	**APPLICABLE FOR**
• At initial review/appointment • At reappointment, recredential, or reapproval	• Medical staff and AHPs as applicable (hospital) • Physicians, other LIPs, and providers (managed care) • Providers (managed care)
ADDITIONAL COMMENTS, CONSIDERATIONS, AND ISSUES	
• The Joint Commission requires that the medical staff bylaws, rules and regulations, or policies define the information on the application to include challenges to or relinquishments of licensure or registration; termination; limitation, reduction, or loss of privileges at another hospital; and involvement in a professional liability action. • NCQA requires an application that includes a statement regarding reasons for any inability to perform the essential functions of the position, lack of present illegal drug use, history of loss or limitation of license and/or privileges or disciplinary activity, felony convictions, and an attestation. A faxed, photocopied, scanned or electronically reproduced attestation is acceptable to NCQA, but a stamped signature is not. • At reappointment or recredentialing, many organizations will use a computer software program profile that is sent to each practitioner in lieu of a blank form to be completed. The practitioner makes any corrections to the form, attests to its accuracy with no corrections or as corrected, and returns it to the appropriate source.	

Board Certification Status

PURPOSE/DESCRIPTION	
To verify that a practitioner is board certified, has recertified, or has been accepted to sit for the boards in the appropriate specialty.	
SOURCES FOR VERIFICATION/INFORMATION	**ACCREDITATION**
• ABMS Directory of Board Certified Medical Specialists (Compendium) • AMA Physician Masterfile	• The Joint Commission does not require board certification, but if a physician is certified or "qualified," the intent state-

• AOA Physician Masterfile or AOA Director of Osteopathic Physicians (NCQA) • Confirmation from appropriate specialty (written or verbal) • Confirmation from the state licensing agency if the managed care organization provides recent evidence that the state agency conducts primary verification of board statutes (NCQA) • Primary source website (NCQA)	ments for the standards related to relevant training, experience, and competence mention board certification/qualification and the sources to verify. • NCQA does not require board certification but does require primary source verification if the practitioner is board certified. The only exception is that board certification is not applicable for chiropractors.
FREQUENCY	**APPLICABLE FOR**
• At initial review/appointment • At reappointment, recredentialing, or reapproval if recertification was due to expire during cycle	• Medical staff (hospitals) • Physicians (managed care)

ADDITIONAL COMMENTS, CONSIDERATIONS, AND ISSUES

- NCQA requires that if a document source (e.g., ABMS) is used for verification, this source must be the most current available. The verification date is the date that the source is accessed. This is good for as long as the certification is current.
- Organizations will need to monitor those specialties whose boards require recertification. This information is available from each specialty board.
- Most specialty boards do not acknowledge the term *board eligible,* but it is still used by some hospitals in bylaws and/or privilege delineation. The term is often used by older practitioners who have completed a training program but have not chosen to sit for the boards. Many boards specify a time period after which the practitioner is no longer eligible to apply to take the boards without some continuing medical education and in some cases a formal training program of some length determined by the board. Because of these time elements (and additional requirements in some cases), it is difficult to track eligibility.
- Some boards require a waiting period of several years after postgraduate training is completed before a physician can qualify to apply to take the boards. Therefore, if a hospital's clinical privileges are worded such that board certification is required, it must also identify the time line to take the boards and/or become certified. If this is the case, it must also define what happens if the boards are taken and failed. This may not necessarily mean that privileges are revoked, but the physician may require additional medical education, additional proctoring, a reduction in privileges previously granted, and/or a focused peer review to determine equivalent qualifications.
- NCQA considers a letter from the Accreditation Council for Graduate Medical Education (ACGME) acceptable to confirm foreign board certification if the MCO also has a letter from the ACGME that states the foreign board primary source verifies training and education for each physician.

Civil and Criminal History

PURPOSE/DESCRIPTION	
Some states require completion of a form and/or an inquiry regarding past criminal history or convictions as part of employment and/or the credentialing process.	
SOURCES FOR VERIFICATION/INFORMATION	**ACCREDITATION**
• State-specific records • Statement of applicant on the application form • Criminal record check by an investigative firm	• The Joint Commission and NCQA accreditation standards do not specifically address verification of civil and criminal history.
FREQUENCY	**APPLICABLE FOR**
• Per state-specific statutes • Per organization bylaws or policies	• State-specific statutes indicate applicability.
ADDITIONAL COMMENTS, CONSIDERATIONS, AND ISSUES	
• A state-specific requirement to obtain a criminal history may also include a requirement to obtain a civil and/or financial crime history. • A release form or a disclaimer that a criminal history will not necessarily disqualify a job applicant may be required. • Pending Health Care Financing Administration (HCFA) changes to Medicare conditions of participation for home health care require a criminal background check for home health aides. All Medicare conditions of participation should be checked for applicability.	

Clinical Privileges

PURPOSE/DESCRIPTION	
To verify that a practitioner has clinical privileges in good standing and/or to obtain documentation to support a request for specific clinical privileges.	
SOURCES FOR VERIFICATION/INFORMATION	**ACCREDITATION**
• Hospitals where clinical privileges have been granted (written or verbal with documentation) • Training programs (written or verbal with documentation) • Programs that offer limited training for specific privileges, such as new procedures (certificate of completion or letter outlining training as defined in criteria)	• The Joint Commission requires primary source verification of current competence in teaching facilities or other hospitals for clinical performance, partly related to clinical privileges granted at those institutions. • NCQA requires verification from the practitioner's primary inpatient admitting facility that the practitioner has clinical privileges in good standing, including any

	restrictions on the scope of privileges. NCQA does not require the practitioner to have clinical privileges, only that they be verified if they exist.
FREQUENCY	**APPLICABLE FOR**
• At initial review/appointment • At reappointment, recredential, or reapproval or for renewal or revision (addition) of individual clinical privileges	• Medical staff and AHPs who have clinical privileges (hospital) • Physicians and other independent practitioners who have or are requesting admitting privileges (managed care)

ADDITIONAL COMMENTS, CONSIDERATIONS, AND ISSUES
• Also see the section "Hospital References" below for additional information. • If a practitioner does not have clinical privileges, the managed care organization should have a written statement describing the inpatient coverage arrangement and should credential/recredential those providing the coverage. • NCQA does not require verification of hospital privileges for dentists if they have a strictly office-based practice. • The 180-day verification time limit by NCQA applies to this element (120 days for NCQA-certified CVO).

Continuing Medical Education

PURPOSE/DESCRIPTION
To identify and collect information relating to continuing medical education as an adjunct to maintaining clinical skills and current competence.

SOURCES FOR VERIFICATION/INFORMATION	**ACCREDITATION**
• List of continuing medical education courses/hours that is submitted in those states that require continuing medical education hours to renew a license • List provided by hospital to practitioner of continuing medical education activity provided by the hospital • Copies of continuing education units (CEU) certificates from courses attended • List of continuing medical education courses/hours submitted to AMA for Physician Recognition Award	• The Joint Commission requires that individuals with clinical privileges participate in continuing education. • NCQA does not have a continuing medical education requirement.

FREQUENCY	APPLICABLE FOR
At reappointment, recredential, or reapproval, or for renewal or revision of individual clinical privileges	• Medical staff and AHPs who have clinical privileges (hospitals)
ADDITIONAL COMMENTS, CONSIDERATIONS, AND ISSUES	
• At least some of the continuing medical education that practitioners participate in should relate to the privileges granted. • Physicians may apply for the AMA's Physician Recognition Award, which requires 150 hours of continuing medical education for a three-year period. The list that is sent to the AMA may be submitted with a reappointment and application as long as it includes a time period that coincides with the two years being evaluated at reappointment. The AMA award certificate itself should not be accepted as evidence of continuing medical education, since there is no way to evaluate the type of education received (i.e., whether anything learned relates directly to the clinical privileges granted). The same is the case for those state-licensing boards that require CEUs to renew a license. The list that is submitted to the state is acceptable. Department chairs can then compare CEUs with the privileges requested.	

Disciplinary Actions

PURPOSE/DESCRIPTION	
A regulatory and accreditation requirement to identify practitioners and providers with disciplinary actions (sanctions and/or limitations on scope of practice) that might affect ability to render competent, quality patient care/services.	
SOURCES FOR VERIFICATION/INFORMATION	**ACCREDITATION**
• State licensing boards • Organization taking action • National Practitioner Data Bank (NPDB) • Federation of State Medical Boards (FSMB) database • AMA Physician Masterfile (Joint Commission)	• The Joint Commission references medical staff bylaw requirements, the NPDB query, and verification of state license. • NCQA requires that applicants provide information regarding history of loss or limitation of previous five years or disciplinary activity; obtain information from state board or FSMB; complete NPDB query; and check for Medicaid/Medicare sanction.
FREQUENCY	**APPLICABLE FOR**
• At initial review/appointment • At reappointment, recredential, or reapproval	• Medical staff (hospitals) • Physicians and other LIPs (managed care) • Others required by statute, accreditation, or organization bylaws, policies, and procedures • Providers (if specified in policy)

ADDITIONAL COMMENTS, CONSIDERATIONS, AND ISSUES
• An NPDB query may reveal disciplinary actions. This information should be clarified with the practitioner and the organization that imposed the action before any decision about the possible impact on privileges or affiliation. • Primary source verification of disciplinary actions is required only for state board actions. • NCQA does not currently recognize NPDB as an acceptable verification source for state board queries and actions. • The 180-day verification time limit by NCQA applies to this element (120 days for a CVO).

Drug Enforcement Administration (DEA) Certificate and State Pharmacy Certificate

PURPOSE/DESCRIPTION	
To verify practitioner registration with the DEA and, if applicable, with the state pharmaceutical licensing agency. A DEA certificate authorizes a practitioner to prescribe controlled substances. Some, but not all, states also require a state pharmacy license.	
SOURCES FOR VERIFICATION/INFORMATION	**ACCREDITATION**
• Copy of certificate from practitioner (NCQA) • Documented visual inspection of original certificate (NCQA) • Confirmation with CDS (NCQA) • National Technical Information Service tape: printout or on line with documentation (NCQA) • Confirmation with the state pharmaceutical licensing agency, where applicable (NCQA)	• The Joint Commission requires primary source verification of current license or registration, but its intent statements reference only state licensure. The only standard reference to DEA is the requirement for the applicant to provide any information on previously successful or currently pending challenges on DEA license or the voluntary relinquishment of such license. • NCQA does not require primary source verification of current certificate or registration.
FREQUENCY	**APPLICABLE FOR**
• At initial review • At reappointment, recredential, or reapproval—DEA must be current at time of peer review (NCQA) • At time of expiration—every three years	• Every practitioner who administers, dispenses, or prescribes a controlled substance must be registered with the DEA.

ADDITIONAL COMMENTS, CONSIDERATIONS, AND ISSUES

- A DEA certificate may be obtained by a physician, dentist, podiatrist, or other practitioner who is authorized by the jurisdiction in which he or she is licensed.
- Documentation of visual inspection should include date of inspection and name or initial of inspector.
- In the hospital setting, the hospital pharmacy may maintain copies of the DEA certificate or other accepted form of DEA verification.
- NCQA does not require that the 180-day verification limit be applied to DEA verification, but the DEA must be effective at the time of the credentialing decision.
- State pharmacy certificates are not applicable for chiropractors or dentists; DEA is not applicable for chiropractors, but it may be for dentists.
- A practitioner may request registration for all or part of the five DEA schedules. If all five schedules are not listed (II, IIN, III, IIIN, IV, and V), the practitioner may not prescribe in unlisted categories. Most organizations require that practitioners have all schedules.
- If a practitioner dispenses and/or administers narcotics in more than one office, he or she must have a DEA for each location. Only one certificate (copy) is generally collected or verified.

Definition of DEA Schedule Codes

- *Schedule I:* No accepted medical use in the United States (e.g., LSD)
- *Schedule II:* Substances with high abuse potential and with severe psychic or physical dependence liability (e.g., opium, morphine, codeine)
- *Schedule II N:* Non-narcotics with high abuse potential (e.g., amphetamine, pentobarbital)
- *Schedule III:* Substances with less abuse potential than those in Schedules I and II (e.g., suppository forms of secobarbital)
- *Schedule III N:* Non-narcotics with less abuse potential than those in Schedules I and II (e.g., derivatives or barbituric acid)
- *Schedule IV:* Substances with less abuse potential than those in Schedule III (e.g., barbital, phenobarbital)
- *Schedule V:* Substances with less abuse potential than those in Schedule IV (e.g., narcotics used for antitussive and antidiarrheal purposes)

Hospital References

PURPOSE/DESCRIPTION

To verify current competence and/or to verify that a practitioner has clinical privileges in good standing in a hospital.

SOURCES FOR VERIFICATION/INFORMATION	ACCREDITATION
• Letters from hospitals • Documented verbal hospital references • Hospital roster, provided that it includes a cover letter stating that the practitioner is in good standing and including any restriction on the scope of privileges (or separate letter on restrictions, etc. is attached)	• The Joint Commission requires verification of current competence from authoritative sources on applicant's scope and level of performance. Hospitals can comment on clinical performance in general terms, satisfactory discharge of professional obliga-

	tions as a medical staff member, and ethical types of operative procedures/complications/outcomes for surgeons of record and applicant's clinical judgment and skills. • NCQA requires oral or written confirmation from practitioner's primary inpatient facility that the practitioner has clinical privileges in good standing.
FREQUENCY	**APPLICABLE FOR**
• At initial review/appointment • At reappointment, recredential, or reapproval	• Medical staffs and AHPs with clinical privileges; other AHPs optional (hospital) • Physicians and other LIPs (managed care)

ADDITIONAL COMMENTS, CONSIDERATIONS, AND ISSUES

- Hospitals have the option of whether to request letters of reference from hospitals at reappointment. Some request letters only if a practitioner is not active at the hospital and they have little or no performance activity to evaluate. Other hospitals want to obtain references from all current hospital affiliations. The argument for not obtaining references from all hospitals is that any required adverse action would be contained in an NPDB report, and the hospitals would not be gaining much by also soliciting information from other hospitals. The other argument is that many hospitals use a generic letter for routine responses, which provides very little information. The best methods to obtain the needed valuable information are asking hospitals to complete a questionnaire that provides more specific information than a generic letter (assuming that the hospital will complete the questionnaire); asking the appropriate questions on the application regarding actions taken by hospitals; and obtaining NPDB reports.
- As verification requests for hospital references increase, and because NCQA addresses the acceptable use of rosters (with qualifications), many hospitals are now willing to provide a partial roster or list of medical staff to requesting organizations. The rosters/lists should contain the practitioner's name, license (MD, DO, etc.), appointment date, and staff category. Any practitioners on the list with adverse actions should be underlined or otherwise marked with a notation in the cover letter that a practitioner release is required before further information is provided. Some hospitals do not want to use rosters and/or require a release form for every practitioner. Other hospitals are comfortable with providing the very basic/in-good-standing information suggested above without a signed release. Some of these hospitals include in their "consent to release of information" a statement like "From time to time, this hospital receives requests from other health care organizations to verify your membership/clinical privileges inclusive in a roster provided by this hospital. Your signature on this release allows that information to be released. If any adverse action has been taken against you, a specific release signed by you will be required from the requesting hospital." Check with legal counsel for assistance in wording the release.
- NCQA states that verification of privileges at a designated participating hospital may be interpreted by the MCO as verification of status at the MCO's designated participating hospital or the primary admitting hospital of the practitioner.

Licensure

<table>
<tr><th colspan="2">PURPOSE/DESCRIPTION</th></tr>
<tr><td colspan="2">To verify current licensure to practice and previous current state sanctions, restrictions, and/or limitations on scope of practice.</td></tr>
<tr><th>SOURCES FOR VERIFICATION/INFORMATION</th><th>ACCREDITATION</th></tr>
<tr><td>• State licensing board via printout, letter, modem, verbal (documented), or licensing board reports for license and/or disciplinary actions depending upon state resources available
• At reappointment, viewing the applicant's current original license (Joint Commission)
• FSMB (disciplinary actions)
• AMA Physician Masterfile (Joint Commission)</td><td>• The Joint Commission requires verification of current licensure, including any disciplinary actions. Also, each applicant (for appointment and reappointment) must provide information related to previously successful or currently pending challenges or voluntary relinquishment of licensure.
• NCQA requires verification of current licensure, previous or current sanctions, restrictions, and/or limitations on scope of practice. Review of information should be for a five-year period and should include all states.</td></tr>
<tr><th>FREQUENCY</th><th>APPLICABLE FOR</th></tr>
<tr><td>• At initial review, appointment
• At reappointment, recredential, or reapproval
• At time of expiration (see issues below)</td><td>• Medical staff and licensed AHPs (hospitals)
• Physicians and other licensed practitioners (managed care)</td></tr>
<tr><th colspan="2">ADDITIONAL COMMENTS, CONSIDERATIONS, AND ISSUES</th></tr>
<tr><td colspan="2">• The 180-day verification time limit by NCQA applies to the element (120 days for CVO certified by NCQA), and the license must be in effect at the time of the credentialing decision.
• Each state has different methods available for verification and reporting of disciplinary actions. And some states license everyone through one board, while others have a licensing board for each category.
• If a practitioner is licensed in more than one state, each current license should be verified or at least the FSMB should be queried and/or the NPDB report should be reviewed (if the organization is qualified to do this) for any disciplinary action.
• Licenses expire at different times (annually, on birth date, etc.) and are valid for different lengths of time (one to three years usually).
• Even though licenses are verified at initial appointment and reappointment/recredentialing, licenses should be reverified (with the state licensing board) at time of expiration. Many organizations collect copies of a license but a copy from the practitioner does not constitute verification.
• The Joint Commission requires evidence of a current verified license at all times.</td></tr>
</table>

Malpractice History

PURPOSE/DESCRIPTION	
To identify the professional liability claims history of a practitioner or provider.	
SOURCES FOR VERIFICATION/INFORMATION	**ACCREDITATION**
• Malpractice carrier • NPDB • The application form identifies history	• The Joint Commission requires that bylaws, etc. define the information to be obtained related to professional liability action(s) and, at a minimum, final judgments or settlements are reported. • NCQA requires verification of malpractice settlements or judgments paid by or on behalf of the practitioner.
FREQUENCY	**APPLICABLE FOR**
• At initial review/appointment • At reappointment, recredential, or reapproval	• Medical staff (hospitals) • Physicians and other LIPs (managed care) • Providers (see below)
ADDITIONAL COMMENTS, CONSIDERATIONS, AND ISSUES	
• NCQA requires either an NPDB query or written confirmation of the past five years of malpractice settlement history from the malpractice carrier; NPDB is not recognized as a source for dentists, podiatrists, or chiropractors. • The 180-day verification time limit by NCQA applies to this element (120 days for a CVO). • At the time of reappointment or recredentialing, only history for the past cycle is applicable; information reviewed previously should not be re-reviewed. • If the past five years include residency or fellowship covered by hospital insurance policy, it is not required by NCQA that information be obtained from that carrier. • A practitioner does not have to be convicted of malpractice for an organization to use malpractice information as part of the credentialing decision. • If a provider is not accredited, the organization's standards of participation may address malpractice history even though Joint Commission does not require verification of the malpractice history; industry standard includes verification either through the malpractice carrier or the NPDB.	

Medical Record Review

PURPOSE/DESCRIPTION
Evaluation of medical recordkeeping practices and practitioner documentation in medical records.

<table>
<tr><th>SOURCES FOR VERIFICATION/INFORMATION</th><th>ACCREDITATION</th></tr>
<tr><td>• Medical records—hospitals
• Medical records—physician office (NCQA)
• On-site evaluation of recordkeeping practices—physician office (NCQA)</td><td>• The Joint Commission requires medical staff involvement in the accurate, timely, and legible completion of records.
• NCQA requires documentation of an evaluation of medical recordkeeping practices.</td></tr>
<tr><th>FREQUENCY</th><th>APPLICABLE FOR</th></tr>
<tr><td>• At initial review
• At reappointment, recredential, or reapproval</td><td>• Medical staff (hospital)
• Primary care practitioners (PCPs) and obstetrics/gynecologists and high-volume specialists at time of recredentialing for medical recordkeeping practices and of primary care for medical record documentation (managed care)</td></tr>
<tr><th colspan="2">ADDITIONAL COMMENTS, CONSIDERATIONS, AND ISSUES</th></tr>
<tr><td colspan="2">• The Joint Commission outlines the information to be included in the medical record review in its information management standards.
• Only individuals with appropriate qualifications should evaluate medical practice and health management.
• The Joint Commission requires that medical staff provide leadership for the measurement, assessment, and improvement of the accurate, timely, and legible completion of patient medical records and that records be reviewed at least quarterly.
• Ambulatory documentation and recordkeeping practices should be reviewed with office staff, including
– forms and methods used for medical record file/filing system
– means of ensuring confidentiality
– organization of files and forms within the file
– documentation practices
• NCQA
– states that high-volume specialists are determined by the managed care organization
– allows a site visit/medical record review to occur within a two-year period before the credentialing decision
– indicates that the managed care organization should have specific standards by which the medical record is reviewed</td></tr>
</table>

Medicare and Medicaid Sanction Activity

<table>
<tr><th colspan="2">PURPOSE/DESCRIPTION</th></tr>
<tr><td colspan="2">Identification of sanctions imposed by the Office of the Inspector General (OIG), which may be criminal with a fine and /or imprisonment, civil monetary, civil liability, or exclusion from Medicare or Medicaid programs, due to such offenses or fraud, excessive claims, failure to furnish medically necessary items, default on a health education loan, or violation of limitations on physician charges.</td></tr>
<tr><th>SOURCES FOR VERIFICATION/INFORMATION</th><th>ACCREDITATION</th></tr>
<tr><td>• NPDB (as of March 3, 1997, the NPDB established a data link with the OIG to provide cumulative sanction information)
• Cumulative Sanctions Report—Internet
• FSMB
• Medicare intermediary
• Medicaid agency or intermediary
• Medicare and Medicaid sanction report distributed to federally contracted managed care organizations</td><td>• The Joint Commission standards are silent in relation to verification or collection of information about Medicare or Medicaid sanctions.
• NCQA standards require managed care organizations to review for previous sanction activity by Medicare and Medicaid.</td></tr>
<tr><th>FREQUENCY</th><th>APPLICABLE FOR</th></tr>
<tr><td>• At initial review
• At reappointment, recredential, or reapproval</td><td>• Managed care organization physicians and other LIPs</td></tr>
<tr><th colspan="2">ADDITIONAL COMMENTS, CONSIDERATIONS, AND ISSUES</th></tr>
<tr><td colspan="2">• In 1976, Congress established the OIG at the Department of Health and Human Services (DHHS). The OIG is charged with identification and elimination of abuse fraud and waste in DHHS programs. OIG work is carried out through inspections, audits, and investigations.
• Query is not applicable for dentists.
• The NCQA 180-day verification time limit applies to this element (120 days for CVO certified by NCQA).
• Verbal verification requires a dated and signed/initialed note in the credentials file indicating source (how and who).
• Verification by review lists or information on line should be documented in the credentials file to include date, signature/initials of staff member, source, and report date if applicable.
• As with other NPDB information, if a report states "no information found," it may be assumed that the practitioner has not had Medicare or Medicaid sanction activity; a specific statement will not be found.</td></tr>
</table>

Member Satisfaction/Member Complaint Information

PURPOSE/DESCRIPTION	
Data that may be incorporated into an NCQA-accredited managed care organization's decision-making process for PCPs.	
SOURCE FOR VERIFICATION/INFORMATION	**ACCREDITATION**
• Members enrolled in the managed care organization	• The Joint Commission is silent on the topic of collection and use of information related to satisfaction or complaints. • NCQA requires that three of six sources of information be used at the time of recredentialing; complaints and satisfaction are two of the six identified sources.
FREQUENCY	**APPLICABLE FOR**
• At reappointment, recredentialing, or reapproval	• PCPs only
ADDITIONAL COMMENTS, CONSIDERATIONS, AND ISSUES	
• There should be documentation of an affirmative assessment even if there are no findings (e.g., if member complaint information is reviewed as part of a practitioner's recredentialing evaluation and no documented complaints are found, the absence should be documented).	

NPDB Query

PURPOSE/DESCRIPTION	
The Health Care Quality Improvement Act of 1986[5] established NPDB as an information clearing house. NPDB is primarily an alert or flagging system that assists in review of credentials through collection and release of certain information related to the professional competence and conduct of physicians, dentists, and some other health care practitioners. State medical and dental boards, hospitals and other health care entities, professional societies, and medical malpractice payers must report certain actions that relate to competence and conduct and payments made for a claim or judgment against a practitioner. Hospitals *must* query NPDB, and other eligible entities *may* query when they employ or contract with a practitioner. To be eligible, the entity must provide health care services and engage in professional review activity through a formal review process.	
SOURCES FOR VERIFICATION/INFORMATION	**ACCREDITATION**
• The only source is NPDB. Fees are charged for all queries, except for self-query by a practitioner. Queries are completed electronically using a modem and QPRAC, the software developed by NPDB.	• The Joint Commission mentions the requirement for hospitals and encourages a query in a timely manner to ensure that all relevant information is available before appointment or granting of privileges.

	• NCQA has a specific standard that the managed care organization has received information from the NPDB and includes it in the file.
FREQUENCY	**APPLICABLE FOR**
• At time of initial application and every two years • If practitioner wishes to add or expand existing privileges at a hospital • At time of application for temporary privileges • At time of application for locum tenens privileges	• Medical staff (hospitals) • Physicians and other licensed independent practitioners (managed care) • May be applicable for some licensed AHPs (with clinical privileges)

ADDITIONAL COMMENTS, CONSIDERATIONS, AND ISSUES
• The 180-day verification time limit by NCQA applies to this element (120 days for CVO). • The NPDB help line at 1-800-767-6732 accepts calls seven days a week, 24 hours a day (excluding federal holidays) and includes recordings for common topics. Weekdays from 8:30 A.M. to 6:00 P.M. (5:30 P.M. on Fridays) Eastern Time, an information specialist is available for questions. • Hospitals do not have to query NPDB on medical and dental residents, interns, or staff fellows (house staff) in structured programs of supervised graduate medical education. But if a resident, intern, or fellow is appointed to a medical staff or is granted privileges to practice outside of the education program, a query must be completed. • NCQA standards note that an NPDB query is not required for chiropractors and podiatrists. • The NPDB query is a federal regulation; hospitals must query at least every two years regardless of accreditation status or affiliation. • A self-query by a practitioner does not constitute a required query by an organization. • Only eligible entities or their authorized agent may query NPDB. The report may *not* be shared with any other entity, organization, or agent. Reports may be shared only when two or more hospitals share a single, unified medical staff and shared peer review process with a joint governing board. Improperly sharing information could result in an $11,000 fine for each offense.[6]

Office Assessment/Site Review

PURPOSE/DESCRIPTION
To assess an applicant's office setting; to evaluate the site against managed care organization standards.

SOURCES FOR VERIFICATION/INFORMATION	ACCREDITATION
• On-site review of the facility in which care is provided	• Joint Commission: not applicable • NCQA: requires initial visit to offices of all potential PCPs, obstetricians/gynecologists and, at recredentialing, a visit to all PCP offices in which there are more than 50 members and obstetrician/gynecologists (if considered PCPs) and other high-volume specialists (as identified by the organization)
FREQUENCY	**APPLICABLE FOR**
• At initial review/appointment • At reappointment, recredential, or reapproval	• PCPs • Obstetricians/gynecologists • High-volume specialists (as determined by managed care organization)

ADDITIONAL COMMENTS, CONSIDERATIONS, AND ISSUES

NCQA standard rationale indicates that

- review should be structured
- review should be focused on the quality of the facility
- assessment of the following should be included:
  - –physical accessibility
  - –physical appearance
  - –adequacy of waiting and exam room space
  - –availability of appointments
- criteria should have goals or standards for acceptable performance

- If a practitioner practices at more than one location, each location should be reviewed by the managed care organization.
- A separate site visit for each practitioner in a medical group at one location is not required.
- The recredentialing site visit is focused on changes in the facility, equipment, and staffing.
- The managed care organization develops the site visit tool, and it is to be completed at the time of or shortly after the visit. No standard or example format is provided by NCQA.
- The site visit should occur before the initial decision and then within a two-year cycle before the recredential decision.
- For practitioners affiliated with a facility accredited by AAAHC or the Joint Commission, the managed care organization may use accreditation in lieu of a site visit; if the MCO obtains a copy of the survey report, the report clearly includes the office, that the survey meets the MCO quality assurance criteria, and that the survey was conducted during the two previous years. This is not interpreted by NCQA to be a delegation.
- Use of information from statewide site visit programs (such as currently established in Oregon and Washington) is considered to be delegation by NCQA.

Peer References

<table>
<tr><th colspan="2">PURPOSE/DESCRIPTION</th></tr>
<tr><td colspan="2">To obtain recommendations from individuals in the same discipline (e.g., physician and physician, podiatrist and podiatrist) who have firsthand knowledge of the practitioner.</td></tr>
<tr><th>SOURCES FOR VERIFICATION/INFORMATION</th><th>ACCREDITATION</th></tr>
<tr><td>• Reference letter (Joint Commission)
• Documented phone conversation (Joint Commission)
• Internal medical staff committee performance improvement, credentials, and executive committees (Joint Commission)</td><td>• The Joint Commission requires peer recommendations as part of the credentialing process and should refer to relevant training or experience, current competence, fulfillment of obligations as a medical staff member, and any effect of health status on the privileges being recommended.
• NCQA does not address peer references.</td></tr>
<tr><th>FREQUENCY</th><th>APPLICABLE FOR</th></tr>
<tr><td>• At initial appointment
• At reappointment, recredential, or reapproval</td><td>• Medical staff and AHPs with clinical privileges (hospital)</td></tr>
<tr><th colspan="2">ADDITIONAL COMMENTS, CONSIDERATIONS, AND ISSUES</th></tr>
<tr><td colspan="2">• If no peer exists within the hospital environment, a recommendation is obtained externally.
• When possible, the Joint Commission recommends that the peer be in the same specialty, but this is not required.
• Some hospitals opt to get peer references at reappointment as well as at the initial peer review process. The only time that is necessary (other than if it is stated policy) is when there are no peers who are part of the department/committee review process.</td></tr>
</table>

Professional Liability Insurance Coverage

<table>
<tr><th colspan="2">PURPOSE/DESCRIPTION</th></tr>
<tr><td colspan="2">Verification that the practitioner has coverage for professional liability with limits to comply with organizational standards.</td></tr>
<tr><th>SOURCES FOR VERIFICATION/INFORMATION</th><th>ACCREDITATION</th></tr>
<tr><td>• Insurance carrier
• Copy from malpractice insurance carrier that is provided by the practitioner
• Copy from practitioner</td><td>• The Joint Commission does not specify professional liability insurance coverage but does require compliance with bylaws, rules and regulations, and policies. In most</td></tr>
</table>

	areas, it is a community standard to require some level of coverage. • NCQA specifies verification of current adequate malpractice insurance according to the managed care organization policy.
FREQUENCY	**APPLICABLE FOR**
• At initial review/appointment • At reappointment, recredential, or reapproval	• Medical staff (hospitals) • Allied health, if specified in bylaws or policies (hospitals and managed care) • Practitioners (managed care) • Providers, if specified in policy
ADDITIONAL COMMENTS, CONSIDERATIONS, AND ISSUES	
• Coverage must be effective at time of the credentialing decision. • Copy should indicate dates and amount of coverage.	

Quality Performance Improvement Activities/Data

PURPOSE/DESCRIPTION	
At time of reappointment/recredential/reapproval, information from performance or quality improvement activities is considered as part of the decision-making process and in support of evaluation of competence for granting privileges.	
SOURCES FOR VERIFICATION/INFORMATION	**ACCREDITATION**
• Practitioner-specific information identified as part of performance improvement activities (hospital) • Practitioner-specific information identified as part of quality improvement activities (managed care)	• The Joint Commission requires that the results of peer review activity be considered at reappointment and that findings of the assessment process that relate to individual practitioners be used in evaluation, renewal, or revision of privileges. • NCQA requires the managed care organization to use performance monitoring information when recredentialing PCPs. Use of three of six sources of information, one of which is information from quality improvement activities, is required.
FREQUENCY	**APPLICABLE FOR**
• at reappointment, recredential, or reapproval	• Medical staff and AHPs with clinical privileges (hospitals) • PCPs (managed care)

ADDITIONAL COMMENTS, CONSIDERATIONS, AND ISSUES
• Practitioner-specific information identified during quality/performance improvement activities should be used in determination of competence. • The Joint Commission identifies several processes that are to be measured and assessed that are usually practitioner specific, including: –medical assessment and treatment of patients –use of medications –use of blood and blood components –use of operatives and other procedures –efficiency of clinical patterns –significant departures from established patterns of clinical practice • NCQA does not require that recredential files contain actual quality review documents. A checklist that includes an affirmative statement related to review of information is acceptable. • If members are assigned by group rather than individual physician, quality data by practice may be used at time of recredentialing.

Training—Professional and Postgraduate School

PURPOSE/DESCRIPTION	
To verify the medical, dental, or other postgraduate training (following four-year undergraduate degree) of practice credentials, e.g., MD (medical doctor), DO, (doctor of osteopathy), DDS (doctor of dental science), DMD (doctor of medical dentistry), DC (doctor of chiropractic), and DPM (doctor of podiatry medicine).	
SOURCES FOR VERIFICATION/INFORMATION	**ACCREDITATION**
• Directly from the medical or professional school or degree-granting institution (letter of confirmation, phone verification acceptable) • For foreign medical graduates, ECFMG confirmation of certificate for those licensed after 1986 • AMA Physician Masterfile • AOA Physician Masterfile (NCQA residency) • Confirmation from state licensing agency if managed care organization provides recent evidence that the state agency conducts primary source verification of residency training (NCQA)	• The Joint Commission requires primary source verification of medical or professional school or degree-granting institution. • NCQA requires primary source verification of highest educational level attained per NCQA guidelines for each practitioner category. If MD, DO, DDS, or DMD is not boarded or residency trained, this is required.

<table>
<tr><th>FREQUENCY</th><th>APPLICABLE FOR</th></tr>
<tr><td>• At initial review/appointment</td><td>• Medical staff, other LIPs and/or AHPs according to bylaws, policies
• Physicians and other licensed, certified, or registered independent practitioners (managed care)</td></tr>
<tr><th colspan="2">ADDITIONAL COMMENTS, CONSIDERATIONS, AND ISSUES</th></tr>
<tr><td colspan="2">• This verification is considered a "static" credential, so there are no time limits for verification. Once verified, this information can be used again for future verifications on the same individual (e.g., by a CVO that processes a practitioner multiple times for different clients).
• ECFMG is an acceptable primary source verification for foreign medical graduates. The ECFMG number given by the physician must be verified by ECFMG, which assesses the readiness of graduates of foreign medical schools to enter residency or fellowship programs in the United States that are accredited by the Accreditation Council for Graduate Medical Education (ACGME).

A foreign medical graduate, as defined by ECFMG, is a physician whose basic medical degree or qualification was conferred by a medical school outside the United States, Canada, and Puerto Rico. The medical school must be listed in the World Directory of Medical Schools published by the World Health Organization. U.S. citizens who have completed their medical education in schools outside the United States, Canada, and Puerto Rico are considered foreign medical graduates. Foreign nationals who have graduated from medical schools in the United States, Canada, and Puerto Rico are not. ECFMG certification is also a prerequisite required by most states for licensure to practice medicine in the United States. Eligibility for certification requires passing the medical school application, passing the ECFMG English test, and documenting the completion of all educational requirements to practice medicine in the country in which the medical education is received.

To verify an ECFMG certificate, include physician name, date of birth, and ECFMG number. Faxed requests and telephone inquiries are not accepted. Responses take approximately two weeks.

• Sometimes it can be difficult, even impossible, to verify education, especially for foreign medical graduates. With NCQA, there are other options, such as verification of the board or residency programs. The Joint Commission will accept a documented effort to obtain information. Also, it accepts the verification from ECFMG for a medical school without further verification.</td></tr>
</table>

Training—Internship, Fellowship, Residency, Postdoctoral

<table>
<tr><th colspan="2">PURPOSE/DESCRIPTION</th></tr>
<tr><td colspan="2">To verify training beyond medical school that may include a rotating internship followed by specialty training.</td></tr>
<tr><th>SOURCES FOR VERIFICATION/INFORMATION</th><th>ACCREDITATION</th></tr>
<tr><td>• Directly from the training program (letter of confirmation or evaluation form, phone verification acceptable)
• AMA Physician Masterfile (NCQA, Joint Commission)
• AOA Physician Masterfile (NCQA residency)
• ADA Masterfile (NCQA residency)
• Confirmation from state licensing agency if the managed care organization provides recent evidence that the state agency conducts primary verification of residency training (NCQA residency)</td><td>• The Joint Commission requires primary source verification of all relevant training or experience from the primary source whenever feasible.
• NCQA requires primary source verification of medical school or highest level attained (residency or board certification) (MD, DO); dental school or residency (DDS, DMO); or podiatry medical school or residency (DPM). If boarded in a podiatry specialty, board must provide evidence that the certifying board conducts primary source verification of podiatry school graduation and/or completion of residency.</td></tr>
<tr><th>FREQUENCY</th><th>APPLICABLE FOR</th></tr>
<tr><td>• At initial review/appointment</td><td>• Medical staff (hospitals)
• LIPs and/or AHPs according to bylaws, policies (hospitals)
• Physicians (managed care)</td></tr>
<tr><th colspan="2">ADDITIONAL COMMENTS, CONSIDERATIONS, AND ISSUES</th></tr>
<tr><td colspan="2">• NCQA refers to medical school, residency, and/or board certification only in its education and training section. It does not acknowledge confirmation of internship or fellowship.
• If recently out of a training program, hospitals should send a copy of the requested privilege delineation with the verification request and ask if the privileges requested relate to the training received. It is also a good idea to ask if the program was completed and if not, why not. Confirm the month as well as the year of program length to assist in identifying any gaps in time.
• This verification is considered a "static" credential, so there are no NCQA time limits for verification.</td></tr>
</table>

Utilization Management

PURPOSE/DESCRIPTION	
At time of recredentialing, information from utilization management activities may be considered as part of the decision-making process.	
SOURCES FOR VERIFICATION/INFORMATION	**ACCREDITATION**
• Practitioner-specific information identified as part of utilization review activities	• The Joint Commission requires collection of data related to the appropriateness of admissions and hospital stays but does not specify that data must be used as part of the credentialing process. • NCQA requires the managed care organization to use performance monitoring information when credentialing PCPs. Use of three of six sources of information, one of which is utilization management data, is required.
FREQUENCY	**APPLICABLE FOR**
• At reappointment, recredential, or reapproval	• Admitting practitioners (hospitals) (managed care) • PCPs only
ADDITIONAL COMMENTS, CONSIDERATIONS, AND ISSUES	
• Documentation of review of objective criteria may be used regardless of whether any problems or issues are identified.	

Work History/Experience

PURPOSE/DESCRIPTION	
To be aware of gaps in reported work history and/or to gather additional information through references.	
SOURCES FOR VERIFICATION/INFORMATION	**ACCREDITATION**
• Information included on the application form (NCQA) • Curriculum vitae (NCQA) • Telephone verification of gaps (must be documented) (NCQA) • Letter of reference (hospitals)	• NCQA requires a minimum five-year work history, but no verifications are required from primary source. • Joint Commission standards do not address work history.

FREQUENCY	APPLICABLE FOR
• At initial review	• Physicians and other LIPs (managed care; hospitals optional)

ADDITIONAL COMMENTS, CONSIDERATIONS, AND ISSUES

- NCQA standards indicate that any gaps longer than six months be investigated; oral verification is acceptable.
- Some managed care organizations use this information to determine the private practice or employment in which the practitioner has been involved in order to match experience with needs of the organization.
- Even though the Joint Commission does not require any work history, hospital application forms may ask for any group affiliations and choose to solicit professional references from these groups or individuals named. Reference letters ask for any comments relative to communication and working relationships with others.

RESOURCES

Table 5–2 lists resources that the credentialing professional will find helpful with the activities of verification and information-gathering activities.

Exhibit 5–10 lists contact information for ABMS.

DEA office addresses can be found in Exhibit 5–11.

Table 5–2 Verification and Information-Gathering Resources

Resource	*Information or Service Provided*	*Contact Information*
Directory of American Medical Education (Association of American Medical Colleges [AAMC])	Listing of medical schools	AAMC 1 DuPont Circle, N.W. Washington, DC 20036
Association for Certification of Nurse Midwives (ACNM) Certification Council	Certification of nurse midwives	ACNM 8401 Corporate Drive, Suite 470 Landover, MD 20705 Phone 301-459-1321
Allied Health Education Directory (American Medical Assocation [AMA])	Occupational descriptions Educational program information	AMA Medical Education Group 515 North State Street Chicago, IL 60610 Phone 312-464-4956

continues

Table 5–2 continued

Resource	*Information or Service Provided*	*Contact Information*
AMA Masterfile	Verification source for MD and DO of • board certification • internship/residency • licensure status (most states) • medical school • sanctions	AMA 515 North State Street Chicago, IL 60610 Phone 800-665-2882 http://www.ama-assn.org
American Association of Nurse Anesthetists (AANA)	Certification of nurse anesthetists	AANA 222 South Prospect Avenue Park Ridge, IL 60069-6968 Phone 847-692-7050
American Board of Medical Specialties Reference Handbook (American Board of Medical Specialties [ABMS])	Purpose of ABMS Listing of ABMS boards with addresses Certification/recertification requirements	ABMS 1007 Church Street, Suite 404 Evanston, IL 60201 Phone 708-491-9091
ABMS Compendium (ABMS)	Verification source for board certification	Published by Marquis Who's Who 121 Chanlon Road New Providence, NJ 07974 Phone 800-521-8110
American Hospital Association (AHA) *Guide to the Health Care Field*	Information and addresses for: • hospitals in the United States • national organizations	AHA 1 North Franklin Chicago, IL 60606-3401 www.aha.org
American Nurses Credentialing Center (ANCC)	Verification for nurse practitioners	ANCC 600 Maryland Avenue, S.W. Suite 100W Washington, DC 20024-2571 Phone 202-554-4444
American Osteopathic Association (AOA), Credentials Services	Verification source for • board certification of osteopathic physicians • AOA-accredited continuing medical education	AOA 142 E. Ontario Street Chicago, IL 60611-2864 Phone 312-280-5800 or 800-621-1773
American Podiatric Medical Association (APMA) Masterfile	Verification source for podiatrists of • podiatry school and residency • board certification if primary source verification by certifying board	APMA 9312 Old Georgetown Road Bethesda, MD 20814 Phone 301-571-9200
Cumulative Sanction Report	Exclusion actions and monthly updates in the form of lists from the *Federal Register*	Website through the Office of Enforcement and Compliance of the HHS Office of the Inspector General at www.Sbaonline.Sba.gov/ignet/internal/hhs/oec.html

continues

Table 5–2 continued

Resource	*Information or Service Provided*	*Contact Information*
Directory of Medical Schools Worldwide, 5th ed.	International institutions that teach (the art and science of) medicine	U.S. Directory Services 655 N.W. 128th Street Miami, FL 33168 Phone 305-769-1700
Education Commission for Foreign Medical Graduates (ECFMG)	Provides confirmation for international medical graduates licensed after 1986	ECFMG 3624 Market Street Philadelphia, PA 19104 Phone 215-386-5910
Federation Credentials Verification Service (FCVS)	Verifies "core" credentials in six categories: • identity • medical education • postgraduate training • examination history • ECFMG certification • board action history	Federation of State Medical Boards Federation Place 400 Fuller Wiser Road, Suite 300 Euless, TX 76039-3855
Federation of Chiropractor Licensing Boards (CINBAD) Chiropractor Information Network/Board Action Database	Information source for chiropractors on • sanctions • licensure restrictions • limitations of scope of practice	CINBAD 901 54th Avenue, Suite 101 Greeley, CO 80634 Phone 970-356-3500
Federation of Podiatric Medical Boards (FPMB)	Information source for podiatrists on • sanctions • licensure restrictions • limitation on scope of practice	Federation of Podiatric Medical Boards 1729 Gladstonberry Road Potomac, MD 20854 Phone 301-424-1001
Federation of State Medical Boards (FSMB)	Information source for physicians on • sanctions • licensure restrictions • limitation on scope of practice	FSMB 6000 Western Place Fort Worth, TX 76107-4618 Phone 817-868-4000 http://www/usmle.org/boards.htm
Medicare/Medicaid Sanctions and Reinstatements Report—not available to general public. Cumulative Sanctions Report may be available.	Information source related to Medicare/Medicaid sanctions	Office of Inspector General Office of Enforcement and Compliance N2-01-26 7500 Security Blvd. Baltimore, MD 21244-1850 http://www.sbaonline.sba.gov/ignet/internal/hhs/invlis.htrml

continues

Table 5–2 continued

Resource	*Information or Service Provided*	*Contact Information*
National Commission for the Certification of Acupuncturists (NCCA)	Organization that certifies acupuncturists	NCCA 1424 16th Street, N.W., Suite 501 Washington, DC 20036 Phone 202-232-1404
National Board of Medical Examiners		http//www/nbme.org
National Commission of Certification of Physician Assistants (NCCPA)	Organization that certifies physician assistants	NCCPA 6849 B2 Peachtree Bunwoody Road Atlanta, GA 30328 Phone 770-399-9971
National Practitioner Data Bank (NPDB)	Required query for hospitals; other eligible entities may query	NPDB P.O. Box 10832 Chantilly, VA 20151 Helpline 800-767-6732
National Register of Health Service Providers in Psychology	Verification of • license • doctoral degree in psychology • supervised, experienced	National Register for Psychologists 1120 G Street, N.W., Suite 330 Washington, DC 20005 Phone 202-783-7663
National Technical Information Service (NTIS)	Verification of DEA	NTIS 5285 Port Royal Road Springfield, VA 22161 Order—703-487-4650 Other—703-487-4808

Exhibit 5–10 ABMS Contact Information

American Board of Allergy and Immunology
University City of Science Center
3624 Market Street
Philadelphia, PA 19104-2675
(215) 349-9466
http://www.abai.org

American Board of Anesthesiology
The Summit, Suite 510
4101 Lake Boone Trail
Raleigh, NC 27607-7506
(919) 881-2570

American Board of Colon and Rectal Surgery
20600 Eureka Road, Suite 713
Taylor, MI 48180
(313) 282-9400

American Board of Dermatology
Henry Ford Hospital
1 Ford Place
Detroit, MI 48202-3450
(313) 874-1088

continues

Exhibit 5–10 continued

American Board of Emergency Medicine
3000 Coolidge Road
East Lansing, MI 48823
http://www.abem.org

American Board of Family Practice
2228 Young Drive
Lexington, KY 40505-4294
(606) 269-5626
www.abfp.org

American Board of Internal Medicine
University City Science Center
3624 Market Street
Philadelphia, PA 19104-2675
(215) 243-1500 (800) 441-ABIM
http://www.abim.org

American Board of Medical Genetics
9650 Rockville Pike
Bethesda, MD 20814-3998
(301) 571-1825
http://www.laseb.org/genetics/abma/abmgmenu.htm

American Board of Medical Specialties
1007 Church Street, Suite 404
Evanston, IL 60201-5913

American Board of Neurological Surgery
Smith Tower, Suite 2139
6550 Fannin Street
Houston, TX 77030-2701
(713) 790-6015
http://www.abns.org

American Board of Nuclear Medicine
900 Veteran Avenue, Room 12-200
Los Angeles, CA 90024-1786
(310) 825-6787

American Board of Obstetrics and Gynecology
2915 Vine Street
Dallas, TX 75204
(214) 871-1619
http://www.melronel.com/rhino

American Board of Ophthalmology
111 Presidential Blvd., Suite 241
Bala Cynwyd, PA 19004
(610) 664-1175
http://www.abop.org

American Board of Orthopaedic Surgery
400 Silver Cedar Court
Chapel Hill, NC 27514
(919) 929-7103

American Board of Pathology
P.O. Box 25915
Tampa, FL 33622-5915
(813) 286-2444
http://www.abpath.org

American Board of Pediatrics
111 Silver Cedar Court
Chapel Hill, NC 27514-1651
(919) 929-0461
http://www.abp.org

American Board of Physical Medicine and Rehabilitation
Suite 674, Norwest Center
21 First Street, S.W.
Rochester, MN 55902
(507) 282-1776

American Board of Plastic Surgery
Seven Penn Center, Suite 400
1635 Market Street
Philadelphia, PA 19103-2204
(215) 587-9322

American Board of Preventive Medicine
9950 W Lawrence Ave., Suite 106
Schiller Park, IL 60176
(847) 671-1750

American Board of Psychiatry and Neurology
500 Lake Cook Rd., Suite 335
Deerfield, IL 60015
(847) 945-7900
http://www.abpn.com

American Board of Radiology
5255 E Williams Circle, Suite 6800
Tucson, AZ 85711
(520) 790-2900

continues

Exhibit 5–10 continued

American Board of Surgery
www.absurgery.org

(847) 475-1520
-abts_evanston@msn.com

American Board of Thoracic Surgery
1 Rotary Center, Suite 803
1560 Sherman Ave
Evanston, IL 60201

American Board of Urology
31700 Telegraph Road, Suite 150
Bingham Farms, MI 48025
(810) 646-9720

Exhibit 5–11 DEA Offices

ATLANTA DIVISION OFFICE
Attn: Registration
75 Spring St, SW, Room 740
Atlanta, GA 30303

Georgia	(404) 763-5908
North Carolina	(404) 763-5909
South Carolina	(404) 763-5909
Tennessee	(404) 763-5908

BOSTON DIVISION OFFICE
JFK Federal Building Room E-400
15 New Sudbury Street
Boston, MA 02203-0131

Connecticut	(617) 557-2200
Maine	(617) 557-2200
Massachusetts	(617) 557-2200
New Hampshire	(617) 557-2200
Rhode Island	(617) 557-2200
Vermont	(617) 557-2200

CARIBBEAN DIVISION OFFICE
2432 Loiza Street
Santurce, PR 00914

Puerto Rico	(787) 253-4230
Virgin Islands	(787) 253-4230

CHICAGO DIVISION OFFICE
230 S. Dearborn Street, Suite 1200
Chicago, IL 60604

Illinois	(313) 353-1234
Indiana	(313) 353-1236
Minnesota	(313) 253-1236
North Dakota	(313) 253-1234
Wisconsin	(313) 253-1236

DALLAS DIVISION OFFICE
1880 Regal Row
Dallas, TX 75235

Oklahoma	(214) 640-0849
Texas	(214) 640-0849

DENVER DIVISION OFFICE
115 Inverness Drive East
Englewood, CO 80112

Colorado	(303) 705-7323
New Mexico or	
Utah	(800) 326-6900
Wyoming	

DETROIT DIVISION OFFICE
431 Howard Street
Detroit, MI 48226

Kentucky	(313) 234-4302
Michigan	(313) 234-4302
Ohio	(313) 234-4302

HOUSTON DIVISION OFFICE
1433 West Loop South, Suite 600
Houston, TX 77027

Texas	(713) 793-3660

LOS ANGELES DIVISION OFFICE
255 E. Temple Street, 20th Floor
Los Angeles, CA 90012

California (South Central)	(888) 415-9822
Hawaii	(888) 415-9822
Nevada	(888) 415-9822
Trust Territory	(888) 415-9822

continues

Exhibit 5–11 continued

MIAMI DIVISION OFFICE
8400 N.W. 53rd Street
Miami, FL 33166

Florida	(305) 590-4880

NEW ORLEANS DIVISION OFFICE
Three Lake Way
3838 N. Causeway Blvd., Suite 1800
Metairie, LA 70002

Alabama	(504) 840-1063
Arkansas	(504) 840-1063
Louisiana	(504) 840-1063
Mississippi	(504) 840-1063

NEW YORK DIVISION OFFICE
99 Tenth Avenue
New York, NY 10011

New York	(212) 337-1593

NEWARK DIVISION OFFICE
80 Mulberry Street
Newark, NJ 07102

New Jersey	(201) 645-3501

PHILADELPHIA DIVISION OFFICE
William J. Green Federal Building
600 Arch Street, Room 10224
Philadelphia, PA 19106

Delaware	(215) 597-9536
Pennsylvania	(215) 597-9536

PHOENIX DIVISION OFFICE
3010 N. 2nd Street, Suite 301
Phoenix, AZ 85012

Arizona	(602) 664-5831

SAN DIEGO DIVISION OFFICE
4560 Viewridge Avenue
San Diego, CA 92123-1672

California (Southern)	(619) 616-4542

SAN FRANCISCO DIVISION OFFICE
450 Golden Gate Avenue
P.O. Box 36035
San Francisco, CA 94102

California (Northern)	(415) 436-7905

SEATTLE DIVISION OFFICE
220 West Mercer Street, Suite 104
Seattle, WA 98119

Alaska	(206) 553-4040
Idaho	(206) 553-4040
Montana	(206) 553-4040
Oregon	(206) 553-4040
Washington	(206) 553-4040

ST. LOUIS DIVISION OFFICE
United Missouri Bank Building
7911 Forsyth Blvd., Suite 500
St. Louis, MO 63105

Iowa	(314) 425-3241
Kansas	(314) 425-3241
Missouri	(314) 425-3241
Nebraska	(314) 425-3241
South Dakota	(314) 425-3241

HEADQUARTERS
U.S. Department of Justice
Drug Enforcement Administration
Central Station, P.O. Box 28083
Washington, DC 20038-8083
(800) 882-9539

WASHINGTON, DC, DIVISION OFFICE
400 6th Street, S.W., Room 2558
Washington, DC 20024

District of Columbia	(202) 401-7360
Maryland	(202) 401-7360
Virginia	(202) 401-7360
West Virginia	(202) 401-7360

NOTES

1. *1998 Surveyor Guidelines* (Washington, DC: National Committee for Quality Assurance, 1997), 356.
2. *1998 Hospital Accreditation Standards* (Oakbrook Terrace: IL: Joint Commission on Accreditation of Heathcare Organizations), 298.
3. *AMA Primary Source Physician Information for Credentialing* (Chicago, IL).
4. *AMA Primary Source Physician Information for Credentialing.*
5. 42 U.S.C. §§ 11101–11152.
6. *NPDB News* (U.S. Department of Health and Human Services) (February 1998), 1–4.

Chapter 6

Privileging and Proctoring

OVERVIEW

The Joint Commission on Accreditation of Healthcare Organizations (Joint Commission) defines clinical privileges as "authorization granted by the appropriate authority (for example, a governing body) to a practitioner to provide specific care services in an organization within well-defined limits, based on the following factors, as applicable: license, education, training, experience, competence, health status, and judgment."[1] Privileging is defined as "the process whereby a specific scope and content of patient care services (that is, clinical privileges) are authorized for a health care practitioner by a health care organization based on evaluation of individual's credentials and performance"[2] and delineation of clinical privileges as "the listing of the specific clinical privileges an organization's staff member is permitted to perform in the organization."[3]

The underlying purpose for delineation of clinical privileges is to ensure that patients are receiving quality care by practitioners qualified to treat a specific illness or perform a specific procedure. Accreditation standards may have a direct effect on whether organizations delineate clinical privileges, but even organizations whose accrediting bodies do *not* require this process can choose to delineate privileges. Hospitals that are in compliance with Joint Commission standards are required to delineate clinical privileges for licensed independent practitioners (LIPs) who provide patient care services in a hospital. In addition, Joint Commission standards for networks require that a process be developed for privileging of physicians in the private office setting. Most managed care organizations at this time do not delineate clinical privileges in the office setting, primarily because the National Committee for Quality Assurance (NCQA) accreditation process does not require privilege delineation for the office environment.

Clinical privileges must be based on specific criteria, and those criteria must be met to apply for the privileges. Practitioners can request privileges by choosing from categories, lists, or other means of delineation according to their specialty, training, and experience. There is a broad spectrum of criteria as well as privilege delineation formats that an organization may use. Formats and types of privileges will be discussed later in this chapter. It is the *responsibility of the applicant* to provide evidence of the necessary education, training, and experience to be granted requested privileges. The application form should outline criteria and required evidence of competence. Information submitted is evaluated against the criteria that were established by clinical departments and approved by the governing body.

Organizations that require privilege delineations must update and revise those delineations on an ongoing basis to stay current with newer forms of treatment and procedures as well as to define the criteria for those desiring to obtain or maintain these privileges. This review process will also ensure that privileges are specific to the current services provided by the organization.

Privileges initially granted a practitioner may be subject to a specific evaluation within a two-year period or other evaluation as described in the designated section.

GRANTING CLINICAL PRIVILEGES

Joint Commission hospital medical staff standards require anyone who practices independently in an organization to have delineated clinical privileges. These privileges are not limited to physicians, dentists, and/or other medical staff members but may be extended to those allied health professionals (AHPs) who by law and by permission of the hospital are able to practice independently. Privileges must also be granted to those individuals (physicians, AHPs) who contract with or otherwise provide services independently to a hospital and are not necessarily members of the medical staff—for example, emergency department physicians. Generally, those AHPs who cannot by law or by permission of the hospital practice independently and who require supervision by a physician (direct or indirect) within an institution have defined job descriptions or practice parameters that outline the scope of services that can be performed. This will be discussed further in this chapter.

Managed care organizations do not commonly privilege practitioners, as NCQA does not have any standards requiring privileges. Managed care contracts/agreements with individual or group practitioners typically include provisions that, in effect, define the scope of activity in the physician office. These provisions address compensation, service provision, utilization review mechanisms, quality assurance processes, licensing and credentialing requirements, termination of care, and continuity of care. The contract/agreement will require or limit care in the practitioner office through service provisions and the payment mechanism. For example, a practitioner agreement may not allow reimbursement for an invasive cardiology procedure performed in his or her office. Refusal of payment is an effective tool in limiting scope of practice.

There are numerous possibilities for privileging in ambulatory care settings. Joint Commission-accredited organizations for the most part are required to delineate privileges. Ambulatory surgical units will most likely have a process that models that of the hospital. Accreditation and setting and level of clinical activity will, in most cases, direct the privileging process.

Some state statutes include language directing clinical privilege delineation. Each organization should be cognizant of all applicable standards and statutes affecting this process.

CREATING AND APPROVING CLINICAL PRIVILEGES

Initial recommendations for criteria and delineated clinical privileges should be approved by the clinicians involved in the specialty area to be defined. Joint Commission hospital medical staff standards for department leadership require that the clinical departments make recommendations to the medical staff for criteria and privileging that are then approved by the governing board for implementation. If medical staff departments are large and include multispecialty groups, clinical departments may opt to appoint a task force of specialists to develop criteria and make recommendations for approval by the department as a whole that are then forwarded to the medical staff executive committee and ultimately the governing board for approval.

Nondepartmentalized medical staffs develop recommended criteria and privileges as a medical staff of the whole (through the executive committee) and forward the recommendations to the governing board for approval.

Joint Commission requires privileges to be "hospital specific," meaning that privileges may be granted only for those procedures, illnesses, and treatments that are provided by the hospital.

For example, if a hospital does not provide obstetrical services, an obstetrician/gynecologist cannot apply or be granted obstetrical privileges, even though that individual is trained and most likely qualified to do obstetrics. As the service is not offered, no criteria are available to determine qualifications. It is important that privileges be cross-referenced with services to ensure that they relate to the services provided by the hospital. If a hospital is part of an integrated system, privileges need to be approved specifically for each location, since not all locations may offer the same services. The privileges form can be an integrated one that is formatted so that, for example, a procedure is checked off for each location where it is available and where the practitioner will be working (single or multiple locations).

TYPES OF CLINICAL PRIVILEGES

A variety of methods may be used to delineate clinical privileges. The most common are categories or levels, laundry/menu lists, core privileges/bundling of privileges, and a combination of these methods. When developing or reviewing methods, types of privileges, and the formats in which they are delineated, it is recommended that organizations first choose a standardized terminology and format. This should be used by all departments and sections involved to the extent possible. If standardized definitions and a standardized format are used, the review and processing of privilege requests will be much easier to standardize among all of the groups that need to review the information—departments, committees and boards. If an organization is using several formats and/or sets of terms it should identify and choose the format that is the easiest to understand and will be the most adaptable to various departments' delineations. If one department is using the term *categories* and another uses *levels*, consensus should be obtained from the departments, and one term used. If consensus cannot be obtained between departments, a credentials committee or executive committee may be asked to approve a standardized format and terminology.

Category or Level

The category or level method of developing privileges is generally defined by the degree of complexity or level of training and/or experience needed to qualify for a category/level. The following example of categorization indicates both a degree of complexity and the training or experience that would be required to qualify for that level:

- *Category I:* Illness or problem that will require skills acquired during postgraduate training in internal medicine or as a consequence of experience to treat. Consultation must be obtained when the patient is seriously or critically ill and the diagnosis is in doubt, when improvement in therapy is not soon apparent (except in irreversible or terminal illness), or when specialized therapy or diagnostic procedures are to be used. The practitioner cannot admit to intensive care or coronary care without consultation. Board certification is not required. At least one year of postgraduate training is required in general medicine (examples could include asthmas, bacterial pneumonia, dehydration, and hypertension).
- *Category II:* Illness or complex problem representing an immediate or serious threat to life. This category requires board certification in internal medicine or completion of residency program, and the applicant must fall within time guidelines of the waiting period to take the boards. Physicians in category II may act as consultants to others and should request consultation when diagnosis or management is in doubt, when unexpected complications arise, or when hazardous procedures or treatment are contemplated (examples could include multiple organ system disease, acute myocardial infarction, and diabetic ketoacidosis).

- *Category III:* Illness or problem requiring an unusual degree of expertise or competence in a subspecialty area acquired through subspecialty training. Board certification is required in the subspecialty area, or required training programs must be successfully completed, and the applicant must fall within time guidelines of the waiting period before taking the boards. The practitioner is expected to act as a consultant in his or her field and in turn to obtain consultation whenever other subspecialty skills are needed.[4] (Examples may include multi-system failure, acute leukemia, complicated myocardial infarction, respiratory failure, and procedures such as angiography and endoscopy.)

Use of the category or level method alone can be ambiguous without specific examples and is generally used by organizations that do not want to be very definitive about their privileging. Exhibit 6–1 is an example of a privilege format using categories and using training and/or board certification to distinguish between the categories.

Exhibit 6–1 Internal Medicine Delineation of Privileges

Privileges in the Department of Internal Medicine shall be granted to physicians on the basis of the following qualifications as set forth in Categories 1 through 4 below. It is understood that those applying for privileges in the Department of Internal Medicine shall have met all other qualifications for appointment to the Medical Staff of Penrose-St. Francis Hospitals, whether this relates to initial appointment or reappointment. It is also understood that in addition to assigned privileges, emergency privileges shall be granted in all cases. Any member of the Medical Staff is authorized in an emergency to do everything necessary to save the life of any patient who is in immediate danger, when any delay in administering treatment would increase the danger of acute worsening of that patient's condition, or of the likelihood of his death. This listing of privileges for which approval is required is not all inclusive and may be changed from time to time through addition or deletion, or changes to this delineation of privileges. Privileges granted to a physician are not permanent and may be changed at each reappointment period if required documentation or qualification changes.

______ **CORE 1**

Illness or problem requiring skills acquired during appropriate and sufficient post-graduate training in Internal Medicine or as a consequence of experience. Appropriate post-graduate training is defined as that obtained in an approved IM training program in good standing. Sufficient time spent in residency is that which with an additional year or less spent in continued training would have qualified the applicant to sit for board examination. Consultation *must* be obtained when the patient is seriously or critically ill and the diagnosis is in doubt, improvement with therapy is not soon apparent (except in irreversible or terminal illness), or when specialized therapy or diagnostic procedures are to be used. *Cannot admit to ICU/CCU without consultation. Board certification not required.*

______ **CORE 2**

Illness or complex problem representing an immediate or serious threat to life, and requiring skills achieved during training sufficient *such that physicians are either certified by the American Board of Internal Medicine or fall within time guidelines of waiting periods prior to taking the boards and can submit copy of notification that they have been accepted to take the boards.* Physicians in Category 2 may act as consultants to others, and in turn should request consultation when diagnosis or management is in doubt, when unexpected complications arise or when hazardous procedures or treatment are contemplated. The AOBIM will not

continues

Exhibit 6–1 continued

be universally accepted as equivalent to ABIM in the determination of qualification for Category 2 and higher Internal Medicine privileges. However, on an individual basis, the application from an applicant with AOBIM certification will be judged based on specific relevant training and experience. Only in cases where the applicant's training and experience are judged to be adequate will AOBIM certification be considered acceptable in lieu of ABIM certification for purposes of considering Internal Medicine privileges of Category 2 and above.

If the applicant fails to pass the boards or if the time for which he has been approved to take the boards has expired, then his privileges shall terminate unless the Credentials Committee approves his continuation based on the applicant's current clinical competence, ethics, good character and reputation, ability to work harmoniously with others and the needs of the Hospital. In unusual circumstances where an individual has additional Internal Medicine training at a minimum of 2 years beyond internship and at least five (5) years practice experience in Internal Medicine, at least 2 years of which are in the Penrose-St. Francis Hospital System (documented satisfactorily by letters from at least 2 members of the Penrose-St. Francis System Departments of Medicine), such individuals may be considered for Category 2 privileges by the appropriate mechanisms of review through the Department Chief and the Credentials Committee. These individuals may also be eligible for Special Procedures Requests authorized for Category 2 only on a physician-by-physician basis, given appropriate experience and demonstrated competence.

______ **CORE 3**

Illness or problems requiring an unusual degree of expertise or competence in a sub-specialty area, acquired through sub-specialty training, *resulting in certification in the appropriate sub-specialty of the American Board of Internal Medicine or falling within the time guidelines of waiting periods prior to taking the boards and can submit a copy of notification from the sub-specialty board that he has been accepted to take the boards.* The physician in this category is expected to act as a consultant in his field and, in turn, to obtain consultation whenever other sub-specialty skills are needed. If failure to pass boards occurs or persists, requested privileges may be considered individually by the Credentials Committee based upon prior training, documented current competence and recommendations from 2 members of the Penrose-St. Francis Healthcare System Medical Staff who have privileges for the procedure(s) requested.

______ **CORE 4**

Physicians who are board certified or can provide evidence from the respective board of intent to take the boards, falling within guidelines established in the specialties of Neurology, Dermatology, Occupational Medicine, Physical Medicine and Rehabilitation, may apply for Category 4 privileges in their specialties. They must document that they meet all of the certifying criteria of their respective Specialty Boards and be within required time frame for certification. If failure to pass the boards occurs or persists, privileges will be considered individually by the Credentials Committee based upon prior training, documented current competence and recommendations from 2 members of the Penrose-St. Francis Healthcare System Medical Staff who have privileges for the procedure(s) requested.

SPECIAL PROCEDURES—Department of Medicine

Please check those procedures for which you are applying.

If qualified for Category 2 privileges only, you are responsible for providing Penrose-St. Francis Hospitals with verification from training programs for specific privileges requested. This information must be received prior to consideration of these privileges being granted. (Where minimum numbers per year are required to maintain competence,

continues

Exhibit 6–1 continued

and the member does not meet the minimum number, the member may provide evidence to support competency based on cases at other hospitals, recent training, or special experience. The numbers may be modified by the Credentials Committee to conform to the recommendations of the American College of Physicians.)

Minimum Criteria: Core 2

Procedures:

____ **CENTRAL VENOUS CATHETER INSERTION**

____ **ELECTIVE CARDIOVERSION** (Documentation of training required.)

____ **SWAN-GANZ CATHETER INSERTION** (Minimum of 3 performed per year. Documentation can be provided by other hospitals for this procedure during reappointment, but must be done at Penrose-St. Francis during initial probation with a minimum of the first 3 cases reviewed by preceptor.)

____ **PLEURAL BIOPSIES** (With documentation of performance of these procedures numbering not less than 5 during the training program.)

____ **CLOSED CHEST DRAINAGE** (Tube) (With documentation of performance of these procedures numbering not less than 10 during training program.)

____ **MANAGEMENT OF VENTILATORS**—Limited to patients requiring or expected to require mechanical ventilator support less than 24 hours. Consultations for mechanical ventilatory support should be performed by credentialed Category 3 internists. Management of ventilators may be performed on primary admissions with assurance of 24-hour coverage for the ventilator. (With documentation of training in ICU setting with rotation on a sub-specialty service such as Pulmonary Medicine which allowed hands-on experience with at least 20 patients needing respirator.)

____ **PERCUTANEOUS LIVER BIOPSY** (Minimum of 5 procedures done yearly to maintain competence.)

____ **FLEXIBLE SIGMOIDOSCOPY** (Documentation of performance of these procedures numbering not less than 6 during training program. Minimum of 6 procedures done yearly without assistance to maintain competence. Physicians performing colonoscopy can use colonoscopy to meet this criterion.)

____ **REHAB ADMITTING** (See attached criteria and submit the required documentation.)

____ **STRESS TESTING** (treadmill or bicycle ergometer with or without nuclear isotopes) (Board certified Internists can apply for privileges if they can document training in treadmills under supervision. If privileges are granted, a minimum of 25 must be performed yearly.) Interpretation of Nuclear Medicine Scans requires special credentialing.

____ **EKG—Panel reader only; must apply through Medical Staff Services**.

Minimum Criteria: Core 2, 3, 4

____ **CONSCIOUS SEDATION**—For initial applications, must provide documentation of physician specialty training during residency. If procedure is not a normal part of physician training, physician must review the education packet and pass the test. Procedure is then considered part of physician's core privileges. For reappointment, physician must reapply for the privilege, but no additional exam or documentation is required.

As stated, the following special procedures require board certification in the designated specialty. Individuals are also eligible if they fall within time guidelines of waiting periods prior to taking their boards as well as submitting a copy of notification from the sub-specialty board that they have been accepted to take boards. If failure to pass

continues

Exhibit 6–1 continued

boards occurs or persists, privileges will be considered individually by the Credentials Committee.

Minimum Criteria: Board Certification in Cardiology

Procedures:

____ **LEFT HEART CATH (50/yr)**
____ **INTRA-AORTIC BALLOON PUMP**
____ **TEMPORARY PACEMAKER INS.**
____ **RIGHT HEART CATH**
____ **PULM. ANGIOGRAMS**
____ **PERICARDIOCENTESIS**
____ **ECHOCARDIOGRAMS** (Board certified internists must have documentation submitted verifying 3 to 4 months of a formal training program with 200 studies. Post-graduate requirements would optimally be a 3- to 4-month training program, but a minimum requirement would include 6 weeks of formal training to include 200 studies performed under supervision and an additional 150 studies to be reviewed by a preceptor at the Penrose-St. Francis Hospitals. Persons qualified to read echos are also qualified to perform stress echo studies, either exercise or pharmacologic. (Must apply through Medical Staff Services.))
____ **TRANSESOPHAGEAL ECHOCARDIOGRAPHY** (Must show completion of approved course related to transesophageal echocardiography performance and interpretation. A minimum of 6 TEE procedures must be evaluated by a qualified preceptor skilled in endoscopy to ensure appropriate intubation and associated anesthetic technique. At least the initial procedure must be observed by the preceptor(s).)
____ **PERMANENT PACEMAKER INSERTIONS** (Probation to include a minimum of 5 generator implants to include placement of at least 3 atrial and 3 ventricular leads. To maintain these privileges, one would have to perform at least 3 procedures a year. Documentation can be provided from other hospitals for these procedures.)

Minimum Criteria: Privileges in Left Heart Cath

Procedures:

____ **PERCUTANEOUS TRANSLUMINAL CORONARY ANGIOPLASTY**

1. Requirements to perform PTCA include full cardiovascular training program, meeting requirements for Board certification to include 12 months of catheterization experience with participation in at least 300 cases and performance as primary operator in at least 200 cases. In addition, physician should have had an additional year of PTCA training by being involved in more than 125 cases and primary operator in more than 75 cases.
2. A second route to qualify for PTCA involved those cardiologists already out of training. These physicians should:
    a) have performed more than 500 coronary angiography cases with acceptable results documented by the catheterization lab director;
    b) have special instruction in regard to PTCA in excess of 50 hours; and
    c) have been involved in the performance of 125 PTCAs and primary operator in at least 75 cases with documented acceptable results. (In order to maintain PTCA privileges, a minimum of 25 procedures must be performed annually.)

Minimum Criteria: Privileges in Percutaneous Transluminal Coronary Angioplasty

Procedures:

____ **CORONARY ATHERECTOMY** (Must have completion of an approved course for atherectomy. Preception is not required for

continues

Exhibit 6–1 continued

those physicians with full privileges in PTCA.)

___ **LASER** (Attendance at an interventional meeting that involves discussion of laser angioplasty within the preceding year. This course should be of at least 2 days' duration. Laser safety course and hands-on experience with the machine through the Spectranetics Company in Colorado Springs.)

___ **STENTS** (Completion of an approved course specifically for stent placement.)

___ Similar course documentation for other new devices as they become available.

Minimum Criteria: Board Certification in Clinical Cardiac Electrophysiology

Procedures:

___ **SIGNAL AVERAGED ELECTROCARDIOGRAM (SAECG)** (Board certified cardiologists may apply if they provide documentation of cognitive training and clinical exposure in the area of SAECG testing (provisional, pending review of credentials including documentation of interpretation of 10 SAECG recordings).)

___ **HEAD-UP TILT (HUT) TILT TABLE** (Board certified electrophysiologists and cardiologists must provide documentation of performing HUT studies. Board certified cardiologists may apply if they provide documentation of cognitive training and clinical exposure in the area of HUT testing. Cognitive training may be experienced during EP or cardiology fellowship or training by another cardiologist or EP who is credentialed and has reviewed at least 3 procedures and written a letter of reference to the Credentials Committee. Board certified internists may apply with documentation of cognitive training and clinical exposure in the area of HUT testing (provisional as above). PLUS successful completion of probation period where HUT studies are supervised and/or "overread" by a qualified interpreter.)

___ **INVASIVE CARDIAC ELECTROPHYSIOLOGIC (EP) STUDIES** (Board certified electrophysiologists must provide documentation of performing 150 "first operator" EP studies during training (automatic). Board certified cardiologists may apply if they provide documentation of cognitive training and clinical exposure during this training in the area of clinical cardiac EP (provisional, pending review of credentials including documentation of performance and interpretation of at least 150 EP studies).)

___ **LEAD EXTRACTION** (Board eligible/certified electrophysiologists must provide documentation of participation in an acceptable course in lead extraction. Preception is not required.)

___ **DIRECTOR CURRENT (DC) OR RADIOFREQUENCY (RF) CATHETER ABLATION FORTHETREATMENT OF SUPRAVENTRICULAR OR VENTRICULAR TACHYCARDIAS** (Board certified electrophysiologists must provide documentation of performing at least 50 "first operator" ablation studies during training or under supervision of a preceptor trained in the field of clinical cardiac EP and having expertise in the field of catheter ablation techniques.)

___ **IMPLANTATION OF ANTITACHYCARDIA DEVICES (PACING CARDIOVERTER DEFIBRILLATOR; ANTITACHYCARDIA PACEMAKER, ETC.) IN THETHERAPY OF SUPRAVENTRICULAR OR VENTRICULAR ARRHYTHMIAS** (Board certified electrophysiologists must provide documentation of participation in implantation and follow-up of antitachycardia devices during training or under the supervision of a preceptor trained in the field of clinical cardiac EP and having expertise in the area. Board certified cardiologists may apply if they can document cognitive training and clinical exposure during this (or supplemental) training in the area, documentation of involvement in implantation, programming and follow-up. PLUS initial supervision and validation of skills by a physician trained and privileged in antitachycardia device therapy.)

continues

Exhibit 6–1 continued

Minimum Criteria: Formal Fellowship or Residency Training in Gastroenterology Board Certification or Eligibility in Gastroenterology Provide Documentation from Training of Procedures as Follows:

	Standard Procedures	*Number of Cases Required*
___	Diagnostic EGD	100
___	Total colonoscopy	100
	Snare polypectomy	20
___	Nonvariceal hemostasis (upper) and lower; (includes 10 active bleeders)	20*
___	Variceal hemostasis (includes 5 active bleeders)	15
___	Esophageal dilation with guide wire	15
___	Flexible sigmoidoscopy	25
___	PEG	10
	Advanced Procedures	
___	ERCP (Diagnostic)	75
___	ERCP (Therapeutic)	25#
___	Tumor ablation, laser (Yag)	20
___	Pneumatic dilation for achalasia	5
___	Laparoscopy	25
___	Esophageal stent placement	10

*Included in total number

#Includes 20 sphincterotomies and 5 stent placements and is in addition to the 75 diagnostic ERCP procedures.

REAPPOINTMENT CRITERIA:

	Procedures	*Number of cases required per 2 yrs.*
___	Upper endoscopy (Must include at least 6 therapeutic endoscopic procedures, e.g., dilation, foreign body removal, sclerotherapy or esophageal banding, and laser or coagulation methods to control hemorrhages.)	50
___	Colonoscopy	40
___	Peritoneoscopy	12
___	Esophageal dilatation	24
___	ERCP	24
___	ERCP sphincterotomy	12
___	Endoscopy-polypectomy	24
___	Esophagoscopy and variceal sclerotherapy/banding	12
___	Endoscopy with laser (must provide documentation of course attendance)	6
___	PEG	6
___	Esophageal stent placement	4

continues

Exhibit 6–1 continued

NEW PROCEDURES (for Gastroenterology):

As endoscopy evolves, new procedures develop for which privileges may be requested. The process for credentialing depends on the background skills and privileges of the applicant and whether the new procedure is a minor or major variant of established techniques. For minor extensions of demonstrated skills, reading or viewing videotapes may be sufficient training. Some new procedures may require formal training or "hands-on" equivalent supervised experienced with adequate written documentation. Endoscopic sphincterotomy is an example of an extremely complex and high risk procedure requiring extensive training and experience. Therefore, privilege granting for endoscopic sphincterotomy requires documented competency.

Guidelines for re-credentialing standards for GI endoscopy are developed in accordance with ASGE principles and per Joint Commission guidelines and must be uniform for all utilizers, within the Department of Medicine, of the endoscopy lab and equipment. These apply for all levels of endoscopic credentials. Credentialing for advanced endoscopic procedures (therapeutic EGD, colonscopy, ERCP, laparoscopy, and liver biopsy) may be limited to those in the Department of Medicine meeting ASGE guidelines with specific training and board certification in gastroenterology.

Minimum Criteria: Board Certification in Medical Oncology

Procedures:

___ **INTRA-VENOUS CHEMOTHERAPY***
___ **INTERPERITONEAL CHEMOTHERAPY***

*A minimum of 12 procedures per year must be performed to maintain competency in these areas. However, any combination of these 2 chemotherapies will be sufficient.

Minimum Criteria: Board Certification in Nephrology

Procedures:

___ **HEMODIALYSIS** (Minimum of 100 treatments performed per year.)
___ **PERITONEAL DIALYSIS**
___ **RENAL BIOPSY** (Minimum of 3 procedures performed per year.)

Minimum Criteria: Board Certification in Neurology or Physical Medicine and Rehab

Procedures:

___ **ELECTROMYOGRAPHY/NERVE CONDUCTION STUDIES** (No preception required. At reappointment, a minimum of five (5) procedures must be performed within the last two years.)
___ **EVOKED POTENTIAL STUDIES** (No preception required. At reappointment, a minimum of five (5) procedures must be performed within the last two years.)
___ **INTRA-OPERATIVE EVOKED POTENTIAL MONITORING** (At initial appointment, physician must have observation by qualified preceptor. At reappointment, a minimum of three (3) procedures must be performed within the last two years.)
___ **MOTORPOINT/NEUROLYTIC BLOCKS** (At initial appointment, physician must have observation by a qualified preceptor. At reappointment, a minimum of 5 procedures must be performed within the last two years.)
___ **POLYSOMNOGRAPHY** (No preception required. At reappointment, a minimum of five (5) procedures must be performed within the last two years.)

Minimum Criteria: Board Certification in Pulmonary Medicine

Procedures:

___ **PULMONARY FUNCTION STUDIES** (By application to Respiratory Services.)
___ **FIBEROPTIC BRONCHOSCOPY** (Approved training in program which includes 50 procedures performed. Minimum of 20 to be performed per year.)
___ **LASER** (Course attendance with documentation. If privilege is granted, 3 procedures per year done to maintain competence.)

continues

Exhibit 6–1 continued

___ **MECHANICAL VENTILATORS** (Minimum of 20 performed per year.)

___ **POLYSOMNOGRAPHY** (By application to Respiratory Services.)

OTHER NON-INVASIVE PROCEDURES (please list):

____

____

ELEANOR CAPRON REHABILITATION CENTER ADMITTING PRIVILEGES, INPATIENT UNIT

The admitting physician must be a member of the Penrose-St. Francis Healthcare System staff. The physician must submit an application to the Credentials Committee. The Commission on Accreditation of Rehabilitation Facilities requires that "the physician responsible for the person's rehabilitation program should possess training and/or experience in rehabilitation." The minimum standards to meet this requirement include any one of the following:

A) Experience:
   The physician must have admitted or participated in the management of the rehabilitation care of at least 3 patients in one of the following categories; stroke, spinal cord injury, closed head injury, amputations, polyarthritis, burns, other neurologic diseases, congenital deformities, or major multiple trauma.

B) Training:
   1) Have completed a physical medicine and rehabilitation residency and be board certified or within the guidelines of waiting to take the boards.
   2) Have had a residency in neurology, neurosurgery, orthopedic surgery or rheumatology and have had a three-month rotation on a rehabilitation unit during that residency.
   3) Have had another type of residency including a six-month rotation on a rehabilitation unit during that residency.
   4) Have had a 12-month rehabilitation fellowship.

If a physician meets only *one* of the above criteria, this shall be deemed satisfactory to meet the requirements for "training and/or experience."

Physicians' admitting privileges are to be reviewed biannually by the Credentials Committee, and continued privileges to admit to the inpatient unit will depend on compliance with the following standards:

A) Must have a minimum of 95% compliance with the rules and regulations established by the Federal Government and by the Colorado Foundation for Medical Care for Medical Rehabilitation units.

B) Must have pre-screened *ALL* admissions to the unit and documented this in the rehabilitation chart.

In order to have privileges renewed on a biannual basis, the physician must be in compliance with both of the standards delineated above.

Signature: ______________________________

Date: ____________________

Revised:

Note: IM, internal medicine; AOBIM, American Osteopathic Board of Internal Medicine. ABIM, American Board of Internal Medicine; EKG, electrocardiogram; EP, electrophysiologic, electrophysiology; EGD, esophagogastroduodenoscopy; PEG, percutaneous endoscopic gastrostomy; ERCP, endoscopic retrograde cholangiopancreatography.

Courtesy of Penrose-St. Frances Healthcare System, Colorado Springs, Colorado.

Laundry/Menu Lists

Laundry or menu list privilege formats attempt to be inclusive of every cognitive and procedural privilege in a specified area, usually a department and/or specialty. Traditionally, organizations using only a laundry list to define privilege delineation do not specify training or experience requirements for specific procedures or illness management. With this method, it is routine for practitioners to check off every procedure listed because they have been trained to do that procedure, not necessarily because they intend to perform all listed procedures or plan to maintain current competence. A problem inherent with this method relates to determination of competence at time of reappointment. Many organizations cannot or do not track how many of the procedures listed, requested, and approved were actually performed over a period of time (e.g., between reappointments) and therefore have no basis to determine the practitioner's current experience or competence for renewal of that privilege. Although not required by the Joint Commission, a tracking mechanism can be very useful.

If this laundry list methodology is preferred, the organization may develop and use guidelines that evaluate part of the competency for obtaining and maintaining privileges based on experience with a certain procedure or groups of procedures over a period of time. This will be discussed in more detail later in the chapter.

Exhibit 6–2 shows a sample laundry or menu list of privileges.

Core Privileges/Bundling of Privileges

In recent years, the concept of "core privileges" or "bundling of privileges" has been introduced as an effective means of delineating clinical privileges. Regardless of the term used, the concept refers to grouping together privileges that might require a similar education, training, or skill to be performed. Privileges can also be related by organ systems, pathophysiology, diagnostic/therapeutic principles, or anatomic relationships. A core group would *not* include procedures or cognitive privileges that require special training different from that generally associated with any type of residency or fellowship. Procedures or privileges that require special training would be listed separately, not in a core group.

One of the benefits of grouping privileges into core groups or bundles is that it eliminates the need for a seemingly endless laundry list of procedures that are ordinarily included in a fully completed training program. Instead, a representative sample is listed for a defined group of privileges, and the practitioner checks only once to request that group of general privileges in a specific specialty area. The privileges included in the core group are the procedures most commonly performed or the diagnosis most commonly treated in the facility or organization.

It is important that when this method is used the clinical areas of the organization where these procedures are performed understand that all procedures will not be requested individually. If there is doubt in the clinical area about a specific procedure, clarification should be sought if someone schedules a procedure that

- is not on the privilege delineation that might be considered a special procedure or
- is not considered to be part of a core group of procedures (every procedure is not listed)

Departments such as surgery, cath lab, and gastroenterology lab are common areas where these questions may arise. If personnel frequently question a procedure that is not specifically listed in a core group, it is probably necessary to add that procedure to either the core group or an individual list of special procedures. This is particularly important when scheduling personnel may be new and unfamiliar with procedures that might be included in a core group of privileges as opposed to unique or special procedures.

Just as physicians need to identify criteria, categories, and/or lists of procedures to be used

Exhibit 6–2 Ambulatory Surgery Delineation of Privileges

Applicant's Name ____________________

Board Certification:
Specialty: ____________________ Date ________
____________________ ________
____________________ ________

Recertification:
Specialty: ____________________ Date ________
____________________ ________

Criteria for privileges: Physicians requesting privileges in Surgery should have completed the requirements for specialization by the American Board of Surgery or the equivalent, as defined by the Clinical Chief.

The following constitute outpatient and inpatient privileges of physicians of the Surgical Service.

Requested	Granted	
____	____	1. To ADMIT any patient, adult or adolescent with a surgical or surgery-related problem, if necessary after ambulatory surgery
____	____	2. To CONSULT on any patient, adult or adolescent with a surgical or surgery-related problem
____	____	3. To ORDER any diagnostic studies and procedures on any patient, adult or adolescent with a surgical or surgery-related problem
____	____	4. To TREAT any patient, adult or adolescent with a surgical or surgery-related problem
____	____	5. To PERFORM all diagnostic and therapeutic procedures usually considered within the sphere of surgery as initialed below. Privileges in these special procedures will be granted individually by the Director of Surgery on recommendation from or in consultation with the appropriate Division Chief. Special procedures may be added to or deleted from this list by the Division Chiefs of the Surgical Service. Request for any alteration in the list of Special Procedures can be initiated by the Director of the Surgical Service.

Requested	Granted	
____	____	Excision of Skin and Subcutaneous Lesions
____	____	Biopsy of Skin and Subcutaneous Lesions
____	____	Biopsy/Excision of Breast Lesions
____	____	Excision/Removal of Finger/Toe Nail
____	____	I/D of Superficial Abscesses
____	____	Sigmoidoscopy—Flexible & Rigid
____	____	Colonoscopy

Requested	Granted	
____	____	Excision of Ano-Rectal Lesions
____	____	Biopsy of Ano-Rectal Lesions
____	____	Removal of Foreign Body—Skin/Subcutaneous
____	____	Hernia—Inguinal
____	____	—Ventral
____	____	—Umbilical
____	____	Burns—FTSG
____	____	—STSG
____	____	Myringotomy & Insertion of Ventilating Tube
____	____	Antrotomy

continues

Exhibit 6–2 continued

Requested	Granted	
____	____	Submucous Resection or Septoplasty
____	____	Excision of Benign Lesions of Oral Cavity & Tongue
____	____	Direct Laryngoscopy
____	____	Nasal Fracture Reduction
____	____	Salivary Gland Calculus Removal
____	____	Excision of Benign Soft Tissue Lesions & Repairs
____	____	Biopsies
____	____	Skin Tumors
____	____	Lacerations
____	____	Endoscopies
____	____	Cervical Esophagectomy with Neck Dissection
____	____	Nasal Septoplasty
____	____	Osteoplastic Frontal Sinusectomy
____	____	Frontal Sinus Ablation
____	____	Grafts
____	____	Skin
____	____	Bone
____	____	Cartilage
____	____	Fascia
____	____	Dermis or Fat
____	____	Tendon
____	____	Nerve
____	____	Prep of Tube or Pedicule Flaps
____	____	Transfer of Direct or Delayed Flaps
____	____	"Z", "V-Y" Plastic Scar Revisions and Dermabrasion
____	____	Excision of Small Tumors
____	____	Benign
____	____	Immediate Repair
____	____	Malignant (small)
____	____	Immediate Repair
____	____	Neck Dissection
____	____	Fractures
____	____	Nose
____	____	Face
____	____	Mandible
____	____	Lacerations
____	____	TMJ Exploration
____	____	Excision Skin Lesions
____	____	Scar Revision
____	____	Dermabrasion (Head & Neck)
____	____	Liposuction (Head & Neck)

Requested	Granted	
____	____	Nose
____	____	Rhinoplasty
____	____	Reconstruction
____	____	Partial
____	____	Complete
____	____	Cleft Lip Repair
____	____	Primary
____	____	Secondary
____	____	Cleft Palate Repair
____	____	Primary
____	____	Secondary
____	____	Ear
____	____	Partial Reconstruction
____	____	Total Reconstruction
____	____	Aesthetic Repositioning of Ear
____	____	Eyelid Plastics
____	____	Cysts of the Neck
____	____	Thyroglossal
____	____	Branchial
____	____	Other
____	____	Hair Transplantation
____	____	Malar
____	____	Malar with Orbital Floor
____	____	Orbital Blowout
____	____	Mandibular—closed
____	____	—open
____	____	Pedicle Flap Procedures
____	____	Chest
____	____	Neck
____	____	Shoulder/Neck
____	____	Forehead/Scalp
____	____	Cheek
____	____	Free Flap Procedures
____	____	Chemical Peel
____	____	Facial Sling Procedures
____	____	Blepharoplasty
____	____	Prognathism Correction
____	____	Retrognathism Correction
		LASER SURGERY*
____	____	CO_2
____	____	Nd Yag
____	____	Argon
____	____	KTP/YAG

*<u>**Check requested privilege and complete appropriate form attached.**</u>

continues

Exhibit 6–2 continued

________________________________ ________________
Signature of Applicant Date

Privileges recommended: ______ as requested
______ with modifications

Statement of clinical privileges: The clinical privileges requested are authorized and consistent with the provisions of the Medical Staff Bylaws, Rules and Regulations. We attest that in recommending these privileges due consideration has been given to the applicant's professional performance, judgment, and technical skill.

______________________ _____ __________________ _____
Signature, Credentials Committee Chair Date Signature, Surgeon-in-Chief Date

Please indicate any change in privileges:

____

Courtesy of University Hospital, State University of New York at Stony Brook, Stony Brook, New York.

by applicants, it is important that each specialty identifying a core group of privileges decide what should be included and then review inclusions on a regular basis.

The potential difficulty of classifying privileges into bundles or core groups is that as training programs evolve, what once was classified as a special procedure requiring training outside of a fellowship or residency may become part of the general training process. One solution for this problem can be a space on the privilege checklist for special procedures for the practitioner to indicate if this was included in the applicant's training program. If the applicant indicates that a procedure was not included in the training program, additional documentation is then required. Depending upon competency verification procedures, the organization may or may not request confirmation from the training program that this training was, in fact, included in the applicant's program.

The section "Review and Revision of Privilege Delineation" contains additional information related to changes to core privileging.

Exhibits 6–3 through 6–5 are examples of core/bundling privilege formats.

Combination of Categories and Lists

Many organizations combine the category method with the laundry/menu list method. This allows better definitions of the intent of each category used, and laundry/menu lists are used in one or more categories based on skills acquired that are defined in the category. Depending upon the criteria that are developed for a particular category or list of privileges, organizations may want to limit which privileges or procedures someone requests on the basis of the category for which they qualify (see earlier definition of categories that differentiate among skills). For example, a physician boarded in internal medi-

Exhibit 6–3 Anesthesia Department Request for Clinical Privileges

QUALIFICATIONS:

Licensed physician who has completed a residency program necessary for or who has board certification in anesthesiology.

DESCRIPTION OF SECTIONS:

PART A: Includes a representative but of necessity not exhaustive list of anesthesia cognitive privileges.

PART B: Includes a listing of procedural skills for Anesthesiologists. Part B represents procedures and conditions normally taught in an Anesthesiology residency training program. Applicants shall provide documentation of having achieved satisfactory proficiency from their residency training program and/or by having regularly exercised these procedures at previous hospital affiliations.

PART C: Represents procedures defined as specialty clinical areas. Specific, designated training and/or previous clinical activity may be required in order to be eligible to apply for these privileges. *The specific documentation, if required, is listed within this document. Only those privileges with documentation submitted will be considered.*

Procedures other than those listed must be obtained on an individual basis through the appropriate department(s) of the hospital upon recommendation of the Section Chief of Anesthesia.

PART A:
EXPLANATION OF COGNITIVE PRIVILEGES FOR ANESTHESIOLOGISTS
(See attached check-off form to request the following)

Privileges to provide medical management of patients who are rendered unconscious or insensible to pain and emotional stress during surgical, obstetrical, and certain other medical procedures; the protection of life functions and vital organs; and the management of problems in pain relief, cardiopulmonary resuscitation, pulmonary care, and critically ill patients in special care units. Privileges to admit patients, perform and document history and physical information, and order diagnostic studies/procedures.

continues

Exhibit 6–3 continued

PART B:
EXPLANATION OF GENERAL PROCEDURAL PRIVILEGES FOR ANESTHESIOLOGISTS
(See attached check-off form to request the following)

CORE I

GENERAL ANESTHESIA: Inhalation, Mask, Endotracheal, Intravenous

CARDIOPULMONARY RESUSCITATION—Tracheal Intubation, Ventilation, Basic and Advanced CPR monitoring techniques

CARDIOPULMONARY BYPASS ANESTHESIA

PEDIATRIC ANESTHESIA (Including Neonatal Resuscitation)—Intravenous line placement, central venous line placement, arterial line placement, pulmonary artery catheterization, tracheal intubation (oral and nasal)

Minimum Requirement for Core I Privileges Is Collective Performance of 50 of the Above Noted Procedures within the Last Two Years

CORE II

REGIONAL/LOCAL ANESTHESIA—Spinal, Epidural, Lumbar, Thoracic, Sacral, Nerve Block, Plexus Block, Field Block, Intravenous Regional (Bier Block), Local Infiltration

CHRONIC PAIN THERAPY—Diagnosis and treatment of such chronic painful conditions as posttraumatic musculoskeletal pain, myofacial pain syndromes, cancer pain, reflex sympathetic dystrophies by the use of nerve blocks, physical and drug therapy

ACUTE PAIN MANAGEMENT—Prescribing the use of epidural narcotics, intravenous narcotics, patient-controlled analgesia on a consulting basis

Minimum Requirement for Core II Privileges Is Collective Performance of 50 of the Above Noted Procedures within the Last Two Years

CORE III

ANALGESIA SEDATION—Intravenous, Inhalation

CONSCIOUS SEDATING DRUGS
Use of conscious sedating drugs per hospitalwide policy

Minimum Requirement for Core III Privileges Is Collective Performance of 25 of the Above Noted Procedures within the Last Two Years

continues

Exhibit 6–3 continued

PART C:
ADDITIONAL PROCEDURAL SKILLS FOR ANESTHESIOLOGISTS
(Specific Documentation Required)

INTERPRETATION OF TRANSESOPHAGEAL ECHOCARDIOGRAPHY

1. Documentation of training in Conventional Echocardiography during residency **OR**
2. Evidence of training through an AMA-approved CME Course

Minimum Requirement for Interpretation of Transesophageal Echocardiography Privileges Is Performance of 10 Procedures within the Last Two Years

SECTION OF ANESTHESIA PRIVILEGE DELINEATION

CHECK-OFF FORM

PART A:
COGNITIVE PRIVILEGES FOR ANESTHESIOLOGISTS

YES OR NO COLUMN MUST BE CHECKED

YES	NO	Physicians in the Section of Anesthesia may apply for the following privileges:	Approved with No Restrictions	Approved with Conditions (See Below)	Denied (See Below)	Documentation Not Received, Voluntary Withdrawal
		Cognitive Privileges For Anesthesiologists				

COMMENTS:

___

___

continues

Exhibit 6–3 continued

PART B:
GENERAL PROCEDURAL SKILLS FOR ANESTHESIOLOGISTS

YES OR NO COLUMN MUST BE CHECKED

YES	NO	Physicians in the Section of Anesthesia may apply for the following privileges:	Approved with No Restrictions	Approved with Conditions (See Below)	Denied (See Below)	Documentation Not Received, Voluntary Withdrawal
		CORE I—General, Cardiopulmonary Resuscitation, Cardiopulmonary Bypass Anesthesia, Pediatric Anesthesia				
		CORE II—Regional/Local Anesthesia, Chronic Pain Therapy, Acute Pain Management				
		CORE III—Analgesia Sedation, Conscious Sedating Drugs				

I HAVE MET THE MINIMUM PROCEDURE REQUIREMENTS FOR THE CATEGORIES I HAVE REQUESTED: YES ____ NO ____

COMMENTS:

____

____

PART C:
ADDITIONAL PROCEDURAL SKILLS FOR ANESTHESIOLOGISTS
(Specific Documentation Required)

YES	NO	Physicians in the Section of Anesthesia may apply for the following privileges:	Approved with No Restrictions	Approved with Conditions (See Below)	Denied (See Below)	Documentation Not Received, Voluntary Withdrawal
		Interpretation of Intra-Operative Transesophageal Echocardiography				

continues

Exhibit 6–3 continued

I HAVE MET THE MINIMUM PROCEDURE REQUIREMENTS FOR THE CATEGORIES I HAVE REQUESTED: YES ____ NO ____

COMMENTS:

____

____

I hereby certify that I have reviewed each cognitive and procedural privilege request as supported by documentation of training and experience and clinical competence and feel the applicant is qualified to perform privileges as designated above.

____

Proctor Assignment

____

Section Chief Signature *Date*

FOR NEW APPLICANTS:
Temporary Privileges Recommended (If Requested) Yes ____ No ____

By signing below, I acknowledge that I have read and understand the Cognitive and Procedural Standards for privileging that I am requesting.

____

Applicant's Signature *Date*

FOR NEW APPLICANTS:
Temporary Privileges Requested:
Yes ____ No ____
(Temporary privileges are considered following Credentials Committee review, and applicant will be notified when effective)

Note: AMA, American Medical Association; CME, continuing medical education; CPR, cardiopulmonary resuscitation.

Courtesy of St. Francis Cabrini Hospital, Alexandria, Louisiana.

Exhibit 6–4 General Surgery Clinical Privileges

CLASSIFICATION OF PRIVILEGES:

Initial applications and reapplications to the Medical Staff and/or additional clinical privileges requested at other times must be accompanied by documentation of training and/or experience, where indicated.

REQUESTED		DIVISION OF SURGERY CLINICAL PRIVILEGES SECTION OF GENERAL SURGERY	NUMBER PERFORMED LAST 2 YRS	RECOMMENDED		DENIED	VOLUN. W/DRAW
CHECK ONE				NO RESTRICT.	CONDITIONS SEE BELOW	SEE BELOW	SEE BELOW
YES	NO	CATEGORY I: COGNITIVE/INTERPRETIVE					
		CORE PRIVILEGES					
		(LIST PRIV.) ______ ______ ______ ______ ______					
		INDIVIDUAL PRIVILEGES					
YES	NO	CATEGORY II: GENERAL PROCEDURES					
		CORE PRIVILEGES					
		(LIST PRIV.) ______ ______ ______ ______ ______					
		INDIVIDUAL PRIVILEGES					
		INDIVIDUAL PRIVILEGES					

continues

Exhibit 6–4 continued

REQUESTED		DIVISION OF SURGERY CLINICAL PRIVILEGES SECTION OF GENERAL SURGERY	NUMBER PERFORMED LAST 2 YRS	RECOMMENDED		DENIED	VOLUN. W/DRAW
CHECK ONE				NO RESTRICT.	CONDITIONS SEE BELOW	SEE BELOW	SEE BELOW
YES	NO	CATEGORY III: SPECIAL PROCEDURES					
		1. Must be credentialed to perform the same procedure surgically; **and** 2. Must provide adequate documentation of current competence; **or** the first five (5) laparoscopic cases for each procedure requested will be observed by a Retreat Hospital credentialed physician with laparoscopy experience of more than 25 cases; **and** 3. Must provide evidence of successful, recent completion of training in the performance of laparoscopic procedure requested by providing documentation of: a. Approved CME course that specifically includes the laparoscopic procedure; or b. Applicant must have received instruction in the laparoscopic procedure as routine part of residency program and provide letter of certification from the program's chief.					
		LAPAROSCOPIC HERNIORRHAPHY—SEE ABOVE CRITERIA					
		LAPAROSCOPIC BOWEL RESECTION—SEE ABOVE CRITERIA					
		INDIVIDUAL PRIVILEGES: LIST SPECIFIC CRITERIA					

Note: CME, continuing medical education.

Courtesy of Columbia Retreat Hospital, Richmond, Virginia.

Exhibit 6–5 Request for Gynecologic Clinical Privileges

(1–) ______________________ Date

Are You Applying for This Category/Privilege?	Privilege/Category	Education	Training	Certification	Experience	References/ Observations
☐ YES ☐ NO Recommendation: ☐ APP ☐ Denied COMMENTS: ________	**CATEGORY I—GYNECOLOGY PRIVILEGES** • Breast biopsy • D and C, with or without cervical biopsy • Biopsy of vulva, and/or perineum • Evacuation of retained products of conception (uterus less than 12 weeks size) • Marsupialization of Bartholin cyst (abscess) • Culdocentesis	MD, DO	Successful completion of a family practice residency	Board certified or seeking certification by the American Board of Family Practice	Perform 24 within the last two years to maintain privileges	
☐ YES ☐ NO Recommendation: ☐ APP ☐ Denied COMMENTS: ________	**CATEGORY II—GYNECOLOGY PRIVILEGES** • D and C, with or without biopsy • D and C, with or without conization • Laparotomy • Operations for removal of uterus, cervix, oviducts, ovaries & appendix; abdominal or vaginal • Diagnostic laparoscopy • Tubal fulguration • Operations of treatment of urinary stress incontinence; vaginal approach, retropubic urethral suspension or sling procedure • Fistula repairs; vesico-vaginal, recto-vaginal, or uretero-vaginal • Tuboplasty; micro, macro, fimbrioplasty • Hernia repair; incisional or umbilical • Operations for treatment of noninvasive carcinoma of: vulva, vagina, uterus, ovary, cervix • Repair of rectocele, enterocele • Vaginectomy; total or partial	MD, DO	Successful completion of an OB/GYN residency	Board certified or seeking certification by the American Board of Obstetrics and Gynecology	Perform 24 within the last two years to maintain privileges	

continues

Exhibit 6–5 continued

Are You Applying for This Category/Privilege?	Privilege/Category	Education	Training	Certification	Experience	References/ Observations
	• Colpocleisis • Strassman procedure (metroplasty) • Myomectomy • Incidental appendectomy • Node dissection; superficial inguinal, pelvic, paraaortic • Use of hysteroscope; diagnostic, therapeutic • Second trimester abortion by suction & curettage and/or D and C (> 12 weeks, but < 20 weeks)					

Note: D and C, dilatation and curettage.

Courtesy of Columbia-Continental Division, Denver, Colorado.

cine (category II) but not in the subspecialty of cardiology (category III) may not be able to request cardiology procedures requiring category III designation.

Exhibits 6–6 and 6–7 are examples of privilege formats combining the category/level and laundry/menu methods.

DEVELOPMENT OF CRITERIA FOR CLINICAL PRIVILEGES

Criteria for clinical privileges are those requirements to be fulfilled before one can be considered for privileges requested. Criteria for privileges should be clearly defined so that the

Exhibit 6–6 Medicine Service Clinical Privileges Request

MEDICINE SERVICE CLINICAL PRIVILEGES REQUEST

☐ **New Applicant** ☐ **Reappointment** ☐ **Additional Privileges**

Physician Name ______________________________ Date ___________

Please indicate a divisional affiliation only if you plan to be active in clinical, educational, and/or research activities:

☐ Allergy
☐ Cardiovascular Medicine
☐ Clinical Pharmacology
☐ Endocrinology
☐ Family Medicine
☐ Gastroenterology
☐ General Internal Medicine
☐ Gerontology
☐ Hematology
☐ Immunology/Rheumatology
☐ Infectious Diseases
☐ Nephrology
☐ Oncology
☐ Pulmonary and Critical Care Medicine
☐ No Divisional Affiliation

Please indicate the Medical Staff classification you are requesting by checking the appropriate box.

☐ **Active Medical Staff**—I request approval to admit patients and/or furnish care as indicated on this form.
☐ **Courtesy Admitting Medical Staff**—I request approval to admit patients and/or furnish care as indicated on this form.
☐ **Courtesy Teaching Medical Staff**—I request approval to admit patients and furnish care as indicated on this form in relation to my clinical teaching appointment.

I understand that I may request additional privileges at a later date.

GENERAL ADMITTING CATEGORIES

☐ **CATEGORY 1. REFERRING PHYSICIAN**

Physicians in this category are affiliated with Stanford University School of Medicine through either teaching appointments or use of faculty as consultants. They do not anticipate providing care for patients in SUH, although they may send patients for admission here and follow their care after admission.

continues

Exhibit 6–6 continued

☐ **CATEGORY 2. LIMITED HOSPITAL PRACTICE**

Physicians in this category may be specialists in Internal Medicine or Family Medicine or general practitioners, allergists, etc., with practices that are primarily ambulatory. They would limit their supervision of hospital care to common conditions in patients who are mildly to moderately ill (e.g., asthma, bacterial pneumonia, venous thrombosis, urosepsis, dehydration, hypertension). This category of medical staff membership requires consultation with other specialists for hospital patients with unusual or complex conditions for uncertain diagnoses or when patients do not improve as expected. In general, these physicians do not perform moderate or high-risk procedures that require special clinical privileges or provide care for patients in the intensive care units.

☐ **CATEGORY 3. EXTENSIVE HOSPITAL PRACTICE**

Physicians in this category may be specialists or subspecialists in Internal Medicine who have major inpatient practice. They may perform lower risk procedures requiring special clinical privileges (e.g., arthrocentesis, lumbar puncture), maintaining adequate activity to ensure high quality. They care for a broader range of diagnoses and severity of illness than category 2 physicians (e.g., moderately to severely ill patients with multiple organ system disease, acute myocardial infarction, diabetic ketoacidosis, bacterial endocarditis, sepsis without shock). Despite their in-hospital experience, these physicians would also exercise good judgment, utilizing consultative physicians appropriately in unusual cases for uncertain diagnoses, or when patients fail to improve as expected. In general, they would not provide sole care for patients in the intensive care units.

☐ **CATEGORY 4. HIGH-RISK HOSPITAL PRACTICE**

Physicians in this category have the most active inpatient practices, will usually be subspecialists, and provide care for critically ill patients in specialized care units (e.g., multi-system failure, septic shock, complicated myocardial infarction, respiratory failure, acute leukemia, cancer requiring chemotherapy). These physicians perform higher risk diagnostic and therapeutic procedures requiring special clinical privileges (e.g., angiography, endoscopy), maintaining adequate activity to ensure high quality.

MEDICINE SERVICE DELINEATION OF PRIVILEGES

Please indicate below those privileges you request and procedures you wish to perform/supervise at Stanford University Hospital. Please state the number of treatment/procedures done in each category/class by you in the past two years (or past 5 years if new applicant) and the number of major complications experienced (describe any such complications on a separate page). New applicants and applicants for credentials in a new procedure must submit written verification of training and experience in the performance of specific procedures.

continues

Exhibit 6–6 continued

	NUMBER DONE Past 5 yrs (New Apps)	Past 2 yrs (Re-apps)	Major Complications
Category I. General Diagnostic and Therapeutic Procedures			
☐ A. Class I—Miscellaneous Procedures			
☐ Lumbar puncture	____	____	____
☐ Skin biopsy	____	____	____
☐ Rigid proctosigmoidoscopy	____	____	____
☐ Fiberoptic sigmoidoscopy			
___ Diagnostic only	____	____	____
___ With biopsy	____	____	____
☐ Bone marrow biopsy and aspiration	____	____	____
☐ B. Class II—Minor Vascular Procedures	____	____	____
☐ Arterial puncture			
☐ Arterial line placement			
___ Percutaneous			
___ Cutdown			
☐ Central venous line placement			
☐ Venous line placement by cutdown			
☐ Femoral vein venipuncture			
☐ C. Class III—Minor Centeses	____	____	____
☐ Diagnostic paracentesis			
☐ Therapeutic paracentesis			
☐ Diagnostic thoracentesis			
☐ Aspiration of intra- and sub-cutaneous cysts, furuncles, etc.			
☐ D. Class IV—Joint Procedures	____	____	____
☐ Arthrocentesis, large joint			
☐ Arthrocentesis, small joint			
☐ Therapeutic injection, large joint			
☐ Therapeutic injection, small joint			
Category II: Cardiovascular Medicine			
☐ A. Class I	____	____	____
☐ Temporary transvenous pacemaker placement			
☐ Placement of flotation right heart catheter			
☐ Pericardiocentesis			
☐ Subclavian venous access			
☐ Elective electrical cardioversion			
☐ B. Class II—Please note: Procedures are subject to controlled access to special laboratories			
☐ A. Left and right heart catheterization, cardiac and/or coronary angiography	____	____	____

continues

Exhibit 6–6 continued

	NUMBER DONE		
	Past 5 yrs (New Apps)	**Past 2 yrs (Re-apps)**	**Major Complications**
☐ B. Coronary interventional techniques, including angioplasty	________	________	________
☐ C. Coronary atherectomy	________	________	________
☐ D. Intracardiac electrophysiology			
___ Diagnostic studies	________	________	________
___ Catheter ablation	________	________	________
___ Testing of antitachycardia/ defibrillator devices	________	________	________
☐ E. Trans-septal left heart catheterization	________	________	________
☐ F. Myocardial biopsy	________	________	________
☐ G. Elective cardiac pacemaker placement	________	________	________
Category III: Endocrinology			
☐ Thyroid biopsy, percutaneous	________	________	________
Category IV: Gastroenterology			
☐ A. Class I—Esophagogastroduodenoscopy (EGD)			
___ with biopsy	________	________	________
___ polypectomy and fulguration	________	________	________
☐ B. Class II—Endoscopic retrograde cholangiopancreatography (ERCP) (select one)			
___ Diagnostic studies only	________	________	________
___ With sphincterotomy, stone extraction and stent placement	________	________	________
___ Manometry	________	________	________
☐ C. Class III—Colonoscopy	________	________	________
___ With biopsy, polypectomy and fulguration			
☐ D. Class IV—Other specialized invasive procedures			
☐ Sclerotherapy for esophageal varices	________	________	________
☐ Percutaneous endoscopic gastrostomy	________	________	________
☐ Heater probe coagulation	________	________	________
☐ Bi-polar cautery	________	________	________
☐ Laser coagulation (separate form required)	________	________	________
☐ Esophageal stent placement	________	________	________
☐ Pneumatic dilation for achalasia	________	________	________
☐ E. Class V—Other Procedures			
☐ Liver biopsy, percutaneous	________	________	________
☐ Small bowel biopsy	________	________	________

continues

Exhibit 6–6 continued

	NUMBER DONE		
	Past 5 yrs (New Apps)	**Past 2 yrs (Re-apps)**	**Major Complications**
☐ Esophagogastric balloon tamponade	______	______	______
☐ Esophageal dilation	______	______	______
___ Rigid	______	______	______
___ Balloon	______	______	______
☐ Duodenal drainage	______	______	______
☐ Endoscopic ultrasound	______	______	______
☐ Esophageal manometry	______	______	______
☐ Rectal manometry	______	______	______
Category V: Hematology			
☐ Bone marrow transplant	______	______	______
Category VI: Immunology & Rheumatology			
☐ Synovial biopsy, percutaneous	______	______	______
Category VII: Renal			
☐ A. Class I	______	______	______
☐ Renal biopsy			
☐ Transplant kidney biopsy			
☐ B. Class II	______	______	______
☐ Hemodialysis			
☐ Peritoneal dialysis			
☐ Shiley catheter placement			
☐ Continuous A-V filtration			
Category VIII: Pulmonary and Critical Care			
☐ A. Class I—Emergency procedures			
☐ Endotracheal intubation	______	______	______
☐ Thoracostomy tube placement	______	______	______
☐ B. Class II—Bronchoscopic procedures			
☐ Rigid bronchoscopy and biopsy	______	______	______
☐ Flexible bronchoscopy and biopsy	______	______	______
☐ C. Class III—Management of controlled ventilation			
☐ With neuromuscular blocking agents	______	______	______
☐ Without neuromuscular blocking agents	______	______	______
☐ D. Class IV—Miscellaneous elective procedures			
☐ Endotracheal intubation (elective)	______	______	______
☐ Thoracostomy tube placement	______	______	______
☐ Placement of flotation right heart catheter	______	______	______

continues

Exhibit 6–6 continued

	NUMBER DONE Past 5 yrs (New Apps)	Past 2 yrs (Re-apps)	Major Complications
☐ Percutaneous pleural biopsy	______	______	______
☐ Percutaneous lung aspiration	______	______	______
☐ Trans-tracheal aspiration	______	______	______

Signature of Applicant ____________________ Date ______

☐ **Privileges approved as requested**

☐ **Privileges approved with the following limitations and/or restrictions:**

____

☐ **Privileges Denied**

Reviewed by Medicine Credentials Committee ____________________ Date ______

Signature of Approval ____________________ Date ______
Division Head

Signature of Approval ____________________ Date ______
Chief, Medicine Service

Note: SUH, Stanford University Hospital.

Courtesy of UCSF Stanford Health Care, Stanford, California.

applicant understands any prerequisite and any "maintenance" requirements. After reviewing the criteria, the applicant may decide that he or she does not qualify and may choose not to apply for those privileges as opposed to requesting the privileges and being denied due to lack of the necessary qualifications. Clinical privilege criteria should be defined *before* an application for specific privileges is given to an applicant.

Joint Commission hospital medical staff standards for department directors' responsibilities include recommending criteria for clinical privileges relevant to the care provided by those with clinical privileges in that department. A broad spectrum of criteria can be defined for clinical privileging. This spectrum can range from a board certification requirement with specific numbers of performed procedures to a broad, generic statement such as "In the specialty requested, consideration will be given to special, documented qualities of training or experience that are desirable to the department." This latter criterion statement basically implies that anyone can apply for privileges within a department and that no specific qualifications are defined. If the latter of the two examples is the approach used for privilege delineations, the organization should consider defining these "special documented qualities" in order to avoid a subjective evaluation that could lead to arbitrary decisions that might then be subject to due process.

Criteria should be defined for each individual or groups of clinical privileges; for example, internal medicine or gastroenterology. Consideration of the following should be made when developing criteria:

1. The required license (MD, DO, DDS, DPM, other).
2. The level of training and education ordinarily expected for someone applying for this procedure or group of privileges (e.g.,

Exhibit 6–7 Psychiatry Privileges and Qualifications

_______________________________ PRIVILEGES
NAME

____
BOARD ISSUED: _______ YEAR

PRIVILEGES CATEGORY 1	QUALIFICATIONS/CRITERIA USUAL AND CUSTOMARY PRIVILEGES	
	QUALIFICATIONS 1. Board certification by or current active participation in examination process leading to certification by the American Board of *Psychiatry*; OR 2. Successful completion of an approved training program; OR 3. Demonstrated acceptable practice in the privileges being requested for a minimum of ten (10) years.	
CATEGORY 2	**NOT USUAL AND CUSTOMARY PRIVILEGES*** *(*Procedures rarely performed, requiring special expertise, and/or requiring documented special training and/or certification when it exists)*	
	QUALIFICATIONS 1. Board certification by or current active participation in examination process leading to certification by the American Board of *Psychiatry*; OR 2. Experience in adolescent inpatient psychotherapy. Includes equivalent of a full year of supervised inpatient work with adolescents and ongoing continuing education in the area of adolescent inpatient psychotherapy, at least two such continuing education experiences per year. 3. Evidence of supervised experience and training in medical management of patient requiring detoxification. 4. Completion of a course of training and/or an acceptable intensive supervision from a clinician experienced with ECT. 5. Past experience under supervision and/or cumulative successful experience with Sodium Amytal interviews. 6. Completion of a course in or a period of supervision from a licensed clinician experienced in Hypnotherapy. 7. Certification in biofeedback.	

continues

Exhibit 6–7 continued

PRIVILEGE NUMBER	CATEGORY 1 - COGNITIVE PRIVILEGES	REQUESTED YES	REQUESTED NO
	Admit patients, perform history and physical exam, order diagnostic studies and procedures, treat and manage patients with psychiatric related problems.		
PRIVILEGE NUMBER	**CATEGORY 1—USUAL AND CUSTOMARY PRIVILEGES**	**REQUESTED YES**	**REQUESTED NO**
	1. Diagnostic evaluation		
	2. Pharmacotherapy		
	3. Dynamic psychotherapy for ages 18 onward		
	4. Crisis intervention		
	5. Consultation and/or therapy with family members		
	6. Behavioral therapy		
	7. Group therapy		
	8. Staff consultation/education		
	9. Forensic decision:		
	a. Ordering 72-hour holds, 14-day holds		
	b. Requesting conservatorship		
	c. Assessing competence		
	10. Planning for after-care		
	11. Requesting appropriate medical/surgical consultation		
	12. Ordering appropriate psychological and/or neuropsychological studies		
PRIVILEGE NUMBER	**CATEGORY 2—NOT USUAL AND CUSTOMARY PRIVILEGES**	**REQUESTED YES**	**REQUESTED NO**
	1. Electric convulsive therapy		
	2. Sodium amytal interviews		
	3. Hypnotherapy		
	4. Biofeedback		
	5. Treatment of adolescents, 15 and older, only		
	6. Bioethical consultation		
	7. Detoxification		

Note: ECT, electroconvulsive therapy.

Courtesy of UCSF Stanford Health Care, Stanford, California.

completed residency, fellowship, internship, other). The minimum number of years' training being required should be specified.

3. Any required reference letters from training program director or other peers who exercise these privileges and have firsthand knowledge of the candidate's training and/or competence.
4. Any board certification, qualification, or recertification requirements. Note that most boards recertify every 7 to 10 years. It is important to include a statement if recertification is necessary to maintain current privileges without additional review.
   - If board certification (and not just successful completion of a postgraduate training program) is required, it is important that bylaws or specific privilege delineations define the consequences of obtaining board certification after the allowed "grace period." Some options are:
     - Privileges shall terminate if board certification is not acquired within the acceptable time frame of the specialty board and/or medical staff bylaws.
     - The applicant will be reviewed on the basis of current clinical competence, equivalent training, and results of quality monitoring activities, and a recommendation will be on the basis of the outcome of this review.
   - With the second of these options, an organization may be more specific about criteria to be reviewed and what those outcomes should be in order to maintain the clinical privileges previously granted. It is possible that a board examination will be taken and failed subsequent to granting of privileges. This should also be addressed either as part of the options above or separately.
     - Specific observation for a certain number of cases (define the number) may be conducted to determine equivalent expertise without board certification.
     - Specific continuing medical education (CME) may be required (number of hours defined) within a stated time frame (retrospective and/or concurrent).
   - If specialty boards are to be a part of criteria, it is necessary to identify the boards that will be considered, namely those approved by the Accreditation Council for Graduate Medical Education (ACGME), Canadian boards, and equivalent American Osteopathic Association (AOA) boards. Boards may be listed that will *not* be considered in lieu of ACGME.
   - If recertification of boards is required, a procedure will be necessary for tracking recertification requirements and compliance. Software programs can track this information, or a manual system may be necessary. The system will need to track each practitioner the year board certification expires so that the board can be contacted to confirm recertification (via letter or access to the board directories such as American Board of Medical Specialties [ABMS], AOA, or the physician contacted to provide the information on recertification). Again, it is important to define what the options and/or consequences will be if recertification is not obtained.
5. Other privileges the practitioner must have to qualify for the privileges being evaluated (prerequisites); for example, privileges in percutaneous transluminal coronary angioplasty required for applying for coronary atherectomy privileges.
6. Specific proctoring requirements, such as observation, retrospective review and the number to be involved in the review (can be defined as a specific number or a range).
7. Any previous or required ongoing continuing medical education program to obtain and/or maintain the privileges and what the information about this education is to include (e.g., documented hours of continu-

ing medical education activity, type of activity (hands on, didactic), written confirmation from any proctoring involved in the program).

8. Any required number of procedures previously performed. This may apply to appointment and/or reappointment. If a specific number of procedures is required, the method for acceptable reporting of this information (e.g., in-house statistics, documentation from other accredited facilities) must be specified. Previously performed procedures are used to help determine competency and do not necessarily apply to every privilege/procedure. If a specific number of previously performed procedures will be included in criteria, it will be necessary to identify steps if the minimum number is not met. The following options might be considered.
   - acceptance and reevaluation in one year
   - recent, related continuing medical education in lieu of meeting minimum numbers
   - observation required for the first procedure (or other number defined)
   - if, after a defined period of time none of the above are met, the individual would voluntarily relinquish the privilege with no adverse effect or reporting requirement to the National Practitioner Data Bank (NPDB)
9. The setting in which the procedure can/will be performed and the patient age restrictions. It is possible that internal medicine privileges will be limited to age 12 and older or that general pediatric privileges will be limited to treatment of patients who are 18 and younger.

Deciding whether to attach a minimum number of procedures to be performed before *obtaining* privileges (appointment) and potentially a required number of procedures to be performed in order to *maintain* those privileges (at reappointment) may result in some controversy. If a requirement for a minimum number of procedures is used, and if the procedure is delineated in more than one department or specialty, there should be agreement by all departments or specialties involved as to the minimum number required to obtain or maintain the privileges. Is that always practical? The minimum number required could vary from one specialty to another depending on the extent of the training program and how many procedures are performed within that program. Training varies in the various specialties. For example, a gastroenterologist will have performed more flexible sigmoidoscopies in a training program than a family practitioner. An option for this scenario might be that the family practitioner be proctored (or obtain additional proctoring if the gastroenterologist also requires initial proctoring). On the other hand, if the family physician has considerable experience, has been out of training for a period of time and can document enough cases, the proctoring requirements could be equivalent to those of the gastroenterologist. Numbers performed to show experience should be *minimum* but at the same time should coincide with how many the department or specialty believes are necessary to maintain the skill needed. Some benchmarks for number of procedures to be performed annually to maintain competence (e.g., for heart surgeries) may be available from specialty boards.

In trying to decide whether numbers should be assigned to a specific procedure for reappointment purposes, the clinical department needs to decide if procedure competency is "static" or not: that is, whether repetition is necessary to maintain the skill. If it is static, numbers probably do not need to be used beyond what was included in a formal training environment. If numbers are defined, it is necessary to determine how those numbers are going to be collected within the reappointment time frame. In-house departments may generate those statistics via computer, or the involved department may have a manual compilation of the data. It will also be necessary to determine what is acceptable documentation from other facilities if the minimum numbers are not met within one's own organization. See Exhibit 6–8 for a sample privilege form that

Exhibit 6–8 Medicine Department Privilege Supplement

INSTRUCTION FOR COMPLETION:

The following privileges may be requested from your division via this form. Please check the privilege(s) you are requesting and submit with documentation noted below:

REQUESTS FOR PRIVILEGES MUST INCLUDE DOCUMENTATION, EITHER A LETTER FROM THE TRAINING DIRECTOR OR OTHER EVIDENTIARY BASIS, PRIOR TO CONSIDERATION.

It is the individual physician's responsibility to maintain a record of procedures performed. Failure to meet criteria for maintenance will result in reproctoring.

Privilege	Parent Division	Category	# to Apply	# to Be Proctored	# Per 2 Yrs. to Maintain	Yes	No	Granted
Flexible Sigmoidoscopy	GIM	1	10	5	12*			
Insertion of Femoral Lines for Dialysis	NEPH	1	10	3	5			
Percutaneous Renal Biopsy	NEPH	1	10	5	4			
Endotracheal Tube Placement	GIM	2	10	10	10			
Intrathoracic CVP Placement	GIM	2	10	3	5			
Paracentesis	GIM	2	5	3	2			
Thoracentesis	GIM	2	5	4	4			
Fine Needle Aspiration of Thyroid	ENDO	2	10	1	1			
Electric Cardioversion	CARD	2	10	3	2			
Right Heart Cath.	CARD	2	20	3	5			
Temporary Transvenous Pacemaker Placement	CARD	2	20	3	5			
Permanent Pacemaker Placement	CARD	2	50	5	10			
Intracoronary Thrombolysis	CARD	2	20	5	3			
Right Ventricular Endomyocardial Biopsy	CARD	2	5	2	3			

*4 at hospital, 8 may be outpatient, office, other facility, with documentation/attestation.

Note: CVP, central venous pressure; GIM, gastrointestinal medicine; NEPH, nephrology; ENDO, endocrinology; CARD, cardiology.

Courtesy of Cedars Sinai Medical Center, Los Angeles, California.

defines numbers (Exhibit 6–1 is also an example).

When an organization is identifying and defining privilege criteria, very often privileges will cross over from one department to another. This can cause "turf battles" among the various specialties or departments, as arguments develop as to who is qualified: For example, gastroenterologists and family physicians doing flexible sigmoidoscopy, cardiologists and surgeons doing pacemaker insertions, or family physicians doing obstetrics. There is no clear formula as to how these issues of privileging criteria should be resolved within the medical staff. Training programs may be difficult to evaluate for different specialties in separate departments. Very often, organizations do not have procedures for how to resolve privileging issues. Community standards of care may be identified, but it can be difficult to define a "community standard of care" when various specialty groups are disagreeing over who should have the ability to perform a specific procedure or maintain privileges.

When these issues arise, the involved departments should be asked to

- meet together for the purpose of resolving differences
- review their respective department's recommended criteria for the overlapping procedures
- make a unified recommendation (or separate recommendations if no resolution is found) to the medical executive committee

The medical executive committee should review, make a recommendation, and refer to the governing board for approval. This approach may sound easier than it really is. Steps 2 and 3 may require several meetings and/or time to gather supporting data to substantiate the recommendation. If different recommendations are received by the medical executive committee, additional time may be required at that level before agreement is reached for a recommendation to the board.

As with any request for privileges, those applying for overlapping privileges should understand that if the defined criteria are met, they are not automatically qualified for the privilege. Additional peer review that may include such items as malpractice history and reference letters must also be considered. If there is any possibility that exceptions will be made to the defined criteria, the bylaws, policies, and procedures could require a statement that applicants who do not meet the criteria may still be considered for the requested privileges "after review of their equivalent training and experience." Consideration must be given to every applicant who does not meet the defined criteria, and the process used must be consistent.

The first step in developing criteria for clinical privileges will be to identify each area and/or category for which privileges are granted. Once this is accomplished, the criteria categories listed previously can be outlined in a format such as that found in Exhibit 6–9. The department (or specialty) then identifies the specific requirements. Specialty boards may have information that is helpful in defining criteria, especially for high-risk and/or high-volume procedures.

ADDITION OF NEW PRIVILEGES

In General

As new procedures develop, privileges need to be added to current privilege delineations. When that happens, a process should be identified and followed to determine criteria for that specific privilege before it is added to the privilege delineation.

It is important to remember that criteria should be established for the new procedures or treatment methodology before the privileges are granted. Often physicians return from a brief training program for a specific procedure and are very anxious to be able to use what they have learned as soon as possible. There should be a general understanding among the medical staff that any new privileging criteria to be added must

Exhibit 6–9 Criteria Development for Privilege Delineation

SPECIFIC PROCEDURE: ______________________________
CLERICAL DEPARTMENT(S): ______________________________
DESCRIPTION OF PROCEDURE: ______________________________

1. License Required	
2. Training and Education	______________ years postgraduate education in ______________ and ______________ or ______________ Special education or CME required: ______________ Fellowship/other in: ______________
3. Experience/Competence	Will evidence of current competence and/or experience be required? _____ yes _____ no Will references be required? _____ yes _____ no if yes: Number? ______________ By whom? ______________ Will evidence of number of procedures performed be required? _____ yes _____ no If yes: Number? ______________ Reporting method? ______________
4. Board Certification/Status	Current Board Certification in ______________ required or certification in ______________ to be obtained within ______________ (time frame) Consequences if not obtained will be ______________
5. Prerequisite Privileges	Must have been granted ______________ privileges needed in order to apply for this privilege
6. Required Documentation	
7. Proctoring	Proctoring of ______________ (number) of procedures within ______________ (time frame) by ______________ (who)
8. Reappointment	Competence at time of reappointment will be measured by: (Options) Minimum number performed ______________ CEU Requirements ______________ Other ______________

Approvals (Board Dates):
Original: Revision:

Note: CME, continuing medical education; CEU, continuing education units

Courtesy of C. Mobley & Associates, LLC, and Quality Management Options, LLC, Colorado Springs, Colorado.

go through the process of being evaluated, written, and approved before the privileges can be requested. There is great risk to the organization if a practitioner exercises privileges that have not yet been granted or for which the criteria have not been defined and approved.

Exhibit 6–10 is a sample policy and procedure for this process.

TELEMEDICINE

Questions have been raised about whether to privilege those physicians involved in telemedicine. Telemedicine is basically using video or other technology to assist hospitals in making a proper patient diagnosis. This is being used in many of the nation's rural hospitals that do not have the expertise locally to help them diagnose some of their patients' conditions.[5] Since the individuals providing the expertise on the video or other technology are not actually on site and are not providing direct hands-on patient care, the question arises as to whether these people need to be privileged. This situation differs from that in hospitals that have any kind of contract with physicians who come into the hospital to provide the services. Such physicians must be credentialed. In 1997, the Joint Commission stated that physicians who provided only consultation by telephone, interactive telecommunications or other modes from a remote location other than where the patient is being treated do not need to be privileged by the organization that is seeking consultation from them. However, "those physicians who provide consultation that the hospital follows for patient care must be privileged."[6] For example, the Joint Commission stated that if an electrocardiogram (EKG) interpretation service provides a report and then the receiving organization enters that report into the medical record, the LIP giving the interpretation should be privileged.[7]

At a minimum, it is suggested that any practitioner who provides this type of consultation via video or other technology should be a qualified health care practitioner who is acting within the scope of his or her expertise. The credentialing professional or medical staff office can check with the hospital where this practitioner has privileges to confirm that he or she is in fact a licensed provider of care. The other alternative would be to query the state licensing board in the state where the practitioner resides to verify current licensure. More definitive standards or guidelines may be forthcoming as this mode of medicine continues to develop and increase in use across the country.

The following should be considered if an organization is considering participation in the use of telemedicine:

- What is the scope of the relationship between the host site and the off-site practitioners?
- Who are the people at the other end of the line offering advice? If they are providing the service to patients in your facility, you need to credential them.
- Do the off-site specialists have privileges at their home base medical center to validate their consultation?
- Does the hospital want to obtain copies of off-site practitioners' malpractice insurance?
- Will all parties share culpability in the event of a lawsuit?[8]

Hospitalists

Another new type of practitioner providing services in the hospital is referred to as a hospitalist. These are physicians who may work primarily with medical groups in a managed care contract environment and are responsible for making rounds on the hospitalized patients. By doing this, they free up more time for the specialists to see and treat patients in their office environment. These physicians are usually internists or general practitioners who make rounds on hospitalized patients, write orders, and discharge the patients. In general, their privilege delineation remains the same as if they were private admitting doctors, although they may need

Exhibit 6–10 New Procedures Approval (Nonexperimental)

GENERAL STANDARDS:

1. Develop standards before applicant's request is processed or accepted.
2. Determine which major specialty(ies) is(are) to develop the standards.
3. Standards are reviewed by multidisciplinary Credentialing Committee "to assure the same level of quality of patient care by all individuals with delineated clinical privileges, within Medical Staff departments, across departments/services, and between members and nonmembers of the medical staff who have delineated clinical privileges." (Joint Commission)
4. Standards must be approved by the Medical Executive Committee and Board prior to implementation.
5. The potential applicant is provided with the specific standards developed for the clinical privileges he or she is requesting.

GUIDELINES FOR APPROVING NEW PROCEDURES (NONEXPERIMENTAL):

I. The request must first be forwarded to the appropriate department chairman to determine whether procedure is general or special with the following outcome:
   A. If it is determined that the procedure is a general procedure and experience is obtained through residency training, the department may recommend addition of procedure to delineation of privileges without outlining specific guidelines.
   B. If it is determined to be a special procedure, the following must be defined by the department:
      1. Is special education/training required? If so, what kind?
         Hands-on training
         Didactic course
         Special certification
         Board certification
         Demonstration of previous performance (supervised, numbers performed, outcome)
      2. Do ongoing minimum competency requirements need to be defined (for reappointment)? If so, define.
      3. Is proctoring required? If so,
         Concurrent or retrospective
         Minimum number required
         By whom
      4. Outline for monitoring of new procedure:
         Indications for use of procedure
         Expected results
         Potential complications and anticipated complication rates
         Other pertinent information reported in medical literature
      5. Those procedures with significant risks should be monitored for a six- to twelve-month period to evaluate the results. A focused review should be done and reported to the credentials and/or quality management committee and department for information.

II. If more than one specialty is involved in the procedure, an ad hoc committee appointed by the chief of staff, with representation by all appropriate specialties, will be used to establish guidelines.

III. Route the proposed standards to the multidisciplinary credentials committee for "one level of care" determination.

IV. Send recommended standards to the Medical Executive Committee and Board of Directors for final approval. Once approved, add to the delineation of privileges form and include criteria concerning privileges to departmental rules/regulations.

V. To be eligible for consideration for the clinical privilege(s) specified, the applicant must provide information demonstrating that he or she meets the standards. If the applicant does not supply the required information, the request will be considered incomplete and will not be processed.

Courtesy of C. Mobley & Associates, LLC, and Quality Management Options, LLC, Colorado Springs, Colorado.

to restrict what privileges they are requesting since their practice will be general and they will not be performing invasive procedures. The basic qualifications remain the same, but a definition of how a hospitalist will have access to patient care when admitted by another physician may need to be spelled out in medical staff policies and/or rules.

As the managed care concept continues to expand, there will most likely be increased use of hospitalists. Managed care organizations believe that hospitalists save the primary care practitioner time as well as reducing time for patients in the hospital. In early 1998, it was reported by the Philadelphia-based National Association Inpatient Physicians' Medical Society for Hospitals that there are nearly 1,500 hospitalists in the country.[9]

TEMPORARY PRIVILEGES

Many organizations use temporary privileges, the nemesis of the medical staff services professional. The granting of these privileges is hospital specific and is outlined in the bylaws, policies, and procedures. Hospitals are not required to grant temporary privileges or prohibited from granting them in the case of any of the temporary privileges described below. Temporary privileges can be defined for a variety of situations. They should be granted only for a specific period of time that needs to be stated in the bylaws (by Joint Commission standards), with any provision for extension of those temporary privileges to be documented. In the information that follows, the same principles can apply to AHPs. Appropriate language should be included in the AHP plan and rules. NCQA does not recognize temporary privileges. Practitioners are expected to be fully credentialed and the review/decision process completed before any contract or agreement allowing them to see patients.

Pending Application

Temporary privileges can be approved while an applicant's file is being verified and completed. The bylaws need to define what information has to be submitted, reviewed, and/or verified before the granting of temporary privileges. It is common to require that the application form be completed and that specific information such as licensure, Drug Enforcement Administration (DEA), license malpractice insurance, and completion of a clinical privilege delineation form has been submitted before approval for temporary privileges. Other medical staffs require the application to be processed through the credentials committee before temporary privileges will be considered.

Standards require and bylaws should state that the information is reviewed by the department chairman and/or chief of staff, following which temporary privileges are granted by the chief executive officer (or his/her designee).[10]

For Care of a Specific Patient

Temporary privileges can be granted to an individual for care of a specific patient. The practitioner is not an applicant to the medical staff but possesses specific expertise that is not currently available through the medical staff and therefore is requested to perform a specific procedure or treatment for an individual case. The bylaws will define what information needs to be received before the granting of temporary privileges (e.g., license, malpractice insurance, description of services to be provided, and any requested documentation for competency evaluation). Policies should describe content of the form to be completed for a one-time-only temporary situation. The information may be documented from a phone conversation between the medical staff office person and the physician requesting the privileges or may require more extensive information gathering. At minimum, information such as license, DEA, and insurance coverage can be faxed to the medical staff office. This request for temporary privileges should also include a written request (or documented verbal request) from the physician on the medical staff who is asking the "outside" physician to participate in patient care.

Temporary privileges can be granted for one-case-only situations to qualified individuals to admit and/or treat a patient. These individuals may possess specific expertise or may otherwise need to admit and/or treat a patient in a hospital where they do not normally practice. In this case, bylaws may allow for a one-case temporary privilege but limit the number of times this can occur in a 12-month period. Many bylaws state that after three or four requests for temporary privileges in a given period of time, the individual must make application to the medical staff. This keeps practitioners from requesting privileges numerous times when they do not want to be on the medical staff but have patients they want to admit to the hospital. Information to be obtained from the requesting practitioner would be the same as mentioned earlier. Approval of these privileges is granted in the same manner as described in the application pending section. Exhibits 6–11 through 6–13 show a sample protocol and forms (one for medical staff and one for AHPs).

Locum Tenens

Locum tenens is the term used for a physician who is going to cover a medical staff member's practice for a temporary period. The reasons vary,

Exhibit 6–11 Temporary Privilege Protocol

CATEGORY ONE

A **Category One** temporary privileges request applies to physicians who: (**1**) Consult on a patient; (**2**) Are Fellows (physicians in training) who will cover a CSMC physician's practice, or (**3**) Possess a special expertise that is not otherwise available at CSMC. **Category One** temporary privileges may not exceed 3 requests during any 12-month period, unless an application for medical staff membership accompanies the third request.

Steps Required:

1. Applicant completes Part I of the Request for Temporary Privileges Form.
2. A Letter of Justification applies to physicians who:
   - (a) *Consult on a patient:* This letter comes from the patient's primary physician.
   - (b) *Are Fellows:* This letter comes from the applicant's Training Director/Instructor giving permission to moonlight as well as verification of date of graduation and their standing in the training program.
   - (c) *Possess a special expertise:* This letter comes from the patient's primary physician.
3. Applicant provides copy of current California license.
4. Applicant provides current DEA Certificate or copy of application or renewal if DEA has expired.
5. All applicants must provide evidence of current Professional Liability Insurance (minimum acceptable limits of liability are $1 million per occurrence/$3 million per aggregate).
   - (a) Physicians who will consult or possess a special expertise must provide a copy of their *own* insurance.
   - (b) Fellows must provide a copy of the policy of the doctor they are covering for as well as a letter from that doctor's insurance company stating "locum tenens" coverage is in effect.
6. Applicant returns the above documentation to the department of his or her specialty.
7. Department completes Part II of the Request/Authorization and submits to Medical Staff Services.
8. *Upon receipt of the Request/Authorization, Medical Staff Services will review for completeness. If incomplete, Medical Staff Services will return the Request/Authorization to the department.*

continues

Exhibit 6–11 continued

9. Medical Staff Services obtains computerized certification of California license with MBC.
10. Medical Staff Services queries National Practitioner Data Bank.
11. Medical Staff Services contacts facilities where the practitioner:
    (a) Is a member and
    (b) Has the privileges that are being requested.
12. Medical Staff Services obtains approval from Chief Executive Officer or designee.
13. Medical Staff Services informs applicant of approval or denial request of temporary privileges.

CATEGORY TWO

A **Category Two** temporary privileges request applies to physicians who will function independently and who: (**a**) Are full-time employees of, or under contract with, Cedars-Sinai Medical Center; (**b**) Are physicians who will be part of a preceptorship program (preceptorship must be (1) an approved program of a department director; (2) approved by the Dept. of Medical Education Office; and (3) approved for continuing medical education credit); or (**c**) Are physicians to be evaluated in the Dept. of Emergency Medicine or Dept. of Anesthesia before formal application for staff membership.

Steps Required:

1. Applicant completes Steps 1 through 6 in Category One.
2. Full-time employee applicants (Category 2a) shall have *executed an employment contract* with Cedars-Sinai Medical Center and shall submit a Medical Staff application and delineation of privileges form.
3. All applicants' requests for temporary privileges must receive preapproval from the chairman of the Credentials Committee or designee.
4. The chairman of the applicant's department shall assign a qualified proctor.

CATEGORY THREE

A **Category Three** temporary privileges request applies to physicians who are applying for Medical Staff Membership and will function independently while their application is in process.

Steps Required:

1. Applicant completes Steps 1 through 6 in Category One.
2. Applicant submits a completed medical staff application and delineation of privileges form.
3. The application must be approved by the Credentials Committee before temporary privileges can be granted.
4. Temporary privileges requested *prior* to recommendation by the Credentials Committee must be accompanied by a letter of justification from the applicant's department chair or designee, and must receive pre-approval from the chairman of the credentials committee or designee.
5. The chairman of the department, or designee, assigns a qualified proctor.
6. Category Three temporary privileges will be granted for a period not to exceed 90 days and may be reviewed for renewal at 90-day increments.

NOTE: Temporary privileges may only be granted after approval by the Chief Executive Officer, or designee. *Completion of the Temporary Privileges Request form alone does not grant privileges.*

Courtesy of Cedars-Sinai Medical Center, Los Angeles, California.

Exhibit 6–12 Request for Temporary Privileges

PART I—TO BE COMPLETED BY PRACTITIONER REQUESTING PRIVILEGES

Practitioner's Name	Specialty
Office Address	Telephone
City ZIP	Date of Birth Social Security #
Medical School	Date Graduated
License # Expiration Date	DEA # Expiration Date
Malpractice Carrier	Amounts of Coverage

CURRENT HOSPITAL AFFILIATION

Primary Hospital: ____________________ Category: ____________________

All other Hospital Affiliations (attach separate sheet if necessary)

Hospital: ____________________ Category: ____________________

Hospital: ____________________ Category: ____________________

LICENSURE/DEA/MALPRACTICE (Append copies of License, DEA & Malpractice):

YES ☐ NO ☐ 1. Have your privileges at any hospital ever been voluntarily or involuntarily suspended, diminished, revoked or not renewed, or is any such action pending? **(If "yes," please submit details on a separate sheet)**

YES ☐ NO ☐ 2. Have you, within the last five (5) years, ever had any settlements or judgments (including claims which were not the subject of a lawsuit) paid by you or on your behalf in relationship to your practice of medicine? **(If "yes," please submit details on a separate sheet)**

I request temporary privileges in the ____________________ ____________________

Division Department

for the following Level of care (check one box only). Refer to Temporary Privilege Protocol for definition of Levels.

☐ Level One ☐ Level Two ☐ Level Three

I hereby release from liability all representatives of the Hospital and its Medical Staff for their acts performed in good faith and without malice in connection with evaluating my application and my credentials and qualifications, and I hereby release from any liability any and all individuals and organizations who provide information to the Hospital, or its Medical Staff, in good faith and without malice concerning my professional competence, ethics, character and other qualifications for staff appointment and clinical privileges, and I

continues

Exhibit 6–12 continued

hereby consent to the release of such information. ***NOTE: Temporary privileges become effective only AFTER approval by the Chief Executive Officer, or designee. Completion of this form alone DOES NOT grant privileges.***

Applicant's Signature ____________________ Date ____________

PART II—TO BE COMPLETED BY THE DEPARTMENT

A. *TEMPORARY PRIVILEGES are recommended as follows:*

Name: ____________________ Specialty: ____________

Level 1 (check one box only)

☐ **To consult with attending physician** (name) ____________
in the care of (Patient's Name): ____________
Physician will not be writing orders or performing procedures.
TEMPORARY PRIVILEGES WILL EXPIRE UPON DISCHARGE OF PATIENT.

☐ Temporary Administrative Privileges to cover the practice of ____________
From: ____________ To: ____________

Level 2 (check one box only)

☐ **For direct patient care responsibilities by virtue of acknowledged special expertise for this patient only.** TEMPORARY PRIVILEGES WILL EXPIRE UPON DISCHARGE OF PATIENT.
Patient Name: ____________
Special Expertise: ____________

☐ Preceptorship/Contract Department (circle one)
Name of Preceptor or Department: ____________
From: ____________ To: ____________

Level 3

☐ **To admit and care for patients pending final approval of application for Staff membership.**
Date reviewed by Credentials Committee: ____________
Date interviewed by Division/Department Chairman: ____________
Not to exceed pendency of application: YES ____ NO ____
If NO, provide dates: From: ____________ To: ____________

B. IN ACCORDANCE WITH THE TEMPORARY PRIVILEGES PROTOCOL, I HAVE REVIEWED AND SUPPORT THE ABOVE REQUEST, AND RECOMMEND APPROVAL OF TEMPORARY PRIVILEGES.

Name of Assigned Primary Proctor ____________________ Date ____________

Department Chairman or Designee ____________________ Date ____________

continues

Exhibit 6–12 continued

PART III—TO BE COMPLETED BY CHIEF EXECUTIVE OFFICER

☐ TEMPORARY PRIVILEGES—**APPROVED**
I have reviewed and support the above request and recommend that temporary privileges be granted for the above physician. The term of these temporary privileges shall be:
FROM: ________________ TO: ________________________
☐ UPON DISCHARGE OF PATIENT

Any extension or renewal of these privileges requires a formal request be submitted.

☐ TEMPORARY PRIVILEGES—**DENIED**
Reason for Denial: ______________________________

______________________________ ________________
Chief Executive Officer/or Designee Date

Courtesy of Cedars-Sinai Medical Center, Los Angeles, California.

Exhibit 6–13 AHP Application for Temporary Privileges

REQUEST RECEIVED: ______________________ EFFECTIVE DATE(S): ____________
AHP CATEGORY: ______________________________
Name: ______________________________ PIN # ______ UPIN # ______
Date of Birth: ___/___/___ PROFESSIONAL SCHOOL: ____________ GRAD. DATE: ____
Internship: ______________________________ **DATES:** ________
Internship: ______________________________ **DATES:** ________
OFFICE ADDRESS: ______________________________ TEL. # ________
RESIDENCE ADDRESS: ___________________________ TEL. # ________
Department: ____________________ Division: ____________________

A	B	C
___ Application Pending ___ Service/DOP Attached	___ Locum Tenens Coverage for: ____________ ___/___/___ TO ___/___/___ Time period requested.	___ Specialized Care of Patient/ Shift or Unit Coverage PATIENT'S NAME PROCEDURE ___/___/___ TO ___/___/___ Time period requested.

continues

Exhibit 6–13 continued

FOR "B" OR "C", Attach Current Copies of:

1. _____ MA Medical License # ________________ Expires: __/__/__
2. _____ Malpractice Insurance Carrier: ________________ Expires: __/__/__
3. _____ Written Prescriptive Guidelines/DEA: MCS Cert.: Expires: __/__/__
4. Supervising Physician: ________________
5. _____ Delineation of Specified Services/Privileges (if more than one procedure)

By applying for Temporary Specified Services/Privileges at Saint Vincent Hospital, I hereby:

- **authorize the Hospital to consult with my current associates regarding my professional competence and qualifications,**
- **acknowledge that I have been given access to the Policies Governing Allied Health Professionals and related Medical Staff governance manuals, Rules and Regulations and agree to be bound by the terms thereof,**
- **acknowledge that these services/privileges will expire in 120 days, unless specified.**

APPLICANT'S SIGNATURE: ________________ **DATE:** ________

FOR "B" OR "C", Director/Chief must obtain a reference re: ability in procedure(s) requested from medical staff authority at primary institution:

Name: ________________

Title/Dept.: ________________

Institution: ________________

Telephone No.: ________________

Reference obtained was:
POSITIVE: ____ **NEGATIVE:** ____

APPROVED BY:

____
HOSPITAL MANAGER DATE

____
DIVISION DIRECTOR DATE

____
DEPARTMENT CHIEF DATE

____
VICE PRESIDENT/MEDICAL AFFAIRS DATE

TO BE COMPLETED BY MSS STAFF:

License Verification: __/__/__

Form B Sent: __/__/__

PMF #: __/__/__

Entered CACTUS: __/__/__

Letter Sent/Copies Distributed: __/__/__

________________ __/__/__
MSS Representative DATE

Note: UPIN, unique provider identification number; DOP, delineation of principles; MSS, medical staff services.

Courtesy of St. Vincent Hospital, Worcester, Massachusetts.

but examples are illness, extended vacation, or educational pursuits. Bylaws or policies outline the specific process, which may be similar to that for initial appointment. Except for illness, the medical staff member knows in advance that he or she will be taking a leave of absence; this should allow ample opportunity for application to be made by the locum tenens physician. Ninety days is an average time for locum tenens privileges to be in effect, with extensions as defined in the bylaws.

Medical staff members should be encouraged to request locum tenens coverage as soon as possible to allow the time needed for the process. The locum tenens physician needs to meet the same qualifications for credentialing and privileges as any medical staff member in the same specialty. Also, proctoring requirements may apply to locum tenens depending upon procedures followed for new medical staff members with clinical privileges.

Emergency Privileges

An emergency is usually defined as an unanticipated condition that could result in serious or permanent harm to a patient if a delay in administering treatment occurred that would add to that harm or danger. Emergency privileges are defined when there is no immediately available, qualified appointee to the medical staff or when a physician who is currently appointed to the medical staff does not have the privileges granted but is permitted to exercise the privileges necessary.

Regardless of these two situations, when the emergency situation no longer exists, the physician should request and receive temporary privileges if necessary to continue to treat the patient. Another physician member of the medical staff with clinical privileges might also take over the care and avoid the need for additional temporary privileges for the original treating physician.

If the treating physician does not require privileges to continue to treat the patient, a simple temporary privilege form can be filled out, and the routine information can be requested to have on file for that emergency case.

NPDB Query

Whenever temporary privileges are granted, the NPDB must be queried. The data bank query will be part of the application process for a "pending application process." Individual requests for one time only or locum tenens may not be processed the same way but do require a data bank query. Please note that a *response* from NPDB is not required before the granting of temporary privileges, but the query must be made at the time the temporary privileges are requested. However, the hospital-specific policy and procedures may require the response from NPDB before any privileges are granted. The NPDB electronic query response time is usually within 48 hours, so the requirement for a response is not unreasonable if electronic query is used.

PATIENT MANAGEMENT VERSUS PATIENT ADMISSION PRIVILEGES

When defining privileges and criteria, it is important to identify any difference between privileges to admit patients and privileges to manage patients. Patients may be admitted to special care units as well as to the hospital, and a physician may have hospital admission privileges but not admitting privileges for a special care unit. A physician on call for the emergency department or a physician treating a patient for a diagnosis that results in complications requiring treatment by another specialist would not necessarily have the privileges to treat those additional complications or to admit to a special unit. This differentiation between management and admitting privileges most likely occurs in areas like special care units, including intensive and coronary care.

COMMUNICATING INFORMATION ABOUT PRIVILEGES

The Joint Commission hospital medical staff standards for privileges require those with clinical privileges to practice only within the scope of the privileges that have been granted to them. It is also incumbent on the hospital that practitioners not be allowed to practice any privileges that have not been granted. Generally, the medical staff office is the source for information about who has what privileges. There also needs to be a mechanism in place for key areas in the hospital to be informed of what privileges the practitioners have. Areas that usually have a need to know include surgery, admissions, cath lab, gastroenterology lab, and other areas performing invasive procedures. Communication can be accomplished in one of several ways. A copy of the privilege form or a form generated from the privilege list can be distributed to areas in the organization identified as having a need to know who has privileges for which procedures. These can be kept in a notebook alphabetically by last name of practitioner. In large organizations, this can be very cumbersome and difficult to keep current. Some organizations access privileges through the in-house computer system. Privileges are accessed when the need to know arises. In this situation, it must be a "read-only" access so that no one else within the organization can make changes to those privilege lists. The availability of on-line information is especially helpful with temporary privileges that may not yet be in the system.

Whatever communication procedure is used, it should include practitioners with temporary privileges and locum tenens privileges. If, for some reason, the privileges granted to a temporary or locum tenens practitioner are not entered into the computer system or distributed for the hard copy notebook immediately, medical staff office personnel or the person responsible for such privileges being granted will have to communicate with all areas that the practitioner will be accessing (e.g., surgery, invasive lab).

If hard copies of privilege lists are distributed, it is important that the lists be updated on a continuing basis—at time of reappointment, at resignation/termination, or whenever privileges are added or deleted. It is also important that department personnel be aware of the importance of keeping lists current and available for staff to reference. Other areas that may benefit from having privilege lists or access to the lists in the system are administrative personnel (for the administrator on call) and nursing administration (for the nursing supervisor in charge). This is especially helpful at night or on weekends when the medical staff office is closed. If hard-copy privilege list distribution is the method used, the medical staff office or credentialing coordinator may want to conduct periodic quality checks in the areas that maintain copies of privileges to ensure that they are using the most current information. Or the medical staff office may want to distribute the copies themselves and replace outdated pages so they know that units/departments have the most current copy. See Exhibit 6–14 for a sample protocol.

Communication of and access to privilege information is an area that is often checked during Joint Commission hospital surveys. The physician surveyor will ask personnel in procedure areas how they determine whether or not someone who is scheduling a procedure has the privileges to do so. *Do not get caught on this one.*

If it is determined that a practitioner wishes to schedule a procedure or is performing procedures or treating patients without the appropriate privileges, an administrator and/or a medical staff office person should be contacted. The hospital bylaws, policy, or procedure should identify the process and accountability for contacting the practitioner to inform him or her that he or she is not credentialed for that privilege. The practitioner may then be referred to credentialing, and staff privileges need to be requested.

The practice of practicing without privileges and/or proper credentialing is a major risk liability for the organization and for the practitioner. Even if a practitioner is fully trained and competent, the lack of specific privileges will put both the organization and individual at substantial risk in a court of law if a malpractice case evolves.

Exhibit 6–14 Policy for Distribution and Maintenance of Physician Privilege Books

POLICY:

It is the policy of Desert Regional Medical Staff Services Department to distribute binders containing Medical Staff Member privilege lists to specific Hospital Departments/Units that require such information. Such information will be distributed monthly immediately following the Hospital Branch Committee meeting. All privilege lists will contain the signatures of the medical staff member and Clinical Department Chairperson. It will be the responsibility of the Director or Manager of these Hospital areas to replace it with the updated list.

PURPOSE:

To assure that all individuals with clinical privileges provide services within the scope of privileges granted.

Physician privilege lists are to be distributed as follows:

Department:	**Privilege Lists/Specialty:**
Perioperative Services:	Anesthesiology All Surgical Subspecialties Critical Care Medicine Family Practice* Obstetrics/Gynecology Pain Management
Emergency Department:	All Medical Staff Members Privilege Lists
Patient Care Management Services (After Hours Nursing Supervisor):	All Medical Staff Members Privilege Lists
Critical Care/ICU Unit:	All Medical Staff Members Privilege Lists
Labor and Delivery:	Obstetrics/Gynecology Family Practice* Perinatology
Infants and Children:	Pediatrics Neonatology Pediatric Cardiology Family Practice*
Gastroenterology:	Gastroenterology Internal Medicine*

continues

Exhibit 6–14 continued

Department:	**Privilege Lists/Specialty:**
Cardiac Catheterization Laboratory:	Cardiology General Surgery* Cardiovascular Surgery Thoracic & Vascular Surgery
Cardiac Services:	Cardiology General Surgery* Cardiovascular Surgery Thoracic & Vascular Surgery
Pulmonary Function Laboratory:	Pulmonology Internal Medicine*
Radiology:	Radiology Radiation Oncology

If a discrepancy is identified between a Medical Staff Member's privilege list and what is scheduled or performed the Director of the Medical Staff Services Department should be contacted. The Director of the Medical Staff Services Department will seek clarification from the appropriate Department Chairperson as necessary and will report back to the Clinical Area. If it is after 5:00 P.M. or on the weekend contact the Director of the Medical Staff Services Department (the operator can call the Director at home); if the Director of the Medical Staff Services Department cannot be reached, contact the After Hours Nursing Supervisor, who will proceed as follows:

- Continue to page or phone the Director of Medical Staff Services at home
- Contact applicable Clinical Department Chairperson (refer to attached list)
- Contact President of the Medical Staff

*If privileges are applicable to the Clinical Area.

Courtesy of Desert Regional Medical Center, Palm Springs, California.

PRIVILEGING IN PHYSICIAN OFFICE/AMBULATORY CARE PRACTICE

Until the early 1990s, most managed care plans, integrated delivery systems, and medical group practices were not required to do any type of privileging in the office practice setting. However, the Joint Commission standards for all accreditation programs require privileging of LIPs. Joint Commission network standards are now requiring privileging in integrated delivery systems that participate in network surveys. The standards require development of a privileging process for those LIPs who practice in settings "other than the network component."[11] This includes private physician offices that are part of a hospital network and clinics that are part of the delivery system. The standards also require that practitioners practicing in a network component be granted privileges by that component in the type of care, service, and setting.[12] On the other hand, NCQA standards do not require office practice privileging. Since the primary purpose of credentialing and privileging should be "to protect the patient," some organizations are considering privileging in the office setting even if their accreditors do not require it. With high-risk and high-technology procedures being performed in places other than in acute care settings, it may become increasingly important to consider privileging practitioners in non–acute care environments such as the physician office.

The process of privileging practitioners in an acute care setting to ensure that they are practicing only those privileges for which they are qualified also applies to privileging in the non–acute care setting. Once an organization identifies the services and/or technologies it will be providing, and in what setting, it needs to determine the qualifications or criteria that practitioners who are part of its organization must have in order to practice in these areas. The following outline may be useful in determining *what criteria* should be developed for privileges in outpatient or non–acute care settings:

- basic education (MD, DO, other)
- minimal, formal training (completion of specific training programs, residency, fellowship, etc.)
- required experience (demonstration of certain number of procedures previously performed; reference letters from residency directors, chiefs of programs, or department chairs in hospitals, certificates of completion of specific procedures not necessarily included in a formal residency program)
- peer references—related to competency

If the core privilege method is used, a list of general types of privileges or procedures that could be performed in the office or outpatient setting need to be listed. Included in core privileges might be the ability to admit to an inpatient setting (if appropriate), do workup of patients, or provide consultation. Specific privileges for procedures that might require additional evaluation would be applied for separately.[13] Because physician offices that may be part of a network will be an accredited component of that network, it is important that some guidelines be in place to ensure that physicians are not performing procedures or treating problems for which they may not be qualified. Once privileges are granted, an audit of the network physician's claims and billing can identify activity procedures performed in the office.

Exhibit 6–15 is a sample privilege format that could be used in the office environment. It is specific for pediatrics.

PRIVILEGING ACROSS THE CONTINUUM

With the onset of the Joint Commission's requirement for office practice privileges and/or the credentialing of various components within a health care delivery system, more systems are developing privilege forms that reach across the continuum or across all practice areas within the system. This is an excellent alternative to multiple privilege forms that often contain the same information such as criteria, procedures, and treatments. It is important, however, that if a combined privilege form is used, any requirements or procedures/treatments unique to any one component within the system be identified as such. This can be accomplished by blocking certain privileges that will not be granted in certain components.

Exhibit 6–16 is a sample format of a privileging form that easily identifies where in the system (hospitals and ambulatory clinics) specific obstetrics and gynecology privileges can and cannot be requested and what the criteria are for these privileges. This format will meet the Joint Commission standard related to hospital-specific privileges being granted.

If a system is considering a combined privilege form such as the one in Exhibit 6–16, the following steps are suggested:

1. Representatives from each involved network or system component/setting are identified, including a credentialing coordinator, or person responsible for the credentialing process for each component;

Exhibit 6–15 Pediatric Primary Care (External Clinics) Core Privileges

Practitioner: ______________________

Criteria:

Practitioners requesting clinical privileges in primary care pediatrics must:

- be an MD or DO
- have completed an ACGME approved residency program in pediatrics
- be board certified in pediatrics
- present letter from chairman of the training program or, if training was longer than five years ago, a letter from the chief of staff where the applicant practices these privileges attesting to the applicant's competence

Core Privileges:

Preliminary diagnosis, initial treatment, management, and use of consultants for the management of medical disorders of children age birth to 18 years in an outpatient setting.

Diagnostic or Therapeutic Procedures:

- lumbar puncture
- initial interpretation EKG
- initial interpretation:
  - chest X-ray
  - abdominal X-ray
  - I&D of superficial abscesses
  - splinting or stabilizing extremity FX
  - suture closure of 1° layer wounds
  - intravenous infusion
  - eye irrigation
  - local infiltration anesthesia

USE OF CONSCIOUS SEDATION IN THE OFFICE SETTING IS EXCLUDED.

Comprehensive examination, diagnosis, and management of:

- Uncomplicated gynecological problems in adolescent females, including vaginitis and sexually transmitted disease, contraception advice, prescription of oral contraceptives, screening pelvic examination.
- Uncomplicated internal medicine problems including cardiac disease, rheumatic disease, gastrointestinal disease, hepatic disease, hematological disease, pulmonary disease, renal disease, endocrine disease, infectious disease, dermatologic disease, neurology disease, and thyroid disease.
- Uncomplicated orthopedic problems including muscle strain, sprains, low back pain, bursitis, tendinitis, and minor musculoskeletal trauma.
- Uncomplicated otolaryngologic problems including otitis media and externa, cerumen occlusion of canal, pharyngitis, laryngitis, removal of nasal or auditory canal foreign body, nosebleed, and sinusitis.
- Uncomplicated urologic problems, including cystitis, epididymitis, and sexually transmitted disease.
- Uncomplicated behavioral problems including crisis intervention, short-term individual counseling for difficulty with interpersonal relationships or adapting to authority, and problems related to substance use and abuse.
- Uncomplicated ophthalmologic problems including conjunctivitis, visual acuity tests, corneal abrasion, and conjunctival foreign body.

Proctoring/Provision Requirements:

- concurrent observation of five procedures for the supplemental privileges granted
- retrospective review of medical records of ten cases
- monitoring through the departmental quality assessment activities

Reappointment:

- confirmation of five cases within the past 12 months for supplemental privileges granted with a complication rate less than the department average

continues

Exhibit 6–15 continued

- confirmation of ten patients treated within the past 12 months provided at an acceptable standard of care as determined through peer review mechanisms
- documentation from an accredited health care facility of #1 or #2 above for practitioners who fail to meet numeric requirements at this hospital
- documentation confirming ten hours of CME activity during the previous 24 months related to the privileges requested

I have read and understand the criteria for core and supplemental privileges in primary care pediatrics and request that such privileges be delineated. Documentation as outlined in the criteria is attached to support this request.

______________________ __________
Practitioner Date

I have reviewed the documentation submitted in support of the practitioner's request for core privileges in primary care pediatrics. On the basis of this documentation of experience and demonstrated competence I __________ recommend __________ do not recommend that these privileges be granted. If privileges are recommended, the following conditions apply: (if none, so state)

____

____

______________________ __________
Division Chief Date

I have reviewed the documentation submitted in support of the practitioner's request for core privileges in primary care pediatrics as well as the recommendation from the division chief. On the basis of this documentation of experience and demonstrated competence I __________ recommend __________ do not recommend that these privileges be granted. If privileges are recommended, the following conditions apply: ______________

______________________ __________
Department Chairman Date

Recommendation for Clinical Privileges presented to:

Medical Director	Approved	Not Approved	Date	Signature
Credentials Committee	Approved	Not Approved	Date	Signature
Med. Exec. Committee	Approved	Not Approved	Date	Signature
Board of Managers	Approved	Not Approved	Date	Signature
Board of Directors	Approved	Not Approved	Date	Signature

Note: FX, fracture; I&D, irrigation and debridement; CME, continuing medical education; EKG, electrocardiogram.

Courtesy of Alfred I. duPont Hospital for Children, Wilmington, Delaware.

Exhibit 6–16 Obstetrics and Gynecology Delineation of Privileges

Applicant's name (please print): ______________________________

Threshold criteria for requesting core privileges:

Basic Education: MD or DO

Formal Training: Successful completion of an ACGME or AOA approved Obstetrics and Gynecology training or residency program *or* the international equivalent in the specialty of Obstetrics and Gynecology.

Board Certification: Certification by the ABMS approved American Board of Obstetrics and Gynecology or the American Osteopathic Board of Obstetrics and Gynecology *or* meet the qualifications required to take the board examination. If qualification to take the exam has expired, the applicant may apply for a *waiver* from the Board of Directors at each Fairview entity to which the applicant is applying.

Sub-specialty Cores: Applicant must meet the above criteria and be certified in, or meet the qualification to take the exam for, each sub-specialty requested. If qualification to take the exam has expired, the applicant may apply for a *waiver* from the Board of Directors at each Fairview entity to which the applicant is applying. *****Applicants requiring *ADMITTING* privileges *must also obtain privileges* in the *General* Obstetrics or Gynecology core.**

If the above criteria are met, you may request the following specific **core** *privileges:*

CORE PRIVILEGES

Ambulatory Core: *A representative, but not complete, identification of procedures to be performed* ***in a Fairview clinic setting only*** *is given within this core. Other procedures of similar complexity will fall within these privileges unless otherwise identified.*
(Please note: An additional form is required for this core.)

In-patient Cores: *A representative, but not complete, identification of procedures is given in the cores. Other procedures of similar complexity will fall within these privileges unless otherwise identified.*

Special requests within each core require specific documentation.

continues

Exhibit 6–16 continued

I hereby request the following **core** Obstetrics and Gynecology privileges:

General Inpatient Core

REQUESTED FACILITY*
N/A *indicates that privilege is not available at the specific entity;* ***AF*** *indicates that an additional form is required for the specific entity.*

	FUMC	FSH	FRH	FNH	EBN	FLR
Obstetrics Core:					N/A	

Privileges include admission, evaluation, consultation, diagnosis, and treatment of female patients of all ages presenting in any condition of pregnancy or illnesses, injuries, or disorders of the obstetric system. These privileges also include vaginal delivery, breech, cesarean section, vacuum extraction, forceps, cerclage placement, circumcision of the newborn, resuscitation of infant, amniocentesis, and other procedures related to normal and complicated delivery. *Core privileges* ***do not include*** *laser, operative laparoscopy, or any of the following special requests.*

Special Requests: *Each of the following privileges requires documentation of training and/or experience specific to the privilege requested.*

	FUMC	FSH	FRH	FNH	EBN	FLR
2nd trimester D & E					N/A	
Chorionic villus sampling					N/A	
Fetal umbilical cord blood sampling					N/A	
Intrauterine transfusions					N/A	
Level II ultrasound					N/A	
Critical care	AF	AF	AF	AF	N/A	AF

**FUMC* = Fairview University Medical Center, *FSH* = Fairview Southdale Hospital, *FRH* = Fairview Ridges Hospital, *FNH* = Fairview Northland Hospital, *EBN* = Ebenezer, *FLR* = Fairview Lakes Regional

continues

Exhibit 6–16 continued

General In-Patient Core

REQUESTED FACILITY*
N/A *indicates that privilege is not available at the specific entity;* ***AF*** *indicates that an additional form is required for the specific entity.*

	FUMC	FSH	FRH	FNH	EBN	FLR
Gynecology Core:					N/A	

Privileges include admission, evaluation, consultation, diagnosis, and pre-, intra, and post-operative care and treatment of female patients of all ages presenting with illnesses, injuries, and disorders of the gynecological system and nonsurgical treatment of illnesses and injuries of the mammary glands and urinary tract. Privileges include standard gynecological procedures involving the vulva, vagina, urethra, cervix, uterus, ovaries, and fallopian tubes as well as other pelvic procedures, appendectomy, lymph sampling, basic pelviscopy, diagnostic hysteroscopy, repair of bladder injury, repairs for pelvic relaxation, and evaluation and treatment of stress urinary incontinence. *Core privileges* ***do not include*** *laser, or any of the following special requests.*

Special Requests: *Each of the following privileges requires documentation of training and/or experience specific to the privilege requested.*

	FUMC	FSH	FRH	FNH	EBN	FLR
Advanced pelviscopy					N/A	
Enterotomy repair and other GI procedures					N/A	
Operative laparoscopy					N/A	
Laser	AF	AF	AF		N/A	
Operative hysteroscopy					N/A	
Tubal microsurgery					N/A	
Critical care	AF	AF	AF	AF	N/A	AF

**FUMC* = Fairview University Medical Center, *FSH* = Fairview Southdale Hospital, *FRH* = Fairview Ridges Hospital, *FNH* = Fairview Northland Hospital, *EBN* = Ebenezer, *FLR* = Fairview Lakes Regional

continues

Exhibit 6–16 continued

In-Patient Sub-Specialty Core	*REQUESTED FACILITY**
Applicant must be certified in, or meet qualifications to take the exam for Gynecologic Oncology ***or*** *request a waiver.*	***N/A*** *indicates that privilege is not available at the specific entity;* ***AF*** *indicates that an additional form is required for the specific entity.*

	FUMC	FSH	FRH	FNH	EBN	FLR
Gynecologic Oncology Core:					N/A	

Privileges include evaluation, consultation, work-up, diagnosis, and provision of surgical and therapeutic treatment to women with malignant diseases, including carcinomas of the cervix, uterus, vulva, and vagina. Also included within this core are radical hysterectomy with lymph node dissection, retroperitoneal surgery for cancer, microsurgery, chemotherapy, pelvic exenteration, vulvectomy, and the performance of procedures on the bowel, urethra, and bladder as indicated. *Core privileges* ***do not include*** *laser, or any of the following special requests.*

Special Requests: *Each of the following privileges requires documentation of training and/or experience specific to the privilege requested.*

	FUMC	FSH	FRH	FNH	EBN	FLR
Laser	AF	AF	AF		N/A	
Operative laparoscopy					N/A	

In-Patient Sub-Specialty Core	*REQUESTED FACILITY**
Applicant must be certified in, or meet qualifications to take the exam for, Maternal and Fetal Medicine ***or*** *request a waiver.*	***N/A*** *indicates that privilege is not available at the specific entity;* ***AF*** *indicates that an additional form is required for the specific entity.*

	FUMC	FSH	FRH	FNH	EBN	FLR
Maternal and Fetal Medicine Core:					N/A	

Privileges include evaluation, consultation, the ability to perform chorionic villus sampling, intrauterine transfusion, fetal umbilical cord blood sampling, and level II ultrasound for the obstetric patient. *Core privileges* ***do not include*** *laser, or any of the following special requests.*

Special Requests: *Each of the following privileges requires documentation of training and/or experience specific to the privilege requested.*

continues

Exhibit 6–16 continued

	FUMC	FSH	FRH	FNH	EBN	FLR
Operative laparoscopy					N/A	
Laser	AF	AF	AF			N/A

*FUMC = Fairview University Medical Center, FSH = Fairview Southdale Hospital, FRH = Fairview Ridges Hospital, FNH = Fairview Northland Hospital, EBN = Ebenezer, FLR = Fairview Lakes Regional

In-Patient Sub-Specialty Core
Applicant must be certified in, or meet qualifications to take the exam for, Reproductive Endocrinology and Infertility ***or*** *request a waiver.*

REQUESTED FACILITY*
N/A *indicates that privilege is not available at the specific entity;* ***AF*** *indicates that an additional form is required for the specific entity.*

	FUMC	FSH	FRH	FNH	EBN	FLR
Reproductive Endocrinology and Infertility Core:					N/A	

Privileges include consultation, evaluation, diagnosis, and treatment for patients presenting with infertility and/or illnesses, injuries, and disorders of the reproductive endocrine system. Privileges also include tubal microsurgery and reanastomosis, GIFT procedure, in vitro fertilization, and operative hysteroscopy, laparoscopy, and the ability to do advanced surgeries for infertility evaluation. *Core privileges* ***do not include*** *any of the following special requests.*

Special Requests: *Each of the following privileges requires documentation of training and/or experience specific to the privilege requested.*

	FUMC	FSH	FRH	FNH	EBN	FLR
Laser	AF	AF	AF		N/A	

*FUMC = Fairview University Medical Center, FSH = Fairview Southdale Hospital, FRH = Fairview Ridges Hospital, FNH = Fairview Northland Hospital, EBN = Ebenezer, FLR = Fairview Lakes Regional

I understand that by making this request, I am bound by the applicable bylaws or policies of the entity at which the privileges are requested. I also attest that my professional liability insurance covers the privileges I have requested.

Signature ____________________ Date ____________________

continues

Exhibit 6–16 continued

Ambulatory Core: *A representative, but not complete, identification of procedures to be performed* ***in a Fairview (FV) clinic setting only*** *is given within this core. Other procedures of similar complexity will fall within these privileges unless otherwise identified.*

Ambulatory Core *Procedures performed in a* ***Fairview clinic setting only;*** certain procedures may not be available at some clinic sites.	**Credentialing Department use only:** CLINIC NAME: ____________________ ____________________________

	FV Clinics
Ambulatory Obstetrics and Gynecology Core:	

Privileges include evaluation, diagnosis, and treatment, including consultation, of patients presenting with conditions of pregnancy and/or illnesses, injuries, or disorders of the obstetric or gynecological system. Privileges also include the ability to perform a history and physical examination, gynecological examination, management of prenatal care, and infertility testing; to order appropriate lab work; and to provide necessary and appropriate follow-up care. *Core privileges* ***do not include*** *laser, or any of the following special requests:*

Special Requests: *Each of the following privileges requires documentation of training and/or experience specific to the privilege requested.*

	FV Clinics
Level II ultrasound	
Artificial insemination	

I understand that by making this request, I am bound by the applicable bylaws or policies of the entity at which the privileges are requested. I also attest that my professional liability insurance covers the privileges I have requested.

______________________________________ ____________________

Signature Date

Note: GI, gastrointestinal; GIFT, gamete intrafallopian transfer.

Courtesy of Fairview System Credentialing, Minneapolis, Minnesota.

credentials committee chairs, medical directors, or vice presidents of medical affairs from each component; and any department chairs that represent a major privileging overlap among the components.
2. Current criteria for each privilege or core group of privileges are reviewed to determine similar or identical criteria and those that differ.
3. Agreement is reached on criteria that should be the same throughout all components/settings using the privilege. The "community standard" concept (components within a close geographic proximity) may be used even if system components are not all located in the same geographic area.
4. Agreement is reached on a format to be used that will identify activities in each component/setting, the standard criteria for all components/settings, and specific criteria for one or more individual components/settings. The format must include shaded or blocked areas for any activity or component/setting that will not be allowed a privilege.
5. Obtain the approval of the medical staff, health plan (if included), and governing body.

REVIEW AND REVISION OF PRIVILEGE DELINEATION

With so many new procedures and treatments being developed and used, organizations that privilege practitioners should review their privilege delineations at least annually. Any procedure that is added during a practitioner's reappointment cycle should be added to the privilege form that the practitioner is asked to complete for the current reappointment. Even an annual review of privileges may not be often enough to keep the forms updated. A good rule of thumb is that the practitioner should never have to "write in" a requested privilege at reappointment more than one time. By the next cycle, any new privileges should have been added to the form. The medical staff office or staff responsible for credentialing can use write-in requests as a start when working with departments to update their lists. The write-in can be included either in the core list (if used) or on the menu list for special procedures requiring separate requests.

Keeping an ongoing list of new procedures and requests for privileges not on the current forms will make the job of revising and updating lists easier. The medical staff office can review this list with the department chair (or chief of staff if no department), make appropriate changes, and obtain approval from the department, medical staff, and governing board annually. As with any department-specific privileges, any related criteria for appointment and/or reappointment are defined as part of the update.

There are no accreditation requirements to revise privilege lists within a specific time period. As with other medical staff standards, the Joint Commission will expect an organization to follow the organizational bylaws, rules, or policies. Therefore, any written requirement for privilege delineation review must be followed.

If a number of years have elapsed since a complete review of privileges has been conducted with subsequent revision of privilege delineations and/or a decision has been made to redesign privilege delineations, the following steps may be helpful:

1. A small task force or committee should be identified to work on the project. This group will conceptualize, review the current information, make recommendations for standardization of format and definitions, assist the clinical departments or areas in their individual reviews, and prepare the revised privilege lists for the approval process. The credentialing professional should be closely involved throughout this project with appropriate practitioner involvement at various stages. Individual departments or areas that support this project should be included in the first phases, as they will be

champions in working with others who disagree with change or require more assistance.

2. Current lists are revised to determine which, if any, formats and definitions of criteria are standard among departments.
3. A standardized definition of categories/levels to be used by each department is identified. Usually, categories or levels start with those requiring the least amount of qualifications and relating to less critical treatment. They increase in qualifications and related treatments or degree of illness (e.g., class I requires the fewest qualifications, and class III covers board-certified specialists).
4. Each clinical department reviews and/or further identifies and defines qualifications required to obtain/maintain privileges in that specific department or section. These will include formal training, boards, and/or experience; completed training programs (residency, fellowship); and board certification/eligibility. Included in the qualifications is any documentation of clinical competency required to accompany requests for granting and/or renewal of specific privileges. (See the earlier section "Development of Criteria for Clinical Privileges.")
5. Any new services offered since the date of last review are added to the "scope of care" based on the services offered by the organization.
6. The core or bundling approach is used to identify which procedures and/or treatments can be grouped together according to volume performed and/or risk involved. It is understood that some procedures will need to be listed separately from a core group because of specific training or experience required. One option for grouping may be to separate cognitive from procedural privileges. Cognitive privileges can be grouped by age definition, organ system, pathology conditions, and so forth.
7. Once core groups or individual privileges have been identified, consideration is given to required minimum clinical activity that can be documented by
   - actual reported numbers performed in each core group or for each individual procedure listed, or
   - attestation by the physician that the minimum activity requirement was met (see the earlier section "Development of Criteria for Clinical Privileges").
8. If procedures, diagnoses, or treatments cross specialties, all groups involved come to agreement on the appropriate qualifications and category.
9. The format for privilege forms to be used by all departments is identified, and approvals obtained from the appropriate bodies.
10. A draft revision of the privilege is completed to encompass the information covered in previous steps, and the draft is reviewed by the involved clinical department(s).
11. Once the review is complete and revisions are drafted, the formal review and approval process follows. If a small task force or subcommittee in a clinical department was charged with the initial review, the draft is next forwarded to the clinical department. The approval process used for new applicants or reappointments would also be used in the recommendation and approval of the revised clinical privileges (e.g., clinical department to credentials committee to executive committee to governing board).
12. When final approval has been granted by the governing board, copies of the revised and approved privileges are used for new applicants or those reapplying for renewal of privileges. The revision and approval date should always be included on the form so that there is never any question as to which form is the most current.
13. Those holding privileges are notified of changes specifically that might affect practitioners during the reapproval process. If any qualifications change during the process, the criteria should indicate whether those currently holding the privileges will

be grandfathered (considered according to the criteria in place when they initially applied for the privileges). If they must meet new qualifications, all old and outdated blank privilege forms should be discarded to avoid sending the wrong form to applicants.

PRIVILEGES IN MORE THAN ONE DEPARTMENT

By program and form design, an individual may need to request privileges in more than one department. This will depend on how the process is designed, how categories are identified, and what format is used. For example, a family physician might need to apply for obstetrical privileges through the ob/gyn department or through the family practice department if privileges might include specific criteria for obstetrics (consistent with the obstetrics department).

Another issue to be addressed if privileges fall into two or more departments is proctoring. If an applicant gains privileges through another department (such as obstetrical privileges for a family physician), the applicant will be proctored by someone in that other department or by someone in his or her specialty who currently has unrestricted privileges in the other department. This should be defined in a policy and communicated to the applicant at the start of any application or required review process.

Another consideration when privileges overlap between departments is the process for monitoring and evaluation. Generally, the department that delineates the privileges is responsible for monitoring and evaluating those privileges. However, if a problem or concern arises regarding a practitioner from another department, it is recommended that once the monitoring department does its review and has any recommendations for improvement, those recommendations also be forwarded to the practitioner's primary department for review.

It is essential for departments to have good working relationships with each other where members of one department may be practicing privileges that are defined primarily by another department. If departments cannot agree on such matters as criteria and evaluations, the executive committee may be asked to intervene and make recommendations once both sides have had an opportunity to present their recommendations.

PRIVILEGES FOR AHPs

As defined in Chapter 3, AHPs are those individuals who provide patient care services with or without supervision and who are not members of the medical staff. They are defined by the organization. Whether they have licenses and the authority by law *and the hospital* to practice independently will determine if they should have delineated clinical privileges or job descriptions.

There are no hard and fast rules about whether AHPs are handled through the medical staff or a hospital process. (See Chapter 3 for more information on determining options.) It is recommended that unless clinical privileges are required, a simpler and quicker process be designed for these individuals. That is, once the forms have been reviewed and approved through whatever defined mechanism, a non–medical staff credentialing process be used.

Although the Joint Commission does not specifically address AHPs in its medical staff standards, it does require that any individual permitted by law *and the organization* to provide care and services without direction or supervision and within the scope of the individual's license have delineated privileges. The privileging process for these individuals, such as clinical psychologists and podiatrists, is the same as that for physicians. Examples may vary from organization to organization or from state to state, since each state licensing board defines the scope of licensure granted. As discussed earlier in this chapter for medical staff members, the designated AHPs complete a privilege form and provide any additional documentation required. Criteria should be defined that the AHP needs to meet before requesting the privileges. The recredentialing process should require the AHP to review and, if applicable, to update the privilege form (same process as the medical staff). See the sample in Exhibit 6–17.

For those independently licensed individuals defined by the state who are not MDs, DOs, or DDSs, the organization must determine whether they are going to be considered independent within the organization and, on the basis of that decision, whether they will be eligible to apply for clinical privileges (and go through the medical staff credentialing process) or whether they will be given a job description/scope of services and processed through the medical staff, human resources, or some other mechanism (e.g., nursing). This is done by the organization defining the scope of services to be provided by these individuals. If there is a category of AHP that parallels a hospital employee position, it is recommended that the qualifications and job description or clinical privileges be adapted for the AHPs to ensure the same level of patient care services provided regardless of how they enter the organization.

The following is a list of items to include in a job description for AHPs:

- name of the AHP category
- qualifications, if any, required for this category (license, continuing education units, certification, malpractice insurance coverage, demonstrated competence, cardiopulmonary resuscitation training, education, other)
- verifications required, if any, of qualifications listed above
- job duties, tasks (what they are able to perform in this capacity)
- level of supervision and from whom (employer, department supervisor, other)
- working conditions (standing, sterile environment, other)
- any probationary requirements (proctoring, initial evaluation)

See Exhibit 6–18 for a sample job description.

If there is no corresponding employee job description for an AHP category, there are several ways to develop one. Using the information listed above, use an AHP or interdisciplinary committee, if one exists, to discuss and recommend the components. If no one on the committee is knowledgeable about the particular category, find someone who is and ask him or her to participate. A physician employer or supervisor may be helpful in this process also. Network with colleagues in nearby hospitals to find out if any of them are willing to share their forms. If no AHP committee exists, work with a supervisor in the area where the AHP will be working, and/or ask input from a department chair or other physician knowledgeable in this particular area. The AHP committee, or whatever group or individual drafted the job description, should recommend approval of the job description, qualifications, and so forth to the appropriate medical staff groups, if required, for information or recommendation (whichever is required by the AHP policies or rules) and to the board for approval. An AHP committee functioning in an organization where nonindependent licensed or unlicensed individuals are not processed through the medical staff serves a very useful purpose. The process can be handled administratively within the hospital and can generate information reports to the medical staff and board. Medical staff review and board approval of the final form (job description, scope of services) are still suggested.

Just as the medical staff should do an annual review of privilege delineation criteria and forms, it is also a good idea to review any job descriptions/clinical privileges for AHPs annually. Any job description that has a corresponding hospital employee job description should be compared to be sure that no changes have been made to the hospital form, criteria, or job functions.

Exhibit 6–17 Clinical Psychology Section

REQUEST FOR PRIVILEGES: LICENSED PSYCHOLOGY

NAME: ________________________________ DATE: ________

By applying for these privileges, I certify that my training and/or experience is commensurate with my request and that I will furnish evidence of this as may be required by the appropriate hospital medical staff committees.

	Requested	Approved
CATEGORY I: PSYCHOTHERAPY		
Individual psychotherapy of children and adolescents.	________	________
Group psychotherapy, children or adolescents.	________	________
Family psychotherapy.	________	________

CATEGORY II: PSYCHOLOGICAL EVALUATION

General psychological assessment of children and adolescents (this includes, but is not limited to, fully competent evaluations for children's emotional, social, learning, and cognitive functioning).	________	________

To obtain privileges in this category, please submit two case reports that document demonstrated experience in the diagnosis and psychoeducational treatment of children's learning disorders.

CATEGORY III: NEUROPSYCHOLOGICAL EVALUATION

Neuropsychological assessment and evaluation.	________	________

To obtain privileges in this category, please document completion of course work or post-graduate experience in neuropsychology, including basic and advanced course work, and provide two case reports documenting experience in neuropsychological assessment or related fields.

CATEGORY IV: HYPNOTHERAPY

Hypnotherapy for use with children and adolescents.	________	________

To obtain privileges in this category, please

1. Document either one graduate course in hypnotherapy or one full post-graduate course or workshop and appropriate education or training;

OR

2. Document appropriate education, training, and experience by letter from training program director, supervisor, or other appropriate individual who has direct knowledge of your performance in a hospital setting;

AND

3. Document two years of clinical experience in hypnotherapy.

continues

Exhibit 6–17 continued

	Requested	Approved
CATEGORY V: BIOFEEDBACK		
Biofeedback for use with children and adolescents	________	________

To obtain privileges in this category, please provide

1. evidence of supervision and training by a licensed supervisor who is credentialed in biofeedback;

OR

2. a letter of recommendation from a licensed supervisor credentialed in biofeedback verifying the level of competence of the applicant psychologist;

AND

3. documentation of two years of clinical experience in biofeedback.

OTHER PRIVILEGES: (Please be specific. Attach separate page if necessary)

________________________________ ____________ ____________

____

____

________________________________ DATE ____________
APPLICANT'S SIGNATURE

________________________________ DATE ____________
CHIEF OF LICENSED PSYCHOLOGY SECTION

________________________________ DATE ____________
CHAIRPERSON, ALLIED HEALTH PROFESSIONAL COMMITTEE

________________________________ DATE ____________
CHAIRPERSON, PSYCHIATRY DEPARTMENT

Courtesy of Children's Hospital, San Diego, California.

Just as it is important in the medical staff privileging process not to grant privileges before criteria have been developed and approved, no classification of AHPs should be credentialed or processed until criteria for either privilege delineation or job description/scope of services are defined. If a request is made for an allied health category that does not exist, the individual should be requested either to write a letter or to have a supervising physician write a letter detailing the type of patient care service that the individual wishes to offer and educational/licensing requirements for that category of AHP. That request is channeled through either an allied health committee or other mechanisms that are defined in the AHP policies.

PRIVILEGES FOR CONTRACTED SERVICE

If the organization uses a contracted service, how the contract defines the individual's func-

Exhibit 6–18 Qualifications and Description of Practice Prerogatives for Registered Nurse Practitioner

REGISTERED NURSE PRACTITIONER (RNP) CATEGORY DEFINITION

A Registered Nurse Practitioner (RNP) is a licensed registered nurse with additional skills in physical diagnosis, psychosocial assessment, and management of health-illness needs in primary care and is registered as an RNP with the California Board of Registered Nursing.

The term *supervising physician* means any physician currently licensed by the State of California who is a current member, in good standing, of the medical staff of Western Medical Center Hospital Anaheim who has completed proctoring requirements.

QUALIFICATIONS

In addition to meeting the General Requirements as outlined in the Allied Health Professionals Rules and Regulations, the RNP shall do the following in order to provide services:

- Provide and maintain current licensure with the California Board of Registered Nursing
- Submit annually documentation of a minimum of 15 units of continuing education relating to the field of RNP
- Have a supervising physician who:
  - Is a physician currently licensed by the State of California
  - Is a current member in good standing of the medical staff at Western Medical Center Hospital Anaheim

VERIFICATION OF QUALIFICATIONS

The following will be verified at the time of appointment and annually thereafter:

- Written verification of current licensure directly from the California Board of Registered Nursing
- Written documentation of current professional liability insurance coverage and claims history directly from the carrier
- Query of the National Practitioner Data Bank
- Documentation from the Medical Staff Services office of current medical staff membership in good standing and completion of proctoring requirements of supervising physician
- Written verification of current competence for initial appointment:
  - Verify education and experience
  - Verify any hospital affiliations
  - Contact references
- The supervising physician accepts full responsibility for the performance of all professional activities of the RNP

continues

Exhibit 6–18 continued

PRACTICE PREROGATIVES WHICH MAY BE PROVIDED BY THE RNP

Because an RNP practice is directed by a supervising physician, an RNP acts as an agent for that physician; the orders given and the tasks performed by an RNP are considered the same as if they had been given and performed by the supervising physician. Unless otherwise negated in treatment protocols submitted by the supervising physician, the following prerogatives may be initiated without the prior patient-specific order of the supervising physician:

- Take a patient history, perform a physical examination, and make an assessment and diagnosis based on this information. The supervising physician will confirm the findings of the H&P and will sign within 24 hours of admission or before any procedure is performed.
- Transmit an order for X-ray, other studies, therapeutic diets, physical therapy, occupational therapy, respiratory therapy, and nursing services as outlined in the delegation of services.
- Transmit an order for, perform, or assist in the performance of laboratory procedures, screening procedures, and therapeutic procedures as outlined in the delegation of services.
- Initiate arrangements for admissions, complete forms and charts pertinent to patient medical records, and provide services to patients requiring continuing care.
- Recognize and evaluate situations which call for immediate attention of a physician, and institute, when necessary, treatment procedures essential for life of the patient.
- Instruct and counsel patients regarding matters pertaining to their physical health. Counseling may include topics such as medications, diets, social habits, family planning, normal growth and development, aging, and understanding of and long term management of their diseases.
- Initiate and facilitate the referral of patients to the appropriate health facilities, agencies, and resources of the community.
- Transmit, orally or in writing on a patient record, a prescription from the supervising physician to a person who may lawfully furnish such medication or medical device. A supervising physician's prescription, transmitted by the RNP, shall be based on a patient-specific order by the supervising physician.

The RNP may not provide the following services:

- may not admit or discharge patients
- may not transmit orders for drugs for the purpose of sedating a patient for a procedure
- may not administer medications
- may not perform invasive procedures

SPECIFIC RULES/REGULATIONS/POLICIES WHICH APPLY TO THE REGISTERED NURSE PRACTITIONER

The RNP shall practice only under the direction and supervision of a supervising physician.

The RNP shall perform only those tasks or functions which have been approved by Western Medical Center Hospital Anaheim.

continues

Exhibit 6–18 continued

Medical record entries made by an RNP must be reviewed, signed, and dated within 48 hours of the entry. H&Ps must be reviewed, signed, and dated within 24 hours of the entry. All orders written by an RNP shall be confirmed by the supervising physician by countersignature in the medical record within 24 hours.

In order to continue the team approach for continuous quality of care, the RNP will inform and involve hospital personnel when appropriate.

Supervision Required:

A supervising physician shall be available in person or by electronic communication at all times when the RNP is caring for patients.

A supervising physician shall delegate to an RNP only those tasks and procedures consistent with the supervising physician's specialty or usual and customary practice and with the patient's health and condition.

A supervising physician shall observe or review evidence of the RNP's performance of patient care services.

The supervising physician has continuing responsibility to follow the progress of the patient and to make sure the RNP does not function autonomously. The supervising physician shall be responsible for all services provided by the RNP under his/her supervision.

The Medical Staff Services Office shall be immediately notified in the event the RNP leaves the employ of the supervising physician, at which moment the RNP's ability to practice at the Hospital is ended.

The RNP shall at all times be identified as an RNP by means of a conspicuous badge stating the nurse's name, title, and name of the supervising physician.

REQUIREMENTS FOR COMPLETION OF ONE-YEAR PROBATIONARY PERIOD

The RNP shall have satisfactorily completed a performance evaluation process and satisfactorily completed proctoring requirements. A minimum of 6 cases shall be retrospectively reviewed to assure that the RNP is adequately supervised and does not exceed the scope of his or her practice. Any member of the Department to which the supervising physician is assigned and who has completed proctoring requirements may serve as a proctor.

METHOD FOR EVALUATING COMPETENCY TO PERFORM PRACTICE PREROGATIVES

A performance evaluation will be performed at the end of the one-year probationary period and annually thereafter. The evaluation process shall include a review of data provided by the Quality Management Department, information provided by the supervising physician and director of the appropriate patient care area, and documentation of satisfactory completion of the annual unit-based update.

continues

Exhibit 6–18 continued

SIGNATURES

I am applying for membership to the Allied Health Professionals Staff in the category of *Registered Nurse Practitioner.* By signing below, I acknowledge that I have read and understand the documents entitled "Qualifications and Description of Practice Prerogatives for Registered Nurse Practitioner" and "Allied Health Professionals Rules and Regulations."

Applicant's Signature	Printed Name of Applicant	Date
Sponsoring Physician Signature	Printed Name of Sponsoring Physician	Date

=For Medical Staff Services Use Only=

Approval for Non–Behavioral Health Practitioners:

Director, Medical Staff Services	Or Designee	Date

Approved: Reviewed/Revised:

continues

Exhibit 6–18 continued

INITIAL APPLICATION CHECKLIST FOR AHP CATEGORY: REGISTERED NURSE PRACTITIONER

Name of Applicant: ______________________________ App Fee Ck. #: __________

Date App Recv'd Complete: ____________________ All Reqd Signatures: [ ] Yes [ ] No

[ ] License/Certification/Registration
[ ] Current Insurance Certificate
[ ] CEUs: ________ for yrs.: ________
(a minimum of 15 units is required annually)

[ ] Three References
[ ] Written Delegation of Service Agree:
[ ] Cross Coverage: ________________

Verifications Sent:		**1st**	**2nd**	**3rd**	**Rec'd**	
Training/Experience	________	____	____	____	____	
	________	____	____	____	____	
Three References	1. ________	____	____	____	____	
	2. ________	____	____	____	____	
	3. ________	____	____	____	____	
Hosp. Affiliations	________	____	____	____	____	
	________	____	____	____	____	
NPDB Query	________	____	____	____	____	Clear [ ] Y [ ] N
License:	Cal. Brd. of Reg. Nursing	____	____	____	____	Clear [ ] Y [ ] N
Prof. Liab. Ins./Claims	________	____	____	____	____	Clear [ ] Y [ ] N

Number of claims, if any: ____________________ Overviews Received [ ] Y [ ] N

Supervising Physician:

Number of claims, if any: ____________________ Overviews Received [ ] Y [ ] N

Med. Staff Mbr: [ ] Yes [ ] No In Good Standing? [ ] Yes [ ] No

Proctoring Completed: [ ] Yes [ ] No

Health Screening Requirements: ***(for all Direct Patient-Care Providers as outlined in AHP Rules and Regulations)***

[ ] Completed Health Screening Form
[ ] Rubella Titer

[ ] PPD or Chest X-Ray
[ ] Varicella Titer

Orientation:

Gen. Hosp. Orientation: Date Completed: __________ Name Badge: Date Issued: _____

Dept. Specific Orientation: Date Completed: __________ Parking Tag: Date Issued: _____

Note: H&P, history and physical; CEU, continuing education unit.

Courtesy of Western Medical Center, Anaheim, California.

tion in the organization, scope of services, and licensure will determine whether clinical privileges or job descriptions are necessary. A contract service may include physicians who require clinical privileges but not necessarily medical staff membership as defined by the contract. For example, a contracted service to supply emergency physicians may not include medical staff membership, especially if individuals are used short term. These individuals, like anyone else who has delineated clinical privileges, must be processed through medical staff mechanisms.

As discussed in Chapter 3, contracted services or individuals may require delineated clinical privileges through the medical staff or may require a scope of practice to be defined through the contract and/or through a human resource mechanism. If the individual is a physician and/or is licensed and contracted to perform independently, the applicable privilege delineation form will be provided to the individual for completion and processed through the medical staff and governing board. If, on the other hand, the license and/or scope of services to be provided are more restrictive, the organization has three options.

1. If a similar or identical class of employee exists within the organization, an abbreviated process can be used that requires the individual to complete an application form and/or the contracted services to submit a current curriculum vitae on each individual along with copies of any current licenses or other formal training certificates for the services to be provided. Long-term contracted services should also be evaluated internally by the department or area using the contracted service.
2. The organization can have language provided in a contract that outlines payment as well as specific services to be provided. Also, the contract should specify
   - the qualifications of the individuals who will be coming to the hospital through the contracted service
   - the information that is verified by the contract service for each individual or groups of individuals (licensure, education, previous employment)
   - how the information is verified (copy of the license or verification with the licensing board)
   - the scope of services to be provided
   - any health screening requirements and frequency
   - how the individuals will be supervised, if applicable
   - any orientation needed by hospital personnel
   - competency evaluation
   - how the hospital may provide information for an evaluation process[14]

   The organization can choose to audit the contracted agency annually to ensure that all personnel provisions are in compliance with the contract. The medical staff should be reviewing appropriate clinical contract services.
3. If there is no similar or identical class of employees and/or the contracted service is not providing any credentialing information, the hospital needs to collect and verify pertinent information and credential/process the individuals internally.

Internal human resource processes are not necessary if the contract is explicit about the qualifications of the contracted personnel coming into the organization and the commitment of the contracted agency to provide those individuals who meet the stated qualifications. If the contract language only provides for a financial relationship and does not address qualifications, some kind of internal evaluation should be instituted. Otherwise, the risk to the organization in not knowing or holding anyone accountable for the performance and qualifications of the health care providers is much greater.

Every hospital should have some process in place that reviews contracts on at least an annual basis and incorporates or deletes any organization-specific requirements as necessary. To avoid any duplicative processes between internal mechanisms and what the contracted service is providing, the two groups need to work together so that the contracted service provides the information needed to demonstrate that its employees are competent.[15]

The organization can choose to audit the contracted agency annually to ensure that all personnel provisions are in compliance with the stated contract. Because the governing body of the organization is responsible for all services provided, it is also important for the governing body to review and approve a contract service review system and to be given information annually with regard to the contracted service's performance.[16]

PRIVILEGES FOR MOONLIGHTERS

Moonlighter is a term used to identify practitioners who are used by organizations to work in areas that cannot be filled by full-time physicians and/or member staff members. They differ from locum tenens staff in that they often work at an organization longer than locum tenens staff (who are taking the place of a medical staff member for a specific period of time). They are often residents in their third or fourth year who are being paid extra to work outside of their residency programs. They may also be physicians who earn extra income by working shifts in addition to their usual practice. Moonlighting often includes work in the emergency department or anesthesia call for obstetrics. Small, rural hospitals often have a need for moonlighters because of the difficulty of recruiting and/or maintaining permanent staff.

Moonlighters differ from house staff, who are residents that participate in patient care under direction of LIPs in the same discipline with clinical privileges and medical staff membership. Moonlighters must have clinical privileges, since they are working independently from any postgraduate program. Clinical privileges for those still in residency programs must be carefully defined to ensure that the privileges reflect only those areas for which the individual has already been trained. Organizations can get assistance and/or approval from a training program to define privileges. Privileges may include access to a medical staff member via telephone should questions arise.

Credentialing should include full licensure and additional malpractice (from that of a residency program). References from program directors can serve as a peer reference and training verification. Moonlighters who are still in a residency program should not be granted medical staff membership. They are granted privileges, and their privileges should expire when they have completed their training program. At that time, they either relocate or apply for membership and clinical privileges that will reflect a fuller scope of practice. Moonlighters do not need to be mentioned in the bylaws if they are not considered members of the medical staff, but they are included in the clinical privilege classification wherever clinical privileges are defined.

PROCTORING

Proctoring is a means of formal evaluation of a practitioner, usually as part of the provisional appointment or as a result of corrective action. The different types of proctoring that can be instituted in hospitals will be discussed in this section. The parameters should be outlined in the bylaws or in proctoring protocols of a credentialing policy and procedure manual.

If a formal proctoring program exists, the hospital uses specific proctoring/evaluation forms to be completed by an assigned proctor or whatever means the hospital defines for a written evaluation. Depending upon the type of proctoring that is being done, proctoring can include a specific time period and/or a specific number of cases (in general or listed by specific procedure), or a combination of both. Again, the bylaws or policies will outline the requirements. The credentialing professional in the medical staff office is often responsible for coordinating the proctoring program. This can be accomplished by distributing the proctoring forms to the practitioner being proctored and making sure that forms are available in the areas of the hospital where the proctoring will be completed (surgery, unit offices, invasive areas, etc.). The completed forms should be returned to the medical staff office so that personnel can track the completion of forms and route them to the appropriate department or committee at the time specified for overall review and recommendation. It usually is the responsibility of the individual being proctored to be sure that the proctor completes the form.

A variety of types of forms can be used to complete an evaluation on a practitioner being proctored. These forms can relate directly to the patient care being provided. They can also relate to interaction with colleagues, staff, patients, and other factors. Exhibits 6–19 through 6–21 can be considered in choosing a format as well as the type of information to be evaluated.

New Applicant Proctoring

The Joint Commission standards do not require a formal proctoring program. However, the standards state that the initial appointment is for a provisional period that is specified or defined in the medical staff bylaws.[17] Some hospitals actually assign the category "provisional" to all new applicants to the medical staff. Following successful completion of a proctoring program or probationary/provisional status, the applicant is assigned to another staff category. Other hospitals have other categories that new applicants are assigned to and do not use the term *provisional*, but it is understood that all new applicants are provisional regardless of whether there is a separate category for new members. Because of the lack of any definitive accreditation standards, hospitals can determine whether they want to have a formal proctoring program for new members that differs from their routine monitoring and evaluation of all practitioners on the medical staff through their ongoing performance improvement program. Some states may have specific requirements with regard to proctoring that must be researched individually. In California, for example, the state does not require proctoring; however, the California Medical Association guidelines include the provision for a proctoring program in California hospitals.

The following is information that should be included in proctoring protocols (or wherever proctoring is defined):

- duration of a proctoring program
- items to be proctored (may be department or specialty specific)
- number of cases to be proctored
- requirements for successful completion of proctoring (including responsibilities of the practitioner being proctored and responsibilities of the proctoring practitioner)
- consequences of noncompletion
- extension

Temporary Privilege Proctoring

There are several types of temporary privileges, in which proctoring may or may not be a requirement depending upon the circumstances and bylaws.

New Applicants

If a hospital has a formal proctoring program, the procedures need to address proctoring those with temporary privileges. It should be understood by the applicant who has temporary privileges and outlined in writing that if there are any problems with the provision of patient care during this temporary period, the temporary privileges can be revoked without due process being afforded the applicant, since the applicant is not yet an approved member of the medical staff. The department chair is responsible for proctoring any new applicants who have been granted temporary privileges until the application process is completed, unless the chair assigns someone else. This is especially important if there is no formal proctoring program in which there is a provision for review of care for the individual who has not completed the application process.

Exhibit 6–19 Pediatrics Proctoring Form

[ ] Concurrent
[ ] Retrospective

PEDIATRICIAN: ______________________ SUBSPECIALTY: ______________________

PROCTORING M.D.: __________________ PATIENT#: ______________________
(Medical Record Number)

TYPE OF ACTIVITY BEING PROCTORED: DATE OF ACTIVITY: __________________
[ ] Direct Admission as Attending (Date of Admission)
[ ] Consultation OR ______________ to ________________
(Time Period of Consultation)

ADMITTING DIAGNOSIS: ____

LENGTH OF STAY: __________________ [ ] Appropriate [ ] Not Appropriate *Explain below

CHECK AS APPLICABLE:	YES	NO	*Explain below	Not Applicable
ADMISSION OR CONSULTATION				
Appropriate	[ ]	[ ]		[ ]
Note Written	[ ]	[ ]		[ ]
HISTORY AND PHYSICAL EXAM				
Appropriate	[ ]	[ ]		[ ]
Complete	[ ]	[ ]		[ ]
Timely	[ ]	[ ]		[ ]
HOSPITAL CARE				
Appropriate Orders	[ ]	[ ]		[ ]
Adequate Progress Notes	[ ]	[ ]		[ ]
Appropriate Use of Lab and X-Ray	[ ]	[ ]		[ ]
Appropriate Use of Consultation	[ ]	[ ]		[ ]
Good Interaction with Staff	[ ]	[ ]		[ ]
PROCEDURES: ______________________				
Appropriate	[ ]	[ ]		[ ]

DISCHARGE DIAGNOSIS: ____
DATE OF DISCHARGE: ____

	YES	NO		Not Applicable
Appropriate	[ ]	[ ]		[ ]

*PLEASE EXPLAIN ANY "NO" ANSWERS, NOTING PROBLEMS IF ANY: ______________
____

OVERALL SUMMARY OF QUALITY OF CARE PROVIDED: ______________________
____

SIGNATURE OF PROCTOR: ______________________ DATE: __________
FORM REVIEWED BY: ______________________ DATE: __________
Chairperson, Department of Pediatrics

Courtesy of Children's Hospital, San Diego, California.

Exhibit 6–20 Anesthesia Proctoring Form

P Patient MR# ______
R Surgeon ______
I Date of Surgery ______
N Length of Surgery [ ] hrs [ ] min
T **ANESTHESIOLOGIST:** ______
PROCTOR: ______
L Primary procedure: ______
E Secondary procedure(s): ______
G Type of anesthesia: ______
I
B PREANESTHESIA WORKUP:
L [ ] good [ ] satisfactory [ ] needs improvement
Y EVIDENCE OF UNDERSTANDING OF COMMON PEDIATRIC PROBLEMS

[ ] yes [ ] no Comments: ______

PATIENT AND PARENTS WELL INFORMED AS TO PROCEDURES AND RISKS

[ ] yes [ ] no

PROPER ANESTHESIA CHOSEN FOR CASE

[ ] yes [ ] no

ANESTHESIA TECHNIQUE:

proper monitoring	[ ] yes	[ ] no	[ ] N/A
good IV technique	[ ] yes	[ ] no	[ ] N/A
acceptable maintenance anesthesia with mask	[ ] yes	[ ] no	[ ] N/A
acceptable intubating technique	[ ] yes	[ ] no	[ ] N/A
appropriate use of fluids and blood products	[ ] yes	[ ] no	[ ] N/A

Comments: ______

ADEQUATE RECOVERY ROOM MANAGEMENT

[ ] yes [ ] no [ ] N/A

POST-ANESTHESIA MANAGEMENT:

post-anesthesia visit made and documented in patient record

[ ] yes [ ] no [ ] N/A

POST-ANESTHESIA ENTRY IN MEDICAL RECORD DESCRIBING PRESENCE OR ABSENCE OF ANESTHESIA-RELATED COMPLICATIONS:

[ ] yes [ ] no [ ] N/A

Comments: ______

RECOMMENDATION:

[ ] FURTHER PROCTORING REQUIRED

Explanation: ______

[ ] REFER TO SUPERVISORY COMMITTEE AS ACCEPTABLE

SIGNATURE OF PROCTOR ______ DATE: ______

Courtesy of Children's Hospital, San Diego, California.

Exhibit 6–21 Cardiology Proctoring Form

Cardiologist: ______________________________

Date: ______________________________

Procedure: ______________________________

Diagnosis: ______________________________

Medical Record/Patient Name: ______________________________

Proctor: ______________________________

Powers of Observation	Satisfactory	Unsatisfactory	Comments
Diagnostic Accuracy			
Clinical Judgment			
Technical Expertise			
Personal Interaction Patients/Family Physicians/Nurses/Technicians			
Input from Other Physicians/ Staff			

Conclusion: ☐ Acceptable ☐ Unacceptable
☐ Acceptable with the following recommendations/limitations:

____

____

Comments: ______________________________

Signature of Proctor: ______________________ Date: ____________

Department Chairman: ______________________ Date: ____________

Courtesy of Columbia Medical Center–West, El Paso, Texas.

One-Time Temporary Case/Single-Case Privileges

The bylaws may allow for one-time temporary privileges for care of a specific patient. Due to the nature of these temporary privileges, it would not be feasible for any kind of formal proctoring program to take place. However, if concerns regarding the care provided by a one-time temporary practitioner are identified during the routine peer review process, that information should be recorded so that if the practitioner applies for temporary privileges again or for medical staff membership at some future date, this information is reviewed during the application process. It could also be cause to deny any future temporary privileges to this individual.

Locum Tenens

A practitioner receiving locum tenens privileges can usually practice at the hospital for a specified period of time, usually less than one year. In hospitals with formal proctoring programs, physicians should be included in the proctoring program and should follow any of the outlined procedures that the medical staff has for proctoring. If no formal proctoring program exists, such practitioners' care is reviewed in the general course of peer review, and any concerns or problems identified can justify revocation of locum tenens privileges.

Focused Proctoring

Focused proctoring is used when the peer review process identifies concerns about an individual already on staff. Through investigation and recommendation, the individual is placed on a focused proctoring program. The proctoring may relate to a specific privilege or group of privileges or may encompass all privileges granted the practitioner to be reviewed for a specific period of time. The type of focused proctoring will determine whether or not a specific evaluation form is used for each admission, treatment, and/or procedure and whether the review will be retrospective or prospective. In general, the steps that are taken in the focused proctoring are as follows:

1. A peer review/investigation of concerns is completed that includes the reason for these concerns and any detail involving the questionable case or cases involved.
2. A recommendation is made through the peer review process to the department and then either to the credentials committee and executive committee or directly to the executive committee. (Individual protocols will define whether the credentials committee function includes review of peer review concerns that are not directly linked to the initial appointment or reappointment process.)
3. The outcome of the review investigation is conveyed to the practitioner. The letter to the practitioner should include
   - the reason for placement on focus proctoring
   - terms of the focus proctoring (time involved and what will be evaluated)
   - responsibility of both the practitioner being proctored and the practitioner who will be proctoring, or other responsibilities defined
   - consequences of noncompliance with the focused proctoring recommendation

Unless the proctoring limits in any way the practitioner's ability to continue with the privileges initially granted, the information at this point is not reportable to NPDB. If, however, a practitioner is able to admit or treat a patient or perform a procedure without another individual reviewing the situation and permitting treatment to take place, this is a change in the way the practitioner can practice, and it is reportable to NPDB. (See NPDB guidelines for additional information.)[18]

Focused proctoring, or a decision to place a practitioner in a formal proctoring review process, is not an action that necessarily needs approval by the governing board. Only if a recommendation is made following the proctoring review that changes in any way the clinical privileges or practice of the affected practitioner will this information need to go to the governing board. Before that happens, the practitioner is usually given the opportunity to request a fair hearing. (In some hospitals, the action is taken by the board before the physician is given the opportunity for a fair hearing. If the physician does not exercise his or her right to a fair hearing, the decision of the board stands. Otherwise, the board decision is reevaluated following the fair hearing process.)

Requirements of the Practitioner Being Proctored

As mentioned earlier, the method for proctoring practitioners will vary greatly. Some medical staffs assign a proctor or proctors to the individual being proctored. In other situations, it is the responsibility of practitioners being proctored to find someone to evaluate or observe the work that they are doing. Procedures need to be outlined and made available to the practitioner being proctored. The following possibilities should be considered when defining the responsibilities of the practitioner being proctored:

- notification to the assigned proctor for each admission or consultation or scheduled procedure (the proctored practitioner can do this by making a phone call or filling out a portion of the evaluation form and then getting it to the proctor)
- making arrangements with a proctor for any direct observation of procedures, treatments, or admissions
- keeping a record of all admissions/consultations/outpatient procedures/other performed at the hospital (to assist in tracking cases that will help to determine if evaluations have been made that reflect all of the care being provided)[19]

Requirements of the Proctoring Practitioner

Just as there are responsibilities for the practitioners being proctored, policies should define those requirements of the assigned proctor/s. They may include the following:

- Review care concurrently and/or retrospectively as appropriate per written guidelines. (If retrospective, a guideline such as "within one month of discharge" can be used. Concurrent review can be defined as done within 24 hours of the admission or procedure in question.)
- Complete appropriate report forms, and submit those forms to the medical staff office or wherever directed.
- Report any poor or significant substandard performance immediately to the department chair (as opposed to waiting for the formal evaluation to take place).
- Be available for immediate consultation with any concurrent review within a certain number of hours.
- Be present during a procedure that requires observation.[20]

The rules and policies should outline the proctoring practitioner's responsibilities with regard to intervening at any time during an observation if this is in the patient's best interest. Check with legal counsel on liabilities for the proctoring practitioner if that individual feels the need to step in and assist or take over the immediate care of the patient.

Policies should also define who is eligible to be a proctor. For example, can a practitioner's associates or partners do any proctoring? Also, can proctoring evaluations be used from another facility (if facilities are willing to share those evaluations) and if so, what percentage of the required number of evaluations (if there is a defined number) can be accepted from elsewhere? If evaluations can be used from elsewhere, are there requirements such as that the proctor at the other hospital must be on active staff at both places. Legal advice should be sought if this possibility is a consideration. Most hospitals prefer to keep the proctoring internal.

Exhibit 6–22 is a sample release of observation reports.

Proctoring of AHPs

Proctoring of AHPs for any of the categories outlined above for medical staff members can have the same or similar guidelines. Proctoring

---

Exhibit 6–22 Authorization for Release of Proctoring Reports

I hereby authorize *Accredited Healthcare Facility* and its representatives to release to the following hospital(s) and its representatives all observation report forms originated at *Accredited Healthcare Facility* that are contained in my credentials file.

List Hospitals

Hospital:	Contact Person:
____________________	____________________
____________________	____________________
____________________	____________________

By my signature I release from legal liability and hold harmless *Accredited Healthcare Facility* and its representatives from any and all claims, suits, actions, and legal liability by providing the requested reports to the hospital(s) and its representatives listed above.

____
Physician's Name (please print)

______________________________ _______________
Physician's Signature Date

-For Medical Staff Services Use Only-

Date Forwarded:
By:

Date Forwarded:
By:

Date Forwarded:
By:

Courtesy of C. Mobley & Associates, LLC, and Quality Management Options, LLC, Colorado Springs, Colorado.

Exhibit 6–23 Perfusionist—Proctor Report

Observed AHP: ______________________ Proctor: ______________________

Medical Record Number: ______________________ Date of Surgery: ______________

Procedures: ____

____

1 = did not meet minimum job requirements
2 = met most, but not all job requirements, needs improvement
3 = met all job requirements
4 = exceeded job requirements
5 = made outstanding performance contribution

	Unacceptable		Satisfactory			Not Applicable
TECHNICAL ABILITY IN OPERATING THE HEART-LUNG MACHINE, THE INTRA-AORTIC BALLOON OF BLOOD GASES	1	2	3	4	5	X
PREPAREDNESS FOR CASE	1	2	3	4	5	X
COMMUNICATION WITH SURGEON	1	2	3	4	5	X
ABILITY TO INTERACT WITH OTHER HEALTH CARE PROFESSIONALS	1	2	3	4	5	X
OVERALL ABILITY & PERFORMANCE	1	2	3	4	5	X
COMPETENCE/SKILL	1	2	3	4	5	X
DOCUMENTATION/RECORDKEEPING	1	2	3	4	5	X
RELATIONSHIP WITH PATIENTS	1	2	3	4	5	X
COMPLIANCE WITH HOSPITAL AND MEDICAL STAFF POLICIES & PROCEDURES	1	2	3	4	5	X

OTHER COMMENTS: ____

____

______________________________ ______________
Signature of Proctor Date

______________________________ ______________
Signature of Department Chairman Date

CONFIDENTIAL—DO NOT COPY. Complete and return to the Medical Staff Office.

Courtesy of The Hospital of the Good Samaritan, Los Angeles, California.

AHPs is usually limited to those AHPs who are licensed by law and allowed by the hospital to practice independently and would mirror the process used for the medical staff. If a formal proctoring process is not used for hospital medical staff members, more than likely it is not used for AHPs. For those AHPs who are directly or generally supervised by physicians, a formal proctoring program is not necessary, since there is a direct responsibility for patient care by the employing or supervising physician for these individuals. In this scenario, the only evaluation that is suggested is at the time of reconsideration of a continued relationship with the AHP (annual or biannual reappraisal).

Exhibit 6–23 is an example of an evaluation format that can be used for AHPs.

As with the medical staff evaluations, AHPs should be evaluated on the direct patient care that they give as well as on their relationships with others in the hospital that they come in contact with during the course of patient care.

NOTES

1. *1998 Hospital Accreditation Standards* (Oakbrook Terrace, IL: Joint Commission on Accreditation of Healthcare Organizations), 283.
2. *1998 Hospital Accreditation Standards,* 298.
3. *1998 Hospital Accreditation Standards,* 285.
4. *Medical Staff Management* (Gaithersburg, MD: Aspen Publishers, Inc., 1995), 2–2:29.
5. *Credentialing across the Continuum* (Marblehead, MA: Opus Communications) (February 1997), "JCAHO interpretation covers telemedicine." Vol. 1, No. 2: 9.
6. *Credentialing across the Continuum* (Marblehead, MA: Opus Communications) (February 1997), "JCAHO interpretation covers telemedicine." Vol. 1, No. 2: 9.
7. *Credentialing across the Continuum* (Marblehead, MA: Opus Communications) (February 1997), "JCAHO interpretation covers telemedicine." Vol. 1, No. 2: 7.
8. *Synergy* (Lombard, IL: NAMSS) (February 1998), Vol. 25, No. 2: 9.
9. *Synergy* (March 1998), 34.
10. *1998 Hospital Accreditation Standards,* 260.
11. *1998 Accreditation Manual for Healthcare Networks* (Oakbrook Terrace, IL: Joint Commission on Accreditation of Healthcare Organizations), 75 (draft standards).
12. *1998 Accreditation Manual for Healthcare Networks,* HR4-HR5.
13. *Practice Privileges Handbook* (Marblehead, MA: Oreeley Associates), 1994).
14. *Health Care Competency and Credentialing Report* (June 1997), Vol. 1, No. 4, 7.
15. *Health Care Competency and Credentialing Report,* Vol. 1, No. 4: 7.
16. *Health Care Competency and Credentialing Report,* Vol. 1, No. 4: 7.
17. *1998 Hospital Accreditation Standards,* 257.
18. NPDB guidelines.
19. *Medical Staff Briefing* (Marblehead, MA: Opus Communications) (September 1996), 12.
20. *Medical Staff Briefing* (Marblehead, MA: Opus Communications) (September 1996), 12; *Medical Staff Briefing* (Marblehead, MA: Opus Communications) (May 1997), 7.

Chapter 7

Committee Involvement in the Credentialing Process

OVERVIEW

Numerous committees may be involved in the credentialing process and associated activities. Most organizations establish a standing review or credentials committee. Peer review or (in hospitals) department committees may assist with the review, screening, or evaluation of credentials and/or competence. Hospital medical executive committees are charged by the Joint Commission to review applications and credentials, and in managed care, the medical management or peer review committee may be involved in review and decision. Performance improvement/quality management committees commonly provide information related to recredentialing. To ensure a smooth review and decision process, it is important to address committee function and structure.

The credentials review committee considers applications (new and reapplication) in relation to organizational standards, criteria, and requirements. In the hospital, recommendations are made to the medical executive committee which, following consideration, makes recommendations to the governing body. In managed and ambulatory care, the credentialing decision is commonly made by a review or credentials committee that reports its decision to the governing body.

Members of committees involved in credentialing should understand and be supportive of the concept of credentialing and be educated in applicable accreditation requirements, internal organization requirements, and effective meeting structure. They should be willing to devote the time and attention necessary to the thorough review of information submitted by applicants and gathered by the credentialing staff. And they must be willing to investigate, evaluate, and use reasonable judgment in drawing conclusions and making recommendations or decisions.[1] This chapter provides information relevant to effective committee meetings.

COMMITTEES INVOLVED IN CREDENTIALING

Other than the National Committee for Quality Assurance (NCQA), organizations that accredit health care organizations do not specifically require a credentials committee but have standards requiring a mechanism for carrying out the credentialing function. The function is most often accomplished by a designated committee. NCQA requires accredited managed care organizations to designate a credentialing committee.

In the Hospital

The Joint Commission on Accreditation of Healthcare Organizations (Joint Commission) requires a medical executive committee (MEC) that has primary authority over activities of performance improvement for the professional services provided by practitioners with clinical privileges. The standards also require that this committee make recommendations directly to the governing body related to

- the mechanism for review of credentials and delineation of individual clinical privileges
- individuals eligible for medical staff membership
- individuals eligible for delineated clinical privileges[2]

Because of the scope of work assigned to the MEC, many hospitals organize a credentials committee that reports to it.

Information concerning competence and privilege delineation is to be obtained from peers. The Joint Commission defines a peer to be an "individual from the same discipline (for example, physician and physician, dentist and dentist) and with essentially equal qualifications."[3] Therefore, medical service departments/section chairs review and report on the individual practitioner performance competency and make recommendations related to delineation of privileges as a part of their regular function and activities. These recommendations may be made directly to the MEC or to it through the credentials committee. The MEC assumes responsibility for all aspects of credentialing activities and functions in a hospital with no medical departments/sections and no credentials committee.

In Managed Care

The National Committee for Quality Assurance (NCQA) requires that a credentials committee with participating practitioner representation receive and review credentials and make recommendations. Organizations that are not seeking NCQA accreditation establish a review body or delegate the review function to an existing committee.

In Ambulatory Care

Large organizations commonly designate a credentials committee. Smaller organizations may choose to delegate activities and functions to an existing management group or committee.

Other Committee Involvement

As already noted, numerous committees may be involved in various aspects of credentials review. Information related to evaluation of competence at the time of recredentialing may be obtained from performance improvement, quality management, utilization management, medical management, or peer review committees. It is important that an organization identify all committees that play a role in the credentialing/recredentialing process and clearly outline the related functions, requirements, and lines of communication. As various committees evaluate the delivery of health care, any information or determination that is practitioner specific may be applicable for inclusion in a practitioner profile. Because the profile becomes the basis of the recredentialing decision, it is important that data be appropriately communicated between committees reviewing care and those responsible for profile development and recredentialing.

THE CREDENTIALS COMMITTEE

Purpose

The primary purpose of a credentials committee is to review information related to the credentials and privileges of practitioners who are applying for membership, affiliation, or a contractual relationship with the organization. Activities normally performed by the credentials committee include

- ensuring that all applicants are reviewed against minimum standards (hospitals) or criteria (managed care) and are treated fairly and objectively
- determining whether there is adequate/sufficient information to evaluate and make a determination/recommendation
- evaluating information presented

- making recommendations or decisions related to participation, appointment, privileges, or relationship[4]

The committee may be charged with other responsibilities, including

- implementation and ongoing review of a standard credentialing and privileging process (privileging is not currently performed in most managed care settings)
- assurance that the credentialing process conforms with applicable accreditation standards and other regulatory requirements
- development of credentialing criteria for determination of a contract offering (in the managed care or ambulatory setting)

Numerous considerations are related to a well-organized, functional committee meeting; these include

- committee structure
- meeting preparation
- meeting procedure
- follow-up

Committee Structure

The major elements to be considered in relation to committee structure are membership, accountability, and frequency of meetings.

Credentials Committee Membership

Credentials committees should be composed of a workable number of members. A workable number can be defined as a group that provides appropriate representation from the scope of services provided and can complete all required functions in a timely manner. Committee membership, including the term of membership, should be defined in the organization's bylaws or policies and procedures. Important attributes of a committee member are

- an interest in the committee and its activities, responsibilities, and functions
- ability to commit to active participation
- prior experience in some aspect of the credentialing function
- professional respect[5]

In the Hospital. The bylaws and/or credentialing policy and procedure manual for the hospital medical staff should define the membership of the credentials committee. The number of medical staff departments/sections and the size of the organization often determine membership. If the credentials committee's primary function is to review administrative or citizenship issues after obtaining recommendations from departments/sections related to the clinical privileges, it is not necessary to have representation from each department/specialty. Members should be chosen from active medical staff members of the organization who are interested in and supportive of having a quality medical staff. Because credentialing is a crucial component of quality within the hospital setting, it is important that responsible, knowledgeable individuals be recruited for membership on this committee. Bylaws or rules will often require that future leaders, past leaders, or a combination of these individuals serve on the credentials committee. Physicians who are current, voting members of the executive committee should not be voting members of the credentials committee (the credentials committee chair is excluded) to avoid having the same person vote twice on any recommendations. (This would not apply to the chief of staff or president of the medical staff, who is normally an ex officio member without a vote.)

Some hospitals will ask a current chief or the president-elect, with no prior experience on a credentials committee, to chair the committee in an effort to involve him or her in leadership functions of the medical staff organization. This is not recommended because the individual chairing this committee must fully understand the responsibilities and options available for all recommendations made. These are learned through committee membership and participation in the process. In some hospitals, membership on the credentials committee is a prerequisite for a leadership role. A chief or president-elect of the medical staff with no prior experience on a credentials committee should be appointed as a nonvoting member of the committee in order to assist in his or her orientation before beginning their elected leadership but should not be appointed chair unless there are no other options available. Optimally, the chairmanship of the credentials committee is reserved for an immediate past president/chief of the medical staff or someone who has served as a chief/president of the medical staff during the past five years. Such an individual has already obtained a full understanding of the responsibilities and options associated with this important function.

Some hospital bylaws still include a committee attendance requirement. This involves attendance at a specified number of medical staff, department, and other committee meetings as a component of continued membership (i.e., 50 percent of all scheduled credentials committee meetings per year). Although the current trend is for hospitals to reduce or eliminate the meeting requirement, we suggest that if requirements exist, they should be focused on committee involvement rather than on attendance. Members of the medical staff should take it upon themselves to be active in the organization. Members who are appointed to and agree to serve on a specific committee, including the credentials committee, should meet the obligation of attending the committee meetings that are held during their tenure. Policy and procedure or bylaws should address the process of replacing a member who cannot serve out his or her appointment or who is unable to regularly attend meetings or fulfill obligations.

Generally, an administrative representative (the chief executive officer, vice president for medical affairs, or other designated administrative representative) is appointed to the credentials committee as a member without a vote. A member of the governing body may also attend meetings as an ex officio nonvoting member. This involvement can contribute to increased trust by the board in the medical staff review and recommendation process.

In Managed Care. The composition of the credentials committee in the managed care setting may be entirely different from that in hospitals. One factor affecting membership relates to the number of physicians who are available for, and interested in, committee involvement and willing to actively participate. Additionally, there are rarely enforceable requirements for committee involvement and activity in managed care contracts. Therefore, there may be more administrative and support staff who are active, voting members of the committee than there are practitioners. The committee membership may consist entirely of organizational employees such as the plan administrator, the director/manager of provider relations, the quality improvement director/coordinator, the plan medical director, credentialers, and other staff involved in network development. If the credentials committee membership does not include practitioners (in addition to the plan medical director), peer recommendation must be obtained from another source, such as a peer review committee or a medical management utilization committee whose membership is primarily composed of practitioners.

NCQA-accredited organizations must include participating practitioners in the credentials committee membership. Physician membership must be representative of the primary care and specialty makeup of the organization including internal medicine and/or family practice, pediatrics, and other specialties that treat significant numbers of members, if the organization is to be compliant with NCQA standards. Separate review bodies for each specialty or type of practitioner will also meet the intent of the standard.

Attendance at committee meetings raises specific issues that are not usually encountered in hospitals. Practitioners are usually asked to volunteer for committee membership for a term of one to two years and they may decline to be involved in the process. To increase involvement, incentives may be offered, including

- provision of meals with the meeting
- meetings held in a location that is easily accessible and attractive to members—

maybe in hospitals where members are normally making rounds at the time of the meetings or in a hotel meeting room with a catered meal
- payment for attendance; committee members frequently receive a stipend or payment for attendance at meetings in managed and ambulatory care organizations

In Ambulatory Care. Credentials committee membership will differ on the basis of the type of setting, the relationship to other organizations, and the accrediting body. Many of the issues raised in the membership in hospitals and in managed care will be applicable.

Accountability

Activities for which the committee is accountable should be outlined in bylaws, the policy and procedures, or the credentials plan document. A copy should be provided to new members and reviewed by the committee as a whole on a periodic basis. All members should have a clear understanding of their role and responsibility for the decision-making process, actions, recommendations, and confidentiality.

Frequency of Meetings

Although there are no accreditation or standard requirements related to frequency of meetings, most organizations have a policy that requires a timely credentialing process. Meetings may be held on a monthly basis or as often as necessary, depending on the amount of work the committee has on the agenda. If the organizational policy allows flexibility, meetings are scheduled by the chair in consultation with the individuals responsible for the agenda development. If a flexible schedule is available and there are few actions on the agenda, the policy may allow for file review with recommendation by telephone poll or for a recommendation by the department chair/credentials committee chair if specific criteria have been met. See the sections on express credentialing in Chapters 3 and 4 for more information about this process.

The hospital credentials committee meeting may need to be scheduled on a regular basis to ensure that recommendations are documented and ready for review at scheduled medical executive committee meetings. Special meetings may be held in ambulatory and managed care organizations if there is a large influx of applications or if important contracts are pending.

Meeting Preparation

Preparation for a meeting includes

- development of an agenda
- notification of members
- preparation of files and other packets of information to be distributed and/or presented
- arrangements for meeting space, food, audiovisuals, room setup, etc.
- applicant interviews (hospital)

Agenda Development

Development of the agenda is the first step in the preparation for the credentials committee meeting. The purpose of an agenda is to focus discussion on the topics or issues requiring discussion or action. A policy and procedure that addresses agenda content, distribution, and time lines ensures that the agenda will be a valuable tool in meeting management. The policy and procedure should include

- agenda format (with an example attached)
- time line for agenda preparation
- process for agenda review and sign-off
- method for handling unfinished business
- distribution (before or at the start of meeting)
- deadlines, if any, for submission of issues to be included on the agenda

Common credentials committee agenda components are

- call to order/approval of previous minutes
- unfinished/incomplete items from last meeting

- items for announcement/information only
- applications for initial provisional/probationary status (hospitals)
- credentials applications (managed and ambulatory care)
- applications for reappointment
- requests for change in category of membership, such as associate to active (hospitals)
- requests for change in privileges, such as new privileges or deletion of privileges not being used (as applicable)
- terminations or resignations from the staff or plan
- special discussion/individual performance
- other business[6]

There are numerous acceptable formats for agendas. An agenda may be developed from a software template (Exhibit 7–1) or in accordance with policy to include required organizational components. Exhibit 7–2 is a sample agenda format for a hospital credentials committee meeting.

Because confidentiality of information is crucial to most credentialing activities, agendas that specify individual names should not be developed for distribution before the meeting.

Meeting Notices

The committee chair and membership usually determine the time frame for notices to be sent to members. One to two weeks is a standard time frame for the notice or meeting reminder. Meetings are often prescheduled on a yearly basis, with the master list of dates distributed to committee members upon appointment. To ensure attendance, several methods of notification may be used. In addition to a master calendar and a written notice before the meeting, a medical newsletter, e-mail, telephone calls, and faxes are commonly used for meeting reminders. Without multiple notices, organizations often experience a decrease in meeting attendance. Due to confidentiality, it is strongly recommended that no materials for review be distributed with the meeting notice.

Members of the credentials committee may be expected or asked to review files before the meeting. If so, additional notice should be given to committee members assigned to review files before the credentials committee meeting. These reviews are usually completed in the credentials office or the office of the reviewer.

File Preparation

A file should not be added to the agenda until it has been reviewed and met all criteria for a complete file. The components required for a complete file are usually listed on a summary sheet. The credentialer completes the summary sheet as information and verifications are received. Files are organized in a standard order with information requiring further review highlighted. The final file review by the credentialing staff should be completed by an auditor, manager, or credentialer other than the individual who worked the file. This review ensures that the summary sheet is complete and accurate and that all information required for an action or recommendation is present and clearly identified.

If all criteria are met, it may not be necessary to take the credentials files to a committee meeting. Summary sheets completed by the reviewer may be submitted to the committee for recommendation without discussion. If this method is used, policies and procedures must address the activity in detail.

The committee must determine the benefits of file review by a committee member before the meeting versus time required during the meeting to complete a review of the files. Use of a premeeting review process may depend on the number of files or issues to be evaluated. Organizations having large numbers of files reviewed by the committee on a regular basis may find a premeeting file review by a committee member to be a significant time saver. If a premeeting review process is used, a review form should be completed by the reviewer and used to present

Exhibit 7–1 Credentials Committee Meeting Agenda

Agenda

Credentials Committee Meeting

Date: ________

1:00 P.M. to 1:30 P.M.

Building 1, Conference Room

Meeting called by:
Type of meeting:
Facilitator:
Note taker:
Timekeeper:

Attendees:
Please read:
Please bring:

Agenda Topics

1:00–1:10 P.M. Meeting Overview

Discussion:

Conclusions:

Action items:	Person responsible:	Deadline:

1:10–1:30 P.M. New Applications

Discussion:

Conclusions:

Action items:	Person responsible:	Deadline:

Note: Format by Microsoft Word version 6.0, Agenda Wizard.

Courtesy of C. Mobley & Associates, LLC, and Quality Management Options, LLC, Colorado Springs, Colorado.

Exhibit 7–2 Agency Format for Credentials Committee

Date:

Location:

Time:

Contact Person:

AGENDA ITEMS

I. Call to Order

II. Minutes Approval

III. Old Business
   A. Previously Reviewed: Additional Information
      1. Dr. ____________________________
      2. Dr. ____________________________
   B. Final Reappointment Notices

IV. New Business
   A. Leave of absence
      1. Dr. ____________________________
   B. Resignations
      1. Dr. ____________________________
   C. New Applicants—Attachment A
   D. Reappointments—Attachment B

V. Next Meeting

Note: LOA, leave of absence.

Courtesy of C. Mobley & Associates, LLC, and Quality Management Options, LLC, Colorado Springs, Colorado.

any information requiring discussion at the committee meeting. If this process is used, a policy should be developed that addresses

- who may review files
- expectations for outcome of file review
- format for documentation of findings
- location of file review (to ensure confidentiality of information in the file)
- time frame for notification and review before the meeting

Applicant Interviews (Hospital)

New applicants at a hospital may be interviewed as part of the credentialing process (see Chapter 3 for additional information). The interview policy may require that all new applicants be interviewed, or the interview may be optional at the discretion of the credentials committee or medical executive committee. If interviews are conducted, the new applicants are usually asked to present a summary of their training and experience. This is followed by an exchange of questions between the applicant and the committee members. This approach can be beneficial for both the committee, to gather information, and the individual, to obtain answers about his or her potential relationship with the organization and the medical staff. It also allows the hospital and medical staff an opportunity to give the applicant information related to medical staff member expectations. Interviews afford the potential member an opportunity to meet the leadership of both the medical staff organization and the hospital administration. Following a formal interview process, a hospital representative may take the group of applicants on a tour of the hospital departments and areas relative to their practice.

If new applicants are interviewed as part of the credentialing process, the interview schedule is developed and coordinated with the credentials committee schedule. The candidate is then notified of meeting date, time of arrival, expected length of interview, location, and other pertinent information. If interviews are conducted before the committee meeting date, the interviewer completes an interview assessment form for inclusion with the file and then summarizes information at the committee meeting.

Location/Meeting Space

Meeting preparation includes

- identification and scheduling of the location and meeting room
- provision for room setup
- coordination of audiovisual and other equipment needs
- arrangements for food service
- accommodations for file transport to the meeting room

Responsibility for each aspect should be assigned and a checklist noting the status and completion maintained (see Exhibit 7–3 for a sample meeting preparation worksheet). Once the meeting date(s) and times are identified, the location is often reserved for 6 to 12 months in advance. The reservation should be confirmed before distribution of the individual meeting notices.

The credentials committee function lends itself to a room setup with tables facing each other to facilitate discussion. A "U" or square table configuration is a common setup for this committee. Files should be delivered to the meeting location at the start of the meeting and collected as discussion is completed. No files should be taken to, or left in, the meeting room unattended.

The last step of meeting preparation is discussion with, and preparation of, the committee chair. The chair should complete the final review of the agenda and review the last meeting minutes to ensure that no outstanding items are left unreviewed. Additionally, if information or files will be presented that have "caution flags" or possible noncompliance issues, the committee chair should be well versed in the issues and the options available for decision before the meeting.

Meeting Procedure

The major aspects of meeting procedure are

- conducting the meeting
- file presentation
- role identification

Conducting the Meeting

When starting a meeting, key issues to address are time frames, identification of attendance, and role identification.

Bylaws and policies and procedures may require a quorum in order to proceed with a meeting or make decisions. A quorum may be defined as

- a specific percentage of voting members
- all voting members present at the meeting
- a percentage of the voting members that are present at the meeting

If a quorum is required and defined, documentation of attendance should include a state-

Exhibit 7–3 Meeting Preparation Worksheet

MEDICAL STAFF MEETINGS FOR THE MONTH OF

Committee	Meeting Date, Time, and Place	Date of Meeting	Day Runner	Classroom Schedule	Reminder of Meeting	Minutes to Meeting in . . .	Minutes Reminder	Food	Sent to Med Exec. Comm.

Courtesy of Columbia Retreat Hospital, Richmond, Virginia.

ment of "quorum present" or "quorum not obtained."

Time frames for the meeting should be identified and communicated to the membership before the meeting. Members should be in agreement with time frames and with the action that will be taken if a time frame is exceeded by discussion. As a general rule, meetings should be completed in one hour. Credentials committee meetings can become very lengthy when the discussion is not structured or the committee chair does not maintain control. The chair should be well versed in meeting management and should be willing to cut off discussion that is not to the point or is not moving toward a conclusion or recommendation. A well-structured agenda and premeeting file review usually allow completion of business within the one-hour time frame.

Identification of attendance is important if members are being reimbursed or are being monitored for compliance with attendance requirements. This can be accomplished through use of a sign-in sheet or by documentation in the minutes. It is common practice to identify members who are not in attendance if there are questions related to reimbursed amount or allegation of unfair decisions.

Role identification for the committee functions is the responsibility of the committee chair. A secretary/recorder should be designated to take and produce minutes. Some committees also have designated roles of timekeepers and/or facilitators.

File Presentation

Numerous options are available for actual review and presentation of file content during the committee meeting.

1. Probably the most common method of file review and presentation involves review, presentation, and discussion at the meeting. Files are brought to the meeting and distributed to the members who are present for review. Each member verbally summarizes information from the file(s) he or she reviewed. Other members ask questions or raise concerns as appropriate, and the committee comes to an agreement for a recommendation or decision.
2. A second option makes use of a file summary sheet that is attached to the front of the file. Files are brought to the committee meeting (by a credentialer and/or physician reviewer who completed a premeeting review) with a summary that notes compliance or noncompliance with required criteria and/or standards. Missing, negative, and questionable information and noncompliance with criteria are highlighted on the summary sheet and become the focus of the discussion at the committee meeting.
3. A method more common to managed care settings separates files by category. Files that meet all criteria and include no negative, questionable, or missing information are placed in a category of "clean" files. Those that do not meet one or more criteria, have missing information, or questions have been raised are placed in a review category. When this method is used, the files that meet all criteria are not brought to the committee meeting. Summary sheets are presented, and practitioners are approved in a consent vote. The remaining committee time is spent reviewing, discussing, and making determinations for each review file.
4. A fourth option is to bring all files to the committee meeting. Each file is circulated and reviewed by each member. This is a very time-consuming process but results in a very detailed and thorough review.

Each of these options can occur with or without a premeeting review process. A determination of which option will be chosen is usually guided by the numbers of files, the time frame for the meeting, the number of committee members, and the comfort level of the chair and committee members related to need for personal review of the files. In general, the meeting should not exceed one hour; therefore, the time frames and frequencies of the meetings often dictate the method chosen.

Decision-Making Process, Actions, and Recommendations

Either bylaws, policy and procedure, or the chair determines the process by which decisions and determinations will be made. Discussion and determinations may follow a strict parliamentary procedure or a process that is less formal but clearly outlined and understood by all members. Voting options include consensus, majority of the membership, majority of those in attendance, or a quorum. If decisions are based on a quorum or percentage of the membership, it is important the minutes reflect that the requirement was met before decisions, discussion, and recommendations were initiated.

The chair is responsible for control of discussion to the extent that no recommendations or decisions are made that are not within the scope of the committee. For example, if membership or information submitted does not include peer input, the committee cannot render any recommendation related to clinical competence. In the hospital, the credentials committee can make a recommendation to the medical executive committee pertaining to membership and clinical privileges of new applicants and those reapplying. The scope of actions available is outlined in the bylaws or policies and procedures and may include

- recommendation for membership and the privileges requested
- recommendation for membership and the privileges requested with restriction (e.g., probation, proctoring, or limitation of requested privileges)
- decision tabled until information can be clarified or additional information obtained
- establishment of an ad hoc committee to further review credentials, information, or requests
- recommendation for denial of membership and privileges

In managed and ambulatory care, the scope of committee actions may be somewhat different from that in a hospital. The governing body may delegate the credentialing and recredentialing decision to the credentials committee and allow contract execution before governing body review. In this case, determination by the committee may include

- compliance with credentialing criteria; initial contract offered
- noncompliance with one or more criteria; exception documented, initial contract offered
- noncompliance with one or more criteria; initial contract offer denied
- compliance with recredentialing criteria; continued relationship
- noncompliance with one or more recredentialing criteria; exception noted
- noncompliance with recredentialing criteria; termination

All actions, determinations, and recommendations made by the credentials committee are documented in the meeting minutes.

Parliamentary Procedure

Committees may choose to use a formal process for decision making. The most common form of parliamentary procedure is outlined in *Robert's Rules of Order*. A summary of rules of motions, according to *Robert's Rules of Order*, follows.[7]

Action or Desired Activity	Statement	Is a Second to the Motion Required?	May the Motion Be Debated?	What Vote Is Required?
Adjourn the meeting (takes precedence over others)	"I move that we adjourn"	Yes	No	Majority
Amend	"I move that we add/ strike out/change _____ and that this motion be amended by . . ."	Yes	Yes	Majority
Call to order	"I call the _________ to order"	No	No	No vote
Consider an item out of its scheduled order	"I move that we suspend the rules and consider . . ."	Yes	No	2/3 vote
End debate or discussion	"I move the previous question"	Yes	No	2/3 vote
Introduce business	"I move that . . ."	Yes	Yes	Majority
Limit debate	"I move that we limit the (number or length) of . . . "	Yes	No	2/3 vote
Object to procedure or to a personal affront	"Point of order"	No	No	No vote, chair decides
Postpone consideration	"I move that we postpone consider-ation of this matter until . . ."	Yes	Yes	Majority
Recess the meeting	"I move that we recess until . . ."	Yes	No	Majority
Reconsider a matter already closed	"I move to reconsider our action relative to . . ."	Yes	Yes	Majority

continues

Action or Desired Activity	Statement	Is a Second to the Motion Required?	May the Motion Be Debated?	What Vote Is Required?
Refer to another committee	"I move that we refer this issue to the _____ committee"	Yes	Yes	Majority
Request information	"Point of information"	No	No	No vote
Table or suspend further discussion or consideration	"I move that we table . . ."	Yes	No	Majority
Vote on a ruling by the chair	"I appeal the chair's decision"	Yes	Yes	Majority

Source: Data from *Robert's Rules of Order,* © 1982, Bantam Books.

Follow-Up

Follow-up activities at the conclusion of a meeting include

- completion of minutes
- follow-up for decisions, actions, and recommendations made at the meeting

Meeting Minutes

Minutes provide documentation that the meeting occurred and should reflect the core content of the discussion and action taken. The minutes are used as evidence of committee activity. They may also be forwarded to the medical executive committee and/or governing body as a report of recommendations and actions. None of the accrediting organizations mandate specific formats or information that must be included in minutes. However, the minutes should clearly and concisely document the deliberations of the committee and include enough information that those referencing them at a later date can understand the key content of discussion, concerns, recommendations, and actions.

Numerous formats are available for documentation of minutes. Whatever format is used, the minutes should include

- name of organization (may be noted by use of letterhead stationery) and name of committee
- date, time frame, and location of meeting
- attendance, including designations (chair, recorder, etc.), absent members, and statement regarding quorum or participation
- discussion as appropriate and actions taken for all items appearing on the agenda

Highlights or specific headings may be used for each action taken to facilitate review of the minutes by the committee membership, governing body, surveyors, and regulators. Exhibits 7–4 and 7–5 are common minutes formats used for credentials committee minutes.

During or at the end of the meeting, the recorder should ask for clarification if a conclusion, recommendation, or planned follow-up has not been clearly articulated.

General rules and guidelines for writing minutes are as follows:

Exhibit 7–4 Committee Minutes Format—Sample 1

Confidential and Privileged Information Protected by ____________________ (Reference-Specific Peer Review Statutes)

Department/Committee:
Meeting Date:
Attendance:

Signature: ____________________________

Date: ____________________________

Topic	Discussion/Conclusion	Recommendation	(Responsibility/ Time Frame) Action	Follow-Up/ Evaluation

Courtesy of C. Mobley & Associates, LLC, and Quality Management Options, LLC, Colorado Springs, Colorado.

Exhibit 7–5 Committee Minutes Format—Sample 2

(NAME OF HOSPITAL)

MEETING: (Name of Meeting)

DATE: TIME: LOCATION:

PRESENT:

ABSENT:

RECORDED BY: APPROVED BY ____________________
(Name of Chair)

Agenda Item	Discussion/Conclusion/Recommendation	Action/Follow-Up

Courtesy of C. Mobley & Associates, LLC, and Quality Management Options, LLC, Colorado Springs, Colorado.

1. Minutes should be developed from notes taken by the recorder during the meeting.
2. Minutes should be transcribed within the week following the meeting to ensure that all information is as accurate as possible.
3. Documentation should be brief and concise and should clearly represent action taken.
4. Lengthy discussion and disagreements among members should not be documented. The minutes should reflect and focus on action, not discussion.
5. Names of members making motions, drawing conclusions, or contributing to the discussion are not necessary.

If a role call vote is held, members' names with their vote are included in the minutes. Exhibit 7–6 is an example format for the minutes of the meeting of a committee hospital credentials committee that allows for completion of action items by the medical executive committee and governing board using the same document. The minutes and disk are forwarded by the credentials committee recorder to the recorder for medical executive committee, who completes that committee's action column rather than reproducing the entire document.

Once the draft minutes are complete, they are sent to the chair for review. Upon completion of the chair's review, the minutes are produced in final form. The chair signs the minutes as approved, usually at the next meeting. The minutes are maintained and distributed according to the bylaws and policy and procedures of the organization. Once the minutes are approved, no corrections or changes may be made without documentation of the change at a subsequent meeting. In general, minutes should not be widely distributed. If copies are required, they should be stamped as confidential and numbered. The distribution list should be maintained with the original minutes. Minutes are retained in accordance with the applicable state regulations and/or the bylaws, policies, and procedures of the organization. These requirements may be outlined in a minutes distribution policy and procedure. Exhibit 7–7 is a sample policy.

Follow-up on Decisions, Actions, and Recommendations

At the close of the meeting, all materials and files are collected. It is important that members understand that any material with an applicant or peer name should be immediately returned to the credentials or quality files. As minutes are transcribed, the recorder should prepare a list of all items that require further action or follow-up. These items will also be placed on the next agenda. A follow-up log (see Exhibit 7–8) or monitoring form (see Exhibit 7–9) should be maintained that identifies the person responsible for follow-up and the time frame for action.

All committee actions, including recommendations to the medical executive committee or governing body, are documented and forwarded to the appropriate entity. If the credentials committee is responsible for the credentialing decision, letters to practitioners indicating action taken are completed and signed by the committee chair or other person designated to do so by policy and procedure. If additional information or action is required, a referral is completed (see Exhibit 7–10).

ALLIED HEALTH OR INTERDISCIPLINARY PRACTICE COMMITTEE

Large organizations or those having a significant number of allied health practitioners may establish an allied health credentials subcommittee. In some states, an interdisciplinary practice committee may be required by state regulations. This committee is composed of allied health practitioners and makes recommendations to the credentials committee, the medical executive committee, and/or the governing board. Additional information related to interdisciplinary practice committees may be found in Chapter 3 of this book.

Exhibit 7–6 Sample Hospital Credentials Committee Minutes

Date: dd/mm/yy Time: 7:00 A.M.–8:15 A.M. Location: Governors Conference Room

Present: C.J. Moberly, MD; S.D. Dutch, DO; G. Alverez, MD; L. Buchan, MD; C.O. Harley, MD

Absent: M. Jones, MD

Recorded By: M. Secretary Approved By: G. Chair ______________________

(Typed name of Chair) Signature

Agenda Item	Discussion/Conclusion/Recommendation	Action/Follow-Up
1. Call to order		
2. Minutes of meeting dd/mm/yy	Minutes approved as written	None indicated
3. Old business		
3.1 Previously revised:		
3.1.a A.B. Goodfellow, MD—DEA certificate	3.1.a Dr. Goodfellow has submitted a current DEA certificate with a local address and full schedule.	3.1.a Recommend approval of reappointment
3.1.b M. Finkelstein, MD—Malpractice history	3.1.b Dr. Finklestein has provided a detailed account of malpractice history. The committee has serious concerns about number and outcome of cases.	3.1.b Recommendation to MEC that appointment and privileges not be granted
4. New business		
4.1 LOA/Resignations		
4.1.a B.J. Smith	4.1.a Dr. Smith as submitted a letter of resignation due to relocation out of state.	4.1.a MEC will be notified of resignation
4.2 New Applicants	4.2 See attachment A: each applicant's credentials and delineation of privileges were reviewed.	4.2 Per attachment A
4.3 Reappointments	4.3 See attachment B: quality profiles, updated credentials, and delineation of privileges were reviewed.	4.3 Per attachment B
5. Next meeting	5. The next meeting will be held on mm/dd/yy in the Governors Conference Room	

continues

Exhibit 7–6 continued

ATTACHMENT A: NEW APPLICANTS

Name, Title, Specialty **Address** **Associated with:**	**Professional Diploma** **Residency** **Fellowship** **Board Status**	**Comments**	**Credentials Committee** **Recommendation** **mm/dd/yy**	**MEC** **Recommendation**	**Governing** **Board Action**
Harrison, Joe, MD Family Practice xxxx Main St. Anywhere, USA Solo Practice	Univ. of Colorado—1982 St. Anywhere Hospital—1982–83 F.P.-Jons Hosp.—1983–86 No fellowship Certified Family Practice	Requesting appointment and privileges in F.P. department. No evidence of adverse information in file.	Recommend appointment to provisional active status with privileges as requested.		
James, Madeleine, DO Family Practice xxxx Right Street Anywhere, USA Joining F.P. of America	Univ. of Tenn.—1989 Naval Hospital, San Diego, CA 1989–93 No fellowship Certified Family Practice	Requesting appointment and privileges in F.P. department. No evidence of adverse information in file.	Recommend appointment to provisional active status with privileges as requested.		

continues

Exhibit 7–6 continued

ATTACHMENT B: REAPPOINTMENTS

Name, Title Department Specialty	Last Reappointment Date Current Status	Comments	Credentials Committee Recommendation mm/dd/yy	MEC Recommendation	Governing Board Action
Abel, John, MD Medicine Dermatology	mm/dd/yy Provisional	Activity level qualifies change in status to consultant	Reappointment to consultant status with privileges as requested.		
Harrison, James, MD Surgery General Surgery	mm/dd/yy Active	Four suspensions for medical records during past 18 months; no other adverse information.	Reappoint to active status with letter of admonition related to medical records.		
Jones, Mike, MD Surgery Cardiovascular Surgery	mm/dd/yy Active	No adverse information noted. Changes in privileges as requested.	Reappoint to active status with changes in privileges as requested.		
Wong, Peter, MD Medicine Neurology	mm/dd/yy Consultant	Two malpractice suits. Settled during reappointment period.	Reappoint to consultant status with privileges as requested.		

Note: LOA, leave of absence; MEC, medical executive committee; DEA, Drug Enforcement Administration; F.P., family practice.

Courtesy of C. Mobley & Associates, LLC, and Quality Management Options, LLC, Colorado Springs, Colorado.

Exhibit 7–7 Minutes Distribution Policy

It is the policy of XYZ Organization to maintain confidentiality of committee minutes to the fullest extent possible.

In an effort to minimize loss of discovery protection for peer review activities, the following policies/procedures address how minutes will be distributed/collected/disposed of.

1. Minutes will not be distributed prior to any meeting. Minutes will be available in the _____________ office prior to any meeting if committee members wish to review them prior to the meeting.
2. Minutes will be copied for distribution at the meeting.
   a. Minute takers will take minutes to the meeting, distribute at the meeting, and collect at the end of the meeting. Minutes are not to be taken out of the meeting room by anyone other than the minute takers.
   b. Other personnel transporting minutes to any meeting will be instructed to follow directions in (a) above. Minutes will be returned to the _____________ office at the end of the meeting for disposal.
3. Committee minutes will be available to committee members, medical officers, department chairmen, quality assurance personnel, and senior management only. Other persons desiring to review committee minutes must make a written request stating reason for reviewing minutes. The request will be reviewed by the committee chairman and permission will be granted or denied.
4. All minutes will be transcribed in the _____________________ office in an effort to maintain confidentiality. Other personnel taking minutes can submit a written draft or a cassette tape to _____________ office personnel.

Courtesy of C. Mobley & Associates, LLC, and Quality Management Options, LLC, Colorado Springs, Colorado.

CLINICAL DEPARTMENT MEETINGS (HOSPITAL)

If hospital clinical departments/sections hold regular meetings and are charged with review of clinical competence and/or support of clinical privilege delineation, information, actions, and/or recommendations are documented using the same guidelines outlined in the previous section titled "Follow-up on Decisions, Actions, and Recommendations."

Discussion of performance and competency at department/section meetings usually relates to

- evaluation of findings from a performance improvement activity or study that may or may not include practitioner-specific results
- findings related to an indicator or a required performance improvement activity (e.g., blood usage, medical record completion) that may or may not be reported as practitioner specific
- individual case review (e.g., concern related to inappropriate or untimely intervention by a practitioner)
- identification of appropriate skills, training, and education for specific privileges considered to be common to the department
- recommendations and actions that involve privileging

PROFESSIONAL REVIEW (MANAGED CARE)

If the credentials committee does not include or address professional review through its membership and function, the review must be assigned to another committee that is composed primarily of practitioners. Peer review related to credentialing and recredentialing may include

Exhibit 7–8 Meeting Status Report/Follow-up Log

Meeting of the: ______________________

Date Discussed	Description of Issue	Action To Be Taken	Responsible Person	Status

Courtesy of C. Mobley & Associates, LLC, and Quality Management Options, LLC, Colorado Springs, Colorado.

Exhibit 7–9 Monitoring of Issues Form

DEPARTMENT/COMMITTEE

MEETING DATE	MSS REP

REFERRED TO (Department/Committee and Meeting Date if Known)

DATE REFERRED	REFERRED BY

IDENTIFIED ISSUE

DISPOSITION (Description of Follow-up and/or Referral Needed/Accomplished)

TRACKING

- ☐ Follow-up completed
- ☐ Policy drafted
- ☐ Procedure drafted
- ☐ To department/committee for review: Approval date ______________________
- ☐ To MSEC for review: Approval date: ______________________
- ☐ Follow up (See Above)
- ☐ To Board of Directors
- ☐ Final drafts signed
- ☐ Final location: ______________________

Note: MSEC, medical staff executive committee; MSS, medical staff services.

Courtesy of Children's Hospital, San Diego, California.

Exhibit 7–10 Committee Referral

MEDICAL STAFF

________________ **HOSPITAL**

TO ________________________________ FROM ________________________________

CASE # ________________________ CHAIRMAN ________________________________

Referring Remarks/Questions: Date: ________________

Reply: Date: ________________

____
Signature

Action by Referring Committee: Date: ________________

Note: This form is for use by departmental committees of the medical staff:

1. In referring medical records to responsible medical staff member for completion, clarification, or further documentation.
2. In referring medical records to other committees of the medical staff or hospital staff for review and comment.

Courtesy of C. Mobley & Associates, LLC, and Quality Management Options, LLC, Colorado Springs, Colorado.

- individual practitioner training, education, and competence related to the requested scope of practice
- individual case review
- knowledge of competence during term of relationship with the organization
- standard of care and practices

REPORTING THROUGH THE ORGANIZATION

Actions and recommendations taken by the committees responsible for credentialing and privileging must be reported to the governing body. In hospitals, the governing body receives recommendations from the medical executive committee. In managed and ambulatory care, credentialing decisions and/or recommendations are forwarded to the governing body from the credentials committee or other designated group. Activity may be documented on a tracking form (see Exhibit 7–11).

RELATIONSHIPS AMONG COMMITTEES AND WITH THE GOVERNING BODY

In some organizations, few committees are involved in the credentials decision. At its simplest level in a hospital, a department chair may make recommendations to the medical executive committee that are then forwarded to the governing body. More common are hospitals with numerous departments/sections and committees or hospitals that are part of a system or network. Managed and ambulatory care may be part of a network or tied to a system with numerous geographic locations and/or contracted relationships. As size and relationships increase, the credentialing function often becomes more complex. There may be several credentials committees within a system having one governing body. Despite the complexity of the organization or system, the credentialing and privilege function should involve the fewest possible steps, people, and number of committees or levels of review. Re-review by committees is seldom productive and rarely results in a recommendation change. The credentialing structure, numbers of individual committees, and relationships between committees should be based upon a clear understanding of credentialing and privileging and should be clearly outlined in the organization's bylaws, rules, or policies and procedures.

Executive Committee (Hospital)

The executive committee of the medical staff is the only medical staff committee required by the Joint Commission. The MEC receives information from review bodies, the credentials committee, departments/sections, and/or others with regard to initial appointment, reappointment, and other related credentialing actions. This information may come in the form of one recommendation or a combined recommendation from the medical staff department and the credentials committee (if they both exist). A clinical department/section may make recommendations concerning privileges directly to the MEC, and the credentials committee may make a separate recommendation concerning membership, administrative, or citizenship issues. In this situation, if one of the recommendations is positive and the other adverse, the medical executive committee (by definition in the bylaws) has to review each recommendation and, on the basis of that review, make one recommendation to the governing body. The MEC may request or require additional information from the applicant, department, and/or credentials committee before making its recommendation to the governing body.

An interview process may be initiated by the MEC if it appears that an adverse recommendation will be made to the governing board. Should a recommendation to the governing board from the MEC be adverse, the fair hearing process in the medical staff bylaws must be followed. In an organization with a nondepartmentalized medical staff and no credentials committee, the MEC collects and reviews information. Privilege and

Exhibit 7–11 Monthly Standing Committee Tracking Form

Month: ______________________ **Year:** ______________________

Committee	**Meeting Date**	**Date Minutes Approved**	**Date to Q.I. (If applicable)**	**Date to Dept. (If applicable)**	**Date to MEC**
Other Sub or Ad Hoc Mtgs This Month:					

Note: Q.I., quality improvement; MEC, medical executive committee.

Courtesy of Children's Hospital, San Diego, California.

competence are addressed by the MEC, which has representation from major services.

Governing Body

The governing body is considered the final authority for granting privileges and medical staff membership in a hospital and for approving credentialing and recredentialing decisions in managed and ambulatory care. A recommendation is made by a peer review body to the governing body (in hospitals, the MEC and in managed and ambulatory care, the credentials committee or other designated body). The governing body may return recommendations to the committees making a recommendation for additional information. It also has the option of interviewing the applicant if there is a question related to qualifications or the information submitted. In hospitals, the application or reapplication processes are basically considered incomplete up to the time that the governing body makes a decision. If the governing board has delegated the credentialing decision in a managed or ambulatory care organization, the process is considered complete at the time of the credentials committee decision.

Actual involvement and hands-on review of files by the governing body varies. In some organizations, the governing body reviews information from a consent agenda as infrequently as once or twice a year. In other organizations, the governing body may choose to become more involved, including doing actual review of individual files, with meetings as frequent as monthly. The governing body may have committees that act on its behalf; that is, the credentialing action may be delegated to an executive or to a quality committee of the board.

OTHER CONSIDERATIONS

Chair's Orientation

For chairpersons to be effective, they must clearly understand their role and the requirements related to their committee. Orientation is usually conducted to ensure that a new chair is familiar with all key aspects of this important position. Orientation can be a formal process or can be conducted on an informal basis. Orientation of a new chair should involve the previous chair and/or the vice-chair or chair-elect for the following term. It includes

1. review and overview of all written material that relates to the committee function
2. information related to minutes
3. review of minutes from the previous year
4. introduction to basic meeting management techniques, including
    - starting the meeting at the scheduled time
    - support for discussion that is informative and leading toward a decision or recommendation
    - limitation of discussion that is not supportive of the objective
    - presentation of options available for recommendation or discussion
    - summarization of actions, recommendations, decisions, and required follow-up
5. agreement on a communication plan (the communication plan includes formalizing of premeeting activities and the sharing of information between the credentialing staff and the chair)

Committee Orientation

The chair is usually accountable for orientation of new committee members. This orientation can occur on an annual basis in a formal setting or can be completed during informal meetings throughout the year. The orientation of new members should focus on

- confidentiality aspects, including signing of a confidentiality statement
- committee functions
- procedure used for making decisions
- legal aspects of committee function and membership

Table 7–1 Cost of a Meeting

Activity	*Time*	*Person*	*Pay/Hour**	*Cost*
Schedule the meeting (phone calls to identify available dates, etc.)	45 min	Scribe and committee members or their contact person	$10.00	$7.50
Reserve room, food arrangements, etc.	15 min	Scribe	$10.00	$2.50
Draft and finalize agenda	2 hours	Scribe	$10.00	$20.00
	15 min	Chair	$125.00	$31.25
Notify members	1½ hours	Scribe	$10.00	$15.00
Identify, collect, and create attachments and handouts	3 hours	Scribe	$10.00	$30.00
Make copies of packet (avg. 12 packets/20 pages each)	1 hour	Scribe	$10.00	$10.00
			$.05/plus page	$12.00
Reminder calls and notices	30 min	Scribe	$10.00	$5.00
Meeting**	2 hours	Physician	$125.00	$2000.00
		Management	$20.00	$120.00
		Scribe	$10.00	$20.00
Food				$100.00
Follow-up	3 hours	Scribe	$10.00	$30.00
	30 min	Chair	$125.00	$62.50

Cost for one committee meeting	$2,465.75
Cost for committee to meet 11 times in one year	$27,123.25
Cost for 15 committees to meet 11 times in one year	$406,848.75

*Pay estimates based upon salary and benefit average for secretary and management—direct costs to organization and loss of potential income and/or pay for physician members.

**Average attendance 12 (eight physicians, three management level, and scribe), two hours each, including travel time, meeting time, and time wasted before and after meeting.

Courtesy of C. Mobley & Associates, LLC, and Quality Management Options, LLC, Colorado Springs, Colorado.

- rules for committee membership and behavior
- overview of actions and activities during the previous year

The credentialing staff member(s) who support(s) the credentials committee function is very instrumental in scheduling and helping to facilitate orientation for new committee chairs and other members.

Cost of a Meeting

It may be beneficial to identify the cost of holding meetings if it is determined that lack of attendance prevents action or that time is being wasted through poor meeting management. Table 7–1 includes a breakdown of meeting activities and time/cost estimates related to each activity. This type of outline with time/cost estimates can be a very effective tool when evaluating committee functions and the need for change.

ADDITIONAL RESOURCES

A number of resources provide good information related to meeting management. These include the following:

- *Credential Committee Self-Assessment Manual,* 1996, published by Opus Communications, Inc., P.O. Box 1168, Marblehead, MA 01945, phone (800) 650-6787. Lists 79 questions in seven different categories for credentials committees to use as a self-evaluation. Use of this tool should enhance committee effectiveness.
- *How to Make Meetings Work,* by Michael Doyle and David Straus, 1976, published by the Berkley Publishing Group, 200 Madison Ave, New York, NY 10016. A helpful guide for committees that need ideas or are not functioning effectively.
- *The Medical Staff Leader's Practical Guide,* by Richard E. Thompson, MD, 1993, published by Opus Communications, Inc., P.O. Box 1168, Marblehead, MA 01945, phone (800) 650-6787. A good guide for hospital medical staff leadership, especially those new to their position.
- NAMSS Guidebook*: Developing a Policy and Procedure Manual for the Medical Staff Services Department,* by Christine Mobley, 1995, published by the National Association Medical Staff Services, 631 E. Butterfield Rd., Suite 311, Lombard, IL 60148, phone (630) 271-9814. Chapter 5, "Medical Staff Meeting Management." Includes good resource materials for general meeting management.
- *The Skilled Facilitator,* by Roger Schwarz, 1994, published by Jossey-Bass, Inc., 350 Sansome St., San Francisco, CA 94104. Information for facilitating meetings can be applied to committee chair activities.
- *The Team Handbook*, by Peter Scholtes et al., 1988, published by Joiner Associates Inc., 3800 Regent St., P.O. Box 5445, Madison, WI 53705, phone (800) 669-8329. A classic for committees that are accomplishing work through use of a team concept.

NOTES

1. F. Rozovky, L. Rozovsky, and L. Harpston, *Medical Staff Credentialing: A Practical Guide* (Chicago: American Hospital Publishing, 1994), 25–32.
2. *1998 Hospital Accreditation Standards* (Oakbrook Terrace, IL: Joint Commission on Accreditation of Healthcare Organizations), 228–229.
3. *1998 Hospital Accreditation Standards,* 237.
4. *Medical Staff Briefing* (Marblehead, MA: Opus Communications), Vol. 6, No. 6 (June 1996), 12.
5. *Credentials Committee Self-Assessment Manual* (Marblehead, MA: Opus Communications, 1996), 6.
6. *Developing a Policy and Procedure Manual for the Medical Staff Services Department* (Lombard, IL: National Association of Medical Staff Services, 1995), 95.
7. *Robert's Rules of Order* (New York: Bantam Books, 1982).

Chapter 8

Performance Assessment and Improvement

OVERVIEW

Quality of care is a major focus in all health care settings. The purpose of an organizational performance improvement or quality management program is to ensure the quality of patient care. Today, performance improvement programs are referred to by numerous titles including *quality management, quality improvement, quality assessment or assurance, performance improvement, total quality management, continuous quality improvement,* and *quality control*. The National Committee for Quality Assurance (NCQA) uses the terms *quality management* and *quality improvement* when referring to these programs, while the Joint Commission on Accreditation of Healthcare Organizations (Joint Commission) currently uses the terms *performance improvement* and *improving organizational performance*. In this chapter, the term *performance assessment and improvement (PA&I)* will be used when referring to any activity that is designed to determine the level of care delivery, provide feedback, or control or change practitioner behavior. PI committee will refer to the committee charged with the responsibility of reviewing data and information related to performance and for ensuring that appropriate action is taken. Improving organizational performance is a broad topic and involves numerous activities. This chapter addresses only the aspects of PA&I activities that relate to credentialing.

An effective recredentialing program is one in which performance improvement activities and credentials review are very closely affiliated. Staff responsible for PA&I and credentialing should report along the same organizational lines, should be strongly committed to the same goals and outcomes, and should have a shared understanding of both performance improvement and credentialing processes. Despite the overlap of the two functions, many organizations have not provided for strong integration of activities, especially in relation to the easy transfer of, and access to, PA&I information that is required during the recredentialing process. PA&I data and information is an essential element in the credentialing process. A positive credentialing/reappointment decision is equal to an organizational certification that reasonable care has been exercised to ensure that each practitioner has both the knowledge and the skills necessary to render appropriate patient care.

Performance improvement information, which may be collected, summarized, and submitted for review during the credentialing process, includes

- medical record review findings
- practitioner-specific information from quality improvement and performance improvement and assessment activities
- patient/member satisfaction survey results (more common in managed care)
- patient/member complaints (managed care)

- utilization management data
- peer review findings
- clinical practice competence evaluation
- clinical outcomes
- results of (accreditation-required) clinical evaluation activities

A practitioner-specific PA&I report, often referred to as a *profile*, can be developed in a database or as a hard-copy file. As it relates to competency assessment of individual physicians, the profile is presented to the credentials reviewer in support of the credentialing and privileging decision. Other independent processes such as peer review, contract evaluation, or human resource employment decisions may also be considered. A well-developed process, using a profile that captures all necessary information, has grown in importance in light of developing networks, mergers, and other integrated relationships that require collection and review of data to make valid credentialing and privileging decisions.

PA&I PROGRAM

The key components of the PA&I program and activities are

- performance assessment and measurement
- performance improvement
- peer review

The outcome of these PA&I activities that relate to credentialing is the data and information that can be retrieved in association with an individual practitioner name. This allows for development of the individual practitioner profile that is used in reappointment and recredentialing.

Most health care organizations have individuals who are responsible for PA&I activities and for compliance with related accreditation standards. In large organizations, it is not uncommon to find a PA&I department managing all activities relating to collection and evaluation of data, accreditation compliance, and implementation of quality improvement initiatives. Small organizations may designate a single individual as a manager of all performance improvement activities and requirements. Regardless of accreditation, size of department, or placement in the organization, the current trend in PA&I is a focus on organizationwide process improvement. This focus causes a problem in terms of credentialing when little or no practitioner-specific information is collected. Although the process improvement approach has resulted in positive changes and improved outcomes in many organizations, it has negatively affected credentialing activities in others. Development of a practitioner profile continues to be a key component of PA&I activities and cannot be effectively accomplished by credentialing professionals alone. The PA&I program must support and must ensure that information related to evaluation of competency is available to those responsible for credentials decisions.

PURPOSE AND ROLE OF PA&I IN CREDENTIALING

Most accrediting bodies require that PA&I data be used as part of the recredentialing process. Historically, in many organizations, once the initial appointment/credentialing process was completed, there was no formal reappointment process. A physician's privileges, appointment, employment, or contract continued as long as both parties were happy with the relationship. Unless there was a major occurrence related to quality or a serious difference related to performance, no systems automatically triggered review of the relationship. Currently, such a practice is considered unacceptable. Accreditation standards for hospital ambulatory and managed care organizations require that the credentialing decision be re-reviewed every two years. As in the initial application process, an application for reappointment or a recredential questionnaire must be completed. Information related to practitioner activities during the prior two-year period is collected and evaluated. In the hospital, physicians must provide evidence of current clinical competence for the privileges that they wish to continue or add. If they cannot demonstrate performance either within the organization or through another organization, then continued affiliation may be denied.

As in the initial application process, both objective and subjective criteria are used during the recredentialing process. Information supplied by the practitioner and obtained from external and from internal sources is reviewed against these criteria. Firsthand assessment of practitioner activity is hopefully available, since the organization has had direct experience with the practitioner. A review of actual activity related to privileges requested in the hospital or activity related to care rendered in the ambulatory care setting provides information for the reappointment or recredentialing decision.

The practitioner profile reflects activity over time and should include any identified practice issues, corrective action taken, and results of follow-up monitoring related to that corrective action. The profile may document enough information to support the credentialing process, or it may act as a mechanism to trigger a more in-depth review of PA&I files, committee minutes, or other material available within the organization. Figure 8–1 outlines the basic steps in a recredentialing process and shows how the performance improvement process relates to recredentialing.

Information collected and entered on a profile may be manual, computerized, or a combination of both. It is commonly obtained by PA&I staff from numerous departments, databases, and quality activities and is compiled into a single database or file. As information is collected, it is reviewed against preestablished criteria, and a decision or determination is made related to compliance with the criteria or thresholds. Various committees may act upon information before it is entered into individual profiles. Should a problem be identified through peer review, it may result in specific action and proctoring or follow-up. Corrective action related to information is entered in the quality file or profile as it occurs and does not take place at the time of reappointment or recredentialing. Trends and major quality concerns should be identified by the PA&I process and addressed as appropriate. Information in the profile/quality file is a summary report of activities and actions taken.

PRACTITIONER PROFILES

For purposes of a common understanding, the term *profile* or *quality file* in this chapter will refer to a written outline or *summary* of objective, practitioner-specific information and data that are developed for and used in the credentials review process. Information included in a profile is both positive and negative as applicable and addresses credentials as well as quality review information. The steps in the development of a profile are

- determining data and information to be collected
- acquiring information
- managing information
- identifying development method and format
- using comparative data
- addressing confidentiality concerns

Determining Data and Information To Be Collected

The first step in the development of a profile is identification of the data and information that will be collected and reported. Much PA&I information is collected on a departmental, organizational, or diagnosis basis and is not reported out in such a way as to identify individual practitioner activity. Therefore, it is necessary to initially identify data that (1) can be easily obtained on a practitioner-specific basis and/or (2) must be practitioner specific due to accreditation or other organization requirements. When identifying information that will be collected or reported, the following should be considered:

- accreditation requirements—both Joint Commission and NCQA have specific requirements for information that must be

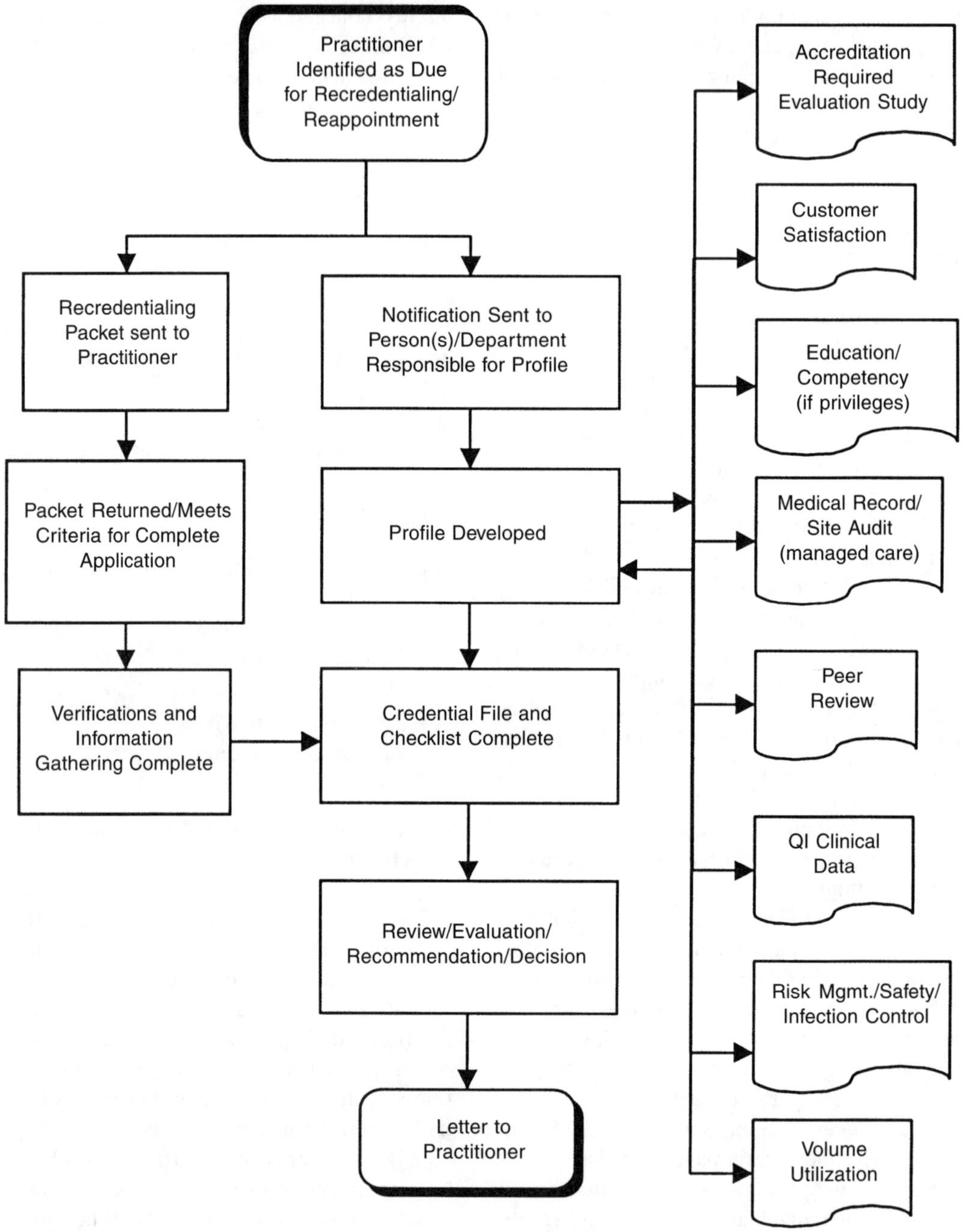

Note: QI, quality improvement.

Figure 8–1 Recredential Process with Development of Profile. Courtesy of C. Mobley & Associates, LLC, and Quality Management Options, LLC, Colorado Springs, Colorado.

collected and reported specific to individual practitioner activity (see the section "Accreditation" later in this chapter for more specific information)
- meaningfulness of the data in terms of the ability of the organization to draw conclusions, take action, and make changes that will have an impact on the outcome of patient care
- the ability and ease of acquiring information
- the ability to measure outcomes objectively
- dimensions of performance considered by the organization to be important to measure

Performance measures that may be considered include

- customer satisfaction
- education/competency
- outcomes
- process improvement activities in which individual practitioner information is identified
- risk management/safety/infection control
- volume/utilization/cost/productivity

When identifying information and data that will be collected, it is important that the focus not relate to only a few areas of performance. Determination and agreement as to the specific data that will be collected and included in the profile for the purpose of the recredentialing decision should be made by the credentialing department working with the PA&I department and should include the key practitioners that will be involved in the review process. If a profile has been developed and in use for some time, it is wise to periodically review the format, reasons why specific information and data are being collected, and the possible need to delete or add additional information.

Acquiring Data and Information

Once the information to be collected has been identified, the second step in development of a profile is the collection or acquisition of the information. These are the functions of systematically acquiring and aggregating information. It should be recognized and understood that data can and should be collected by numerous people in the organization, including staff from medical records, utilization review, those involved in peer review processes, and credentialing and PA&I staff. There are numerous methods of data collection including surveys, audits, run charts, and graphs. The method used will depend upon the size, maturity, and the complexity of the organizational PA&I process. Sometimes direction for data acquisition may come from the PA&I department with little involvement by the credentials staff and other departments. In other organizations, credentials staffs are responsible for collection and documentation of the information. Ideally, data acquisition is a joint effort by all who are in a position to identify practitioner-specific information, with either PA&I or credentials staff taking the lead to ensure an organized, timely process.

Managing Information

As information is acquired, it is stored or maintained in a computer system, a hard-copy file, or a combination of both. Since the profile is only one component of PA&I activity, profile information is often integrated into the PA&I system and is produced at the time the profile is requested by the credentials staff. A summary of the functions, activities, and accountability related to the development and use of profiles is found in Figure 8–2.

Identifying Method and Format

The format or appearance of a profile and the development method are as varied as the organizations that produce them. Development should take into consideration

- capability of the system in which the information is stored to produce reports

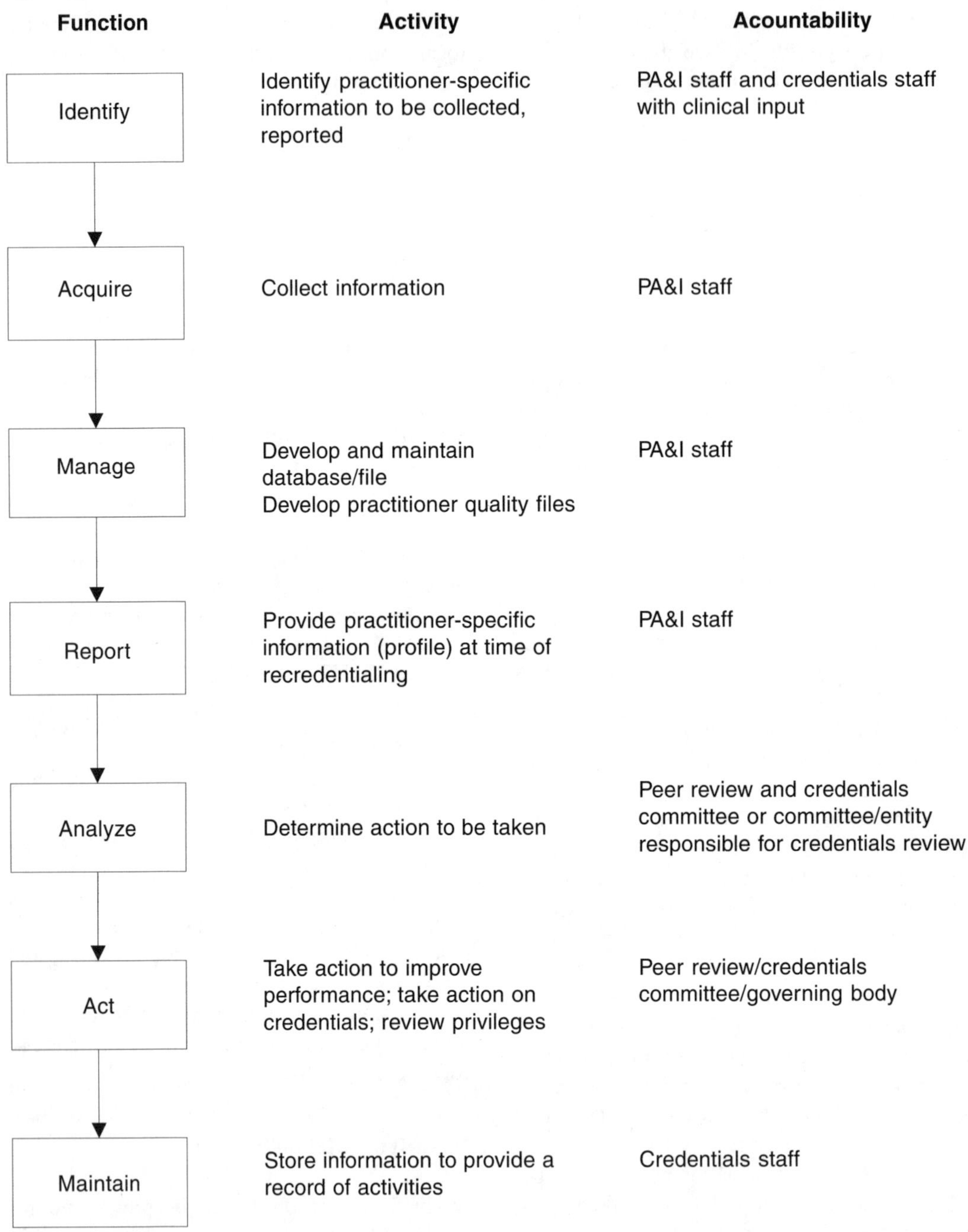

Figure 8–2 Development and Use of PA&I Practitioner Profile. Courtesy of C. Mobley & Associates, LLC, and Quality Management Options, LLC, Colorado Springs, Colorado.

- staff time and productivity to transfer hard-copy information from minutes, quality files, and other reports into a computer or onto a hard-copy profile
- length or size of completed profile
- readability
- availability of information/ data that is practitioner specific
- ability of receiver to draw objective conclusions from the information presented

If most of the information and data to be entered on a profile is stored in a computer system, the system capability to produce reports will be a key factor in the development of reports. There are PA&I and credentialing software programs available that produce a standard profile or one that can be customized by the organization. Some organizations use word-processing and database software rather than systems developed specifically for maintaining quality data. In this situation, practitioner-specific information and data are usually collected and stored in a hard-copy quality file. A profile is developed at time of recredentialing, using the information available in the file, or the quality file is forwarded for review along with the credentials file. All computer-based programs require data entry. Some sophisticated networks now have computer programs that draw utilization data from claims or encounter data to prepopulate a profile. This type of system still requires data entry of PA&I information that is practitioner specific.

Development of a profile is a time-consuming process no matter which development method is used. "Need to know" should dictate content rather than desire for "nice-to-know" information. The length of the profile, its readability, and the quality of its information will determine the reviewers' willingness to carefully evaluate the information.

A profile commonly includes basic demographics such as

- practitioner's name
- identifying number
- specialty
- date of appointment/affiliation; date of last review
- dates covered by profile
- number of admissions (hospital) or other identified activity
- member count (managed care)

Exhibit 8–1 is an example of a profile that is completed by staff at the time of recredentialing. It includes common required elements. Information available in a quality file provided by PA&I staff is used, and demographics are obtained from reports requested from the information systems department. Minutes are retrieved for results of required functions (blood usage, pharmacy and therapeutic, medical records). This format uses the approach of "no news is good news." In other words, if there are no reports of findings specific to a practitioner, he or she is considered to be competent and have no quality problems for that function.

Completion of a profile such as the one in Exhibit 8–1 is time consuming for staff involved, and as there is no comparative information, it is difficult for a reviewer to draw conclusions about the scope of any identified problems. Objective information about the competency of a practitioner is minimal.

Using Comparative Data

A complicated matrix with large amounts of comparative data usually results in more questions than thoughtful conclusions. However, to draw conclusions, individuals responsible for recredential or reappointment review should be provided some comparative data. This may be in the form of volume of activity (maximum or minimum acceptable), volume numbers, thresholds, benchmark (best practice) information, comparable data from other organizations, peer activity, or previous activity of the practitioner for the same element or component. For example, hospital medical record completion data would include both the number of times suspended and a comparison group number for the same period.

Exhibit 8–1 Reappointment Physician Performance Profile

Evaluation Period: ______________________

Name: ______________________ Specialty: ______________________

Physician #: ______________________ DOB: ______________________

Department: ______________________ Current Staff Category: ______________________

Requesting change in status to: ______________________

LICENSURE/CERTIFICATION

State license verified:	Expiration Date: ________	☐ Yes	☐ No
Restrictions to license		☐ Yes	☐ No
DEA certificate current	Expiration Date: ________	☐ Yes	☐ No
Restrictions to DEA		☐ Yes	☐ No
Board certification in ______________________; verified		☐ Yes	☐ No
Change since last review		☐ Yes	☐ No

VOLUME/ACTIVITY/UTILIZATION

	Year ______	Year ______
Number of inpatient admissions	______	______
Number of outpatient encounters	______	______
Number of referrals/consultations	______	______
Number of surgeries/invasive procedures		
Inpatient	______	______
Outpatient	______	______
Number of inpatient admission denials	______	______

MEMBERSHIP/EDUCATION

	Year ______	Year ______
Number of hours of continuing medical education	______	______
Meeting attendance (% attended)	______	______
General medical staff	______	______
Department	______	______
Committee (optional)	______	______

MEDICAL RECORD COMPLETION/REVIEW

	Year ______	Year ______
Completion of medical records:		
Number of suspensions	______	______
Number of cases reviewed for clinical pertinence	______	______

continues

Exhibit 8–1 continued

RISK MANAGEMENT

Malpractice cases filed since last review	☐ Yes	☐ No
NPDB expiration date: ____ NPDB reports/actions since last review	☐ Yes	☐ No
Clear of Medicare/Medicaid sanctions	☐ Yes	☐ No
Malpractice insurance with appropriate coverage amounts	☐ Yes	☐ No

BLOOD AND BLOOD PRODUCTS UTILIZATION

	Year ______	**Year** ______
Completed transfusion ratio	______	______
Number of adverse reactions	______	______
Number of peer review cases	______	______
Appropriateness of review	______	______

MEDICATION USAGE

	Year ______	**Year** ______
Number of adverse drug reactions	______	______
Number of peer review cases	______	______
Appropriateness of review	______	______

OPERATIVE AND OTHER INVASIVE PROCEDURES

	Year ______	**Year** ______
Number of normal tissue identified	______	______
Number of peer review cases	______	______
Appropriateness of review	______	______

ADDITIONAL INFORMATION TO BE CONSIDERED

Note: DEA, Drug Enforcement Administration; NPDB, National Practitioner Data Bank.

Courtesy of Columbia Miami Heart Institute, Miami, Florida.

The comparison group might be an average of all practitioners in the same department. In managed care, the element of member grievances might be reported in the form of number of grievances per 1,000 members. Exhibit 8–2 demonstrates use of comparative data in a hospital profile, and Exhibit 8–3 demonstrates use in a managed care profile.

Obviously, use of comparative data involves collection of very specific data. This approach is seldom seen in manual systems, where no large amounts of comparative data are available. In managed care, NCQA expects that significant amounts of data will be collected and tracked as part of the quality management program. In this case, comparative information should be readily available.

Addressing Confidentiality Concerns

Crucial to PA&I activities is maintaining strict confidentiality of information. This extends to the information included in an individual practitioner quality file and/or a practitioner profile that is shared with medical staff and others involved in credentials review. A policy outlining all aspects of information development, storage, and access should be developed to address confidentiality and applicable peer review provisions

Exhibit 8–2 Cross Section of Physician Performance Profile (Hospital) Using Comparative Data

Required Component	Threshold (Desired Outcome)	Findings	Peer Review*
Medication Usage			
Adverse drug reactions as % of annual admissions	<6%	14.6%	D
Blood Usage			
Number of units cross-matched		20	
Number of units transferred		10	
Completed transfusion ratio	<2.0	2.0	A
Medical Records			
Total number of admissions		116.0	
Total number of delinquent record notices as % of admission	<10%	4%	
Continuing Medical Education			
Number of hours completed	>25 hours	40	

*A = findings acceptable; no follow-up; B = findings outside of standard; letter to physician; C = findings caused concern; physician requested to formulate an action plan; D = findings unacceptable; corrective action plan initiated by peer review in conjunction with department.

Courtesy of C. Mobley & Associates, LLC, and Quality Management Options, LLC, Colorado Springs, Colorado.

Exhibit 8–3 Cross Section of Physician Performance Profile (Managed Care) Using Comparative Data

PATIENT SATISFACTION WITH MEDICAL CARE

Mail-in Survey Results		
	1998	1999
Number returned		
Overall score (1–5 poss.)		
Mean (for PCPs in same dept.)	4.10	
Goal	4.5	4.6

Complaints and Grievances		
	1998	1999
Number of complaints per 1,000 members		
Number of grievances per 1,000 members		
Goal	<2:1000	<1.5:1000

Mammography		
	1998	1999
Eligible members		
% compliance		
Department average	71%	
Goal	>80%	>82%

Childhood Immunization		
	1998	1999
Eligible members		
% compliance		
Department average	92%	
Goal	>90%	>92%

Medical Recordkeeping			
Goal	*Previous Score*	*Review Date*	*Score*
90%	88%		

Site Review			
Goal	*Previous Score*	*Review Date*	*Score*
85%	92%		

Note: PCP, primary care practitioner.

Courtesy of C. Mobley & Associates, LLC, and Quality Management Options, LLC, Colorado Springs, Colorado.

(which might be governed by state statutes). All related forms and information should be marked or stamped as confidential. If protected by peer review statutes, the profile and any other information forwarded by PA&I should include a statement to that effect with reference to the specific statute. Confidentiality should be addressed as part of the orientation of credentials committee members, department chairs (in hospitals), and others involved in these reviews.

DEVELOPMENT OF A PROFILE, START TO FINISH

An organization that wishes to develop profiles or one that requires revision of its current profile would follow these five steps:

1. Identify data.
   - Identify regulatory and accreditation requirements for performance evaluation elements.
   - Identify data and information considered by the organization to be essential for performance evaluation.
   - Identify the source and availability of data and information listed.
   - Identify accountability and method for obtaining information for each element on a practitioner-specific basis.
2. Identify comparative data.
   - For each element or component determine availability of comparative volume data.
   - Identify a threshold or benchmark for each element in terms of acceptable practice or goal/best practice. Use of thresholds usually results in peer review referrals if the threshold is exceeded.
3. Develop profile format.
   - If the profile will be completed manually, any format that is readable and allows ease of review can be used.
   - If profile will be produced (all or in part) from a computer database, the software program will dictate the format.
4. Identify communication links.
   - Identify method and turnaround time standards for notification by credentials staff that profile needs to be updated or produced.
   - Identify method and turnaround time standards for performance improvement, peer review, and other information to be reported to PA&I staff.
   - Identify method to enter data or compile hard copy to support development of a profile.
5. Initiate process.

Performance Evaluation

At the time of reappointment, the major question answered in the credentialing process is whether the applicant for recredentialing meets all of the standards and criteria that are required by the organization to continue the relationship. It is important to maintain fairness for all applicants and, in light of current legal activity, to ensure a performance evaluation process that provides objective information for recredentialing.

The first step in performance evaluation is the compilation of information included in the practitioner profile. The collection and use of outcome data in the health care field has taken many forms and has been applied to practitioners in numerous ways, including evaluation of utilization and attempts to influence practitioner behavior. Development of a useful profile requires that objective criteria be used to the greatest extent possible and that the information be gathered and made available in a format that is practitioner specific. A vast amount of information is available in health care settings that can be included in practitioner profiles and used for performance evaluation. Information may address not only clinical competence but also the practitioner's willingness and ability to work with others and to fulfill the requirements of the relationship. Table 8–1 outlines the various categories and examples of information that may be collected and used in development of a practitioner profile.

Access/Availability

Access and availability information has historically been connected with the managed care environment. NCQA requires collection of data related to access to services or patients' ability to obtain care. The information is usually obtained during the physician site visit audits and may address phone service, parking, language accommodations, and geographic convenience. Availability relates to office hours and ability to obtain an appointment. Appointment availability surveys (usually phone surveys) are often used by managed care organizations to determine availability of appointments in various categories such as emergency, nonemergency, routine, and preventive categories. Whether a

Table 8–1 Information To Consider for Use in Development of Practitioner Profiles

	Hospital	*Managed Care*
Access/Availability		Access to services Access compliance; site visit audit Appointment availability
Citizenship	Compliance with bylaws, policies, rules and regulations Reports of disruptive behavior Meeting attendance (if required)	Compliance with contract provisions Reports of disruptive behavior
Clinical Competence	Evaluation by peers/department chair	Peer evaluation
Medical Record	Timely completion of records	Compliance with medical record audit criteria
Peer Review	Identified concerns/actions Number of cases reviewed with findings	Identified concerns/actions Number of cases reviewed and findings
Performance Improvement	Functions: Efficiency of clinical practice Medical assessment patterns and treatment Use of blood and blood components Use of medications Use of operative and other procedures Autopsy results	HEDIS criteria compliance in the categories of Effectiveness of care Satisfaction with the experience of care Health plan stability Use of services Cost of care Informed health care choices Descriptive information
Risk Management	Trending of incident reports Litigation information Verification of liability coverage Data bank report	Litigation information Verification of liability coverage Data bank report
Satisfaction	Patient satisfaction	Member satisfaction PCP changes Member complaints
Utilization	Inpatient denials Outpatient denials	UR committee: Overutilization Underutilization

continues

Table 8–1 continued

	Hospital	*Managed Care*
Volume	Ambulatory cases Inpatient admissions Discharges/DRG Consultations Surgical cases/procedures Length of stay	Enrollment Disenrollment Hospital admissions Bed days Specialist referrals
Other	CME Board certification	CME Board certification

Note: HEDIS, Health Plan Employer Data and Information Set; DRG, diagnosis-related group; CME, continuing medical education; UR, utilization review; PCP, primary care practitioner

Courtesy of C. Mobley & Associates, LLC, and Quality Management Options, LLC, Colorado Springs, Colorado.

physician's practice is "open" (i.e., whether he or she is accepting new patients) may also be an indicator of availability.

Citizenship

Citizenship refers to compliance with bylaws, rules, and regulations. Determining compliance with citizenship categories may be more subjective than for other categories. Hospitals traditionally have included required meeting attendance as a citizenship component of their bylaws. If an organization has this requirement, the profile should include a statement of compliance with the specific requirements. Compliance with other aspects of bylaws, rules and regulations, and policies may also be included. Common examples are committee assignments, participation in general education offerings, and ethics and conduct. Information related to interpersonal relationships can cause great difficulty if not presented appropriately. The purpose behind criteria related to interpersonal relationships is to ensure that the practitioner can work within his or her department or assigned situation and be considered a desirable asset to that team. Additional questions may relate to interpersonal relations with support staff, courtesy, respect, response, and the absence of any disruptive behavior. Before any negative information is reported on the practitioner profile, the organization's policy for dealing with disruptive behavior should have been followed.

Clinical Competence

Clinical competence is another category that is more subjective than objective. Information related to clinical competence is usually obtained from peers and, in the hospital setting, from a department chair. Traditionally, a format of questions and answers is developed and forwarded to the department chair or peers working most closely with the practitioner and to other organizations or institutions where the practitioner practices. Appropriateness and timeliness of professional judgment, demonstration of an acceptable level of technical skill, demonstration of an acceptable level of patient management, and acceptable outcomes are commonly addressed. Exhibit 8–4 is a sample competence questionnaire sent to another organization. Exhibit 8–5 is a sample review and recommendation summary to be completed by a department chair/section chief. It may be used if the practitioner has a low level of activity during the reappointment period.

Exhibit 8–4 Peer Evaluation of Competence

Date: ______________________

Name: ______________________

Address: ______________________

Re: ______________________
Physician Name

Dear Dr. ______________________,

The above-named physician has applied/is reapplying for appointment and privileges at *Accredited Health Care Facility.* Enclosed is a copy of the applicant's Delineation of Privileges Checklist and a Release from Liability statement. Please provide us with the following information.

1. Dates of Dr. ______________'s affiliation with your hospital.
2. Department assignment ______________________
3. Current medical staff category ______________________
4. Have the applicant's appointment or clinical privileges at your hospital ever been reduced, suspended, or changed in any way? ☐ **Yes** ☐ **No**
5. Have any disciplinary actions ever been taken? ☐ **Yes** ☐ **No**
6. Considering the requested privileges, please rate the following:

	Excellent/ Superior	**Average**	**Poor**
Basic medical knowledge	☐	☐	☐
Clinical competence	☐	☐	☐
Technique/skill	☐	☐	☐
Professional judgment	☐	☐	☐
Quality of documentation	☐	☐	☐
Patient and staff interaction	☐	☐	☐

Activity level (patient contacts, both inpatient and outpatient) during the past two (2) years. Please check one. ☐ **0–25** ☐ **26–50** ☐ **51–100** ☐ **100+**

______________________ ______________________ ______________________
Signature Title Date

Courtesy of C. Mobley & Associates, LLC, and Quality Management Options, LLC, Colorado Springs, Colorado.

Exhibit 8–5 Department Chairperson Review and Recommendation Summary

PHYSICIAN NAME: ________________________ REVIEW PERIOD: ________ to ___________

Consider this physician's performance since his/her last reappointment, and indicate response in the appropriate column. Provide an explanation for any "no" answer.

	YES	NO
1. Has this practitioner exercised the privileges granted at the time of last appointment/reappointment to the extent that you are able to assess current competence, skill, and judgment based upon demonstrated proficiency?	☐	☐
If no, does the file contain sufficient evidence of activity at another local facility to support the requested privileges?	☐	☐
2. On the basis of your observation and other information presented, does the practitioner's professional judgment, clinical competence, experience, qualifications, and professional performance appear to be consistent with the requested privileges?	☐	☐
3. To the best of your knowledge is this practitioner free of any physical or mental disability including possible dependence on drugs or alcohol, which would prevent him or her from carrying out responsibilities to patients?	☐	☐
4. Have you observed or are you aware of any evidence of general uncooperativeness and/or inability to communicate with patients, peers, or staff?	☐	☐
5. To the best of your knowledge, has this practitioner been compliant with the bylaws, rules and regulations, and applicable policies of the medical staff?	☐	☐
6. Are you aware of any evidence of breach of ethics or other related matters?	☐	☐
7. As a result of your review, are there any peer review, quality, or other findings, trends, or patterns of care that should affect reappointment?	☐	☐

On the basis of my review of the quality profile, requested clinical privileges, and other information included in the credentials file:

☐ I recommend renewal of privileges as requested
☐ I recommend modification or addition of privileges as requested
☐ I do not recommend the requested changes in privileges due to ____________________________
☐ I do not recommend reappointment due to ____

Section Chief ____ Date _____________

continues

Exhibit 8–5 continued

On the basis of my review of the quality profile, requested clinical privileges, and other information included in the credentials files:

- ☐ I recommend renewal of privileges as requested
- ☐ I recommend modification or addition of privileges as requested
- ☐ I do not recommend the requested changes in privileges due to ______________________
- ☐ I do not recommend reappointment due to ______________________________

Department Chair ____ Date ____________

Courtesy of C. Mobley & Associates, LLC, and Quality Management Options, LLC, Colorado Springs, Colorado.

In managed care settings, clinical competence is usually rated by the number of formal peer review actions rather than by questionnaires on clinical competence that are completed by peers.

Medical Records

In hospitals, accurate, timely, and legible completion of medical records is required by Joint Commission standards. The following information may be included in a profile:

- number of times suspended
- diagnosis incomplete at time of discharge
- history and physicals incomplete at time of discharge
- surgical dictation incomplete at time of discharge
- discharge summaries not dictated within a specified number of days from discharge

In managed care, those organizations that are accredited by NCQA have completed required medical record audits for primary care physicians. The medical record criteria are identified by the organization before the site visit, along with threshold of compliance. Results of the audit are reported as part of the profile. Refer to the section "Facility site visit and medical record audits" in Chapter 4 of this book for more details on this topic.

Peer Review

Peer review results are often reported on the profile. Most organizations use a grading system for rating the severity of peer review findings. The scoring system may be two tiered, with one tier addressing standard of care and one addressing outcome. A rating for standard of care might be: A = acceptable, B = questionable, and C = unacceptable. A rating for severity of outcome might be: 0 = no adverse outcome, 1 = potential for adverse outcome, and 2 = adverse outcome. Table 8–2 shows a five-level peer review grading system.

When peer review action occurs, it is reported (along with the clinical competence rating, if applicable) on the profile. Table 8–3 shows a cross section from a profile noting peer review actions. The profile may reflect only the occurrence of a peer review action rather than any information related to severity or outcome. If this method is used, the minutes and/or quality file that contains details related to peer review is presented or forwarded by PA&I to the reviewer.

Performance Improvement

NCQA-accredited managed care organizations collect information specific to Health Plan Employer Data and Information Set (HEDIS) criteria (see the section "Accreditation Require-

Table 8–2 Five-Level Peer Review Grading System for Rating the Severity of a Quality Problem

Performance Grade	*Finding*
0	No quality problem identified/meets standard of care
1	• No adverse patient outcome or no actual detrimental effect • Often done by practitioners in field but not in total compliance with indicator • Possible documentation or system failure
2	• Potential for adverse patient outcome, but no or minimal actual detrimental effect occurred, and/or • Practice differs from usual approach but special mitigating circumstances present
3	• Adverse patient outcome and/or detrimental effect that requires additional medical or surgical treatment/moderate adverse effect, and/or • A significantly unusual approach
4	• Adverse patient outcome that requires significant medical or surgical attention or treatment/significant adverse effect, and/or • A frankly unusual approach that is never or rarely used by other practitioners in the field
5	• Adverse patient outcome resulting in death, permanent loss or disability, or an imminent danger to body or mind, and/or • Inappropriate and contraindicated approach

Courtesy of C. Mobley & Associates, LLC, and Quality Management Options, LLC, Colorado Springs, Colorado.

Table 8–3 Cross Section from Practitioner Profile Reporting Peer Review Activity

Peer Review		*Total # Cases Reviewed This Time Period*						
		*Number of Cases at Each Performance Grade**						
Element	*Number Referred for Peer Review*	*0*	*1*	*2*	*3*	*4*	*5*	*Action/Follow-up*
Adverse drug reaction	2	1		1				Letter
Sentinel event	3	1			1	1		Corrective action plan
Adverse event during anesthesia	1		1					Letter

*For performance grade definitions, see Table 8–2.

Courtesy of C. Mobley & Associates, LLC, and Quality Management Options, LLC, Colorado Springs, Colorado.

ments," subsection "NCQA," later in this chapter). HEDIS information, if collected and entered into a data system allowing for the identification of individual practitioners, should be included in the practitioner profile. Information from quality studies or initiatives to improve performance of a system or process, or to address other identified problems, may also be included if practitioner-specific information is available.

Joint Commission hospital accreditation standards specify review of the use of

- blood and blood components
- medications
- operative and other procedures that place patients at risk

The standards require medical staff to provide leadership for process measurement, assessment, and improvement for these activities. The hospital is to collect data and use a systematic approach to assess the data. The standards also specifically require intensive assessment of

- confirmed transfusion reactions
- significant adverse drug reactions
- significant medication errors
- major discrepancies, or patterns of discrepancies, between preoperative and postoperative diagnosis
- adverse events or patterns of adverse events with anesthesia use
- pathologic review of specimens removed during surgical or invasive procedures that involve a discrepancy with a preoperative diagnosis
- sentinel events (unexpected occurrences or variations involving death, serious injury, or risk of death or serious injury)[1]

In past years, these activities were most frequently addressed in medical staff department meetings or in committees specifically formed to review use of blood, medications, and medical procedures. When the Joint Commission's performance improvement model changed, the requirements continued, but the method for complying with them changed. Any organization that is not collecting data related to *all* of the above should immediately evaluate its current performance improvement process and make changes to ensure compliance. All of the listed performance improvement activities lend themselves to data collection with specific practitioner identification. Both overall volume (comparative data) and activity per practitioner should then be reported on profiles.

Risk Management

Any litigation that is new within the previous two-year period, as well as verification of liability coverage and information contained in the data bank report, may be considered a risk management issue and is commonly included in both hospital and managed care profiles. If the information gathered was fully reviewed and acted upon at the last credentialing or recredentialing decision, it is not necessary to include it in the current profile unless a trend has been identified.

A sentinel event is defined by the Joint Commission as "an unexpected occurrence involving death or serious physical or psychological injury, or the risk thereof. Serious injury specifically includes loss of limb or function." The event is called "sentinel" because it sends a signal or sounds a warning that requires immediate attention.[2] Most sentinel events result in completion of an incident or occurrence report. The risk manager should be educated regarding the need to refer practitioner-specific information for peer review and for inclusion in the profile.

Satisfaction

Patient satisfaction with practitioner services may be collected, compiled, and submitted to the performance/quality improvement department and included in the profile. Customer service/satisfaction surveys are commonly distributed in hospitals. Recognizing the need for improved relationships, some specify physician interaction.

If obtained, this information is applicable for inclusion in a profile. In managed care, primary care practitioner (PCP) changes, member complaints, appeals, and grievances, in addition to results of the member satisfaction surveys, may be included in this category. Disenrollment surveys, if they include questions related to satisfaction with practitioner services, may also be included.

Utilization

Historically, utilization data are closely linked with the concept of economic credentialing, which tends to be viewed negatively. Nonetheless, they are still frequently used and can be very helpful when used comparatively. In the hospital, both inpatient and outpatient denials may be reported. Utilization review committees in managed care organizations that review specific cases may report decisions related to over- and underutilization of services, including pharmacy, laboratory, hospitalization and other ambulatory care services. In most cases, utilization data in managed care are reported per member/per month.

Volume

Traditionally, volume statistics are reported in great numbers because of the ease of collecting the information. In hospitals, the number of inpatient and outpatient cases, discharges, consultations, surgical cases and procedures, breakdowns by diagnosis-related group (DRG) and length of stay are routinely collected and reported. In managed care, volume statistics related to membership, disenrollment, hospital admissions, bed days, and number of referrals are commonly collected. Use of the information should be clearly identified, and information presented in the profile should be either related to thresholds or used for comparative purposes.

Other

Additional information that may be collected and reported on a profile includes involvement in continuing medical education (CME) and board certification. Both may relate to competence for specific privileges requested in the inpatient and outpatient settings. CME is often dictated by the state licensing requirements but should also relate to specialty or to specific privileges.

Summary

The profile, once completed, should present a picture that allows the credentials or review committee body to compare activity against preestablished thresholds, criteria, and/or benchmarks and to draw a conclusion as to the practitioner's judgment, clinical decisions, citizenship, and overall competence. Issues that influence the development of a practitioner profile include the following:

1. Practicing physicians should be involved in all aspects of implementation and evaluation of the data and information to be collected and presented and of the criteria, guidelines, and thresholds by which it will be measured.
2. It is vital that the system and all information be fully protected and that confidentiality be maintained.
3. Information should be nonjudgmental, and reviewers should be able to make comparative decisions derived from population-based analysis, adjusted measures, and other clinical performance information obtained through community standard and/or benchmarks.
4. The data and information collected and the decisions made should provide educational feedback as to any adverse actions as well as to positive recredentialing decisions.
5. Profiles should never be released to the public on a physician-specific basis.

ORGANIZATIONAL ISSUES OF PA&I

The organization identifies and defines roles and responsibility for PA&I as they relate to credentialing. These include

- roles, activities, and responsibilities of the governing board members
- authority, accountability, and roles of medical/peer review (department chair, committee chair, and/or medical director)
- authority, accountability, and roles of PA&I staff/manager
- the role and responsibilities of the credentials committee or body responsible for credentials review
- establishment of support mechanisms and lines of communication related to PA&I information

Governing Body

The governing body of an organization is responsible for numerous aspects of PA&I activities. It

- ensures quality patient care by requiring and supporting the organizationwide PA&I program
- ensures the development of a written plan for the PA&I program that describes the program organization, scope, objectives, evaluation process, and activities
- identifies operational linkages between functions related to clinical aspects of patient care
- provides resources and support systems for functions

Medical/Peer Review

The role of medical leadership is key to the effective function of the PA&I program. Leaders should be accountable for ensuring that the PA&I program is implemented and properly functioning. They usually assume accountability for troubleshooting, answering questions, and supporting a smooth-running process and ensuring open communication between required functions and departments. Leadership responsibilities for PA&I include

- assurance of the quality and appropriateness of patient care provided within the organization or under the scope and responsibilities of the organization
- recommendation of clinical privileges (hospitals and other settings as appropriate)
- accountability for the professional and administrative activities
- surveillance of performance of individuals who are members of or affiliated by contract with the organization
- assurance that the individual practitioner profiles are developed and that information is reported along appropriate channels

PA&I Department or Designated Individual

The PA&I department or designated individual is responsible for

- identification of required data and functions
- collection of data
- identification of practitioner-specific trends
- development of practitioner-specific profiles

Credentials Committee or Other Designated Review Body

The credentials committee is responsible for

- analysis of information (provided or referenced in the profile) to ascertain if issues have been identified that would, could, or should affect the credentials decision
- management of the lines of communication and flow of information
- review, approval, and/or recommendation related to criteria and review methods
- evaluation of effectiveness of activities on an annual basis

Support Functions

The organizational support of the PA&I program includes provision of appropriately trained individuals and resources allocated to perform activities. Numerous organizational programs and departments may be assigned various responsibilities related to the PA&I process. These include

- utilization review or utilization management department or function
- medical staff/credentials staff office
- medical records/health information department
- provider relations and/or recruitment department

Each department or function must clearly understand its role, responsibilities, and accountabilities relating to obtaining, storing, and disseminating information and must be willing to interface in a timely manner. Organizations vary widely in structure and reporting requirements. Figure 8–3 outlines the common structuring of the major functions and activities related to PA&I activities and credentialing.

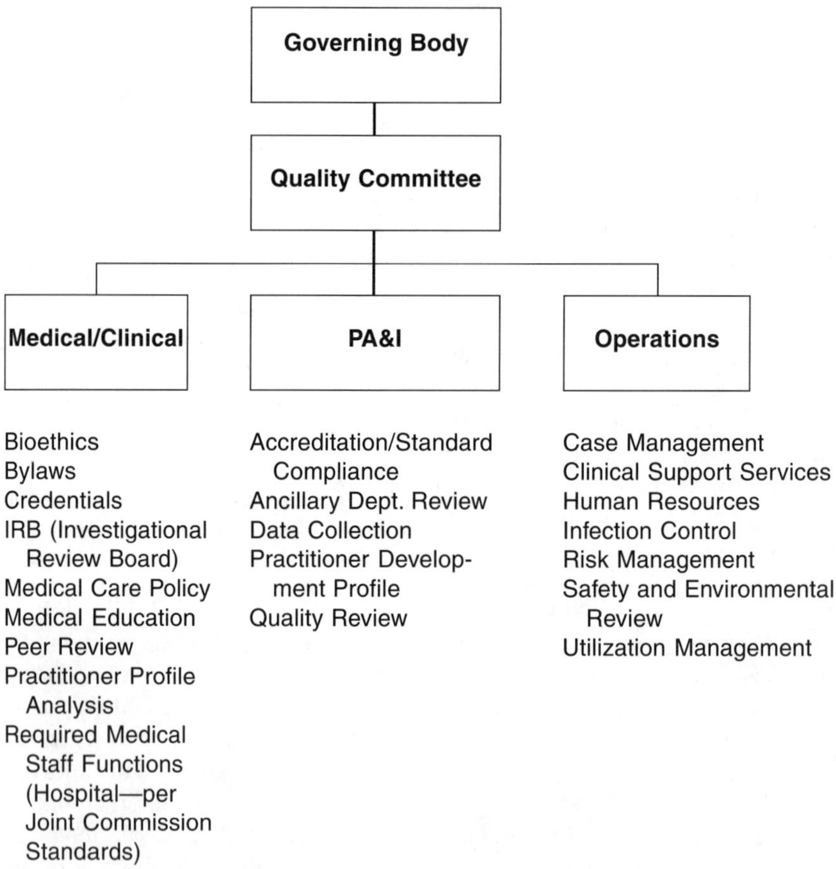

Figure 8–3 Organizational Structure and Reporting Mechanism. Courtesy of C. Mobley & Associates, LLC, and Quality Management Options, LLC, Colorado Springs, Colorado.

ACCREDITATION REQUIREMENTS

Both the Joint Commission and NCQA require reappointment or recredentialing to occur every two years and have specific standards addressing a tie-in to performance information. Joint Commission standards require the process to include criteria directly related to quality of care. Additionally, specific performance improvement functions require medical staff participation, including use of medications, blood and blood components, and operative and other invasive procedures. This information is often used as a component in demonstration of current competence. NCQA addresses performance monitoring to reappraise professional performance, judgment, and clinical competence and specifies that this monitoring must include at least three of six sources; member complaints, information from quality improvement activities, utilization management, member satisfaction, medical record reviews, and site visits.

Table 8–4 identifies accreditation requirements as they relate to PA&I and credentialing activities.

Joint Commission

The Joint Commission has a quality improvement framework that stresses the link between an organization's performance of important functions and care outcomes, costs involved in achieving these outcomes, and judgments related to the quality and value of services.[3] The Joint Commission also defines specific dimensions, functions, and processes. It has identified dimensions of performance that affect the quality of outcomes and resource use. A *function* is defined as a group of processes with a common goal, and a *process* is defined as a series of linked goal-directed activities.[4] The current focus of the performance improvement activities required by the Joint Commission is on processes rather than individual performance. This approach is compatible with continuous quality improvement and total quality management strategies, which were developed by Juran and Deming and are currently used in health care settings. It must be noted that the process/outcome emphasis does not negate the organization's responsibility for review of *individual* professional competence, judgment, and skills. The next evolution in Joint Commission accreditation involves integration of performance measurement into the accreditation process.[5] This initiative has been given the designation of *ORYX*.[6] Implementation of the new data-driven accreditation process that focuses on outcomes will be incremental. Accredited hospitals and long-term care organizations must have enrolled in a performance system and identified at least two clinical measures that address at least 20 percent of the organization's patient population in the first phase. Data will be collected related to the chosen measurements, clinical measures, during 1998 and will be submitted by March 31, 1999, to the Joint Commission through the facility-specific performance measurement system (which is ORYX approved).[7] During 1999 and 2000, the Joint Commission will expand the scope of measurement, and it anticipates that accredited hospitals and long-term care organizations will have a total of four clinical measurements that address at least 40 percent of the organization's patient population.[8]

The performance measures will

- address at least one of the following performance categories: clinical, health status, satisfaction, administration/financial
- not address individual practitioner performance exclusively
- be related to at least one of the Joint Commission's accreditation programs: ambulatory health care, behavioral health care, home care, hospital, pathology and clinical laboratory services, long-term care, or health care network

In light of the Joint Commission's new initiatives and current framework that relate to processes and outcomes rather than specifically focusing on individual practitioner activities, the task of identifying current competence has be-

Table 8–4 PA&I Credentialing Accreditation Requirements

	Joint Commission—Hospitals	*NCQA—Managed Care*	*AAHCC/URAC*	*AAAHC*
	Source: *1998 Hospital Accreditation Standards*	Source: *1998 NCQA Surveyor Guidelines for Accreditation of Managed Care Organizations*	Source: *National Health Care Practitioner Credentialing Standards, Version 1.0*	Source: *Accreditation Handbook for Ambulatory Health Care, 1998–99* edition
Terminology	Performance improvement evaluation	Quality management and improvement	Quality management	Quality management and improvement and quality of care provided
Activities	The executive committee makes recommendations to the governing body pertaining to the participation of the medical staff in organizational performance improvement activities.	The program provides the framework within which the managed care organization assesses and improves the quality of clinical care and the quality of service.	Outcome and performance measurements used in credentialing/recredentialing of health care practitioners are included in the written credentialing plan as applicable.	Appointment/reappointment and clinical privileges are based upon professional peer evaluation.
Who is responsible	When medical staff clinical departments exist, the director of each department is responsible for • clinically related activities • continuing surveillance of the professional performance of all individuals in department who have delineated clinical privileges	The credentialing committee or other review body designated by the governing body is responsible for evaluation of information as it relates to recredentialing.	Not defined in standards	The governing board may be involved directly or may delegate to a peer-based quality management and improvement program.

	• recommending clinical privileges for each department member • continued assessment; improvement of quality of care and services Each department makes recommendations regarding professional criteria for privileges that pertain to current competence and the ability to perform the requested privileges. (If departments do not exist, the responsibility is the executive committee's.)	The quality improvement function is responsible for collection and sharing information related to • credentialing • member complaints • utilization management • medical records review		
Who is reviewed	Current competence is evaluated for all medical staff members and all others with delineated clinical privileges who are subject to department bylaws, rules, regulations, etc., at time of reappointment.	The scope of practitioners is defined by the managed care organization. It must include but is not limited to • MDs • DOs • DDSs • DPMs • DCs	As defined in the organization's written credentialing plan	Each member of the health care organization, including allied health practitioners

continues

Table 8–4 continued

	Joint Commission—Hospitals	*NCQA—Managed Care*	*AAHCC/URAC*	*AAAHC*
		• Other licensed independent practitioners with whom it contracts or whom it employs and who treat members outside the inpatient setting		
When/how often the activity occurs	Every two years as part of recredentialing Continuous assessment and improvement of quality of care and services	Every two years as part of recredentialing Ongoing development of practitioner's profile	As defined in the organization's written credentialing plan	Every two years as part of reappointment Peer evaluation of current competence
How reviewed	Department chair evaluation Individual case review (peer review) Profiles Outcome studies Other performance improvement activities	Profiles Quality improvement activities Peer review	Not defined in standards	Not defined in standards
What is reviewed	Demonstration of current competence is based upon • results of performance improvement activities • peer recommendation • department or clinical service recommendation	Performance monitoring information that is collected to reappraise professional performance, judgment, and clinical competence must include at least three of the following six sources:	Not defined in standards	The standards specify specific quality improvement activities but do not require that results be incorporated into the reappointment review.

Performance improvement functions requiring medical staff participation include

- medical assessment and treatment of patients
- use of medications
- use of blood and blood components
- use of operative and other procedures
- efficiency of clinical practice patterns
- significant departures from established patterns of practice
- education of patients and families
- coordination of care
- accurate, legible, timely completion of medical records

Appraisal for reappointment is based on ongoing monitoring of information concerning

- professional performance
- judgment
- clinical or technical skills

- member complaints
- information from quality improvement activities
- utilization management
- member satisfaction
- medical record reviews
- site visits

Courtesy of C. Mobley & Associates, LLC, and Quality Management Options, LLC, Colorado Springs, Colorado.

come more difficult for the PA&I and credentialing staff. The Joint Commission standards for reappointment specifically require information related to current competence that is based on ongoing monitoring of information concerning

- professional performance
- judgment
- clinical or technical skills

Additionally, there is a requirement for peer recommendation. Some hospitals have adapted a "no news is good news" approach and state that if nothing was reported out of a required function, the physician has no problems with activity. This is not always considered an acceptable approach by surveyors and does not result in a clear picture of competence.

NCQA/HEDIS

NCQA has developed the standardized performance measurements set, which is called Health Plan Employer Data and Information Set (HEDIS). HEDIS 2.0 was released by NCQA in 1993 and was a result of efforts by employers and health plans to identify an integrated set of uniform standardized performance measures that could be used to document the quality and value of health plans. The plan was to allow for comparisons between competing plans. HEDIS 2.5, released in 1995, updated the earlier version to allow for easier collection of data and greater standardization. In 1997, additional changes were made, resulting in HEDIS 3.0, which was implemented in 1998.[9] These elements will be introduced into *the 1999 Managed Care Organization Accreditation Standards.*

The HEDIS 3.0 data collection categories are

- effectiveness of care
- access /availability of care
- satisfaction with the experience of care
- health plan stability
- use of services
- cost of care
- informed health care choices
- health plan descriptive information

The measures in each category are as follows:

1. Effectiveness of Care
   - childhood immunization
   - adolescent immunization
   - advising smokers to quit
   - flu shots for older adults
   - breast cancer screening
   - cervical cancer screening
   - prenatal care in the first trimester
   - low–birth weight babies
   - checkups after delivery
   - beta blocker treatment after a heart attack
   - eye exams for people with diabetes
   - health of seniors
   - follow-up after hospitalization for mental illness
2. Access/Availability of Care
   - adult access to preventive/ambulatory health services
   - children's access to primary care providers
   - availability of primary care providers
   - availability of mental health/chemical dependency providers
   - availability of obstetrical and prenatal care providers
   - initiation of prenatal care
   - low–birth weight deliveries at facilities for high-risk deliveries and neonates
   - availability of dentists
   - annual dental visit
   - availability of language interpretation services
3. Satisfaction with the Experience of Care
   - member satisfaction survey
4. Health Plan Stability
   - disenrollment
   - provider turnover
   - years in business/total membership
   - indicators of financial stability
5. Use of Services
   - well-child visits in the first 15 months of life
   - well-child visits in the third, fourth, fifth, and sixth years of life

- adolescent well-care visits
- frequency of ongoing prenatal care
- frequency of selected procedures
- inpatient utilization—general hospital/acute care
- ambulatory care
- inpatient utilization—nonacute care
- discharge and average length of stay—maternity care
- Caesarean section rate and vaginal birth after Caesarean section rate
- births and average length of stay, newborns
- mental health utilization—inpatient discharges and average length of stay
- mental health utilization—percentage of members receiving inpatient, day/night care and ambulatory services
- readmission for selected mental health disorders
- readmission for chemical dependency

6. Cost of Care
   - rate trends
   - high-occurrence/high-cost DRGs
7. Informed Health Care Choices
8. Health Plan Descriptive Information
   - board certification/residency completion
   - provider compensation
   - arrangements with public health, educational, and social service organizations
   - total enrollment
   - enrollment by payer
   - unduplicated count of Medicaid members
   - diversity of Medicaid membership
   - weeks of pregnancy at time of enrollment in the health plan

Many managed care organizations collect and report HEDIS data in such a way that individual practitioner information can be reported for inclusion in an individual practitioner profile that is reviewed at the time of reappointment. In addition to the HEDIS data, the quality improvement function in the managed care setting accredited by NCQA is responsible for collecting and sharing information related to

- member complaints
- utilization management
- member satisfaction
- information from quality improvement activities
- medical record review
- site visits

Use of three of the six sources meets the standard.

PEER REVIEW

Peer review may be defined as an evaluation by unbiased practitioners (peers). Some organizations define a peer to be someone of the same background as the practitioner being reviewed (e.g., an MD reviewing MD practice, a DO reviewing DO practice). Others may be narrower in definition, requiring the same specialty and background. This is an ongoing issue of discussion, as many practitioners feel that only someone of their particular specialty is capable of rendering a decision as to quality. The Joint Commission defines *peer* to be an individual from the same discipline and with essentially equal qualifications.[10] This is often interpreted as meaning an individual with the same professional initials (e.g., MD, PhD, DPM). NCQA defines a peer to be one with similar types and degrees of experience.[11]

Table 8–5 outlines differences between peer review, performance assessment and measurement, and performance improvement activities.

Peer review is used in the review of credentials, development of criteria, and review of performance. An organization may have a peer review committee or may accomplish individual case review through retrospective case or file review. Most organizations have a specific process, policy, and procedure that outlines peer review and/or review of clinical cases. Exhibit 8–6 is a sample case review worksheet used for peer review.

Table 8–5 Differences between Peer Review, Performance Assessment and Measurement, and Performance Improvement Activities

	Peer Review	*Performance Assessment and Measurement*	*Performance Improvement*
Definition	An objective review by a peer of the case rendered	Data collection and monitoring of performance that may identify areas for improvement	Actions taken to change the process or function and improve the outcome
Focus	Practitioner	Function and process	Function and outcomes and process
Target	Practitioner competency	High-risk, high-volume, problem-prone processes	Process variation
Purpose	Ensuring	Determining	Improving
Goal	Control	Identify	Change
Practitioner involvement	High	Low	Moderate
Desired results	Determination of practitioner competency	Identification of conformance with indicators or requirement for improvement	Improvement or positive change in outcome

Courtesy of C. Mobley & Associates, LLC, and Quality Management Options, LLC, Colorado Springs, Colorado.

Exhibit 8–6 Case Review Worksheet

COMMITTEE NAME: ______________________ Meeting Date: __________

Patient's Name: ______________________________ M.D.: _____ / _____ / _____

M.R. Number: ____________________ Age: ___

QIC NUMBER						

Admission: __________ Discharge: ____________

Referral Source: ____

Reason for Review/Pertinent Information: ______________________

____

____

Procedures/Dates: ____

____

REVIEW OF COMPLICATION: ☐ N/A Date: __________

Was the complication a result of the care that was given?	☐ Yes	☐ No	
Was the complication a known, possible result of the care that was given?	☐ Yes	☐ No	☐ N/A
Was death or major disability the result of this complication?	☐ Yes	☐ No	☐ N/A

CASE MANAGEMENT:

Were the following indicated and timely:

Drug Therapy?	☐ Yes	☐ No	☐ N/A
Treatments?	☐ Yes	☐ No	☐ N/A
Laboratory Tests?	☐ Yes	☐ No	☐ N/A
Diagnostic Procedures?	☐ Yes	☐ No	☐ N/A
Surgical Procedures?	☐ Yes	☐ No	☐ N/A

DOCUMENTATION:

Was chart documentation clinically pertinent to the patient's condition?	☐ Yes	☐ No
Was chart documentation adequate?	☐ Yes	☐ No

REVIEWER'S SUMMARY:

_____ No further review needed. Clinical management acceptable.

_____ Further review requested.

_____ N/A — Continue to back of worksheet.

continues

Exhibit 8–6 continued

Reviewer's Comments: (If necessary, explain above determination.)

____
____
____
____
____

Reviewer's Signature __________ Date __________

Date Closed:
M.D. Educ.: Y N

COMMITTEE REVIEW SUMMARY

COMMITTEE COMMENTS/FOLLOW UP:

(Including specific questions to be answered, if letter sent.)

____
____
____
____
____

COMMITTEE CONCLUSION: (Check one)

/__/ 1. Management acceptable
/__/ 2. Management unconventional, but acceptable
/__/ 3. Management unacceptable

Committee Member's Signature __________ Date __________

COMMITTEE ACTIONS:

FOR OFFICE USE ONLY

Inquiry/ Referral to	Date	Reply Requested	Date Reply Received	Comments	C
		☐ Y ☐ N			
		☐ Y ☐ N			
		☐ Y ☐ N			
		☐ Y ☐ N			
		☐ Y ☐ N			
		☐ Y ☐ N			
		☐ Y ☐ N			

Courtesy of Cedars-Sinai Medical Center, Los Angeles, California.

COMMON ISSUES AND PROBLEMS

Reappointment of Low-Volume Practitioners

Determination of competence at reappointment is made more difficult if a practitioner has had little activity or is considered to be a low-volume practitioner. A required component of the reappointment process is review of current competence (Joint Commission, for hospitals). If the practitioner has had so little activity that no information has been identified for the profile or is available from peers in the organization, another method must be developed. The most common alternative is to use information from another organization in which the practitioner has had significant activity during the previous two years. The practitioner may be required to obtain specific information if he or she wishes to be reappointed, including

- evaluation by chief executive officer at the organization where primary practice/activity occurred
- clinical activity summary from organization(s) where primary practice/activity occurred
- information regarding medical records violations from primary practice organization
- evaluation of competence from department chief at primary practice organization

This information is then used along with the information provided by the applicant's certificates (termination, limitation, reduction or suspension of license, memberships, or professional liability action) to determine compliance with criteria for reappointment.

Quality Files

Organizations have developed numerous methods for developing, maintaining, and storing files containing results of performance evaluation activities. Some integrate all information into the credentials file, while others place it in a quality file that is stored with the credentials file. Still others maintain quality files in an area separate from all other files and do not allow access by anyone other than PA&I staff. State statutes related to peer review should be consulted and legal counsel obtained before a determination is made related to files containing performance review and evaluation material. Storage of quality information in the credentials file may allow access to the information by review bodies, regulators, and staff from other departments such as utilization review, provider relations, or medical records. The policy that directs the development, access to, and storage of credentials files should also address the practitioner profile and other performance evaluation materials used in the credentialing process.

Developing Profiles for Allied Health Professionals

Frequently the profile and formal evaluation of the competency of allied health professionals (AHPs) at the time of reappointment is inadequate or not completed at all. The practitioner may be contracted, with no competency evaluation because of a belief that the organization is not responsible for it; or he or she may be employed, with the competency evaluation tied into an employment evaluation or supervision by a physician that results in only a supervisor evaluation. If a practitioner is credentialed and privileged through the medical staff process or is listed as an independent practitioner by a managed care organization, a profile should be developed. Information related to supervised, dependent, employed nonlicensed AHPs is found in Chapter 3 of this book. Information that may be included in an AHP profile includes

- licensure, certification, and registration
- supervisor evaluation (as applicable)
- continuing education related to specialty or privileges requested

- peer review findings
- individual findings related to any performance or quality studies
- disciplinary actions
- results of patient satisfaction survey/patient complaints

Exhibit 8–7 is a sample profile for an AHP.

Using Computers for Profiling

As health care organizations grow, there is increased use of computers and networked systems. This often allows for identification of volume and utilization data from the organization's information system. Many managed care organizations have computerized systems that provide information such as

Exhibit 8–7 AHP Quality Profile

NAME: __________ TITLE: __________ CATEGORY: __________

RESPONSIBLE/SUPERVISING PHYSICIAN: __________

DATE OF APPOINTMENT OR LAST REAPPOINTMENT DATE: __________

TIME PERIOD COVERED BY PROFILE: from __________ to __________

	YES	**NO**
Changes requested in privileges?		
Any change in licensure?		
Any change in certification?		
Supervisor evaluation attached?		
Any problems identified in application, attestation, or other information collected?		

Complaints	**Number**	
Patient complaints		
Staff complaints		
Physician complaints		
Quality Care Assessment	**Number**	**Outcome**
Clinical Pertinence Review	**Number**	**Outcome**
Blood		
Medications		
Operative/other procedures		

Additional information relevant to performance during this period:

Reviewed by __________ Date: __________

Courtesy of C. Mobley & Associates, LLC, and Quality Management Options, LLC, Colorado Springs, Colorado.

- number of members assigned to practitioner
- number of inpatient admissions
- number of office visits (for enrolled members)
- number of admissions per 1,000 covered lives
- average length of stay per admission
- average charges per patient/diagnosis
- average referrals per 100 office visits

Hospitals commonly obtain the number of inpatient and outpatient admissions per practitioner along with numbers of surgical and other invasive procedures. The quality initiatives of the Joint Commission (ORYX) and NCQA (HEDIS) require computer support, and in the future we should obtain more practitioner-specific information. Numerous software companies have developed PA&I software that allows identification of practitioner-specific information. Few of these programs integrate with organizational information systems; thus, they require significant data input.

Concerns about confidentiality, peer review protection, economic credentialing, risk adjustment of outcomes, and use of information have slowed the evolution of computer support for practitioner profiles. But since we live in an ever increasing computerized environment, PA&I and credentials professionals will find themselves more involved in electronic production of information.

NOTES

1. *Joint Commission Perspectives* (Joint Commission on Accreditation of Healthcare Organizations) 18 (March/April 1998), Vol. 5, No. 2; PI11–PI12.
2. *Joint Commission Perspectives,* PI2.
3. *Performance Improvement in Ambulatory Care* (Oakbrook Terrace, IL: Joint Commission on Accreditation of Healthcare Organizations, 1997), 3–5.
4. *Performance Improvement,* 11.
5. *ORYX: The Next Evaluation in Accreditation* (Oakbrook Terrace, IL: Joint Commission on Accreditation of Healthcare Organizations, 1997), PM-1.
6. *ORYX,* PM-2.
7. *ORYX,* PM-2.
8. *ORYX,* PM-2.
9. *1998 Questions and Answers about the Committee on Performance Measurement (CPM) and HEDIS 3.0* (Washington, DC: National Committee for Quality Assurance).
10. *1998 Hospital Accreditation Standards* (Oakbrook Terrace, IL: Joint Commission on Accreditation of Healthcare Organizations), 255.
11. *Surveyor Guidelines for Accreditation of Managed Care Organizations, 1998* (Washington, DC: National Committee for Quality Assurance, 1998).

CHAPTER 9

Legal Issues and Documents

Christina Wiggins-Giles

OVERVIEW

There are legal implications to many aspects of the credentialing process. Credentialing policies and procedures, activities, and forms are affected by the Health Care Quality Improvement Act of 1986,[1] the Americans with Disabilities Act,[2] and state regulations relating to peer review and confidentiality of information. The Health Care Quality Improvement Act outlines professional review requirements that have been incorporated into most hospital medical staff bylaws and most fair hearing plans, and into credentials plans in hospitals and managed and ambulatory care organizations.

Maintaining confidentiality of information is a concern for all credentialing professionals as more requests for information are received and sent to other organizations. State peer review laws may allow exchange of peer review information between hospitals, but most do not address disclosure between hospitals and ambulatory or managed care organizations. Maintaining peer review privileges of confidentiality and immunity requires both knowledge of and compliance with statutes.

Dealing with an impaired practitioner and use of drug testing as part of the application process are issues that now must be addressed by health care organizations. The credentialing professional is often responsible for staying abreast of changes as well as for implementing these policies and procedures. This chapter addresses the legal aspects of these issues and credentialing activities.

The references to laws and legal requirements in the following pages have been summarized by the authors, who are not legal professionals. The information is provided only as a reference for aspects of credentialing that should also require legal review by counsel for the organization. Appropriate legal counsel should always be obtained for review of bylaws, policies and procedures, forms, and other documents that have legal implications.

CONFIDENTIALITY

The word *confidential* is defined as information protected from being revealed.[3] As it relates to credentialing, confidentiality represents the issue of information being available to a group or health care entity that would possibly be harmful or prejudicial to a particular individual or group. The issue is whether material is discoverable (allowing access to documents or witnesses) or admissible (whether documents, objects or testimony may be admitted into evidence at trial.)[4] Information may be discoverable but not admissible. The law varies by state, and the federal courts have separate rules regarding discovery and admissibility that will override the state law. A state or federal court order may order a hospital to release medical records or other confidential information.

There is wide variance in state law concerning peer review privileges of confidentiality and immunity. In general, to be protected, information must be obtained from activities involving review by peers. Credentials review is usually considered to be a peer review activity. Some states provide that credentials committee records are not subject to subpoena, discovery, or disclosure; others state that such records are not discoverable but are defined as confidential. Many states contain an exception allowing discovery of records of committees that deal with issues of staff privileges or membership when a physician is contesting termination, suspension, or limitation of privileges.

Numerous types of documents can be considered peer review documents; some are protected, some are not. All the documents listed below should be treated as confidential, and language should be adopted from state law and incorporated into the bylaws and relevant policies to identify those documents that are protected under the law. "Treated as confidential" means that the documents should be stamped confidential, access should be limited to individuals authorized to see or use the information (and the authority should be defined in a policy), maintenance areas should be secure, and documents should not be put into the mail or faxed. Minutes should be numbered, distributed at the meeting, and collected at the end of the meeting. All hospital and medical staff individuals who will be participating in a committee that handles such information should be educated as to the importance of following any policies or procedures specified for this information. Treating the material as confidential and ensuring that all individuals who come into contact with it are fully informed of their responsibilities enforce the official peer review status of the information and should qualify the information for maximum protection under the relevant state law.

Examples of confidential documents are: patient/member complaints; practitioner profile data; audit/outcome reports; medical records; incident or occurrence reports; National Practitioner Data Bank (NPDB) inquiries and reports; utilization review, quality assessment, case management and performance improvement data; and committee minutes.

Examples of documents that are commonly considered to be nonconfidential are delineation of privilege forms, screening criteria, application materials, policies, release forms, corporate bylaws, medical staff bylaws, rules and regulations, department policies, and fair hearing plans.[5]

It is recommended that any document that the organization wishes to protect under applicable state statutes be

- clearly marked as "confidential" using the applicable statute language
- distributed only on a "need-to-know" basis
- identified in policy and procedures as privileged and confidential pursuant to the applicable statute
- filed and maintained separately from nonconfidential documents

CONFIDENTIALITY POLICY

A confidentiality policy should be developed to address the information collected and maintained for credentialing purposes, quality review/performance improvement activities and findings, risk management activities and findings, and all relevant committees authorized to review and make recommendations based upon those findings.

A confidentiality policy should contain the following:

- a policy statement clearly stating the purpose of the policy
- information/documents that are covered by the policy and are considered peer review documents
- individuals and groups (committees/governing body) allowed access to the information, under what circumstances they are allowed access and why, and when and where they are allowed access (including whether the individual practitioner is al-

lowed access to his or her own file, whether he or she can obtain copies of all documents in the file, and how he or she could request to add an item of information to the file)
- location of files, both paper and computerized
- security of files and areas where files are kept
- computerized security and access, backup protection
- identification of any codes used in the files, and location of the code key and accountability for codes and keys
- information that will be released over the telephone versus information that will require a written release form (identify the release/authorization form to be used and when it will be obtained and maintained)
- information that will be made available to third parties, regulators, accreditation surveyors, managed care plans

Exhibit 9–1 is an example policy addressing the confidentiality of hospital medical staff records.

A related policy that should be developed along with the confidentiality policy is a retention policy. A retention policy should specify what documents are collected and used in the credentialing/quality/performance improvement system, where and how they are maintained, and how long they will be retained. If there is a backup system for retaining records, such as microfiche, microfilm, or a computerized scanning program, the policy should specify at what point the information is transferred and what happens to the paper copies. Accreditation, state statute, corporate policy, and individual counsel may affect the determination of what will be retained and for how long.

THE HEALTH CARE QUALITY IMPROVEMENT ACT'S REQUIREMENTS FOR REVIEW ACTIONS

The Health Care Quality Improvement Act of 1986 includes standards for professional review actions. This federal law requires that professional review actions must be taken

1. in the reasonable belief that the action was in the furtherance of quality health care
2. after a reasonable effort to obtain the facts of the matter
3. after adequate notice and hearing procedures are afforded
4. in the reasonable belief that the action was warranted by the facts[6]

Additionally, the Act requires the following:

- The physician must be given notice that a professional review action has been proposed, including reasons for the proposed action.
- The physician has the right to request a hearing on any proposed action and to be informed of the time limit in which to request the hearing (may not be less than 30 days).
- A summary of rights.
- If a hearing is requested, notice of its location, date (to be no more than 30 days from date of notice), and time must be given to the physician along with a list of the witnesses (if any) expected to testify on behalf of the professional review body.
- The hearing must be held before an arbitrator mutually acceptable to the physician and the health care entity, before a hearing officer, or a panel appointed by the entity who is not in direct economic competition with the involved physician.
- The physician involved may be represented by an attorney of other person of his or her choice; have a record made of the proceedings; call, examine, and cross-examine witnesses; present evidence; and submit a written statement at the close of the hearing.
- At completion of the hearing, the physician has the right to receive the written recommendation along with the basis for the recommendation and to receive a written decision from the entity.[7]

Exhibit 9–1 Confidentiality of Medical Staff Records

SUBJECT: Confidentiality of Medical Staff Records	NO.

POLICY: All medical staff records will be consistently handled and maintained in a confidential manner.

PURPOSE: To ensure that all medical staff records maintained by or on behalf of the Medical Staff will be handled and preserved according to the procedures outlined in this policy.

DEFINITIONS:

MEDICAL STAFF RECORDS shall include but not be limited to: records of meetings, proceedings, interviews, reports, communication (written and oral), memoranda, statements, recommendations, findings, evaluations, opinions, conclusions, actions, data, credentials files, peer review files, and patient care/risk management files that relate to Medical Staff members and their responsibilities.

INFORMATION shall include but not be limited to: physician specific demographics, medical staff rosters, listings of departmental members, etc.

ACTIVITIES shall include: all documents and proceedings related to the quality management, utilization review, risk management/patient care assessment, and credentialing processes.

PERSONNEL shall include: all hospital personnel, members of the Medical Staff and governing body.

IMPLEMENTATION

BREACH OF CONFIDENCE

A breach of this policy by any of the personnel listed above would include but not be limited to the intentional release or exchange of any oral or written information to any person/group/agency not directly involved in the work related to the areas in this policy.

Any person found to violate this policy will be subject to immediate disciplinary action and/or dismissal.

CONFIDENTIALITY STATEMENT

All involved hospital personnel, members of the Medical Staff and governing body will be requested to sign a confidentiality statement (see Medical Staff Services Department Confidentiality Statement). These statements will be maintained in the appropriate department.

Written by:	Issued by:	Approved by:	Date Issued:	Page
____________ Director Medical Staff Serv.	____________ Vice President Medical Affairs	____________ Chief Executive Officer	Supersedes Date:	

continues

Exhibit 9–1 continued

LOCATION AND SECURITY PRECAUTIONS

MEDICAL STAFF SERVICES (MSS)

The minutes and records of all medical staff committees, subcommittees, and ad hoc committees supported by MSS personnel and credentials files shall be maintained in the department of Medical Staff Services under the custody of the director or authorized representative.

QUALITY MANAGEMENT SERVICES (QMS)

The minutes and records of all Medical Staff quality management committees, subcommittees and ad hoc committees supported by QMS personnel, quality and utilization data, and peer review files shall be maintained in QMS under the custody of the director or authorized representative.

RISK MANAGEMENT SERVICES (RMS)

The minutes and records of all committees, subcommittees and ad hoc committees supported by RMS personnel, variance or occurrence reports, complaints, patient care assessment reports and documents pertaining to patient compensable/clinical events shall be maintained in RMS under the custody of the director or authorized representative.

In all cases, active and inactive medical staff records and files shall be kept locked when authorized representatives are not present. All active and inactive files shall be permanently maintained in the appropriate department or in an officially designated safe storage area.

IDENTIFICATION SYSTEM

Records of quality review data and reference to individuals in peer review minutes shall be coded to protect the identity of the practitioner, patient, and medical record. The director of QMS, in concert with the direction of MSS and RMS, is responsible for establishing and maintaining the integrity of the identification system.

COMPUTERIZED DATA

Precautions for data processed or stored in a computer shall include:

1. Limited access through the use of passwords and individual levels of security.
2. Daily backups to magnetic disk or tape shall be performed.
3. Files on diskettes shall be kept in a locked, secure file.
4. Refer to Administrative Policy Manual, Information Services, Ad Hoc Reporting Policy 7.1.2 for process to request and/or release computerized data.

ACCESS TO MEDICAL STAFF RECORDS

A. MEANS OF ACCESS

All requests for information by persons within the hospital shall be presented in writing to the director of QMS, MSS, or RMS, as appropriate. A record of all requests made and granted shall be maintained in the appropriate department.

continues

Exhibit 9–1 continued

Those requests which require notice to, or approval by, other officials shall be forwarded to those persons.

A person permitted access under this policy shall be allowed to inspect the records in question in the presence of an appropriate authorized departmental representative and to make notes regarding them, but will not be allowed to remove or make copies of them.

B. ACCESS BY PERSONS PERFORMING OFFICIAL FACILITY OR MEDICAL STAFF FUNCTIONS:

1. Access to information contained in medical staff records to the extent necessary to perform official functions:

   Hospital President
   Vice President Medical Affairs
   Patient Care Assessment Coordinator
   Medical Staff President
   President-Elect Medical Staff
   Clinical Department Chiefs/Division Directors

2. Access to information contained in medical staff records to perform committee or governing body functions:

   Voting Members of:
   Credentials Review Committee
   *Medical Executive Committee
   *Professional Affairs Committee
   *Board of Trustees

   *Any requests to review files by members of these committees/governing bodies will have such request noted.

3. Access to information contained in medical staff records to the extent necessary to prepare documents, reports, profiles:

   Medical Staff Services Personnel
   Quality Management Personnel
   Risk Management Personnel
   Chairs of Patient Care Assessment, Utilization Review, Clinical Monitoring and Clinical Risk Committees

4. Statistical information may be provided to the Planning and Marketing Department in accordance with guidelines established by the Medical Staff and Administration.

C. ACCESS BY INDIVIDUAL PRACTITIONER:

A practitioner may view his or her entire file in the presence of the Director or designees of the Department where the file is maintained. The practitioner may not remove the file or any part of the file or make copies of any portion of the file except for copies of certificates, clinical privileges, CME documentation, and application which were provided by the applicant. Copies of any other documents (credentials, peer review and risk files) must be requested in writing. The reason for the request must be stated and such requests must be approved by the Chief of the Department in which the physician is a member and by the Vice President of Medical Affairs [VPMA].

If the practitioner disagrees with the inclusion of an item in his or her file, he or she may request in writing an amendment to add a document to the file or to request the removal of a document from the file. The decision to amend the file or remove an item from the file requires the consensus of the Chief of the Department in which the physician is a member, the Medical Staff President, and the VPMA.

continues

Exhibit 9–1 continued

D. BY PERSONS OR ORGANIZATIONS OUTSIDE OF ST. VINCENT HOSPITAL:

1. Credentialing or Peer Review at other Health Care Facilities.

   All requests for practitioner information shall be in writing on the requested hospital's stationery. The request must include the reasons and a statement signed by the practitioner specifically releasing St. Vincent Hospital from liability and dated within the previous 12 months.

   All requests for information from other hospitals will be responded to with the provision of the most recently completed reference request form (Appendix B). Any request for additional information will require that the practitioner be contacted and an additional release signed by the practitioner prior to the information being released. Requests for information about practitioners whose file contains adverse information (having negative effect on a practitioner's membership or privileges) should be reviewed by legal counsel.

E. TELEPHONE REQUESTS:

Only confirmation or acknowledgment of a specific practitioner's period of affiliation, staff category and department/division membership and place of medical, podiatric, dental, or other appropriate training, all internships, residencies, fellowships, and board certifications may be released upon telephone request. All such requests should be referred to the Department of Medical Staff Services. All other requests for information contained in the medical staff records by persons or organizations outside the hospital shall be in writing and forwarded to the Chief Executive Officer of the hospital or his designee. The release of any such information shall require the concurrence of the Chief Executive Officer of the hospital, Vice President of Medical Affairs and the President of the Medical Staff.

This does not preclude Department Chiefs/Division Directors and Medical Staff officers/leaders from responding to legitimate telephone inquiries concerning Medical Staff and/or physicians who have trained at St. Vincent in order to provide a personal reference or to expand upon written information already provided.

F. SUBPOENAS:

All subpoenas of medical staff records involving potential liability shall be referred to the Director of Risk Management Services, who will notify the Massachusetts Medical Professional Insurance Association and the physician(s) involved. The MMMJUA will determine legal counsel involvement and shall so advise the Director of Risk Management Services. The Director of Risk Management Services will simultaneously advise and consult the Chief Executive Officer, VPMA, Chief Operating Officer or President of the Medical Staff as appropriate to the particular situation.

G. REQUEST BY FACILITY SURVEYORS:

Facility Surveyors (from the Joint Commission on Accreditation of Healthcare Organizations, State Department of Public Health, Federal Health Care Finance Administration, or any other facility surveyors) shall be entitled to inspect records covered by this policy on the facilities' premises in the presence of appropriate hospital or medical staff personnel provided that (1) no originals or copies may be removed from the premises, (2) only with the concurrence of the Chief Executive Officer or his designees, or the VPMA or his designee.

Note: Adapted format from InterQual, Inc., North Hampton, New Hampshire.

Courtesy of St. Vincent Hospital, Worcester, Massachusetts.

If an adverse determination is made on the decision to credential, grant privileges, or recredential, the fair hearing requirements of the Health Care Quality Improvement Act may apply. Since the consequences of noncompliance with the Act are significant, it is wise to periodically review corrective action, due process and fair hearing processes with legal counsel.

CORRECTIVE ACTION AND FAIR HEARING—HOSPITAL

The Joint Commission includes in its Medical Staff Standards specific requirements for the executive committee of the medical staff to provide

- fair hearing and appellate review mechanisms for medical staff members and other individuals holding clinical privileges, and
- mechanisms for corrective action, including indications and procedures for automatic and summary suspension of an individual's medical staff membership or clinical privileges[8]

On the basis of the Joint Commission's required provisions, and because all hospitals and medical staffs should be concerned with providing a fair and consistent set of rules and requirements that allow each medical staff member or applicant due process, the medical staff bylaws or fair hearing plan should contain the fair hearing procedure to be used by the medical staff in a hospital. Many hospitals have begun to separate the documents to include bylaws, fair hearing plan, credentials procedures, rules and regulations, and policies governing allied health professionals.

Corrective action in the hospital may be categorized as automatic, summary, or routine. Automatic action occurs when a practitioner fails to comply with specific provisions of membership and privileges; for example, loss of license or other required certificate such as a Drug Enforcement Administration (DEA) certificate, no malpractice insurance, or incomplete medical records. The medical staff bylaws outline those situations in which automatic corrective action will occur. Summary action is initiated for situations in which there is reasonable belief that there is a threat to the well-being or safety of a patient or patients (e.g., an impaired practitioner, a perceived impairment, or a sentinel event in the operating room). It is taken to correct the immediate problem and results in suspension of some or all clinical privileges until a full investigation can be completed. Routine action occurs when the practitioner is notified of an impending investigation, allegations, and/or procedural rights that may or may not result in any adverse action taken. An example is a trend or concern identified by, or referred to, a medical staff department leader, committee, or ad hoc group that further investigates. Findings are reported or recommendations made. The practitioner is often interviewed or counseled as part of this process, and under these circumstances (defined in the bylaws), interviews are considered informal and not a formal hearing. All meetings and interviews should be documented; this may be helpful if a more formal action is taken later. Grounds for corrective action must be specified in the bylaws or a related document; they commonly address such issues as

- failure to comply with medical staff bylaws, rules and regulations, and applicable policies and procedures
- medical practice that is not considered to be in accordance with community, standard, customary, or generally accepted professional standards
- violation of professional ethics or unprofessional conduct
- impairment that affects the ability of the practitioner to care for patients

If routine corrective action will adversely affect the practitioner's ability to exercise clinical privileges, he or she is afforded the right to a hearing. Summary action also affords the right to hearing when the suspension is upheld and adverse recommendation is made as the result of an investigation. Privileges may be suspended or affected until the process is completed. Automatic suspension does not entitle the practitioner to a hearing due to the nature of its defined grounds in the bylaws.

Due process is defined as the right of fundamental fairness in proceedings. Procedural due process requires that notice and right to a fair hearing be afforded before an action that might deprive.[9]

The Corrective Action and Fair Hearing Plan

The corrective action and fair hearing plan or some similar section in the medical staff bylaws should address the following:

1. Allowance for an informal investigation into the situation before initiating a formal corrective action. The individual(s) or committee(s) authorized to conduct the informal investigation should be identified. If a committee is authorized, the plan should cover appointment of the members, identification of individuals who may or will participate in the investigation, method of contact and notification of the medical staff member being investigated, whether there will be formal documentation of the investigation, where that documentation will be maintained, and who will receive the outcome report.
2. Who can initiate an investigation—either individuals or committees who have the authority to initiate corrective action with respect to a member of the medical staff.
3. The reasons why investigation and corrective action can be initiated. Typically, they may include situations in which a practitioner with a staff appointment or clinical privileges
   - engages in acts, statements, demeanor or professional conduct (either within or outside of the hospital) that is contrary to the bylaws, rules, and policies or standards of the hospital or medical staff
   - engages in acts that are detrimental to patient safety or to the delivery of quality patient care
   - fails to act in accordance with standards of medical practice, with detrimental results to patient care and/or safety
   - is disruptive to the hospital operations such that the quality or efficiency of patient care is, or is likely to be, affected
   - is in violation of state or federal criminal statutes or is engaged in conduct that violates standards of ethical conduct governing his or her practice
   - has been disciplined by another state or federal agency
   - has committed a felony or other act involving dishonesty, fraud, deceit, or misrepresentation
   - fails to respond to requests for an interview, or to investigational questioning
4. How all requests and notices concerning the corrective action will be handled.
5. How the official investigation will be handled, including:
   - review of medical records
   - interviews with the practitioner involved
   - interviews or information collection from the individual or group making the request for corrective action or with any other individuals who may have knowledge of the events involved
6. The actions that the medical executive committee may take after the conclusion of the investigative process, including the time frame within which it must take action. Actions may include
   - rejection or modification of the request for corrective action
   - a verbal warning or formal letter of reprimand (which does not evoke the right to a hearing)
   - additional education or training
   - recommendation of medical/psychiatric treatment

- recommendation of a probationary period of prescribed duration with a review of all cases, required consultation or direct supervision, suspension of appointment prerogatives, and limitation of the right to admit patients
- recommendation for reduction, suspension, or revocation of all or part of the clinical privileges
- recommendation for suspension or revocation of medical staff appointment

7. Acknowledgment of the procedural rights to be afforded to the practitioner based on the recommendation or type of action taken by the medical executive committee and any other action that could be taken, if not included in the procedural rights.
8. Criteria for which a summary suspension may be imposed and the persons or bodies entitled to impose summary suspension. Such action is usually imposed in severe cases when the practitioner's conduct requires that immediate action be taken to prevent danger to life or injury to the practitioner or others.
9. Criteria for which an automatic suspension may be imposed and the persons or bodies entitled to impose automatic suspension. Such action is usually imposed when
    - a practitioner's license to practice has expired or been revoked, limited, or restricted in any way that would affect the practitioner's ability to perform clinical privileges granted or has been suspended, or placed on probation
    - a practitioner's drug enforcement number expires or is revoked, restricted or limited, suspended, or placed on probation
    - felony conviction
    - failure to complete medical records within the required time frame after receiving adequate warning
    - failure to maintain the minimum level of professional liability insurance as required by the hospital
    - failure to appear at a meeting of any committee of the medical staff in order to discuss proposed corrective action

    Automatic suspension does not entitle a practitioner to a hearing. Reinstatement of membership or privileges may be allowed in specific cases that can be rectified such as obtaining the minimum level of professional liability insurance.

Fair Hearing

When the medical executive committee or the board of trustees recommends an action that is deemed "adverse" or affecting membership or privileges, the practitioner may be afforded the right to fair hearing procedures or due process. It is important that the medical staff bylaws clearly state that the practitioner will be limited to only one hearing and one appellate review on any specific set of facts. The following actions are examples of those that would initiate the hearing procedure if recommended by the medical executive committee or the board of trustees:

- denial of initial staff appointment if denial relates to the practitioner's competence to practice medicine
- denial of reappointment
- suspension of appointment
- revocation of appointment
- reduction in staff category if based on professional competence or professional conduct of the practitioner
- special limitation of the right to admit patients not related to standard administrative or medical staff policies
- denial or restriction of requested clinical privileges
- involuntary reduction of clinical privileges
- suspension of clinical privileges (provided that summary suspension entitles the practitioner to request a hearing)
- revocation of clinical privileges

Some types of actions or recommendations typically would not entitle the practitioner to hearing procedures:

- a verbal warning or formal letter of reprimand
- a monitoring or consultation requirement attached to the exercise of clinical privileges imposed during a provisional period
- corrective counseling
- a recommendation that the medical staff appointee be directed to obtain retraining, additional training, or continuing education
- imposition of a defined period of time involving the review of cases or a specific number of cases
- expiration without renewal of a contract or employment arrangement to provide specific clinical services
- reduction in staff category based upon noncompliance with medical staff policies
- denial or revocation of temporary privileges in accordance with the bylaws
- limitations on the exercise of privileges resulting from a board decision to enter into an exclusive contractual arrangement for the provision of specific clinical services

Hearing Prerequisites

Notification. Due process requires that the physician be given adequate notice of the recommended adverse action as soon as proposed, except in instances of summary suspension. This notice must contain the place, time, and date of the hearing. The date of the hearing must not be less than 30 days after the date of the notice of the proposed action. The hearing notice must also include a concise statement of the practitioner's alleged acts or omissions, a list of the specific medical records in question, and a list of witnesses who are expected to testify (reciprocal guidelines may apply). This information should be detailed in the fair hearing plan or the medical staff bylaws. State statutes should also be reviewed to ensure that there are no additional requirements imposed by state law relevant to the hearing notification process.

Waiver of Rights. The practitioner always has the right to waive his or her hearing rights. Should this occur, the governing body may consider the recommended adverse action without the input of a hearing panel. The fair hearing plan or medical staff bylaws should contain a provision clearly stating that if the practitioner fails to request a hearing to which he or she is entitled, that shall be deemed a waiver of the right to such a hearing and to any appellate review.

Conduct of Hearing

The fair hearing plan or medical staff bylaws should contain provisions that outline

- how witnesses will be handled
- how the hearing committee will be appointed and what types of individuals should be members
- action if any of the parties fail to appear
- who shall act as the hearing officer and his or her duties
- a requirement of the personal presence of the practitioner in question
- the format for the presentation of information and the rights of all parties
- a description of the procedure and evidence that may be introduced, as well as the admissibility of the evidence (Note: The hearing does not necessarily follow the court rules of evidence.)
- the burden of proof and what must be proven (The burden of proof may vary depending on the type of adverse action involved. In many instances, the practitioner will have the burden of proving that the recommended action against him or her is arbitrary and capricious.)
- how the records of the hearing will be kept and by whom
- available action(s) if a postponement is requested by either party

- a requirement that the majority of the hearing committee be present throughout the hearing and deliberations in order to vote
- allowance for recesses and adjournment
- time frame within which the hearing committee must provide a report of its findings and to whom it shall forward the report
- the body that will accept the hearing committee's report and recommendation, the time frame within which it shall render its decisions, and to whom it will render its decision
- contents of hearing report, including the basis for the recommendation, the recommendation, and the decision
- right of the practitioner to obtain a copy of the hearing records
- notification of the action, whether it is favorable or unfavorable to the practitioner, and any right of appeal

Appellate Review

If the result of hearing activities is adverse to the practitioner, then the practitioner has a right to request an appellate review. The appellate review is used to determine if the due process was handled according to policy and was not arbitrary. The fair hearing plan or medical staff bylaws should define

- the process for providing notice of time and place for appellate review
- who will compose the appellate review body—typically the board of trustees or several board members
- who will act as the presiding officer of the appellate review body
- a requirement that a majority of the members be present throughout the review and deliberations in order to be allowed to vote
- possible actions to be taken:
  - If it is determined that policy was followed, corrective action is immediately effective.
  - If it is determined that policy was not followed, a plan is made to rectify and is referred to a special combined council (equal numbers of medical staff and board of trustees) to consider the issue(s).

Use of Attorneys

There should be a statement in either the fair hearing plan or the medical staff bylaws that addresses whether the practitioner and the hospital and medical staff representatives are to be allowed to have attorneys at the hearing and appellate review. It is usually recommended and most hospitals unilaterally allow both parties to have access to attorneys. If one party requests an attorney, it should notify the other party in advance.[10]

Exhibit 9–2 is a sample scheduling protocol for due-process proceedings, and Exhibit 9–3 is a due-process checklist.

CORRECTIVE ACTION, APPEALS, AND TERMINATION IN MANAGED CARE AND AMBULATORY CARE SETTINGS

The National Committee for Quality Assurance (NCQA) includes in its credentialing standards for managed care organizations requirements for

- policies and procedures for altering the conditions of the practitioner's participation based on issues of quality of care and service, and for defining the range of actions that may be taken to improve performance before termination[11]
- procedures for reporting to appropriate authorities serious quality deficiencies that could result in a practitioner's suspension or termination[12]
- an appeal process for instances in which the managed care organization chooses to alter the conditions of the practitioner's participation on the basis of issues of quality of care and/or service and informs practitioners of the appeal process[13]

Exhibit 9–2 Scheduling Protocol for Due-Process Proceedings

Physician name: ____________________

I. **DATE OF NOTICE FROM DEPARTMENT RECOMMENDING GROUNDS FOR HEARING:** ____________________

Vice President for Medical Affairs is notified regarding recommendation which is grounds for a hearing in accordance with the Bylaws. Vice President will determine if action is justified and if the recommendation is appropriate according to the Bylaws. Vice President will consider alternatives to a hearing, if possible. Vice President will seek legal counsel, if necessary.

SUMMARY SUSPENSION: ____________

OTHER RECOMMENDATION: ____________

a. ________ Denial of Membership
b. ________ Denial of Requested Rank Change
c. ________ Denial of Reappointment
d. ________ Demotion of Rank
e. ________ Termination of Membership
f. ________ Denial of Requested Privileges
g. ________ Change of Professional Privileges
h. ________ Suspension of Professional or Other Medical Staff Privileges
i. ________ Requirement of Consultation

DATE NPDB DUE: ____________

DATE NPDB SENT: ____________

IF SUMMARY SUSPENSION, NPDB REPORTS FILED. NOTIFY HOSPITAL DEPARTMENTS.

II. **DATE OF NOTICE APPOINTING MSREP:** ____________

Vice President of Medical Affairs appoints Medical Staff Representative and provides Job Description.

III. **DATE OF NOTICE "RECOMMENDATION NOT UPHELD":** ____________

Recommendation not upheld by Vice President for Medical Affairs. Referred back to Committee.

IV. **DATE OF NOTICE "RECOMMENDATION UPHELD":** ____________

Vice President of Medical Affairs upholds recommendation. Notice of Charges is sent in accordance with Bylaws.

a. ________ *Affected Practitioner notified by Certified Mail/Return Receipt requested (Summary Suspension—Notify by Hand Delivery and Certified Mail)*
b. ________ *Department Chair (assists with drafting Notice of Charges)*
c. ________ *Chief of Staff*
d. ________ *Medical Staff Coordinator responsible for affected practitioner's department*
e. ________ *Legal Affairs/in-house counsel*
f. ________ *Medical Staff Representative*

continues

Exhibit 9–2 continued

V. **NOTICE OF CHARGES**

Medical Staff Coordinator drafts Notice of Charges which is reviewed and signed by Vice President of Medical Affairs (under certain circumstances, is first reviewed by Legal Affairs).

INCLUDED IN NOTICE:

a. ___________ *Actions proposed to be taken and nature of the charges.*

b. ___________ *Provides 30 days to request a hearing.*

c. ___________ *Advises re: filing of Adverse Action Report to NPDB.*

d. ___________ *Summary of hearing rights.*

e. ___________ *Intent for legal representation (time frame).*

f. ___________ *Requests that practitioner responds to Vice President of Medical Affairs in care of Medical Staff Director.*

VI. **DATE NOTICE OF CHARGES RECEIVED BY PRACTITIONER: ___________**

Medical Staff Coordinator monitors for return of certified receipt by practitioner within 5 to 7 days of date Notice of Charges sent.

VII. **DATE RECEIVED REQUEST FOR A HEARING: ___________**

REQUEST MUST BE RECEIVED BY: ___________

Receipt of Request for a Hearing by the Vice President for Medical Affairs (must be within 30 calendar days following practitioner's receipt of Notice).

VIII. **DATE SENT RESPONSE TO REQUEST FOR A HEARING: ___________**

Acknowledge Receipt (Response to) of Request for a Hearing. Text includes Article XIII, Section 7(e) "Representation and Notice of Representation," which includes the requirement of the practitioner to give a 30-day notification to the Medical Staff if the practitioner is not to be represented by legal counsel; Section 7(f) "Right of Inspection and Identification of Documents," that also allows the practitioner, with a 30-day notification prior to the hearing, to have access to documents relevant to the practitioner (does not allow access to confidential material involving other staff members). Also, the practitioner may request, within 10 days before the hearing, access to documentary evidence that will be presented at the hearing.

IX. If no Request for a Hearing is received within the time frame established by the Constitution:

a. ___________ **DATE ACTION BECOMES FINAL**

Action becomes final upon expiration of 30-day period. (See NPDB Reporting.)

X. **NOTIFICATION OF REQUEST FOR A HEARING**

a. DATE CHIEF OF STAFF NOTIFIED: ___________
Chief of Staff is notified by Vice President of Medical Affairs immediately upon receipt of request.

b. DATE MSC NOTIFIED: ___________
Medical Staff Coordinator is notified re: Receipt of Request for Hearing.

c. DATE LEGAL AFFAIRS NOTIFIED: ___________
Legal Affairs

continues

Exhibit 9–2 continued

d. DATE VP OF MED. AFFAIRS NOTIFIED: ____________
Vice President of Medical Affairs

e. DATE DEPT. CHAIR NOTIFIED: ____________
Department Chairman

f. DATE MSREP NOTIFIED: _____________
Medical Staff Representative

XI. **DATE RECEIVED REQUEST FOR HEARING:** ___________
SCHEDULE HEARING BY: __________
Hearing Committee appointed to convene within 60 calendar days following receipt of Request for Hearing. (NOTE: Eight or nine members of the attending staff selected randomly from numerical listings; at least one should be the same medical specialty as physician requesting the hearing.) Verify with Medical Affairs regarding the Hearing Committee involved in the case.

XII. **HEARING COMMITTEE SELECTION PROCESS:**

a. __________ *Random list is compiled by Director of MSS.*

b. __________ *Verify eligibility of Hearing Committee members selected with the MSC responsible for the department of the practitioner.*

c. __________ *Memo directed to Chief of Staff for approval of Hearing Committee Members.*

XIII. **DATE SENT APPOINTMENT LETTERS:**
Hearing Committee Appointment Letters marked "CONFIDENTIAL" and which include the paragraph from the Notice of Charges is sent by the Chief of Staff.

XIV. **DATE RESPONSE TO APPOINTMENT DUE:** __________
Response to Notice of Appointment due from Hearing Committee members within 5 business days.

XV. **DATE FOLLOW-UP PHONE CALLS TO HEARING COMMITTEE COMPLETED:**
____
Follow-up telephone calls to Hearing Committee members who have not responded to appointment.

XVI. **OPTION DATES:** _______, _______, _______, _______.
Hearing dates must be coordinated with (select variety of dates. Ask when not available).

XVII. **PARTICIPANTS**

a. Affected Practitioner ___________________________________
_______ ________ ________

b. Hearing Officer ____
(Confirm with Legal Affairs to arrange orientation. NOTE: If the Hearing Officer is not acceptable to practitioner, the practitioner is provided with a list of three names and is requested to choose two out of the three.)
__________________ ____________________ ____________________

c. Hearing Committee Members
1. ____
______________ _______________ _______________

continues

Exhibit 9–2 continued

2. ______________________________
______ ______ ______

3. ______________________________
______ ______ ______

4. ______________________________
______ ______ ______

5. ______________________________
______ ______ ______

6. ______________________________
______ ______ ______

7. ______________________________
______ ______ ______

8. ______________________________
______ ______ ______

d. *Medical Staff Representative(s): (Is informed of responsibilities—includes the right of Medical Staff Representative to request a witness to be excused.)*

1. ______________________________
______ ______ ______

2. ______________________________
______ ______ ______

e. *Witnesses*

1. ______________________________
______ ______ ______

2. ______________________________
______ ______ ______

3. ______________________________
______ ______ ______

4. ______________________________
______ ______ ______

f. Legal Counsel ______________________________
(Verify with Legal Affairs.)
______ ______ ______

g. Practitioner's Legal Counsel ______________________________
______ ______ ______

h. Medical Staff Coordinator ______________________________
______ ______ ______

i. Court Reporter ______________________________
______ ______ ______

XVIII. **DATE CONFIRMED ROOM ARRANGEMENTS:** ______________

______________ *Location*
______________ *Contact*
______________ *Extension*

continues

Exhibit 9–2 continued

XIX. **DATE MAILED NOTICE OF HEARING: ___________**

Vice President of Medical Affairs sends Notice of Hearing to (modified from Notice of Charges):

a. ___________ *Affected Practitioner (Certified Mail—Return Receipt Requested)*

b. ___________ *Chief of Staff*

c. ___________ *Chairman of Department*

d. ___________ *Division Director*

e. ___________ *Medical Staff Representative*

f. ___________ *Practitioner's Representative*

g. ___________ *Legal Affairs*

h. ___________ *Outside Legal Counsel*

i. ___________ *Practitioner's Legal Counsel*

j. ___________ *Hearing Officer*

k. ___________ *Hearing Committee Members*

l. ___________ *Witnesses*

m. ___________ *Court Reporter*

n. ___________ *Medical Staff Coordinator/Director*

XX. **DATE MAILED MATERIAL TO HEARING OFFICER: _________**

Hearing Officer Receives:

a. ___________ *Bylaws of the Medical Staff*

b. ___________ *Medical Staff Rules and Regulations*

c. ___________ *Notice of Charges*

d. ___________ *Department/Division Rules and Regulations*

e. ___________ *Hearing Manual*

f. ___________ *Other:* ____

____

XXI. **DATE SENT CATERING REQUEST: ___________**

Catering request completed.

XXII. **DOCUMENTATION**

The manner in which proceedings shall be recorded:

__________ *Court Reporter* ___________ *Video Tape*

__________ *Audio Tape*

XXIII. **DATE OF OBJECTION(S): ___________**

Objections received from affected practitioner relative to:

a. __________ *Hearing Date*

b. __________ *Committee Members*

c. __________ *Manner of Recording*

d. __________ *Other:* ____

____

____

continues

Exhibit 9–2 continued

Resolution: ____
____
____
____

Postponements must be requested in writing supported by a written factual showing good cause. The Hearing Officer may postpone in accordance with the Bylaws.

Postponement Requested ____________________

By ____

Reason ____

Postponement Approved ____________________

By ____

Postponement Denied ____________________

By ____

Reason for Denial ____________________
____
____

DATE HEARING RESCHEDULED: __________

__________ *Catering Contacted*

__________ *Room Arrangements Confirmed*

Notification of Postponement/Rescheduled Hearing is sent to distribution list as in XIX/a-n, of this protocol.

XXIV. __________ **DOCUMENTARY EVIDENCE**

Prepared for presentation at hearing as required by Hearing Manual. Evidence is prepared in consultation with other pertinent departments.

XXV. **DATE COMPLETED COURTESY REMINDER CALLS:** __________

Courtesy reminder calls 5 days before hearing date to:

a. Committee Members
b. Witnesses
c. Medical Staff Representative
d. Legal Counsel
e. Hearing Officer
f. Court Reporter
g. Confirm Room Arrangements

XXVI. **HEARING CONVENED:** __________ **DATE:** __________

Quorum is 3 members

Failure to appear or refusal to attend the hearing without good cause, by the practitioner, will be deemed acceptance of recommendation of actions involved which shall become final immediately upon the Hearing Committee's determination of a lack of good cause for failure to appear. Chief of Staff, Vice President of Medical Affairs will evaluate the requirement of attendance regarding the Hearing Officer, Medical Staff Representative, Legal Counsel, and the Medical Staff Coordinators.

continues

Exhibit 9–2 continued

XXVII. CONTINUATION DATE ________ DATE NOTIFICATION SENT __________

CONTINUATION DATE ________ DATE NOTIFICATION SENT __________

CONTINUATION DATE ________ DATE NOTIFICATION SENT __________

CONTINUATION DATE ________ DATE NOTIFICATION SENT __________

(See distribution list in XIX/a-n, as above.)

XXVIII. **DATE HEARING ADJOURNED: ___________**

XXIX. **DATE HRG COMMITTEE DECISION DUE TO MEC: ___________**
DATE RECEIVED HRG COMMITTEE DECISION: ___________
MEC receives written decision (within 30 calendar days after final adjournment or 15 calendar days if practitioner is under suspension).

a. **DATE CONTACTED HEARING OFFICER: ___________**
Hearing Officer contacted to present report to MEC.

b. **DATE MEC MEETING: ___________**

XXX. **FINDINGS AND RECOMMENDATIONS OF MEC:**

__________ *Hearing Committee Report upheld by MEC*

__________ *Hearing Committee Report overturned by MEC*

Comments: ____

____

____

____

XXXI. **DATE FINAL REPORT DUE TO PRACTITIONER: __________**
Decision and report to affected practitioner with rights of appeal included. Sent by Vice President of Medical Affairs by Certified Mail/Return Receipt Requested (must be within 15 days of MEC meeting).

DATE SENT FINAL REPORT TO PRACTITIONER: ___________

LAST DATE DUE FOR REQUEST FOR AN APPEAL: ___________
(30 calendar days of Receipt of Notice [of final report].)

XXXII. **MEC'S REPORT TO EXECUTIVE COMMITTEE OF THE BOARD: ________**
Medical Executive Committee's decision and report to Executive Committee of the Board (for information only).

XXXIII. **DATE RECEIVED APPEAL: ___________**
Appeal requested. (Request for Appeal must be received within 30 calendar days of Receipt of Notice [final report to practitioner].)

XXXIV. **GROUNDS FOR APPEAL**

____

____

____

____

continues

Exhibit 9–2 continued

a. **DATE SENT NOTIFICATION OF REQUEST FORAPPEAL TO BOARD:________**
Notification of Request for Appeal to President of Board from Vice President for Medical Affairs.

1. ___________ *Date notified Legal Affairs*

2. ___________ *Date notified in-house counsel*

b. **DATE DUE FOR SCHEDULING APPEAL COMMITTEE:** ___________
Appeal Committee Hearing (must be scheduled within 30 calendar days of receipt of request).

1. _________________ *Date*

2. _________________ *Time*

3. _________________ *Location* _________ *confirmed*

4. Committee

_________________________________, *Chairman*

_________________________________, *Member*

_________________________________, *Member*

5. _________________ *Catering* _________ *confirmed*

c. **DATE SENT NOTIFICATION TO PRACTITIONER RE: APPEAL COMMITTEE HEARING:** ___________

Notification to Affected Practitioner regarding Appeal Committee Hearing (cc: Appeal Committee Members and Vice President of Medical Affairs).

d. _________ DATE CONTACTED COURT REPORTER

e. _________ DATE CONTACTED OUTSIDE LEGAL REPRESENTATIVE

f. _________ DATE PREPARED DOCUMENTS FOR APPEAL COMMITTEE MEMBERS

g. _________ DATE SET FOR APPEAL COMMITTEE MEMBERS' ORIENTATION WITH LEGAL COUNSEL

XXXV. **DATE APPEAL COMMITTEE CONVENED:** ____________

XXXVI. **DATE APPEAL COMMITTEE ADJOURNED:** ____________

XXXVII. **DATE BOARD RECEIVED APPEAL COMMITTEE REPORT:** ___________
Board of Directors receive conclusion of the Appeal Committee (shall not exceed 45 calendar days from adjournment of Appeal Committee).

XXXVIII. **DATE BOARD TAKES FINAL ACTION:** ___________
Board of Directors takes final action:

1. ___________ *Render final decision in writing.*

2. ___________ *Remand back to MEC.*

3. ___________ *Remand back to Hearing Committee.*

continues

Exhibit 9–2 continued

XXXIX. **DATE FINAL DECISION DELIVERED TO PRACTITIONER: ________**
(Certified Mail/Return Receipt Requested.)

XL. **DATE FINAL DECISION DELIVERED TO MEC: _________**

XLI. **DATE ADVERSE ACTION REPORT FILED: __________**
In accordance with the Health Care Quality Improvement Act, if applicable, an Adverse Action Report should be filed with the Medical Board of California (MBC) within 15 days of final action by the hospital's Board of Directors. MBC then has 15 days within which to forward the Adverse Action Report to the National Practitioner Data Bank.

REASON NOT FILED: ______________________________

NOTE: In accordance with the Bylaws, the practitioner does not have any further appeal rights within the hospital medical staff structure. The next level in the appeal process would involve the filing of a Writ of Mandamus in Civil Court.

Note: NPDB, National Practitioner Data Bank; MSC, medical staff coordinator; MSS, medical staff services; HRG, hearing; MEC, medical executive committee; MSREP, medical staff representative.

Courtesy of Cedars-Sinai Medical Center, Los Angeles, California.

- The credentialing process document, which defines
  - the practitioner's right to review information submitted in support of his or her application
  - the process for notifying the practitioner of any information obtained during the managed care organization's process that varies substantially from that submitted by the practitioner
  - the practitioner's right to correct erroneous information[14]

Similarly, the NCQA standards for the certification of physician organizations include requirements for policies and procedures for altering the conditions of the practitioner's participation.

Joint Commission standards for ambulatory care require "defined procedures for discontinuing appointments and curtailing clinical privileges, and consideration of appeals on decisions to discontinue appointment or denial of privileges."[15] The intent of the standard states that the procedure for handling appeals includes

- a mechanism for scheduling hearings
- the procedures to be followed at a hearing
- composition of the hearing panel
- an agenda for the hearing[16]

Other accrediting and certifying bodies also require such policies and procedures. Before the establishment of these various bodies, most group practices and physician organizations did not have formal policies and procedures in place concerning fair hearing and due process. Most difficult situations were handled as they appeared and were probably not handled consistently. Ini-

Exhibit 9–3 Due-Process Review Checklist

PRACTITIONER/lawyer:

Hearing Officer:
MS Rep:
MSO:

NPDB: due ____________ NPDB: filed ____________ Board copies: ____________

~ ______	DUE DATE FOR	SUMMARY SUSPENSION: Memo notifying departments of removed privileges (to distribution)	DATE [ ] ______
~ ______	DUE DATE FOR	SUMMARY SUSPENSION: [ ] REF TEXT to ADMINISTRATION [ ] PROFILE TO ADMINISTRATION	DATE [ ] ______
______	DUE DATE FOR	MS Rep appoint/call Department Chair Dr. [ ] is appointed	DATE [ ] ______
______	DUE DATE FOR	MS Rep appoint/FAX Dr. -ACCEPTS -CALL FOR MEETING WITH	DATE [ ] ______
______	DATE SENT	Notice of charges/Certified receipt #	DATE [ ] ______
______	DUE DATE FOR	Notice of charges/Certified receipt returned	DATE [ ] ______
______	DUE DATE FOR	Request for Hearing/NOT RECEIVED (30 days from notice of charges)	DATE [ ] ______
~ ______	DUE DATE FOR	Request for Hearing/NOT RECEIVED; Notification Memo—REQUEST FOR HEARING NOT RECEIVED to distribution	DATE [ ] ______
~ ______	DUE DATE FOR	Request for Hearing/NOT RECEIVED; LETTER to practitioner/RECOMMEND ACTION BECOMES FINAL	DATE [ ] ______
______	DUE DATE FOR	Request for Hearing/RECEIVED: due 30 days from date on returned certified receipt to Medical Staff Office	DATE [ ] ______
~ ______	DUE DATE FOR	Request for Hearing/RECEIVED: Memo notifying practitioner's request for hearing sent to distribution	DATE [ ] ______
~ ______	DUE DATE FOR	Response to Request for hearing/DRAFT VP SIGN MAIL	DATE [ ] ______
______	DUE DATE FOR	Request for documentation (e.g., witnesses, documents) due 30 days before hearing date	DATE [ ] ______
______	DUE DATE FOR	Intent for no legal representation (per practitioner) due 30 days before hearing date	DATE [ ] ______
______	DUE DATE FOR	Request for documents/evidence: presented at hearing due 10 days before hearing date	DATE [ ] ______
______	DUE DATE FOR	Setting hearing date: due more than 30 days but less than 60	DATE [ ] ______
______	DUE DATE FOR	Hearing Officer appointment/Call suggested Hearing Officer	DATE [ ] ______
______	DUE DATE FOR	Hearing Officer appointment/Call Hearing Officer to meeting with:	DATE [ ] ______
~ ______	DUE DATE FOR	Hearing Officer appointment/Notice of charges, e.g., sent to Hearing Office	DATE [ ] ______
______	DUE DATE FOR	Hearing Committee appointment/Compile random list	DATE [ ] ______
~ ______	DUE DATE FOR	Hearing Committee appointment/Memo to Chief of Staff CoS approves:	DATE [ ] ______
~ ______	DUE DATE FOR	Hearing Committee appointment/Appointment letters sent	DATE [ ] ______
______	DUE DATE FOR	Hearing Committee appointment/Appointment letters response (5 days from appointment letters sent)	DATE [ ] ______
______	DUE DATE FOR	Hearing Committee appointment/EXCUSE letters [ ] transfer to "dump" list	DATE [ ] ______
______	DUE DATE FOR	Hearing Committee appointment/Preliminary meeting with: Call/schedule meeting:	DATE [ ] ______
______	DATE FOR	HEARING	DATE [ ] ______
~ ______	DUE DATE FOR	Notice of hearing/DRAFT VP SIGN SENT	DATE [ ] ______
______	DUE DATE FOR	Notice of Hearing/Certified receipt returned from practitioner	DATE [ ] ______

________	DUE DATE FOR	Hearing/Room—catering booked	DATE [ ] ________
________	DUE DATE FOR	Notice of hearing/Confirmations	DATE [ ] ________
________	DUE DATE FOR	Hearing/Exhibits for committee, e.g., compiled	DATE [ ] ________
________	DUE DATE FOR	Request for postponed/rescheduled hearing received from practitioner	DATE [ ] ________
~ ________	DUE DATE FOR	Response to request for continuance of hearing	DATE [ ] ________
________	DATE FOR	Notice of POSTPONED/RESCHEDULED HEARING:	DATE [ ] ________
________	DUE DATE FOR	Response to request for continuance of hearing	DATE [ ] ________
________	DATE FOR	HEARING 2	DATE [ ] ________
________	DATE FOR	HEARING ADJOURNED	DATE [ ] ________
________	DUE DATE FOR	MEC/Hearing Committee decision to Medical Staff Office/30 days after adjourned; 15 days if suspended.	DATE [ ] ________
________	DUE DATE FOR	MEC/Hearing officer contacted/scheduled to present report to MEC	DATE [ ] ________
________	DUE DATE FOR	MEC/Post hearing: DO/NEED/GET:	DATE [ ] ________
________	DATE FOR	MEC meets/adjourns	DATE [ ] ________
~ ________	DUE DATE FOR	MEC/DECISION OF MEC IN THE MATTER OF M.D. DRAFTED PRINTED SIGNED	DATE [ ] ________
~ ________	DUE DATE FOR	MEC/MEMO RE DECISION OF MEC w/ HEARING COMMITTEE REPORTS sent to Board (for fyi)	DATE [ ] ________
~ ________	DUE DATE FOR	MEC/NOTICE OF MEC RECOMMENDED DECISION sent to practitioner (15 days after MEC adjourns)	DATE [ ] ________
________	DATE SENT	Notice of MEC's recommended decision/certified receipt #	DATE [ ] ________
________	DUE DATE FOR	Notice of MEC's recommended decision/certified receipt returned	DATE [ ] ________
________	DUE DATE FOR	IF NO APPEAL/MEMO to Exec Chair = [ ] M.D., NO APPEAL REQUESTED (30 days from date on certified receipt)	DATE [ ] ________
________	DUE DATE FOR	IF NO APPEAL/final letter to practitioner "no appeal requested, recommended charges final"	DATE [ ] ________
________	DUE DATE FOR	if SUMMARY SUSPENSION: to Medical Board/Notices, Charts, Exhibits, NPDB, letter. etc.	DATE [ ] ________
________	DUE DATE FOR	if SUBPOENA/ 1. [ ] initial material to Medical Board 2. [ ] final material to Medical Board	DATE [ ] ________
________	DUE DATE FOR	FINAL/ [ ] HEALTH USER MAINTENANCE FORM TO ADMINISTRATION [ ] UPDATE MASTERLIST [ ] CLOSE OUT ELECT FILE	DATE [ ] ________
________	DUE DATE FOR	FINAL/REFERENCE LETTER TEXT DRAFTED	DATE [ ] ________
________	DUE DATE FOR	SETTLEMENT [ ] AGREEMENT [ ] MEMO NOTIFYING DIST (NO HEARING HELD) [ ] PROFILE [ ] F. LETTER	DATE [ ] ________
________	DUE DATE FOR	IF NO APPEAL/Letter to practitioner "no appeal/recom act final" cc: chair/Exec Comm/Brd/CoS	DATE [ ] ________
________	DUE DATE FOR	Appeal/Certified receipt returned from practitioner	DATE [ ] ________
________	DUE DATE FOR	Appeal/Request for appeal: 30 days after practitioner receives MEC decision	DATE [ ] ________
________	DUE DATE FOR	Appeal/Request for appeal: Set appeal hearing date by (30 days from "request for appeal")	DATE [ ] ________
~ ________	DUE DATE FOR	Appeal/Memo notifying Appeal Committee Chair of request for hearing sent	DATE [ ] ________

continues

Exhibit 9–3 continued

~ ______	DUE DATE FOR	Appeal/Response to request for appeal sent	DATE [ ] ______
______	DUE DATE FOR	Appeal/Committee members selected	DATE [ ] ______
~ ______	DUE DATE FOR	Appeal/Memo to Chief of Staff re: Appeal Committee members	DATE [ ] ______
~ ______	DUE DATE FOR	Appeal/Appointment to Appeal Committee members letters sent	DATE [ ] ______
______	DUE DATE FOR	Appeal/Preliminary committee meeting/meet with:	DATE [ ] ______
______	DUE DATE FOR	Appeal/Preliminary committee meeting/Calls: coordinate preliminary meeting	DATE [ ] ______
~ ______	DUE DATE FOR	Appeal/Notification of hearing sent	DATE [ ] ______
______	DUE DATE FOR	Appeal/Room-catering booked	DATE [ ] ______
______	DUE DATE FOR	Appeal/Hearing transcripts xeroxed/Exhibits compiled	DATE [ ] ______
______	DUE DATE FOR	Appeal/CONFIRMATIONS	DATE [ ] ______
______	DUE DATE FOR	HEARING/Appeal	DATE [ ] ______
______	DUE DATE FOR	Request for postponed/rescheduled appeal hearing received from practitioner	DATE [ ] ______
~ ______	DUE DATE FOR	Response to request for continuance of appeal hearing	DATE [ ] ______
______	DUE DATE FOR	POSTPONED/Rescheduled	DATE [ ] ______
______	DUE DATE FOR	HEARING-2/Appeal	DATE [ ] ______
______	DUE DATE FOR	POSTPONED-2/Rescheduled	DATE [ ] ______
______	DATE FOR	Appeal/APPEAL COMMITTEE MEETS/ADJOURNS	DATE [ ] ______
______	DUE DATE FOR	Appeal/Committee Chair contacted for follow-up re: decision	DATE [ ] ______
______	DUE DATE FOR	Appeal/APPEAL COMMITTEE REPORT AND RECOMMENDATION	DATE [ ] ______
______	DUE DATE FOR	Appeal/Appeal Comm. report & recomm. to BOARD (45 days from Appeal Comm. adjournment)	DATE [ ] ______
______	DATE FOR	Board/Adjourns	DATE [ ] ______
~ ______	DUE DATE FOR	Board/FINAL WRITTEN DECISION OF THE BOARD OF DIRECTORS: DRAFT Pres's signature:	DATE [ ] ______
______	DUE DATE FOR	Board/final written decision sent to practitioner (no time limit) [ ] CC: LAWYERS	DATE [ ] ______
______	DUE DATE FOR	Board/DATE ACTION BECOMES FINAL (date final decision sent to practitioner)	DATE [ ] ______
~ ______	DUE DATE FOR	Board/MEMO from Board Chair—Notifying MEC of FINAL DECISION	DATE [ ] ______
______	DUE DATE FOR	Board/[ ] HEALTH USER MAINT. FORM TO ADMIN [ ] UPDATE MASTERLIST [ ] CLOSE OUT ELECT FILE	DATE [ ] ______
______	DUE DATE FOR	Board/Remand to MEC	DATE [ ] ______
______	DUE DATE FOR	Board/Remand to Hearing Committee	DATE [ ] ______
______	DUE DATE FOR	if SUMMARY SUSPENSION: to Medical Board/Notices, Charts, Exhibits, NPDB, letter. etc.	DATE [ ] ______
______	DUE DATE FOR	if SUBPOENA/[ ] final material to Medical Board	DATE [ ] ______
______	DUE DATE FOR	REFERENCE LETTER TEXT DRAFTED	DATE [ ] ______

~COMPLETE PROTOCOL CHECKLIST

Final: keep in hearing file: copies
transfer to credential file: originals

A. from Judicial Hearing
1. MEC's final letter to practitioner
2. Hearing Committee Report to MEC
3. Notice of hearing
4. Response to request for hearing
5. Request for hearing

B. Appeal
1. Board's final letter to practitioner
2. Appeal Comm. report to Board
3. Notice of hearing—Appeal
4. Request for Appeal

C. LOG IN MASTER LIST

SETUP

MASS II
1. Create electronic folder
2. Create list (copy variables/Hearing)
   a. enter charges, addresses known, etc.
3. copy Judicial Review/Protocol = fill out top/print
4. DUE DATE CHKLIST/update
5. STAT/LOG/update
6. make GRID/individual
7. GRID ALL/update

FILES
1. Labels/hearing book/due date bk/folder
2. Label folder

Note: MEC, medical executive committee; CoS, chief of staff; NPDB, National Practitioner Data Bank.

Courtesy of Cedars-Sinai Medical Center, Los Angeles, California.

tial policies and procedures used by managed care organizations have been much less formal and detailed, providing fewer procedural rights than the processes detailed in the hospital setting. With the advent of accreditation standards, these processes are being revised by managed care organizations and are becoming more formal.

By establishing a detailed, fair process, a managed care organization will ensure that objective standards are used in making credentialing decisions and will satisfy the participating practitioner's need and expectation for a fair process, as has been established in the hospital setting for many years. Additionally, it will allow qualification for immunity as outlined by the Health Care Quality Improvement Act as long as the organization has a process that fully complies with the act's procedural requirements:

- Peer review action is taken in the reasonable belief that the action was in the furtherance of quality health care.
- Action is taken only after reasonable effort is made to obtain the facts of the matter.
- The affected physician is provided adequate notice and hearing procedures.
- There is a reasonable belief that the action is warranted.[17]

Many of the components outlined in the hospital setting for corrective action could also be used in the managed care setting. At the minimum, an investigation and corrective action policy should include

1. Types of behavior that would initiate an investigation—that is, anything that could be detrimental to the quality of patient care or safety, the organization's operations, or the community's confidence in the organization
2. How an investigation may be initiated and by whom, whether the request must be in writing, to whom it should be submitted, the required attached documentation, and the time frame in which the medical director or other identified person must respond
3. If a group or another individual (other than the medical director) conducts the investigation, a written report and a time frame for submitting the report
4. If an initial interview with the practitioner in question is allowed, the parameters of that interview, including who would be allowed to conduct it, what information should be provided to the practitioner before the interview, whether a written record will be maintained of the interview, where the final record will be kept, who will be allowed access to the report, and repercussions to the practitioner for failing to participate or declining the interview
5. Actions available to the medical director after the initial interview or at the conclusion of the investigation, which may include:
   - rejection of the request for investigation
   - formal warning letter or reprimand
   - probationary period with retrospective review of cases, without special requirements for concurrent consultation or direct supervision
   - suspension of the practitioner's participation in the group or plan or for the treatment of specific types of patients or diagnoses
   - requirements for direct supervision or consultation
   - reduction, suspension, or limitation of the practitioner's participation or practice in providing care for the plan's patients
6. A description of any deferral options available to the medical director, including a description of the situations in which a deferral would be possible and an accompanying time frame for deferral before reconsideration
7. A definition of the procedural rights that will be afforded the practitioner if the medical director recommends removal from the member panel or suspension or

limitation of the practitioner's participation in the plan

8. A definition of "other actions" that the medical director might take that would not afford the practitioner any procedural rights, possibly including:
   - a warning or reprimand
   - required additional education or training or counseling
   - reduction of prerogatives that would not affect the practitioner's practice
   - probation with retrospective monitoring
9. A listing of issues that would initiate an automatic suspension of the practitioner, who is authorized to suspend, what type of notice should be provided, and how it should be delivered to the practitioner; the listed issues would be similar to those for hospitals, including
   - revocation, suspension, restriction, or probation of practitioner's state license to practice or federal or state drug enforcement certificate
   - failure to maintain adequate professional liability insurance
   - failure to comply with the managed care organization's policies and procedures relevant to office requirements or medical records maintenance
   - failure to respond to requests for an interview or to investigational questioning
   - loss of hospital privileges or membership for quality-of-care or professional conduct reasons
   - failure to maintain compliance with general criteria
   - engagement in conduct that violates state law or standards of ethical conduct governing his or her practice
   - commission of a felony or other act involving dishonesty, fraud, deceit, or misrepresentation
10. A listing of issues that would initiate a summary suspension of the practitioner, who has the authority to suspend, what type of notice needs to be provided to the practitioner, and how it should be delivered; the listed issues would be similar to those for hospitals, including conduct requiring that immediate action be taken to prevent danger to life, or injury to the practitioner, patients, employees, or other persons present in the organization's facilities
11. Actions by the medical director relevant to the suspended practitioner's patients (i.e., notification of the suspension, provision of an alternate practitioner, and time frame for action)
12. What the practitioner must do, or period of time that must pass before reapplying for participation (e.g., "Practitioner must wait at least 12 months before reapplying after being disciplined or suspended")[18]

All corrective actions are based upon "peer review" activities of the organization. Peer review may be defined and structured very differently in managed and ambulatory care than in a hospital. How peer review is conducted is determined by the state law requirements, the market conditions, and the control of the organization. Typically, the ambulatory or managed care organization establishes a quality assessment/performance improvement plan that includes peer review process and policies and procedures and further defines the corrective action process. When a provider contracts with the organization, he or she should be made aware of the relevant components of the plan and be informed of the corrective action process. The contract should also include the requirement that he or she will agree to fully participate in and cooperate with the credentialing, quality assessment/performance review, and utilization management programs. It is important that the physician contract wording be coordinated with the corrective action procedure to ensure that there is only one way for a specific issue to be handled and that the practitioner is clear about his or her rights and the procedures that must be followed.

AMERICANS WITH DISABILITIES ACT

The Americans with Disabilities Act is a comprehensive federal law designed to eliminate discrimination on the basis of disability. Title I of the act prohibits discrimination by a covered entity against a qualified individual with a disability because of the disability, in relation to application procedures, hiring, compensation, training, advancement, and other aspects of employment.[19] The question that each health care entity must answer is whether to modify its credentialing procedures to conform to the requirements of the Act. The Act may have implications for all health care settings, and several accrediting organizations reference it.

The Joint Commission standards specify four major professional criteria to be used in the assessment of an applicant requesting clinical privileges: current licensure, relevant training or experience, current competence and ability to perform the privileges requested. Before the 1997 standards, the last criterion listed by the Joint Commission was "health status." The change in wording to "ability to perform" was implemented in response to the Americans with Disabilities Act. The 1998 Joint Commission Hospital Accreditation Medical Staff Standards include the following comments relevant to the Act:

> The Americans with Disabilities Act (ADA) bars certain discrimination based on physical or mental impairment. Toward preventing such discrimination, the Act prohibits or mandates various activities. Hospitals need to determine the applicability of the ADA to their medical staff. If applicable, the hospital should examine its privileging or credentialing procedures as to how and when it ascertains and confirms the ability of an applicant to perform the privileges requested. For example, the act may prohibit inquiry as to the physical or mental health status of an applicant prior to making an offer of membership and privileges, but may not prohibit such inquiry after an offer is extended (contingent on the ascertainment of health status). The Act does not appear to prohibit inquiry as to the ability of the applicant (without specified reference to health matters) to perform the specific privileges requested. Thus, this latter inquiry may be made and confirmed as a component of the applicant process. The Joint Commission cannot provide legal advice to hospitals. However, the Joint Commission has and will absolutely construe MS 5.4 through MS 5.4.3, MS 5.10.1, and MS 5.10.1.1 in such a manner as not to be inconsistent with hospital efforts to comply with the ADA.[20]

The Joint Commission still requires verification of current health status. Because of the Americans with Disabilities Act, the interpretation for the standard requiring verification of current health status has been more flexible; however, most surveyors still expect to see some comment on the health status of an applicant. Health status can be verified by the director of a training program, the chief of service or chief of staff from another hospital where the applicant holds privileges, or a currently licensed physician designated by the hospital.

NCQA also has specific wording concerning the status of an applicant in its credentialing standards. Criteria 4.1 and 7.7.1 state, "The applicant completes an application for membership. The application includes a statement by the applicant regarding reasons for any inability to perform the essential functions of the position, with or without accommodation" and Criteria 4.2 and 7.7.2 stipulate "lack of present illegal drug use."[21]

Although, on its face, the Americans with Disabilities Act appears to apply only to employees, many legal counsels have concluded that the courts will interpret the provisions of this law to protect all members of a hospital medical staff, whether employed or not. The issue for health care organizations then becomes whether they will consider the questions that practitioners can be asked about their health status, as well as the questions that can be asked on reference questionnaires regarding the health status of applicants and, in hospitals, the questions that can be asked of department chiefs with regard to observed performance in the reappointment process.

Legally, there is strong support that the courts will interpret the law to apply to practitioners who have staff privileges, or who are affiliated with a managed care organization, as if they are employees. For that reason, most hospitals and managed care organizations have adjusted what was previously known as "the health status questions" that were included on the applications for appointment and reappointment.

The Americans with Disabilities Act prohibits discrimination against "qualified individuals with disabilities." A qualified individual with a disability is defined as "an individual with a disability who meets the skill, experience, education and other job-related requirements of a position held or desired, and who, with or without accommodation, can perform the essential functions of the job."[22] The Act is very specific concerning the definition of an individual with a disability: It is a person who has a physical or mental impairment that substantially limits one or more of his/her major life activities, has a record of such impairment, or is regarded as having such an impairment."[23] An applicant may not be asked about the existence, nature, or severity of a disability but may be asked about his or her ability to perform specific functions.

After an initial offer to join the medical staff or to become a participating practitioner is made, the health care organization can make medical inquiries or conduct a medical examination. The offer to join the medical staff or become a participating practitioner can be conditioned on the results of a medical examination or inquiry, but only if it is required of all physicians seeking staff appointment, privileges, or affiliation.

What Do *Reasonable Accommodation* and *Undue Hardship* Mean?

Under the Americans with Disabilities Act, *reasonable accommodation* is defined as any change in the work environment or in the way things are typically done that results in equal employment opportunity for an individual with a disability. Examples might be modifying work schedules, acquiring or modifying equipment or devices, and job restructuring.

Undue hardship is defined as an action that is excessively costly, extensive, substantial, or disruptive or that would fundamentally alter the nature or operation of the business.

IMPAIRED PRACTITIONER

Dealing with an impairment or with alcohol or drug misuse is a very uncomfortable situation for everyone involved. Medical staff leaders do not want to admit that such situations could involve practitioners, so they are not always willing to initiate policies for handling them. Two things should be stressed when initiating these discussions: (1) consistency is the best approach, ensuring that there is no difference in how employees and medical staff members are treated when such situations occur; (2) practitioners are human beings and are often troubled with the same problems as everyone else. By developing policies to address these situations before they arise, the medical staff can avoid taking the "look-away" approach and can instead offer a fair, consistent, positive approach that will help the individual in question to obtain the help required for rehabilitation while ensuring that the leaders in the organization are taking the appropriate steps to protect the patients and other health care workers.

Practitioner drug and alcohol abuse is of great concern to health care organizations during the credentialing process, since such abuse could pose a great threat to patient safety. The Americans with Disabilities Act does permit an employer to ensure that the workplace is free from the illegal use of drugs and alcohol. However, the ADA also provides protection from discrimination for those physicians recovering from drug or alcohol addiction. A health care organization may inquire about and refuse to appoint or associate with individuals who are currently engaged in the illegal use of drugs. However, if the individual is undergoing or has undergone treatment or rehabilitation for drug use, he or she is protected under the Americans with Disabilities Act.

An alcoholic is a person with a disability and is also protected by the ADA if he or she is qualified to perform the essential functions of the job. However that physician may be disciplined, terminated, or denied employment or association if his or her use of alcohol adversely affects the exercise of clinical privileges or practice. Alcoholism is a disability under the ADA, but alcohol use that affects job performance is not. Unsatisfactory behavior such as absenteeism, tardiness, poor job performance, or accidents caused by alcohol or illegal drug use need not be accepted or accommodated.

Health care organizations are also grappling with the issue of physicians who may be HIV positive or have other infectious diseases. Most of these diagnoses will qualify as a disability, so can the health care organization restrict or limit the infected physician's privileges or practice? The key issue is whether there is an impairment that results in a direct threat to the health and safety of others, including patients, in the workplace. The courts will look to current medical and scientific data and the judgment of public health officials in assessing such situations. Unfortunately, the opinions of courts on such issues have not been consistent.[24]

Issues of impairment are not easily handled. The best that a health care organization can do is establish a fair process that may include

- Asking a simple, law-abiding health question on the application such as "Are you able to perform the privileges you are requesting?" In a managed care setting, there will also need to be a direct question concerning the current use of illegal drugs as well as a rewording of the question to reflect practice rather than "privileges."
- Establishing a process that would enable a medical examination or health status inquiry to take place after the offer is made. This could be instituted at some point after the credentials committee has made a conditional recommendation of acceptance of the application. Some organizations initiate a thorough health status questionnaire at this point; others wait until the application has been approved by the governing body before initiating the health questionnaire. Consistency is the key—everyone must be questioned at the same time in the process, with the same questions.
- Establishing a process that will help deal with issues as they arise—for example, initiating a practitioner well-being committee (physician health committee separate from the credentials committee) to which all health-related issues will be forwarded for consideration. The organization must be prepared to further investigate a health-related issue if one becomes apparent.
- Ensuring that the process is reviewed by legal counsel and that the group identified to handle health care issues is sufficiently educated and supported so that they thoroughly understand their role and accountability and feel comfortable with their responsibilities.
- Developing a model health policy with the goal of maintaining and improving the quality of patient care through the support and encouragement of good health among medical professionals.

The components of the policy (most likely found in the hospital setting) could include

1. Definition of an "impaired" physician—for example, "one who is unable to practice medicine with reasonable skill and

safety to patients because of a physical or mental illness, including deterioration through the aging process or loss of motor skill, or excessive use/misuse of drugs, including alcohol"

2. Support of the peer review and quality assessment/performance improvement processes of the medical staff through functions that evaluate the health of its members
3. Provision of an informal system for assistance at initial stages
4. Provision of a structured system for the support and enhancement of the health of a physician who has experienced a failure of performance associated with a health-related problem; this system should include the requirement that a verbal or written report be submitted to the department chair, the medical director/vice president of medical affairs, or the chief executive officer and that the investigation process and who will participate be defined.
5. Options for investigation, including
   - forming an ad hoc committee
   - use of a formal, organized physician health committee
   - engaging an outside consultant
   - directing a review by another individual
   - taking immediate action regarding the physician in question concerning privileges or practice allowances
6. Identification of what will happen to the report after the investigation, who shall be informed, and where the report will be maintained
7. Permission for the authorized medical staff leader(s) to require immediate physical or mental health examination or a blood test for substance abuse
8. Description of the options, based on the severity of the problem and the nature of the impairment:
   - requiring the practitioner to undertake a rehabilitation program
   - imposing appropriate restrictions on privileges or practice related to plan members
   - immediately suspending privileges/practice until rehabilitation has been accomplished
9. Identification of the point at which hospital legal counsel should be contacted
10. Establishment of the parameters of rehabilitation
11. Identification of the procedure for reinstatement after rehabilitation:
    - what letters of reference will be required, and from whom
    - required assessment from the physician's primary care physician
    - requirement that the practitioner identify two other physicians who will assume responsibility for his or her patients in the event of a relapse or unavailability
    - monitoring requirements, if so designated
    - time periods for additional testing
    - how requests for information from other health care entities concerning the physician will be handled (e.g., all to be handled by the medical director)

Exhibit 9–4 is a sample policy addressing impaired practitioners.

DRUG TESTING FOR APPLICANTS AND MEDICAL STAFF MEMBERS (HOSPITALS)

Many organizations have chosen not to confront the issue of drug testing for either employees or medical staff applicants or members. Other organizations have developed very specific policies that apply to both employees and medical staff members, including preemployment, premedical staff membership screening and required screening upon suspicion of use.

If the organization chooses to develop a drug test policy, the following items could be addressed:

Exhibit 9–4 Policy Regarding Impaired Practitioners

9.11.1 *Policy Regarding Members and Those Holding Clinical Privileges*

9.11.1.1 In formulating and pursuing any policy regarding impaired physicians, the following considerations should be borne in mind and set the tone for how we approach the issues. Doctors have devoted their study, skills and efforts to the treatment of persons' illnesses and the relief of their pain. They have also vowed to do no harm. Though impairment by an illness can render doctors ineffective or likely to do harm, their impairment is usually due to an illness which is treatable. The success rate for the treatment of impaired physicians "tends to run . . . higher . . . than for like disorders in the lay population, with reliable figures reported in the area of 78% to 87% success after five or more years of follow-up." (Walze, Robert S., M.D., J.D., "Impaired Physicians: an Overview and Update of the Legal Issues," *Journal of Legal Medicine* 11:131–198, 1990). Additionally, the return of a competent recovered physician results in significant economic savings over the training of a new practitioner. Further, an impaired physician deserves the same confidentiality as would be afforded any other patient, except where counterbalanced by the duty to protect others. There will always be a countervailing dynamic between the duty of his colleagues and his hospital to protect others and the right of the impaired physician to confidentiality. Those opposing dynamics will remain no matter what policies and rules are formulated and need careful attention from all the individuals entrusted to deal with all the issues of each impaired physician's situation.

9.11.1.2 This policy is directed to incidents which may occur at or affect the hospital; however, it is emphasized that physicians who have reasonable suspicion to believe a fellow physician is impaired, in or out of the hospital setting, may refer that physician directly to the Colorado Physician Health Program ("CPHP") for diagnosis and treatment.

9.11.1.3 Referring a physician under this policy or to CPHP does not discharge a physician's reporting obligations under the Colorado Medical Practice Act (12-36-118(3)). The duty to report to the Colorado Board of Medical Examiners must be evaluated on a case by case basis, preferably in consultation with legal council.

9.11.2 *Report & Investigation*

9.11.2.1 If any individual working in the hospital has a reasonable suspicion that a Medical Staff member, Medical Associate, or Medical Assistant (Practitioner) may be impaired because of mental or physical disability, including substance abuse, the following steps should be taken:

9.11.2.1.1 An oral or, preferably, a written report shall be made to the Chief Executive Officer or the Vice President of Medical Affairs. The report shall include a description of the incident(s) that led to the conclusion that the practitioner may be impaired. The report must be factual. The individual making the report does not need to have proof of the impairment, but must state the facts leading to reasonable suspicion.

9.11.2.1.2 If, after discussing the incident(s) with the individual who filed the report, the Chief Executive Officer or Vice President of Medical Affairs believes there is enough information to warrant an investigation, the Chief Executive Officer or Vice President of Medical Affairs shall direct that an investigation be instituted and a report thereof be rendered by one of the following:

(A) the Chief of Staff

(B) the Vice President of Medical Affairs

continues

Exhibit 9–4 continued

(C) a standing committee of the Medical Staff

(D) an outside consultant such as the Colorado Physician Health Program

(E) another individual or individuals appropriate under the circumstances

9.11.2.1.3 The CEO or the investigating person or body may require any medically appropriate testing including dementia screens. If a reasonable suspicion of impairment due to drug or alcohol abuse exists, the Chief Executive Officer, his designee including the Administrator on call, or any of the above investigators shall require appropriate laboratory testing of the suspected individual by a reference laboratory certified by CAP, NIDA, or other acceptable certifying agency chosen by the hospital. Testing procedures shall follow portions of the *Mandatory Guidelines for Federal Workplace Drug Programs* as published in the *Federal Register* Volume 53, Number 69, of April 11, 1988. The applicable portions are Subpart A 1.2, Subpart B 2.2, 2.3, 2.4(a)-(g)(5), 2.4(g)(8), 2.4(h)(i)(k), 2.7. The following cut off levels are established; levels above which are considered positive for reporting purposes.

(A) Alcohol 50 mg/dl (blood alcohol)

(B) Marijuana Metabolites 100 ng/ml

(C) Cocaine Metabolites 300 ng/ml

(D) Opiate Metabolites 300 ng/ml

(E) Phencyclidine 25 ng/ml

(F) Amphetamines 1,000 ng/ml

(G) Benzodiazepine 300 mcg/ml

(H) Barbiturates 300 mcg/ml

(I) Demerol—There is no present screening procedure available so the presence of the drug is considered positive.

Testing for any other drugs may be performed as deemed appropriate under the circumstances of the suspicion. Cut off levels for drugs not listed here shall be determined by the Medical Review Officer.

9.11.2.1.4 Failure of the practitioner to cooperate with this testing will be grounds for summary suspension as provided for in the Bylaws of the Medical Staff.

9.11.2.1.5 If, after the investigation, it is found that sufficient evidence exists that the practitioner is impaired, the Chief Executive Officer shall meet personally with that practitioner or designate another appropriate individual to do so.

9.11.2.2 The practitioner should be told that the results of an investigation indicate that the practitioner suffers from an impairment that affects his or her practice. The practitioner should not be told who filed the report or the specific incidents contained in the report.

9.11.2.3 Depending upon the severity of the problem, and the nature of the impairment, the hospital has the following options:

(A) Require the practitioner to undertake a rehabilitation program as a condition of continued appointment and clinical privileges.

(B) Impose appropriate restrictions on the practitioner's practice.

continues

Exhibit 9–4 continued

(C) Immediately suspend the practitioner's privileges in the hospital until rehabilitation has been accomplished if the practitioner does not agree to discontinue practice immediately.

9.11.2.4 If the matter cannot be handled internally or jeopardizes the safety of the practitioner, patients or others, the hospital shall seek the advice of hospital counsel to determine whether any conduct must be reported to law enforcement authorities or other governmental agencies and what further steps must be taken; however, the hospital will comply with all reporting requirements imposed on it by law.

9.11.2.5 The original report and a description of the actions taken by the Chief Executive Officer or Vice President of Medical Affairs shall be included in the practitioner's peer review file. If the investigation reveals that there is no merit to the report, the report should be removed from that file and kept in a separate confidential record in the Office of Medical Affairs. If the investigation reveals that there may be some merit to the report, but not enough to warrant immediate action, the report shall be included in a confidential peer review portion of the practitioner's personnel file and the practitioner's activities and practice shall be monitored until it can be established that there is, or is not, an impairment problem.

9.11.2.6 The Chief Executive Officer or Vice President of Medical Affairs shall inform the individual who filed the report that follow-up action was taken.

9.11.2.7 Throughout this process, all parties should avoid speculation, conclusions, gossip, and any discussions of this matter with anyone outside those described in this policy.

9.11.2.8 In the event of an actual or apparent conflict between this policy and any part of the Medical Staff Bylaws, Rules and Regulations, or other policies of the hospital or its Medical Staff, including the due process, hearing and appeals procedures, then the provisions of this policy shall control.

9.11.3 *Rehabilitation*

Hospital and Medical Staff leadership shall assist the practitioner in locating a suitable rehabilitation program. A practitioner shall not be reinstated until it is established, to the hospital's satisfaction, that the practitioner has successfully completed a program in which the hospital has confidence.

9.11.4 *Reinstatement*

9.11.4.1 Upon sufficient proof that a practitioner who has been found to be suffering an impairment has successfully completed a supervised rehabilitation program, the hospital, in its sole discretion, may consider that practitioner for reinstatement to the Medical Staff.

9.11.4.2 In considering an impaired practitioner for reinstatement, the hospital and its Medical Staff leadership must consider patient care interests paramount.

9.11.4.3 The hospital must first obtain a letter from the physician director of the rehabilitation program where the practitioner was treated. The impaired practitioner must authorize the release of this information. That letter shall state:

(A) whether the practitioner is participating in the program

(B) whether the practitioner is in compliance with all of the terms of the program

(C) whether the practitioner attends AA or similar meetings regularly (if appropriate)

(D) to what extent the practitioner's behavior and conduct are monitored

continues

Exhibit 9–4 continued

(E) whether, in the opinion of those doctors, the practitioner is rehabilitated

(F) whether an after care program has been recommended to the practitioner and, if so, a description of the after care program

(G) whether, in his or her opinion, the practitioner is capable of resuming medical practice and providing continuous, competent care to patients

9.11.4.4 The practitioner must inform the hospital of the name and address of his or her primary care physician and must authorize that physician to provide the hospital with information regarding his or her condition and treatment. The hospital has a right to require an opinion from other consultants of its choice at any time it deems such opinions necessary.

9.11.4.5 From the primary care physician the hospital needs to know the precise nature of the practitioner's condition, and the course of treatment as well as the answers to the questions posed above.

9.11.4.6 Assuming all of the information received establishes that the practitioner is rehabilitated and capable of resuming care of patients, the hospital must take the following additional precautions when restoring clinical privileges:

(A) The practitioner must identify two similarly credentialed practitioners who are willing to assume responsibility for the care of his or her patients in the event of his or her inability or unavailability.

(B) The practitioner shall be required to obtain periodic reports for the hospital from his or her primary physician—for a period of time specified by the Chief Executive Officer and the Vice President of Medical Affairs—stating that the practitioner is continuing treatment or therapy, as appropriate, and that his or her ability to treat and care for patients in the hospital is not impaired.

9.11.4.7 The practitioner's exercise of clinical privileges in the hospital shall be monitored by the department chairperson or by a practitioner appointed by the department chairperson. The nature of that monitoring shall be determined by the Credentials Committee after its review of all of the circumstances.

9.11.4.8 The practitioner must agree to submit to an alcohol or drug screening test (if appropriate to the impairment) at the request of the Chief Executive Officer, his designee including the administrator on call, the investigators designated in 9.11.2.1.2 who have reasonable suspicion that the physician may be under the influence of drugs or alcohol. In the case of impairment due to alcohol or drug abuse, the practitioner shall be subject to random drug/alcohol screening for the entire duration of affiliation with the hospital.

9.11.4.9 All requests for information concerning the impaired practitioner shall be forwarded only to the Vice President of Medical Affairs or Chief Executive Officer for response.

9.11.5 *Physicians Health Committee*

The Physicians Health Committee, a sub-committee of the Credentials Committee, shall be established to receive all reports from monitors of impaired physicians, access the quality and adequacy of the recovery/monitoring program, report to the Credentials Committee, and assist all impaired physicians to re-integrate into the Medical Staff. The committee shall coordinate education on impairment for the Medical Staff. The membership of the Physicians Health Committee shall be appointed by the Chief of Staff from the active Medi-

continues

Exhibit 9–4 continued

cal Staff to serve staggered terms of at least two years. The committee shall include a majority of members who are also members of the Credentials Committee including the Vice President of Medical Affairs. The chairman of the Physicians Health Committee shall be a member of the Credentials Committee. The committee shall meet as needed at the call of the chairman.

9.11.6 *Policy Regarding Drug Testing of Applicants for Medical Staff Membership and Clinical Privileges*

9.11.6.1 Applicants are required to refrain from the use of illegal drugs and the improper use of legal drugs. The granting of appointment and clinical privileges in the Penrose-St. Francis Healthcare System affects the health and safety of others. Therefore, all applicants shall be tested for the presence of illegal drugs and the improper use of legal drugs in their system.

9.11.6.2 Clear, advance notice of this policy shall be given all applicants during the pre-application phase of credentialing. Test results shall be kept strictly confidential.

9.11.6.3 Upon receipt of an application and the applicant's physical presence in Colorado Springs, the Vice President of Medical Affairs shall inform the applicant of the time and place for testing. The applicant shall have no more than 8 hours after notification to present himself for testing.

9.11.6.4 Prior to testing the applicant will be required to identify any prescribed or over-the-counter drugs, or other substances which might be present in his body fluid and to provide confirmation of such prescriptions by his physician. The applicant will be given an opportunity to disclose any other appropriate information which may affect the results of his screening.

9.11.6.5 All test samples shall be given under controlled conditions and sealed for testing by the testing facility. Each sample must be analyzed by a reference laboratory certified by CAP, NIDA, or other acceptable certifying agency chosen by the hospital. Each sample is to be split and if the first aliquot yields positive results for any illegal drug or improperly obtained prescription drug, a second aliquot is to be tested by an appropriate different test method being at least as sensitive as the initial testing method. In the event of a positive test result, the pertinent sample is to be frozen or otherwise appropriately preserved by the laboratory for the purpose of furthering testing. Testing procedures shall follow the previously outlined portions of the *Mandatory Guidelines for Federal Workplace Drug Programs* as published in the *Federal Register* Volume 53, Number 69, of April 11, 1988. The applicable portions are Subpart A 1.2, Subpart B 2.2, 2.3, 2.4(a)-(g)(5), 2.4(g)(8), 2.4(h)(i)(k), 2.7. The following cut off levels are established; levels above which are considered positive for reporting purposes.

(A) Alcohol 50 mg/dl (blood alcohol)

(B) Marijuana Metabolites 100 ng/ml

(C) Cocaine Metabolites 300 ng/ml

(D) Opiate Metabolites 300 ng/ml

(E) Phencyclidine 25 ng/ml

(F) Amphetamines 1,000 ng/ml

(G) Benzodiazepine 300 mcg/ml

continues

Exhibit 9–4 continued

(H) Barbiturates 300 mcg/ml

(I) Demerol—There is no present screening procedure available so the presence of the drug is considered positive.

9.11.6.6 Test results shall be returned confidentially to the Vice President of Medical Affairs for inclusion with the application. The Vice President of Medical Affairs shall forward the test results to the applicant. Those applicants who test negative shall be considered for appointment and/or clinical privileges. Those who test positive without adequate pre-existing explanation based on a physician's prescription or other information provided shall not be considered further for appointment or clinical privileges at this time. The applicant who tests positive shall be referred to the Colorado Physicians Health Program for evaluation. Following evaluation by the Colorado Physicians Health Program, at the sole discretion of the Credentials Committee of the Medical Staff, the applicant may then be considered.

9.11.6.7 If the Credentials Committee elects not to consider the application, the applicant shall have none of the right of hearing and appeal provided by the Bylaws of the Medical Staff but shall be considered to have provided an incomplete application.

Courtesy of Penrose–St. Francis Healthcare System, Colorado Springs, Colorado.

1. A statement of policy reflecting the organization's commitment to maintaining a safe, healthful, and efficient environment that is drug and alcohol free and giving reasons why the policy was developed (e.g., to detect users and remove abusers and to prevent the use and/or presence of those substances in the workplace)
2. Identification of those who will be included in the policy (e.g., all employees, applicants to and members of the medical staff, residents)
3. Definitions of terms such as *under the influence, illegal drugs, controlled substances, legal drugs, abuse* of any legal drug, *reasonable suspicion,* and *possession*
4. Alcohol and/or drug use prohibitions
5. Individuals who will be tested and when follow-up testing, additional testing, refusal to test, the types of drug/alcohol tests that will be administered, how specimen collection will take place and where, which laboratory will be used, and technical help for the applicant regarding prescription and nonprescription medications and their effects on the test
6. Test results reporting, to whom the information will be sent, how the person tested will be informed of the findings, and the process for challenging the test results
7. Procedures to be followed before requesting screening (these should be specific and provide help to the supervisor in determining whether there is a situation of possible drug or alcohol use in the workplace); possibly also an addendum that provides a list of problem indicators for supervisors to assist them in assessing a situation
8. If the organization has an organized, formal education program concerning alcohol or drug use, such as a drug-free awareness program, a description of this program, as well as a description of the Employee Assistance Program available to the employee (if the organization provides a separate route of assistance for

physicians, such as a physician well-being committee and/or participation in a state medical society program, then the policy should also include reference to those resources)

9. A rehabilitation section outlining what the employee/physician must do while receiving help for the problem (e.g., request a leave of absence without any disciplinary action taken as long as the employee/physician continues to participate in the program; sign an agreement/contract that specifies the actions required of the employee/physician; options for employees/physicians whose impaired status was discovered under conditions that threatened their own, patients', or other employees' safety (in this case, in a hospital setting, the medical staff bylaws or fair hearing plan could be referenced concerning summary suspension)
10. Involvement of law enforcement agencies/licensing agencies—when such referrals will be made and by whom
11. A statement referencing federal and state reporting requirements
12. A statement placing the responsibility for maintaining a drug- and alcohol-free workplace on all members of the management team and medical staff

Exhibit 9–5 is an example policy for drug testing.

Exhibit 9–5 Medical Staff Member/AHP Applicant Protocol for Drug/Substance Testing

I. **Applicant Notification**

Medical Staff Office will notify applicants within (   ) days after arriving in **(city)** and advise them that they have an appointment with **(name of test facility)** designated by the **(name of hospital, individual)** for a pre-appointment drug screen, which will include a blood alcohol and urine test.

If applicant states he/she is unable to make the appointment, applicant will be advised that submitting to a drug screen is a requirement for application to be accepted by **(name of hospital)**. This notification shall be confirmed by letter to the applicant. The call should then be referred to CEO, Administrator on Call, other.

II. **Facility Notification**

Medical Staff Office will call **(name of facility)** and let them know that applicant has been notified and is expected to be there within the next 8 hours for the pre-appointment drug screen.

III. **Applicant Identification of Drug/Substance Use**

Prior to testing, the applicant will be required to identify any prescribed or over-the-counter drugs, or other substances which might be present in his body fluid, and to provide confirmation of such prescription by his physician. The applicant will be given an opportunity to disclose any other appropriate information which may affect the results of his screening.

IV. **Testing Procedure/Cut off Levels**

Testing procedures shall follow the *Mandatory Guidelines for Federal Workplace Drug Programs* as published in the *Federal Register* Volume 53, Number 69, of April 11, 1988. The applicable portions are Subpart A 1.2, Subpart B 2.2, 2.3, 2.4(a)-(g)(5), 2.4(g)(8), 2.4(h)(i)(k), 2.7. The following cut off levels are established; levels above which are considered positive for reporting purposes.

continues

Exhibit 9–5 continued

A. Alcohol 50 mg/dl (blood alcohol)
B. Marijuana Metabolites 100 ng/ml
C. Cocaine Metabolites 300 ng/ml
D. Opiate Metabolites 300 ng/ml
E. Phencyclidine 25 ng/ml
F. Amphetamines 1000 ng/ml
G. Benzodiazepine 300 mcg/ml
H. Barbiturates 300 mcg/ml
I. Demerol—There is no present screening procedure available so the presence of the drug is considered positive.

V. **Collection of Specimens**

A. Collection will be done at **(name of testing facility).**
B. Collection will be done by **(name of testing facility)** employee who is fully trained in urine drug screen collection.

VI. **Transport of Specimens**

The collector will take the sealed specimens from **(name of testing facility)** at the close of each day's screenings and send via lab courier to the Toxicology Lab at **(name of hospital).**

VII. **Paperwork from the Chain of Custody Form**

A. The "Laboratory" copy will be sealed with the specimen and sent to the laboratory.
B. The "Donor" copy will be given to the applicant at the time of collection.
C. The "Collector" copy and the "Company" copy of the Chain of Custody form will be retained at **(name of testing facility)** to be filed under lock.

VIII. **Test Results**

A. Test results will be sent to **(name of testing facility)** via lab courier in a sealed envelope to be opened only by the Drug Screen Coordinator.
B. Test results will be reviewed and verified by the Drug Screen Coordinator at **(name of testing facility).**
C. Verified result (negative or positive) will be sent in a sealed tamper-evident envelope to the CEO **(or other designated individual)** or by secure electronic FAX.
D. A copy of the result must then be sent certified to the applicant. In the event of a positive result, the applicant will then be asked to meet with **(designated individual)** personally and he will recommend the applicant contact the **(state)** Physician Health Program, or other appropriate program.
E. Applicants who test positive without adequate pre-existing explanation based on a physician's prescription or other information provided shall not be considered further for appointment or clinical privileges at this time. The applicant who tests positive shall be referred to the **(state)** Physicians Health Program for evaluation.

   Following evaluation by the **(state)** Physicians Health Program, at the sole discretion of the Credentials Committee of the Medical Staff, the applicant may then be considered.

continues

Exhibit 9–5 continued

IX. **Turnaround Time**

A. Twenty-four hours on negative results to **(name of testing facility)**

B. Thirty-six hours on negative results to CEO **(other designated individual)**

C. Positive results up to five (5) days to **(name of testing facility)**

D. Positive results up to six (6) days to CEO **(other designated individual)**

X. **Storage of Results**

The lab report of test results, the "Company" and "Collector" copies of the Chain of Custody form will be filed at **(name of testing facility)** under lock.

Courtesy of Penrose–St. Francis Healthcare System, Colorado Springs, Colorado.

NOTES

1. 42 U.S.C. §§11101–11152.
2. Act of July 26, 1990. Pub. L. No. 101-336.
3. G. Pozgar, *Legal Aspects of Health Care Administration,* 6th ed. (Gaithersburg, MD: Aspen Publishers, Inc., 1996), 699.
4. Pozgar, *Legal Aspects,* 685.
5. P. Younger et al., *Physician Credentialing and Peer Review Answer Book* (Gaithersburg, MD: Aspen Publishers, Inc., 1995), 119–127.
6. 42 U.S.C. §11112.
7. 42 U.S.C. §11112.
8. *1998 Hospital Accreditation Standards* (Oakbrook Terrace, IL: Joint Commission on Accreditation of Healthcare Organizations), MS2.3–2.3.2.
9. *Lexikon: Dictionary of Health Care Terms, Organizations, and Acronyms for the Era of Reform* (Oakbrook Terrace, IL: Joint Commission on Accreditation of Healthcare Organizations, 1994), 271.
10. Younger et al., *Physician Credentialing,* 89–127.
11. *1998–1999 Surveyor Guidelines for the Accreditation of Managed Care Organizations* (Washington, DC: National Committee for Quality Assurance, 1998), 173.
12. *1998–1999 Surveyor Guidelines,* 173 (CR 11.1).
13. *1998–1999 Surveyor Guidelines,* 173 (CR 11.2).
14. *1998–1999 Surveyor Guidelines,* 141 (CR 1.5–1.7).
15. *1998–1999 Comprehensive Accreditation Manual for Ambulatory Care, 1998–99* (Oakbrook Terrace, IL: Joint Commission on Accreditation of Healthcare Organizations), 451 (HR 7.3–7.3.1).
16. *1998–1999 Comprehensive Accreditation Manual,* 451.
17. 42 U.S.C. §§11101–11152.
18. P. Younger et al., *Legal Answer Book for Managed Care* (Gaithersburg, MD: Aspen Publishers, Inc., 1995), 173–190.
19. Pozgar, *Legal Aspects,* 573–574.
20. *1998 Hospital Accreditation Standards,* 251.
21. *Surveyor Guidelines.*
22. Pozgar, *Legal Aspects*, 573–574.
23. E. Jones et al. (Boston, MA: Mintz, Levin, Cohn, Ferris, Glovsky and Popeo, PC).
24. Younger et al., *Physician Credentialing,* 64–66.

CHAPTER 10

Delegated and Centralized Credentialing

OVERVIEW

As the scope of credentialing activities has grown, the number of practitioners and providers being credentialed has increased. As the number of organizations involved in credentialing has expanded, obtaining help, becoming more cost-effective, and decreasing duplication have become priorities for many organizations. Delegation of credentialing activities, specifically obtaining verifications from credentials verification organizations (CVOs), is now commonplace.

There are numerous possibilities for delegation. Quality management and improvement and utilization management may be delegated along with all aspects of credentialing. This chapter will address only credentialing. The possibilities of delegated credentialing activities include the following:

- An organization delegates its credentials verification activities to a medical society or commercial CVO, which may or may not be certified.
- The credentialing process is fully delegated to another organization.
- A network or an organization with several facilities or components delegates credentials verification or other components of credentialing to a centralized, internal unit.
- An organization that performs credentialing activities acts as a delegated organization for another organization.
- An organization uses a company specializing in data collection (such as site and medical record review).

The possibilities for delegation are as broad as the number of relationships an organization has, or is willing to consider. Both the National Committee for Quality Assurance (NCQA) and the Utilization Review Accreditation Commission (URAC) have standards specific to delegation and have developed certification programs to support the process.

The delegation process consists of

- identification of potential delegated organizations
- review of credentialing practices, policies, and procedures
- on-site audit to determine compliance with requirements
- approval of delegation
- execution of contract or letter of agreement
- oversight by the delegating organization

Many credentialing professionals continue to express concern about the practice of delegation. Concerns center on lack of control, cost, timeliness, and possible loss of work. Supporters of delegation reference efficiency, cost savings, productivity, physician convenience, and the specific expertise available.[1]

DELEGATION

What Is Delegated Credentialing?

A credentialing delegation process occurs when a health care organization grants authority for credentialing functions to another organization. The delegated organization might be a CVO, physician group practice, health plan, hospital, subcontracted network, or other health care organization that has a credentials process that meets or exceeds the standards of the delegating organization.

NCQA defines delegation as "a formal process by which a managed care organization (MCO) gives another organization the authority to perform certain functions on its behalf" and states that "although an MCO can delegate the authority to perform a function, it cannot delegate the responsibility for assuring that the function is performed appropriately."[2]

Hospitals may use the term *outsourcing* to refer to an agreement with a CVO to provide verification services. The term *outsourcing* may be used when referring to delegation activity, but regardless of the terminology used, the same requirements and principles apply.

What Can Be Delegated?

Credentialing functions and activities that can be delegated include

- verification
- collection of information that is used in the credentialing process but not verified (e.g., site visits or medical record review)
- the credentialing and recredentialing process, including the decision (managed and ambulatory care only)
- monitoring of performance for recredentialing

Delegation of verification to CVOs or centralized credentialing units is the most common form of delegation today. Data collection can also be delegated. A developing field in managed care is site visits and medical record audits. Data collection for site and medical record reviews may be delegated to a CVO or other organization performing visits and reviews. NCQA and URAC allow all or part of the credentialing and recredentialing process (including the decision) to be delegated to another organization. This involves a number of requirements that will be discussed in detail later in this chapter. Delegation can also be used for a specific category of practitioners. Possibly an organization will delegate credentialing activities only for behavioral health practitioners or alternative care practitioners and providers but do no other delegation.

Who Can Delegate?

Basically any health care organization can delegate verification activities. Data collection is delegated only for those organizations that have specific requirements to collect data as part of their credentialing activities—most commonly managed care organizations and hospitals. The entire credentialing process is delegated only by organizations that are accredited by AAAHC , URAC, or NCQA or that have no accreditation status and choose to delegate.

Who Can Be a Delegated Organization?

Any organization that is engaged in credentialing activities and functions, is willing to enter into a delegation agreement, and meets the standards set forth by the organization seeking to delegate can be a delegated organization. Although there are many outstanding delegated entities, not everyone does a good job. Carefully developed standards, evaluation visits, a good contract or letter of agreement, and oversight of the process are vital elements in a successful delegation.

ACCREDITATION POSITIONS RELATED TO DELEGATION

The major health care accrediting organizations that address delegation are

- Accreditation Association for Ambulatory Health Care (AAAHC)
- Joint Commission on Accreditation of Healthcare Organizations (Joint Commission)
- National Committee for Quality Assurance (NCQA)
- Utilization Review Accreditation Commission (URAC)

AAAHC

AAAHC, which accredits ambulatory care organizations (for more detail, see Chapter 2 of this book), allows delegation of credentialing by the organizations it accredits. The 1998–99 standards state that "credentialing of a health care practitioner by another health care organization other than the accreditable organization, such as by a hospital, may be utilized as part of an overall independent process of credentialing by the accreditable organization, but is not relied upon exclusively."[3]

Joint Commission

Joint Commission accreditation standards for hospitals and for health care networks do not specify provisions of delegated credentialing activities but do reference delegation to external agencies to collect the information needed for primary source verification. The Joint Commission developed a set of principles for evaluating credentials verification organizations. (These are found in the Credentials Verification Organization section later in this chapter.) Hospitals that are accredited by the Joint Commission may use and in fact historically have frequently used medical societies, other hospitals within a system, CVOs, the American Medical Association (AMA) verification service, and other external agencies to obtain and support their activities related to verification. The Joint Commission does not offer a certification for the verification process, so the hospital or other organizations accredited by the Joint Commission are required to have evidence of verification in the credentials files when they are surveyed.

The Joint Commission's *Comprehensive Accreditation Manual for Health Care Networks* references delegated activity in the Management of Human Resources Standards. If the network uses the credentialing process and decisions carried out by a component hospital, as part of its contract the network requires

- that the hospital appointment process meet applicable network standards, including verification
- that, if requested, the hospital will provide a letter confirming use of the same appointment process for each licensed independent practitioner (LIP) applicant
- that the hospital notify the network when it changes the appointment status of an LIP
- that the hospital allow review of credentials files[4]

NCQA

NCQA, in its standards for accreditation of managed care organizations, has the most detailed information relating to delegation. In addition to the standard specific to delegation of credentialing and recredentialing activities (CR13), the scoring interpretation for each credentialing standard specifies delegation requirements. NCQA considers delegation to have occurred if an organization that is not the MCO conducts any part of the credentialing process. There is no delegation if the MCO or its parent company conducts all of the credentialing functions. Surveyors consider both delegated and nondelegated activity and identify any findings that are different between the two. The standard that governs delegation includes requirements for

1. oversight of the delegated activity
2. a mutually agreed-upon document that includes
   - description of the responsibilities of both parties
   - the delegated activities
   - the process by which the MCO will evaluate the delegated entity's performance
   - the remedies, including revocation of the delegation, that are available to the MCO if the delegated organization does not fulfill its obligations
3. the MCO to retain the right, based on quality issues, to approve, terminate, or suspend individual practitioners. (Therefore, a delegated organization such as a hospital may approve and privilege a practitioner for medical staff membership and privileges at that hospital but the MCO organization may choose not to include the practitioner in the network or plan because of noncompliance with its quality criteria.)
4. the MCO to evaluate the delegated organization's capacity to perform before delegation and evaluate on an annual basis whether the performance continues to be conducted in accordance with NCQA standards and the expectations of the MCO[5]

If a delegated organization in turn delegates to another organization, a subdelegation has occurred. With a subdelegation, the MCO must either conduct oversight or verify that the delegated organization is performing its own oversight audit.[6]

NCQA also offers a certification service to CVOs that, when obtained, relieves some of the oversight requirements for delegating organizations (discussed in more detail later in this chapter).

URAC

URAC, which provides accreditation for health care networks, defines delegation as "a transfer of authority and responsibility that occurs when a network contracts with a third party to perform credentialing functions as outlined in the agreement. (The third party can include, but is not limited to, an IPA [independent practice association], hospital, or CVO.)"[7]

The standards for the URAC network credentialing program reference both delegation and subdelegation of credentialing activities and note that

- the network is not required to maintain credentials files for delegated or subdelegated practitioner activity
- the delegated organization is required to complete primary source verifications per URAC standard requirements
- a CVO may be used for verifications
- recredentialing may be delegated or subdelegated
- time frames for verification (180 days) are applicable to delegated entities
- the network must retain authority and maintain oversight of all delegated activities
- there must be a contractual agreement in which the delegated or subdelegated organization agrees to maintain the standards of both the network and URAC
- the network must retain final authority over acceptance and denial of practitioners
- the network must review quarterly status reports from the delegated organization
- random audits of each delegated organization must be completed on an annual basis[8]

Accreditation and Delegation

It is to be expected that delegation activities will grow and undergo much more development and refinement during the next few years. As networks grow and develop, individual practitioners are contracted with numerous agencies, and as credentialing staff seek ways to increase their productivity and decrease duplication, delegation may provide answers.

CONSIDERATIONS RELATED TO DELEGATION

Aspects of delegation to be considered and evaluated before determination to pursue a delegation agreement are

- differences between requirements and activities in hospitals and managed care
- legal issues
- confidentiality
- recredentialing
- National Practitioner Data Bank (NPDB) query
- cost benefit analysis

Differences between Requirements and Activities in Hospitals and Managed Care

As outlined in Chapter 1, there are numerous differences between credentialing activities in hospitals and in managed care. These need to be identified and clearly understood if any delegation is considered between organizations that are not of the same type or with an organization providing the majority of services to either hospitals or managed care. A network, ambulatory, or managed care organization considering delegation of the credentialing or recredentialing process to a hospital will need to negotiate those requirements that are not normally encompassed in hospital credentialing, such as the 180-day verification time frame. A hospital that is considering use of a CVO whose major client base is managed care should ensure the CVO's ability to verify all training and education and to obtain information related to competency before contracting. Allied health practitioners (AHPs) are used in different ways by hospitals and managed care. Some managed care organizations now use physician assistants and nurse practitioners as primary care providers. These categories are usually not considered LIPs in hospitals and as such are not always subject to peer review and credentialing activities to the extent that physician primary care practitioners are.

Legal Issues

To date, there has not been significant case law relating to delegation activities, but by its very nature delegation can be a high-risk activity. Delegation of the credentialing process does not relieve the delegating organization of the responsibility to ensure that only fully qualified practitioners and providers are included in their network or Plan. NCQA standards state that a managed care organization delegating the credentialing/recredentialing decision may need to provide performance monitoring information to the delegated organization for use in the recredentialing decision. Many states have peer review statutes that may direct or affect the sharing of peer review information. Legal counsel should be obtained for determination of the effect of this aspect of delegation activity, with the appropriate language included in the delegation contract or agreement.

Of importance in terms of legal consideration is the fact that the delegating organization maintains and is ultimately accountable for all functions, regardless of whether the functions are performed internally or by a delegated or subdelegated organization. Some organizations that have accepted delegation do not understand that the delegating organization is still accountable for the process. This is a very important concept in terms of contract language and the right of the delegating organization to audit files and obtain copies of credentials files and related information. NCQA differentiates between *author-*

ity and *accountability*, stating that "authority to act on behalf of" can be delegated, but not "accountability" for a function's being properly carried out.[9]

Confidentiality

Inherent in delegation activities is the requirement for access to practitioner information, patient records, and performance improvement or peer review information. The delegation assessment and contract/agreement language should carefully consider protection of confidentiality of all information that may or will be disclosed or exchanged. The release signed by the practitioner as part of the application process should address release and exchange of information with delegated entities, including sharing of peer review or performance improvement information.

Most contracts executed between managed care organizations and practitioners include a provision that the MCO will be allowed access to the medical records of its members, and to the office for the purpose of evaluating the delivery of care. The contract language may need to be expanded to cover delegated agreements. Patient authorization forms may also need to be expanded to cover delegated activities and access to medical records. Some states have statutes specific to the medical records of patients with diagnosed substance abuse, psychiatric diagnosis, sexually transmitted diseases, and AIDS/HIV. Access to these records should be specified in contract language and delegation contracts/agreements.

The following are points to consider when developing a delegated agreement:

- All applicable state regulations should be identified and addressed.
- If state statutes limit access to any information, the contract/agreement language should address disclosure or restriction of disclosure of that information.
- Practitioner contracts, patient authorizations, and delegation contracts/agreements should include language designating the delegated entities as "agents" of the delegating organization.
- The contract/agreement should include provisions that specifically address confidentiality, disclosure of information, and maintenance of information and of confidentiality by the delegated organization.

Recredentialing

If the credentialing process decision is delegated, the delegated organization will probably (by contract) be responsible for recredentialing. Delegated recredentialing requires the managed care organization or delegating organization to ensure that the necessary-quality information is incorporated into the decision-making process. If quality, utilization, member service, and medical records activities are performed internally, the organization must have a mechanism for sharing the information with the delegated organization performing the credentialing. If these activities have also been delegated, the delegate must have a method of capturing and sharing the relevant information at the time of recredentialing.[10]

National Practitioner Data Bank (NPDB) Query

If the delegation is to include verification activities and the delegating organization is eligible to query NPDB, a determination will have to be made as to who will complete queries. If the delegated organization is to do queries, it must:

- be designated (by written agreement) as an "authorized agent" by the delegating organization
- understand that query responses may not be shared among organizations

Cost Benefit Analysis

A consideration of benefits and disadvantages should address the issues from the standpoint of the organization, the practitioner, and the delegated organization. These may be

- duplication of activity
- collaboration/communication
- cycle time
- staff available for evaluation/oversight
- risk

The major considerations in delegation of activities are cost savings and reduction of activity within the organization. To make a determination of the extent of the impact that delegation will have, a cost benefit analysis should be completed. The first step is identification of all credentialing activity with time involved in each step, which is multiplied by the number of current and projected practitioners and providers. (More information on an analysis can be found in Chapter 11 of this book.) The cost of current activities is calculated using budget analysis data, and a cost is assigned to activities for which delegation is being considered. When identification and solicitation of potential delegation entities begin, specific credentialing activities are outlined in the Request for Proposal (RFP). Evaluation of responses to RFPs against internal costs (identified initially) provides information as to the cost-effectiveness of delegation.

Some aspects of an analysis go beyond costs. These include evaluation of quality, resources, and support services. All required services should be clearly identified and included in the RFP. These aspects may be more difficult to quantify than costs but should not be ignored.

EVALUATION OF A POTENTIAL DELEGATE

Evaluation of a potential delegate should include

- review of the potential delegate's policies and procedures
- an on-site audit of activities and documentation
- comparison of results of review of policies and procedures and results of on-site audit with preestablished criteria

The review of policies and procedures and the on-site audit take place before contract negotiation. The auditing organization may be asked to sign a confidentiality statement and/or nondisclosure statement. Review for delegation of the credentials/recredentialing process, including the credentialing decision, should include

1. Policies, procedures, minutes, and any other documents applicable to credentialing activities
   - steps outlining the initial application, credentialing/recredentialing of practitioners
   - criteria and exceptions to criteria
   - mechanism for review/revision of policy and procedures
   - time frame for verification and procedures to ensure compliance with time frames
   - time frame for recredentialing activities
   - accreditation requirements addressed in policy and procedures or other written documents
2. Governing board or governing body
   - the governing board/body approves credentialing policies, procedures and processes
   - documentation is given if the governing board has designated all or part of the approval process (not applicable for hospitals)
   - evidence of credentials review and approval is provided in board minutes
3. Minutes review
   - committee(s) meets as frequently as defined in the policy and procedure
   - composition of the review committee includes peers
   - minutes reflect compliance with the criteria and process as outlined in the policies, procedures, and other documents
   - minutes reflect the discussion and conclusions when a criterion is not met

- minutes reflect evidence of follow-up
- there is evidence that recredentialing is performed within specified time frames and in compliance with the existing policies, procedures, standards and other directives.

4. Hard-copy credentials file and file storage
   - confidentiality policy and procedure for the credentials files
   - security of the credentials files
   - access to the files
5. Application form
   - all components required by accreditation bodies and other information are applicable to all entities using it
6. Policies and procedures for reducing, suspending, or terminating appointment/privileges
   - policies and procedures that define what will result in a suspension or termination
   - evidence if practitioners have been suspended or terminated in the past
   - evidence that quality deficiencies were reported to appropriate agencies per policy or regulatory requirement
   - outline or summary of process by which the delegated organization will report back to the delegating organization if any actions are taken against the organization's practitioners
   - due process if the delegated organization reduces, suspends, or terminates privileges or status
7. Delegation of any activities (which would result in a subdelegation arrangement)
8. Database function
   - access/security
   - information available
   - data integrity
   - transmission of data
9. Credential file audit
   - license to practice
   - hospital privileges
   - Drug Enforcement Administration (DEA)/Controlled Dangerous Substance (CDS) certificate
   - board certification/residency/education
   - malpractice insurance
   - malpractice claims history
   - NPDB query
   - sanctions against license
   - Medicare/Medicaid sanctions

If the potential delegation relates only to verification activities, then the delegating organization should not have access to any information related to peer review, quality, quality profiling, or the recredentialing decision. Review of an organization for performance of verification would include

1. Scope of services
   - processes for data collection and information development and verification
2. Policy and procedures
   - provisions for periodic review
   - evidence of review and approval by governing body
   - disclosure of disciplinary actions
3. Internal quality improvement/control processes
   - quality assessment/improvement structure
   - minutes
   - evidence of activities
   - customer satisfaction evaluation and improvement
   - complaint process
4. Credential file audit
   - verification time frames
   - license to practice
   - hospital privileges
   - DEA/CDS certificate
   - board certification/residency/education
   - malpractice insurance
   - claims history
   - NPDB query
   - sanctions against license
   - Medicare/Medicaid sanctions
5. Confidentiality
   - confidentiality policy and procedure for the credentials files
   - security of the credentials files
   - access to the files

6. Application form
7. Database function
   - access/security
   - information available
   - data integrity
   - transmission of data

Once all information has been identified and gathered and an on-site audit has been completed, results are compared with preestablished criteria. The criteria should include all applicable accreditation and regulatory requirements. Results of this comparison will indicate the feasibility of pursuing a delegated relationship.

CONTRACT/LETTER OF AGREEMENT

A contract or letter of agreement should be executed between the organization that is delegating activities and the delegated organization. This document serves as the understanding between the two parties. It outlines requirements and consequences of noncompliance with requirements and identifies the scope of the relationship. Contracts differ significantly in that accreditation requirements and negotiations between organizations result in different language.

Key elements of contract language for delegated credentialing are

- effective dates
- responsibilities of the delegating organization
- responsibilities of the delegated organization (including compliance with criteria, standards, and requirements)
- time frames and method for submission of data (practitioner and provider demographics) by the delegating organization to the delegated organization
- time frames and method for submission of information by the delegated organization to the delegating organization
- specification of information that the delegate collects and verifies
- right of access by the delegating organization to files, minutes, and other documents for purposes of evaluation and oversight of process, and the process by which the delegates' performance will be evaluated
- statement that the delegated organization will act as "an agent for" and "on behalf of" the delegating organization
- maintenance and storage of hard copy of file
- confidentiality provisions
- method for handling case-specific data
- ownership and distribution of hard copy of file and any other information obtained by delegated organization upon termination of the contract
- remedies, including revocation of delegation if obligations are not fulfilled
- as applicable, the right of the delegating organization to reach a decision independent of that of the delegate

Exhibit 10–1 is a sample contract for delegation of credentials verification services. Exhibits 10–2 and 10–3 are sample contracts between a hospital and an independent practice association with a physician release.

STEPS IN A DELEGATION PROCESS

The steps in the delegation process are:

1. identification of need or interest in delegation
2. development of decision criteria
3. development of delegation criteria
4. identification of potential delegated entities or receipt of request for delegation
5. RFP development and distribution (optional)
6. comparison of RFP response with decision criteria (optional)
7. on-site audit, review of policy and procedures, and file evaluation
8. evaluation of audit results against delegation criteria
9. approval of decision to pursue agreement

Exhibit 10–1 Agreement To Delegate Credentialing Verification

This **Agreement** is made this ________ day of ____________________, 19_____

BY AND BETWEEN

____ PHYSICIAN HOSPITAL ORGANIZATION (hereinafter called "PHO")

AND

_____________________________________, CREDENTIALS VERIFICATION ORGANIZATION (hereinafter called "CVO").

WHEREAS PHO is a health care organization that engages in the credentialing of its physicians and other licensed health care practitioners, including verification of credentials from original sources, and wishes to delegate to CVO the function of verifying credentials of PHO professionals, in accordance with the terms and conditions of this Agreement; and

WHEREAS, CVO is an organization that engages in verification of credentials from original sources, of physicians and other licensed health care professionals and is willing to accept the function of verifying the credentials of PHO practitioners in accordance with the terms and conditions of this Agreement;

NOW, THEREFORE, in consideration of the mutual covenants, promises, and agreements contained herein and other good and valuable considerations, the sufficiency of which is hereby acknowledged, PHO and CVO agree as follows:

1. RECITALS: The above recitals are true and correct and are incorporated as part of this Agreement.

2. DEFINITIONS: When used in this Agreement, the term "practitioner" shall mean a physician (MD, DO, DDS) or other licensed healthcare professional who is currently a member or has submitted an application for medical staff membership and privileges at PHO.

3. SERVICES:

3.1. CVO agrees to provide credentialing and recredentialing primary source credential verification services to PHO, according to Joint Commission and NCQA standards, for all existing practitioners and those seeking initial or renewal of clinical privileges in PHO in accordance with the terms of this Agreement. CVO shall not have the right or responsibility to initiate or deny clinical privileges at PHO or to take any professional review action on behalf of PHO, which decisions shall be the sole right and responsibility of PHO.

CVO services shall include (a) verification from original sources of practitioner's professional licensure, education, training and/or experience, malpractice claims history, professional review actions, and other items relevant to practitioner's credentials and qualifications. Appendix A, attached to and incorporated into this Agreement, outlines acceptable verification sources. For every practitioner, CVO agrees to certify that the information was verified with primary sources and to indicate the date of the verification; (b) absent causes beyond control of CVO, CVO will provide the information in its possession regarding

continues

Exhibit 10–1 continued

each practitioner on or before ninety (90) days following receipt by CVO of a completed request form from PHO; (c) notification to PHO by CVO of licensure expiration, revocations, or sanctions imposed on practitioner will occur within two weeks of receipt by CVO; (d) CVO will act as a designated agent for the required National Practitioner Data Bank query and forward original response from NPDB to PHO; and (e) CVO shall provide copies to PHO of all other primary source documents obtained by CVO.

3.2. PHO agrees to obtain from practitioners a signed release form permitting and authorizing CVO to provide to PHO information about the practitioner and releasing from liability all individuals involved in the credentialing process and provide CVO with copy of such release. PHO agrees to maintain all credentialing information received from CVO in strict confidence in accordance with applicable state law. (a) PHO agrees to notify the CVO within ten (10) days of any termination of a practitioner application. (b) PHO will authorize CVO to act as a designated agent for querying the National Practitioner Data Bank. Query responses will be forwarded directly to PHO by CVO.

3.3. CVO will not subdelegate any activity or function without the prior written approval of PHO.

4. CONFIDENTIALITY: Both parties will use all reasonable efforts to ensure the confidentiality of credentialing information obtained and/or maintained. Information will be released only pursuant to the written release of information forms signed by the practitioner whose credentials are being verified.

5. FEES: As compensation for CVO services under this agreement, PHO shall pay to CVO a fee per practitioner, as set forth in Exhibit B attached to and incorporated into this agreement. Fees shall be paid concurrent with CVO's submission of a monthly bill for each practitioner request forwarded to PHO. The monthly fee per practitioner as set forth in Exhibit B shall entitle PHO to updates and mutually agreed-on periodic reports.

6. TERM AND TERMINATION: This Agreement shall remain in force until terminated by mutual agreement of both parties. Either party may terminate the Agreement upon ninety (90) days' written notice. In the event of termination of this Agreement, the parties shall have no further obligation to each other except for those obligations accrued prior to termination and the obligation to protect confidential and proprietary information.

7. DISPUTE RESOLUTION; REMEDIES: PHO and CVO agree to resolve any controversy, claim or dispute arising out of or relating to this agreement in accordance with the dispute resolution procedures as set forth in Exhibit B attached to and incorporated into this Agreement.

8. MUTUAL AGREEMENT AND OBLIGATIONS: It is understood that this Agreement may not be assigned by either party without the written consent of the other party. This Agreement may be amended at any time by mutual agreement of the parties, provided that it shall have been written and signed by both parties. This Agreement constitutes the entire agreement between the parties. Nothing in this Agreement shall be construed as creating or giving rise to any rights in any third parties or any persons other than the parties hereto.

PHO address:

CVO address:

continues

Exhibit 10–1 continued

IN WITNESS WHEREOF, the parties have caused this Agreement to be executed the day and year first written above.

Date:_______________ Signature:_______________________________ Title:____________

Witness: __________________ By: _______________________________________

Date:_______________ Signature:_______________________________ Title:____________

Witness: __________________ By: _______________________________________

Courtesy of C. Mobley & Associates, LLC, and Quality Management Options, LLC, Colorado Springs, Colorado.

Exhibit 10–2 Agreement between Hospital and Independent Practice Association (IPA)

In consideration of the mutual covenants herein contained, and intending to be bound, the parties agree as follows:

I. DEFINITIONS

The following terms shall be referred to as follows in this Agreement:

__________ IPA, referred to as _____IPA
__________ Hospital, referred to as _____H
Medical Staff of _____, referred to as MS__.
Department of Medical Affairs, referred to as DMA.

II. RESPONSIBILITIES

The parties shall have the following responsibilities under this Agreement:

__________ **IPA**

A designated contact person will be identified to the DMA to maintain communication of application updates. This physician member will be the President of the _____IPA or his or her designee.

Members of the _____IPA will agree to sign a release for __________ Hospital to provide utilization review, quality assurance, risk management, patient or staff complaints, credentialing information (to include denial, reduction, revocation of privileges); signature shall release _____H and its agents from any and all liability or damages. _____IPA will reciprocate and provide practice information to _____H. President of the _____IPA and his or her designee will educate all members with regard to access of information process. Further, potential recruits will be referred to the Credentialing Assistant in DMA for the credentialing process and appropriate forms.

continues

Exhibit 10–2 continued

Credentialing and Quality Assurance processes will be consistent with the Bylaws, Rules, and Regulations of the MS_.

__________ **Hospital**

A release form will be provided to any potential _____IPA recruits; it will be attached to the Medical Staff preapplication form.

Credentialing assistant will provide application status updates to the potential recruit and, if requested, to the president of _____IPA or his or her designee. Credentialing assistant will be the key contact person in DMA.

MS_ Quality Assurance coordinator will be the contact person with regard to physician quality assurance activities.

The Director of Medical Affairs of _____H will be the contact person with regard to utilization of services through the Atlas information database.

Medical Staff Coordinator will be the contact person with regard to corrective action updates of _____IPA members after any restrictions, revocations, denial of privileges instituted by the Governing Board of _____H.

In Witness Whereof the parties have executed this Agreement on the dates set forth below.

__________ IPA

By: ______________________________ ______________________
President, _____IPA Date

__________ Hospital

By: ______________________________ ______________________
President, MS_ Date

By: ______________________________ ______________________
President, _____H Date

Courtesy of Boulder Community Hospital, Boulder, Colorado.

10. negotiation and execution of contract
11. identification of process for information exchange
12. monitoring and oversight of process

DELEGATION PLAN

Organizations that decide to fully delegate the credentialing/recredentialing process should develop a delegation plan document. The plan should address

1. scope of delegation activities
2. policies and procedures
   - responsibility for all credentialing actions
   - audit process
   - decision-making process
   - oversight/quality management/evaluation
   - process for corrective action and revocation of delegation if obligations are not met

Exhibit 10–3 Physician Release

The undersigned hereby releases, indemnifies, and holds the Hospital and its board members, agents, medical staff appointees, and employees harmless to the full extent provided by law from any and all liability arising out of the provision of information about me to _____IPA and to _____H, including but not limited to information concerning professional review actions involving me and my other activities at the Hospital.

The undersigned also authorizes _____IPA to request such information about me from the Hospital.

_______________________________ _______________________________

Signature Date

____

Printed Name

Courtesy of Boulder Community Hospital, Boulder, Colorado.

3. criteria/standards
4. forms and tools used in evaluation and oversight activities
5. management of the delegation process
6. job description for staff managing delegations

THE HOSPITAL MEDICAL STAFF OFFICE AS A DELEGATED ORGANIZATION

Managed care organizations may request that a hospital medical staff office accept delegation if a significant component of their panel is affiliated with the hospital. This arrangement relieves the requirement for practitioners to complete two applications and related credentialing processes. In this type of delegation arrangement, the MCO must perform annual evaluations of the medical staff credentialing function (if required by its accreditation). This evaluation may be viewed as unnecessary by the medical staff office due to compliance with the Joint Commission and a belief that the hospital process is more detailed than that of MCOs. Communication should occur to assure that both parties understand the process. Identification of requirements should address authorization to review files

- MCO does not review files of nonparticipating practitioners
- MCO should not have access to performance or quality data
- MCO is not required to maintain a hard-copy file with copies of information found in hospital file, profile is the only required document

SUBDELEGATION

Subdelegation occurs when an organization delegates credentialing activity to another organization, which itself delegates a part of the credentialing activity. This most commonly occurs when an organization delegates to a hospital or other organization that is using the services of a CVO. Thus, the verification is a subdelegated service for the first organization. Subdelegation is accepted practice and is addressed by both URAC and NCQA standards. A subdelegation agreement does not change responsibility for compliance with standards, but initial evaluation and oversight may be accomplished by one rather than both of the delegating organizations (if information is shared).

ENSURING QUALITY

A significant aspect of delegation is the oversight or continued assurance that contract requirements are met. An annual assessment of the delegated organization process is required by NCQA to determine whether the delegated activities are being carried out in accordance with standards.

Oversight Activities

NCQA requires an evaluation process no less than annually for delegates that are not NCQA accredited or certified. The evaluation should include an audit of credentials files (either 5 percent or 50 files, whichever is less). The file audit should be structured to ensure that information is being appropriately verified. At minimum, the audited files should include 10 credentialing and 10 recredentialing files.

The evaluation is usually conducted on site, but some components may be conducted by phone and review of documents forwarded by the delegated organizations. The evaluation should be based upon the requirements outlined in the contract or letter of agreement. The file audit format should mirror the NCQA standards. Although the requirement is for an annual evaluation, if problems are identified or the scope of the activity is significant, more frequent evaluation may be warranted. If the delegation is for verification only and the delegated organization is an NCQA-certified CVO, the oversight requirement is restricted to elements not certified. This is discussed in more detail later in the chapter.

Key Elements of a Successful Delegation

A successful delegation will reduce duplication of verifications and provide an opportunity to collaborate and ensure a quality network. Elements of a successful delegation include

- a well-written, easily readable contract or letter of agreement that addresses all aspects of the relationship
- an evaluation process and audit tool that addresses all key elements of the process
- open communication—all results, concerns, and work well done are shared
- schedule oversight review with documented results provided to the delegated organization
- provision of a copy of the contract or letter of agreement to a subdelegate

CREDENTIALS VERIFICATION ORGANIZATIONS (CVOs)

A CVO is an organization or independent contractor that performs primary source verification, gathers information related to a practitioner's credentials for initial credentialing and/or recredentialing, and provides the information to another entity or network component. Some CVOs also conduct physician office visits and medical record review. In the past, CVOs, often medical societies, performed verification, but those organizations normally performed it only for hospitals in their local geographic area. Current CVOs perform activities for entities willing to contract with them that require primary source verification or support in acquiring information.

Types of CVOs

Many types of CVOs currently exist. These include

- Independent, privately owned CVOs that are for-profit and have been organized specifically to perform verification functions.
- Medical societies that perform verification services. In the past, these societies have had hospitals as their primary clients, but as

health care is developing, many are adding networks and accommodating requests from managed care and other organizations involved in credentialing activities.

- Hospital systems/health care networks' internal centralized verification services. Such services usually provide primary source verification, application services, etc., only to the hospitals and related entities within that system or to related health plans and do not normally provide services to external entities on a for-profit basis.
- The AMA and the American Osteopathic Association (AOA) have developed practitioner profiles but are not considered to be true CVOs.

Advantages of Using a CVO

A major advantage of using a CVO is the decrease or elimination of duplication of information that is required of the practitioner. If a CVO processes the majority of practitioner applications in one area, the practitioner may be required to complete only one application and potentially one recredentialing application. This saves time for both the practitioner and all of the organizations that would otherwise be processing individual applications.

Other advantages include

- *Positive impact on productivity, ability to use information in a standardized manner, and decrease in time spent obtaining missing information.* Use of a CVO is a distinct advantage for organizations that do not have personnel knowledgeable about the credentialing verification process or sufficient staffing to include the verification/reverification process. CVOs usually have significant expertise because verification is their only job.
- *CVOs' cycle time.* CVOs are usually able to complete the verification process more quickly due to use of on-line and tape-to-tape verifications.
- *Reduction of overall paperwork,* especially for managed care organizations. The CVO maintains the hard copies and gives the managed care organization a profile summary of information received, including the date; only adverse information, such as any sanctions, NPDB adverse reports, malpractice payments, or anything other than a "clean" hospital reference (current and in good standing), is forwarded in hard copy to the managed care organization. (See Chapter 3 for more information on paperless credentialing.)

Cost may be an advantage or a disadvantage, depending on the number of practitioners and scope of activities.

Disadvantages of Using a CVO

Some disadvantages of using a CVO may be perceived rather than real. Disadvantages may include

- *Loss of control and increased cost.* CVOs can find it difficult to convince organizations that their service can be cost-effective and be done at the same level of quality and timeliness as it would be done internally. The contractor should deal with frequency and type of communication related to status of verifications and other concerns to maintain good working relationships.
- *Compliance with the 180-day verification time frame.* This becomes an issue when an NCQA-accredited MCO delegates to a noncertified CVO. A delegated CVO is allowed 120 days to provide information to the client, allowing the client or organization 60 days for review and approval. If the delegated organization is unable to consistently comply with the 120-day turnaround time, the relationship can clearly be a disadvantage for the managed care organization.

- *Standardized forms.* Many CVOs have standardized application forms and form letters. If a delegating organization has specific information that it needs to collect that is unique to that organization, the organization may need to request that information on its own or pay extra to have it collected by the CVO.
- *Cycle or schedule.* The cycle or schedule used by the CVO may not fit the organization's schedule for processing. This most often occurs with the recredentialing cycle. A delegating organization may renew by appointment date, while a CVO may renew information only on practitioner birth dates.
- *Staffing.* Some organizations believe that delegating to a CVO may be used as justification to reduce the number of full-time employees (FTEs) in the hospital medical staff office. The medical staff or credentialing office can justify the use of a CVO while maintaining the same staffing. The use of a CVO allows the medical office staff to concentrate on the evaluation of information and collection of additional information where problems may exist. In general, use of a CVO does not mean an automatic reduction in staffing but does mean that office staff time is more productive. This is an *advantage*.
- *Exchange of information.* If the computer systems of the two organizations cannot communicate, there is a possible problem in relation to the ability to provide or access information. The delegating organization will have to provide lists of practitioners, etc.; a hard copy becomes a much more time-consuming process, although it can be overcome through use of disks, downloading, and so forth.

Key Functions Performed by CVOs

CVOs do not perform credentialing by definition. Credentialing includes review, evaluation and approval, or other decision. CVOs do not evaluate competency, make judgments, or render decisions related to inclusion of a practitioner in a panel or on a medical staff. Therefore, the functions performed by the CVO are specifically limited to the three areas of

- application and gathering of data
- primary source verification
- site reviews, including medical record evaluation

CVO Evaluation

To determine the viability and benefit of outsourcing to a CVO, it is necessary to obtain information about the internal cost of verification. This information may then be used for cost comparisons in review of CVOs. It is also good practice to identify and define all specific activities that might be delegated or outsourced.

If an organization determines that it will consider a CVO, it should identify

- capability of the CVO to provide service for the organization. This relates specifically to the scope of practitioners, both number and type, including allied health.
- costs and fees (what is included in the fee and all add-on costs)
- information about the computer and software system and ability of the organization's computer and software systems to communicate with those of the CVO under consideration
- services provided by the CVO, including requirements for application, types of verification, and availability of office site and medical record reviews if applicable
- availability of management reports that reflect status, work in progress, and compliance with standards
- certification status

The Joint Commission has outlined principles for evaluation of agencies providing centralized credentials services. These are shown in Exhibit 10–4.

CVO Certification

In 1996, NCQA initiated its first "derivative" program by surveying CVOs for the purpose of certification. This program, modeled after managed care organization accreditation was designed to provide some relief for delegation oversight to accredited managed care organizations' 10 elements of application and verification. NCQA-accredited managed care organizations that delegate their verification to certified CVOs are not subject to oversight requirements and file verification during survey. The certification might also be considered a benchmark and as-

Exhibit 10–4 Principles for Evaluation of Agencies Providing Centralized Credentials Services

1. The agency makes known to the user what data and information can be provided by it.
2. The agency provides documentation to the user describing how its data collection, information development, and verification process(es) are performed.
3. The user and agency agree on the format for the transmission from the agency of credentials information about an individual.
4. The user can easily discern what information, transmitted by the agency, is from a primary source and what is not.
5. For information that can become out of date (e.g., licensure, board certification), the agency will provide the date that the information was last updated from the primary source.
6. The agency certifies that the information transmitted to the user accurately presents the information obtained by it.
7. The user can discern whether the information transmitted by the agency from a primary source is **all** the primary source information in the agency's possession pertinent to a given item or, if not, where additional information can be obtained.
8. The user can engage the quality control processes of the agency when necessary to resolve concerns about transmission errors, inconsistencies, or other data issues that may be identified from time to time.

Definitions

agency: Any entity used by a health care organization to obtain information, including from primary sources, for the purpose of verifying an individual's credentials.

credentials: Documented evidence of licensure, education, training, experience, or other qualifications.

primary source: The original source of a specific credential that can verify the accuracy of a qualification reported by an individual health care practitioner. (Examples include medical school, graduate medical education program, and state medical board.)

Source: Data from *1998 Comprehensive Accreditation Manual for Hospitals: The Official Handbook,* MS-36, © 1998, Joint Commission on Accreditation of Healthcare Organizations.

sures potential clients that the CVO is in full compliance with specific standards. Therefore, it may be advantageous for organizations that are not accredited by NCQA to consider using certified CVOs. For a CVO to be eligible for review, it must

1. verify credentials for any of the following practitioner types:
   - MD, DO
   - DPM, DDS, DC
   - behavioral health
2. have at least a six-month track record

Individual elements that are eligible for certification are

- practitioner application processing
- license to practice
- hospital privileges
- DEA/CDS registration
- board certification/completion of residency
- malpractice insurance
- malpractice claims history
- NPDB query
- sanctions against licensure
- Medicaid/Medicare sanctions

The NCQA review of a CVO considers

- policies and procedures
- quality improvement process
- data security and integrity
- ongoing reporting of disciplinary information
- practitioner application
- appropriate verification and documentation that is in compliance with MCO credentialing standards

Validation of compliance is determined through an audit of completed credentials files with identification that

- individual queries are made to primary source as required
- verification is completed within 120 days (allowing 60 days for MCO to complete evaluation and make a decision)

Duration of the CVO certification by NCQA is two years.

URAC has just announced a program to certify CVOs. The reader will need to determine status, applicability, and activity from this organization.

PHYSICIAN ORGANIZATION CERTIFICATION

NCQA developed the physician organization certification program to help streamline the accreditation process for managed care organizations and the physician organizations affected by it. The program involves a review by NCQA of a physician organization instead of numerous reviews by MCOs that are NCQA accredited. The program works in much the same way as CVO certification in relief of the oversight requirements.

Organizations that are eligible to participate in the physician organization certification program include

- primary care and multispecialty groups and networks
- independent practice associations
- physician hospital organizations
- integrated delivery systems
- organizations that provide management services and that contract with or are able to contract with a licensed MCO to provide delegated services

The areas available to physician organizations for certification are

- credentialing and recredentialing
- member rights and responsibilities
- medical records
- preventative health
- quality management and improvement
- utilization management

Certification may be obtained for any or all of the areas, and the standard categories are the same as NCQA's MCO accreditation.

CENTRALIZED OR UNIFORM CREDENTIALING AND/OR VERIFICATION SERVICES

Centralized or uniform credentialing or verification services are frequently developed for

- large health care systems (i.e., those health care systems with multiple hospitals)
- health care systems with hospital(s), providers, and managed care products
- hospitals that own or manage multiple ambulatory care services, including physician offices
- multiple hospital affiliation

A centralized uniform function is beneficial in that it

- ensures standardization of processes
- allows for one application form, saving time for the practitioner
- is cost-effective to reduce duplication of activity
- may minimize liability

All or part of credentialing may be consolidated when creating a centralized system, including

- application form and application packet distribution
- credentialing plan, policies and procedures, and documents used during the credentialing process
- verification
- development of criteria for privileges and delineation of privileges forms
- review and evaluation of credentials
- decisions related to participation, affiliation, membership, status or privileges
- corrective action, due process, fair hearing

Figure 10–1 outlines a centralized verification process and its reporting structure in the organization.

Components that must be addressed when developing a centralized uniform credentialing and/or verification process include

1. determination of which elements of the credentialing process will be centralized
2. organizational structure, including decision-making authority
3. use of a joint application, which may need to be expanded to meet managed care or other requirements
4. legal issues
   - release form for sharing information
   - confidentiality of information
   - peer review immunity
   - location, storage, and sharing of peer review information
   - obtaining and use of NPDB
   - antitrust implications of uniform decision making
   - corrective action process
   - sharing of information
   - required changes to bylaws and other governing documents
5. development of shared policies, procedures, and other documents
6. development of privileging criteria and delineation of privileges
7. communication, maintenance, and storage of all credentialing documents, information, and files

Organization/CVO receives request for an application via mail or telephone.

↓

All appropriate entities are notified when request is received, and appropriate privilege checklists are forwarded to the CVO (if applicable).

↓

Application packet is sent to applicant.

↓

CVO receives application and reviews it for completeness. If application is not complete, a letter is sent regarding the incomplete information.

↓

Copies of application are made and forwarded to entities, and applicant's credentials are entered into software program.

↓

Requests for primary source verifications and other information are mailed out.

↓

Primary source verification and information are received and entered into computer.

↓

Thirty days after initial query (option—status letter forwarded to the applicant requesting assistance), second requests initiated for information not received.

↓

Copies of all verifications are made and forwarded with applicable privilege forms to each entity that the physician is applying to.

↓

Once applicant is approved, the designated entity(ies) sends notification of approval to CVO for database entry.

↓

Database is updated, noting date of appointment, status, and category. Information is updated and entered per contract requirements.

Note: Entities refers to those organizations having a contract with the CVO.

Figure 10–1 Centralized Verification Process for Initial Application Using One Application Form. Courtesy of C. Mobley & Associates, LLC, and Quality Management Options, LLC, Colorado Springs, Colorado.

NOTES

1. C. Mobley, "CVO Utilization Survey Results" (paper presented at the meeting of the Medical Society Credentials Verification Organization of America, Washington, DC, March 1998).
2. *1998 Surveyor Guidelines for the Accreditation of Managed Care Organizations, 1998* (Washington, DC: National Committee for Quality Assurance, 1998), 353.
3. *1998–1999 Accreditation Handbook for Ambulatory Health Care* (Skokie, IL: Accreditation Association for Ambulatory Health Care, 1998), 22.
4. *Comprehensive Accreditation Manual for Health Care Networks, 1998–2000* (Oakbrook Terrace, IL: Joint Commission on Accreditation of Healthcare Organizations, 1998), HR3.8–HR3.12.
5. *1998 Surveyor Guidelines*, 180–186 (CR13).
6. *1998 Surveyor Guidelines*, 85.
7. *National Health Care Practitioner Credentialing Standards, 1997* (Washington, DC: Utilization Review Accreditation Commission, 1997), 6.
8. *National Health Care Practitioner,* 6.
9. *National Health Care Practitioner,* 370.
10. *National Health Care Practitioner,* 377.

CHAPTER 11

Roles and Relationships

OVERVIEW

Every health care organization that credentials practitioners has its own process and procedures. The department or area in the organization responsible for credentialing varies greatly in terms of roles, reporting relationships, responsibilities, and titles. Generally, a group, committee, or individual who compiles and initially reviews applications for initial credentialing and recredentialing forwards this information to a group, committee, or board that ultimately makes the final decision. Regardless of where the credentialing activities and decisions take place, relationships are important to the success of the credentialing program. This chapter will explore the roles of those most directly involved in the credentialing process and the relationships among all of the groups, departments, and individuals involved.

It is important that everyone involved, directly or indirectly, in credentialing have a good understanding of the entire process. Knowledgeable individuals better understand how their actions affect all of the other components of the credentialing process. Knowledge also enables people to cooperate and work together so that the process can work smoothly. For example, in managed care, staff responsible for recruiting practitioners must understand the timing of the credentials, verification, and approval process in order to keep the practitioner informed and to plan for execution of a contract. This is essential to ensure that the credentialing process is complete before patient contact. Staff unfamiliar with credentialing procedures may relay an expectation that "a little bit of paperwork" has to be completed before a practitioner can actually begin seeing patients. This situation may set unreal expectations for both the credentialing area and the potential practitioners.

Often, managers and leaders in an organization will have little knowledge of the time, scope of activities, and potential risks inherent in the credentialing process. Staff responsible for the process should be the experts and should be responsible for educating other members of the organization.

Teamwork and cooperation among departments, individuals, and committees are essential to a smooth credentialing process. If a large number of practitioners are going to be processed within a short time, the credentialing area must gear up and plan for the increased workload. Additional personnel may be required to assist with an influx of new applications. Ongoing communication and cooperation will support a timely process. If the departments and individuals responsible for credentialing and quality activities are not integrated, cooperation is essential to ensure that quality information is communicated for use in the recredentialing process.

DEPARTMENTS INVOLVED IN THE CREDENTIALING PROCESS

A medical staff (hospital) or provider credentialing (ambulatory/managed care) office or department has responsibility and accountability for numerous activities, including credentials verification, file development, review of information, processing privileges, and recredentialing. Depending on the organization, other functions such as committee support, development of emergency department on-call schedules, calendars, and newsletters or other communications to practitioners may also be assigned to the medical staff/provider credentialing office or department. The organization's size, relationships with other facilities, and scope of services offered will affect the function of the office.

Although there is no "typical" organizational chart for a hospital or managed care company, there are models that have proven to be effective. The credentialing function may be performed in a credentialing department as part of an integrated department (e.g., administration, quality management) or in an office with one or several people having reporting relationships to key decision makers.

The credentialing professional may have learned how to perform the function through on-the-job training or by a combination of on-the-job training, education (course work or seminars), and certification. Credentialing has become increasingly more complex, and it is essential that staff responsible for daily activities be qualified.

Regardless of the position of the credentialing function in the organization, the structure should support the information collection, review, and approval process. Table 11–1 outlines key aspects of a structure for the credentialing process.

Table 11–1 Structure for Credentialing Process Steps

Responsible Party	***Process Step***
Credentialing coordinator/department	• Preapplication • Distribution of application
Credentialing coordinator/department	• Data collection and verification • File development • Initial evaluation
Department review (hospital)	• Competency evaluation for privileges requested
Credentialing committee	• Review against criteria • Decision or recommendation to board (managed care) • Recommendation to medical executive committee (hospital)
Medical executive committee (hospital)	• Review recommendations from departments, credentials committee • Recommendation to governing body
Governing board	• Approval

Courtesy of C. Mobley & Associates, LLC, and Quality Management Options, LLC, Colorado Springs, Colorado.

In Hospitals

In hospitals, the credentialing function can be assigned to numerous areas. If the hospital is fairly small, there is seldom a medical staff office or department. The credentialing will be accomplished by administrative personnel or by a person assigned to carry out medical staff services. Credentialing may be done in a department such as quality management, administration, or medical records or in an integrated department performing numerous functions such as medical staff, quality improvement, risk management, or case management. Credentialing is commonly performed in a department that provides many services to the medical staff organization such as a medical staff office, medical affairs department, or medical staff department. With larger integrated delivery systems, there is a move to centralize some of the credentialing functions, such as verification, at a system level. In this case, rather than being located in a credentialing office within the confines of hospital parameters, credentialing is located in or falls under the auspices of a systems department.

Figures 11–1 and 11–2 show, respectively, a single and an integrated approach to medical staff support personnel reporting relationships.

In Managed Care

Managed care organizations may have a credentialing office or department that reports to quality management, administration, or provider services, or the credentialing function may reside in the provider contracting or provider relations department. The number of contracted practitioners and providers will often determine whether the function is stand-alone or integrated

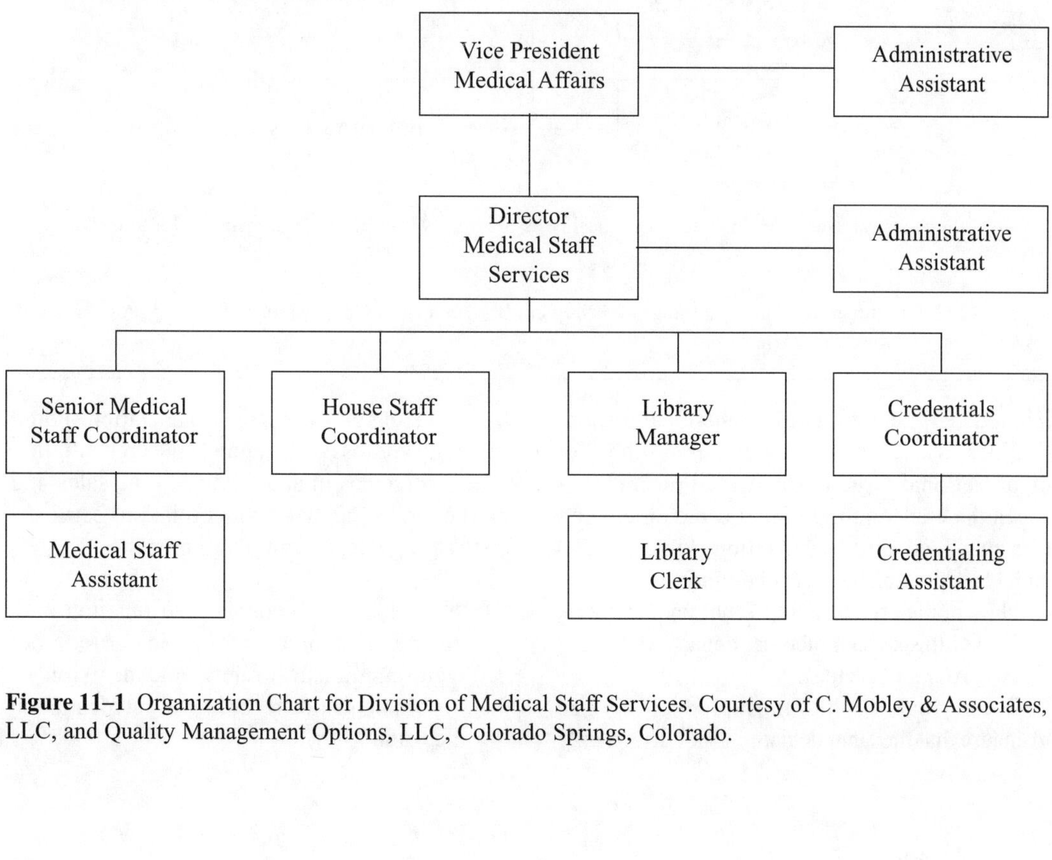

Figure 11–1 Organization Chart for Division of Medical Staff Services. Courtesy of C. Mobley & Associates, LLC, and Quality Management Options, LLC, Colorado Springs, Colorado.

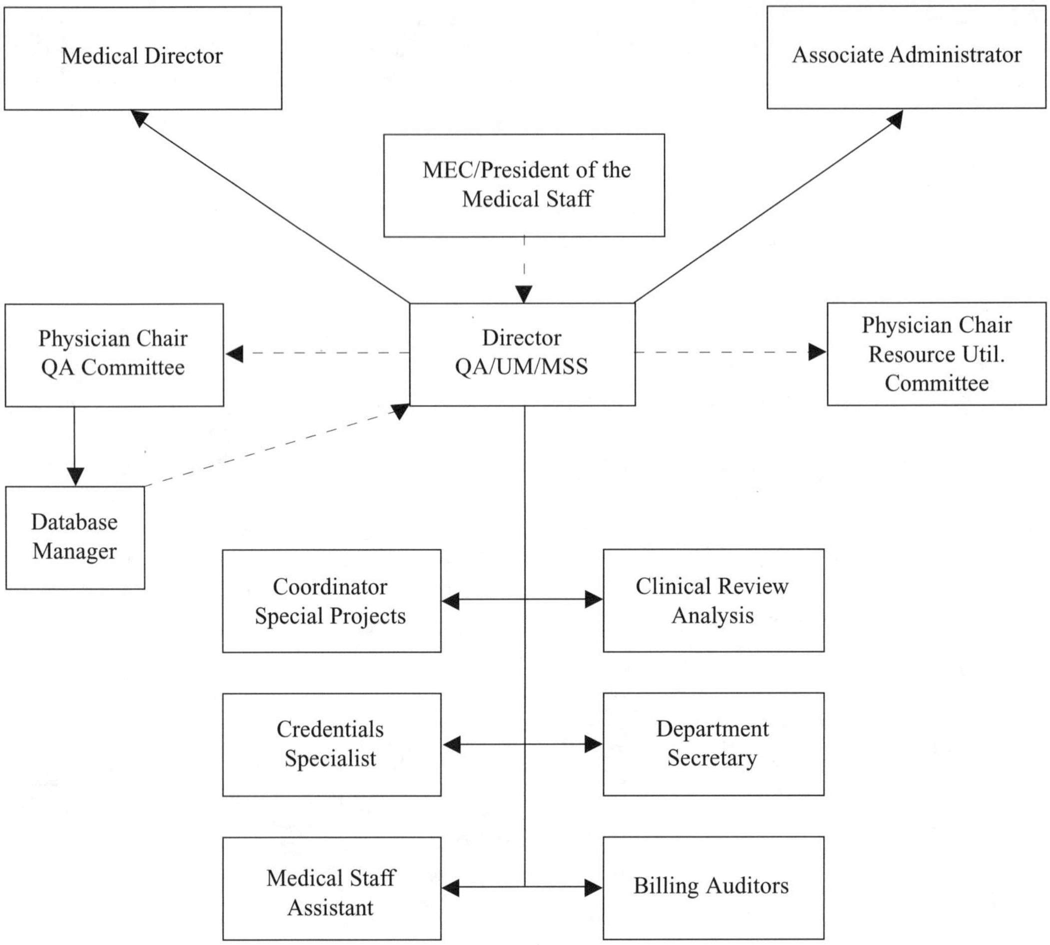

Note: MEC, medical executive committee; QA, quality assurance; UM, utilization management; MSS, medical staff services.

Figure 11–2 Organization Chart for Integrated Medical Staff Services.Courtesy of Alfred I. duPont Hospital for Children, Wilmington, Delaware.

into a department with other functional responsibilities. There are numerous possibilities for organizational structure and relationships between the credentialing function and other parts of a managed care organization. Figures 11–3 and 11–4 demonstrate two common structures. As shown, the credentialing function can reside in the health services/medical department or relate to provider services.

To carry out activities most productively and to ensure that the final decision is not driven only by marketing concerns, the organization should carefully address placement. If the credentialing function resides in and reports to the sales and marketing and/or the provider relations/services/contracting department, there must be

- a mechanism to connect the function with the medical director for policy criteria development, file review, and decision or recommendation regarding the credentialing decision

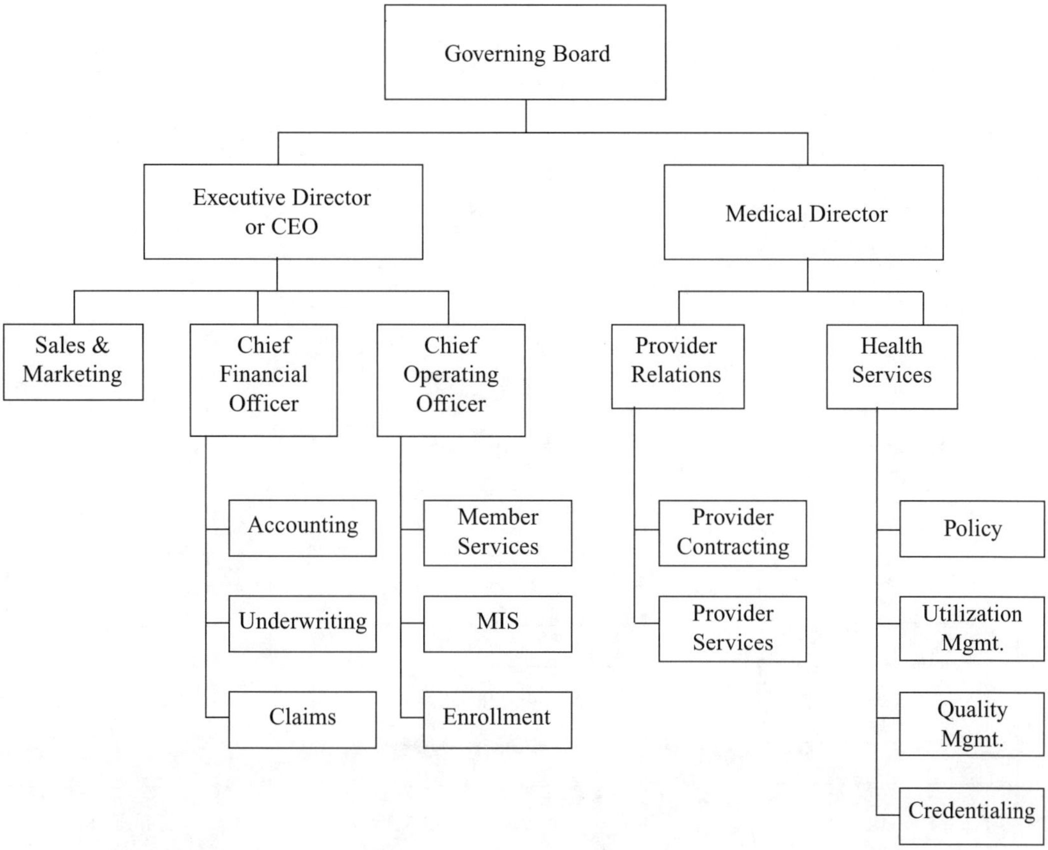

Note: MIS, Management Information Systems.

Figure 11–3 Organization Chart for Managed Care—Example 1. Courtesy of C. Mobley & Associates, LLC, and Quality Management Options, LLC, Colorado Springs, Colorado.

- assurance that recruitment and network development efforts do not influence the process or final decision
- a process to protect the confidentiality of information in the credentials and provider quality files

In Ambulatory Care

In ambulatory care, there is rarely a credentialing department. The function is commonly carried out within the administrative or business offices or in conjunction with the medical director. In ambulatory care, a significant component is focused on response to insurance requests for information. An administrative secretary or insurance clerk may carry out many of the credentialing activities.

In Credentials Verification Organizations

In contrast, a credentials verification organization (CVO) is in the business primarily to do credentials verification. Therefore, the entire company centers on a verification time cycle. Information is provided to clients who pay for credentialing verification services. Like other organizations where credentialing is performed

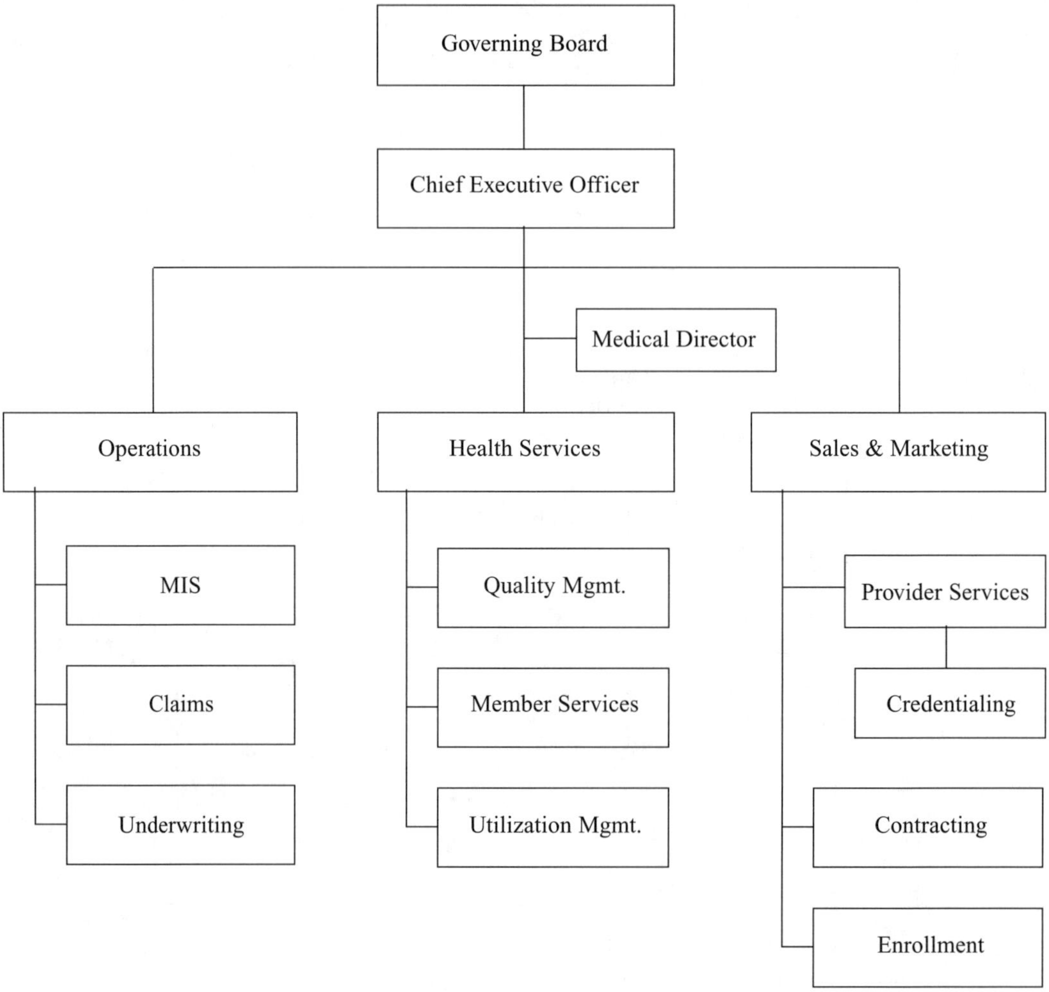

Note: MIS, Management Information Systems.

Figure 11–4 Organization Chart for Managed Care—Example 2. Courtesy of C. Mobley & Associates, LLC, and Quality Management Options, LLC, Colorado Springs, Colorado.

by a small department or by an individual within that organization, CVOs have a separate function responsible for gathering and reporting information. Figure 11–5 is an organizational chart for a CVO.

In Centralized Credentialing

In some networks or systems, credentialing is done at a centralized location. This may be in the city, in the region, or at the corporate offices. The advantage to centralizing credentialing or a component of credentialing such as verification is that it can eliminate duplication of effort across a system with multiple entities performing the same function. As long as there is good communication and appropriate data are available to the individual organizations in the system, there is no real detriment to having a part or all of the credentialing done off site. As systems and or-

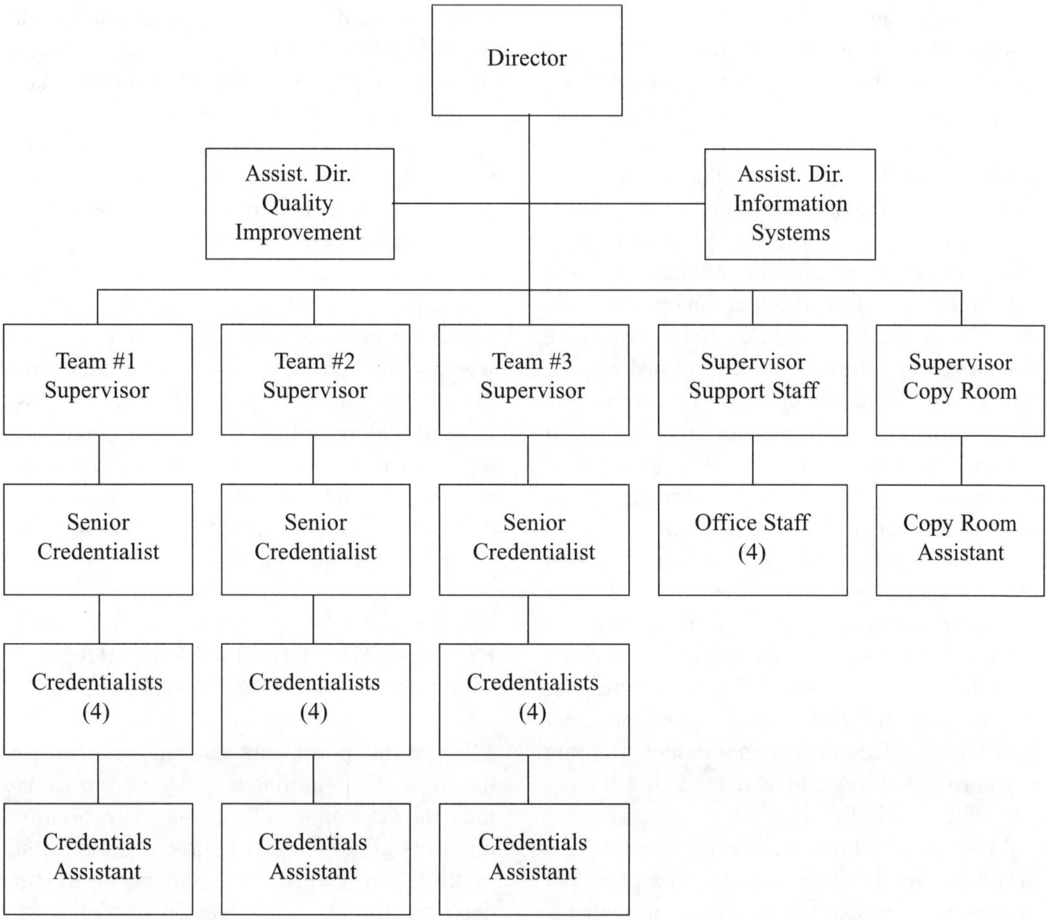

Figure 11–5 CVO Organization Chart. Courtesy of Greater Arizona Central Credentialing Program, Phoenix, Arizona.

ganizations continue to seek ways to consolidate functions, they are moving away from the more traditional system in which credentialing is done within the institution where the provider will be practicing or in the local managed care office. For many, this is a real paradigm shift and has been met with much questioning and resistance from those who have been used to having the information physically available in hard-copy format on site. Technology allows for computer status reports that are easily available, and in many cases, the information can be scanned, downloaded, or copied many times, with the original being retained in a central location. This can be a very productive, cost-effective approach.

STAFF POSITIONS INVOLVED IN THE CREDENTIALING PROCESS

The size of the organization and amount of work required to credential all practitioners will determine the type and number of staff positions needed to support this function. In organizations that have a department specifically responsible for a credentialing function, there is commonly a director or manager who has the overall responsibility for ensuring that the credentialing policies and procedures are carried out. Often this is a supervisory position because multiple people are employed to perform certain aspects for credentialing. In departments that are involved in more than credentialing, there will probably be a credentialing coordinator position responsible for everything related to credentialing and not directly involved in other functions of the department, such as meetings, bylaws revision, or contracting. Larger organizations may require several coordinators who are each responsible for a segment of the physician, practitioner, or provider population—for example, by letter in the alphabet, by specialty, by department, or by some other system. Titles such as *credentialing assistants* or *data coordinators* may also be used in the credentialing field. Regardless of the size of the organization, someone in the group discussed above will be responsible for working with the individuals who must review the credentials files and make recommendations and/or decisions affecting the appointment, granting of clinical privileges, and recredentialing of practitioners.

At the senior administrative level, many organizations have a medical director, vice president of medical affairs, or some other position that is either medical-administrative or purely administrative. Such senior-level individuals may have other responsibilities in addition to overseeing credentialing activities. They are not necessarily involved in the day-to-day credentialing activities but act in an advisory capacity when issues arise that may require involvement by a physician and/or administrator. Directors and managers of a credentialing process directly responsible for daily operations commonly report administratively to a senior management position.

In managed care organizations, the medical director will often be involved in the recruitment, review, evaluation, and approval of a practitioner making application to the plan. If this person makes the final decision, there must be input from a credentialing committee or another review body of participating practitioners. This position differs from that of a medical director in a hospital environment because the standards of the Joint Commission on Accreditation of Healthcare Organizations (Joint Commission) require department and executive committee recommendation to a board for final approval.

As can be seen from the previous organization charts, there are a variety of reporting relationships within an organization for those involved in credentialing. What also varies is whether the person to whom the credentialing manager or director reports has a basic knowledge of the credentialing function. Often these reporting relationships are administrative only and lack the support and/or expertise of the individual responsible at the credentialing level within the organization.

INVOLVEMENT OF THE PHYSICIAN OR HEALTH CARE PRACTITIONER

Up to this point, this chapter has addressed the roles of the individuals involved in gathering data, developing a credentials file, performing oversight of the review process, and recommending and approving the credentialing decision. But the health care practitioner who submitted information for review and approval also has responsibilities in the credentialing process. Often the health care practitioner is asked to supply information, such as copies of malpractice insurance, Drug Enforcement Administration (DEA) certificates, and documentation of specific education or training as it relates to clinical privileges requested as an attachment to the application. When information is requested from verifying organizations or individuals and is not received in a timely manner, the physician or practitioner may be requested to assist in having that information forwarded to the requesting organization.

Physicians and practitioners may also be required or requested (depending upon bylaws or policy and procedure) to appear before review bodies for an interview. Interviews may include questions related to their application or other action involving peer review activities. Once a request is made for additional information on an application or reapplication, failure to respond could result in action that would stop the review process from continuing further. This could mean that the practitioner would lose the opportunity to be associated with the organization.

As mentioned earlier, the credentialing decision in managed care organizations can be made at the credentials committee level or at an individual medical director level with input from other plan practitioners. Even if the decision is made at an individual or committee level, it is suggested that the governing board of the managed care organization be informed as an information item that practitioners have been credentialed or recredentialed.

ROLE OF THE GOVERNING BOARD

The role of the governing board in credentialing activities for a hospital is very clearly defined in the Joint Commission Standards for the Governing Body.[1] According to these standards, the governing body is ultimately held accountable and is the approval body for all credentialing decisions. Some governing boards receive the information from the medical staff organization in the form of a board report listing those practitioners and the credentialing recommendations that have been reviewed by the medical staff departments and committees. Detail of the report varies. It can be a list of the physicians and recommended actions, or it can be more detailed, including a profile of the practitioner who is being recommended. In some cases, the entire credentials file is available for review by the board members. Boards may have a quality committee that is charged with reviewing the actual recommendations and either taking action on behalf of the board or forwarding its recommendations to the board as a consent agenda item.

In managed care organizations, a governing board may or may not be directly involved in the credentials approval process. The standards of the National Committee for Quality Assurance (NCQA) do not require specific board action. Therefore, many organizations have delegated approval to a credentials committee. Even if the credentials committee is given the authority to make credentialing decisions, the approvals may be reported at a future board meeting for information. As in hospitals, the managed care approval body may review a list of the practitioners (previously reviewed by the medical director) or may review the entire credentials files.

Board composition varies from one organization to another and may include several members who are lay people and are not necessarily involved in health care as a profession. There are usually several physician members as well as others with health care and administrative experience. Board members should be oriented to the credentialing function and educated about their responsibility and accountability for making credentialing decisions or recommendations. Even if lists of practitioners are submitted with recommendations for action, boards always have the right to request additional information if they have questions or concerns, believe that something is missing, or believe that more information is necessary before they are comfortable making a final decision.

Even though hospital boards are given the ultimate authority to make the final decisions regarding practitioners, they must be able to depend on everyone involved in the process to carefully fulfill all requirements of his or her assigned responsibility. The board will still be held ultimately accountable, but it can certainly delegate all of the verification, reviews, and so forth to the medical staff who have expertise in evaluating their peers. Boards should be very interested in the process that the medical staff use to make their recommendations to the board. Often, the chief of staff or president of the medical staff will be a board member and can provide that liaison between the organized medical staff and the governing board. The vice president of medical affairs or the medical director is also a position that can provide that liaison with and/or education to the board so that board members better understand the processes being followed.

As is the case in both managed care and hospitals, boards may not meet often enough for timely decisions on credentialing recommendations. Therefore, a credentialing committee or medical director in a managed care organization, or, in hospitals, a quality committee of the board that meets more frequently, can be empowered to make these decisions, with decision information forwarded to the board when they meet.

Credentialing professionals can play a role in educating boards about the credentialing processes by participating in their orientation. Flowcharts for the various credentialing processes can be valuable tools used for board education. Orientation should take place at least annually and should include new board members as well as a review for ongoing board members.

FUNCTIONS OF THE MEDICAL STAFF OFFICE—HOSPITAL

As stated earlier, a hospital medical staff office or department has credentialing as one of many functions supporting the medical staff organization. The components of the credentialing process that the medical staff office performs may vary among organizations; for example, verifications may be outsourced to a commercial CVO, a medical society CVO, or somewhere else within the health care delivery system. Regardless of whether the verifications are done internally or externally, usually the initial contact by the prospective practitioner comes to the medical staff office of the hospital where the practitioner intends to practice. Following that initial contact, either an application is sent from the medical staff office, or notification is made to a CVO or other component within the system to forward information to the prospective applicant.

Once the verifications have been completed and all data obtained for a prospective applicant, the credentialing personnel will review the information, determine if additional information is needed, and then proceed with the review process, including medical staff committee, department, and/or executive committee reviews, after which recommendations are forwarded to the governing board for the final decision. If additional information is requested of the prospective applicant, credentialing personnel will be responsible for sending letters or faxes or making phone calls in an attempt to gather that information.

After the decision is made by the governing board to approve or disapprove the applicant, the medical staff office has the responsibility of notifying the applicant. Additionally, it notifies departments within the organization that need to know that a new practitioner has been added to the medical staff organization or allied health staff. This may be done in the form of hard-copy memos and/or computerized programs that distribute the information to those who need it. The process is basically the same for a reappointment process or change in clinical privileges. If an adverse recommendation is made, the medical staff office will be instrumental in facilitating the fair hearing process.

Other credentialing functions performed in the medical staff office include

- processing temporary privileges
- monitoring a provisional period for new practitioners or provisional status for other practitioners who have been placed on probation for specific procedures and/or treatments
- processing reference requests by other organizations
- documenting the process and/or notifying appropriate individuals regarding disciplinary action which may or may not involve a fair hearing process, and assisting in the facilitation of a fair hearing process with regard to revocation, denial, suspension, or limitation of clinical privileges and/or medical staff membership

FUNCTIONS OF THE CREDENTIALING OFFICE—MANAGED CARE

Activities in a managed care provider credentialing office are much the same as credentialing activities in a hospital medical staff office. Although there is no organized medical staff function in managed care, the credentialing staff is responsible for gathering and verifying information and developing a file for all practitioners and providers who will be or are contracted with the plan. Most plans will have a significantly larger number of contracted practitioners and providers than are found in a hospital medical staff organization. The credentialing function may be stand-alone or may be integrated into another department. Either way, it will generally be responsible for gathering information that is needed from the practitioner, verifying the information, and preparing the documentation for review by individuals and designated committees.

In a managed care environment, it is possible for the verification component to be outsourced. Once the information has been received and the internal review process has begun, additional information may be requested or required before any final decision. If practitioners are employed, the hiring process may be integrated with credentialing, or the two processes may be conducted independently. If the process is integrated, it is important to clearly delineate the purpose and requirements of each step. If independent, it is important to address duplication of efforts and timeliness of process to allow for identification of a credentialing start date that coincides with completion of credentialing. Practitioners in managed care may contract with the health plan and/or be employed.

NCQA allows managed care organizations to delegate all or part of the credentialing function to an external organization such as a hospital. In a delegated arrangement, the verification, as well as the review and approval process, performed by the hospital may be accepted in its entirety by the managed care organization as long as the hospital process includes all required elements. The managed care organization delegating a significant component of its activities will have different structure and staffing than one that does not delegate.

FUNCTIONS OF A CVO

CVOs are composed mostly of individuals who will be responsible for some component of credentials verification. In larger CVOs, numerous individuals may perform the same function but may divide the work by alphabet or according to verification components. For example, one individual may do all data bank queries; another may do all licensure verifications. If individuals are doing just one type of verification, it is fairly easy to train and orient new employees. The advantage of having an organization largely composed of people doing only verifications is that on-the-job training may be sufficient. Hiring people with previous managed care or hospital credentialing experience is very helpful. Regardless of the verification function or other functions performed, employees' health care experience will give them a better understanding of how their particular function feeds into the overall credentialing process. By understanding the entire credentialing process, they can better appreciate the importance of the function they perform as individuals.

ORGANIZATION OF A "TYPICAL" OFFICE RESPONSIBLE FOR CREDENTIALING

This is an intriguing title for this section, since it is difficult to determine whether there is a "typical" organization of an office that is responsible for credentialing. Managed care organizations and hospitals are diverse in their internal organization, and many organizations outsource a portion or all of the credentialing function. It may, in fact, be difficult to find a "typical" credentialing office.

The Medical Staff Office—Hospital

In hospitals, the credentialing function can be part of a medical staff office with multiple employees; a single individual who is part of administration, quality management, or medical records (commonly occurs in smaller hospitals); or, more recently, part of a system credentialing or medical staff department. The single individual who is part of another department may be a dedicated person to medical staff support or may have only a portion of his/her responsibilities dedicated to medical staff support or a portion of medical staff support such as credentialing. Within a multiple-person department, one person can be assigned the primary credentialing responsibilities. If the department is large enough, several people given different tasks may be responsible for credentialing, or one individual may be assigned to all credentialing tasks for a department or other defined group. It is possible to have a credentialing manager or supervisor in addition to a department director in larger organizations. Other models may exist, but the ones mentioned are the most common (see organization charts in Figures 11–1 and 11–2).

If the hospital outsources its verification component of credentialing, someone internally is still responsible for receiving and reviewing the information and facilitating the medical staff/board recommendation and approval process. If a health care delivery system (with multiple hospitals, clinics, etc.) has a centralized credentialing office, the data collection (verification) and/or the initial review can all occur at that level and then be forwarded to the individual components within the system for further process with the medical staff. If any component of the credentialing process occurs in more than one area of a department, a hospital, or a system, it is important that the function be well coordinated by knowledgeable individuals who communicate effectively with all involved.

The Credentialing Office—Managed Care

In managed care organizations, the provider credentialing department or credentialing function may be part of medical management, provider relations, or even sales and marketing. As in hospitals, access to individuals or groups who need to review the information is most important.

If the function is staffed with three or more employees and performs little or no delegation, the structure of the office may look like the one shown in Figure 11–6.

The department or activity may be organized to perform on a functional or a task basis. A functional organization would specify credentialing activities such as initial application, recredentialing, and facility site review and would assign them to specific employees. In this structure there may be little continuity, and employees can become very specialized. This can be beneficial, as the employee becomes very competent in performance of the activity, but it can be problematic if only one employee is knowledgeable about an activity.

If the organization is task based, the credentialing activities may be identified and assigned differently. One coordinator might be responsible for all credentialing tasks and activities for any practitioner whose last name falls into a specified group of letters, or for all practitioners whose offices are located in a specified geographic area.

Regardless of how the credentialing department or function is organized, the key to performance will be the employee's ability to effectively interact with the practitioners and external organizations or entities. The structure should ensure that interactions can occur easily and in a timely manner.

In some managed care organizations, the process allows a contract or employment agreement to be executed before the credentialing process is fully completed. This may result from internal

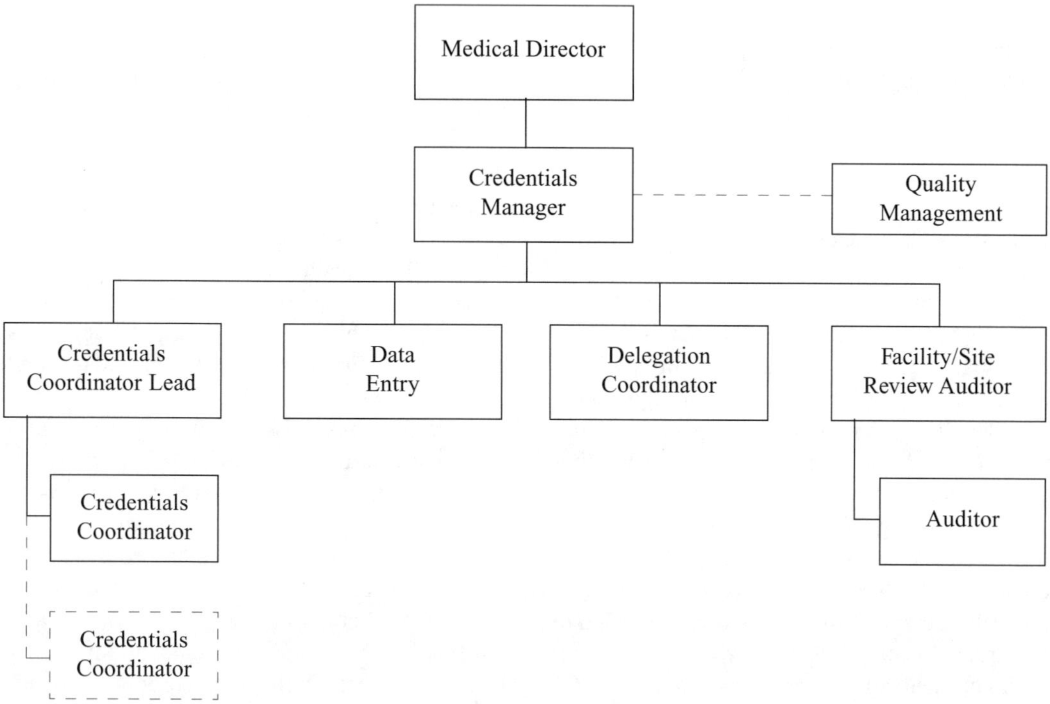

Figure 11–6 Sample Structure for Credentials Function in a Managed Care Organization. Courtesy of C. Mobley & Associates, LLC, and Quality Management Options, LLC, Colorado Springs, Colorado.

marketing and/or recruitment pressures or from insufficient knowledge of the risks involved when practitioners are allowed to see patients before completion of credentialing. If the credentialing function is part of the marketing or provider relations departments, the pressure on credentialing employees may be increased. Administration should be aware of this possibility and take steps to ensure that all practitioners and providers are credentialed appropriately, with as much support given to credentialing as to recruitment. Note that NCQA does not allow temporary privileges.

While hospitals obtain direction from bylaws, rules, and regulations, managed care organizations have policies and procedures that outline and direct the credentialing process. These policies and procedures should outline criteria, process timing, and options, thus allowing appropriate access to key individuals in the organization by those doing daily work.

QUALIFICATIONS OF THE CREDENTIALING PROFESSIONAL

Because there is little formal education available for individuals in the credentialing profession, individuals enter the profession with different backgrounds from both inside and outside health care. A number of health care educational and/or professional organizations offer credentialing seminars that range from beginning "how to" courses for those directly involved in credentialing to advanced courses offering information related to credentialing standards and procedures for administrators and physician leaders within an organization.

Education/Certification

The National Association Medical Staff Services (NAMSS) in Lombard, Illinois, is the professional organization for those involved in credentialing and offers certification programs specifically for credentialing specialists and those in medical staff services. The credentialing certification is *certified provider credentialing specialist* (CPCS). Prerequisite criteria include formal education as well as direct experience in credentialing. NAMSS also offers a certification that is broader in terms of scope and knowledge required. Credentialing is only one component of this certification; others include medical staff law, administration/management, medical/health care terminology, accreditation, and medical staff organization. The designation is *certified medical staff coordinator* (CMSC).

A few community colleges nationwide offer an associate degree in medical staff service science that includes credentialing in the curriculum. Other organizations, such as the Healthcare Assembly, located in Portsmouth, New Hampshire, offer a credentialing certificate program.

It is a distinct advantage for credentialing professionals to have specific training through seminars or course work in order to be most proficient and knowledgeable in their job. Certification (through NAMSS) is a distinction that indicates relevant knowledge to an organization that desires specific credentialing expertise. Many organizations are supportive of membership in NAMSS as well as continuing education in order to remain current with accreditation/federal/state standards, common practices, and problems arising within the credentialing environment. What once was a fairly simple process has become increasingly complex as the types of organizations that are required to credential individuals increase, as well as number of accrediting organizations. It is possible for some organizations to be surveyed by more than one accrediting body. As noted in Chapter 2 of this book, credentialing standards are a part of all major accreditation organizations. There must be a mechanism within each health care organization for those involved in credentialing to keep abreast of all changes that occur and then to revise internal policies, procedures, and/or bylaws to be in compliance with all of the standards and other changes.

As individuals cross over from hospitals into managed care and vice versa, it is important that they understand the differences in credentialing activities and accreditation standards and not assume that the standards and procedures applicable in one area of health care will necessarily work in another organization.

Most job descriptions for credentialing positions will reflect the experience required. NAMSS certification may also be required. Some job descriptions may indicate that education and/or certification is preferred and that those individuals with the higher qualifications will be considered first or that certification must be obtained within a specified time period following employment. Today, there are more positions available than qualified individuals to fill them. Unfortunately, not all organizations understand the importance of hiring individuals with specific expertise and training in the credentialing field. Many people have been hired into credentialing positions and have subsequently left because they were initially unaware of the complexity of the credentialing function within an organization. In small organizations, there may be no one else in the organization who has background or experience, and it is even more difficult for a person new to the credentialing field to understand and learn all of the components of a credentialing program. Organizations with little or no true understanding of credentialing processes may hire individuals without the necessary knowledge or expertise. Unfortunately, these organizations often do not realize their error in hiring the wrong people until they are close to an accreditation survey or until a legal situation related to credentialing arises.

Most organizations complete a mock survey or survey preparation review in the 6 to 12 months before a scheduled accreditation visit. This review may be the first time an organization identifies that the credentialing function is not in compliance with standards or internal policy. This results in a crisis situation that is usually very costly to resolve. Hiring experienced competent staff decreases the possibility of this situation.

The type of position may determine the degree of experience, including supervision or management of a credentialing department. If an individual is coming into a managed care organization or a hospital with experience from the "other side" (managed care organization or hospital), there should be an agreement that the individual be willing to attend educational conferences or seminars and/or undertake self study in order to understand the differences in procedure and certainly the accreditation standards with regard to credentialing.

Job Descriptions

There are a number of key elements to be considered in the development or update/revision of a job description for personnel responsible for credentialing activities. These include

- *Education.* It is common for larger institutions or organizations to require a bachelor's degree in a health-related field. This is also true if the position will involve management of personnel and/or the overall process. If the position is at a system director level, a master's degree in health care, business or information systems may be preferred. As previously stated, certification (CPCS or CMSC) is an indication of knowledge and education and may be required at time of hire or within a specified period of time following hire date.
- *Experience.* Generally one to two years of experience in credentialing is indicated for any position in which the individual will be working independently or in small organizations where only one individual will be doing credentialing activities.
- *Knowledge.* The job description commonly includes areas in which the applicant should be able to demonstrate knowledge. These areas might include the accreditation process and applicable standards, regulatory agency requirements, quality and process improvement concepts and processes, fluency in medical health care terminology, and credentialing software. The typical knowledge base in a job description for someone in managed or ambulatory care includes initial credentialing and recredentialing, delegated credentialing (if that organization uses delegation), and the appropriate accreditation standards. Typical for a hospital knowledge base would be initial appointment, reappointment, temporary privileges (if applicable), provisional monitoring (if it exists), clinical privileges, the appropriate accreditation standards (Joint Commission, American Osteopathic Association [AOA]), and bylaws.
- *Skills.* Skills may be categorized as hard or soft. Hard skills are those that can be measured, such as word processing or database management. Soft skill requirements, or those that cannot be easily measured, are more common. These include interpersonal skills, problem solving, decision making, and customer relations skills.

The job description may briefly address these elements or may be very detailed. An example of a brief statement would be "Demonstrates skill and proficiency in applying the techniques, concepts and principles that are central to the credentialing function." The sample job descriptions, Exhibits 11–1 to 11–5, are for a variety of credentialing positions in hospitals and managed/ambulatory care and could be adapted to many organizations.

Exhibit 11–1 Job Description for Manager, System Credentials Department

TITLE: Manager

POSITION CODE:

PAY GRADE:

REVISED DATE:

REPORTS TO: Director, System Medical Staff Services

POSITION SUMMARY

Provides direction for and management of the Systems Credentials Department.

POSITION ACCOUNTABILITIES AND PERFORMANCE CRITERIA

1. Assures the sound fiscal operation of the department, including the timely, accurate, and comprehensive development of an annual budget. Monitors operating budget and staffing levels. (5)
    - Demonstrates responsibility for the containment of costs through appropriate ordering of supplies, recovery of service charges, and conservation of supplies.
    - Responds promptly to changes in workload, adjusting assignments as necessary to achieve optimal productivity and efficiency.
    - Monitors department expenditures to ensure compliance with budget limits.
2. Establishes and maintains department policies and procedures, quality improvement programs, and safety objectives. Ensures that operations conform with local, state, and federal governmental regulations. Directs the preparation and maintenance of department reports. (2)
    - Demonstrates accurate knowledge of relevant laws, policies, regulations, and standards affecting decisions and interpretations.
    - Communicates new or modified policies and procedures to appropriate personnel thoroughly and promptly.
    - Observes, implements, and clarifies policies, procedures, and regulations to facilitate department operations that are consistent with legal and organization guidelines.
3. Ensures the delivery of quality services in area of operations. Acts as an educational resource and is available for consultation to departmental and system staff members. Develops and maintains effective working relationships with department staff, system staff, directors, managers, physicians, and other internal or external customers. Fosters a smoothly functioning, efficient operation through timely and effective resolution of employee or operational issues. (1, 3, 5)
    - Develops systems, processes, and quality monitors.
    - Regularly updates knowledge of techniques, guidelines, and regulations.
    - Communicates technical information in a manner appropriate for the intended audience.
    - Demonstrates attitude of cooperation and professionalism at all times.
    - Interacts with other levels of management on a regular basis for planning and coordination.
4. Selects, educates, orients, and assigns department staff (either directly or through others). Develops standards of performance, evaluates performance, and initiates or makes recommendations for human resource actions. (3, 5)
    - Demonstrates knowledge of human resources functions, considering theory and actual practice results.

continues

Exhibit 11–1 continued

- Provides leadership development to supervisory staff for effective problem identification and resolution and for efficient day-to-day operations.
- Assigns work to departmental staff, provides direction, and reviews all work as necessary.
- Determines staff learning needs and schedules inservice education programs.
- Responds to all task- or performance-related questions patiently and thoroughly, providing context as well as direction.
- Determines the qualifications and competence of staff who provide credentialing services.

5. Provides leadership example by demonstrating exceptional standards in issues such as teamwork and through interpersonal relationship development, reliability and attendance, professional appearance, and commitment to and participation in the business quality improvement programs. Participates in staff meetings as necessary. Attends and serves on professional/civic service organizations as a system representative. (2, 3, 5)
   - Performs job duties within legal and professional regulations and guidelines.
   - Maintains harmonious relationship with coworkers, providing support and assistance to coworkers to ensure quality patient care.
6. Maintains an acute awareness and accurate interpretation of the credentialing policies, procedures, rules, and regulations. (4, 5)
   - Demonstrates accurate knowledge of relevant laws, policies, regulations, and standards affecting decisions and interpretations.
   - Researches all available options and makes appropriate recommendations.
   - Communicates technical information in a manner appropriate for the intended audience.
   - Serves as a resource to other employees.
   - Communicates updated or new guidelines and regulations to appropriate personnel.
7. Coordinates the processing of medical staff and allied health professional applications for distribution to system facilities. (1, 3, 5)
   - Performs job duties within legal and professional regulations and guidelines.
   - Researches all available options and makes appropriate recommendations.
   - Communicates technical information in a manner appropriate for the intended audience.
   - Interacts with other levels of management on a regular basis for planning and coordination.
8. Coordinates the communication of information between credentials department and system facilities.
   (a) The performance of this function is the reason that the job exists.
   (b) There are limited employees among whom the performance of this function can be distributed.
   (c) This function occupies a great deal of the employee's time.
   (d) This function is highly specialized. Employees are hired for the skill/ability to perform this function.
   (e) Failure to perform this function may have serious consequences.

POSITION QUALIFICATIONS

Minimum Education: Associate degree in medical staff service science, business, or a related field of study or an equivalent combination of training and experience. Bachelor's degree in business administration/management preferred. CMSC or CPCS required within one year of date of hire, or within time period specified by the System Director. (CPCS preferred.)

continues

Exhibit 11–1 continued

Minimum Experience: Five years' comprehensive credentialing experience in an acute care hospital setting and three years' management and supervisory experience.

Skills, Other: Computer skills, i.e., word processing, database, spreadsheet. Excellent organization and public relations skills, ability to work independently and under pressure while subject to frequent interruptions. Statistical, analytical, and problem-solving skills. Ability to communicate, both orally and in writing, with all levels of personnel. Must work well as a member of a team.

Physical Demands: Mostly sedentary work. Some bending, light lifting.

I have read and understand my job description.

____________________ ____________________

Signature Date

KEY TO NUMBERED CRITERIA

1) The performance of this function is the reason that the job exists.
2) There are limited employees among whom the performance of this function can be distributed.
3) This function occupies a great deal of the manager's time.
4) This function is highly specialized. Employees are hired for the skill/ability to perform this function.
5) Failure to perform this function may have serious consequences.

Courtesy of Columbia Continental Division, Denver, Colorado.

STAFFING ANALYSIS

A frequent concern of administration is the appropriate number of full-time equivalents (FTEs) required to maintain the credentialing function. This is a complex topic and requires specific data and research due to many variables related to the way information is verified and obtained within an organization.

In the past, industry standards estimated between 14 and 17 hours for processing an initial application in a hospital and approximately 8 to 11 hours for a reappointment. This included all aspects of credentialing a physician, from first contact until decision was communicated. The same time frame may be applicable today; however, those using improved technology such as on-line services can reduce the time significantly, depending on the technology used.

Calculating Time To Process an Application

The first step in determining appropriate staffing is identification of the time involved in pro-

Exhibit 11–2 Job Description for Credentials Manager

Job Title: Credentials Manager JC# 4278

Working Title: Credentials Manager Page 1 of 5

Department: Medical Staff Services CC# 148678 Date:

Ratings Guide: 4 = Consistently Exceeds 3 = Often Exceeds
2 = Generally Meets 0 = Does Not Meet

Major Area of Responsibility	Rating

I. Responsible for managing legal aspects of Credentialling, especially as it relates to aspects of litigation, in working closely with medical staff, senior management and Legal Counsel. (weight = 40%)

a. Works with Senior Vice President and Legal Counsel in coordination of disciplinary, medico-administrative and medico-legal proceedings with appropriate communications to State Board of Medical Examiners and National Practitioner Data Bank of any disciplinary/adverse actions taken, impairment. _______

b. Works closely with Legal Counsel and Risk Management in responding to subpoenas and preparation for Depositions. _______

c. Monitors medical staff for adherence to medical staff bylaws, state and federal regulations and Joint Commission requirements, and communicates noncompliance to SVPMS and Chief of Staff; and interprets these regulations to the medical staff and hospital staff when required. Maintains expertise in these areas. Provides education to MSS/QI staff when required. _______

d. Serves on Task Force designed to transition & re-engineer Medical Staff Structure throughout the state and to facilitate streamlined management of credentialling and privileging data across the organization. _______

e. Provides Delegated Credentialling services to managed care payors, being aware of restrictions and prohibitions regarding the nature of material being disclosed, and serves as liaison with others in their work with managed care payors. _______

f. Analyzes and participates in recommendations for changes in the medical staff bylaws on an ongoing basis to conform with internal and external changes. _______

Comments: ____

____

____

____

_____	/	_____	=	_____	×	_____	=	_____
Sum of Ratings		# of Stds.		Avg. Rating		Weight		Points

continues

Exhibit 11–2 continued

Major Area of Responsibility	Rating
II. Directs the Health System Credentials Program, to assure its integrity in maintaining a state of readiness for licensing and accrediting agencies, and management of daily operations of the Medical Staff Services Department, to assure effective/efficient systems to support the credentialling process and the medical staff organization. (weight = 40%)	
a. Manages the Application and Reappointment processes to include research and analytical responsibility for all credentials documentation to ensure that the program's objectives are accomplished per the Bylaws, Rules and Regulations.	_______
b. Advises the SVPMS, Chief of Staff or Credentials Committee of problems with physicians, non-physicians, credentials files or application process.	_______
c. Daily management of departmental operations to ensure that smooth operations, excellent customer service, and legal objectives are met.	_______
d. Directs Medical Staff Services Department in area of Medical Staff Joint Commission standards, especially in credentialling, to assure readiness for accreditation surveys and other regulatory agency requirements.	_______
e. Manages all activities of the Credentials, Medical Executive, Bylaws and Physicians Health Committees to include advising Chief of Staff, Committees and Chiefs on credentialling, Bylaws issues and physician monitoring, to include coordination of investigative proceedings.	_______
f. Researches and develops criteria for privileging for medical staff departments to assure state-of-the-art privileging in meeting Joint Commission standards and Bylaws requirements.	_______
g. Responsible for preparation of Medical Staff report to the Board of Directors assuring the integrity of the report and ensuring that actions are communicated appropriately by MSS personnel.	_______
h. Assures development and maintenance of a credentialling link to quality improvement activities and works closely with QI Coordinators in coordinating efforts between QI and MSS functions.	_______
Comments: ____ ____ ____ ____	
_____ / _____ = _____ × _____ = _____ Sum of Ratings / # of Stds. = Avg. Rating × Weight = Points	

continues

Exhibit 11–2 continued

Major Area of Responsibility	Rating
III. Actively seeks to promote and helps to maintain through interactions with all others within and outside the department a positive, professional, team-oriented, and service-conscious environment which contributes to the goals of the department and reflects the values of the System. (weight = 20%)	
a. Demonstrates a respect for the human dignity of all individuals (employees, physicians, peers, volunteers, customers, visitors, etc.); helps to create and maintain team work within the work environment; practices good negotiation skills for resolving conflicts.	_______
b. Consistently insures a customer service orientation with regard to requests, customer problems, complaints, suggestions, etc.; follows through with and/or resolves while presenting an image of professionalism.	_______
c. Nurtures an atmosphere of collaboration and team oriented interpersonal relationships, communication flow and information sharing between depts.	_______
d. Contributes toward the delivery of quality health care with a concern for the well-being of those served.	_______
e. Complies with all departmental and hospital policies and procedures; uses good judgment in questioning them when appropriate.	_______
f. Participates in community activities related to area of responsibility; presents in-services; serves on professional committees.	_______

Comments: ____

____

____

_____	/	_____	=	_____	×	_____	=	_____
Sum of Ratings		# of Stds.		Avg. Rating		Weight		Points

POSITION SUMMARY

Responsible for directing, managing, creating and monitoring systems related to Medical Staff Services. Management of Healthcare System Credentials Program to assure the program's integrity according to Medical Staff Bylaws, Joint Commission Standards and other regulating agencies. Involved in legal aspects of credentialling, especially as they relate to aspects of litigation, and works closely with Medical Staff, officers, and legal attorneys in coordination of disciplinary and legal proceedings. Management of daily operations of the Medical Staff Services Department to maintain effective/efficient systems to support the medical staff organization, to include ongoing monitoring of departmental systems. Provide consultative expertise to the Medical Staff, senior management and hospital staff on Bylaws, Rules/Regulations and regulatory standards.

continues

Exhibit 11–2 continued

KNOWLEDGE, SKILLS AND ABILITIES

1. Certification, Registration or Licensure

   Certification by National Association of Medical Staff Services (NAMSS) as Medical Staff Coordinator Required.

2. Minimum Education

   Bachelor's Degree.

3. Minimum Experience

   3–5 years in a Medical Staff Services Department with high level of responsibility for credentialling, legal and disciplinary proceedings.

4. Other Knowledge, Skills or Abilities Not Listed Above

   Must demonstrate understanding of the medical staff organization responsibilities and its related bylaws; rules and regulations that govern the organization; Joint Commission standards/survey process/scoring guidelines; other regulatory agency requirements/standards; an integrated credentialling/quality management system; and medico-legal issues and laws relating to medical staff organizations; must be familiar with clinical information systems and data management techniques. Exposure to and responsibility for handling confidential information with high degree of sensitivity and diplomacy. Professional attitude and appearance at all times.

SUPERVISION

1. Received: Senior Vice President for Medical Services

2. Given: Day-to-day management/responsibility for department activities to assure direction/coordination of smooth MSS operations for the credentialling process, legal and regulatory requirements and maintenance of excellent customer service.

INTERPERSONAL SKILLS

Requires excellent oral communication skills, analytical abilities, creativity, strong interpersonal skills, and ability to manage complex systems. Works effectively, confidently and pro-actively with the Medical Staff, Hospital Staff, senior management, hospital directors, external agencies, Medical Education, Medical Records, ISG, Medical Staff Services and Quality Improvement. Position further requires independent problem-solving, decision-making and negotiating abilities. Must be able to develop trusting relationships with medical staff and department personnel.

MENTAL AND PHYSICAL EFFORT

1. Mental Effort Requires on-going flexibility as well as ability to address issues that arise demanding immediate attention and/or continued surveillance with effective results. Must be able to balance these interruptions with routine schedule of on-going responsibilities and assist staff to do same.

continues

Exhibit 11–2 continued

Must be able to work under pressure with deadlines and maintain confident composure through criticism/demands from the Medical Staff, senior management, department directors and/or others. The Credentials Manager must have a disciplined mind and systematic thinking capacities in order to attend to details related to Medical Staff as defined by State/Federal requirements and Bylaws, Rules/Regulations, adapt and interpret established practices and procedures to address problem situations, and make judicious decisions when faced with exceptions to the written rules.

2. Physical Effort Must be mobile and able to travel to all sites, other hospitals and corporate offices as required. Hours of work will vary. Ability to sit for long periods, use computer equipment, and reach and lift heavy files and notebooks.

IMPACT

The Credentials Manager is responsible for directing, managing, creating and monitoring systems related to Medical Staff Services. The impact of this position involves high level legal, financial, quality and regulatory implications. This person is involved in legal aspects of credentialling and works closely with medical staff, senior management and attorneys in the coordination of disciplinary and legal proceedings. Further responsibilities include acting in a liaison role between hospital staff, medical staff, and senior vice president for Medical staff services streamlining of MSS systems, and increasing effectiveness and customer service with the medical staff.

Note: SVPMS, Senior Vice President of Medical Services; MSS, Medical Staff Services; QI, quality improvement; ISG, Information Service Group.

Courtesy of Penrose–St. Francis Healthcare System, Colorado Springs, Colorado.

cessing an initial application. Calculating the time for processing an application can be difficult, especially if many individuals are involved in the process. It will be necessary to break down each specific component in the process and then have each employee identify the average time it takes to complete the task.

Significant factors affecting activity are whether a computer software system is used to manage the process and generate letters and forms and whether the verification (and, in the case of managed care, even the credentialing evaluation) is delegated to another entity and/or outsourced to a CVO.

Initial Application

Following are routine components of processing an initial application, along with issues to be considered in terms of time evaluation.

1. Preapplication
   - Is a preapplication process used (method to determine if individual is eligible to receive application)?
   - Is the process completed as a telephone interview, a written communication, or a combination of the two?
   - How extensive is the preapplication process? Does it apply to all practitioners or only in certain circumstances?
   - If written, what time is involved in mailing/faxing the questionnaire, obtaining and reviewing the information, and communicating with the prospective applicant?
   - If the preapplication process is a telephone interview, what is the average time it takes to ask the questions and document the answers provided by the

Exhibit 11–3 Job Description for Credentials Coordinator (Lead)

JOB CONTENT QUESTIONNAIRE

Job Title: Credentials Coordinator (Lead)

Name:

Department: Provider Credentialing

Facility:

Phone Number:

Today's Date:

Name of Person to Whom You Report:

That Person's Job Title: Manager, Network Credentialing

Position Purpose: Completes and coordinates completion of provider credentialing process for identified segment of health plan credentialing needs. Provides direct file completion as well as process oversight and coordination, audit, reporting, and assures quality and timeliness of outcomes.

WHERE DOES YOUR JOB FIT IN THE ORGANIZATION? Complete the structure using job titles only.

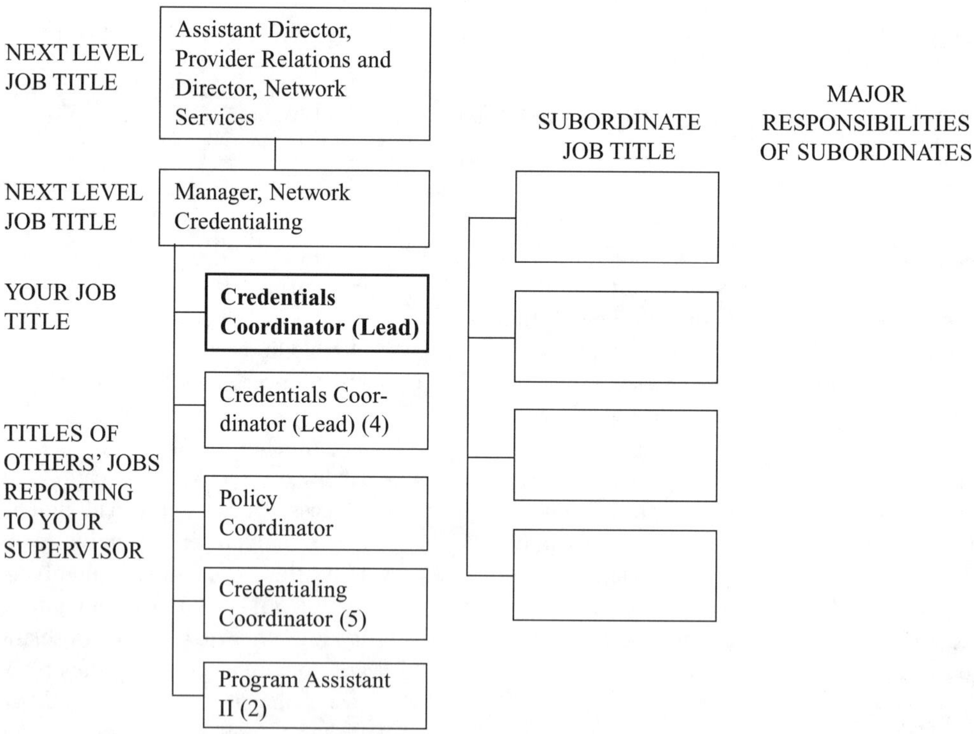

continues

Exhibit 11–3 continued

WHAT ARE YOUR JOB'S MAJOR RESPONSIBILITIES AND END RESULTS?	List brief statements that describe what you do (end results), how you do it (action taken), and how you know you've done it well (ways to measure accomplishment).		
% Time	**What You Do (End Result)**	**How You Do It (Action Taken)**	**Ways To Measure Accomplishments of End Result**
1. 55%	Coordinates accurate verification of provider files for initial appointment and for reappointment within established time frames and in accordance with the standards required by the accrediting/ regulatory agencies.	• Determines that provider applicant meets initial criteria. • Determines that application form/attachments are complete prior to processing. Coordinates completion of files with Provider Contracting staff. • Oversees creation of applicant file, including electronic and computer-generated verifications. • Monitors status of verified information and provides information to appropriate personnel as designated by policy. • Analyzes verifications for content and generates follow-up requests for additional information if necessary and/or requested. • Advises manager of any adverse or questionable information received and recommends follow-up action, which may include review by risk management or legal department. • Promotes and maintains confidentiality of provider files and all information related to the credentialing process.	• Application not processed if criteria not met. • Applications returned to Provider Relations for follow-up with prospective provider. • Criteria for complete application are met prior to processing. • Data are compiled that facilitate review and appropriate action by peer review bodies that include verifications dated within acceptable timeline according to NCQA standards. • Provider Relations receives regular status reports according to established policy. Other personnel receive prompt and accurate status reports when requested. • All verification sources required by NCQA and the Joint Commission are included in the applicant file. • Additional information needed is identified, requested, and received prior to individual and committee process. • Potential quality issues are identified, resulting in all information necessary being available for individual and committee review. • No breach or violation of confidentiality is reported or identified.

continues

Exhibit 11–3 continued

% Time	What You Do (End Result)	How You Do It (Action Taken)	Ways To Measure Accomplishments of End Result
2. 20%	Activates the peer review/committee process once the verification component is completed and the file is complete.	• Notifies individual and/or committee of files ready for review. • Meets with individual reviewers as necessary and attends committee meetings to provide needed information. • Advises peer reviewers of applicant's credentials with questionable or adverse information received and provides guidance to committee in their review, analysis, and recommendations for applicants. • Reviews all applicable committee minutes to ensure that action taken is appropriately documented. Advises recording personnel of any corrections to be made. • Coordinates notification of Board approvals to applicant and appropriate plan parties. • Provides information/education to personnel at region levels regarding credentialing requirements of regulatory agencies and issues involving outcome of credentialing decisions.	• Files are ready for first review within 60–90 days of attestation date. Credentialing process is in compliance with the 180-day NCQA standard. A variance report is completed for files incomplete within the 60–90-day time frame. • All questions regarding applications are answered to the satisfaction of the individual or group involved. • Committee is knowledgeable regarding all options and outcomes of adverse recommendations based on plan policy, bylaws, accreditations standards, and NPDB guidelines. • Minutes accurately reflect action taken. • Letters to applicants are sent within specified time frame. • Appropriate notification is given to plan personnel as outlined in policy and within specified time frame. • Inservices are given periodically to region personnel.
3. 15%	Oversees database management of demographic information on providers and tracking/updating of expired information to ensure that accurate and current data exist for each provider maintained in the database.	• Monitors reports of expired information and progress in obtaining updated information. • Assists staff with problems in verifications and recommends appropriate action to resolve issues and/or resolves personally. • Provides current, dated information (e.g., licensure, DEA, insurance) to regions for use in recredentialing. • Obtains information from regions relative to recredentialing decisions for data input once process is completed. • Coordinates completion of Board biography information.	• NPDB queries are performed for all physicians and other defined individuals upon application and, at a minimum, every two years. • Other verifications are updated within 30 days of expiration. • Verifications are completed within established time frame and in accordance with NCQA Accreditation Standard time lines. • Regions have necessary information provided in order to facilitate recredentialing process within established time frames.

continues

Exhibit 11–3 continued

% Time	What You Do (End Result)	How You Do It (Action Taken)	Ways To Measure Accomplishments of End Result
			• All provider database files contain date of most recent reappointment. • Bios are forwarded to the appropriate department within specified time frame. All bio information is accurate.
4. 5%	Identifies areas for improvement in the credentialing process and recommends options for consideration.	• Evaluates processes as they exist and measures outcome in terms of accuracy and time lines to determine if need for improvement exists. • Monitors changes in accreditation and regulatory standards through communication with manager and/or other appropriate personnel. • When requested, outlines key components of a new or existing policy/procedure for policy coordinator to update.	• Recommendations are acted upon with documented performance improvement. • Updated procedures reflect changes in standards or requirements. • Policy/procedure manual reflects changes and/or additions.
5. 5%	Maintains up-to-date knowledge regarding credentialing processes and related accrediting and regulatory standards.	• Networks with colleagues in the profession. • Reads industry information relative to credentialing. • Shares knowledge gained with others.	• Record of CEUs for attendance at state, local, and/or national conferences to meet NAMSS requirements for ongoing certification (30 hours for every 3 years). • Routing slips on reading material signed off. • One inservice provided at meetings involving Provider Credentials staff, Provider Relations staff, regional personnel, or others as requested.

WORK ASSIGNMENTS Describe how your work is structured. How are assignments given, monitored, and reviewed?

Coordinator is accountable for all process activities for a designated portion of the provider network, as determined by the Manager, Provider Credentialing.

GUIDANCE AND AUTHORITY Describe the authority permitted to your position. Note specific budget, staffing, and technical decisions for clarification. Specify only those decisions that are made by you versus those referred to others (i.e., your supervisors) or governed by policies and procedures.

continues

Exhibit 11–3 continued

The coordinator is accountable for departmental and interdepartmental process coordination related to creating completed provider credentialing. The coordinator either completes process steps him/herself or delegates and monitors completion of work by other staff, as available. In addition, the coordinator facilitates interdepartmental communication and activities related to file completion. The coordinator is accountable for decision making regarding whether the provider meets credentialing criteria, for completion of all steps in the verification processes, and for coordination or tracking of the review process. The coordinator works independently to complete verification process, utilizing risk management or legal consultation per the procedural framework when problems are encountered. The coordinator is accountable for determining work priorities in consultation with the contracting team customer and ensures that work activities are clearly in line with plan policies and procedures as well as consistent with contract development plans. The coordinator must have thorough knowledge of NCQA/Joint Commission standards.

WHAT ARE THE MAJOR CHALLENGES OF YOUR JOB? Describe the most difficult problems you have to solve and how to solve them.

Most Difficult Challenges	Typical Solutions
Meeting customer expectations within a complex, distributed credentialing system.	• Facilitate and participate in cross-departmental, cross-regional development teams. • Maintain content knowledge/certification to create a context for meeting customer expectations. • Frequently communicate with medical staff leadership, contracting team members, and direct team members.
Adhering to quality standards regardless of pressure to bend rules to accommodate network development need.	• Work within a documented framework for policy management, including exception management. • Monitor policy compliance, providing feedback and issues escalation to the appropriate leadership level.
Coordinating case completion and approval/disapproval when information regarding applicant is adverse.	• Consult with legal and risk management staff. • Consider other sources of information on the provider. • Represent plan policy when determining approval/denial.
Ensuring that credentialing systems meet NCQA requirements at all times, regardless of resource constraints.	• Continuously monitor system outputs and process points against NCQA standards. • Provide leadership in interpreting standards.
Developing and implementing work to meet customer requirements.	• Meet with customer to clarify expectations. • Document expectations. • Explore options for implementation with appropriate plan leaders and identify best option. • Coordinate process requirements among process participants. • Direct, monitor, and evaluate effectiveness of implementation and give feedback to individuals accountable for implementation.

Note: NPDB, National Practitioner Data Bank; CEU, continuing education unit.

Courtesy of Group Health Cooperative, Seattle, Washington.

Exhibit 11–4 Job Description for Credentials Delegation Coordinator

JOB CONTENT QUESTIONNAIRE

Job Title: Credentials Delegation Coordinator

Name:

Department: Provider Credentialing

Facility:

Phone Number:

Today's Date:

Name of Person to Whom You Report:

That Person's Job Title: Manager, Provider Credentialing

Position Purpose: Coordinates completion of provider credentialing process for identified segment of health plan credentialing needs. Provides direct file completion as well as process oversight and coordination, audit, reporting, and assures quality and timeliness of outcomes.

WHERE DOES YOUR JOB FIT IN THE ORGANIZATION? Complete the structure using job titles only.

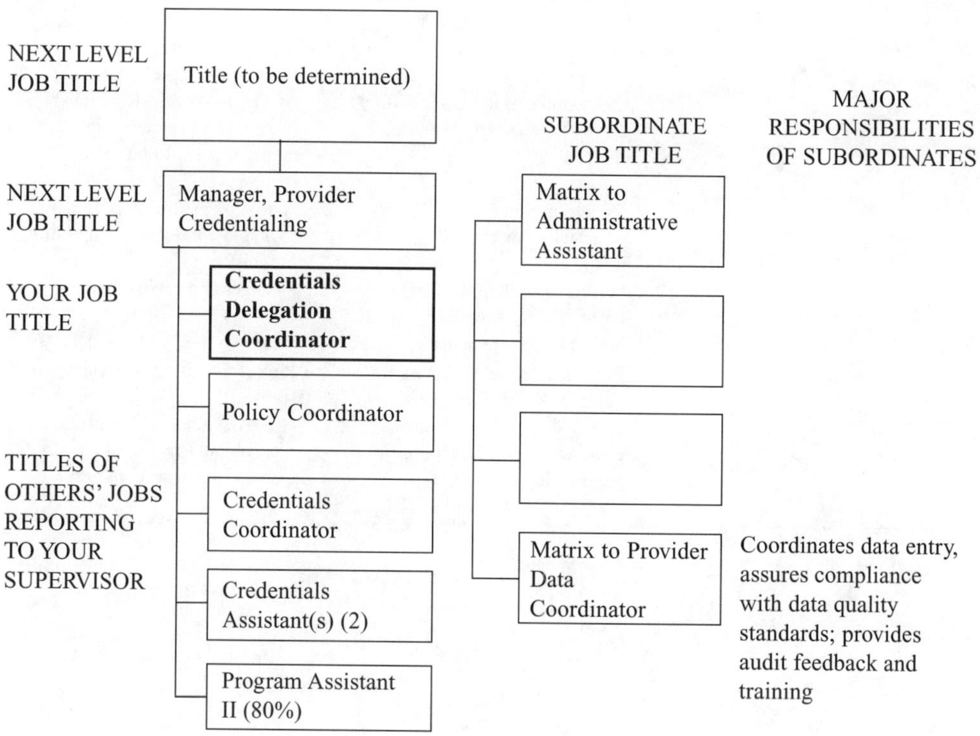

continues

Exhibit 11–4 continued

WHAT ARE YOUR JOB'S MAJOR RESPONSIBILITIES AND END RESULTS?	List brief statements that describe what you do (end results), how you do it (action taken), and how you know you've done it well (ways to measure accomplishment).		
% Time	**What You Do (End Result)**	**How You Do It (Action Taken)**	**Ways To Measure Accomplishments of End Result**
1. 50%	Schedules and performs due diligence reviews of credentialing activities for potential clients who have been requested to provide contract service, resulting in detailed analysis report of findings and recommendations relative to delegated status.	• When notified of request of pending audit, determination is made if prospective client meets criteria for delegation review.	• Manager and Provider Relations are notified that criteria are or are not met. If met, reviews are scheduled within time frames specified in policy relative to date of request and scheduled review date.
		• Performs delegation review of credentialing activities using approved audit tool that reviews for verification information in credentialing files, committee minutes, policies, and procedures and for effectiveness of credentialing processes.	• Delegation review accomplished according to established policy and in accordance with NCQA standards for oversight of contracted activity.
		• Writes detailed report including findings and recommendations that is maintained along with a copy of the completed audit tool.	• Report and audit tool show statistical sample required by NCQA standards. Reports are received and reviewed by manager prior to committee review.
		• Creates action plan with prospective or current clients whose review identifies deficiencies that must be corrected or excluded from delegated components.	• Action plans are identified and re-audits conducted to monitor progress with outcome reports to manager and review bodies.
		• Performs annual audits of current clients to monitor effectiveness of delegates' credentialing and reappointment or recent processes.	• Report and audit tool show statistical sample required by NCQA standards. Reports are received and reviewed by manager prior to committee review.

continues

Exhibit 11–4 continued

% Time	What You Do (End Result)	How You Do It (Action Taken)	Ways To Measure Accomplishments of End Result
2. 25%	Maintains effective working relationships with delegation clients, provider coordinators and review bodies, and other departments or individuals involved in delegated activities.	• Motivates the review process once the delegation audit report is completed by notifying individuals on committees involved according to established policy. • Summarizes findings for review individuals or bodies, noting any particular concerns or issues with the audit outcome. • Notifies prospective or current delegation clients of final outcome of review process. • Promotes customer service with ongoing contracts with the delegation clients to determine any change in provider base or other action that could affect delegation status. • Meets periodically with provider coordinator to update status with delegation client. • Meets as necessary with personnel who may be auditing same clients for other delegation status.	• Reviews result in approval, partial approval, or denial of delegated status. • Reviewers are knowledgeable regarding audit outcomes based on policy, bylaws, and NCQA standards on delegation. • Letters to clients are sent within specified time frame. • Appropriate notification is given to personnel as outlined in policy and within specified time frame. • Contracts are made at least quarterly and documented, and current client rosters are obtained. • Meetings are documented and provider coordinators receive information on current status of delegation client. • These meetings result in increased understanding of all delegated functions that, in turn, should benefit the client due to joint efforts to minimize disruption and/or eliminate any duplication of effort.
3. 15%	Oversees database management of information on delegated providers and clients to ensure that accurate and current data exist in the database.	• All clients and delegation providers are entered with appropriate information. • Updates are made to database as information changes and/or annual audits are completed. • Provides current information to personnel requiring the data.	• All data are entered within established time lines and current information can be retrieved. • Updates are entered within established time lines and current information can be retrieved. • Requests for information are processed and received to the satisfaction of requesting party.

continues

Exhibit 11–4 continued

% Time	What You Do (End Result)	How You Do It (Action Taken)	Ways To Measure Accomplishments of End Result
4. 5%	Identifies areas for improvement in the delegation process and recommends options for consideration.	• Evaluates processes as they exist and measures outcome in terms of acceptable time lines to complete audits and report writing. • Evaluates data collection tool/ related forms and recommends revisions. • Monitors changes of NCQA/ other regulatory agencies and recommends necessary changes to meet standards/requirements. • When requested, outlines key components of new or existing policy for policy coordinator to update.	• Recommendations are acted upon with documented performance improvement. • Changes made result in improved performance measurement of delegation client's credentialing activities. • Updated procedures reflect current accreditation or regulatory requirements. • Policy/procedure manual reflects changes and/or additions.
5. 5%	Maintains up-to-date knowledge regarding delegation audits and related accrediting and regulatory standards.	• Networks with colleagues in the profession. • Reads industry information relative to credentialing. • Shares knowledge gained with others.	• Record of CEUs for attendance at state, local, and/or national conferences and meet to NAMSS requirements for ongoing certification (30 hours for every 3 years). • Routing slips on reading material signed off. • Inservice provided at meetings involving Provider Credentials staff, Provider Relations staff, regional personnel, or others as required.

WORK ASSIGNMENTS Describe how your work is structured. How are assignments given, monitored, and reviewed?

Work priorities are identified by the Manager, Provider Credentialing, based on input from the assistant medical director of clinical planning and improvement, regional chiefs of staff, provider relations managers; director, Clinical Planning and Improvement; and vice presidents with accountability for Operations Credentialing.

GUIDANCE AND AUTHORITY Describe the authority permitted to your position. Note specific budget, staffing, and technical decisions for clarification. Specify only those decisions that are made by you versus those referred to others (i.e., your supervisors) or governed by policies and procedures.

Weekly meeting with Manager, Provider Credentialing, to review workload priorities and to review and confirm policy drafts and implementation of delegation activities.

continues

Exhibit 11–4 continued

WHAT ARE THE MAJOR CHALLENGES OF YOUR JOB?	Describe the most difficult problems you have to solve and how to solve them.
Most Difficult Challenges	**Typical Solutions**
Planning and coordinating work to meet customer and plan credentialing requirements for delegation.	• Meet with customer to clarify expectations. • Document expectations. • Explore options for implementation and identify best option. • Present expectations, options for implementation, and best option to leadership bodies with a specific request for action. • Monitor and evaluate effectiveness of implementation and give feedback to individuals accountable for implementation.
Meeting customer expectations within a complex, distributed credentialing system.	• Facilitate and participate in cross-departmental, cross-regional development teams. • Maintain content knowledge/certification to create a context for meeting customer expectations. • Frequently communicate with medical staff leadership, contracting team members, and direct team members.
Adhering to quality standards regardless of pressure to ensure that contractual and delegation conditions are met.	• Work within a documented framework for policy management, including expectation management. • Monitor policy compliance, providing feedback and issues escalation to the appropriate leadership level.
Coordinating case completion/subsequent re-audits approval/disapproval when information regarding applicant is adverse.	• Consult with legal and risk management staff. • Consider other sources of information on the provider. • Represent plan policy when determining approval/denial.
Prospective or current delegation client that plan is anxious to contract with fails audit; subsequent corrective action plans.	• Provider files would need to be credentialed in-house with subsequent plan approval of individual providers. • Refer provider files to a CVO for verification process with subsequent plan approval of individual providers.

continues

Exhibit 11–4 continued

QUANTITATIVE DATA List all the significant data that will provide an indication of the size of the area upon which your position has impact.

No. of Projects:	Number of people you supervise directly or through subordinates:
Avg. Project Budget:	Total annualized payroll of your unit or department:
Other Measures—Specify Type	Total annualized operating budget of your unit or department:
Coordinator participates in professional groups at state level and maintains CMSC credentials.	Services provided by external providers account for some $X million of the medical staff budget.
Coordinator assists manager in evaluation of credentials assistant.	

WHAT ARE YOUR JOB'S PRIMARY WORKING RELATIONSHIPS? List major interactions, frequency, and purpose of contracts.

Other Cooperative Employees	Frequency and Purpose of Contact	People Not Employed by the Cooperative	Frequency and Purpose of Contact
Title TBD, Provider Relations	Occasional meetings to clarify expectations.	Customer Leaders	Contact as needed to set data and credentialing priorities.
Manager, Provider Credentialing	Weekly meetings to establish priorities and resolve issues.	NAMSS meetings	Monthly, to gain information re: NCQA and other professional standards.
Medical Directors	Contact as needed for direction for specific priorities.	External hospitals and HMOs	Contact as needed to survey, gather information, and act as consultant regarding policy and procedure.
Medical Director, Clinical Planning and Improvement	As needed for coordination of issues.	State and NPDB representatives	Contact as required to report privileges and membership sanctions.
Regional Medical Directors, other Staff Leaders, Operations Leaders, Board members	As requested to serve as process consultant, establish credentialing priorities.		
Regional Administrators	As needed to serve as process consultant, establish credentialing priorities.		

continues

Exhibit 11–4 continued

Other Cooperative Employees	Frequency and Purpose of Contact	People Not Employed by the Cooperative	Frequency and Purpose of Contact
Regional Representatives involved in reappointment process	Frequent contact to discuss/coordinate reappointment process for individual practitioners.		
Data Team Representatives	Contact as needed to obtain data support.		
Provider Relations Managers and Coordinators	Routine meetings (monthly or more often) to coordinate credentialing and contracting activities.		
Legal Counsel and Director of Risk Management	Contact as needed to consult regarding nonconforming review elements.		
Clinical Planning and Improvement Representatives	Contact as needed to coordinate credentialing and quality improvement activities.		

WORKING CONDITIONS Describe your working conditions, paying particular attention to physical and/or exposure to hazardous or danger conditions.

Normal office environment

EMPLOYEE COMMENTS

Signature

SUPERVISOR'S COMMENTS

Signature

Note: NCQA, National Committee for Quality Assurance; CEU, continuing education unit; NAMSS, National Association Medical Staff Services; CVO, credentials verification organization; CMSC, certified medical staff coordinator; HMO, health maintenance organization.

Courtesy of Group Health Cooperative, Seattle, Washington.

Exhibit 11–5 Job Description for Medical Staff Credentialing Coordinator

POSITION TITLE: Medical Staff Credentialing Coordinator

Reporting Relationship/Organizational Structure:
Reports to: Director Medical Staff
Others Reporting to Same Supervisor: Medical Staff Meeting Coordinator
Medical Staff Secretary
CME Coordinator
Supervises: Volunteers

POSITION PURPOSE:

To provide support to the medical staff and AHP credentialing process under the supervision of the Medical Staff Director.

KEY RESPONSIBILITIES/ESSENTIAL FUNCTIONS:

- Processes new medical staff and allied health applicants for initial appointments, provisional reviews and re-appointments.
- Assures confidentiality of medical staff activities as they relate to the functions and responsibilities of the Medical Staff.
- Assists Department Chairs' research and development of criteria for privileging guidelines for respective departments. Initiates review and any revision at least annually.
- Prepares board reports, follow-up action after meeting, including correspondence and privilege checklist distribution to appropriate hospital departments.
- Drafts minutes done within 72 hours (weekdays) of meetings.
- Prepares agendas, meeting minutes, correspondence and other follow-up, location and meals for credentials committee meetings.
- Maintains up to date computer program for all currently approved appointees and statistical data needed for appropriate in-house departments.
- Serves as facilitator and recorder for Credentialing Committee and related committees as assigned.
- Responsible for Quarterly Department of Health Report.
- Responsible for revisions and distribution of the Medical Staff roster to all Department Directors quarterly.
- Directs physician complaints, peer review issues and/or quality management issues to Director, appropriate administrative personnel or medical staff leadership.
- Adheres to hospital and department safety policies and procedures. Monitors and records adherence to fire drills conducted by the hospital.
- Demonstrates Customer Service/Service Plus principles and behaviors consistent with organization's vision and values.

OTHER RESPONSIBILITIES:

- Provides backup for Director in MEC, Bylaws and General Staff when necessary.
- Provides backup assistance for the other Coordinator when absent.

continues

Exhibit 11–5 continued

- Performs other duties as assigned to meet department or Healthcare System needs.
- Directs inquiries and coordinates Medical Staff organization functions in Director's absence when requested.

DIMENSIONS:

575 physician reappointments
125 allied health professionals
70 new applicants per year

CUSTOMERS SERVED:

Medical and Allied Health Professional Staff, committees, applicants, visitors, and patients

QUALIFICATIONS:

- Associate degree in related field, a degreed professional or certified Medical Staff Professional or demonstrated equivalent competence.
- 4 years of executive secretarial experience with a minimum of one-year experience in hospital/medical staff background, preferably in a medical staff department.
- Certification (CMSC) or (CPCS) by the National Association of Medical Staff Services preferred.
- Proficiency in word processing, transcription, and minute taking.
- Knowledge of basic recordkeeping and filing systems. Demonstrates skill in written and oral communications and relating to physicians.
- Ability to prepare reports and follow-up with minimal supervision.
- Maintains emotional stability and a calm disposition, and has ability to relate positively with all levels of professionals.
- Ability to adapt to flexible work schedules and frequent interruptions.
- Possesses willingness to improve. Reliable, tactful, honest and discreet, maintains confidentiality at all times.
- Ability to solve problems and make decisions. Work requires consistent exercise of discretion and independent judgment.

OTHER REQUIREMENTS:

SIGNATURES:

Employee: ______________________________ Date: __________

Director: ______________________________ Date: __________

Human Resources Reviewer: ______________________ Date: __________

Note: CME, continuing medical education; AHP, allied health professional; MEC, medical executive committee.

Courtesy of Columbia Medical Center–West, El Paso, Texas.

prospective applicant, review information, and communicate results or next step?
- What other tasks and activities are involved in this application that may take someone's time?

2. Contact with the applicant
   - If a preapplication is used, what is the next contact with the applicant?
   - If a preapplication is not used, what is the average amount of time involved in contact with an initial applicant, determination of eligibility, and communication of request for an application packet?
3. Mailings to the applicant
   - How much time does it take to collect all information and mail the packet to the applicant? (This setup may include contact with a CVO or other entity to forward the information.)
   - Is information entered into a database for tracking the distribution and receipt of applications? If so, how much time is involved in entry?
4. File setup
   - At what point in the process is a file started?
   - What is included in the file? How easy is it to obtain all necessary forms?
   - Do file folders have preprinted tabs for the various sections (application, license information, National Practitioner Data Bank (NPDB), education, training, etc.), or are they typewritten individually?
   - How much time does it take to enter information into the computer (if not done previously)?
5. Verification and gathering of information
   - Are verifications done internally, or are they outsourced?
   - If they are processed internally, and if computer support is available, how much time does it take to set up the computer file and print all the appropriate verification requests?
   - If there is no verification outsourcing and no supporting software, what is the time involved in producing the verification forms, letters, etc.?
   - If the Internet or other on-line source is used to collect any information, what is the average time it takes to request and download that information and place it in the file?
   - Is the American Medical Association (AMA) Physician Masterfile used, and if so, what time is involved in requesting information and filing information when received?
   - How much time does it take to access NPDB for a required query? (Include time to print and file queries.)
6. Second requests
   - What is the average number of second requests for information per application, and what is the average time involved in processing second requests (or third requests)?
   - Are second requests written, or are phone calls made to the applicant if there is missing information? What is the average time for each phone contact and/or written contact?
7. Interview arrangement
   - Are interviews conducted for all applicants, no applicants, or some applicants?
   - How much time is spent arranging the interview (phone calls, room reservation, any orientation materials, confirmation, other steps in the process)?
   - Is any time spent in documenting all or part of interview results?
8. Computer input (this may be included in other components or can be calculated separately)
   - What is the average time for computer input (1) initially when the application is received, (2) as additional information is received, (3) through the review process, and (4) after the final decision is made by the governing body or committee?

9. Temporary privileges
   - If temporary privileges are used, what is the average time it takes to process specific verifications that are required by bylaws or policies?
   - Who must be notified, how are they notified, and what is the average time it takes?
   - What is the ratio of temporary privileges to total number of applicants in any given year? (In a total calculation, an average time for initial applications with temporary privileges and average time without temporary privileges may be identified.)
10. "Caution flag" follow-up
    - What are the average number of applications that require additional follow-up (based on information received that causes concern or requires additional information)?
    - Are phone calls, letters, or other methods involved, and what is the average process time?
11. Initial review; contact with department chair (hospital), medical director, or client (this step will vary according to the setting and the procedure requirements for review)
    - What time is involved in obtaining review by department chair (hospital)?
    - Are phone calls or other contacts made with individuals for prereview before a committee review process?
    - What time is involved in calls and/or assistance with this review?
    - Is there a quality review of the file before it is forwarded to the committee (or in the case of a CVO, before it is forwarded to the client)?
12. Review process (multiple level, committee, board)
    - How many review steps are there? (Include all the levels of review through approval by board or other body.)
    - What is the credentialing staff involvement in the review process?
    - What preparation is required for any or all of the review/approval bodies? (Include time involved in attending meetings, writing minutes, tracking sheets, written reports, other.)
13. Notification (applicant, organization personnel)
    - How are applicants notified of the final decision, and how much time does notification take on the average?
    - Who is notified within the organization, what methods are used, and what is the average time involved?
14. Photocopy time
    - Photocopy time may be significant, and even if it is completed by clerical support, it should be factored into process time. If not integrated into previous activities, time should be calculated.
15. Filing
    - Filing may have been included in other components, or a total time for all filing can be calculated.
16. Site visits (for managed care organizations)
    - If credentialing personnel are responsible for site visits, what is the average time it takes for the site visit and any subsequent reports that are made? Time involved in the contacts with the office staff and travel time should be included in the total calculation.

Reappointment/Recredentialing

The same questions can be used in the reappointment or recredentialing process, taking into account the following activities:

- mailings to practitioner
- verification
- second requests
- computer input
- "caution flag" follow-up
- contact with department chair/medical director/client

- review process
- notification
- photocopy time
- filing
- site visits

In addition, the following calculations need to be completed for the recredentialing process:

1. Practitioner profile
   - Is the practitioner profile developed by the credentialing staff, or is the information gathered from other areas of the organization (quality management, risk management, medical records, pharmacy, etc.)? What is the time involved in notification, collection of material, and printing it in a profile format?
   - Are physician office site visits performed, and what is the time involved?
   - Is time involved in any computer downloads of profile information?
   - Are physician attendance records at medical staff meetings required and/or calculated?
2. Privilege comparisons
   - If new privilege delineations are required, how much time is involved in comparison and/or determination of whether additional review is needed for changes in privileges?
   - Are previous privilege forms copied and sent to each applicant as part of the reappointment packet?
   - What is the average number of applicants that require additional information regarding privilege requests, and how much time does it take to process them?

Temporary Privileges

The same process and questions can be used to determine the number of hours required to process requests for temporary privileges.

Determining Staffing Needs on the Basis of Projections

Once all activities related to the credentialing process have been identified and the times calculated and averaged for each step, it is possible to complete projections to be used in staffing analysis.

The second step in the process of determining appropriate staffing is identification of activity. Most departments will have documentation of activity during the prior year. This documentation may be part of a year-end report or a management report or may be found in minutes. If no documentation can be identified, current activity will have to be tracked for a period of three to six months.

The numbers of preapplications processed, applicants, reapplicants, and temporary privileges granted during the prior 12 months are identified and then multiplied by the number of hours calculated as average for each activity. When added together, this will result in the number of hours needed to complete the process.

To calculate the number of FTE staff needed to complete the work, a total of 2,080 hours (40-hour work week multiplied by 52 weeks) is identified. The average number of hours for holidays, vacation, and sick time allowed by the organization is subtracted. Therefore, if six holidays (48 hours) and three weeks of vacation and sick time (120 hours) are allowed, 1,812 hours will be the starting point of number of work hours available for one FTE. Additional time is usually subtracted, as in all probability no individual will be fully productive for eight hours every day. The resulting number is the number of hours for one FTE. Dividing the number of hours identified to complete the process by the number of hours for one FTE will result in the number of FTEs required to maintain the credentialing process. Note that this calculation did not include components unique to an organization's policies.

Table 11–2 is a sample worksheet projecting the credentialing process for an integrated net-

Table 11–2 Staffing Projections

	Initial Appointment		*Reappointment*	
	In House	***With Use of CVO***	***In House***	***With Use of CVO***
Physician (employed or contracted) w/hospital privileges	13–17 hrs[A]	9–11 hrs	8–10 hrs[B]	5–5 hrs
	15 avg	10 avg	9 avg	5 avg
Contracted physician w/no hospital privileges	11–15 hrs	9–11 hrs	6–10 hrs	3–5 hrs
	13 avg	10 avg	8 avg	4 avg
Nonmedical staff provider being credentialed w/privileges[C]	12–16 hrs	8–10 hrs	7–9 hrs	4–4 hrs
	14 avg	9 avg	8 avg	4 avg
Nonmedical staff provider w/no hospital privileges	10–14 hrs	8–10 hrs	4–8 hrs	1–3 hrs
	12 avg	9 avg	6 avg	2 avg
Certified[D]	2–4 hrs	NA	1.5–3.5 hrs	NA
	3 avg		2.5 avg	

Note: Developed by Chris Mobley and Sheryl Deutsch using NAMSS criteria and other available sources, and based on previous experience with clients. All assumptions are based on implementation of BPR recommendations.

A Assumes direct hours and includes:
File development/management
Verification
Info gathering and clarification
Review and approval process (accompany file)
Preparation of material to Board
All notifications
Use of CVO assumes 4–6 hours for appointment, 3–5 hours for reappointment.

B Does not include collection/follow-up of quality profile.

C Category involves providers that are:
Not members of the medical staff
Are licensed and independent
Are fully credentialed
Majority in this category are Behavioral Health.

D Certified category includes providers who are not being fully credentialed but who are completing an application and submitting a copy of their license. File is initiated.
Category addresses providers that bill independently and must go through a process in order for the hospital to provide information to ______________.

Courtesy of C. Mobley & Associates, LLC, and Quality Management Options, LLC, Colorado Springs, Colorado.

Exhibit 11–6 Sample Annual Report

Department Name ______________________

January, 199_ to December, 199_

Initial Appointments: Medical Staff .... ______
Allied/Behavioral Health .... ______

Locum Tenens Applications Processed .... ______

Temporary Privileges: One-Time Temps (Medical Staff) .... ______
(Allied/Behavioral Health) .... ______

Applicants to Medical Staff .... ______
Allied/Behavioral Health .... ______

Emergency Privileges: .... ______

Practitioners on Provisional Monitoring .... ______

Reappointments: Medical Staff .... ______
Allied/Behavioral Health .... ______

Reference Letters Answered .... ______

Resignations: Medical Staff .... ______
Allied/Behavioral Health .... ______

Leave of Absence Granted .... ______

Deaths .... ______

Total No. of Meetings Supported by Department .... ______

Total Practitioners Maintained in Database: MD, DO, DDS .... ______
AHP, BH .... ______

Phone Calls—Incoming and Outgoing .... ______

OTHER ACTIVITIES/PROJECTS:

Hearings Held .... ______

No. of Emergency Dept. Call Lists Generated (count each separately) .... ______

Bylaws Revision (list extent of involvement)

Privilege Delineation Revision (list specialties)

Joint Commission/NCQA Survey Preparation, Involvement

Newsletters Generated (how many)

New Practitioner/Leadership Orientations (how many)

Special Function (list involvement)

Courtesy of C. Mobley & Associates, LLC, and Quality Management Options, LLC, Colorado Springs, Colorado.

Exhibit 11–7 Medical Staff Services Credentialing Statistics

MONTH: ____________ YEAR: ____________

APPOINTMENTS	IN PROCESS	COMPLETED YEAR-TO-DATE
ANESTHESIOLOGY		
CRITICAL CARE MEDICINE		
EMERGENCY MEDICINE		
FAMILY PRACTICE		
LABORATORY MEDICINE		
MEDICINE		
NEUROLOGY		
OB/GYN		
ORTHOPEDICS		
PEDIATRICS		
PSYCHIATRY		
RADIATION ONCOLOGY		
RADIOLOGY		
SURGERY		
APPOINTMENTS TO CREDENTIALS COMMITTEE		
APPOINTMENTS TO MEDICAL EXECUTIVE COMMITTEE		
APPOINTMENTS TO PROFESSIONAL AFFAIRS COMMITTEE		
APPOINTMENTS TO BOARD OF TRUSTEES		
REAPPOINTMENTS	**IN PROCESS**	**COMPLETED YEAR-TO-DATE**
ANESTHESIOLOGY		
CRITICAL CARE MEDICINE		
EMERGENCY MEDICINE		
FAMILY PRACTICE		
LABORATORY MEDICINE		
MEDICINE		
NEUROLOGY		
OB/GYN		
ORTHOPEDICS		
PEDIATRICS		
PSYCHIATRY		
RADIATION ONCOLOGY		
RADIOLOGY		
SURGERY		
REAPPOINTMENTS TO CREDENTIALS COMMITTEE		
REAPPOINTMENTS TO MEDICAL EXECUTIVE COMMITTEE		
REAPPOINTMENTS TO PROFESSIONAL AFFAIRS COMMITTEE		
REAPPOINTMENTS TO BOARD OF TRUSTEES		
TEMPORARY PRIVILEGES REQUESTED		

Courtesy of St. Vincent Hospital, Worcester, Massachusetts.

work with a managed care organization. These projections are based on work done in house, compared with verification by a CVO.

This exercise provides information as to the actual time involved in the credentialing process and helps determine the required number of FTEs. Once calculated, the information provides justification for an appropriate number of FTEs and for improved technology such as new software programs and/or hardware, outsourcing work such as the verification component to a CVO, and/or helping to redefine work flow among the current staff. It may also be used to determine if redesign, streamlining some of the processes, reengineering the entire process, or eliminating unnecessary processes is indicated.

Regardless of whether an organization is looking to increase or decrease staffing or is considering redesign of the work processes, this is a good exercise to evaluate whether any steps or processes are taking a great deal of time but producing poor or inadequate results. It should be completed on an annual basis. Anther advantage to this analysis, especially if a multiple-person department is involved in the credentialing process, is to determine if a job division among FTEs is equitable. For example, one employee is responsible for all of the initial appointments, and another is responsible for reappointments. A staffing analysis and calculation of time involved in each of the components of the process could indicate an inequity in assignments. Another possible outcome might be the revision of job descriptions to more accurately describe and define the work.

ANNUAL CREDENTIALING STATISTICS

Using the above information as a guide, it is possible to produce a statistical report on at least an annual basis for senior management and/or medical staff organizations to review that recaps the credentialing activity over the past year. Exhibits 11–6 and 11–7 are sample reports showing credentialing activity for the past year that can be used on an annual basis to educate management, administration, board, and/or medical staff organization. This information can also be tracked from year to year to see how much variance occurs, which may be useful for staffing purposes.

NOTE

1. *Hospital Accreditation Standards, 1998* (Oakbrook Terrace, IL: Joint Commission on Accreditation of Healthcare Organizations, 1998), 216–219.

CHAPTER 12

Credentialing Resources and Additional Information

NATIONAL ASSOCIATION MEDICAL STAFF SERVICES

The National Association Medical Staff Services (NAMSS) is the major professional association for those involved in the credentialing field. It is composed of more than 3,700 individuals nationwide providing expertise in areas of provider credentialing, medical staff services, and provider relations. It was formed in 1978 and promotes continuous improvement of quality in health care by providing educational and professional development opportunities for its members.

NAMSS offers two certification programs, with one, certified provider credentialing specialist (CPCS), specifically designed for the credentialing specialist. Certification is the industry standard and serves as a measure of knowledge and experience in the field. Many employers seek certified individuals for positions in their organizations.

Educational opportunities include an annual three-day educational conference (plus two bonus days of additional education) with over 1,000 attendees. State and national seminars are also held throughout the year and throughout the country. Many states are organized to offer educational opportunities; this is helpful to those whose budgets will not allow long-distance travel. In addition, NAMSS offers resource materials written by those with expertise in the profession.

NAMSS also has an Independent Study Program that consists of five modules for learning. The program is accredited, and students can earn college credit for these modules through their local colleges and universities.

NAMSS has a monthly publication, *SYNERGY*, with articles of information and education that the credentialing professional needs to know.

The NAMSS office is located in Lombard, Illinois. For additional information, call (630) 271-9814; fax (630) 271-0295; or email www.namss.org.

EVALUATION OF NEEDS/PURCHASING A CREDENTIALING SOFTWARE SYSTEM[1]

Before deciding to purchase a software system, complete an analysis of need. The steps are as follows:

1. Identify data management needs.
   - Identify why new software is needed.
   - If a replacement software, what do staff like and dislike about current software?
   - Does information systems policy and procedure have requirements that will affect the decision?
2. Identify activities that might be accomplished more efficiently through automation. Examples include
   - verification request correspondence
   - tracking status of verification activities

- committee management/tracking/scheduling/follow-up
- tracking continuing medical education activities for reappointment/recredentialing
- quality assurance peer review tracking system
- corrective action/due-process tracking
- communication of clinical privileges
- electronic query to the National Practitioner Data Bank (NPDB)
- electronic confirmation of state licensure
- tracking proctoring

3. Meet with the information systems department and outline technical issues that must be considered:
   - network versus stand-alone system (if a multiperson department or a centralized department that collects information for other medical staff organizations, a network system is suggested)
   - interface with internal information system department
   - printers
   - multifacility programs (see note under first bullet above)
   - external software versus internal system considerations
4. Make a wish list of features, and talk with internal information systems people to see if they can fulfill the needs or can assist in evaluating commercial software.
5. Identify and list vendors to be contacted.
6. When interviewing vendors, include the following in the discussions:
   - features offered
   - features desired
   - user list for reference (call and talk to the people who have used the system for a more objective evaluation)
   - help lines (turnaround time for request and help)
   - cost, installation, and training
7. Cross-reference list of requirements, needs, and "nice-to-have" features with features identified by vendors.
8. Identify two or three programs that seem to best meet needs, and request trial software or demos.
   - Identify cost factors.
   - Identify installation issues.
   - Determine ability to meet training needs.
9. Identify program for purchase.

PREPARING MEDICAL STAFF FOR JOINT COMMISSION CREDENTIALS INTERVIEW

Use of the following questions can help prepare physicians who will be involved with the credentials interview during a survey by the Joint Commission on Accreditation of Healthcare Organizations (Joint Commission).

1. Describe the appointment/reappointment process.
2. Describe the process of granting/revising/renewing clinical privileges.
3. How do you determine that all medical staff members who have clinical privileges provide services within the approved scope of practice?
4. Does each member of the medical staff agree in writing to be bound by the medical staff bylaws, rules, and regulations?
5. Do radiologists and gastroenterologists at this institution apply for conscious sedation privileges?
6. Do obstetricians require anesthesia privileges?
7. Do podiatrists at this institution perform history and physicals?
8. How do you determine that an applicant is competent to perform requested procedures?
9. Does your application form identify any language for voluntary or involuntary loss of privileges?
10. What is the turnaround time for the credentialing process?
11. Did you have any practitioners who were not reappointed this year? If yes, please describe the reason.

12. In review of a credentials file, please identify the following:
    - verification of current license
    - department chair recommendation
    - basis for reappointment (quality profile)
    - basis for renewal of privileges[2]

ASSESSING THE EFFECTIVENESS AND PRODUCTIVITY OF CREDENTIALING ACTIVITIES

Periodically, the office responsible for credentialing, the medical director, the chief of staff, and the medical staff should review their policies and procedures and evaluate credentialing activities. At this time, revisions should be made to reflect current practice or to improve the process. The following tools can be used to help assess the credentialing activities in an organization.

Practitioner Satisfaction Survey

It is a good idea to survey all or a representative sample of new medical staff members, allied health practitioners (AHPs), or those newly affiliating with an ambulatory or managed care organization. A simple satisfaction survey can be sent with practitioners' letter of appointment/privileges/acceptance for affiliation, asking them to complete the form and return it in an effort to continue to improve the application process.

Some of the questions to ask in such a survey are:

- Did you receive all of the information and instructions you needed to complete the application form and return all the required documents? If not, what could be done better?
- Were you notified in a timely manner (either verbal or written) with regard to any additional information you needed to furnish to complete your application?
- Were you kept informed of the progress of your application?
- Did you need to contact us by phone for any reason? If yes, did you reach someone who was able to help you with a minimum wait time?
- Were medical staff office personnel/credentialing staff friendly and helpful to you during this initial application process?
- Do you believe that your application was processed in a timely manner and that it was coordinated with your practice start date?
- Do you have any suggestions to improve the initial credentialing process?

A similar survey could be developed and used for the reappointment/recredentialing process. It is recommended that a random sampling method be used for this survey.

Productivity Reports

Very often, administrators and/or medical staff leaders are not aware of the volume of credentialing activity that occurs in any given organization. In an effort to educate the administrative and medical staff leadership, it is suggested that an annual report be submitted to administration that summarizes credentialing activity. See Exhibits 11–6 and 11–7 in Chapter 11 of this book for sample productivity/annual reports. This additional information would also be helpful in further educating people about the time involved in credentialing.

File Audits

A file audit can be used in preparation for a survey or at any time if it is believed that complete information may not be available in the credentials file (see Exhibit 12–1 for a sample credentials file audit). For purposes of an accreditation survey, this tool could be used for files that have a high potential of being requested by a surveyor. Such files might include the leadership of the medical staff organization (officers,

Exhibit 12–1 Credentials File Audit

Privileged and Confidential

Practitioner Name: ______________________ Staff Category: ____________________

Department: ______________________ Specialty: ____________________

Leadership Position: ______________________

1. Initial application in file?	Yes ☐	No ☐	Dated:	________
2. Since 1987, primary source verification for education, training, hospital, peer references?	Yes ☐	No ☐		
3. Current state license?	Yes/NA ☐	No ☐	Exp. Date	________
4. Current state pharmacy license?	Yes ☐	No ☐	Exp. Date	________
5. Current DEA license?	Yes ☐	No ☐	Exp. Date	________
6. Current NPDB in file?	Yes ☐	No ☐	Query Date	________
7. Current insurance in file?	Yes ☐	No ☐	Exp. Date	________
8. Boarded? Specialty(ies) ______________	Yes ☐	No ☐	Exp. Date	________

Comments: ____

9. Reappointment current?	Yes ☐	No ☐	Exp. Date	________
10. Current reappointment letter in file?	Yes ☐	No ☐		
11. Physician activity information in file? (PI/QA)	Yes ☐	No ☐		
12. Hospital references (if applicable)?	Yes ☐	No ☐		
13. Peer reference/review for specialty (MD, DPM, etc.)?	Yes ☐	No ☐		
14. CME documentation?	Yes ☐	No ☐		
15. Current dept. chair recommendation?	Yes ☐	No ☐		
16. Current dept. chair comments?	Yes ☐	No ☐		
17. Was last reappointment 2 years or less?	Yes/NA ☐	No ☐		

Comments: ____

*Peer Reference/Review for Specialty (MD, DPM, etc.)

18. Privilege delineation in file?	Yes ☐	No ☐	Dated:	________
19. Department chair signature?	Yes ☐	No ☐		
20. Department chair personal comments?	Yes ☐	No ☐		

Comments: ____

21. Credentialing Committee, MEC, BOT signatures where indicated for ***most recent appointment***? (can be initial or reappointment) Yes ☐ No ☐

File Rating ☐A+ ☐B ☐PF **File Auditors Initials** ____________ **Date:** __________

A+ - All "Yes" answers (exceptions #8, #16, #20)
B - Missing items/information can be completed by ______________.
Date
PF - Problem File

Note: PI, performance improvement; QA, quality assurance; DEA, Drug Enforcement Administration; CME, continuing medical education; MEC, medical executive committee; BOT, board of trustees.

Courtesy of C. Mobley & Associates, LLC, and Quality Management Options, LLC, Colorado Springs, Colorado.

executive committee members, committee chairs, medical directors), initial appointments/credentialing during the last six months, current temporary privileges, anyone with adverse action or a reduction in privileges or staff category for whatever reason, a representative of each of the invasive procedure areas within the hospital, and others as defined by the organization.

If there is concern that many of the credentials files are not in good shape, this audit tool can be used to audit all files. A similar form can be developed for AHPs as well. Once complete, the audit tool can be used as a worksheet if requests are being made to bring the file into compliance.

SKILLS ASSESSMENT

The following skills assessment can be used by the credentialing professional to identify areas of strength and weakness, or by a manager as a needs assessment, or to evaluate knowledge of a new applicant. Questions cover both hospital and managed care credentialing activities and relate to both Joint Commission and National Committee for Quality Assurance (NCQA) accreditations.

Topics

1. Accreditation and Certification
2. Regulatory and Legal Aspects of Credentialing
3. Credentialing
4. Privileging
5. Meeting Management
6. Allied Health
7. Delegation
8. Quality Assurance and Peer Review
9. Information Management
10. Other

Instructions

1. Choose the one **best** answer.
2. Assume that references to managed care are for NCQA-accredited organizations and that Joint Commission references are for accredited hospitals unless otherwise stated.
3. If a question references a medical staff organization, it assumes a hospital setting.

1. Accreditation and Certification

Identify the following acronyms:

1. NCQA ____________________
2. Joint Commission ____________________
3. AMA ____________________
4. POC ____________________
5. NCQA is the only organization that accredits health maintenance organizations.

   TRUE FALSE

6. NCQA, the Joint Commission, and AAHCC accredit hospitals, managed care organizations, and other health care organizations.

   TRUE FALSE

7. Credentialing accounts for what percentage of the NCQA accreditation decision?
   a. 10%
   b. 15%
   c. 20%
   d. 25%
8. NCQA has clarified the term *provider* to mean
   a. any physician affiliated with the plan
   b. any licensed individual who is qualified to practice and wishes to obtain plan affiliation
   c. an organization or institution that provides services to plan members
   d. all of the above
9. NCQA requires that physicians and dentists be board certified within five years of plan affiliation.

   TRUE FALSE

10. Both NCQA and Joint Commission accreditation

a. require that accreditation be obtained within five years of initiation of the organizations' activities
b. have specific standards relating to credentials activities
c. require that all practitioners employed or affiliated with an organization be credentialed and assigned privileges
d. none of the above

11. Both NCQA and the Joint Commission require that a credentials committee review files of all practitioners applying for affiliation or membership.

TRUE FALSE

12. In managed care, policies and procedures define the credentialing process, while in the hospital the process is defined by bylaws.

TRUE FALSE

13. NCQA and Joint Commission standards that address initial credentialing of physicians and other practitioners are quite similar.

TRUE FALSE

14. The AMA profile is considered to be acceptable verification for relevant training by
a. NCQA
b. the Joint Commission
c. both NCQA and the Joint Commission
d. neither NCQA nor the Joint Commission

15. The AMA has a new program that offers accreditation for physician offices.

TRUE FALSE

16. The Joint Commission survey team for hospitals with 100 or more beds is made up of
a. two physicians and a nurse
b. two physicians and an administrator
c. a physician, a nurse, and an administrator
d. a physician and two administrators

17. Joint Commission surveys are designed to determine whether
a. correct processes are performed
b. correct processes are performed well
c. correct processes improve performance
d. all of the above

18. The Joint Commission offers specialty accreditation for
a. respiratory care
b. ambulatory care
c. credentials verification organizations
d. all of the above

19. Random unannounced surveys are conducted by
a. NCQA
b. the Joint Commission
c. both NCQA and the Joint Commission
d. neither NCQA nor the Joint Commission

20. Before Joint Commission surveys, the CEO must sign a certificate attesting that no fraudulent activities have occurred in relation to documents presented in surveys.

TRUE FALSE

21. The Joint Commission reviews medical staff activities through
a. credentials files review
b. bylaws review
c. leadership interview
d. all of the above

22. The Joint Commission identifies credentialing and the medical staff organization to be
a. an organizational function
b. a structure with functions
c. a patient-focused function
d. none of the above

2. Regulatory and Legal Aspects of Credentialing

Identify the following acronyms:

1. NPDB ______________________
2. HCQIA ______________________
3. The party against whom legal action is brought is the
a. defendant
b. plaintiff

c. litigant
d. witness

4. An example of a tort would be
a. a breach of confidentiality
b. falsifying an application
c. assault and battery
d. all of the above

5. "Any-willing-provider" laws are enacted by states to ensure that patients have the right to choose any physician willing to accept new patients.

TRUE FALSE

6. Liability is
a. unlawful restraint and monopolies or unfair business practices
b. an obligation incurred through any act or failure to act
c. a wrong damage done to another
d. professional misconduct

7. The Health Care Quality Improvement Act
a. was driven by the *Patrick vs. Burget* case, in which the court stated that peer review physicians engaged in shabby unprincipled and unprofessional conduct
b. established NPDB
c. provides immunity from liability for damage resulting from good-faith peer review activities involving physicians and dentists
d. all of the above

8. Hospitals may query NPDB whenever they have reason to believe that information has been reported on a health care practitioner who has been granted staff privileges.

TRUE FALSE

9. The Health Care Quality Improvement Act outlines minimum due-process steps that should be offered to a physician who believes that he or she has been treated unfairly during the credentialing process.

TRUE FALSE

10. A summary suspension is
a. suspension of clinical privileges due to incomplete medical records
b. a form of discipline used when a physician's license has been revoked
c. an action taken without affording the affected person the opportunity for a hearing before the suspension
d. none of the above

11. Inability to work with others in the hospital may be used as grounds to terminate a physician from the medical staff.

TRUE FALSE

12. No admissions to the hospital for two years may be used as grounds for
a. denial of reappointment
b. a summary suspension
c. initiation of "any-willing-provider" provisions
d. all of the above

13. Grounds for termination from a hospital medical staff that have been upheld by the courts include
a. criminal activity and loss of federal narcotics license
b. refusal to treat indigent patients
c. failure to purchase malpractice insurance and failure to become board certified
d. all of the above

14. A physician must always be informed when an investigation is initiated to determine whether a disciplinary action is necessary.

TRUE FALSE

15. Hospitals are the only health care entities with mandatory requirements for querying NPDB.

TRUE FALSE

3. Credentialing

Identify the following acronyms:

1. ECFMG ____________________
2. DEA ____________________

3. ADA ______________________________

4. FSMB _____________________________

5. ABMS _____________________________

6. Credentialing applications must include an attestation and release from liability.

   TRUE FALSE

7. Approval of credentialed physicians requesting medical staff membership and clinical privileges in a hospital is the responsibility of
   a. the chief executive officer
   b. the medical executive committee
   c. the governing body
   d. all of the above

8. Hospitals must credential
   a. employed physicians who provide patient care
   b. all members of the medical staff
   c. licensed independent practitioners (as defined by state law and the hospital)
   d. all of the above

9. The purpose of a preapplication process is to
   a. shorten the time required to process an application
   b. evaluate a practitioner's competency before recommending clinical privileges and membership
   c. screen out noneligible applicants through objective review of specific requirements
   d. all of the above

10. If a preapplication process is used, possible candidates for membership or affiliation should be sent a list of criteria and an explanation of the credentialing process.

    TRUE FALSE

11. In a preapplication process, a decision to withhold an application due to noncompliance with a threshold criteria is reportable to NPDB.

    TRUE FALSE

12. In the hospital, an applicant to the medical staff is applying for
    a. delineation of clinical privileges and medical staff membership
    b. designation of a staff category
    c. an assignment to a department (if departmentalized)
    d. all of the above

13. Application for medical staff appointment can be considered "voluntarily withdrawn" if an application is incomplete, information is not forthcoming, or questions are not adequately resolved.

    TRUE FALSE

14. The time frame for receipt of a complete application
    a. is defined by NCQA standards
    b. is defined by Joint Commission standards
    c. is defined by both NCQA and Joint Commission standards
    d. is defined by the organizations' bylaws/policies and procedures

15. The maximum time for processing an application
    a. is defined by NCQA for managed care organizations and by medical staff bylaws for a hospital
    b. is defined by the Joint Commission
    c. is defined by both NCQA and the Joint Commission
    d. is defined by the credentials committee

16. The application should include a statement that privileges will be denied on the basis of provision of false or fraudulent information.

    TRUE FALSE

17. The Joint Commission requires that information
    a. about licensure be primary source verified
    b. about training and experience be primary source verified
    c. about competence be primary source verified
    d. all of the above

18. Reappointment or recredentialing must be completed
    a. on a yearly basis
    b. every two years
    c. every three years
    d. according to the policy of the organization

19. Methods used to verify credentials information may include
    a. internal
    b. centralized
    c. delegated
    d. all of the above

20. Primary source verification may include
    a. a faxed copy
    b. a copy from the practitioner
    c. a copy forwarded by another hospital
    d. none of the above

21. NCQA requires primary source verification of
    a. clinical privileges at primary hospital
    b. all disciplinary actions
    c. peer recommendations
    d. work history

22. Information considered a "caution flag" would be
    a. licensure in more than one state
    b. a missing peer recommendation
    c. missing dates or gaps in practice
    d. all of the above

23. Competency for initial appointment and privileging in the hospital setting can be verified
    a. by the applicable specialty board
    b. through contacting other facilities, training programs, and peer references
    c. by completion of postgraduate training
    d. through licensure

24. For initial appointment, the Joint Commission requires that hospitals primary source–verify medical school graduation and internship/residency through
    a. contact with the highest level of education obtained
    b. board certification
    c. the school or training program
    d. any of the above

25. Hospital appointment and reappointment decisions must consider criteria that are directly related to the quality of care.

    TRUE FALSE

26. The Joint Commission has a standard requiring participation in continuing education.

    TRUE FALSE

4. Privileging

1. Temporary privileges may be granted according to
   a. Joint Commission standards
   b. NCQA standards
   c. Both Joint Commission and NCQA standards
   d. Neither Joint Commission nor NCQA standards

2. The Joint Commission defines clinical privileges as
   a. criteria that the practitioner must meet in order to perform certain procedures in the hospital
   b. permission to provide medical or other patient care services in the granting institution, within well-defined limits, based on the individuals' professional license and his or her experience, competence, ability, and judgment
   c. the level of minimal competence for a beginner treating an average patient
   d. procedures that can be performed by members of different departments

3. Delineation of privileges is
   a. a term used to describe the process of establishing specific criteria that a practitioner must meet to perform specific procedures at a hospital
   b. a term used to refer to the granting of specific privileges to each practitioner

c. the process of measuring practitioners against criteria that have been developed by each clinical department or specialty
d. all of the above

4. A practitioner who requests clinical privileges must prove that he or she is qualified to perform the requested procedures.

   TRUE FALSE

5. Hospitals <u>must</u> have criteria for granting clinical privileges before accepting a request from a practitioner for those specific privileges.

   TRUE FALSE

6. Criteria for granting clinical privileges may include
   a. extent of training and education experience
   b. board certification
   c. minimum number of procedures performed
   d. all of the above

7. A practitioner applies for clinical privileges by completing an application for medical staff membership.

   TRUE FALSE

8. A physician requesting privileges for treating Alzheimer's disease, epilepsy, and neuralgia and to perform EEGs and CTs would probably be
   a. an orthopedist
   b. an endocrinologist
   c. a gynecologist
   d. a neurologist

9. Delineation and granting of clinical privileges is required by
   a. the Joint Commission
   b. NCQA
   c. both the Joint Commission and NCQA
   d. neither the Joint Commission nor NCQA

10. Temporary privileges may be granted
    a. to an applicant for membership in a medical staff whose credentials have not yet been received by the governing body
    b. for a time period defined in the bylaws
    c. in time of emergency or dire need
    d. all of the above

11. NCQA standards do not recognize temporary privileges. To grant them would not be in compliance with the standards.

    TRUE FALSE

12. NPDB must be queried
    a. at the time temporary privileges are requested
    b. at the time one-case privileges are requested
    c. whenever an individual already on staff requests additional clinical privileges
    d. all of the above

13. Provisional privileges are usually defined as
    a. admitting privileges that are limited by specialty or by training education or experience
    b. privileges granted to a new medical staff member, not to exceed two years
    c. the privilege list sent out to applicants, which is limited to hospital-specific privileges
    d. none of the above

14. Clinical departments are responsible for
    a. granting temporary privileges
    b. establishing criteria for privileges
    c. approving medical staff membership
    d. recommending new applicants to the governing board

15. Before granting temporary privileges, the Joint Commission requires primary source verification of <u>at least</u>
    a. DEA certification
    b. current competence
    c. liability and insurance
    d. all of the above

16. Short-term privileges that should be time limited and not extended unless addressed in written policy or bylaws include all but
    a. temporary privileges

b. one-case privileges
c. initial appointment privileges
d. locum tenens privileges

17. Locum tenens privileges are defined as
    a. privileges for a physician who needs to admit only a few of his or her private patients in a year's time
    b. privileges needed during an emergency at a hospital where the physician usually does not practice
    c. privileges for a physician who is temporarily covering another physician's practice for a defined period of time
    d. privileges a physician obtains while his or her application is in process

18. Privileges must be reviewed and updated at time of reappointment.

    TRUE FALSE

5. Meeting Management

Define the following acronyms

1. PDCA ____________________
2. CRAF ____________________
3. Agenda and minutes formats should be consistent throughout an organization because
    a. it is a Joint Commission standard
    b. it creates a common frame of reference and documentation in minutes is standard
    c. both a and b
    d. neither a nor b
4. The purpose of minutes is to
    a. help the decision-making process
    b. direct discussion
    c. prepare participants for business at hand
    d. provide documentation about action taken
5. Confidentiality in minutes is important since they may later be subjected to court scrutiny, or compromised security could result in review of minutes by inappropriate personnel. The best method for keeping names of people protected in a set of minutes is to
    a. use code numbers that are secured with only key authorized people who have access to the cross-reference to names
    b. use last names only
    c. use only the person's initials
    d. use first name and last name initial
6. The proper way to make correction to minutes that have been officially corrected in a subsequent meeting is to
    a. make the correction on the computer, and attach a corrected copy to the original copy of minutes
    b. make the correction on the computer, and replace the original minutes that contained the error
    c. record the correction in the subsequent meeting's minutes, and make the correction in red ink directly on the minutes to be corrected with the chair's initials
    d. not make any correction to the minutes, since no one will probably ever look at those minutes again
7. Committees mandated by the Joint Commission, for involvement with the credentials decision include
    a. credentials committee
    b. peer review committee
    c. medical executive committee
    d. none of the above
8. New applicants for hospital medical staff membership are frequently interviewed by the credentials committee.

    TRUE FALSE

9. All actions and recommendations taken by committees responsible for credentialing and privileging must be reported to the governing body.

    TRUE FALSE

6. Allied Health

Define the following acronyms:

1. AHP ____________________
2. EMT ____________________

3. PA ______________________________

4. CNM ______________________________

5. CRNA ______________________________

6. Joint Commission standards require that the same criteria, policies, and procedures used to credential physicians are used for AHPs.

   TRUE FALSE

7. Mechanisms for providing the competency of all practitioners who provide patient care is required by the Joint Commission.

   TRUE FALSE

8. AHPs who are categorized as independent by law and the organization
   a. do not require clinical privilege delineation in a hospital
   b. are employees of a physician rather than of a hospital
   c. function without the supervision of a physician
   d. do not have to be credentialed

9. The Joint Commission requires that licensed independent practitioners have delineated clinical privileges.

   TRUE FALSE

10. Dependent AHPs
    a. are usually employees of a staff physician
    b. may not be licensed
    c. are not required to have delineated privileges
    d. all of the above

11. Depending on how they function in an organization, the following practitioners would often be categorized as independent AHPs:
    a. clinical psychologists and podiatrists
    b. scrub nurses and nurse surgical assistants
    c. nurse practitioners and physician assistants
    d. speech pathologists and audiologists

12. AHPs who must be credentialed by the medical staff as opposed to the human resources function are
    a. dependent AHPs
    b. independent AHPs
    c. both dependent and independent AHPs
    d. neither category of AHPs

13. A hospital may designate the review of credentials, scope of practice, and competency of dependent AHPs to the Human Resources department.

    TRUE FALSE

14. In the hospital, dependent AHPs cannot be members of the medical staff organization.

    TRUE FALSE

7. Delegation

1. Delegation is
   a. a contract or letter with another organization that defines financial responsibility for all credentialing and recredentialing activities
   b. an activity designed to ensure that each step in the credentialing process has an assigned accountability for all outcomes
   c. a formal process by which a managed care organization gives another entity the authority to perform credentialing functions on its behalf
   d. all of the above

2. NCQA limits the extent to which a managed care organization delegates its credentialing activities.

   TRUE FALSE

3. The Joint Commission has no standards for delegation.

   TRUE FALSE

4. A managed care company is accountable for any credentialing and recredentialing of its practitioners, regardless of the level of delegation.

   TRUE FALSE

5. If a managed care company chooses to delegate <u>all</u> of its credentialing responsibilities to another organization, NCQA requires that
   a. the delegated organization have credentialing policy and procedures that are consistent with those of the managed care company
   b. the managed care company approve the delegates' credentialing policy and procedures
   c. the managed care company retain the right to make final credentialing decisions
   d. all of the above

6. According to NCQA, all delegated credentialing activities must be monitored.

   TRUE FALSE

7. According to NCQA requirements,
   a. the managed care organization must evaluate the performance of a delegate's program on an annual basis
   b. a delegated contract must be revoked if it is determined that the delegate's performance is not meeting standards
   c. no delegation may occur unless the delegate has had a credentialing process in place for at least 12 months
   d. all of the above

8. The managed care organization should retain the right to approve and/or terminate practitioners even in situations where decision making is delegated.

   TRUE FALSE

9. Delegated activities may not be subdelegated to another entity.

   TRUE FALSE

10. NCQA states that it is possible to delegate the entire credentialing process, including the decision.

    TRUE FALSE

8. Quality Assurance and Peer Review

Define the following acronyms:

1. PI ________________________

2. QM ________________________

3. A quality program structure provides for integration of
   a. utilization review
   b. clinical review
   c. credentials review
   d. all of the above

4. Medical staff quality improvement activities usually include review of
   a. blood usage, mortality, and surgical procedure review
   b. credentialing and recredentialing decisions
   c. nursing, lab, and radiology clinical outcomes review
   d. all of the above

5. The Joint Commission requires that the hospitalwide quality improvement committee have physician members representing all major specialties.

   TRUE FALSE

6. Physician profiles or report cards are a common method of reporting individual results of quality activities in the managed care environment.

   TRUE FALSE

7. Peer review differs from quality improvement in that
   a. peer review monitors activities of physicians, while quality improvement is focused on organizational activity
   b. peer review is focused on individual practitioners, while quality improvement focuses on process
   c. peer review identifies "outliers" to standard practice, and quality improvement

determines the process by which the outliers will be addressed
d. there is no difference in the two activities

8. NCQA requires that information from quality improvement activities always be incorporated into its recredentialing decision-making process.

   TRUE FALSE

9. The Joint Commission requires that information from quality improvement activities be incorporated into its recredentialing decision-making process.

   TRUE FALSE

9. Information Management

Define the acronym

1. MIS ______________________________

2. A separate credentials file must be maintained for each credentialed practitioner.

   TRUE FALSE

3. Those who should have access to credentials files are
   a. credentialers, provider relations, and medical staff services personnel
   b. All personnel listed in (a) plus administration
   c. physicians for their own file only, in addition to credentialing staff and administration
   d. anyone with a need to know and who is included in the access policy of the organization

4. Quality improvement information that is specific to an individual practitioner is
   a. never made available to the involved practitioner
   b. maintained in files separate from the credentials file and identified as confidential and peer review protected
   c. confidential and not related to credentialing
   d. made available only to the individual practitioner involved in or affected by the information

5. NCQA has a standard that requires managed care organizations to develop policies and procedures to ensure the confidentiality of all information obtained in the credentialing process.

   TRUE FALSE

6. Credentials files should not leave a secure area unless accompanied by an authorized individual.

   TRUE FALSE

7. Information that would generally be found in a credentials file and not a separate file containing protected peer review information is
   a. department chair review form
   b. all information regarding disciplinary action
   c. letter of appointment to medical staff
   d. NPDB information

8. The length of time that expiring information should be kept in a credentials file
   a. should be defined in a policy developed with legal advice
   b. depends on when you run out of space in the file cabinet
   c. is two reappointment cycles
   d. is determined by the manager of the credentialing department

9. Credentials minutes
   a. are considered confidential, and access is defined by policy
   b. should never be destroyed unless disks are maintained in a secure area or information is transferred to microfiche or scanned on disk
   c. need to reflect recommendations made for approval or decisions on credentialing activities
   d. all of the above

10. NCQA requires an organization to have a disaster recovery procedure in the event that the data system crashes and information on line cannot be retrieved.

    TRUE FALSE

10. Other

Define the following acronyms:

1. HMO ______________________
2. PPO ______________________
3. IPA ______________________
4. NAMSS ______________________
5. CMSC ______________________
6. CPCS ______________________

Answers

1. Accreditation and Certification

1. National Committee for Quality Assurance 2. Joint Commission on Accreditation of Healthcare Organizations 3. American Medical Association 4. Physician Organization Certification 5. False 6. True 7. A. 8. C. 9. False 10. B. 11. False 12. True 13. True 14. C. 15. True 16. C. 17. D. 18. B. 19. B. 20. True 21. D. 22. B.

2. Regulatory and Legal Aspects of Credentialing

1. National Practitioner Data Bank 2. Health Care Quality Improvement Act 3. A. 4. C. 5. False 6. B. 7. D. 8. True 9. True 10. C. 11. True 12. A. 13. D. 14. False 15. True

3. Credentialing

1. Educational Commission for Foreign Medical Graduates 2. Drug Enforcement Administration 3. Americans with Disabilities Act 4. Federation of State Medical Boards 5. American Board of Medical Specialties 6. True 7. C. 8. D. 9. C. 10. True 11. False 12. D. 13. True 14. D. 15. A. 16. True 17. D. 18. B. 19. D. 20. A. 21. A. 22. C. 23. B. 24. C. 25. True 26. True

4. Privileging

1. A. 2. B. 3. D. 4. True 5. True 6. D. 7. False 8. D. 9. A. 10. D. 11. True 12. D. 13. B. 14. B. 15. B. 16. C. 17. C. 18. True

5. Meeting Management

1. Plan, Do, Check, Act 2. Conclusions, Recommendations, Actions, Follow-up 3. B. 4. D. 5. A. 6. C. 7. C. 8. True 9. True

6. Allied Health

1. Allied Health Practitioner 2. Emergency Medical Technician 3. Physician Assistant 4. Certified Nurse Midwife 5. Certified Registered Nurse Anesthetist 6. False 7. True 8. C. 9. True 10. D. 11. A. 12. B. 13. True 14. True

7. Delegation

1. C. 2. False 3. True 4. True 5. D. 6. True 7. A. 8. True 9. False 10. False

8. Quality Assurance and Peer Review

1. Performance Improvement 2. Quality Management 3. D. 4. A. 5. False 6. True 7. B. 8. False 9. True

9. Information Management

1. Management Information System 2. True 3. D. 4. B. 5. True 6. True 7. C. 8. A. 9. D. 10. True

10. Other

1. Health Maintenance Organization 2. Preferred Provider Organization 3. Independent Practice Association 4. National Association Medical Staff Services 5. Certified Medical Staff Coordinator 6. Certified Provider Credentialing Specialist

RESOURCE LIST

Below are listed sources of additional information on Credentialing, Appointment, Recredentialing, Reappointment, Privileging, Profiling, Peer Review, HEDIS, and ORYX.

Accreditation Association for Ambulatory Health Care Inc. (AAAHC), standards manuals for accreditation, 9933 Lawler Avenue, Skokie, IL 60077-3708

Accreditation Council for Graduate Medical Education, 515 North State Street, Chicago, IL 60610; (312) 464-4920; www.acgme.org

American Academy of Nurse Practitioners, P.O. Box 40013, Washington, DC 20016

American Association of Ambulatory Health Care Facilities, 9933 Lawler Avenue, Chicago, IL 60077

American Association of Health Plans (AAHP), 1129 20th Street N.W., Suite 600, Washington, DC 20036-3421; (202) 778-3207

American Association of Preferred Provider Organizations, 601 13th Street N.W., Washington, DC 20005; (202) 347-7600

American Board of Medical Specialties (ABMS), information regarding the specialty boards; 1007 Church Street, Suite 404, Evanston, IL 60201-5913; (708) 491-9091; www.abms.org

American Medical Association, *Graduate Medical Education Directory,* Medical Education Data Service, and AMA Physician Masterfile, 515 North State Street, Chicago, IL 60610; (312) 464-5000; www.ama-assn.org

American Osteopathic Association, *American Osteopathic Association Directory* and physician profile information; 142 E. Ontario Street, Chicago, IL 60611; www.am-osteo-assn.org

Association of American Medical Colleges; www.aamc.org

Briefings on Credentialing, Briefings on JCAHO, Medical Staff Briefing, and *Credentialing across the Continuum;* monthly publications of Credentialing Resource Center/Opus Communications, P.O. Box 1168, Marblehead, MA 01945; www.opuscom.com

Chiropractor Information Network; Federation of Chiropractor Licensing Boards, 901 54th Avenue, Suite 101, Greely, CO 80634; www.sni.net/fclb

Competency and Credentialing, monthly publication available through Ross Communications, 600-A Anton Boulevard #476, Costa Mesa, CA 92626

The Credentialing Desk Reference, 2nd edition; includes addresses and contact information for education, licensure, and specialty board certification; Opus Communications, P.O. Box 1168, Marblehead, MA 01945

Curing Health Care: New Strategies for Quality Improvement, by Donald Berwick, A. Blanton Godfrey, and Jane Poessner; Jossey-Bass Publishers, San Francisco, CA; (800) 956-7739

Graduate Medical Education Directory; American Medical Association Order Department OP416796, P.O. Box 7046, Dover, DE 19903; (800) 621-8335

Guide to Graduate Medical Education, Association for Hospital Medical Education, 1200 19th Street N.W., Suite 300, Washington, DC 20036

Handbook of Medical and Professional Staff Management, 2nd edition, edited by Cindy Gassiot and Vicki Searcy, 1998, published by the Texas Society for Medical Staff Services, 1033 La Posada Drive, Suite 220, Austin, TX 78752

Healthcare Competency and Credentialing Report, William Wrinn, Publisher, P.O. Box 10, Beverly, MA 01915; (508) 524-0230

Joint Commission on Accreditation of Healthcare Organizations; publications including *Joint Commission Perspectives* as well as standards manuals for accreditation and other educational materials and seminars; One Renaissance Boulevard, Oakbrook Terrace, IL 60181; customer service (630) 792-5800; www.jcaho.org

Legal Answer Book for Managed Care, Aspen Publishers, Inc., 200 Orchard Ridge Drive, Gaithersburg, MD 20878

The Managed Health Care Handbook, 3rd edition, by Peter Kongstvedt, Aspen Publishers, Inc., 200 Orchard Ridge Drive, Gaithersburg, MD 20878

Medical Group Management Association; 104 Inverness Terrace E., Englewood, CO 80112-5306; (303) 799-1111

Medical Staff Credentialing: A Practical Guide, by Fay Rozovsky; American Hospital Association, 1 North Franklin, Chicago, IL 60606-3401

Medical Staff Management: Forms, Policies, and Procedures for Health Care Providers, edited by Christine Mobley and Sheryl Deutsch, 1995, with supplements in 1996, 1997, 1998, and 1999; Aspen Publishers, Inc., 200 Orchard Ridge Drive, Gaithersburg, MD 20878

NAMSS Guidebook; Developing a Policy and Procedure Manual for the Medical Staff Services Department; National Association Medical Staff Services, 631 Butterfield Road, Suite 311, Lombard, IL 60148

National Association for Healthcare Quality (NAHQ) publications, including *Journal for Healthcare Quality* as well as an annual conference and educational materials, 5700 Old Orchard Road, First Floor, Skokie, IL 60077-1057; www.ncqa.org

National Association Medical Staff Services (NAMSS) publications, including *SYNERGY* as well as annual conference, educational programs, and resource materials; 631 Butterfield Road, Suite 311, Lombard, IL 60148; www.NAMSS.org

National Committee for Quality Assurance (NCQA) standards manuals for accreditation and information related to HEDIS; 2000 L Street, Suite 500, Washington, DC 20036

National Personnel Records Center for military references, copy of discharge papers (DD214), and Officer Evaluation Report; 9700 Page Boulevard, St. Louis, MO 63112; mark attention to: appropriate branch (e.g., Army)

National Practitioner Data Bank Guidebook, Health Resources and Service Administration, Bureau of Health Professions, Division of Quality Assurance, Parklawn Building, Room 8A-55, 5600 Fishers Lane, Rockville, MD 20875; publication number HRSA-95-255

National Practitioner Data Bank Help Line: (800) 767-6732; npdb.com/npdb.htm

ORYX: The Next Evolution in Accreditation, Joint Commission on Accreditation of Healthcare Organizations, 1997, 1 Renaissance Boulevard, Oakbrook Terrace, IL 60181; ORYX website: www.jcaho.org; ORYX information line, (630) 792-5085

Physician Credentialing and Peer Review Answer Book, Aspen Law Center, 1995; Aspen Publishers, Inc., 200 Orchard Ridge Drive, Gaithersburg, MD 20878

Robert's Rules of Order, Newly Revised, by Henry Robert, William Morrow and Co. Inc., 1350 6th Avenue, New York City, NY 10019

The Juran Prescription: Clinical Quality Management, by Kathleen Goonan; Jossey-Bass Publishers, San Francisco, CA; (800) 956-7739

Total Quality in Healthcare: From Theory to Practice, by Ellen Gaucher and Richard Coffey; Jossey-Bass Publishers, San Francisco, CA; (800) 956-7739

Transforming Healthcare Organizations: How To Achieve and Sustain Organizational Excellence, by Ellen Marszaleck-Gaucher and Richard Coffey; Jossey-Bass Publishers, San Francisco, CA; (800) 956-7739

Utilization Review Accreditation Commission (URAC); standards manuals for accreditation, 1130 Connecticut Avenue N.W., Suite 450, Washington, DC 20036

NOTES

1. V. Jackson and V. Searcy, "Software Evaluation" (paper presented at the annual meeting of the National Association of Medical Staff Services, Pittsburgh, PA, September 1995).
2. K. Morris, Material prepared for JCAHO survey (Miami Beach, FL: Columbia Miami Heart Institute, 1998).

Acronyms/Glossary

AAAHC: Accreditation Association for Ambulatory Health Care.

ACCESSIBILITY: The ability of a managed care member to obtain services at the time they are needed. Accessibility addresses both appointment scheduling and telephone access. Results of accessibility and availability surveys may be taken into account as part of the recredentialing process of an ambulatory or managed care organization.

ACCREDITATION: A voluntary process in which a determination of compliance with standards is made by a health care accrediting organization of an eligible health care organization.

ADA: Americans with Disabilities Act.

ADS: Alternative delivery system.

AHP: See ALLIED HEALTH PROFESSIONAL.

ALLIED HEALTH PROFESSIONAL (synonyms: ALLIED HEALTH PRACTITIONER, ALLIED HEALTH PERSONNEL, LICENSED INDEPENDENT PRACTITIONER, MID-LEVEL PRACTITIONER): A health care practitioner, qualified by license or certificate and training, to assist, support, and complement physicians and other health care professionals. The health care organization (and in some cases the licensing body) determines those practitioners who will be categorized as allied health as well as the degree of their independence to provide services.

AMA: American Medical Association.

AMAP: American Medical Accreditation Program.

AOA: American Osteopathic Association.

APPLICANT: An individual who is applying for affiliation, membership, contract, or other relationship with a health care organization.

APPLICATION FORM: An employment application form is a document completed by an applicant interested in employment, used by the human resource department to obtain information related to employment. A credentialing application is the document completed by a person interested in affiliation with a health care organization and is used to obtain information required to complete the credentialing process. The recredentialing form is the document completed at the time of recredentialing and is used to obtain information required to complete the recredentialing process.

APPOINTMENT: Designation of membership in a medical staff organization. Appointment to the medical staff is common in hospitals and is independent of the process of granting privileges.

AVAILABILITY: The ability of a managed care organization to provide appropriate services by practitioners (number, type, and geographic location) to meet the needs of its members.

BENCHMARK: A measure of best practice. A benchmarking process identifies best practice for a specific activity, process, or outcome; identifies how the practice occurs; and applies the lessons learned to improve performance.

BYLAWS: A document that establishes a governance framework, identifies roles and responsibilities, and grants authority to an organization and its individual members. Governing body bylaws (organizational bylaws) outline the laws or requirements of the organization. The medical staff bylaws are the requirements that regulate the medical staff organization.

CARF: Commission on Accreditation of Rehabilitation Facilities.

CDS: Controlled Dangerous Substance; refers to state pharmacy license for practitioners.

CERTIFICATION: Usually references BOARD CERTIFICATION, which is a professional designation indicating that a physician has passed an examination and met other eligibility requirements of a medical specialty board. NCQA offers a certification program for credentials verification organizations and physician organizations. Individual organizations may also certify providers of care. In this case, certification refers to the process of verifying and certifying that a institutional or facility health care provider meets requirements for quality and service.

CLIA: Certified Laboratory Institution Administration; certifies laboratories.

CLINICAL DEPARTMENT: A hospital medical staff department made up of practitioners who are organized according to specialty, clinical activity, or expertise as defined in the medical staff bylaws.

CLINICAL PRIVILEGES (also see DELINEATION OF CLINICAL PRIVILEGES): The authorization granted to an individual to perform specific patient care functions at a specified site or sites within the delivery system, within the limits of his or her license, registration or certification and in accordance with the bylaws of the organization. According to established criteria, privileges are granted or denied by the organization.

CME: See CONTINUING MEDICAL EDUCATION.

CMSC: Certified medical staff coordinator.

COMPETENCE: The ability of a practitioner to perform required services, make sound clinical judgments, and perform technical skills, based upon education, training, clinical experience, physical and mental health, and proper dexterity.

CONTINUING MEDICAL EDUCATION: Education to update clinical knowledge.

CONTRACTED PROVIDER: An entity, institution, or facility that has a contractual agreement to provide specific services.

CPCS: Certified provider credentialing specialist.

CPI: Clinical performance improvement.

CREDENTIALING: The process of obtaining, verifying, and evaluating information relating to qualifications of a health care practitioner or provider of care and a decision related to compliance with defined requirements. Occurs at time of initial application and every two years thereafter.

CREDENTIALS: Information that demonstrates qualifications. In health care, physician credentials include documentation regarding education, training, license, experience, and other elements identified by the organization.

CREDENTIALS FILE: An individual practitioner/provider record that includes the information relevant to credentialing. The file may be in a hard-copy format, an electronic medium, or a combination of both.

CREDENTIALS VERIFICATION ORGANIZATION: An organization (independent, centralized, for-profit or not-for-profit) that verifies credentials and provides that information to other organizations, entities, or functions.

CRITERIA: Objective, measurable statements or specifications against which health care activity, decisions, processes, and outcomes can be compared.

CVO: See CREDENTIALS VERIFICATION ORGANIZATION.

DDS: Doctor of Dental Science.

DEA: Drug Enforcement Administration.

DELEGATION: The process of giving another entity the authority to perform specific credentialing activities. A common delegation relationship is the use of a credentials verification organization (CVO) to obtain information and verification of credentials.

DELINEATION OF CLINICAL PRIVILEGES (Also see CLINICAL PRIVILEGES): The form used in credentialing licensed independent practitioners that lists those procedures, treatments, modalities, and/or disease management categories that may be requested by a practitioner.

DMD: Doctor of Medical Dentistry.

DO: Doctor of Osteopathy.

DPM: Doctor of Podiatric Medicine.

ECFMG: Educational Commission for Foreign Medical Graduates.

ECONOMIC CREDENTIALING: Measurement of the utilization and the cost-effectiveness of a practitioner's practice as part of the credentialing or recredentialing process.

EOC: See EVIDENCE OF COVERAGE.

EVIDENCE OF COVERAGE: The document provided to a member of a managed care plan that outlines services and benefits covered by the plan.

FSMB: Federation of State Medical Boards.

GOVERNING BOARD: The group (board of trustees, board of directors, governing body) granted the ultimate authority and responsibility for the operation of the organization.

HCQIA: Health Care Quality Improvement Act of 1986.

HEDIS: Health Plan Employer Data and Information Set.

HMO: Health maintenance organization.

IDS: Integrated delivery system.

IPA: Independent practice association.

JCAH: Joint Commission on Accreditation of Hospitals (former name of the Joint Commission on Accreditation of Healthcare Organizations).

JOINT COMMISSION: Joint Commission on Accreditation of Healthcare Organizations.

LIP: Licensed independent practitioner.

LOCUM TENENS: Privileges granted to a practitioner who will be practicing for a defined period of time (usually 30 to 90 days). Used most commonly for coverage of a physician taking a vacation or leave of absence.

MCO: Managed care organization.

MCP: Managed care plan.

MD: Doctor of Medicine.

MEC: See MEDICAL EXECUTIVE COMMITTEE.

MEDICAL DIRECTOR: The physician who is employed by, or contracted with, a health care organization and charged with the management of clinical functions, commonly including credentialing, quality management, risk management, and utilization review.

MEDICAL EXECUTIVE COMMITTEE: An executive function carried out by medical staff representatives who are authorized to act on behalf of the medical staff. The MEC is a Joint Commission requirement for accredited hospitals.

MEDICAL STAFF: The organized group of practitioners permitted by law, accreditation standards, and the health care organization to provide patient care services independently within the organization. The medical staff is charged through the bylaws with the responsibility for the quality of care rendered to patients by those practitioners having clinical privileges.

MEMBER: An individual enrolled for coverage under an Evidence of Coverage by a managed care organization.

MEMBER COMPLAINTS: Concerns and complaints submitted by members of a managed care plan regarding benefits, care, or service. One of six sources of information to be considered (use of three of the six sources meets the standard) in the recredentialing decision-making process for primary care practitioners by an NCQA-accredited organization.

MEMBER SATISFACTION: Data collected from members of a managed care plan regarding satisfaction with benefits, care, and service. One of six sources of information to be considered (use of three of the six sources meets the standard) in the recredentialing decision-making process for primary care practitioners by an NCQA-accredited organization.

MSO: Medical staff organization.

MSS: Medical staff services.

NAHQ: National Association for Healthcare Quality.

NAMSS: National Association Medical Staff Services.

NBME: National Board of Medical Examiners.

NCQA: National Committee for Quality Assurance.

NPDB: National Practitioner Data Bank.

ON-CALL PRACTITIONER: A qualified practitioner who has an agreement to provide medical services on a coverage or on-call basis. Some managed care companies require that contracted practitioners execute coverage agreements only with other contracted practitioners.

PA&I: Performance assessment and improvement.

PCP: See PRIMARY CARE PRACTITIONER.

PEER REVIEW: Review, evaluation, and assessment of the quality, appropriateness, timeliness, effectiveness, and efficiency of care by a practicing peer. *Peer* is often defined as a practitioner of the same specialty.

PHO: Physician-hospital organization.

PLAN: An organization that insures or pays for health care services as outlined in an Evidence of Coverage. Often referred to as a "managed care plan."

PPO: Preferred provider organization.

PRACTITIONER: An individual who is a licensed or certified health care professional.

PRIMARY CARE PRACTITIONER: An individual who provides primary care services to members of a managed care organization. Family practice, internal medicine, and pediatrics are commonly designated as primary care specialties.

PRIMARY SOURCE VERIFICATION (Also see VERIFICATION): Verification of a practitioner's or provider's qualifications and credentials with the source issuing the credential.

PROCTORING: Observation and evaluation of a practitioner for appointment and/or clinical privileges.

PROVIDER: A facility or institution that provides services for patients or members, such as a hospital or a pharmacy.

QA: Quality assurance or quality assessment.

RECREDENTIAL (may also be referred to as RECERTIFICATION or REAPPOINTMENT): The formal process, which occurs at least every two (2) years, of determining changes in nonstatic credentials (e.g., licensure and continuing education) and identifying information related to current competence. The recredentialing process identifies activity and determines competence through review of information collected as part of the quality or performance assessment and improvement activities, peer review, and monitoring of information that relates to judgment, performance, and skills.

RM: Risk management.

RULES AND REGULATIONS: The official statements related to patient care that is provided within the organization. General requirements found in most medical staff rules and regulations address the specific provisions for medical care, admission requirements, consultations, patient discharge information, and autopsy protocol.

SECONDARY VERIFICATION (also see VERIFICATION): Verification of the credentials of a practitioner or provider based upon evidence obtained by means other than direct contact with the issuing source (i.e., a copy provided by the practitioner or the AMA Physician Masterfile) .

SITE VISIT: An on-site review of the facility where care or a service is provided.

SUBDELEGATION: The transfer of activity and responsibility from a delegated entity to another entity—for example, a physician hospital organization's delegation of credentialing to a managed care plan, which in turn delegates verification to a credentials verification organization.

TEMPORARY PRIVILEGES: Privileges granted for specific conditions and for a specified period of time as defined in the medical staff bylaws.

UR/UM: See UTILIZATION REVIEW/UTILIZATION MANAGEMENT.

URAC: Utilization Review Accreditation Commission.

UTILIZATION REVIEW/UTILIZATION MANAGEMENT: The review and evaluation process of the appropriateness, efficiency, and necessity of services and patient care and treatment. UM information is one of six sources of information to be considered (use of three of the six sources meets the standard) in the recredentialing decision-making process for primary care practitioners by an NCQA-accredited organization.

VERIFICATION: The confirmation or validation of information provided by the practitioner applying for affiliation, membership, or clinical privileges.

WORK HISTORY: Information provided by the applicant related to his or her employment, clinical practice, and/or training.

Index

D

N

O

W